UNDERSTANDING BANKRUPTCY

Michael J. Herbert
Professor of Law
University of Richmond,
The T.C. Williams School of Law

LEGAL TEXT SERIES

MATTHEW BENDER

QUESTIONS ABOUT THIS PUBLICATION?

For questions about the **Editorial Content** appearing in these volumes or reprint permission, please call:

Ellen Siegel, J.D., at .... 1-800-252-9257 Ext. 2574
Outside the United States and Canada please call .... (212) 448-2000

For assistance with replacement pages, shipments, billing or other customer service matters, please call:

Customer Services Department at .... (800) 833-9844
Outside the United States and Canada, please call .... (518) 487-3000
Fax number .... (518) 487-3584

For information on other Matthew Bender publications, please call
Your account manager or .... (800) 223-1940
Outside the United States and Canada, please call .... (518) 487-3000

1997 Reprint

Library of Congress Cataloging-in-Publication Data

Herbert, Michael J.
Understanding bankruptcy law / Michael J. Herbert.
p. cm. — (Legal Text Series)
ISBN 0-8205-2868-4
1. Bankruptcy—United States I. Title. II. Series.
KF1524.H427 1995
346.73—dc20 95-18149
[347.30678] CIP

MATTHEW BENDER & CO., INC.
EDITORIAL OFFICES
2 Park Avenue, New York, NY 10016-5675 (212) 448-2000
201 Mission St., San Francisco, CA 94105-1831 (415) 908-3200

TABLE OF CONTENTS

Page

CHAPTER 4
A BRIEF HISTORY OF BANKRUPTCY

CHAPTER 5
BANKRUPTCY JURISDICTION AND VENUE

CHAPTER 6
COMMENCEMENT OF THE CASE

CHAPTER 7
PROPERTY OF THE ESTATE

Page

CHAPTER 11
EXEMPTIONS AND REDEMPTION

CHAPTER 12
DISCHARGE AND REAFFIRMATION

CHAPTER 13
GENERAL AVOIDING POWERS; GENERAL LIMITATIONS ON AVOIDING POWERS

Page

CHAPTER 14
PREFERENCES

CHAPTER 15
FRAUDULENT TRANSFERS AND FRAUDULENT OBLIGATIONS

CHAPTER 16
LIQUIDATION UNDER CHAPTER 7

Page

CHAPTER 17
REORGANIZATION UNDER CHAPTER 11

CHAPTER 18
REORGANIZATION UNDER CHAPTER 13

Page

CHAPTER 19
REORGANIZATION UNDER CHAPTER 12

CHAPTER 20
ROLE OF PROFESSIONALS IN THE PROCEEDING

CHAPTER 21
INTERNATIONAL BANKRUPTCY

CHAPTER 22
SPECIAL USES OF, AND PROBLEMS IN, BANKRUPTCY

INTRODUCTION

This book is designed to provide a basic introduction to bankruptcy and related state debtor/creditor law. It is equally useful in an introductory Creditors' Rights course that emphasizes bankruptcy; a free-standing Bankruptcy course; or an advanced course in Debtor Reorganization. While it does not and cannot pretend to anticipate every question that may arise, it does provide a reasonably detailed discussion of the issues most likely to arise. It is as up-to-date as possible, given the fast-changing nature of the law it examines; for example, it analyzes in detail the Bankruptcy Reform Act of 1994 which was enacted just before the manuscript was due to its publisher.

The primary goal of this book is to bring order and clarity to a body of law that sometimes has neither. Its focus is on the neophyte, who has little or no knowledge of bankruptcy law or practice. In addition, it sketches much of the state commercial law and debtor/creditor law that provide a backdrop to bankruptcy law. It is impossible, for example, to understand many key provisions of the Bankruptcy Code without having at least some knowledge of the state law regarding mortgages, deeds of trust, and security interests.

It is my hope to supplement, not to displace. Ideally, the student looking into this book will also be looking at the statutory provisions and the cases interpreting those statutory provisions. Although this text is useful to those who have not, full understanding requires facility with the Code and the case law.

In the last two decades, bankruptcy has evolved from a somewhat obscure specialty to one of the dominant bodies of law. Traditionally, the bankruptcy bar was divided into two groups—the rather small group that did consumer and small business bankruptcy, and the tiny group that did business reorganizations. Each had certain elements of a club; indeed, many bankruptcy practitioners retain a degree of nostalgia for the days when insolvency lawyers, if somewhat isolated from the profession as a whole, enjoyed (in much of the country at least) the kind of (perhaps imaginary) camaraderie that is usually associated with small-town lawyers.

Much of this has changed. Bankruptcy has become a boom area of practice, one of interest to a growing number of firms. The annual rate of bankruptcy filings has grown rapidly, reaching a recent peak of nearly one million. The administrative and judicial structure of bankruptcy has become elaborate and formalized; the scope of bankruptcy has grown in unexpected directions. Bankruptcy is now a serious matter not only for commercial and insolvency lawyers, but also for tax lawyers, environmental lawyers, tort lawyers, and labor lawyers.

There are many reasons for this transformation. One is a change of attitude—it is widely perceived that, while bankruptcy once carried with it the stigma of failure and dishonesty, it does so no longer. Another is that some alternatives to bankruptcy, especially state insolvency proceedings, have withered away. The Bankruptcy Code itself is in part responsible; it contains a number of legal devices that permit people and companies to achieve—or at least to try to achieve—goals that are simply not achievable under any other body of law. For example, bankruptcy is practically the only method of dealing with "mass torts" in a single consolidated proceeding.

Along with the explosion of bankruptcy litigation has come a parallel explosion of academic interest in bankruptcy. Not long ago, most law schools had little more in their curriculum than a single course in Creditor's Rights, only part of which was taken up by bankruptcy law. Today, many schools have several courses, covering not only basic bankruptcy but reorganization bankruptcy, bankruptcy tax, bankruptcy environmental law, and the like. Similarly, for many years there was only one important secondary source—Collier on Bankruptcy, a venerable treatise first published in 1898 (the 15th edition of which is still the leading authority).[1] Now there are many sources; of special interest to the law school community are the numerous law reviews that specialize in bankruptcy law, and the many articles on bankruptcy published in non-specialist law journals. I have tried to include a fair sampling of these other sources, to which students should turn for further discussion when they find themselves excited by a particular topic.[2]

Bankruptcy has also become a hot topic among legal theorists. Nothing that touches so large a part of the American economy and American society can exist for long without triggering efforts to fit it within larger structures of economic and political thinking. While this book is primarily aimed at giving a basic overview of bankruptcy, it also introduces the reader to the most important theoretical perspectives. Bankruptcy is an area in which there is often little separation of theory and practice, not least because Congress is constantly returning to basic principles as it writes and rewrites bankruptcy law.

Bankruptcy law in this country is federal law. The substantive parts are found almost entirely in the Bankruptcy Code (Title 11 of the United States Code); procedural provisions are found mainly in the Bankruptcy Rules and in various parts of U.S.C. Title 28. Although some state law is directly incorporated into the Code, and other state law indirectly affects rights in bankruptcy, any conflict between state law and bankruptcy is resolved in favor of the latter.

One of the features of federal law is that a wealth of legislative history underlies it. Insofar as the Code is concerned, the primary sources of that history are the House and Senate Reports that accompanied its original enactment. There was also extensive floor debate on some provisions; and most of the subsequent amendments to the Code are supported by similar reports and debates. The weight to be given these sources is today controversial. Several members of the Supreme Court, most noticeably Justice Antonin Scalia, largely reject the use of legislative history in statutory interpretation. This question too is explored in the book.

I end by suggesting one final reason why you should find this one of the most exciting courses you will take in law school. In a practical, if not a de jure, sense,

---

[1] Not coincidentally, Collier's is a Matthew Bender publication.

[2] Yes, some of us do find bankruptcy exciting!

bankruptcy is the court of last resort. In virtually every bankruptcy, there are far more claims than there are assets. Not only is there no free lunch; there is not enough lunch to feed everybody; to continue the metaphor, in most cases there is scarcely any lunch at all. In bankruptcy there is only so much to go around; it is not sufficient; yet it is all there is or will ever be. This means that bankruptcy law must make choices that are both unsatisfactory and final. How should the limited pool be divided up? How do we, how should we, decide between the claim of the mortgage holder to whom the debtor owes money on a loan and the maimed victim of the debtor's intentional tort? How do we also fit in the tax collector, the utility company, the credit card company, and the debtor's unpaid housekeeper? Bankruptcy law again and again forces us to make the hard disagreeable choices that are otherwise too often ignored. You may agree or disagree with the choices that have been made, but you should understand them; you should also understand that a choice is unavoidable.

With all this said, I hope you will find your study of bankruptcy exciting and intriguing. I hope as well you will find this book a helpful guide. Good luck!

ACKNOWLEDGEMENTS

Many thanks to the University of Richmond Law School's research funds and to my able research assistants, Lisa Bingen and Raxa Desai. The Third Floor and the Ad-Hoc Sub-Rosa Acting Committee on Austerity were, as always, an inspiration; so was Berryhill's red Mustang convertible. The folks at Matthew Bender have provided the necessary encouragement and patient editorial work; I have therefore exempted them from the curse I occasionally impose on publishers. Finally, for superb secretarial assistance and complete lack of sympathy for any authorial whining, full credit goes to Nancy E. O'Brien and Anne Yates Reynolds Smith.

I gratefully acknowledge the permission extended to reprint excerpts from the following works:

Ronald J. Bacigal,

The Limits of Litigation: The Dalkon Shield Controversy, 69 (1990). Reprinted with permission of the author.

Jagdeep S. Bhandari and Lawrence A. Weiss,

The Untenable Case for Chapter 11: A Review of the Evidence, 67 Am. Bankr. L.J. 131 (1993). Reprinted with permission of the authors and the American Bankruptcy Law Journal.

James W. Bowers,

Groping and Coping in the Shadow of Murphy's Law: Bankruptcy Theory and the Elementary Economics of Failure, 88 Mich. L. Rev. 2097, 2145 (1990). Reprinted with the permission of the author.

Michael Bradley and Michael Rosenzweig,

The Untenable Case for Chapter 11, 101 Yale L.J. 1043, 1044-45 (1992). Reprinted with permission of the author. Also, reprinted by permission of The Yale Law Journal Company and Fred B. Rothman & Company, from The Yale Law Journal, Vol. 101, pp. 1043-1095.

Jean Braucher,

Lawyers and Consumer Bankruptcy: One Code, Many Cultures, 67 Am. Bankr. L.J. 501, 557-58 (1993). Reprinted with permission of the author and the American Bankruptcy Law Journal.

Irving A. Breitowitz,

New Developments in Consumer Bankruptcies: Chapter 7 Dismissal on the Basis of "Substantial Abuse," 59 Am. Bankr. L.J. 335 (1984). Reprinted with the permission of the author and the American Bankruptcy Law Journal.

David G. Carlson,

Leveraged Buyouts in Bankruptcy, 20 Ga. L. Rev. 73, 80-83 (1985). Reprinted with permission of the author.

Richard E. Flint,

Bankruptcy Policy: Toward a Moral Justification for Financial Rehabilitation of the Consumer Debtor, 48 Wash. & Lee L. Rev. 515, 519-20 (1991). Reprinted with permission of the author and the Washington & Lee Law Review.

Steven A. Karg,

A Bankruptcy Trap for the Unwary Creditor: Equitable Subordination Resulting From Excess Credit Control, 15 Seton Hall Legis. J. 434 (1991). Reprinted with permission of the author and the Seton Hall Legislative Journal.

Donald T. Trautman, Jay Lawrence Westbrook, and Emmanuel Gaillard,

Four Models for International Bankruptcy, 41 Am. J. Comp. L. 573, 625 (1993). Reprinted with permission of the author.

DEDICATION To Will, Sean, Laura, Mary Beth, and Ben

CHAPTER 1

General Principles Underlying Insolvency Law

§ 1.01 The Nature of Insolvency Law

[A]—Introduction: Debtors or Deadbeats?

At the heart of any discussion of insolvency law are at least two insoluble problems. The first is reconciling the use of insolvency law to benefit both the insolvent and the creditors. The second is finding a way to distribute the debtor's inadequate assets among competing meritorious claims. The problems are insoluble precisely because of the insolvency; there is not enough to do everything that would be desirable. It is impossible to square this circle.

On the one hand, bankruptcy is a way out of trouble for hopelessly swamped debtors; on the other, it is an efficient means of collecting obligations. These two goals are in hopeless conflict; what to the debtor is escape is swindle to the creditor, and the creditor's efficient collection is the debtor's peonage. The arguments are old. During the Civil War, it was argued that a pro-debtor law was needed to preserve loyalty to the Union:

> Of what advantage can it be to creditors or to the country that so many tens of thousands of the active men of this country should be held in thralldom?
>
> . . . .
>
> The law formerly in force by which the creditor could keep his debtor in prison for an indefinite period, without relief, has been abolished in all Christian countries. But there may be a punishment of death without the knife, and an imprisonment without the bolts and bars of the jail.
>
> . . . .
>
> What to [the debtors] are the guarantees of the Constitution? Why should they love the Government and yield it a hearty allegiance?[1]

From the debate over the 1984 Amendments to the Bankruptcy Code, which significantly reigned in the perceived pro-debtor bias of the original 1978 Bankruptcy Reform Act, comes a passionate statement of the opposite point of view:

> Mr. Chairman, for the last couple of years in going home, I have been getting many complaints from the owners of small businesses about the large number of persons taking bankruptcy. It was pointed out to me that a number of these persons taking bankruptcy had good jobs. They could

[1] Cong. Globe, 38th Cong., 1st Sess. 2638 (1864) (remarks of Rep. Jenckes).

> pay their obligations, but it was the easier route to go chapter 7 and take bankruptcy and not worry about their debts.
>
> . . . .
>
> Well, something is wrong when the bankruptcy laws encourage people to take bankruptcy and then a small businessman goes before the courts and they tell him, "We can't help you at all."[2]

Not only does the debate deal with the rights of debtor and creditor; there is, in addition, a perpetual struggle over which creditors should be given the best crack at obtaining what assets the debtor does have. There are several tools for giving better treatment to some creditors than others; these include recognition of liens, granting priority in payment from the debtor's assets, and making all or part of a debt non-dischargeable (meaning that the debtor still owes it even after the bankruptcy proceeding is complete). The debate over who gets what is at least as complex, and at least as political, as the debtor/creditor conflict itself.

Over the years Congress has given favored treatment to an amazing variety of creditor groups; in recent years these have included, among others, labor unions, retirees, the victims of drunk (or drugged) drivers, government agencies that guarantee student loans, consumers who buy on layaway plans, ex-spouses, landlords, shopping mall operators, farmers, and the Federal Reserve System. There is sometimes little logic, other than political logic, used in deciding who is in a favored position. Moreover, there is little consistency in the favors granted. For example, some tax claims are protected by giving them priority and by making them non-dischargeable in some but not all forms of bankruptcy. Wage claims are given a priority but are dischargeable. Drunk driving claims are given no priority but are not dischargeable. Student loan claims have no priority but are sometimes dischargeable and sometimes not. Labor contracts are protected in an entirely different way: unlike most other contracts, the debtor must honor them except in limited circumstances. Why a particular creditor is given favored treatment is only half the mystery; why it is given one form of favored treatment and not another is sometimes equally baffling.

There are certainly themes that run through bankruptcy law; some of these are introduced in the next sections of this chapter. However, the term "theme" in this context has roughly the same meaning that it has in a musical or literary text. There are ideas, sometimes conflicting ideas, that recur. However, they are never fully synthesized or played out to their logical conclusion. In short, there is no one concept of bankruptcy that can explicate the Code. The Code is a fundamentally political document which, like most statutes, represents a series of horse-trades (some of which have nothing at all to do with bankruptcy as such). Given the relative completeness of the legislative record, it is possible to trace many of these horse-trades quite specifically; this can be (to say the least) amusing for the amateur student of the legislative process and excellent fodder for more rigorous (or at least more elaborate) schools of analysis, such as public choice.[3] In this book, our analysis must

---

[2] 130 Cong. Rec. H1812 (daily ed. March 21, 1984) (remarks of Rep. G. V. Montgomery).

[3] See, for example, Barry E. Adler, *Financial and Political Theories of American Corporate Bankruptcy*, 45 Stan. L. Rev. 311 (1993).

of necessity be rather limited; however, you should at least keep in mind that the rationale stated in support of one provision may be entirely contrary to the rationale stated in support of another provision. This represents an intellectual incoherence that is not so much due to a lack of congressional cerebral activity as to the way in which bankruptcy law, like nearly all law, is inevitably made.[4]

[B]—The "Fresh Start"

It is common, in discussions about bankruptcy, to see references to the concept of the "fresh start."[5] This concept is absolutely central to modern American insolvency law. The debtor, having surrendered non-exempt assets to the trustee, receives a second (or third or fourth or fifth) chance at making a go of things. Some discussions of the fresh start principle take on almost a mystical quality: bankruptcy is seen as a financial rebirth; after the "estate" (which as in probate law is how we describe the assets) is administered, and the debts discharged, the debtor begins a new financial life, unencumbered by the debts of the old. This financial redemption find roots deep in myths of the American character. It may not be entirely a coincidence that bankruptcy law became a permanent feature of American life only in 1898, roughly the time that the "frontier" was "closed." While the 19th century provided impecunious debtors with migration—with a fresh start in newly opened lands[6] —the 20th century offered bankruptcy instead. And, perhaps, some advance might be noted in the method used for the fresh start; the 20th century version does not dispossess other human societies, it only discommodes banks.

Although most analysts of bankruptcy law are uncomfortable with discussions of morality, rather than of economics, the fresh start occasionally has been the basis for asserting that there is a deep ethical underpinning to debt discharge. In the view of one commentator:

> [T]he central justification for the debtor financial relief provisions of the Bankruptcy Code is founded in a natural law theory of morality. A review of the history of bankruptcy legislation substantiates this moral justification for debtor relief encompassing the attributes of social, distributive, and commutative justice, existing in harmony as a humanitarian response to the financially downtrodden. Thus, the focus of fresh start policy should be on the adequacy of debtor protection, and not upon the economic or political ramifications of that protection. The moral justification for fresh start places certain commutative justice limitations upon the distributive justice aspects of debtor relief depending upon the actions of the debtor vis-a-vis his creditors. These limitations place the focus of

---

[4] The remark that it is always unwise to watch either the manufacture of laws or of sausages is generally attributed to a man who liked the latter rather more than the former, Otto von Bismark.

[5] For a particularly thorough study of the fresh start in the consumer bankruptcy context, see Charles G. Hallinan, *The "Fresh Start" Policy in Consumer Bankruptcy: A Historical Inventory and an Interpretive Theory*, 21 U. Rich. L. Rev. 49 (1986).

[6] More precisely, lands newly opened to European-American settlement.

the resolution of issues involving discharge and dischargeability on issues of fairness.[7]

As nebulous and even quasi-religious as some discussions of the fresh start undoubtedly are, the basic idea is by no means without meaning. Indeed, given the fact that most Chapter 7 bankruptcies result in no recovery to creditors, the fresh start is all that is accomplished in the typical case. Note too that when a U.S. bankruptcy court is considering whether it should allow a foreign bankruptcy court to deal with property located in the U.S., it is expressly commanded to consider whether the foreign proceeding adequately protects the debtor's fresh start.[8] Moreover, there are endless cases that interpret the Code using the debtor's fresh start as a touchstone. One of the classic articulations of the fresh start concept raised it nearly to the level of a fundamental constitutional right:

> One of the primary purposes of the bankruptcy act is to "relieve the honest debtor from the weight of oppressive indebtedness and permit him to start afresh free from the obligations and responsibilities consequent upon business misfortunes."
>
> . . . .
>
> . . .The power of the individual to earn a living for himself and those dependent upon him is in the nature of a personal liberty quite as much as, if not more than, it is a property right. To preserve its free exercise is of the utmost importance, not only because it is a fundamental private necessity, but because it is a matter of great public concern. From the viewpoint of the wage earner there is little difference between not earning at all and earning wholly for a creditor. Pauperism may be the necessary result of either . . .The new opportunity in life and the clear field for future effort, which it is the purpose of the bankruptcy act to afford the emancipated debtor, would be of little value to the wage earner if he were obliged to face the necessity of devoting the whole or a considerable portion of his earnings for an indefinite time in the future to the payment of indebtedness incurred prior to his bankruptcy.[9]

Having said this, it is important to note that there is an undertone of another early American tradition—puritanism—in the analysis of the fresh start. This financial rebirth is to be available to the worthy, not the worthless; to the financially luckless, not the feckless layabouts. The moral strain in fresh start analysis cannot be ignored. Courts are often inclined to stretch a statutory point when they believe they are

---

[7] Richard E. Flint, *Bankruptcy Policy: Toward a Moral Justification for Financial Rehabilitation of the Consumer Debtor*, 48 Wash. & Lee L. Rev. 515, 519-20. (1991).

[8] See Bankruptcy Code § 304(c)(6). For a fuller discussion of international bankruptcy, see Chapter 21 of this book.

[9] Local Loan Co. v. Hunt, 292 U.S. 234, 244-45 (1934) (citations omitted). Note that these words, so supportive of the fresh start, came from a Court that was generally viewed as reactionary, and unsympathetic to the plight of those economically crushed by the ongoing Great Depression.

thereby increasing the chances of a worthy debtor. By contrast, some at least will ignore statutory language when it seems to benefit an artful dodger.[10]

There is also a persistent question about whether the fresh start policy is relevant to courts making decisions (as opposed to Congress passing laws). There is a growing view, at least on the Supreme Court, that bankruptcy policy is for Congress. If Congress wants to focus on giving debtors a fresh start, it is (within the broad limits of the Constitution) free to do so. The job of the judge is rather more circumscribed; the judge is to make a reasonable interpretation of the language that Congress has enacted in the Code. When that language promotes a fresh start, the court should not narrow it; when by contrast it protects the interests of creditors, the court should not ignore it to promote the debtor's interests.

[C]—Creditors' Rights

No bankruptcy law has ever been wholly pro-debtor (despite occasional hyperbole from creditor groups). Indeed, some creditor rights are given rather scrupulous protection in bankruptcy. Most notably, the Code follows the long tradition of giving special status to "property" interests, such as mortgages, security interests, and leasehold rights. Broadly speaking, the debtor cannot claim a fresh start free of those interests, unless their holders have agreed otherwise or been paid in full.

Despite the fresh-start policy, a cursory reading of the Code gives the impression that the rights of creditors are paramount. It is certainly true that more of the statute deals with debt than with discharge. However, as Professor Breitowitz has noted the number of statutory provisions dealing with distribution is at the very least misleading. Reality is discharge:

> One who does nothing more than peruse the provisions of the Code . . . would be blissfully unaware of the economic realities of the typical consumer proceeding. As noted, the Code contemplates the possibility of creditors placing a debtor into bankruptcy involuntarily; sets out detailed provisions regarding creditors' meetings and election of trustees; and specifies priorities in the distribution of assets. In point of fact, involuntary petitions against consumers are virtually unknown; few, if any, creditors even bother to show up at a creditors' meeting; indeed, even the interim trustee who generally does attend may do nothing more than look over the schedules and ask the debtor if the information is accurate, a procedure that typically takes less than 15 minutes. Trustees are seldom elected because of lack of creditor interest notwithstanding the fact that only a minimal indication of such interest is required. Finally, for all practical purposes, the priority and distribution provisions of Chapter 7 are virtually a dead letter; in over 90% of all cases, there are no assets available for distribution after exemptions are claimed.[11]

---

[10] For an example of this, see § 18.08[A][2], which discusses the courts' strained interpretation of the statutory provisions that governed Chapter 13 plan confirmation prior to the 1984 Amendments to the Code.

[11] Irving A. Breitowitz, *New Developments in Consumer Bankruptcies: Chapter 7 Dismissal on the Basis of "Substantial Abuse,"* 59 Am. Bankr. L. J. 335 (1984).

Note especially the fact that unsecured creditors, at least, rarely benefit from bankruptcy. A number of studies have confirmed that in the typical bankruptcy, which is an individual Chapter 7 case, there are no unencumbered, non-exempt assets to distribute to the unsecured creditors. This does not necessarily mean that the debtor retains all of the property. To the contrary, a major reason why there is nothing for unsecured creditors is that there are secured creditors. At least one study found that nearly all non-exempt property was encumbered; thus, many bankruptcies are nothing more than the splitting of the debtor's property between the debtor and the secured creditors, with the latter taking by far the larger share.[12] To the extent this is true, the whole purpose of bankruptcy as a collection device is called into question; secured creditors do not need and generally do not want the assistance of a bankruptcy court in seizing their collateral.

Since 1978, there has been a hit-and-miss tendency to broaden the rights of creditors.[13] Many of the major amendments of the Code since its original enactment in 1978 have been broadly pro-creditor.[14] The 1994 Amendments continued this pattern; although they include a few provisions that aid debtors, they include many more that strengthen the position of creditors, especially lessors and lien creditors. Whether these changes do any good or not is questionable, and one's evaluation depends largely upon one's assumptions. If a substantial number of bankrupts have untapped ability to pay, then it may well be wise to reform the Code still further. To the extent payment can be squeezed out without undue transaction costs, the cost of credit generally should drop because the risk to creditors will drop. Conversely, if there is little left to get, however hard we squeeze, then it is pointless to try.

Finally, bankruptcy may clear off most existing debts, but it does not provide the debtor with an unblotted fresh start. Generally speaking, private companies are not prevented from discriminating on the basis of the debtor's bankruptcy. Lenders may refuse to grant credit, or may do so only on discriminatory terms.[15] The fact of bankruptcy may be kept in the debtor's credit report for 10 years[16] which may reduce access to credit. Bankruptcy is thus by no means cost-free even to the no-asset debtor.

[D]—The Role of Murphy's Law

Professor Bowers has recently published several amusing and provocative articles that remind us of a basic rule of bankruptcy and the rest of life. He begins with Murphy's law: Whatever can go wrong, will go wrong. He proceeds, colorfully but

---

[12] Michael J. Herbert & Domenic E. Pacitti, *Down and Out in Richmond, Virginia: The Distribution of Assets in Chapter 7 Bankruptcy Proceedings Closed During 1984-1987*, 22 U. Rich. L. Rev. 303 (1988).

[13] See Paul M. Black & Michael J. Herbert, *Bankcard's Revenge: A Critique of the 1984 Consumer Credit Amendments to the Bankruptcy Code*, 19 U. Rich. L. Rev. 845 (1985).

[14] A notable exception is the 1986 enactment of Chapter 12, which is decidedly pro-family farmer.

[15] See § 12.10 of this book.

[16] Fair Credit Reporting Act § 605(a)(1), 15 U.S.C. § 1681c(a)(1)(1988).

thoughtfully, to the conclusion that a large part of bankruptcy law may simply be pointless:

> The impulse to have bankruptcy law and to tinker with it after we have it comes not from notions of "equality" or "efficiency" but rather from wishful thinking. We are doomed because we harbor hope, a specific belief in alchemy: that if we are only clever enough, gold can be squeezed from turnips. Our fatal wish is for a world in which disasters don't occur. We don't really care if anybody gets paid "equally" or paid "efficiently." What we really want is a world in which they get paid. Period[17]

While this critique may be somewhat overstated, it is certainly true that in most bankruptcies the only significant difference between the bankruptcy resolution and the non-bankruptcy resolution of financial failure is that in the former, the obligor receives a legally binding discharge.[18] Whether this is sufficient to justify a bankruptcy system is at least debatable.

§ 1.02 Modern Theories of Insolvency Law

[A]—Introduction

For many years, bankruptcy law existed without much of a theoretical context; apart from a few shibboleths, little was said and less was considered by lawyers and judges about the effect and proper role of bankruptcy. There was only one broadly recognized history of bankruptcy law, Charles Warren's Bankruptcy In United States History, published in 1935. This masked a sporadic and informal legal literature that was found in cases, occasional articles, and speeches. There were also studies made from the perspective of other disciplines. However, formal efforts to draw together the disparate strands of bankruptcy thinking were, at least as far as lawyers were concerned, rare.

This is no longer true. Indeed, bankruptcy law may now suffer from a surplus of theories, some of them very worthy and profoundly insightful but perhaps so removed from the realities of practice that even their authors sometimes confess they are unlikely to affect actual practice, at least in the short run. There has also been a renewed interest in bankruptcy history[19] and a rather new effort to gather

---

[17] James W. Bowers, *Groping and Coping in the Shadow of Murphy's Law: Bankruptcy Theory and the Elementary Economics of Failure*, 88 Mich. L. Rev. 2097, 2145 (1990). This article focuses on bankruptcy law generally; for a somewhat similar critique of Chapter 11 see James W. Bowers, *The Fantastic Wisconsylvania Zero-Bureaucratic-Cost School of Bankruptcy Theory: A Comment*, 91 Mich. L. Rev. 1773 (1993).

[18] Michael J. Herbert & Domenic E. Pacitti, *Down and Out in Richmond, Virginia: The Distribution of Assets in Chapter 7 Bankruptcy Proceedings Closed During 1984-87*, 22 U. Rich. L. Rev 303 (1988).

[19] For just a few of the many articles that have blended historical review with analysis of contemporary bankruptcy problems, see John C. McCoid, II, *Pendency Interest in Bankruptcy*, 68 Am. Bankr. L.J. 1 (1994); Charles Jordan Tabb, *Rethinking Preferences*, 43 S.C. L. Rev. 981 (1992); John C. McCoid, II, *Setoff: Why Bankruptcy Priority?*, 75 Va. L. Rev. 15 (1989).

empirical data about bankruptcy practice and the substantive impact of bankruptcy law on real-world behavior.[20] It is certainly true that for the theorist, the historian, and the pragmatist, there is now a wealth of material tackling bankruptcy from almost every conceivable perspective, and nearly every mode of legal writing, from the dryly statistical to the vividly narrative.[21] Almost every current in present legal thought, with the possible exception of Critical Race Theory, is now present in the bankruptcy literature.

It is unfortunately impossible even to sample the full range of this literature. I address, and very briefly, only the two most important strains of bankruptcy theory. These two—which I dub "economic" and "social"—dominate, both in quantity and in influence, the bankruptcy debate. These are not approaches that are in any sense remote from the daily grind of bankruptcy work. They directly influence court opinions and Congressional enactments. While other approaches have their own distinct merits, they have not (as yet) had much impact on the nitty-gritty of bankruptcy work. Even these two approaches are only sketched; it would take at least the full length of the book to evaluate them fully. The next few pages, however, should give both a taste of the work done and references to a few of the most valuable sources.

[B]—"Economic" Theories

Much contemporary legal theory is rooted in the assumption that laws, or at least laws that deal with property rights, should have as their goal the advancement of economic efficiency. Although the law and economics movement is diffuse, and includes scholars of many different political and social perspectives[22] a number of its leading proponents are associated with what is variously referred to in popular parlance as "Chicago School" or "Neo-Classical" economics.[23] Speaking very broadly, this tradition assumes that the primary, if not the only, motivation of individuals is to increase their wealth (a term that sometimes is limited to its ordinary

---

[20] For a few of the most recent efforts in this regard, see Teresa A. Sullivan, Elizabeth Warren & Jay Lawrence Westbrook, *The Persistence of Local Legal Culture: Twenty Years of Evidence From the Bankruptcy Courts*, 17 Harv. J. Law & Pub. Policy 801 (1994); Paul B. Lackey, *An Empirical Survey and Proposed Bankruptcy Code Section Concerning the Propriety of Bidding Incentives in a Bankruptcy Sale of Assets*, 93 Colum. L. Rev. 720 (1993); and Ian Domowitz & Thomas L. Eovaldi, *The Impact of the Bankruptcy Reform Act of 1978 on Consumer Bankruptcy*, 36 J. Law & Econ. 803 (1993). Many other empirical studies are discussed throughout this work.

[21] For an example of a work that contains both the statistics and their dramatization, see Teresa A. Sullivan, Elizabeth Warren & Jay Lawrence Westbrook, As We Forgive Our Debtors: Bankruptcy and Consumer Credit in America (1989).

[22] See, for example, Randy E. Barnett, *Post-Chicago Law and Economics*, 65 Chi.-Kent L. Rev. 3 (1989); Christopher J. Bruce, *A Positive Analysis of Methodology in the Law and Economics Literature*, 12 Hamline L. Rev. 197 (1989).

[23] Note that neither label is entirely satisfactory, since many of the tenants of this approach were first developed in Austria, not Chicago, and their selection of the "classics" is rather narrowly defined. David Ricardo is quintessentially "in" while Karl Marx is definitively "out."

meaning and sometimes defined so broadly as to become merely a synonym for personal preferences). It also assumes that people's choices are made rationally, and that people, when making choices, are highly sensitive to slight marginal advantages.

Although sometimes caricatured as a disingenuous smokescreen for the interests of the business community, neoclassical economics at the very least raises a number of provocative questions regarding many common assumptions about legal policy and legal rules. It also demands a rigorous logic that is not always followed by those who reject its tenets. It is hardly surprising that bankruptcy has attracted much attention from law and economics scholars. It is, after all, in bankruptcy that many economic issues come to a head.

A number of the most distinguished bankruptcy academics of recent years are decidedly in the neoclassical economics mold. To name only two, Thomas Jackson[24] and Douglas Baird,[25] have written, separately and in collaboration, on many bankruptcy issues. They have been particularly influential in their efforts to forge a unifying rationale for bankruptcy law. Among many distinguished judges who broadly adhere to a law and economics approach to bankruptcy law, Seventh Circuit Judge Frank Easterbrook may reasonably take pride of place. He has written a number of important cases that combine rigorous analysis with a lucid and engaging prose style.[26]

The single most influential academic work of this group is Jackson's The Logic and Limits of Bankruptcy, published in 1986. While it is hardly fair to reduce a complex and thoughtful work to a few sentences, its core can be suggested by the following summary. In Jackson's view, the proper function of bankruptcy is to provide a collective creditor proceeding that efficiently enforces existing non-bankruptcy rights. To the extent possible, bankruptcy should not tinker with substantive rights; when it does so, the resultant uncertainty increases costs without correspondingly increasing benefits. Rather, bankruptcy should focus on an inefficiency that is innate to individual, atomistic proceedings. When one creditor sues a debtor, that creditor's only interest is maximizing its own recovery, regardless of whether this is consonant with the greatest possible recovery for creditors as a whole. However, if creditors act collectively, they become concerned about overall recovery. This is not because of altruism. Rather, it is because over time it makes more sense for creditors to share evenly in larger pools of assets from many debtors than to take their chances of being able to seize a disproportionate number of assets from an occasional, and smaller pool of assets owned by a few of its debtors.

For example, imagine creditors A, B, and C, each of whom is owed $1,000 by debtor X, $1,000 by debtor Y, and $1,000 by debtor Z. The value of each debtor's assets depends on the way in which those assets are dealt with. The value is only $1,000 if the debtors are liquidated in a piecemeal fashion but is $2,000 if the debtors are either liquidated in an orderly fashion or reorganized.

---

[24] Currently President of the University of Rochester.

[25] Presently Dean of the University of Chicago Law School.

[26] This is not to denigrate Judge Easterbrook's colleague and sometime soulmate, Judge Richard Posner, who is probably the single best known law-and-economics scholar in the country.

If creditors A, B, and C act independently of each other, then each will attempt to seize all available assets of each debtor. This will cause a disorderly liquidation, thus limiting the value of the assets to $1,000 per debtor. Independent action makes it impossible for the debtors to reorganize or conduct an orderly liquidation; this reduces the value of each debtor's assets. This in turn reduces the total payout to the creditors as a whole.

Suppose that A gets lucky in its independent action against X and collects the entire amount of its debt. This means that B and C get nothing, because A has exhausted X's assets. A has obtained full payment on one debt; and if it gets equally lucky in its actions against Y and Z, it will be paid in full on all three of its debts. The corrolary of this is that if A is three times lucky, B and C get nothing at all from X, Y or Z.

In the example given, it is easy to see why B and C would prefer orderly liquidations: but why would A? The reason is that A has no guarantee that it will be lucky once, let alone three times. Assuming that B and C are equally well situated, A's chance of getting lucky in any action is only 1 in 3; its chance of getting lucky in all (and thus being paid in full) is 1 in 9; and there is an 8 in 27 chance that it will get nothing at all.

By contrast, assume that collective action of the three creditors would permit the debtors to reorganize, or liquidate in an orderly fashion, and thereby increase the value of each debtor's assets to $2,000. Moreover, assume that the $2,000 would be equally divided among the three creditors. In that case, each creditor would receive two-thirds of its claims. This would directly benefit the creditors, who would exchange a remote chance of full payment and a real chance of no payment for a certainty of substantial payment. It would indirectly benefit the rest of the economy; the risk and uncertainty faced by lenders would be reduced and they would in turn be able to make better (and cheaper) decisions about their lending.

For many practical reasons, the three creditors find it difficult or impossible to agree to the efficient model of a collective action. Bankruptcy fills this gap by making the choice for them. It leaves them with their existing rights (thus avoiding an increase in uncertainty) but forces them to exercise those rights in a manner that in every case benefits them as a whole and over time benefits them individually. This is often called the "creditor's bargain"—it is the deal they would make if they could, and is made for them because there are insuperable practical barriers to them making it for themselves. Whatever paternalism is involved in imposing this choice is justified by the fact that this is the choice they would really like to make, and, in a more perfect market, the choice they would make.

Just as it is impossible in a short space to do more than suggest the full dimensions of this theory, it is impossible in even less space to indicate a couple of the criticisms. The Creditor's Bargain is based on a number of assumptions for which there is little systematic empirical evidence. For example, the theory in its simplest form assumes that creditors are similarly situated. Creditors who can systematically secure all of the assets of each of their debtors have little or no incentive to enter into any bargain that would force them to share those assets with other creditors. In addition, the Creditors' Bargain model assumes that collective proceedings result in greater payouts to creditors—while true in some situations, this is clearly untrue in others.[27] For example, if a reorganization increases the value of the debtor's assets by $1,000,000 but costs $1,200,000 the reorganization has in fact subtracted value, not added it, and the creditors would have been better off in liquidation. It is the perception of at least some lawyers and scholars that many Chapter 11 cases have precisely this result.[28] In any event, the Creditor's Bargain theory has sparked lively debate and much dissent.[29]

There is also a purely practical objection to using this theory to explain all bankruptcy law. Like it or not, Congress has never enacted a bankruptcy law that single-mindedly aimed at maximizing return to creditors. Bankruptcy law expresses a series of compromises over a number of issues, not all of them (perhaps not many of them) rooted in the economics of the Creditor's Bargain. And, given the Supreme Court's present penchant for following the "plain meaning" of Congress' enacted statutory language, arguments that the Code's text should be interpreted in accordance with this (or any other theory) are likely to fail.[30] This objection, of course, does not speak to whether the Creditor's Bargain ought to be the touchstone of bankruptcy, but only to whether it is.

Finally, at least some aspects of the economic approach have failed to find support, or at least undisputed support, from empirical data. For example, economic theory indicates that the rate of bankruptcy filings should be closely correlated with the scope of exemptions. Exempt property is the property that the debtor gets to keep, even after bankruptcy; and exemptions vary from state to state. If people are rational wealth-maximizers, they should be attracted to bankruptcy when and where exemptions are extensive (because they can shed debt at little price, that is, with little loss of their assets) and should be less interested in bankruptcy when and where exemptions are low (because the cost of discharging their debts is effectively increased). In fact, what empirical data there is indicates that there is little or no relationship between the rate of filing and the level of exemptions.[31] This of course

---

[27] For an aspect of this, see the criticisms of Chapter 11 reorganization discussed in § 17.01 of this book.

[28] In fairness, this issue may be more of a problem with the Bankruptcy Code's inadequate facilitation of the Creditors' Bargain model than a defect in the model itself.

[29] For just a few of the more interesting critiques of the Creditor's Bargain, see Linda J. Rusch, *Bankruptcy Reorganization Jurisprudence: Matters of Belief, Faith, and Hope—Stepping into the Fourth Dimension*, 55 Mont. L. Rev. 9 (1994); Susan Block-Lieb, *Fishing in Muddy Waters: Clarifying the Common Pool Analogy as Applied to the Standard for Commencement of a Bankruptcy Case*, 42 Am. U. L. Rev. 337 (1993): David G. Carlson, *Bankruptcy Theory and the Creditors' Bargain*, 61 U. Cinn. L. Rev 453 (1992); Donald R. Korobkin, *Value and Rationality in Bankruptcy Decisionmaking*, 33 Wm. & Mary L. Rev. 333 (1992).

[30] For a discussion of the Supreme Court's textualist approach to interpretation, see § 1.03 of this chapter. For a good example of a case in which the Court opted for plain meaning over plausible interpretation based on Jackson's theory, see United Savings Ass'n of Texas v. Timbers of Inwood Forest Assocs., 484 U.S. 365 (1988).

[31] See § 1.02[C] of this chapter.

does not disprove the theory; there are many things that can explain the lack of correlation.[32]

All this having been said, however, it is undeniable that the neo-classical economic analysis of bankruptcy has been influential and has raised many disturbing questions. To some extent at least, bankruptcy laws can encourage unnecessary filings, can impose costly uncertainty, and can result in wastefully increasing the cost of credit. Curiously, although many of the critiques have focused on consumer bankruptcy, the evidence suggests that they are most on point when applied to small business bankruptcies. There is substantial reason to believe that abuse and unnecessary discharge is more likely to occur in that setting.

[C]—"Social" Theories

In contrast to the economic perspective on bankruptcy law is what might reasonably be referred to as the social perspective. In the view of many commentators, bankruptcy is a multi-faceted body of law that both represents a number of political compromises and seeks to achieve a number of not always coherent ends. The social theorists tend to be somewhat more interested in empirical data and pragmatic issues than the economic theorists. They tend to shy away from attempts to formulate fundamental rules and all-encompassing models. This often means that they have a warmer reception among practitioners (pragmatists all) than do the high theorists of neo-classical economics. It also means that their work tends to be "softer"—more nuanced, perhaps, but often a trifle fuzzy in its conclusions.

The sacred text of this approach is undoubtedly As We Forgive Our Debtors.[33] This is a brilliant, readable, and very ambitious book researched and written by two law professors, Elizabeth Warren[34] and Jay Westbrook,[35] plus one sociologist, Teresa A. Sullivan.[36] It attempts a picture of consumer bankruptcy without imposing a firm theoretical model. The work has attained iconic status among those broadly sympathetic to the social theories of bankruptcy; indeed, one can (without bothering to read the text) almost always predict the attitude and conclusions of an author by the number of cites to As We Forgive in the footnotes.

The book debunks a number of significant beliefs about bankruptcy that are based on more myth than fact. For example, consumer debtors come from a broad range

---

[32] For example, there are data that indicate few debtors are able to use all of their exemptions even in a low exemption state; see Michael J. Herbert & Domenic E. Pacitti, *Down and Out in Richmond, Virginia: The Distribution of Assets in Chapter 7 Bankruptcy Proceedings Closed During 1984-87*, 22 U. Rich. L. Rev. 303, 316-17 (1988). If there are indeed only a handful of people who are able to benefit from generous exemptions, the presence of those exemptions would not have any significant effect on filings.

[33] Readers attuned to bias should be aware that I have previously written a favorable review of this book, and am, with some reservations, in agreement with its observations and conclusions.

[34] William A. Schnader Professor of Commercial Law at the University of Pennsylvania.

[35] Benno C. Schmidt Chair of Business Law at the University of Texas.

[36] Professor of Sociology and Law at the University of Texas.

of occupations,[37] they are about as likely to own their own homes as the rest of the population[38] and bankruptcy is generally precipitated by a long period of chronic economic trouble rather than by an acute crisis.[39] According to the book, there is little evidence that consumer bankrupts use the system to gain economic advantage. Bankruptcy recidivism is rare; few people file a second bankruptcy after gaining discharge in a first.[40]

Many other studies support at least some of the contentions made in As We Forgive. For example, there is evidence that bankruptcy filing rates are not much affected by whether applicable exemption law is pro-debtor or pro-creditor.[41] There is plenty of evidence that most bankrupts have few assets.[42] There is also evidence that few debtors are actually able to use all of their exemptions.[43]

Many criticisms can be and have been leveled at the social theories. Although the social theorists have gathered a good deal of empirical support for their view in consumer bankruptcy, the empirical work regarding commercial bankruptcies is both less extensive and more ambiguous. Recently, Professor Warren has attacked the law and economics critique of business reorganizations under Chapter 11. The effectiveness of this critique remains subject to debate.[44]

Even the work on consumer bankruptcy has been critiqued. Most of the studies made have very limited samples. As We Forgive Our Debtors involved only 1529 cases, all filed in 1981, gathered from ten districts in three states.[45] Moreover, the As We Forgive database is now somewhat old[46] and may no longer be representative. The opportunities for abuse under the Code may only gradually have come to the attention of lawyers, and the situation now may be rather different from it was when the data were gathered. Moreover, the studies may not always have been asking the right questions; currently, there is a great deal of concern about the use of bankruptcy for the sole purpose of postponing eviction for a few months. This

---

[37] As We Forgive Our Debtors 85-95.

[38] *Id.* at 129.

[39] *Id.* at 168-69, 305.

[40] *Id.* at 192-95.

[41] U.S. General Accounting Office, Report to the Chairman Committee on the Judiciary, House of Representatives, Bankruptcy Reform Act of 1978 — A Before and After Look (1983); Woodward & Woodward, *Exemptions as an Incentive to Voluntary Bankruptcy: An Emperical Study*, 88 Com. L.J. 309 (1983).

[42] Michael J. Herbert & Domenic E. Pacitti, *Down and Out in Richmond, Virginia: The Distribution of Assets in Chapter 7 Bankruptcy Proceedings Closed During 1984-1987*, 22 U. Rich. L. Rev. 303, 310-11 (1988)

[43] *Id.* at 316-17.

[44] See § 17.01 of this book.

[45] As We Forgive Our Debtors 18-20.

[46] The data were gathered from cases filed less than three years after the Bankruptcy Code was effective, and before a number of important amendments were made. They may thus reflect a less sophisticated practice than has since developed, and do not at all reflect the effect of statutory changes.

is somewhat different from the issue examined in many of the consumer bankruptcy studies: the use of bankruptcy to discharge debt while retaining property.

Most significantly, the social theorists, like the economic theorists, occasionally succumb both to overgeneralization and the desire to make a clear point. If the evidence indicates that bankruptcy abuse is not epidemic, that does not necessarily mean that it is trivial. Even if the claim that a billion or more dollars in debt is unnecessarily discharged each year is exaggerated, that does not mean that there is hardly any unnecessary discharge. While it is certainly true that our credit and banking system has not collapsed because of the Bankruptcy Code, this does not mean that the Code has caused no injury. Finally, the apparently low rate of bankruptcy abuse might be explained as an effect of Congressional and judicial sensitivity to the abuses that the economic theorists warned about.

Be warned: the debates over bankruptcy, which are as old as bankruptcy law itself, are not likely to end in clear victory for any viewpoint. In part, this is due to the incomplete and ambiguous nature of the available information. In greater part, it is due to fundamental differences about the goals to be served. To the social theorists, a bit of economic inefficiency may well be a modest price to pay for the financial (and even psychological) fresh start. To the economic theorists, that inefficiency is an implicit tax on the most productive sectors of society and thus retards the economic prospects of all. This is not a difference in perspective that would be eliminated even by perfect data. The debate over whether debtors are desperate or desperadoes is thus not likely ever to be resolved.

§ 1.03 Interpretation of the Bankruptcy Code

For several generations, it has been a commonplace that many traditional rules of statutory interpretation have outlived their usefulness. Chief among these is what has commonly been known as the "plain meaning" rule. Traditionally, if the text of a statute has a plain, unambiguous meaning that does not produce an absurd or unconstitutional result, that meaning controls and the court will not listen to other sources (such as committee reports, floor debate, and other legislative history). While the court will attempt to make sense of the entire statutory text, and fit the meaning of words and phrases within the entire body of the statute, it will only in rare cases go outside of the text. It is, to a degree, analogous to the parol evidence rule in contracts.

The plain meaning rule has probably remained the primary method of statutory interpretation used by courts, especially state courts. However, weaknesses in the rule have long been noted, and innumerable studies have attacked it as unworkable or incoherent. It has long been true that federal courts (which, unlike most state courts, have available to them abundant legislative history) have largely rejected the plain meaning rule. In the specific context of bankruptcy, there has been a long tradition of paying minimal heed to the statute and maximum attention to perceived bankruptcy policy.[47]

In recent years, however, there has been a revived interest in the plain meaning rule. Spearheaded by Justice Scalia, a number of Supreme Court Justices have insisted that, despite its admitted flaws, the plain meaning rule enforces a more appropriate division of authority between the legislative and judicial branches, and forces the former to do what it ought to do—that is, to say what it means. With an occasional exception[48] the Court has insisted on the primacy of enacted text to determine what bankruptcy law is.[49] This insistence on textualism has yet to transform entirely even the Supreme Court's bankruptcy jurisprudence, let alone that of lower courts. In a number of cases the Court has, rather to Justice Scalia's annoyance, added to its discussion of the text a review of the legislative history; this in the face of that Justice's insistence that the legislative history part of the opinion is but a waste of thought, ink and paper. However, it must be said that the plain meaning rule is at least an honored method of interpretation, and may well become dominant.[50] Throughout this book, we will be examining whether the plain meaning revival will affect unsettled questions or even those that have a long precedential history behind them.

Critics of the plain meaning rule are many. The rule has been attacked as absurd (if for no other reason than that no English word or phrase is entirely without ambiguity). It has been seen as a block to the rational development of bankruptcy law, because Congress cannot constantly revise the statute to make its meaning clearer. Indeed, the great majority of the academic commentary on the rule is hostile.[51]

---

[47] At the risk of again plugging this publisher's product, I recall an incident during my early days in practice. Faced with a tricky question under the old Bankruptcy Act, I was told by my supervising partner to "look it up in Collier's. If you can't find anything, check the statute."

[48] See Dewsnup v. Timm, 502 U.S. 410 (1992), in which the Court made a complete hash of the plain meaning of the phrase "allowed secured claim."

[49] See Patterson v. Shumate, 112 S.Ct. 2242 (1992); Toibb v. Radloff, 501 U.S. 157 (1991); United States v. Ron Pair Enterprises, 489 U.S. 235 (1989).

[50] It has been suggested that the addition of Justice Breyer to the Court may tilt the balance toward more use of legislative history; his Circuit Court decisions and his comments on the use of legislative history have indicated that he is not sympathetic to the plain meaning rule. See Walter A. Effross, *Another Vote for Legislative History? New Justice Breyer's Bankruptcy Decisions*, XIII Am. Bankr. Inst. J. No. 6 1 (July/August 1994).

[51] See, for example, Bradley C. Karkkainen, *"Plain Meaning": Justice Scalia's Jurisprudence of Strict Construction*, 17 Harv. J. Law & Pub. Policy 401 (1994); Frederick Schauer, *Statutory Construction and the Coordinating Function of Plain Meaning*, 1990 Sup. Ct. Rev. 231; Nicholas S. Zeppos, Justice Scalia's Textualism: *The "New" New Legal Process*, 12 Cardozo L. Rev. 1597 (1991). For a balanced, but generally positive review of the plain meaning rule, see Robert K. Rasmussen, *A Study of the Costs and Benefits of Textualism: The Supreme Court's Bankruptcy Cases*, 71 Wash. U. L.Q. 535 (1993).

§ 1.04 Constitutional Limits of Bankruptcy Law

For all of the significance of bankruptcy law, there is surprisingly little delineation of its constitutional boundaries. There has been only one Supreme Court case—a very troublesome case—about the scope of bankruptcy jurisdiction. That case, *Northern Pipeline*, is discussed in the chapter on jurisdiction.[52] Supreme Court pronouncements regarding the substantive scope of bankruptcy law are almost as scarce.

In a way, this is surprising. The power given by the Constitution to Congress, to enact uniform laws on the subject of bankruptcy, carries with it potential powers nearly as broad as those contained in the Commerce Clause. This is not, however, a power without limits.

The same constitution that permits bankruptcy also protects property.[53] At some point, not well defined, substantive bankruptcy law becomes an impermissible deprivation of property rights. For the most part this problem has been dealt with in Congressional debate rather than court decision. Even when it has arisen in bankruptcy litigation, the courts have generally tried to dodge the constitutional issue by interpreting the statutory language in a way that avoids the problem.

Broadly speaking, the general assumption is that Congress may do virtually anything under its bankruptcy power that is reasonably related to dealing with insolvents provided that it acts prospectively. Congress may even deviate from its longstanding tradition of protecting certain property interests in bankruptcy, so long as it does so only with regard to subsequently arising property rights. A constitutional problem does arise if the Congress enacts a bankruptcy law that seriously impairs pre-existing property rights.[54] This attitude conforms to the generally hands-off approach that the Supreme Court has taken toward regulation of property rights since the late 1930's.

§ 1.05 Some Basic Concepts about Business Law

In this section, I briefly discuss some very basic concepts about business and finance law and practice that may be helpful to a student who has no background in either. All of these concepts are important background to bankruptcy law. All of them should be familiar to a student who has taken Corporations or Business Organizations.

"Legal Entity." Under our law, human beings are not the only persons with property and other rights. Artificial entities, created today primarily for business purposes (although including non-profits and municipalities), are also "persons" with names, rights, and obligations. A business corporation is one such entity; it may own property and act in its own right (although those actions, obviously, must be

---

[52] See § 5.03 of this book.

[53] Notably but not exclusively in the Fifth Amendment of the Constitution, which prohibits the federal government from depriving any person of property without due process of law.

[54] See § 11.09 of this book.

through the agency of human beings). It is owned by stockholders; howeve rarely applicable exceptions, these stockholders are not personally liable for the corporation's debts. By contrast, a partnership, while also a legal entity for most purposes, is only partially independent of its owners. Although a partnership can today own property, and act in its own right, ultimately, its general partners are personally liable for its debts. If the partnership has limited partners, however, those partners are more like stockholders in a corporation; they are not personally liable for partnership debts. There are many variations of these basic structures; a recently developed, and very popular, one is the limited liability partnership, which received recognition in the 1994 Amendments to the Bankruptcy Code. The exact attributes of the various types of legal entity, and the circumstances under which an owner is liable for an entity's debts, vary slightly from state to state.

Things are quite different if the business and the owner are one and the same. A business operated by a sole proprietor is not a separate legal entity. The business and its owner are legally identical. The Michael J. Herbert who files a Schedule "C" (business) tax return and receives the occasional small royalty from Matthew Bender & Co. is indistinguishable from the Michael J. Herbert who with pained expression dispatches a monthly check to the bank that has the mortgage on his personal residence. Every business creditor and every personal creditor has the right to pursue both his business and his non-business property.

In bankruptcy, these rules remain. The stockholders of a corporate bankrupt are in nearly all situations protected from personal liability. So too are limited partners. General partners remain residually liable for the partnership's unpaid debts (although the bankruptcy of the partnership does not directly involve the partners, and vice-versa). A proprietorship bankruptcy is the bankruptcy of both business and owner; personal and business debts, personal and business assets are all part of the same pot. There are a few significant differences between the proprietor bankruptcy and a consumer bankruptcy, but these do not relate to legal entity.

"Debt" and "Equity" (or "stock"). Broadly speaking, the financial structure of any business entity is divided into debt and equity. In its most basic form, debt is an absolute obligation owed to another. By absolute, I mean that the obligation exists regardless of the entity's financial health. Even if the entity is losing money, a debt must still be paid according to its terms. By contrast, equity is the ownership of whatever is left after all debts have been paid. If there is nothing left, the equity holder owns nothing. Owning equity is more risky than owning debt, because equity comes behind debt in the pecking order; however, equity holders have a chance for greater profits than debt holders. Generally speaking, a debt holder is entitled to principal plus interest, whether or not the company makes money. An equity holder is entitled to distributions, including dividends, only if the company (1) makes enough money to permit a distribution and (2) chooses to make a distribution. If the company is very successful, the equity holders will have a greater gain than the debt holders. The gain of the debt holder is capped by the interest rate. The gain of the equity holder has no limit; whatever is left after debt belongs to it. Even if the company chooses never to pay a dividend, the equity holder's interest generally grows in value because the net value of the company belongs to the equity holders.

For example, if you had lent $1000 to Wal-Mart in 1970 at 7% interest for 30 years you would still be getting a steady $70 per year and would reasonably expect the repayment of your $1000 principal in 2000. If you had purchased Wal-Mart stock in the same year, your investment would be worth much more than you paid for it and the dividends alone might well exceed your initial investment. In short, equity enjoys the unlimited benefits of success while bearing the greatest risk; debt enjoys lower risk at the cost of limited gain.

"Fiduciary Duty." Most of our law is based on the notion that people are free to act in their own self-interest, so long as certain fundamental rules are obeyed—for example, every adult is obligated to act as a reasonably prudent person, and you do not have the right to poison Uncle Mortimer's tea just because he has left you his vast fortune. However, in some relationships, often but by no means always business relationships, one person owes another a fiduciary duty—which means that he or she must to a considerable degree subordinate self-interest to the interest of the other. Employees owe fiduciary duties to their employers, and thus cannot divert business opportunities to personal benefit; lawyers owe fiduciary duties to clients and thus cannot sell their dirty secrets to the tabloid press. In bankruptcy, this issue becomes important because the trustee and the debtor in possession owe a fiduciary duty to the bankruptcy estate. They are supposed to devote their efforts to the best possible liquidation or reorganization—best possible being largely synonymous with maximum return to creditors.

§ 1.06 Some Interminably Recurring Terms of Art

In this section, I spell out a few bankruptcy terms of art that appear over and over again throughout these materials. Some of these terms are more fully explored elsewhere.

"After notice and a hearing." There are many bankruptcy actions that may be taken only "after notice and a hearing." This phrase does not mean quite what it appears to mean. It does not mean that there must be a hearing; neither does it mean that the hearing or the notice take any particular form. Rather, it means that the court may act only "after such notice as is appropriate in the particular circumstances" and after "such opportunity for a hearing as is appropriate in the particular circumstances."[55] Indeed, if proper notice has been given, the court may act without any hearing at all if the hearing is not requested in a timely fashion by a party in interest or there is not enough time for a hearing.[56] In general, therefore, where I discuss a matter that requires notice and a hearing, I use the more precise phrase, "notice and an opportunity for a hearing."

"Bankruptcy Act" or "Act" refers to the bankruptcy law that was in force from 1898 to 1979.

"Bankruptcy Reform Act" refers to the law that was passed in 1978 to replace the Bankruptcy act and various other related laws.

---

[55] Bankruptcy Code § 102(1)(A).

[56] Bankruptcy Code § 102(1)(B).

"Bankruptcy Code" or "Code" refers to the current substantive bankruptcy law, enacted as part of the Bankruptcy Reform Act in 1978, effective October 1, 1979. It has been frequently amended, most recently in 1994.

"Claim" refers to an obligation of the debtor (or of the estate) that is dealt with in the bankruptcy.

"Debtor" This word has two connected meanings. It refers to an obligor, such as a person who has borrowed money to buy a house or a car. It also refers to the bankrupt—Congress in 1978 banished the term "bankrupt" from bankruptcy law.

"Estate" refers to the legal entity that is created by the bankruptcy proceeding. The estate is not the debtor.

"Interest" sometimes refers to ownership of the debtor and sometimes to ownership of property of either the debtor or the estate. In the former sense, it is essentially the same as "equity."

"Trustee and Debtor-in-Possession" In some bankruptcy proceedings, the property is administered by a trustee; in others, by a debtor-in-possession (meaning the same people who ran the debtor before the bankruptcy). The Code frequently talks about the powers and the duties of the trustee. In point of fact, the debtor-in-possession (or DIP) has nearly all the powers and obligations that a trustee has. In consequence, I generally use the abbreviated phrase "trustee/DIP" when I refer to matters that relate to both the trustee and the debtor in possession. When a particular matter relates to only one or the other, I generally say "trustee" or "debtor-in possession" or "DIP."

"Value" and "Present Value"

Value is perhaps the single most significant word in the Code. The value of property is critical in a number of situations; for example, determining the allowed amount of a secured claim, whether a creditor has adequate protection, when a debtor is insolvent, and whether a plan of reorganization meets the "best interest of creditors" test. Despite this, the term has no fixed definition; rather, value is determined contextually. To take a simple example: what is the value of an inventory of 5,000 widgets? It might be $50,000 (the hypothetical normal retail price), $37,000 (a normal wholesale price), $34,000 (the expected price it would receive in an orderly liquidation) or $20,000 (the expected price that would be received in a quick, knock-down liquidation). Any of these prices might be the value of the inventory in bankruptcy, depending on the context in which the question is being raised. If the debtor is a reorganizing retailer with good prospects, the highest price might be correct; if it is a collapsed wholesaler undergoing an immediate liquidation, the lowest is more likely to be applied.

Present Value. Present value becomes important in measuring the value of property and payments, especially in reorganization plans. Present value is simply a way of describing the value today of payments that are to be made in the future. One million dollars today is worth more than one million dollars a year from now, or than five annual $200,000 payments to be made in the future. The reason is simple. One million dollars today can be invested today, and earn interest, dividends, rents or other profits. One million dollars a year from today cannot be invested until a year from today; thus, broadly speaking, one million dollars a year from today has a present value of one million dollars minus the value of a year's investment income. If we assume that we can invest today and get a total of 5% per annum income, then the present value of one million dollars to be received one year from today is $952,380.95. To put it the other way'round, if you invest $952,380.95 today at 5% per annum simple (that is, not compounded) then exactly one year from today you will have one million dollars.[57]

The calculation of present value is relatively easy, thanks to many excellent reference books and, more recently, personal computers and electronic calculators. The difficult part is determining the "discount rate" used to reduce the future payments to present value. The discount rate should represent the expected yield that would be produced by investment of the property. There are two problems in setting this yield.

First, investment yields are not stable over time. They vary with supply and demand, and are significantly affected by inflation rates.[58] It is difficult to predict interest rates for a five week period, let alone a five year period. The best the court can do is make a reasonable estimate. Inevitably, there will be a degree of error in the calculation; the error generally increases with time. Thus, the chance that payments made over a long period of time will in fact have a present value equal to the stated dollar amount is vanishingly small.[59] For this reason, a court will often be influenced by any interest rate previously agreed to by the parties. If the debt in question bears interest at 10%, a court is likely to use 10% as an appropriate rate for calculating future value for the remaining term of the obligation; it at least reflects the parties' own estimate and risk-allocation.[60]

Second, yields vary with risk, including payment risk. Quite high nominal rates of return can be earned on investments that have a high probability of going into default. However, the real rate of return must be adjusted for the possibility of non-payment. To avoid the additional complexities that this creates, courts usually look to investments that are virtually free of payment risk, such as short-term U.S. government securities.[61] Since default risk is reasonably assumed to be zero, the court does not then have to factor in default risk. Investments with this degree of

[57] Note that this example, like others used in this book, ignores tax effects. At times, it is necessary to make adjustments to offset differences in the tax treatment of the basic payment and the income on that payment. This is a simplifying assumption that does not change the basic issue.

[58] Roughly speaking, high inflation tends to cause investment to move from financial instruments to tangibles, such as real property and non-perishable goods; when the supply of investment capital available to borrowers shrinks, the price (interest) goes up.

[59] Note that there is a way to avoid this problem, although it appears not to be widely used in bankruptcy: the future payments may include a variable rate of interest that increases or decreases in accordance with a set standard, such as the prime rate.

[60] Note that the court is probably not required to use the contract interest rate.

[61] Many courts use a "basket" of several, variably dated government securities and use their average rate of interest to determine the discount rate.

safety carry a lower interest rate than do other comparable investments..Thus, the interest rates used to calculate present value are generally on the low end of those available legally in the market.

CHAPTER 2

Basic Creditors' Rights

§ 2.01 Sources of Creditor's Rights Law

Although the law regarding creditor's rights and debtor's defenses traditionally has been left to the states, this has never been entirely true; indeed, bankruptcy law itself is the most obvious intrusion of federal power into creditor's rights. Moreover, in recent decades, the U.S. government has increasingly regulated the debtor/creditor relationship, especially when the debtor is a consumer. However, most of the remedies available to creditors upon the failure of a debtor to pay are still creatures of state rather than federal law. It is those remedies that are the usual stuff of traditional creditor's rights classes, and thus the subject of this chapter. This is a massive subject in itself, and cannot be fully explored in this book. However, it is possible to sketch out the most important issues—or at least the issues that are most likely to arise in or in the background of a bankruptcy proceeding.

Broadly, creditor's rights can be divided into two general categories. The first deals with the voluntary creation of property rights held by the creditor to protect its interest. These rights includes such things as mortgages, deeds, of trust, and Article 9 security interests. Also included in this chapter is a brief review of leases. Leases, like mortgages or security interests, create divided interests in property; one purpose of that division is to protect the lessor's right to get paid the promised rent. Although not liens in the usual sense of the word, the lessor's rights have some of the same characteristics as liens, and are given somewhat similar treatment in bankruptcy. Similarly, rights of setoff, which are not technically liens, are also included in this chapter. The rights of the offsetting creditor are treated by the Bankruptcy Code as virtual liens; it is therefore appropriate in this introductory material to group them together.

The second category deals with property rights that are created by law. These are sometimes called "involuntary." The term is a trifle misleading. They are involuntary in the sense that the debtor need not explicitly grant them to the creditor. However, in many cases, they arise from voluntary transactions. For example, a voluntarily created contract right, if breached, may lead to the imposition of an involuntary judicial lien.

§ 2.02 Consensual Liens

[A]—Introduction

A consensual lien is one created by the agreement of the person granting the lien. For example, a home mortgage or a security interest in a newly purchased car is a consensual lien. The person who grants the lien is exchanging a limited property interest for some accommodation from the grantee—most typically, an extension of credit. The creditor who obtains the lien nearly always is seeking greater security for payment or performance of an obligation. In its simplest terms, a bank that makes a mortgage loan exchanges a $100,000 loan for not only a promise of repayment but also an interest in the property acquired with that loan—if the promise to repay is not kept, the bank may seize the house that secures repayment.

[B]—Real Estate Mortgages and Deeds of Trust

Generally speaking, interests in real estate as collateral (other than some interests in fixtures) are established by the use of mortgages or deeds of trust.[1] Although there is a great deal of discussion, particularly in older cases, about whether these instruments represent "conveyances" or "liens," the ins and outs of that issue are of no significance to our discussion. Both mortgages and deeds of trust involve two-step transactions. The first step, execution and delivery of the document, establishes the rights between the creditor and the debtor. In most cases, a second step—proper recording of the document—is required to establish rights against third parties, including most subsequent purchasers of the property.[2] Ordinarily, the document itself must be recorded in the real estate records of the county (or in some cases, in the city) in which the real property is located. The mortgage/deed of trust may be valid only for a particular extension of credit or for a particular amount stated in the document itself.

A variation used in some states is the installment land contract, sometimes called a "contract for deed." This is a contract under which the buyer takes possession and makes payments, while the seller retains title until the payments are complete. Traditionally, the contract for deed gave the vendor an exceptionally broad remedy: if the vendee defaulted, the vendor could keep all payments made and recover the property. This rule, which amounted to a forfeiture of the vendee's partial payments, has been whittled away by legislative action and court decision.[3]

Priorities are generally established on a first in time, first in right basis—interests in the property that are recorded first are given first priority. There are many major and minor variations on this pattern; for example, it is often true that a person who has notice of a previous unrecorded interest takes subject to it.[4] However, insofar as bankruptcy is concerned, recordation of the transfer is a virtual necessity. The bankruptcy trustee has the power to avoid any interest in realty that a bona fide purchaser could take free of.[5] Thus, even when a BFP with notice would take

---

[1] One variation on this, used in some states, is the filing of a consent judgment against the property, creating what is in effect a consensual judicial lien that is discharged by paying the obligation according to its terms.

[2] See generally, Roger A. Cunningham, William B. Stoebuck & Dale A. Whitman, The Law of Property §§ 11.9, 11.10 (2d ed. 1993).

[3] See Grant S. Nelson and Dale A Whitman, Real Estate Finance Law §§ 3.26-3.30 (3d Ed. 1994).

[4] See generally, Roger A. Cunningham, William B. Stoebuck & Dale A. Whitman, The Law of Property § 11.10 (1993).

[5] Bankruptcy Code § 544(a)(3); for a fuller discussion of this, see § 13.02 of this book.

subject, the trustee can still avoid; the issue is not whether some BFPs take subject but rather whether any BFP could take free. This issue is determined not by the Code but by the relevant body of real estate law, nearly always state law. At times this determination can be difficult, because in any given state there may be little statute or case law that clearly determines every BFP or other priority issue.

[C]—Security Interests in Personal Property

[1]—Uniform Commercial Code Article 9[6]

Most aspects of the law regarding security interests in personal property are governed by Article 9 of the Uniform Commercial Code, which also has provisions covering security interests in fixtures that arise apart from the real estate to which the fixture is attached. The coverage of Article 9 is determined by the economic substance of the underlying transaction, not by the label attached to it. Article 9 controls if the interest granted is substantively a security interest; that is, if it is a right to seize collateral upon default. Sometimes, a transaction of this type will be called a "lease" by the parties to the transaction; this is done usually for tax reasons. However, if the "lessor" under the "lease" does not retain any valuable reversionary rights then the transaction is a sale plus security interest. For example, if the "lease" allows the lessee to buy the goods for nominal consideration at the end of the lease term, or if the "lease" runs for the entire useful life of the goods, then the "lease" is not a lease.[7] This distinction is very important in bankruptcy. In most cases, a security interest creates a lien that is valid against the bankruptcy trustee/DIP if and only if the security interest is evidenced by the filing of a financing statement. As a general rule, no such filing is required to preserve the lessor's rights in bankruptcy.

The basic Article 9 statutory scheme can easily be divided into two parts. The first, "attachment," deals with the establishment of rights between the creditor (more properly, the secured party) and the debtor. The second, "perfection," deals with the establishment of priorities between the secured party and third parties with regard to the collateral.

Attachment requires three things: agreement, value, and rights.[8] The Article 9 security interest arises only by agreement between the debtor and the secured party. Unless the secured creditor takes physical possession of the collateral, the security agreement must be in writing; it must be signed by the debtor; and it must have a description of the collateral. If the collateral is growing crops or timber to be cut, the security agreement must also include a description of the land on which the crops or timber is located.[9] The secured party must give value for the security interest.[10]

---

[6] Note that the discussion of Article 9 security interests is rather more extensive than that of other liens; this is because many bankruptcy casebooks use more cases and questions drawn from Article 9 than from other bodies of state law creditors' rights.

[7] U.C.C. § 1-201(3); see Thomas D. Crandall, Michael J. Herbert & Lary Lawrence, Uniform Commercial Code § 23.5(1993).

[8] U.C.C. § 9-203(1).

[9] U.C.C. § 9-203(1)(a).

[10] U.C.C. § 9-203(1)(b).

However, this does not mean new value. If the security interest is given by the debtor to secure a debt that the debtor already owes to the secured party, the secured party has given value for it.[11] Finally, the debtor must have rights in the collateral[12] but this does not mean that the debtor must be the only person who has rights. The debtor may be a partial owner or a co-owner; the debtor may even be a lessee of the goods. The key question is whether the debtor has some alienable property interest in the goods.

The security agreement may provide for so-called "after-acquired property"; that is, property that the debtor does not have at the time of the agreement but subsequently acquires.[13] Technically, the security interest does not attach until the debtor obtains some rights in the property; but when the debtor does obtain rights, the security interest attaches automatically, without any further agreement. The security agreement may similarly provide that future advances made to the debtor are secured by both existing and after-acquired collateral.[14] Thus, a single security agreement can cover any number of loans.

Attachment fixes the rights of the secured party against the debtor, most importantly, the right to repossess the property if the debtor defaults, and to resell it to recoup the amount of the debt. However, there may be other persons who also have claims to the collateral. These may include judgment lienholders, other secured creditors, buyers of the collateral, and the like. Attachment alone is not necessarily sufficient to establish the secured party's rights against them.

Generally speaking, the secured party must "perfect" the security interest to establish its priority against third party claimants. Perfection in some cases occurs automatically upon attachment—for example, a purchase money security interest in consumer goods is automatically perfected,[15] which simply means that the secured party need take no other step to establish priority. However, in most types of secured transactions, perfection requires both attachment and some further action. The additional action is designed to give notice to third parties of the existence of the security interest, and thus to avoid the possibility that subsequent lenders or purchasers might be mislead by the debtor's apparent ownership of the collateral.

The most common perfecting act is the filing of a financing statement. Security interests in most types of collateral can be perfected by filing; security interests in some types of collateral may only be perfected by filing.[16] A security interest can also be perfected in most cases by possession; except for intangible property, the secured party perfects its interest by taking physical possession of the collateral. In most cases, of course, it is impractical for the secured party to take possession of

---

[11] U.C.C. § 1-201(44).

[12] U.C.C. § 9-203(1)(c).

[13] U.C.C. § 9-204(1).

[14] U.C.C. § 9-204(3); see Thomas D. Crandall, Michael J. Herbert & Lary Lawrence, Uniform Commercial Code § 24.17(1993).

[15] U.C.C. § 9-302(1)(d).

[16] U.C.C. §§ 9-302(1), 9-304. See generally Thomas D. Crandall, Michael J. Herbert & Lary Lawrence, Uniform Commercial Code §§ 25.1 -25.17(1993).

the collateral, since the debtor still needs to use it. Thus, filing is by far the most common perfecting act.

In some cases, there are special perfection rules. Most notably, security interests in titled vehicles are perfected not by filing a financing statement but by having the security interest listed on the certificate of title. Federal law also prescribes special means of perfection for certain types of property, such as airplanes and intellectual property. Since the U.C.C. is state law, these federal rules supersede.

Broadly speaking, the Article 9 priority rules follow a first-in-time, first-in-right approach—that is, rights prior in time are prior in right. Generally, if either the security interest was perfected or the financing statement was filed before the competing claim arose, the security interest has priority. For example, if a security interest in the debtor's equipment was perfected on January 1, and a judgment lien attached on January 5, the security interest would have priority. When the equipment is sold, the proceeds will be first applied to the debt secured by the security interest. If there is any surplus, the remainder will be applied to the judgment debt.[17]

Insofar as bankruptcy is concerned, the most crucial priority rule in Article 9 is that contained in section 9-301(1)(b). That provision states that an *unperfected* security interest is subordinate to the rights of "a person who becomes a lien creditor before the security interest is perfected."[18] As we will explore in Chapter 13,[19] the bankruptcy trustee or debtor-in-possession has the rights of a lien creditor. This means that the unperfected security interest is of no value in a bankruptcy proceeding.

As indicated above, an Article 9 security interest gives the secured party something that general creditors do not have. The secured party has an actual property interest in its collateral; this property interest coexists with that of the debtor. The key feature of this property interest outside of bankruptcy is that the secured party may seize and sell the property when the debtor defaults. In many cases, no court action is required to establish or enforce the secured party's rights to the collateral; it may be taken by self-help, so long as there is no breach of the peace.[20] In bankruptcy, the secured party, if its interest is perfected, has an even more valuable right. A "perfected security interest" is a property interest recognized and protected in bankruptcy proceedings. Although the secured creditor is by no means unaffected by the bankruptcy, and has no certainty of payment in full, it is almost certain to obtain a much greater payout than is received by unsecured creditors.

---

[17] For a fuller discussion of priorities generally, see Thomas D. Crandall, Michael J. Herbert & Lary Lawrence, Uniform Commercial Code Chap. 26 (1993).

[18] U.C.C. § 9-301(1)(b). A "lien creditor" means a creditor who has a lien created by "attachment, levy, or the like." U.C.C. § 9-301(3).

[19] See § 13.02.

[20] U.C.C. § 9-503. If self-help cannot be accomplished peaceably, the secured party must resort to judicial action, generally by seeking the remedy of replevin or detinue.

[2]—Non-Article 9

There are a number of laws other than Article 9 that deal with consensual security interests in personal property. Some of these laws work in conjunction with Article 9; they supersede part but not all of its rules. Others operate independently. A few of the most important are described in this sub-paragraph.

Even within the Uniform Commercial Code, there are other provisions that deal in part with security interests. Most notably, Article 8, which deals with investment securities (such as stocks and bonds) contains rules that partially pre-empt Article 9. Article 8 divides investment securities into two broad categories—"certificated" and "uncertificated." Certificated securities are the familiar type—stocks or bonds printed on stiff durable paper with scrolls and eagles and proclamations of value. Uncertificated securities are intangible—they exist merely as records of, and claims on, the issuer. A security interest in a certificated security is perfected by possession of the paper. A security interest in an uncertificated security is perfected by registration of the interest with the corporation.[21]

Federal admiralty law governs security interests in registered vessels. A preferred ship mortgage, which will have priority over the trustee or DIP, requires a number of formalities quite alien to the world of Article 9 transactions. Other federal laws only partially preempt Article 9. Security interests in aircraft, for example, are largely covered by the U.C.C., but perfection is governed by federal law, which requires that the security interest be recorded in the F.A.A. Registry in Oklahoma City.

[D]—Real Estate Leases

Generally, long-term leases of real estate require a filing to protect the rights of the lessee against third partes. For example, in a particular state leases of less than 3 years need not be recorded while leases of three years or more must be.[22] In addition, there are special filing rules for leases of "fixtures" that apply regardless of the duration of the lease. Those rules are discussed in the next subsection.

In general, the rights of both the lessor and the lessee are determined on a first in time, first in right basis. Third party rights in the property that exist prior to the lease (or prior to the recording of the lease, if recording is necessary) are prior to those of the parties to the lease; subsequently arising rights are subordinate. Thus, if after the lease the creditors of the lessor obtain a lien on the leased property, that lien will not affect the rights of the lessee.

If a long-term lease is not recorded, the rights of the lessee may be subject to those of a bona fide purchaser. If they are, then the lease may be avoided in bankruptcy.[23] In addition, there are a number of rules in the Bankruptcy Code that deal with the ability of a bankrupt lessee to retain possession of the property leased.[24]

---

[21] U.C.C. § 8-321.

[22] See generally, Roger A. Cunningham, William B. Stoebuck & Dale A. Whitman, The Law of Property § 11.9 (1993).

[23] Bankruptcy Code § 544(a)(3)

[24] See §§ 9.03 and 9.04 of this book.

[E]—Personal Property Leases

Article 2A of the U.C.C. governs personal property leases in nearly all states.[25] Its provisions include coverage of the rights of the lessor and creditors in the leased goods. Those provisions directly and indirectly affect the status of the various interests in bankruptcy. The most important of the rules are sketched out in this paragraph.

Of primary importance, at least to the lessor, is that there is no general requirement that the lessor's interest be recorded. So long as the lease is a "true lease" and not a disguised sale plus security interest in the goods[26] and so long as the lease is not a lease of fixtures, a financing statement is not required. Thus, the typical personal property lease is a one-step transaction; no second step is required to protect the lessor's rights against the trustee/DIP's avoiding powers. The reason for making true leases single-step is simple: the equipment leasing industry, which played a dominant role in the drafting of Article 2A, was adamantly opposed to the imposition of a filing requirement, precisely because of their fear that a failure to file would lead to the loss of the lessor's rights if the lessee filed bankruptcy. They argued, successfully, that avoidance of the lessor's interest because of a failure to file was too steep a penalty.

There is one significant exception to this. Article 2A covers the lease of fixtures.[27] A fixture is created when personal property is so affixed to realty that it becomes part of the realty.[28] For a fixture lessor to have priority over certain third parties, the lessor must file a "fixture filing," that is, a record of the lease in the local real estate records.[29] Note, however, that even if there is no filing, the rights of the lessor are superior to the rights of a creditor who obtains a judgment lien after the lease contract became effective.[30] Thus, the trustee/DIP cannot avoid the lessor's interest in the fixture under its power as a hypothetical lien creditor.[31] The fixture lessor who has not filed remains, however, vulnerable to other lien creditors, such as the holder of a mortgage or deed of trust on the entire property of which the fixture is a part.

Insofar as other Article 2A leases are concerned, the general rule is first in time first in right. Broadly speaking, the rights of both the lessor and the lessee are prior

---

[25] See T. Crandall, M. Herbert, and L. Lawrence, Uniform Commercial Code, § 9.2(1993). As of July 1, 1994, 44 states and the District of Columbia had adopted Article 2A. See Stephen T. Whelan & Robert D. Strauss, *UCC: Leases*, 49 Bus. Law. 1857 (1994).

[26] For a discussion of this, see § 2.02[C][1], above.

[27] U.C.C. § 2A-309.

[28] U.C.C. § 2A-309(1)(a).

[29] U.C.C. § 2A-309(1)(b), (4). For a fuller discussion of this, see Thomas D. Crandall, Michael J. Herbert, and Lary Lawrence, Uniform Commercial Code § 11.7(1993).

[30] U.C.C. § 2A-309(5)(b).

[31] Bankruptcy Code § 544(a)(1). Note that the trustee/DIP also has the rights of a hypothetical bona fide purchaser of real estate—but only of real estate other than fixtures. Bankruptcy Code § 544(a)(3). Because of the exclusion of fixtures from that provision, the trustee/DIP cannot avoid the unfiled fixture lease on that basis either.

to the rights of subsequent creditors, including subsequent lien creditors.[32] Thus, ordinarily a bankruptcy of the lessee does not affect the property rights of the lessor, or vice-versa. However, the ability of a bankrupt lessor or lessee to assume or transfer the contract rights is regulated by sections 363 and 365 of the Code, which are discussed in Chapter 9 of this volume.

§ 2.03 Judicial Liens

[A]—Introduction

Judicial liens are involuntary liens; that is, they arise without the consent of the person whose property is subject to the lien. Specifically, a judicial lien is created by law as a method of giving tangible effect to a money judgment. When A sues B, and obtains a money judgment against B, A does not thereby get any right to any specific property of B. B, now the "judgment debtor" owes the amount of the judgment, but does not generally have the affirmative obligation to pay it. All the judgment establishes is that B owes a stated amount of money to A because of some act or omission. If B does not voluntarily pay the judgment, A will have to take further steps to do so.

A can pursue several routes for collection. These range from dunning letters to involuntary bankruptcy. However, if B has any property, A's most likely step is to impose a judicial lien on that property and then foreclose on that lien. There are many subtle variations on the applicable rules from state to state. However, broadly speaking, liens on real property are obtained by docketing the judgment while liens on tangible personal property are obtained by levy of execution. Although it is impossible in the space available to survey all the state variations, the following sections sketch out the most common rules and the most frequently encountered issues.

[B]—Real Property

A judicial lien on realty is ordinarily established by docketing the judgment. "Docketing" simply means that the judgment is filed in the county where the real estate is located.[33] The main purpose for docketing the judgment is exactly the same as the purpose for filing a mortgage or deed of trust—to protect the interests of subsequent creditors and purchasers against unknown interests.

Broadly speaking, the lien will have priority over subsequently arising interests and will be subordinate to existing interests (other than those of the judgment debtor). Existing interests may or may not include the interests of a person who has an unrecorded interest but is in possession of the property, depending on the state. The general rules regarding foreclosure of the lien are discussed in § 2.07[A] of this chapter.

---

[32] See § 9.04 of this book.

[33] See, for example, Doug Rendleman, Enforcement of Judgements and Liens in Virginia § 4.3 (2d ed. 1994).

Insofar as bankruptcy is concerned, a judicial lien on real property is given essentially the same status as most other liens. If the judgment was docketed prior to the filing, the judgment creditor may have a secured claim. However, it is generally necessary for the docketing to have occurred more than 90 days before the petition was filed, because a judgment lien that first arises during those 90 days will generally be avoidable as a preference.[34]

[C]—Tangible Personalty

Imposing a judicial lien on personalty, especially tangible personalty, generally requires a step beyond the docketing of the judgment: this is usually called "levy," "execution," or (perhaps the most analytically precise) "levy of execution." The reason usually given for this is that there are no centralized records regarding ownership of most types of personal property. This contrasts with real property. Where realty is involved, a buyer or creditor can go to the county records and determine, with a high degree of precision, who owns or has a claim to any realty in that county. There are no corresponding records regarding personalty; thus, there is no place for a creditor or buyer to go to determine what interests exist in personal property. This rationale runs a bit thin today, since there are in fact many public records regarding interests in personalty. For example, we maintain records of Article 9 security interests in personal property; the fact that there is no index of the property itself is irrelevant, since those records are maintained by the name of the owner, not the identity of the property.[35] Another rationale given is that requiring levy places the seizure of property into the hands of the presumably neutral sheriff rather than a potentially vindictive plaintiff. However, this is not a policy followed consistently in the law. There are many circumstances—for example, Article 9 security interests—in which we allow great latitude in seizing property to the creditor. Thus, it is more accurate to say that the continuance of levy of execution is based more on tradition than anything else.

Essentially, levy of execution requires that the sheriff or a designee take an action to seize the property after the judgment has been docketed in the appropriate county. Usually, this seizure is symbolic rather than physical. In many states, the seizure requires only that the property be "tagged"—that is, marked to show that it is subject to a judicial lien. Some states do not even require this rather minimal form of seizure. They require only that the property be in the "view and control" of the sheriff. This means that the sheriff must actually see the property and be able to touch it.[36] No tagging is required; there is thus no effort made to give notice of the lien on the property itself.

---

[34] See § 14.02[F] of this book.

[35] Similarly, note that records of the property levied upon are maintained after the levy is complete.

[36] Needless to say, this leads to a number of interesting cases regarding property that is behind a closed but transparent window.

[D]—Intangible Property

Rights to intangible property of the judgment debtor are generally acquired through garnishment. Whether there is a lien on the property prior to the actual garnishment is a matter over which the states differ. In some cases, only the actual garnishment creates a lien; in others, the lien may arise earlier—for example, when the judgment is docketed.

§ 2.04 Statutory and Common-Law Liens

[A]—Introduction

There are a considerable number of liens that arise without any court action. Some of these are created by the common law; others by statute. Except for construction liens, all of these liens are possessory—the lienholder must have physical possession of the goods. The following sketches out common patterns for the most frequently arising types of liens.

[B]—Construction Liens

A construction lien (also known as a mechanic's or materialman's lien) is a lien designed to protect subcontractors and suppliers of building projects against the default or bankruptcy of the prime contractor. In most construction contracts, the prime contractor is the only person who deals directly with, and is in contractual privity with, the landowner who is having the construction built. The prime contractor, however, parcels out portions of the job to various subcontractors and material suppliers. For example, one subcontractor will do the plumbing; another the electrical work; a third the interior design. The actual goods used will be acquired from building supply companies. Since the plumber, the electrician, the designer, and the supply company have no contracts with the owner, they cannot sue directly if they are not paid by the prime contractor. Construction lien laws protect them by giving them liens on the property for their unpaid contracts.

Typically, the lien arises when the construction begins. The lien is generally perfected by a system of notice to the public and the owner, generally involving the recordation of the lien in real property records and personal service on the owners. It may also be necessary to publish notice of the lien in local newspapers. The period for giving notice is quite short, typically not more than 180 days after the completion of work.[37]

[C]—Repair Liens

Repair liens—also sometimes called mechanic's liens, but not to be confused with construction liens that are called mechanic's liens—are possessory in nature. A person who has repaired personal property and not been paid for it is often given

---

[37] See generally, Grant S. Nelson and Dale A. Whitman, Real Estate Financing Law § 12.24 (1985).

a lien that is perfected merely by possession. These liens are today generally statutory; the scope and priority of the lien depends upon the terms of the statute and vary widely.

§ 2.05 Tax Liens

[A]—Introduction

One area of creditors' rights law often overlooked in law school, although never in the rest of the world, is the power of government to attach and foreclose on property for unpaid tax obligations. Tax liens, particularly federal tax liens, are of great concern to those who own or have extended credit to troubled companies. As one might expect, governments tend to award themselves sweeping rights that can even be superior to those of existing lien creditors.

[B]—IRS Liens

Federal tax liens, commonly referred to as IRS liens, are codified in the federal Tax Lien Act, which, although it attempts to balance governmental and private rights, tips significantly in favor of the former. The Tax Lien Act integrates fairly well, but incompletely, with state law liens. However, in some key respects Congress has deviated from state law priority; those deviations control because of the Constitution's Supremacy Clause.

The IRS lien, like so many other liens, is a two-step interest; the first step establishes rights against the taxpayer while the second establishes rights against other claimants. The first step is the assessment of a deficiency—a formal method of determining the IRS' claim that the taxpayer has not paid all taxes due. The second step, of crucial creditors' rights significance, is the filing of a notice of deficiency. Although the first step "creates" the lien, the lien is largely ineffective against third parties until the second step has been taken. As is true of other filing requirements, the filing is intended to give notice to buyers and creditors of the otherwise secret lien and the IRS' interest is thus generally subordinate to interests that arose before the filing. Notice of the lien is filed on a statewide basis, at a place determined by state law.[38]

The scope of the lien is exceedingly broad. Virtually every interest of the taxpayer in property is subject to it. Moreover, although subject to prior interests, the lien, once notice is filed, has priority over subsequent interests, unless the Lien Act says otherwise. This creates headaches even for existing creditors. For example, as noted in § 2.02[C] [1], an Article 9 security agreement can cover after-acquired property. When that property is acquired, the security interest automatically attaches to it. However, if the property is acquired after the filing of the tax lien notice, the IRS will generally have priority over the security interest. The exceptions are few and limited. The same is true with subsequent advances of credit. A creditor may have

---

[38] See generally, Thomas D. Crandall, Michael J. Herbert & Lary Lawrence, Uniform Commercial Code § 26.22(1993).

an interest in property that has priority over the IRS lien. However, if that creditor makes a further advance of credit after notice is filed, the creditor's priority may only extend to the debt that existed at the time of filing. With a few exceptions, the creditor will not have priority in the property with regard to the subsequent advance.

For example, suppose that River Bank has an Article 9 security interest in all the equipment of Shady Dealings, Inc. As of June 1, 1997, Shady owes River $100,000. On July 1, 1997, notice of an IRS lien is filed. A few days later, Shady acquires a new widget machine for use in its factory. Shortly after that, River loans Shady $30,000 for working capital, secured under the original security agreement (River was not required, however, by the loan agreement to make this loan). River will have priority up to $100,000 in the equipment Shady had prior to July 1, 1997. The IRS will have priority in the new widget machine. It will also have the second priority in the other collateral; it will come after River's original $100,000 loan, but before the River's $30,000 loan.[39]

As noted, there are some exceptions to these rules. Most important are a set of very complex provisions that give significant protection to some rather limited and tightly defined types of security interests in after-acquired property and future advances. These are beyond the scope of this discussion.

For bankruptcy purposes, the key is the filing requirement. It is filing that establishes rights against third parties and thus (indirectly) the trustee/DIP. If notice of the deficiency has not been filed before bankruptcy, the IRS may have a priority unsecured tax claim or a non-dischargeable unsecured tax claim, but it will not have a secured claim.

[C]—State and local tax liens

State and local tax laws also provide for the imposition of liens on property if the taxes are not paid when due. Most of these laws are less sweeping that the IRS lien; in many states, only real property is subject to the lien. There are also many variations about regarding the notice of the lien and the tax authority's rights against third parties.

§ 2.06 Setoff

There is perhaps no right of creditors more obvious or ancient that the right of setoff. This right is rooted in the rather obvious notion that if A owes B, and B owes A, it is logical to permit each to reduce the obligation it owes by the obligation it is owed. If Alice owes Bert $20, and Bert owes Alice $10, then it makes perfect sense to say that Alice may choose to offset Bert's debt to her, pay him $10, and call it quits. Although there are a number of subtle qualifications to this rule[40] that basic insight remains central to it.

---

[39] See generally, Internal Revenue Code §§ 6321-6323.

[40] For example, setoff may not be used if the debt from A to B is a general obligation while the debt from B to A is a "special" obligation, such as an obligation arising from a trustee-beneficiary relationship.

It is surprising, then, that setoff was not at first recognized by the common law (although it was in equity, and received its first statutory codification in Colonial Virginia).[41] In modern times, however, it is so well established that it is likely to be given more weight than potentially conflicting statutes, such as Article 9 of the U.C.C., unless the statute clearly states otherwise.[42] Setoff rights are also largely preserved under the Bankruptcy Code, although the exercise of those rights may be postponed by the Code's automatic stay of actions against the debtor and the debtor's property. Indeed, setoff rights are treated as if they were secured claims.[43]

§ 2.07 Remedies

[A]—Foreclosure on Real Property

Foreclosure on a mortgage or other real property lien often requires, and generally involves, judicial action culminating in a sheriff's sale by auction and an accounting before the court. The debtor generally has the right to redeem the property by paying the obligation in a lump sum. This right of redemption must be exercised within a set period of time, usually less than a year. In some states, there is a non-judicial alternative—a "power of sale" foreclosure, based on a contractual party given to someone (such as the trustee under a deed of trust) to dispose of the property upon default. Although not requiring judicial action, a power of sale foreclosure is subject to judicial review. Moreover, unlike self-help repossession of personal property, foreclosure under a power of sale laws requires substantial prior notice to the mortgagor.[44]

[B]—Self-Help Repossession of Personalty

Self-help repossession (that is, seizure of property without court order or court action) is available under a number of circumstances. The most important are found in Article 2A (Personal Property Leases) and Article 9 (Secured Transactions) of the Uniform Commercial Code. An Article 2A lessor generally has the right to seize leased property upon the lessee's default.[45] Similarly, an Article 9 secured party generally has the right to seize collateral when the debtor defaults.[46] (Note that some states have limited or curtailed this right in consumer transactions.)

"Self-help" means exactly what it says. No notice, no hearing, no court order, no bond, no sheriff, no judicial approval of the sale. This is considered to be constitutional because there is insufficient state action involved to trigger the protections of the Fifth and Fourteenth Amendments.

---

[41] William H. Loyd, *The Development of Set-off*, 64 U Pa. L. Rev. 541 (1916).

[42] See U.C.C. § 9-104(i)(Article 9 does not apply to setoffs).

[43] For a full discussion of setoff in a bankruptcy case, see § 10.09 of this book.

[44] See generally, Grant S. Nelson & Dale A. Whitman, Real Estate Finance Law §§ 3.26 -3.30 (3d ed. 1994).

[45] U.C.C. § 2A-525(2), (3).

[46] U.C.C. § 9-503.

There is one statutory limitation: breach of the peace. The lessor/secured party may use self help only if there is no breach of the peace caused by the repossession.[47] The phrase "breach of the peace" has engendered a wealth of case law. Broadly speaking, it refers not only to actual violence but also to threats of violence, illegal actions (such as breaking into a locked garage), fraudulent actions, or even actions that are resisted in any tangible way by the lessee or debtor.[48] In general, the debtor/lessee can stop a self-help repossession simply by telling the repossessor to go away. However, if there is no resistance of any kind, the repossession may go forward; this may be true even if a prior repossession attempt was blocked by the debtor.[49]

If self-help repossession cannot be accomplished without breach of the peace, then the secured party/lessor must use judicial means to obtain possession, usually replevin. Failure to cease and desist when a breach of the peace occurs may in fact subject the repossessor to liability. In extreme cases, even punitive damages may be awarded for an improper self-help repossession.[50]

[C]—Replevin and Detinue

Replevin (and, in a few states, detinue) is a long-established method of obtaining possession of property wrongfully detained by the defendant. In the context of state creditor's rights, its primary significance is as a judicial alternative to self-help repossession. Broadly speaking, replevin is an action to recover the actual goods, while detinue is an action to recover the goods or their value.

[D]—Pre-Judgment Seizure

In a number of situations, creditors would like to seize or at least to block transfer of the debtor's property before judgment has been entered. Generally, a pre-judgment judicial seizure requires a showing of extraordinary circumstances, such as a risk that the property will be hidden or moved out of state. In addition, over the past few decades, the courts have imposed Constitutional due process requirements on pre-judgment seizure. These are familiar to students who have taken, and who remember, first-year Civil Procedure. At a minimum, there must be some unbiased scrutiny of the creditor's claim that prejudgment seizure is necessary, notice to the debtor whose property is being seized, and an opportunity for a prompt post-seizure hearing. Some states prohibit or restrict pre-judgment seizure, especially in consumer cases. The Bankruptcy Code's automatic stay provisions have

[47] U.C.C. §§ 2A-525(3), 9-503.

[48] See Thomas D. Crandall, Michael J. Herbert, and Lary Lawrence, Uniform Commercial Code, §§ 13.4.3(with regard to leases) and 27.9 (with regard to security interests) (1993).

[49] See Wade v. Ford Motor Credit Co., 668 P.2d 183, 36 U.C.C. Rep. Serv. 1433 (Kan. App. 1983). (Debtor, who was armed at the time, told repo man that if she saw him near her car again she would "leave him laying right where I saw him." Some days later, repo man successfully repossessed during the middle of the night. Held, no breach of the peace.)

[50] See Big Three Motors, Inc. v. Rutherford, 432 So.2d 483, 36 U.C.C. Rep. Serv. 338 (Ala. 1983).

an indirect effect on pre-judgment seizure, because those provisions may require the seizing creditor to return the property.[51]

[E]—Garnishment

Garnishment is the means by which a creditor seizes intangible personal property. Although the term is often associated with the seizure of the debtor's wages, it in fact encompasses other seizures of intangibles, such as a bank account balance. Broadly speaking, garnishment is accomplished through an order of garnishment[52] served on a person who owes the judgment debtor money. For example, the debtor's employer may be served a garnishment order. The order obligates the debtor's debtor to pay over to the court some or all of the money owed to the debtor when the debt becomes due. In the example given, the employer must pay the garnished portion of the wages, but only when those wages are actually payable to the debtor, that is, on payday.

Garnishment of wages has been subjected to a number of statutory restrictions in recent years. Federal law generally prohibits the garnishment of more than a portion an employee's net (post-tax) wages.[53] In addition, there are many state limitations, such as a prohibition on more than one garnishment per month.

[F]—Foreclosure Sale of Personal Property

Under U.C.C. article 9, property seized by the creditor is ordinarily sold by the creditor, not by a sheriff. A secured party may "sell, lease or otherwise dispose of any or all of the collateral."[54] The sale may be either by public auction or by "private" sale (that is, a sale that is specifically negotiated with the buyer. The sale itself must be done in a commercially reasonable manner. In nearly all cases, the debtor must be given prior notice of the sale, and in some cases other secured parties must also be given notice.[55] The proceeds of the sale are distributed first to the costs of the sale, then to satisfying the secured debt, then to satisfying any junior debts.[56] In very rare cases, there is a surplus left from the sale; if the collateral secured a debt, then the surplus goes to the debtor. More commonly, there is a deficiency (that is, the proceeds of sale are insufficient to pay off the obligation); in that case the secured party is entitled to an unsecured "deficiency judgment" for the remainder.[57]

In rare cases, a secured party will elect to keep the property rather than resell it. The secured party must give prior notice of its intention not to sell to the debtor and in some cases to other secured parties. If the secured party receives an objection within 21 days after its sends the notice, the secured party must sell the collateral.

[51] See Chapter 8 of this book.

[52] Sometimes known as a "suggestion" of garnishment.

[53] 15 U.S.C. § 1671–1677.

[54] U.C.C. § 9-504(1).

[55] U.C.C. § 9-504(3).

[56] U.C.C. § 9-504(1).

[57] U.C.C. § 9-504(2). Note that in some states, the failure of the secured party to comply with the Article 9 rules for disposition deprive it of its right to a deficiency judgment.

There are additional restrictions that apply if the collateral is consumer goods. Retention of the collateral satisfies the debt entirely; the secured party cannot obtain a deficiency judgment if it keeps the collateral.[58]

The debtor has a limited right of redemption (that is, a right to recover the property after repossession). This right must be exercised before the secured party does any of the following: (1) disposes of the collateral, (2) enters into a contract to dispose of the collateral, or (2) discharges the obligation by retention of the collateral. To redeem, the debtor must tender full payment. This means that the debtor must tender all of the following:

1. The entire obligation secured (for example, if the obligation is $10,000 and $1,200 accrued interest, the debtor must tender $11,200 to meet this requirement), plus
2. All of the expenses reasonably incurred by the secured as a result of the default, such as the cost of repossession and preparing the goods for sale, plus
3. The secured party's reasonable attorney's fees and legal expenses—but only to the extent that the security agreement (i) provided for the collection of those fees and expenses and (ii) the provision in the security agreement is permitted under the law. (Most but not all states permit a contract to shift attorneys's fees from one party to the other by contract).

This right to redeem may be waived, but only in a writing executed after the debtor went into default (thus, a waiver of redemption rights in the original agreement is unenforceable).[59]

Redemption is an entirely nugatory right for most debtors. The requirement that the debtor pay the entire debt, plus the creditor's expenses and (in many cases) legal fees in a single lump is in nearly all cases an insuperable barrier. Debtors who have access to that much cash rarely default in the first place. Moreover, to redeem the goods the debtor may actually have to pay much more than they are worth, because they may have less value than the amount of the obligation. The Bankruptcy Code provides a slightly more favorable form of redemption for debtors.[60]

[G]—Non-regulatory State Insolvency Proceedings

Non-regulatory state insolvency proceedings fall into two broad types, both of which have become nearly extinct in recent years. The two types are "receiverships" and "assignments for the benefit of creditors." Except for a few specialized areas, such as the reorganization of insurance companies, state insolvency proceedings have almost been replaced by bankruptcy proceedings,[61] because of the many

---

[58] U.C.C. § 9-505.

[59] U.C.C. § 9-506.

[60] See § 11.11 of this book.

[61] Indeed, these remedies have fallen into such disuse that some trial court judges have refused to allow their use. See First National State Bank v. Kron, 464 A.2d 1146 (N.J. App. Div. 1983) (trial court judge gave, as one reason for refusal to appoint a receiver, that the receivership statute had been forgotten and was no longer viable.)

advantages that debtors have in bankruptcy, most particularly the ability to force a discharge of indebtedness. States are precluded from imposing a discharge on an unwilling creditor, because of the so-called Contract Clause of the federal Constitution, which prohibits states from "impairing" obligations of contract. In addition, any state insolvency proceeding that becomes too much like a bankruptcy proceeding is preempted by Congress' Constitutional power to enact uniform laws on the subject of Bankruptcy.[62]

The fundamental difference between a receivership and an assignment is that the former is generally involuntary and the latter is voluntary. In a receivership, a court, upon motion of one or more creditors, appoints a person to take custody of the debtor's non-exempt property, sell the property, and distribute the proceeds to creditors. In general, a receiver will only be appointed if ordinary collection methods have failed. As such, it resembles a Chapter 7 bankruptcy; indeed, the Chapter 7 structure was borrowed from existing state receivership law. As indicated, however, the irreducible difference between the state receivership and the Chapter 7 is that a state cannot grant a discharge—the debtor still owes the unpaid debts.

Assignments for the benefit of creditors are started by the debtor, who assigns his or her non-exempt property to a court-supervised assignee, who liquidates the property and distributes the proceeds. As is true with receiverships, no discharge is granted. However, at least some states have attempted to get around this limitation by giving creditors a choice—they can participate in the distribution only if they agree to waive all future claims against the debtor. If they do not wish to waive, they receive none of the distribution but retain their entire claim.

These are only general models of state insolvency proceedings. There are many variations. They are not here discussed because of their fading significance.

[H]—Regulatory Receiverships

By contrast with ordinary state receivership proceedings, state and federal regulatory receiverships are both common and of great significance. Indeed, to a large degree, they are not affected by bankruptcy law. Many of the types of companies that may be subject to regulatory receiverships are ineligible for bankruptcy.

By long tradition, many financial institutions, especially insurance companies, have been regulated by state rather than federal authorities. Other financial institutions, such as FDIC-insured banks, are subject to a separate set of insolvency laws. Insurance companies and FDIC-insured financial institutions are not permitted to file bankruptcy.[63] Those companies must be liquidated or reorganized under the relevant state or federal regulatory laws.

---

[62] U.S. Const. Art. 1 § 8.

[63] This prohibition is indirect; it is found in Bankruptcy Code § 109, which defines who may be a debtor under the various chapters of the Code and excludes these institutions.

[I]—Cognovit/Confession of Judgment

In a number of states, the use of a so-called cognovit note has traditionally been a device used to simplify the process of obtaining a judgment. A cognovit provision is a voluntary confession of judgment executed by the obligor when the obligation is entered into. It is quite simply a formal admission of legal liability made prior to any default. In those states that recognize cognovits, the creditor, upon actual default, need merely file its complaint and the obligor's admission with the court; judgment against the obligor will be entered perfunctorily.

One form of cognovit with which your author became familiar consisted of a single page divided into four parts. Part one was the note; part two was the lender's complaint; part three was the borrower's answer (in which the borrower admitted everything alleged in the complaint); part four was the court's order granting judgment for the lender. Except for a few dates and the court's order, everything (including the pleadings) was filled in when the loan was made.

Cognovits are obviously fraught with risk of abuse. Because of this, some state prohibit them altogether, or at least in consumer transactions. Others impose restrictions, such as a requirement of notice and a fairly generous opportunity to reopen the judgment if there in fact is a dispute. The Federal Trade Commission also has prohibited the use of cognovits in many consumer transactions.[64]

§ 2.08 Compositions and Workouts

Workouts and compositions are non-judicial methods of dealing with debt that are rooted in the common law of contracts. The term "workout" usually refers to an agreement between the debtor and a single creditor or group of creditors. The term "composition" usually refers to an agreement between the debtor and all of its creditors, or at least all of its significant creditors. These terms are not used with great consistency. However, the key is not the terminology used but rather the legal substance, which is a contract that extends or partially discharges one or more obligations. There have historically been two major conceptual problems: consideration and the effect of these agreements on third parties.

The following is a simple example of a workout between Heep Industries and one of its customers, Micawber & Co.:

> Micawber has been purchasing widgets from Heep for many years. These purchases are on open account credit; Micawber has 30 days to pay for each shipment. During the past few years, Micawber's business has declined; as a result, it has gradually become later and later in its payments. As things now stand, Micawber owes Heep $500,000; $150,000 is at least 90 days overdue, $250,000 is 1 -90 days overdue, and the remaining $100,000 is still current (that is, the 30 day credit period has not yet run). Micawber proposes the following in exchange

[64] Michael J. Herbert, *Straining the Gnat: A Critique of the 1984 Federal Trade Commission Consumer Credit Regulations*, 38 S.C. L. Rev. 329, 336-42 (1987).

> for Heep's promises not to sue and to continue deliveries: (1) Micawber will give Heep a second mortgage on its warehouse and office buildings (Micawber has about a $100,000 equity in them); (2) Micawber will grant Heep a security interest in all of Micawber's inventory; (3) All future shipments will be C.O.D., and (4) Micawber will pay Heep $10,000 per month on the existing debt. Heep agrees.

The workout agreement is nothing more or less than a new contract between Micawber and Heep under which Micawber gives collateral and agrees to new credit terms in exchange for Heep's promise to refrain from suing and to keep shipping. The mutual promises and forbearance provide consideration for the workout contract.[65] Note, however, that Heep has a certain degree of vulnerability should Micawber go into bankruptcy in the near future. The collateral and the $10,000 payments can both be attacked as avoidable preferences,[66] and in extreme and unusual cases, as fraudulent transfers.

The following is a simple composition agreement between Dummey Corp. and its various creditors:

> Dummey Corp. is a small corporation with one unpaid secured creditor and six unpaid unsecured creditors. The secured creditor is River Bank, which is owed $800,000 and has $600,000 in collateral. The six unsecured creditors are suppliers; they are owed respectively $100,000, $50,000, $50,000, $20,000, $20,000 and $10,000. Dummey has no unencumbered assets except for $60,000 of equipment and is unable to pay its debts as they come due. Dummey proposes to pay $25,000 to River Bank in exchange for its promise to reduce the debt to $650,000, reduce the monthly payments, and extend the term of the loan from 5 years to 15 years. Dummey proposes to pay each of the other creditors 10% of the debt immediately, in exchange for their promises to reduce the debt by 50%, accept payment of that reduced amount in 3 equal annual installments, and keep shipping supplies on a C.O.D. basis. Everyone agrees except the creditor who is owed $10,000.

An agreement of this type is binding on all who accept it; the usual theory for enforcement is that the mutual agreement of creditors to "take a haircut" (reduce the debt) creates either consideration for each individual creditor's promise or in the alternative that it creates a promissory estoppel based on detrimental reliance. However, this agreement is not binding on those who do not agree; and, very often, the composition agreement by its own terms will only be binding on those who agree if everybody agrees. Thus, in the hypothetical, Dummey Corp. will either have to get the accepting creditors to agree that the composition is binding on them even though there is one dissenter or, in the alternative, pay off the dissenter. Of course,

---

[65] Note as well that a workout can often be classified as a contract modification. The need for consideration to make a modification enforceable has been considerably diminished in recent decades. See, for example, U.C.C. 2-209(1) and 2A-208(1).

[66] See Chapter 14 of this book.

if Dummey pays off the dissenter, the other creditors might then balk and demand more for themselves. It is this problem that is addressed by Chapter 11 of the Bankruptcy Code; that chapter in effect gives the debtor a way to force dissenting creditors into a composition if a sufficient number of other creditors agree to it.

The composition does have advantages over Chapter 11; the costs of a composition are usually lower than the costs of a Chapter 11 bankruptcy and the composition is not subject to the kind of court scrutiny that the Chapter 11 reorganization plan is. Finally, note that non-bankruptcy compositions and bankruptcy reorganizations are not mutually exclusive. In some cases—often called "prepackaged" Chapter 11s—the debtor and its major creditors will agree to all or most of the reorganization plan prior to filing bankruptcy; the bankruptcy is then filed and the pre-negotiated plan is presented to the court and the other creditors.

§ 2.09 Exemptions

There is a long-standing tradition in the states to permit even the most impecunious debtor to retain some assets. These assets are "exempt" from execution; that is, a creditor seeking to enforce a judgment may not seize them. The fundamental reason for the exemptions is the belief that even the most hopelessly insolvent should not be deprived of the basic necessities of life.

For many years, the exemption laws preserved, as if in amber, a picture of 19th Century rural American life. Thus, a debtor was allowed to keep such things as a cow, a pig, a spinning wheel, and a dozen or more dishes for *him*self, *his* wife and *their* 10 children. In recent years, exemptions have become more realistic; cars have replaced horses and pension rights have replaced farm land.

Broadly speaking, exemptions have fallen into three categories: the homestead exemption, specific exemptions of tangible personalty, and specific exemptions of income equivalents. As suggested by its name, the homestead exemption has protected all or (more typically) a portion of the value of the debtor's home. In most states, the amount of the homestead exemption is too small to permit the debtor actually to keep his or her home; rather, it permits the debtor to keep a portion of the proceeds when the home is sold. The specific exemptions in tangible personalty are likewise often very stingy; there are typically caps on the value of the property that may be protected. Exemptions that encompass earned income substitutes (such as pension or life insurance proceeds) are typically somewhat more generous, in recognition of the debtor's need to have some source of income for personal needs and the support of dependents.

There are considerable variations from state to state. Some states, mainly in the south and southwest, provide extraordinarily generous exemptions. Other provide very little. Moreover, many bankrupts have so little property that they are not even able to take advantage of the exemptions they do have; they simply do not have enough property to exempt.[67]

---

[67] See Michael J. Herbert & Dominic E. Pacitti, *Down and Out in Richmond, Virginia: The Distribution of Assets in Chapter 7 Bankruptcy Proceedings Closed During 1984-1987*, 22 U. Rich. L. Rev. 303, 318-19 (1998).

Exemptions are preserved in bankruptcy. In some states, an individual debtor may choose either the state exemptions to which he or she is entitled or a list of federal exemptions. In most states, the debtor is limited to the state exemptions. This issue, and others related to exemptions, is discussed at length in Chapter 11.

Traditionally, exemptions only protected unencumbered property. If there was a valid lien on the exempt property, the lien was unaffected by the exemption. For example, if the debtor owned a homestead worth $50,000 but subject to a $50,000 mortgage, the debtor could not claim a homestead exemption. If the mortgage was $47,500, the debtor could not claim a homestead exemption for more than the $2,500 equity in the property.

For the most part, the rule that liens have priority over exemptions still applies. There has been a slight movement away from this for certain kinds of liens. For example, under the Code's federal exemptions, and under some state exemption laws, some liens on exempt household goods can be avoided by the debtor. This issue is discussed in greater detail in the material on the federal exemptions.[68]

There has been a great deal of controversy over the effect of exemption laws. According to many economists, generous exemption laws ought to lead to an increase in bankruptcies, because debtors will be able to shed debt without loss of assets. In fact, the evidence does not support the notion that bankruptcy filing rates are significantly affected by exemption laws. It appears that very few bankrupts are influenced on way or another by the amount of property they can retain in the proceeding.[69] There are many explanations for this; the most obvious is probably the fact that most debtors do not have much property to exempt; the fact that one state might permit $1,000,000 in exemptions and another only $10,000 is of no consequence to debtors who have only $8,000 of unencumbered property in the first place.

§ 2.10 Suretyship

In earlier parts of this chapter, I discuss the use of property as a means of ensuring repayment of a loan or performance of some other obligation. Another method, of considerable antiquity, is the creation of a right to sue a person other than the primary obligor. For example, suppose that B wishes to borrow money from River Bank, but is insufficiently credit-worthy. To enable B to get the loan, S guarantees payment; when the loan comes due, both B and S are liable to River. This is the essence of suretyship.

In modern terminology, a surety is a person "who is liable for the debt or obligation of another, whether primarily or secondarily, conditionally or unconditionally."[70] Although there is much old case law distinguishing between contracts

[68] See § 11.09 of this book.

[69] See § 1.02[C] of this book.

[70] Laurence P. Simpson, Handbook on the Law of Suretyship § 4 (1950). Although there is at present an ongoing effort to write a second restatement on suretyship law, for most purposes the Simpson treatise (which despite its age is the most recent general treatise on suretyship law) remains authoritative. See also the Restatement of Security (1941).

of surety and contracts of guaranty, the modern trend is to treat the latter as merely a sub-species of the former. The key elements are (1) at least two obligors and (2) at least one of the obligors is entitled to indemnification from at least one of the other obligors for its payment or performance of the obligation. The latter is what distinguishes the suretyship relationship from other forms of co-obligation. If A and B borrow money for their joint benefit and use, and A pays the entire loan, A is entitled only to contribution—that is, A can get back from B half of what A paid. By contrast, if A is a surety for B and pays the entire loan, A can get back from B the entire amount.

There are always at least three persons involved in any surety transaction. The primary obligor is known as the "principal" or the "principal debtor." The surety goes by a number of names, including "surety," "guarantor," and "accommodation party." The person to whom the obligation is owed is the "creditor." There are in consequence at least three sets of rights and duties: those between principal and creditor, those between surety and creditor, and those between principal and surety. If there are multiple sureties, then there will also be rights and duties between them. Much surety law is still case law, but there are a number of state and federal statutes and regulatory enactments that govern particular suretyship issues or types of suretyship contracts. If the obligation assured by the security is a negotiable instrument (such as a check or certain types of promissory notes) then the applicable law is found primarily in Article 3 of the Uniform Commercial Code.[71] In 1984, the Federal Trade Commission issued a rule that requires certain disclosures for consumer sureties.[72]

Although suretyship issues most often arise in the context of loan transactions, the law is by no means so limited. Many sureties are guaranteeing performance of non-monetary obligations. For example, there is a whole industry build around construction bonds. A construction bond is a suretyship contract under which the bonding company promises to complete a construction project if the building contractor fails to do so. (Of course, the actual construction work will not be done by the pinstriped executives of the bonding company, but by another contractor they hire to complete the work.)

The precise obligations of the surety are ultimately a matter of the contract it makes, but in the absence of express provisions to the contrary there are a number of implied rights and obligations. There are also many nuances and limitations that are not explored in this discussion because of space considerations. Moreover, sureties enjoy a number of defenses that are not available to principals; these too must be left to one side in this work. However, for the purposes of understanding bankruptcy, it is sufficient to sketch out the most important rules. The main types of suretyship contracts assuring the payment of loans, and their primary attributes, are as follows:

---

[71] See U.C.C. §§ 3-419, -605; Thomas D. Crandall, Michael J. Herbert & Lary Lawrence, Uniform Commercial Code § 15.8(1993).

[72] Michael J. Herbert, *Straining the Gnat: A Critique of the 1984 Federal Trade Commission Consumer Credit Regulations*, 38 S.C. L. Rev. 329, 355-59 (1987).

1. Guaranty of Payment. If the suretyship contract uses the word "guaranty" without any further limitation, the contract is normally construed to be a guaranty of payment. This means that the creditor may pursue the guarantor as soon as the obligation is due, without having to first obtain a judgment against the principal.[73]

2. Guaranty of Collection. In rare cases, a guaranty will be "of collection" rather than "of payment." This means that the creditor must in most cases sue the principal and attempt to collect the debt from the principal's assets before pursuing the surety.[74]

3. Accommodation Maker. This is the familiar "cosigner" of a loan—for example, a parent who co-signs an automobile loan with a child, or the president of a small corporation who cosigns with her corporation. The accommodation maker's contract is much like that of a guarantor of payment. If the debt is not paid when due, the accommodation maker may be sued immediately, without any prior recourse against the principal.[75]

It is important to stress that in each of these situations, the surety has a claim for full indemnification against the principal. By contrast, the principal has no right of contribution or indemnification against the surety. The principal was supposed to pay the debt; if the principal does not do so, the surety is entitled to attempt collection against it.[76]

Insofar as bankruptcy is concerned, there are several important suretyship issues. These are:

1. Claims against bankrupt sureties. Ordinarily, a claim of a creditor against a bankrupt surety will be a general unsecured claim. This is not always true; the surety may have both promised to pay the debt and secured that promise with collateral. If there is collateral subject to an unavoidable lien, the claim will be a secured claim.

2. Claims against bankrupt principals by sureties. Ordinarily, the surety's claim for indemnification against a bankrupt principal will be a general unsecured claim; in the rare case that there is collateral for the surety's claim it will be a secured claim. There can be difficult problems if the surety's claim is contingent—that is, if the principal has not yet forced the surety to pay the debt. The subject of contingent claims is discussed more fully in § 10.02[C] of this book.

3. Protection of non-bankruptcy sureties of bankrupt principals. As a general rule, the bankruptcy of the principal does not have any effect on the right of the creditor to sue the surety; indeed, bankruptcy is one of the reasons why a creditor wants to have a surety. However, in Chapter 12 and 13, actions against some sureties are automatically stayed during the

---

[73] Laurence P. Simpson, Handbook on the Law of Suretyship § 6 (1950).

[74] Laurence P. Simpson, Handbook on the Law of Suretyship § 7 (1950).

[75] U.C.C. §§ 3-419(b), -412.

[76] Laurence P. Simpson, Handbook on the Law of Suretyship §§ 47-48 (1950).

proceeding; the court has some discretion to order a similar stay when the automatic stay rules do not apply. This issue is discussed in §§ 8.04 and 8.05.

§ 2.11 Examination of the Debtor

State laws provide for debtor's examinations, which are hearings at which a judgment debtor must give sworn testimony about its assets. This is a device to assist a creditor in locating, seizing, and liquidating the debtor's property. Since the examination is under oath, any lie by the debtor may subject the debtor to prosecution for perjury (although such prosecutions are extremely rare). Upon disclosure of the existence and location of the debtor's assets, it may be possible to seize them immediately. For example, at least one young lawyer was told by his supervising partner to ask the debtor, " 'How did you get to the court?' When he says, 'In my car,' ask the judge to order him to hand over the keys."

§ 2.12 Contempt Sanctions

Under certain circumstances, a debtor may be held in contempt of court for failure to obey a court order in a collection proceeding. For example, it is common in Article 9 security agreements to contractually require the defaulting debtor to assist the secured party in locating and gathering collateral.[77] If the debtor refuses to comply with this provision, the secured party may be able to get a court order for specific performance of the debtor's promise. Further refusal then becomes civil contempt; a court may order the debtor to pay a fine or even suffer imprisonment.[78]

§ 2.13 Seller's Right of Reclamation

Under Article 2 of the Uniform Commercial Code, a seller who discovers that it has delivered goods, on credit, to a buyer who is insolvent has a limited right to reclaim those goods from the buyer. To exercise this right, the seller must make a demand on the buyer within 10 days after the buyer received the goods.[79] Since nearly all reclamations occur in a bankruptcy proceeding, the U.C.C. provision must be read in conjunction with section 546(c) of the Code. That provision broadly validates the reclamation right, but modifies the U.C.C. rules slightly. Under section 546(c), the demand for reclamation must be in writing.[80] The 10 day period given to the seller to make the demand is absolute unless the bankruptcy occurs during

---

[77] Provisions of this sort are specifically validated by U.C.C. § 9-503.

[78] Such imprisonment should not be violative of the widespread prohibitions on imprisonment for debt, because the imprisonment is not on account of the debt but rather for contemptuous refusal to obey the court's order.

[79] U.C.C. § 2-702(2).

[80] Bankruptcy Code § 546(c).

that period, in which case it is extended to 20 days.[81] Under the U.C.C. provision, there is no time limit if the buyer has made a written misrepresentation about its solvency to the seller during the preceding three months.[82] Since section 546(c) is federal law, its absolute 10 -20 day rule supersedes the U.C.C.'s more flexible version. Finally, section 546(c) gives the bankruptcy judge three options: either the goods can be returned, or the seller can be given a lien on property to secure the seller's claim for payment, or the court may grant the seller an administrative priority claim for payment.[83] The last alternative is appropriate only if it is probable that all administrative claims will be paid in full.

Note that section 546 does not create a right of reclamation. It merely recognizes a state-created right:

> [The] Bankruptcy Code does not create any right of reclamation for sellers of goods to insolvent buyers. It merely recognizes such a right to a limited extent in a bankruptcy case, if any such right exists under either common law or statute other than the Bankruptcy Code. Thus, section 546(c) requires as premise that the reclaiming seller have an independent right of reclamation under applicable nonbankruptcy law. Section 546(c) then narrows those nonbankruptcy reclamation rights by imposing additional procedural and substantive requirements before such rights will be recognized in a bankruptcy case.[84]

In short, for reclamation right to be good in bankruptcy, the seller must comply with all the requirements of both the U.C.C. and of the Bankruptcy Code. Compliance with the U.C.C. is required because that establishes the state law right. Compliance with the Bankruptcy Code is required because that provides the protection for the state law right when the buyer has gone into bankruptcy.

---

[81] Bankruptcy Code § 546(c)(1)(B). The additional 10 day period for reclamation was added by the 1994 Amendments.

[82] U.C.C. § 2-702(2). For a fuller discussion, see Thomas D. Crandall, Michael J. Herbert & Lary Lawrence, Uniform Commercial Code § 8.13.3.

[83] Bankruptcy Code § 546(c)(2).

[84] In re Video King of Illinois, Inc., 100 Bankr. 1008, 1013 (Bankr. N.D. Ill. 1989).

the period in which [illegible] it is expected to [illegible] have [illegible] form [illegible] the [illegible] of the buyer [illegible] made [illegible] contrary to the [illegible] during the preceding [illegible] Since section [illegible] [illegible] 10-day [illegible] supersedes the [illegible] [illegible] made by the seller [illegible] or [illegible] contrary to [illegible] the seller [illegible] of payment [illegible] claim the provision. The last alternative is appropriate only if it is [illegible] all [illegible] claims will be paid [illegible].

[illegible] may not [illegible]

[illegible]

[illegible]

CHAPTER 3

A Brief History of Bankruptcy

§ 3.01 The Bankruptcy Clause

The story of the United States Constitution is well known; post-independence concerns about the weakness of the central government led to the drafting in 1787 of a new federal charter to replace the existing Articles of Confederation. After a considerable struggle, the Constitution was adopted by the requisite majority of the states. The enhanced national government was finally organized in the spring of 1789 (although the Constitution was not ratified by all the states until more than another year had passed).

Among the powers bestowed on the national government by the new Constitution was the power to enact "uniform laws on the subject of bankruptcies throughout the United States."[1] Like many of the other powers granted the nascent federal government, the bankruptcy power was largely dormant throughout the nineteenth century. And, like those other powers, it has come into its own in the twentieth. Although it is the commerce clause that has been the primary vehicle for the expansion of federal power over trade and credit, the bankruptcy clause has played a substantial secondary role. To a large and growing degree, the law of debtors and creditors has been federalized; Congress' power over bankruptcies is a major reason why.

§ 3.02 Bankruptcy Law Prior to 1898

During the 19th Century, the Congress exercised its bankruptcy power only sporadically, to meet the periodic crises of a growing market economy. Federal bankruptcy legislation was viewed as a temporary and emergency measure, only appropriate to deal with the aftermath of economic depression. Routine debtor-creditor adjustments were left to the states. In ordinary times, state creditors' rights law was viewed as sufficient to deal with the problems of debtor default. Temporary national bankruptcy laws were in force during 1800 to 1803, 1841 to 1843, and 1867 to 1878.[2]

§ 3.03 The Bankruptcy Act, 1898-1979

The first permanent bankruptcy law was the Bankruptcy Act of 1898. Enacted in the aftermath of the severe 1893 depression, it endured for more than 80 years

---

[1] U.S. Const. Art I, § 8, cl. 4.

[2] Collier on Bankruptcy, 15th ed. (1995), ¶ 1.02[4] [hereafter Collier on Bankruptcy].

with only one major group of amendments. As was true of all the prior bankruptcy acts, the 1898 act was born in controversy.

Two quite different groups were pressing Congress for a bankruptcy act. Debtors, including especially hard-hit farmers, wanted a voluntary act that would provide relief from creditor pressure. Creditors, especially commercial creditors, wanted an involuntary act that could be used to pry assets out of recalcitrant deadbeats. The resultant Act was an uneasy compromise that created both voluntary and involuntary forms of bankruptcy (but protected farmers from the latter), provided both a debtor's fresh start and new collection tools for lenders, and became the basis for a body of substantive and procedural law that is today of far more importance than the enacting Congress could have imagined.[3]

Although there were many amendments to the Act over the years (indeed, the first amendments were enacted just a couple of years after the Act was passed) the core of it remained intact until the Code. There was one very substantial addition—the Chandler Act of 1938, which, in response to another Great Depression, added several Chapters to the Act to deal with business and individual reorganization.[4] The business reorganization Chapters were denoted Chapter X, Chapter XI, and Chapter XII. Only the first two were of much significance (Chapter XII, according to some, was a piece of special legislation tailor-made for one specific company in a district represented by a powerful congressman). Chapter X was designed for the reorganization of large, publicly owned companies; Chapter XI for reorganizing small, closely held ones.[5]

From at least the 1960's onward, there was growing dissatisfaction with the Act. Complaints were many and varied. They included the often opaque language of the statute, which had been so glossed by court decision and scholarly interpretation that the actual words of the Act were often ignored. The division of business reorganizations into Chapters X and XI was viewed as cumbersome and productive of unnecessary and expensive litigation.[6] Chapter XIII seemed to be a failure in all but a few districts.[7] The court system was clumsy, the jurisdictional provisions defied rational analysis, and the entire Act reflected a horse-and-buggy financial world far removed from contemporary life.

Under the sponsorship of Senator Quentin Burdick a commission, known as the Burdick Commission, was appointed to study and recommend revision of the Act.[8] The commission was lightly staffed and funded; perhaps for this reason it did a remarkable job of analyzing existing law and proposing changes. Although many of its recommendations did not survive the legislative process,[9] they served as the framework for Congress' eventual action.

---

[3] Bankruptcy recently peaked at just below 1,000,000 cases per year.

[4] Note that there had earlier been reorganization provisions for railroads and some other businesses—see § 17.01 of this book.

[5] See § 17.01 of this book.

[6] See § 17.01 of this book.

[7] See § 18.01 of this book.

[8] Collier on Bankruptcy ¶ 1.03[2][a].

[9] Collier on Bankruptcy ¶ 1.03[2] -[5].

After much legislative wrangling over both the substance of the Code and its sweeping jurisdictional provisions, the Bankruptcy Reform Act of 1978 (which included both the Bankruptcy Code and a number of related procedural and jurisdictional rules) was enacted. The Bankruptcy Reform Act, or BRA, provides the current framework for bankruptcy law. It is the BRA and its Code, as amended and interpreted, that we study in this book.

§ 3.04 The Bankruptcy Code, 1979-

Few laws that did not involve taxes have been greeted with as much anticipation as the Code. During the final months of the Act, bankruptcy filings dwindled as lawyers waited to take advantage of the new law. A burst of pent-up filings greeted the Code when it came into effect. The most distinguished treatise in the field, Collier on Bankruptcy, was issued in a new (15th) edition specifically designed to deal with the new law.

The Code became effective on October 1, 1979, and almost immediately became the subject of much debate and many calls for revision. The loudest complaints came from the consumer credit industry, which decried the Code as a virtual charter for deadbeats. It may seem odd that so much of the furor centered on the consumer bankruptcy. Chapter 11, a mainly business chapter, is arguably the most pro-debtor chapter in the Code,[10] and the monetary stakes in the typical consumer bankruptcy are negligible. However, consumer creditors were concerned not by any particular bankruptcy, but by the overall effect they saw on consumer borrowers' willingness to repay. It was not the fear of losing $100 that spooked creditors, but the fear of losing $100 a million times over. If indeed the Bankruptcy Code invited and rewarded bankruptcy, then bad debts would rise, profits would fall, the price of credit would be pushed up and the specter of government intervention to cap interests rates would loom.

Whether the Bankruptcy Code was a significant contributing factor to increased bankruptcy is by no means clearly established. It is certainly true that October 1, 1979, marked the beginning of a long period of generally rising bankruptcy filings. The meaning one ascribes to these raw numbers, however, is less clear. The years 1979 through 1982 included a period of considerable economic stress, with a burst of high inflation followed by the worst recession since World War II. With greater prosperity in the mid-1980's, bankruptcy rates stabilized, then fell (although admittedly not to their pre-1979 levels). More economic trouble in the late 1980's and early 1990's led to another surge; the improvement in the economy after 1991 has led to another plateau, and by 1994 filing rates were markedly down. However, while it is true that the rate of bankruptcy closely correlates with the current state of the economy, the secular trend is higher; each peak rises further while each trough is shallower. Clearly, the response to current economic conditions does not entirely explain the steady, if zig-zag, rise in bankruptcy filings since the Code was enacted.

---

[10] For a general critique of Chapter 11's possible pro-debtor tilt, see Lynn M. LoPucki, *The Debtor in Full Control—Systems Failure Under Chapter 11 of the Bankruptcy Code*, Parts 1 & 2, 57 Am. Bankr. L. J. 99, 247 (1983).

It may also be that the increase in consumer bankruptcies is simply reflective of the increase in consumer debt, and that the increase in consumer debt reflects a change in attitudes by lenders. Borrowers might not be more feckless; rather, lenders may have decided to lower their standards, sacrificing collectibility to maintain volume. It may well be that consumer lenders may have decided to cut their average margins on individual loans (by accepting higher default rates) so as to obtain greater numbers of loans overall.

Bankruptcy statistics are a bit like a Rorshach test. They tend to reveal the perspective of the person looking at them. Like the raw data on global warming (or is it cooling?), they can support almost any point of view.

In any event, the struggle over the original version of the Code came to a head in 1982. Much to the surprise of most observers, the United States Supreme Court held that the jurisdictional provisions of the Bankruptcy Reform Act were unconstitutional.[11] Suddenly, the country was faced with the possibility that there would be no bankruptcy system at all.

For two years, while the bankruptcy courts labored under a jury-rigged system of possibly unconstitutional jurisdictional rules, Congress fought over revision of the Code. One of the main struggles was over consumer bankruptcy. Many efforts were made to scale back the relief afforded to consumers, even to force some consumers to reorganize under Chapter 13 rather than to liquidate under Chapter 7.

The most draconian creditor proposals were defeated. What was left was a series of half-measures, which are discussed at various points in this book. Even those half-measures, though, have to a measurable degree made it more difficult for at least some consumer debtors to get discharged. It was not entirely inaccurate to refer to BAFJA, as one wag did, as "Bankcard's Revenge."[12] Of greater significance were other changes made, most notably the new and highly complicated jurisdictional structure discussed in Chapter 5 of this book.[13] Unloved and late, the Bankruptcy Amendments and Federal Judgeship Act of 1984—known to all as BAFJA—came into force in October, 1984.

Almost exactly two years later, Congress sprang yet another October surprise. The Bankruptcy Judges, United States Trustees and Family Farmer Bankruptcy act of 1986 (which alas has no comfortable acronym, since BJUSTAFFBA is a bit hard to pronounce) came into effect in October, 1986. The two most important provisions of this law were nationwide establishment[14] of the previously experimental U.S. Trustee program, and the enactment of Chapter 12, for reorganization of family

[11] Northern Pipeline Construction Co. v. Marathon Pipe Line Co., 458 U.S. 50 (1982), judgment stayed, 459 U.S. 813 (1982). For a detailed discussion of this case, and its effect on bankruptcy law see § 5.03 of this book.

[12] Paul M. Black & Michael J. Herbert, *Bankcard's Revenge: A Critique of the 1984 Consumer Credit Amendments to the Bankruptcy Code,* 19 U. Rich. L. Rev. 845 (1985)

[13] See § 5.04.

[14] Well, almost—two states retain a different system. See § 4.03 of this book.

farms. Perhaps in reaction to the stingy spirit of BAFJA—or perhaps because there are a lot of farm-state senators—Chapter 12 is a thoroughly "pro-debtor" chapter.[15]

There were still many complaints about, and much tinkering with, the Code. Dissatisfaction did not lessen; however, it increasingly focused on business rather than consumer bankruptcy. The hot issues from the mid 1980's through the early 1990's centered around the creative use of bankruptcy to deal with mass torts, labor unions, and declining real estate prices. One hears much less today about forcing consumers into Chapter 13. One hears a great deal about abolishing Chapter 11.[16] We have thus gone in a few years from considering whether it is appropriate to force consumers to reorganize in bankruptcy to considering whether it is appropriate to prohibit businesses from doing so.

A number of ambitious proposals were made to revamp and even to jettison the Code. In the last days of the unlamented 103rd Congress, a grab-bag of amendments squeezed through. The Bankruptcy Reform Act of 1994 continued the recent tradition of being enacted in October at the very end of a legislative session. It was, however, no October Revolution; indeed, it should probably be called the Bankruptcy Trivia Act. It made a number of relatively minor changes, overturned a few controversial court cases, and on the whole tilted the bankruptcy balance slightly in a pro-creditor direction. It strengthened still further the already dominant position of secured creditors, and provided some assistance to institutional lenders. It also forced practically every academic to rewrite his or her Bankruptcy syllabus, since many of the cases overturned were classroom favorites. However, the 1994 Amendments did not have the sweep of the 1978 Act, BAFJA, or even the 1986 Amendments. They did not affect the basic structure of bankruptcy law.

What next? The 1994 Amendments included one provision that could bring substantial change—they provided for a new Bankruptcy Commission that is to study the Code and make recommendations. True, the legislative history calls upon the Commission to be cautious; according to it, "the Commission should be aware that Congress is generally satisfied with the basic framework established in the current Bankruptcy Code. Therefore, the work of the Commission should be based upon reviewing, improving, and updating the Code in ways which do not disturb the fundamental tenents and balance of current law."[17] Whether this injunction will have any effect is unclear. It was, after all, written by staffers for a Democratic Congress; it may not reflect the views of a Republican one. In any event, the stage is set for yet another wrestling match over bankruptcy law. It is for this reason, as much as any other, that students must come to grips not only with the complexities of the Code today but the issues that will underlie the debate over the Code tomorrow.

---

[15] See Chapter 19 of this book.

[16] See § 17.01 of this book.

[17] Bankruptcy Reform Act of 1994, Section-by-Section Description, Title VI.

CHAPTER 4

The Bankruptcy System

§ 4.01 Introduction

Bankruptcy encompasses not only a body of substantive law, but also a set of procedural rules and an entire judicial and administrative system. Various procedural rules are studied throughout this book; however, an entire chapter is necessary to sketch the bankruptcy system. That system includes not only courts and a special appellate process, but also a separate administrative branch of the federal government.

It is remarkable, given the vast responsibilities assigned to the bankruptcy system, that its bureaucracy is small and relatively inexpensive. Moreover, there is a long tradition of making the system, insofar as possible, self-supporting; its costs are largely borne by its beneficiaries, the debtors and the creditors. This does not mean that the system is immune from criticism; a number of reform proposals, many of which will increase costs, are being considered.

§ 4.02 Bankruptcy Courts and Bankruptcy Judges

As noted in Chapter 5,[1] until recently bankruptcy lacked its own clearly defined court system, and its decision makers were low-status "referees" rather than honored federal judges. While it is no doubt true that many referees were of outstanding ability, they were branded with second, if not third, class status. Elements of this remain today; indeed, it is not too much to say that prejudice against bankruptcy judges has been a major factor in the rather jury-rigged system of bankruptcy jurisdiction discussed in Chapter 5.[2]

At present, the bankruptcy court is an autonomous adjunct of the district court. It has its own judges, courtrooms, clerks, and dockets. Its pleadings, orders, and other documents are captioned "U.S. Bankruptcy Court." However, its jurisdiction is essentially derivative of the district court's jurisdiction, and the district court may at any time withdraw part or all of any case from it.[3] The fact that such withdrawals are rare reflects only the practical reality that district court judges are not generally much interested in bankruptcy and are themselves overwhelmed with other litigation.

While exercising considerable independence in nearly all bankruptcy cases, the bankruptcy judge remains somewhat less than a full-fledged federal judge. A

[1] See § 5.02.

[2] See § 5.04.

[3] See § 5.04 of this book for a fuller discussion of the relationship between the district court and the bankruptcy court.

bankruptcy judge, unlike a district judge, is not appointed by the President and is not given life tenure. Rather, the bankruptcy judge is appointed by the judges of the relevant federal Circuit Court of Appeals for a term of 14 years.[4] This appointment can be, and often is, renewed. A bankruptcy judge may be removed during the term by the circuit court judges;[5] a district court judge can only be removed by impeachment in the House of Representatives and conviction by the Senate. The core of all this is that the Congress has given bankruptcy judges only the limited status of "Article I" judges rather than "Article III" judges who have life tenure revocable only upon bad behavior.[6] Life tenured Article III judges have strongly resisted promoting their bankruptcy brethren to the same status; this has created a nearly impenetrable thicket of jurisdictional and constitutional problems.[7] Moreover, rather adding insult to injury, the bankruptcy judge is paid only 92% of a district judge's salary.[8] While it is probably true that most bankruptcy judges enjoy collegial relationships with their district judges, there are occasional horror stories reported—such as the refusal of some district judges to permit their bankruptcy judges to use the same elevator.

Given these problems, it is noteworthy that the quality of the bankruptcy bench is quite high. While there is much grumbling from creditors that too many bankruptcy judges are "pro-debtor," there is much to indicate that there is broad satisfaction with the overall quality of bankruptcy's judiciary, and a perception that it continues to improve. It is likely that the power of the bankruptcy court and the bankruptcy judge will continue its long secular trend of expansion, and that objections to full Article III status will continue to diminish. Whether this will eventually lead to full equality between the district judges and the bankruptcy judges remains to be seen.

---

[4] 28 U.S.C. § 152(a)(1). If a majority of the circuit judges cannot agree on an appointment, the bankruptcy judge is appointed by the chief judge of the circuit. 28 U.S.C. § 152(a)(3). In United States Territories, the district judges serve as bankruptcy judges, unless Congress authorizes the appointment of bankruptcy judges, in which case they are appointed by the Circuit Court within which the territorial district is located. 28 U.S.C. § 152(a)(4).

[5] The grounds for removal, however, are limited and there are procedural protections:

> A bankruptcy judge may be removed during the term for which such bankruptcy judge is appointed, only for incompetence, misconduct, neglect of duty, or physical or mental disability and only by the judicial council of the circuit in which the judge's official duty station is located. Removal may not occur unless a majority of all the judges of such council concur in the order of removal.

28 U.S.C. § 152(e).

[6] Note, however, that bankruptcy judges are "judicial officers of the United States district court established under Article III of the Constitution." 28 U.S.C. § 152(a)(1).

[7] See § 5.01 of this book.

[8] 28 U.S.C. § 153(a).

§ 4.03 United States Trustees

Prior to the Bankruptcy Code, the bankruptcy courts had only a rudimentary administrative structure. Basic issues, such as the appointment and supervision of trustees and creditors' committees were dealt with by the bankruptcy judge, sometimes rather haphazardly. Indeed, it was not uncommon that the judge wore several hats—judicial officer (ruling on contested issues), dispenser of patronage (appointing trustees), and guru (dispensing ex parte wisdom and advice).[9] Although in the view of some there is little evidence that these many roles led to outright corruption or systematic abuse, the inherent conflict in them was one reason for the subordinate status of bankruptcy judges, and one problem the Congress was determined to address in the Code.

The Congressional solution is the United States Trustee (except in a few districts, where the slightly different office of Bankruptcy Administrator is used).[10] The U.S. Trustee was created for the purpose of taking over the administrative functions formerly left in the hands of the judge. Originally a pilot program for only a few districts, the U.S. Trustee program went nationwide under the 1986 Amendments.[11] The United States Trustee is appointed by the United States Attorney General for a term of 5 years (subject, however, to removal at any time, with or without cause).[12] The powers of the U.S. Trustee are broad, and there are proposals to make them still broader. Among (many) other things, the U.S. Trustee does the following:

1. Establishes the panel of trustees available to serve in particular cases.[13]
2. Monitors applications for professional compensation and reimbursement and comments on those applications when appropriate.[14]
3. Monitors Chapter 11 plans and disclosure statements and comments on them;[15]
4. Monitors Chapter 12 and 13 plans and comments on them;[16]

---

[9] Especially to inexperienced young lawyers, such as your humble narrator.

[10] 28 U.S.C. § 581; the Bankruptcy Administrator is used in Alabama and North Carolina and is supposed to be phased out by 2002. The functions of the Bankruptcy Administrator were slightly enhanced by the 1994 Amendments, to more clearly conform to the functions of the United States Trustee.

[11] Michael J. Herbert, *Once More Unto the Breach, Dear Friends: The 1986 Reforms of the Reformed Bankruptcy Reform Act*, 16 Cap. U. L. Rev. 325, 326 (1987).

[12] 28 U.S.C. § 581(b), (c). The same act created the office of assistant United States Trustee, who may appointed when the public interest so requires and serves at the pleasure of the Attorney General. 28 U.S.C. § 582(a), (b).

[13] 28 U.S.C. § 586(a)(1).

[14] 28 U.S.C. § 586(a)(3)(A). For a discussion of professional compensation under the Bankruptcy Code, see § 20.03 of this book.

[15] 28 U.S.C. § 586(a)(3)(B). For a discussion of Chapter 11 plans and disclosure statements, see § 17.11 of this book.

[16] 28 U.S.C. § 586(a)(3)(C). For a discussion of Chapter 12 and 13 plans, see §§ 19.07 and 18.07 of this book, respectively.

5. Monitors creditors' committees;[17]
6. Appoints the interim Chapter 7 trustee;[18] who serves unless and until a trustee is elected by creditors;[19]
7. Appoints the Chapter 11 Creditors' Committee,[20] and
8. Has standing to move for dismissal of a consumer Chapter 7 proceeding on the ground that the filing is a substantial abuse of the Bankruptcy Code.[21]

Many other powers and obligations of the U.S. Trustee will be discussed in this book.

§ 4.04 Standing Trustees (Chapters 12 and 13)

Chapters 12 and 13 utilize trustees in a way that is quite different from Chapter 7. Proceedings under the latter chapter always involve a debtor-in-possession, as do nearly all proceedings under the former. However, all Chapter 12 and 13 cases are assigned to a "standing" trustee whose job it is to supervise cases throughout the court district.[22] The job of the standing trustee is somewhat similar to that of the U.S. Trustee (although the powers are much more limited); the standing trustee is to oversee and comment on cases, not to manage them. Some standing trustees are extremely influential in establishing district-wide standards for such things as the adequacy of the debtor's plan.

§ 4.05 Panel (a/k/a Case) Trustees

A panel or case trustee is the person who is responsible for administering a particular estate on behalf of its creditors.[23] By tradition a lawyer with bankruptcy experience, the panel/case trustee is used in all Chapter 7 cases and in a very few Chapter 11 and 12 cases. It is this trustee who is supposed to find the debtor's assets, abandon those that are of no value, sell the remainder, and distribute the proceeds. The panel/case trustee is also required to pursue preferences, fraudulent transfers,

[17] 28 U.S.C. § 586(a)(3)(E).

[18] Bankruptcy Code § 701(a)(1).

[19] For a discussion of the election of the Chapter 7 trustee, see § 16.05 of this book.

[20] Bankruptcy Code § 1102(a)(1). For a discussion of the Chapter 11 creditors' committee, see § 17.04 of this book.

[21] Bankruptcy Code § 707(b).

[22] See §§ 18.04 and 19.03 of this book.

[23] Case trustees are also referred to as panel trustees, because they are normally appointed from a panel of potential trustees established by the U.S. Trustee. It is more accurate to use the term "panel trustee" only when referring to those on the panel and "case trustee" when referring to the trustee in a particular case; not all trustees serving in a case are appointed from the panel. Chapter 11 trustees, who are rarely appointed, are normally not taken from the panel.

and other avoidable transactions. The trustee is to examine the debtor and where necessary attack the discharge.[24] Curiously, the Chapter 7 panel/case trustee may not attack the filing under section 707(b), which prohibits abusive Chapter 7 filings by consumer debtors.[25]

§ 4.06 Eligibility, Qualification, and Role of Standing and Case Trustees

To be eligible as either a standing trustee or a case trustee, an individual must be competent to perform the trustee's duties[26] and, in a Chapter 7, 12, or 13 case, must either reside in or have an office in (i) the district in which the case is pending or (ii) a district adjacent to the district in which the case is pending.[27] A corporation can also serve as a trustee (although this is rare). To be eligible, the corporation must be authorized in its charter or bylaws to act as a trustee and, in a Chapter 7, 12, or 13 case, must either reside in or have an office in (i) the district in which the case is pending or (ii) a district adjacent to the district in which the case is pending.[28] A person who has served as an examiner[29] in the case may not serve as trustee.[30] The U.S. trustee may serve as trustee in a particular case only "if necessary."[31]

The case trustee must also "qualify." This is another way of saying that the trustee must get a bond ensuring that the trustee will perform the required duties. Within five days after the trustee's appointment, and before the trustee begins official duties, the trustee must file with the court a bond in favor of the United States, conditioned on the faithful performance of the trustee's official duties.[32]

The role of the trustee is representative of the estate.[33] This is a fiduciary duty; the trustee must act for the best interests of the estate. In the typical liquidation case, this translates to obtaining the maximum dividend for creditors.

§ 4.07 The Bankruptcy Estate

Central to all bankruptcy, especially liquidation bankruptcy, is the definition of the bankruptcy estate. This is simply the shorthand term for the property that is administered in the bankruptcy proceeding. Moreover, the value of this property provides the baseline for distribution to creditors. In a liquidation proceeding, the

---

[24] For a fuller discussion of the duties of the panel/case trustee, see § 16.06 of this book.

[25] For a discussion of Bankruptcy Code § 707(b), see § 16.03[B] of this book.

[26] Bankruptcy Code § 321(a)(1).

[27] Bankruptcy Code § 321(a)(1).

[28] Bankruptcy Code § 321(a)(2).

[29] For a discussion of the role of an examiner, see § 17.06 of this book.

[30] Bankruptcy Code § 321(b).

[31] Bankruptcy Code § 321(c).

[32] Bankruptcy Code § 322(a).

[33] Bankruptcy Code § 323(a).

creditors receive either the estate's property or the value of the estate's property. In reorganization, the creditors are entitled to receive at least the value of the property that would have been in the Chapter 7 estate.

Under pre-Code law, only some of the bankrupt's property became part of the estate; for example, exempt property was excluded.[34] The Code takes a somewhat different tack. All of the debtor's property becomes property of the estate when the bankruptcy is filed. Some portion of that property may subsequently cease to be property of the estate, either because of exemptions, abandonment, or transfer. Generally speaking, the scope of the estate is most narrowly circumscribed in an individual proceeding under Chapter 7.

Section 541 defines property of the estate. Insofar as property owned by the debtor prior to the commencement of the case is concerned, the definition is nearly all-inclusive. The estate includes virtually all legal or equitable property interests that the debtor had at the time the case was commenced,[35] including nearly all community property interests of the debtor,[36] property recovered under the trustee's/DIP's avoiding powers,[37] and other property interests. The exact composition of the estate is discussed in full detail in Chapter 7 of this book.

§ 4.08 Debtors and Debtors in Possession

Throughout this book, the terms "debtor" and "debtor in possession" are used. The former term applies to the bankrupt.[38] It is used in lieu of the more familiar term because Congress thought that the word "bankrupt" was unpleasant.[39] The term functions well enough as a politically correct euphemism, but creates occasional slight difficulty as to whether, in any particular context, it refers to an obligor or to the subject of a bankruptcy proceeding.

In a Chapter 7 proceeding, the debtor is usually of little significance in the formal part of the case. Once the petition and schedules are filed,[40] the debtor's only statutory role is loser of its non-exempt property (if any) and winner of discharge. There are exceptions to this; for example, there may be litigation over the dischargeability of particular debts, over whether discharge should be granted, and other matters. However, especially in a consumer bankruptcy where there are few debts, fewer assets, and little likelihood of serious misconduct by the debtor, such litigation is rare.

---

[34] For a discussion of exemptions under the Code, see Chapter 11 of this book.

[35] Bankruptcy Code § 541(a)(1).

[36] Bankruptcy Code § 541(a)(2).

[37] Bankruptcy Code § 541(a)(3).

[38] Bankruptcy Code § 101(13).

[39] "The general term debtor is used . . . for ease of reference . . . and as a means of reducing the stigma connected with the term bankrupt." H.R. Rep. No. 595, 95th Cong., 1st Sess. 310 (1977).

[40] See Chapter 6 of this book.

Some of the debtor's duties are sketched out in section 521. In addition to filing the schedules, the debtor must cooperate with the trustee,[41] surrender property of the estate and relevant records to the trustee,[42] and appear at the discharge hearing (if any).[43] A consumer debtor must also file a statement of intentions regarding encumbered property—specifically, whether the debtor intends to retain the property, surrender the property, claim the property as exempt, redeem the property, or reaffirm the debt that is secured by the property.[44] Ordinarily, the debtor must act on the stated intention within 45 days after filing the notice.[45] This list is by no means exhaustive. Throughout these materials we will we see that the debtor may have many other duties even in a liquidation proceeding.

A "debtor-in-possession" (DIP) is created whenever a debtor files under Chapters 11, 12, or 13. The debtor is a debtor-in-possession because there is normally no case trustee appointed to take over the estate.[46] The term technically applies to the debtor itself, but is often used to describe its management—for example, when ABC Corporation files Chapter 11, its successor in the bankruptcy is ABC Corporation, Debtor-in-Possession—but when people refer to the DIP they may well be referring to Joe Abc, the president of ABC Corporation.

The DIP is a primary participant in the proceedings. The DIP has many of the powers and functions of the trustee,[47] and conducts whatever negotiations precede the filing of the plan of reorganization. The DIP however is not the person who filed, but rather a person created by the filing; ABC Corporation and ABC Corporation Debtor-in-Possession are two different legal entities.[48]

§ 4.09 Creditors, Creditor Examination, and Creditors' Committees

Generally speaking, bankruptcy proceedings are supposed to be for the benefit of two groups: debtors and creditors. The former benefit from discharge and the fresh start; the latter from the presumably efficient and even-handed administration and distribution of the debtor's non-exempt property. The interests of these two groups are inevitably in conflict, especially in Chapter 7 liquidation.

In virtually all cases most creditors play an entirely passive role. Apart from filing a proof of claim and perhaps receiving a distribution, the typical creditor does nothing and pays no heed to what does happen. The reason for this is simple economics; the bankruptcy value of the typical claim is negligible, and creditors who

---

[41] Bankruptcy Code § 521(3).

[42] Bankruptcy Code § 521(4).

[43] Bankruptcy Code § 521(5).

[44] Bankruptcy Code § 521(2)(A).

[45] Bankruptcy Code § 521(2)(B).

[46] There are some situations under Chapters 11 and 12 in which the DIP is displaced by a trustee—see §§ 17.06 and 19.03 of this book, respectively.

[47] See Bankruptcy Code §§ 1107, 1203, and 1303.

[48] For a discussion of some of the implications of this, see § 9.02 of this book.

have already given up hope of collection are rarely interested in sending good money after bad by participating in the case. With rare exceptions, only those creditors whose claims have real value in bankruptcy play an active part; and, in most cases, only creditors with secured claims have claims with real value.

Section 341 requires the United States Trustee to convene and preside at a meeting of creditors within a reasonable time after the order for relief.[49] The U.S. Trustee may also convene a meeting of equity security holders.[50] In a sharp change from the law under the act, the bankruptcy judge may not even attend any meeting convened under this provision;[51] the purpose of this prohibition is to safeguard the impartiality of the judge, who may be called upon to adjudicate matters that might arise at these meetings. The 341 hearing, as it is often called, is open to all creditors, not just those who serve on a creditors' committee.

The single most important function of the section 341 creditors' meeting is to provide a forum for an examination of the debtor. This examination serves the same function as a state law debtor's examination. It gives the creditors the opportunity to probe for the location of assets and into other matters such as fraudulent conveyances, preferences, and the like.[52]

Section 343 states that the debtor shall appear and submit to examination under oath at the section 341(a) hearing. The debtor may be questioned by the creditors, any indenture trustee, the case trustee, an examiner[53] or the United States Trustee.[54] The scope of the examination encompasses "the debtor's acts, conduct, or property, or any matter that may affect the administration of the estate, or the debtor's right to discharge" and in a reorganization case may also include "inquiry into the liabilities and financial condition of the debtor, the operation of his business, and the desirability of the continuance thereof, and other matters relevant to the case and to the formulation of the plan."[55]

The examination must concern matters that are relevant to the bankruptcy itself. Moreover, in at least some circumstances the debtor may refuse to disclose trade secrets and similar proprietary information.[56] However, there is no requirement that the examination comply with strict rules of evidence or that all of the testimony be admissible.[57] The debtor—who has a general duty to surrender books and records to the trustee, if any[58] —may be ordered to produce those books and records for

---

[49] Bankruptcy Code § 341(a).

[50] Bankruptcy Code § 341(b).

[51] Bankruptcy Code § 341(c).

[52] For a discussion of the state law debtor's examination, see § 2.11 of this book.

[53] For the role of the examiner, see § 17.06 of this book.

[54] Bankruptcy Code § 343.

[55] H. R. Rep. No. 595, 95th Cong., 1st Sess 332 (1977); S. Rep. No. 989, 95th Cong., 2d Sess. 43 (1978).

[56] See In re Continental Forge Co., Inc. 73 Bankr. 1005, 1007 (Bankr. W. D. Pa. 1987).

[57] See Collier on Bankruptcy ¶ 343.04.

[58] Bankruptcy Code § 521(4).

a section 341 hearing.[59] The debtor clearly retains its constitutional privilege against self incrimination; however, immunity from prosecution may be granted; if it is, the debtor must testify.[60]

Under some Chapters of the Code, a creditors' committee is organized to supervise the proceeding. Creditors' committees are of greatest significance in Chapter 11; the Chapter 11 rules are discussed in detail in Chapter 17.[61] However, they are also occasionally used in Chapter 7 proceedings—see Chapter 16.[62]

§ 4.10 Lawyers and Other Professionals

It is fair to say that lawyers dominate bankruptcy proceedings. The trustee is usually a lawyer, represented by another lawyer. Although pro se proceedings are permitted, the debtor will usually have a lawyer. A creditors' committee is likely to have a lawyer; so may individual creditors. In large cases there will be a great many lawyers, with correspondingly large fees; the largest business bankruptcies have fees in the tens of millions of dollars.

Other professionals may also be hired. These include accountants, actuaries, and in rare cases business consultants. Their fees too may be very high. Indeed, there is a perception that some cases, particularly some protracted Chapter 11 cases, serve mainly to provide lawyers with large fees at the expense of creditors.

The court exercises control over all fees paid by the debtor or from the estate. The details of this process are discussed in Chapter 20.[63] In addition, that Chapter and others in this book discuss the special professional responsibility issues that may arise in a bankruptcy proceeding.

§ 4.11 Bankruptcy Rules

Bankruptcy is a body of both substantive and procedural law. The procedural aspects of bankruptcy are largely contained in the Bankruptcy Rules and Official Forms. Broadly speaking, the Bankruptcy Rules are divided into three main groupings. The first deals with matters that are specific to bankruptcy—for example, the contents of the petition or the time within which proofs of claim may be filed. The second group deals with adversary proceedings—litigation that occurs during the bankruptcy. Those rules are closely modeled on the Federal Rules of Civil Procedure; indeed, many merely incorporated by reference the relevant FRCP rule, sometimes with minor alterations.[64] The third group deals with bankruptcy appeals.

---

[59] Collier on Bankruptcy ¶ 343.05.

[60] See Bankruptcy Code § 344.

[61] See § 17.04.

[62] See § 16.09.

[63] See § 20.03.

[64] For example, see Bankruptcy Rule 7005, which says, in full:

Rule 7005. Service and Filing of Pleadings and Other Papers

Rule 5 F.R.Civ.P. applies in adversary proceedings.

In addition, there are a large number of official bankruptcy forms for such things as the petition, the schedules, proofs of claim, and the like.

In addition to the general Bankruptcy Rules, there are many local rules that are significant. In some districts, the local rules deal with more than housekeeping matters; for example, there are districts in which the local rules have been used to deal with the problems of small Chapter 11 proceedings. Beyond even these rules, which are at least codified, are innumerable local practice traditions. Despite the Constitutional mandate for a uniform law on bankruptcy, there are wide variations from district to district in the actual application of bankruptcy law.[65]

This book does not deal comprehensively or systematically with the Bankruptcy Rules, let alone local rules and customs. Some of the rules are sketched out, as are some of the better documented district practices. The student of bankruptcy law, however, should be aware from the outset that the academic view is a view from the top—that is, the view from the standpoint of statute and reported case law. The view from the trenches of actual practice is often significantly different.

§ 4.12 Trial Process

A bankruptcy is itself a piece of litigation; indeed, bankruptcy is one of the most common forms of litigation. However, within any proceeding, there may be sub-cases that are themselves litigated. For example, in a single bankruptcy case there may be disputes regarding preferential transfers, liquidation of claims, and requests to lift the automatic stay of actions against the estate's property. If those disputes are not resolved between the parties, then they will have to be tried. Depending on a variety of factors, including the complex jurisdictional rules that apply to bankruptcy cases,[66] the dispute may be tried in the bankruptcy court, in a federal district court, or in state court. It becomes a "case within a case," as is evidenced by the somewhat confusing nomenclature that is generally used. A reported opinion generally carries both the style of the case (for example, In re Styles) and of the specific matter litigated (for example, River Bank v. Landfall, Trustee of Styles, Inc.). The litigated matter may be indiscriminately referred to under either name in subsequent cases and in the commentary. For this reason, a number of bankruptcy cases are known under two different names.[67]

Bankruptcy court litigation within the bankruptcy case itself is generally done through an "adversary proceeding." An adversary proceeding may involve anything from a simple hearing to a full-blown trial. With some exceptions, the Federal Rules of Civil Procedure and the Federal Rules of Evidence apply. In a complex adversary proceeding, there may be extensive discovery and many witnesses; this, however, is not typical.

---

[65] Jean Braucher, *Lawyers and Consumer Bankruptcy: One Code, Many Cultures*, 67 Am. Bankr. L. J. 501 (1993).

[66] See Chapter 5 of this book.

[67] In this book, adversary proceedings within cases are generally cited in full, using both the style of the adversary proceeding and of the underlying case.

The 1994 Amendments have somewhat expanded, or at least clarified, the powers of the bankruptcy court in litigation. In those amendments, the bankruptcy court was specifically given the power to hold status conferences regarding any case or proceeding,[68] previously, there was some debate over the propriety of such conferences. In addition, there is now a statutory process for conducting at least some jury trials in the bankruptcy court.[69] The significance, and indeed the propriety, of the jury trial rules is discussed further elsewhere in this book.[70]

§ 4.13 Appellate Process

Bankruptcy cases are subject to a rather complex set of appellate rules. Some of these rules are jurisdictional; the scope of review depends on whether the bankruptcy judge is acting as a judge who hears and decides cases or as a referee who hears and makes proposed findings of fact. In the former case, the scope of review is limited; in the latter it is de novo. Because these rules are intimately tied to the court's jurisdictional authority, they are discussed in Chapter 5.[71]

Other rules are strictly procedural. In all federal judicial circuits except the 9th Circuit, the first level of appeal has been from the bankruptcy court to the local district court. To some degree at least, this will change, due to the 1994 Amendments. As is true generally in appellate systems, appeals may ordinarily be taken only from final judgments, orders, and decrees. An interlocutory order or decree may generally be appealed only with leave of court.[72]

The Judicial Council of any Federal Circuit has long had the power to establish a somewhat different system for dealing with the initial appeal. The Council could create a bankruptcy appellate panel, comprised of bankruptcy judges from districts within the circuit.[73] The desire of district court judges to retain control over the bankruptcy court greatly limited the effectiveness of this provision. Prior to the 1994 Amendments, only the 9th Circuit established a bankruptcy appellate panel.

The 1994 Amendments have somewhat changed the status of the Bankruptcy Appellate Panel. Under the new provisions, the judicial council of each circuit must establish a Bankruptcy Appellate Panel Service unless it finds that there are insufficient judicial resources available or that the establishment of the BAPS would result in undue delay or increased cost to parties.[74] The ability of the BAPS to hear appeals

---

[68] Bankruptcy Code § 105(d)(1994 Amendments).

[69] 28 U.S.C. § 157(e)(1994 Amendments).

[70] See § 5.04[F].

[71] See § 5.04[E] .

[72] 28 U.S.C. § 158(a). See also, Bankruptcy Rule 8001(b)for the rules relating to an interlocutory appeal. Note that the 1994 Amendments permits an immediate interlocutory appeal of orders increasing or decreasing the period during which a Chapter 11 debtor has the exclusive right to propose a plan of reorganization. 28 U.S.C. § 158(a).

[73] 28 U.S.C. § 158(b)(1). It is also possible to establish a joint bankruptcy appellate panel for 2 or more districts. 28 U.S.C. § 158(b)(2) (amended 1994).

[74] 28 U.S.C. § 158(b)(1).

is dependent in part upon the district court judges and in part upon the parties to the appeal. In any given district, a majority of the district court judges must vote to authorize the BAPS to hear and determine appeals originating from that district.[75] If there is such an authorization, then the first layer of appeal is to a three-judge panel of the BAPS.[76] However, either party to the appeal may elect to have the appeal heard by the district court rather than the BAPS panel.[77]

Under either system, there is a second layer of appellate review. The Circuit Courts of Appeal have jurisdiction over appeals from the district court and the bankruptcy appellate panel. This is an appeal of right that any unsuccessful party may take.[78] It is limited to appeals from final decisions, judgments, orders and decrees.[79]

The final level of appeal is to the United States Supreme Court. In most cases there is no appeal of right. With few exceptions, Supreme Court review may only be sought by petitioning for a writ of certiorari.[80] Traditionally, the Court rarely took bankruptcy cases. In recent years, however, a substantial number of cert petitions have been granted, although the number declined sharply in 1994. Broadly speaking, the Court only accepts certiorari when an important question of statutory interpretation has resulted in a split between Circuit Courts.

---

[75] 28 U.S.C. § 158(b)(6).

[76] 28 U.S.C. § 158(b)(5). Note that none of the three judges may be from the district from which the appeal is being taken.

[77] 28 U.S.C. § 158(c).

[78] 28 U.S.C. § 158(d); see Collier on Bankruptcy ¶ 3.03[1][d][ii].

[79] 28 U.S.C. § 158(d). As is normally the case, however, it is at least possible to seek review of non-final orders through an extraordinary writ.

[80] Collier on Bankruptcy ¶ 3.03[1][e].

CHAPTER 5

Bankruptcy Jurisdiction and Venue

§ 5.01 Introduction

One of the most vexed problems in bankruptcy is, and long has been, the jurisdiction of the court acting in bankruptcy. For generations, lawyers, judges, and academics (not to mention bewildered law students) have complained about jurisdictional rules that are at best prolix and complex, and at worst downright perverse. There are many reasons why problems exist and have never been fully addressed. For the last two decades, however, one has predominated: the unwillingness of Congress to grant, and of much of the federal judiciary to countenance, life-tenured status for bankruptcy judges. The United States Constitution has been interpreted to permit two kinds of federal judges—full, Article III judges, appointed for life, and limited, Article I judges, serving at will or for a term of years.[1] The Supreme Court has decided that the former may exercise a much broader jurisdiction than the latter. This in turn affects bankruptcy, because bankruptcy requires the exercise of a broader jurisdiction than the Constitution allows to Article I judges, which is all that the bankruptcy judges are. Someone must have those broad powers; otherwise, the bankruptcy is unworkable. The conflict between the need for broad powers, and the reluctance to grant them, has led to a Rube Goldberg set of jurisdictional rules that even now may be unconstitutional.[2]

§ 5.02 Bankruptcy Jurisdiction Prior to 1984

Under the old Bankruptcy act, the bankruptcy jurisdiction was exercised in name, if not often in fact, by the district court judge, an Article III life-tenured judge. However, there was much confusion over the distinction between "summary" and "plenary" jurisdiction, a distinction not entirely unlike the current division between "core" and "non-core" proceedings, discussed below. This is now ancient history, except for the fact that Congress, when it enacted the Bankruptcy Reform Act of 1978, made a fatal decision to simplify the rules by granting the newly enhanced bankruptcy courts almost unlimited jurisdiction over matters pertaining to the bankruptcy and the estate, without also giving the bankruptcy judges life tenure. This reform was widely heralded as one of the great advances in bankruptcy law; yet it survived only until 1982, when it was struck down by the Supreme Court.

---

[1] For a further discussion of this issue, see § 4.02 of this book.

[2] It is believed by some bankruptcy professionals that the rules are of doubtful legality—but that the lawyers and judges alike are avoiding litigation over the issue because of an unwillingness to reopen the issue.

§ 5.03 The End of An Experiment: *Northern Pipeline (a/k/a Marathon Pipe Line)*

The effort to bestow broad jurisdiction on bankruptcy judges without granting them life tenure was put to a swift, if uncertain, end by the Supreme Court in 1982. The case was *Northern Pipeline Construction Co. v. Marathon Pipe Line Co.*[3] Much of the Court's reasoning in that case is obscure. However, its one clear and unequivocal message is that the great breadth of jurisdiction given to the untenured bankruptcy judiciary was unconstitutional.[4] The court was especially concerned about the ability of bankruptcy judges to rule on issues of state law. Only a full, life-tenured, Article III judge can be given the power that the Bankruptcy Reform Act gave to deal with matters so far removed from the Bankruptcy Code.

Although the BRA's grant of jurisdiction was utterly unconstitutional, the Court said that this utterly unconstitutional jurisdiction could still be exercised for several months. This stay of unconstitutionality was granted to permit Congress to concoct a solution; and the stay was extended for a further several months when Congress failed to act promptly. Congress, perhaps intrigued by this notion of flaunting constitutionality, or perhaps burdened with more pressing issues than the collapse of a large part of the federal judicial system, tarried beyond the original and the extended deadline, taking no action until 1984. The obvious solution—elevation of bankruptcy judges to Article III status, was rejected, in part because of pressure from Chief Justice Burger and other members of the federal judiciary and in part because a Democratic Congress did not want to give a Republican president the power to hand out some 200 lifetime appointments. A rather desperate, and conceivably constitutional, solution to the problem was devised by the courts themselves, and imposed by emergency rule. Finally, in 1984, as part of the Bankruptcy Amendments and Federal Judgeship Act, Congress acted. BAFJA's solution, which was to a degree modeled on the emergency rule, is controversial and perhaps constitutionally suspect; it is discussed in the next section.

§ 5.04 General Structure of Jurisdiction Since 1984

[A]—Introduction

BAFJA attempted to circumvent *Northern Pipeline* by a simple device: the assignment of jurisdiction to the district court with, however, the expectation that jurisdiction would generally be exercised by the bankruptcy judge. This device is propped up by other provisions that circumscribe the power of the bankruptcy judge (and even in some cases the district judge) to decide contested matters. However, this initial bit of legerdemain is at the core of the BAFJA rules. It is perhaps fortunate

---

[3] 458 U.S. 50 (1982), judgment stayed, 459 U.S. 813 (1982).

[4] As an example of the degree to which this decision came as a shock, I might mention that I was involved in the representation of one of the creditors in that case; and when I and other lawyers in my firm first learned of the constitutional challenge, we thought it was a joke.

that these rules are rarely reviewed with any eye toward strict enforcement of *Northern Pipeline*; if they were, the entire structure of bankruptcy jurisdiction might well be struck down.

[B]—Grant of Jurisdiction to the District Court

Bankruptcy jurisdiction is centered in the district court, of which the bankruptcy court is an autonomous adjunct. Six types of bankruptcy jurisdiction are set out: "cases under" Title 11; "civil proceedings arising under," "civil proceedings arising in," "civil proceedings related to," Title 11; "property of the debtor," and "property of the estate." The first four types are divided between the case itself and specific litigation that might occur under specific provisions of the bankruptcy code (such as preference litigation). The case itself is subject to the court's original and exclusive jurisdiction, as are those other issues that are resolved in the course of the proceeding. Other litigation that occurs during the case is subject to the courts original (but not exclusive) jurisdiction; in some situations, other courts may actually hear these matters. They are subdivided into "arising in," "arising under," and "related to." Roughly speaking, "arising under" refers to matters that are determined under the provisions of the Bankruptcy Code; "arising in" refers to non-Bankruptcy Code matters that come up in a bankruptcy proceeding; "related to" refers to matters that are, at least initially, outside the bankruptcy. In addition, the district court has exclusive jurisdiction of all the "property of the debtor" and all the "property of the estate."[5] Note that exercise of bankruptcy jurisdiction is not subject to the same geographical limitations imposed on state courts and (in most cases) district courts; it extends nationwide.[6]

To put it in chart form, the grants of jurisdiction to the district court are as follows:

EXCLUSIVE: The bankrutpcy case itself	Property of the Debtor
	Property of the Estate
ORIGINAL BUT NOT EXCLUSIVE: Civil proceedings arising under the Code	Civil proceedings arising in the bankruptcy
	Civil proceedings related to the bankruptcy

[5] The relevant provisions of the U.S. Code read as follows:

(a) Except as provided in subsection(b) of this section, the district courts shall have original and exclusive jurisdiction of all cases under title 11.

(b) Notwithstanding any Act of Congress that confers exclusive jurisdiction on a court or courts other than the district courts, the district courts shall have original but not exclusive jurisdiction of all civil proceedings arising under title 11, or arising in or related to cases under title 11.

. . .

(e) The district court in which a case under title 11 is commenced or is pending shall have exclusive jurisdiction of all of the property, wherever located, of the debtor as of the commencement of such case, and of property of the estate.

28 U.S.C. § 1334 (a), (b), (e).

[6] U.S.C. § 1334(e).

Of the various categories of jurisdiction, three are of primary significance, or at least create the most difficulties. These are "arising under", "arising in", and "related to." Those phrases will be used as terms of art in this discussion.

As noted, the district court has original and exclusive jurisdiction of all cases arising under Title 11.[7] Put simply, a bankruptcy case must be filed in the proper federal district court. Remember however that the bankruptcy court is in fact a part of the district court, so that filing a petition with the bankruptcy court is in fact filing a petition with the district court. In a real world context, the actual physical location at which the petition is to be filed is the office of the bankruptcy court clerk.

The district court has original but not exclusive jurisdiction of civil actions arising in, arising under, or related to a bankruptcy.[8] On the face of it, this means that civil actions involving the debtor may be filed in any of a number of courts, which could disrupt the orderly conduct of the bankruptcy. This impression, however, is misleading. Under section 362 of the Code, virtually every court action that could affect the debtor is stayed by the filing of the petition.[9] This means that although another court may have concurrent jurisdiction over the matter, the claimant will be prevented from initiating or continuing litigation in that court, unless the bankruptcy court orders the stay lifted.[10] Without such an order, jurisdiction can only be exercised by the district court/bankruptcy court.

These initial rules skirt the *Northern Pipeline* objection by formalistically placing the bankruptcy case, and all appurtenant matters, into the hands of the district court and its life-tenured judge. The practical exercise of this jurisdiction is quite another matter. This is discussed in the next section.

[C]—The Bankruptcy Judge's Exercise of Jurisdiction—General Order of Reference

The basic jurisdictional grant is a facade. With a few exceptions, the district court judge need not actually hear the bankruptcy or any of the related matters; indeed, the district judge rarely has any interest in doing so. Bankruptcy matters are automatically turned over to the bankruptcy judge under a "General Order of Reference."[11] This is simply a blanket order that bankruptcy matters go to the bankruptcy judge. What does this do to the exclusivity of the district court's jurisdiction regarding the case itself, the debtor's property, and property of the estate? Remember that the bankruptcy court is a part of the district court, and the bankruptcy judge an officer of the district court.[12] The general order of reference

---

[7] 28 U.S.C. § 1334(a).

[8] 28 U.S.C. § 1334(b).

[9] See Chapter 8 of this book for an extended discussion of this automatic stay.

[10] As noted in § 5.05 of this chapter, below, the court might also abstain from the matter and leave it to another tribunal to resolve.

[11] 28 U.S.C. § 157(a).

[12] See § 4.02 of this book.

merely moves the case from one part of the district court to another—from the life tenured Article III judge to the 14-year, 92% pay, Article I judge.

The district judge retains the power to withdraw the reference, in whole or in part, either on its own motion or the motion of any party. The district judge is required to withdraw the reference if determination of a particular matter requires interpretation of a federal statute regulating interstate commerce.[13] Thus, the district judge retains nominal power over the proceeding even when referred to the bankruptcy judge. The power however is rarely exercised. As a practical matter, therefore, it is almost always the non-tenured bankruptcy judge who actually exercises the district court's jurisdiction.

[D]—Cases Under/Core Proceedings Arising Under/Core Proceedings Arising In: Hear and Determine

The nominal power of the district court is further reinforced by the rules regarding review of the bankruptcy judge's decisions. Some decisions are given deference; that is, the bankruptcy judge has the same power as a district judge to make findings of fact, and the review of those findings is under the same standard used when the district court judge's findings are reviewed. Other decisions are given no (formal) deference; the bankruptcy judge is treated as a master or magistrate whose findings are reviewed de novo. In determining which is which, the rules introduce another category to those already studied: core proceedings. Some matters that fit within the "arising under" and "arising in" jurisdiction are further defined as "core proceedings."

Deference is given to the bankruptcy judge in two circumstances. The first relates to the bankruptcy itself; in the words of the statute, the "[bankruptcy judge] may hear and determine all cases under title 11."[14] Thus, the case itself is in the hands of the bankruptcy judge. Similarly, the bankruptcy judge may "hear and determine" the matter when it is a "core proceeding arising under or arising in a case under title 11."[15] When the bankruptcy judge enters an order or judgment regarding the case or in a core proceeding, that order or judgment is subject to normal appellate review.[16] The factual findings of the bankruptcy judge are upheld unless they are clearly erroneous; the court determinations of law are reviewed de novo. This is precisely the same way that a matter determined by a district court in a trial is reviewed by a circuit court.

Roughly speaking, a core proceeding is one that fundamentally involves bankruptcy law and the management of the estate; other law may be involved, but only secondarily. It appears to be similar, though not necessarily identical, to "arising

[13] 28 U.S.C. § 157(d).

[14] 28 U.S.C. § 157(b)(1).

[15] 28 U.S.C. § 157(b)(1).

[16] 28 U.S.C. § 157(b), 158. For those of you who are wondering what happens to an arising under/arising in proceeding that is not a core proceeding, join the club. It is not even clear if there is such a thing; the arising under/arising in categories may or may not be identical to core proceedings.

under/arising in" civil proceedings. Section 157(b)(2) gives an incomplete list of core proceedings; among other things, this list includes the following:

1. Administration of the estate,
2. Allowance of claims,
3. Turnover orders,
4. Exercise of avoidance powers,
5. Objections to discharge,
6. Determining the validity, extent and priority of liens,
7. Automatic stay litigation,
8. Plan confirmations,
9. Use/sale/lease of property[17]

Not all of these matters are unique to bankruptcy—for example, fraudulent transfer litigation is a core proceeding[18] even though the rules applied may in fact be borrowed from state law[19] —but they all are matters of immediate importance to the liquidation or reorganization of the estate.

As is generally true with matters of jurisdiction, the court itself makes an initial determination regarding its authority to hear the matter. On the judge's own motion, or that of a party, the bankruptcy judge determines whether a proceeding is a core proceeding. This determination is not to be based solely on the fact that resolution of the matter may involve state law.[20]

[E]—Non-Core "Related To" Proceedings: Hear and Propose

Northern Pipeline's main objection to the jurisdiction given the bankruptcy court was that it encompassed too many matters that were too remote from bankruptcy law. There is, however, a need to decide many such matters to complete the liquidation or reorganization of debtors. Although these issues are "non-core" they are often as important or more important than the core proceedings.

The bankruptcy judge is not prohibited from hearing non-core proceedings. To the contrary, section 157(c)(1) of Title 28 specifically authorizes the judge to do so, provided that the latter is "related to" a bankruptcy case.[21] For example, the court might well hear a state law contract case that must be resolved to determine the amount of a claim against the estate. However, the bankruptcy judge in such matters ordinarily acts more like a master or magistrate than like an ordinary judge.

---

[17] 28 U.S.C. § 157(b)(2).

[18] 28 U.S.C. § 157(b)(2).

[19] See § 15.03 of this book for a discussion of the bankruptcy use of state fraudulent transfer law.

[20] 28 U.S.C. § 157(b)(3).

[21] 28 U.S.C. § 157(c)(1). Note that there is a gap in the statutory scheme: nothing is said about the role of the bankruptcy judge in determining non-core matters that arise under or arise in a bankruptcy case.

The bankruptcy judge's findings of fact are given no deference. Rather, the judge submits proposed findings of fact and conclusions of law to the district court. The district judge enters the final order or judgment, and only after considering both the proposals of the bankruptcy judge and "reviewing de novo those matters to which any party has timely and specifically objected."[22] Note that the district court judge does not always have to review the matter de novo; if there is no "timely and specific" objection to the bankruptcy judge's proposals, the district court judge may accept them as is.

Another provision, however, makes it possible for the bankruptcy judge actually to "hear and determine" non-core proceedings. If all parties consent, the district court may refer a "related to" matters to the bankruptcy judge to "hear and determine" subject to the ordinary appellate review standards.[23] This provision is odd for a couple of reasons. First, it flatly contradicts the black-letter rule (that you no doubt learned in Civil Procedure) which states that the parties to a dispute cannot consent to expand the subject matter jurisdiction of a court. The ability of a bankruptcy judge to hear and determine non-core proceedings is an issue of subject matter jurisdiction, and yet the parties may, if the district court so permits, consent to the exercise of jurisdiction by a judge who ordinarily may not do so. More significantly, the constitutionality of this jurisdiction is suspect; under one reading of *Northern Pipeline*, this rule leads to the impermissible determination of purely state law matters by untenured bankruptcy judges.

[F]—Jury Trials

One of the most difficult questions that has arisen in recent years is the degree to which jury trials are to be allowed in bankruptcy proceedings. This is deeply entangled with the question of the bankruptcy court's jurisdiction, because it is unclear whether a bankruptcy judge can constitutionally hear a matter if there is a right to jury trial. Broadly speaking, most courts have accepted the notion that if a person has filed a claim in the bankruptcy proceeding, they have in effect consented to the exercise of power by the bankruptcy court over the claim, and thus waived the right to a jury trial of issues related to the claim.[24]

The 1994 Amendments deal in part with this jury trial question. The Amendments do not create a generalized right to jury trial, but they do specify a particular circumstance under which the bankruptcy judge may conduct a jury trial. If there is a right to jury trial in a matter that may heard by a bankruptcy judge, the judge may conduct the jury trial if the district court specially designates him or her to exercise jurisdiction and all of the parties expressly consent.[25] This provision will probably have every little effect. It is rare that all parties to a contested matter in bankruptcy would consent to a jury trial before a bankruptcy judge.

---

[22] 28 U.S.C. § 157(c)(1).

[23] 28 U.S.C. § 157(c)(2).

[24] See Granfinanciera, S.A. v. Nordberg, 492 U.S. 33 (1989).

[25] 28 U.S.C. § 157(e).

§ 5.05 Abstention

[A]—Introduction

Even when the district court has jurisdiction over a matter, it may choose to abstain from exercising that jurisdiction. Indeed, in a few circumstances, it is required to abstain. Abstention is a doctrine that goes well beyond bankruptcy; what is unusual about bankruptcy is that there are specific statutory provisions detailing both permissive and mandatory abstention rules. Those rules are included in the jurisdictional provisions, and provide additional props for their somewhat dubious constitutionality.

[B]—Permissive Abstention

Section 1334(c)(1) of Title 28 specifically permits the district court to abstain from hearing matters that "arise under" "arise in" or are "related to" bankruptcy cases. The court may abstain whenever abstention is "in the interest of justice, or in the interest of comity with State courts, or [out of] respect for State law."[26] This right to abstain exists despite the grant of original but not exclusive jurisdiction over those types of cases. There is no power, however, to abstain with regard to the bankruptcy itself, as that is subject to the original and exclusive jurisdiction of the district court. It appears that permissive abstention is rare; this is probably because of the very practical fact that bankruptcy proceedings ordinarily will be delayed and made more expensive if issues are tried in courts other than the bankruptcy or district court in which the petition was filed.

[C]—Mandatory Abstention

Of greater significance than the permissive abstention rule are the mandatory abstention rules. Under Title 28, the district court must (with one exception) abstain from hearing a proceeding based on a state law claim or a state law cause of action if:

1. A party to the proceeding makes a timely motion for abstention, and
2. The matter is "related to" a bankruptcy case,[27] and
3. The only jurisdictional basis on which the case is in federal court is the bankruptcy jurisdiction, and
4. An action is commenced in a state court of appropriate jurisdiction, and
5. The state court action can be timely adjudicated.[28]

For example, suppose that the proceeding involves a state-law contract claim against the debtor. There are no federal law issues, and the parties are from the same state. The relevant state court could adjudicate the matter without significantly delaying

[26] 28 U.S.C. § 1334(c)(1).

[27] Mandatory abstention never applies to an "arising under" or "arising in" case. 28 U.S.C. § 1334(c)(2).

[28] 28 U.S.C. § 1334(c).

the bankruptcy proceeding. If either party makes a timely motion for abstention, the motion must be granted.

All of the statutory requirements must be met. For example, if the proceeding is a federal antitrust claim, abstention is not mandatory because there is a separate basis for federal jurisdiction—federal question jurisdiction.[29] Similarly, if the parties are from different states, and the amount in controversy is sufficient to meet the amount-in-controversy requirement, abstention is not mandatory because the case is subject to the diversity jurisdiction of the federal courts.[30] Likewise, if a state court trial would significantly delay the liquidation or reorganization of the estate, abstention is not required.[31] In reality, very few proceedings are actually subject to mandatory abstention.

There is a significant exception to the mandatory abstention rules: personal injury claims against the estate. In the list of core proceedings, it is explicitly stated that "the liquidation or estimation of a contingent or unliquidated personal injury tort or wrongful death claims against the estate" is not a core proceeding.[32] However, that particular non-core proceeding is explicitly excluded from the mandatory abstention rules.[33] Thus, if the debtor is in bankruptcy because it ruined the health of thousands of women to whom it sold a defective contraceptive device, the core issues of the case are not core proceedings, but they need not be sent back to the state courts from which they came.[34] A further provision states that personal injury tort and wrongful death claims are to be tried either in the district court in which the bankruptcy is pending or the district court in the district in which the claim arose.[35] The district court where the bankruptcy is pending determines which court will hear the case.[36] The decision to abstain or not to abstain is virtually unreviewable by higher courts.[37]

---

[29] 28 U.S.C. § 1331.

[30] 28 U.S.C. § 1332.

[31] 28 U.S.C. § 1334(c)(2).

[32] 28 U.S.C. § 157(b)(2)(B).

[33] 28 U.S.C. § 157(b)(4).

[34] Note, however, that these claims may be the subject of voluntary abstention; the Code does not prohibit them from being tried in state court. Also note that the rule does not apply to tort claims by the estate against someone else, but only to tort claims against the estate. A personal injury claim by the estate may be subject to mandatory abstention. Although there is ambiguity in the wording of the relevant statutory provisions, it appears that § 157(b)(5), which requires that personal injury cases be tried in district court, applies only if the district court has not voluntarily abstained from hearing the proceeding.

[35] 28 U.S.C. § 157(b)(5).

[36] Id.

[37] 28 U.S.C. § 1334(d) states that "[a]ny decision to abstain or not to abstain made under this subsection (other than a decision not to abstain in a proceeding described in subsection (c)(2)) is not reviewable by appeal or otherwise by the court of appeals under section 158(d), 1291, or 1292 of this title or by the Supreme Court of the United States under section 1254 of this title."

§ 5.06 Venue

As noted in Chapter 6, the case itself must be filed where the debtor is located.[38] Normally, that is also the proper venue for proceedings "arising under", "arising in," or "related to" the case,[39] although in some cases the trustee/DIP has the option to file in other districts, based on non-bankruptcy venue rules.[40] However, a different rule applies to certain small matters. If the proceeding is to recover a money judgment or property worth less than $1,000, or is to recover a consumer debt of less than $5,000, then the proceeding must be in the district where the defendant resides.[41] There is also a provision that permits the court to transfer venue "in the interest of justice or for the convenience of the parties."[42]

---

[38] See § 6.04 of this book.

[39] 28 U.S.C. § 1409(a).

[40] See 28 U.S.C. § 1409 (c)–(e).

[41] 28 U.S.C. § 1409(b).

[42] 28 U.S.C. § 1412.

CHAPTER **6**

Commencement of the Case

§ 6.01 Introduction

Bankruptcy cases are commenced by the filing of a petition in the proper form, with the proper fee, in the proper district. The fee, by the way, is mandatory; except for a small pilot program.[1] neither Congress nor the courts have yet seen fit to permit bankruptcy to be filed *in forma pauperis.*[2] It is thus possible to be too poor to go bankrupt.[3]

The petition may either be voluntary (that is, filed by the debtor) or involuntary (that is, filed by creditors). There are detailed requirements for each type of petition. There are also detailed eligibility requirements for each Chapter; not all persons are eligible for relief under all Chapters, nor are involuntary petitions always permitted.

There is a general requirement, rarely litigated but applicable to all debtors in all Chapters, that the debtor must have significant nexus with the United States. Individual and business entities must either reside in, or have a domicile, place of business, or property in the United States.[4] In addition, political subdivisions or public agencies or instrumentalities of a "State"[5] may be a debtor.[6] There is no requirement, however, that the debtor be a United States citizen.

Another rarely litigated general exclusion from eligibility appears in section 109(g). This provision only applies to individuals and "family farmers" (the definition of the latter term is in section 101(18)). Neither may be a debtor under any Chapter of the Bankruptcy Code if

---

[1] Congress has set up a limited program for in forma pauperis petitions; as of October 1, 1994, this program was authorized for no more than six judicial districts. The program will run for three years. Departments of Commerce, Justice, and State, the Judiciary, and Related Agencies Appropriations Act of 1994, § 111(d)(3), 107 Stat 1165 (1993).

[2] It is, however, possible to pay the fee in installments with permission of the court or the clerk. Bankruptcy Rule 1006(b).

[3] Despite the seeming harshness of this rule, opinion is divided as to its appropriateness. Some commentators have decried it as an unnecessary barrier to badly needed relief. See Karen Gross & Shari Rosenberg, *Reflecting on and beyond United States v. Kras*, 2 Am. Bankr. Inst. L. Rev. 57 (1994) and Henry J. Sommer, *The Time Has Long Since Come*, 2 Am. Bankr. Inst. L. Rev. 93 (1994). Others view it as a necessary curb on abusive filings by those who do not belong in bankruptcy. See Michael C. Markham & Bethann Scharrer, *An Unnecessary Privilege in Bankruptcy*, 2 Am. Bankr. Inst. L. Rev. 73 (1994).

[4] Bankruptcy Code § 109(a).

[5] Except with regard to eligibility for relief under Chapter 9 (Municipal Bankruptcy), the term "State" under the Code includes not only the fifty states but also both the District of Columbia and the Commonwealth of Puerto Rico. Bankruptcy Code § 101(52).

[6] Bankruptcy Code § 109(a).

1. The prospective debtor was a debtor in any bankruptcy case during the proceeding 180 days, and either

2.A. The case was dismissed for willful failure to abide by the orders of the court or to appear before the course to prosecute the case, or

B. The debtor both requested and obtained a voluntary dismissal of the case following the filing of a request for relief from the automatic stay.[7]

This provision is an attempt to prevent repeated abusive filings aimed only at delaying non-bankruptcy proceedings. For example, Sadie Shadie might be facing a real estate foreclosure. To trigger the automatic stay provided by bankruptcy, and thus to stop the foreclosure proceeding in its tracks, she files a petition.[8] However, she has no real intention of pursuing bankruptcy; when a motion to lift the stay is made by the mortgagee, the case is quickly dismissed on Shadie's own motion. The foreclosure proceeding resumes, and Shadie again files within the 180 day period. The second filing may be dismissed under section 109(g), and the mortgagee thus permitted to complete the foreclosure.

§ 6.02 Commencement of a Voluntary Case

[A]—Introduction

A voluntary bankruptcy is commenced when the debtor files a petition with the bankruptcy court.[9] The filing of the petition constitutes the "order for relief."[10] In other words, the court does not have to take any further action for the case to begin. The filing has many other implications. For example, it triggers the automatic stay of other proceedings against the debtor; it also determines many time limits, such as the preference period, the fraudulent transfer period, and the time the debtor has to file various documents with the court. "Commencement of the case," which means filing of the petition, is one of the most important and most frequently used phrases in the Bankruptcy Code.

[B]—Eligibility for Relief

The eligibility of a person to be either a voluntary or an involuntary debtor under the Code varies from Chapter to Chapter. The main rules for voluntary debtors are sketched out below:

Chapter 7 (Liquidation). Virtually any individual or business entity may be a voluntary debtor in a Chapter 7 proceeding. The only exceptions are (1) railroads, (2) most domestic financial institutions, (3) most foreign financial institutions[11] and (4) governmental units.[12] Each of the

---

[7] Bankruptcy Code § 109(g).

[8] For a discussion of the automatic stay, see Chapter 8 of this book.

[9] Bankruptcy Code § 301.

[10] Bankruptcy Code § 301.

[11] Bankruptcy Code § 109(b)(1), (2), (3).

[12] This last exception arises from the fact that only a "person" may file Chapter 7 (Bank-

exclusions reflects the fact that there are other methods for dealing with their insolvencies. For example, there are state and federal institutions and structures, such as the FDIC, to deal with most insolvent financial institutions. There is a special subchapter in Chapter 11 of the Bankruptcy Code for railroads; and Chapter 9 of the Code deals with insolvent municipalities.

This broad eligibility rule must be read in conjunction with the de facto limitation put on consumer debtor eligibility imposed by section 707(b). That provision permits the court to dismiss consumer Chapter 7 filings that it finds abusive. It is discussed in detail in § 16.03[B] of this book.

Chapter 9 (Adjustment of Debts of a Municipality). Chapter 9, which is rarely used, is available only to a municipality, such as a county or city, and only under limited circumstances. The debtor must have been authorized to be a debtor under the law of the state that created it, must be insolvent, and must "desire to affect a plan to adjust" its debts.[13] In addition to those requirements, the debtor must have either (1) have obtained creditor agreement to the filing, (2) have failed to obtain creditor agreement after good faith negotiation, (3) be unable to negotiate with its creditors or (4) reasonably believe that a creditor may attempt to obtain a preference.[14]

Chapter 11 (Reorganization). The eligibility requirements of Chapter 11 are virtually the same as those for Chapter 7. There are only two differences. First, a stockbroker or commodity broker is eligible for Chapter 7 but not for Chapter 11.[15] Second, a railroad, which is not eligible for Chapter 7, is eligible for Chapter 11.[16] Note, however, that railroad reorganizations are subject to a somewhat different set of Chapter 11 rules.[17]

For a number of years, there was uncertainty as to whether the Chapter 11 included an implicit "going concern" requirement. Put simply, could a debtor who had no business operations file Chapter 11? This dispute

---

ruptcy Code § 109(b)) and, with one exception not here relevant, the term "person" does not include a governmental unit. Bankruptcy Code § 101(41).

[13] Bankruptcy Code § 109(c)(2), (3), (4). The requirements for a municipal bankruptcy were tightened by the 1994 amendments. The authorization under state law must be specific rather than general; for example, by naming the specific municipality seeking relief in the authorizing legislation.

[14] Bankruptcy Code § 109(c)(5). Broadly speaking, a preference is a payment that benefits one creditor at the expense of others. For a full discussion, see Chapter 14 of this book.

[15] Bankruptcy Code § 109(d).

[16] Bankruptcy Code § 109(d).

[17] For a brief sketch of those rules, see § 17.19 of this book.

was resolved by the Supreme Court, which, based on the plain language of the statute held that no such requirement existed.[18]

Chapter 12 (Adjustment of Debts of a Family Farmer with Regular Annual Income). With the possible exception of Chapter 9, Chapter 12 has the most complex eligibility requirements under the Code. Most of these requirements appear in section 101 (Definitions), not in section 109 (Who May be a Debtor). A deceptively simple eligibility requirement leads into a complex web of definitions. It is those definitions that actually set the scope of Chapter 12.

Chapter 12 relief is available only to "a family farmer with regular income."[19] A family farmer with regular income is defined rather elaborately as a "family farmer whose annual income is sufficiently stable and regular to enable such family farmer to make payments under" a Chapter 12 plan.[20] From this we move to the definitions of family farmer,[21] farmer,[22] and farming operation,[23] each of which adds its mite to the final result.

Broadly speaking, to qualify for Chapter 12 an individual (or individual and spouse) must be engaged in farming operations and must have no more than $1,500,000 in debt. Generally, at least 80 percent of those debts must arise from the farming operation and more than 50 percent of the income must come from the farming operation. Corporations and partnerships may also qualify for Chapter 12, but only if they are controlled by a single family.[24]

Chapter 13 (Adjustment of Debts of an Individual with Regular Income). Chapter 13 eligibility is also somewhat restricted, but by no means as much as Chapter 12 eligibility. Several requirements must be met. First, the debtor must be either an individual or an individual and spouse. Corporations, partnerships, and other legal entities are not permitted to file.

Second, the debtor (and, where applicable, the debtor's spouse) must have debts less than a specified amount; prior to the 1994 Amendments,

---

[18] Toibb v. Radloff, 501 U.S. 157 (1991); for a discussion of this issue that the *Toibb* court was kind enough to cite with approval, see Michael J. Herbert, *Consumer Chapter 11 Proceedings: Abuse or Alternative?*, 91 Com. L. J. 234 (1986).

[19] Bankruptcy Code § 109(f).

[20] Bankruptcy Code § 101(19).

[21] Bankruptcy Code § 101(18).

[22] Bankruptcy Code § 101(20) Note however that this definition need be looked at only in a negative sense, because the definition of "farmer" does not apply in to determining the meaning of the phrase "family farmer."

[23] Bankruptcy Code § 101(21).

[24] For a more detailed discussion of these very complex rules, see Collier on Bankruptcy ¶ 109.05A.

non-contingent, liquidated, unsecured debts of less than $100,000 and non-contingent, liquidated, secured debts of less than $350,000.[25] This cap was criticized as being too low. In consequence, in the 1994 Amendments, Congress raised the amount. The debtor and spouse now must have non-contingent, liquidated, unsecured debts of less than $250,000 and non-contingent, liquidated, secured debts of less than $750,000.[26] Moreover, these caps will continue to rise in the future. The 1994 Amendments also include an escalator provision that will automatically increase certain dollar limits, including those regarding eligibility for Chapter 13 relief, every three years.[27] These limits were designed to restrict Chapter 13 to relatively small proceedings. There is a fair amount of litigation over them. A particular problem arises if a debt unliquidated at the commencement of the proceeding is liquidated during the proceeding, and the debt pushes the debtor over the Chapter 13 limit. For example, suppose that at the inception of the proceeding, D'Artangan scheduled a disputed tort claim. During the pendency of the case, the claim was determined to be $650,000—thus putting D'Artangan's debts far beyond the statutory cap on unsecured claims. It is reasonably clear that this does not affect D'Artangan's right to continue under Chapter 13, because the statute refers to obligations that existed at the time of the petition.[28]

Third, the debtor must have regular income. There is no requirement that the income be from any particular source. Unlike old Chapter XIII, which required income from wages or salaries, Chapter 13 permits the debtor to use income from such things as pensions, public assistance payments, self-employment, or investments. Neither must the income be entirely steady; reasonably predictable fluctuations, such as those associated with seasonal employment, do not necessarily preclude the debtor from Chapter 13 relief.[29] The only requirement is self-referential; the income must be "sufficiently stable and regular to enable [the] individual to make payments under" a Chapter 13 plan.[30] Since the normal Chapter 13 plan lasts for three years, this translates to reasonably predictable and steady income over that three year period.

---

[25] Bankruptcy Code § 109(e) (amended 1994). In a joint husband/wife case, the debts are aggregated to determine whether the debtors are eligible. There is no requirement, however, that both spouses file, nor that if both file they file jointly.

[26] Bankruptcy Code § 109(e)(1994 Amendments).

[27] Bankruptcy Code § 104(b)(1). The first adjustment will be made on April 1, 1998; each adjustment will be based on the consumer price index for the preceding three years and will be rounded to the nearest $25.00.

[28] Bankruptcy Code § 109(e).

[29] See Collier on Bankruptcy ¶¶ 109.05 and 1300.40[1].

[30] Bankruptcy Code § 101(30).

[C]—Petition and Schedules

Along with the petition, the debtor must file a number of other documents. All of these documents are standardized by the Bankruptcy Rules and Forms; they are designed to be easily completed and for the most part are. Even greater simplicity arises from the fact that there is excellent software available to assist in translating raw information to finished forms. The main purpose of these other documents is to provide the court, the trustee, and the creditors with information about the debtor's financial situation. These documents include, among other things, a list of creditors[31] and a quite a few "schedules" of assets, obligations, and other matters. The schedules are as follows:

> Schedule A—All real property interests of the debtor other than leasehold interests and any encumbrances.
>
> Schedule B—All personal property other than leases or executory contracts. Encumbrances on the property are not included on Schedule B.
>
> Schedule C—All property that the debtor claims as exempt.
>
> Schedules D through F—All Secured, Priority, and General Unsecured Claims
>
> Schedule G—Executory contracts and unexpired leases.
>
> Schedule H—Co-obligors of the debtor.
>
> Schedules I and J—Current income and expenses (for individual debtors only).[32]

Among the other documents an individual Chapter 7 debtor must file is a statement of intention to reaffirm debts, redeem property, or avoid liens on property.[33] An individual Chapter 7 debtor's attorney must file a statement that the debtor has been advised about alternatives to Chapter 7.[34] Corporate debtors must include with their schedules a declaration by an officer or other authorized agent that the schedules are true and correct;[35] individual debtors must sign a similar declaration of their

---

[31] Bankruptcy Rule 1007(a). In a voluntary case, the creditor list is not required if the schedule of liabilities is filed with the petition. Also note that in Chapter 11 and Chapter 9 proceedings there must also be a list of the 20 largest unsecured claims. Bankruptcy Rule 1007(d).

[32] Bankruptcy Rule 1007(b)(1). See also, Official Form 6, which sets out the form of the various schedules.

[33] Bankruptcy Code § 521(2), Bankruptcy Rule 1007(b)(2).

[34] See Official Form 1—note that the debtor must also confirm that he or she is aware of the alternatives and has chosen Chapter 7. These requirements were added by BAFJA in 1984 as part of the effort to encourage consumers to reorganize rather than liquidate. See Paul M. Black and Michael J. Herbert, *Bankcard's Revenge: A Critique of the 1984 Consumer Credit Amendments to the Bankruptcy Code*, 19 U. Rich. L. Rev. 845, 852-55 (1985).

[35] See Official Form 2.

own.[36] Other documents may be required depending on the type of bankruptcy. Generally speaking, these initial documents must be filed within 15 days after the petition.[37]

[D]—Joint Filings

As a practical matter, many individual bankruptcies are in fact rooted in the mutual financial difficulties of a married couple. Because of this, the Code explicitly permits joint filing by spouses.[38] The key advantages to joint filing are lowered costs for both the court and the debtors. A joint case may make possible a more efficient administration; and, at a minimum, it cuts one cost: the fee. In a joint case, only a single filing fee is required.[39]

Joint filing, however, does not necessarily mean consolidation of the cases. Depending on the circumstances—that is, depending upon the amount of joint ownership and joint debt—the court may leave both estates independent of each other, consolidate the estates in part, or consolidate them entirely.[40] For example, if the two spouses held little property in joint ownership, and had few obligations on which both were liable, the court would probably administer the case as two separate estates.

§ 6.03 Commencement of an Involuntary Case

[A]—Introduction

One of the great debates that surrounded the enactment of the 1898 Bankruptcy Act was over involuntary bankruptcy. Those representatives whose chief concerns were for the impecunious, especially farmers, wanted voluntary bankruptcy and its attendant discharge of debt, but opposed involuntary bankruptcy which they feared would be used by banks to force debtors into the clutches of the federal courts. In time a compromise was reached, under which involuntary bankruptcy was permitted, but limited. One of the key protections was that the debtor not only had to be in financial trouble; the debtor also had to do something that either created special risks for the creditor or was considered wrongful. Under the old act, involuntary proceedings were predicated on an "act of bankruptcy," such as making a fraudulent or a preferential transfer.[41]

---

[36] See Official Form 1.

[37] Bankruptcy Rule 1007.

[38] Bankruptcy Code § 302(a).

[39] See generally, Collier on Bankruptcy ¶ 302.02[1].

[40] Bankruptcy Code § 302(b).

[41] Collier on Bankruptcy ¶ 303.06 [4]; see Bankruptcy Act § 3. Note that one of the acts of bankruptcy bore a slight resemblance to the present law, which focuses on the inability to pay debts; the sixth act of bankruptcy was a written admission of the inability to pay debts and a willingness to be adjudicated a bankruptcy. Bankruptcy Act § 3(a)(5).

The 1978 Code abolished this concept almost entirely. There are no acts of bankruptcy. The key to involuntary bankruptcy is simply the general non-payment of debts by the debtor; this is the only issue in almost all involuntary bankruptcy cases. However, other protections, some of which were also found in the Bankruptcy Act remain; these are found in the eligibility requirements. Certain debtors simply cannot be forced into bankruptcy at all, and certain types of bankruptcy may not be involuntarily commenced. An additional, and perhaps even more important, protection is that in most cases three unsecured creditors must join the petition.

It has long been noted that the number of involuntary bankruptcies is much lower than one might expect; indeed, there are now so few that the Administrative Office of the Courts no longer keeps separate records of them.[42] This suggests that the need for involuntary bankruptcy is slight, and that the normal state law creditor remedies are nearly always sufficient. It also reinforces the notion that the almost exclusive function of bankruptcy is to provide relief for the debtor, not collection for the creditor.[43] There are other explanations. Recently it has been asserted that the numbers are not inappropriately low; that various practical and institutional inhibitions, coupled with the desire to settle through out-of-court negotiations, explain the paltry numbers.[44]

[B]—Chapters in Which Involuntary Petition Permitted

One restriction on involuntary bankruptcy is the limitation of the Chapters under which an involuntary petition can be filed. The Bankruptcy Code permits involuntary proceedings only if the case is filed under Chapter 7 or Chapter 11. No involuntary cases are allowed under Chapters 9, 12, or 13. In practice, nearly all involuntary proceedings are Chapter 7 cases.

A Chapter 9 proceeding involves the bankruptcy of a municipality. Since these proceedings directly effect the sovereign powers of the state that created the municipality, they are only allowed if the state permits them.[45] A simple corollary of this is that the case may not be started at the behest of creditors.

Involuntary petitions are not allowed under Chapters 12 because that Chapter is available only to family farmers, and there is a long tradition of prohibiting involuntary petitions against farmers. Chapter 13 cannot be commenced involuntarily for at least two reasons. First, an involuntary Chapter 13 is probably impractical, because that Chapter is available only to individuals, and there is no practical way of forcing an individual to reorganize against her will. Second, Congress was concerned that any attempt to force an individual into reorganization would come

---

[42] See Elizabeth Warren & Jay Lawrence Westbrook, The Law of Debtors and Creditors 410 (2d ed. 1991).

[43] See § 1.01 of this book for a discussion of this issue.

[44] See Susan Block-Lieb, *Why Creditors File So Few Involuntary Petitions and Why the Number is Not Too Small*, 57 Brook. L. Rev. 803 (1991).

[45] See § 6.02[B] of this chapter for a discussion of the requirements for filing a petition under Chapter 9.

perilously close to involuntary servitude.[46] Note, however, that the policies militating against an involuntary Chapter 13 are not followed rigorously. Involuntary Chapter 11 proceedings are permitted, even though the debtor may be an individual.

[C]—Persons Against Whom an Involuntary Petition May Be Filed

Even when the filing is under Chapter 7 or Chapter 11, the debtor must be a person who is (1) generally eligible for relief under that Chapter and (2) a person who may be forced into bankruptcy. Some debtors may be forced in Chapter 7 but not into Chapter 11, and vice-versa. Some debtors may not be forced into bankruptcy, regardless of the Chapter.

Railroads may not file Chapter 7;[47] thus, they may not be forced into Chapter 7.[48] By contrast, all railroads may file Chapter 11, and thus may be forced into it.[49] Many financial institutions are entirely excluded from bankruptcy proceedings because their insolvency is governed by state law or by other federal law; in consequence, they cannot be the subject of an involuntary bankruptcy;[50] the exception is a stockbroker or commodity broker, who can be a voluntary or involuntary bankrupt in Chapter 7 but not Chapter 11.[51]

Farmers, family farmers, and non-profit corporations can never be put into involuntary bankruptcy.[52] The first two categories reflect the fact that, although this has been a predominantly urban nation since 1920, and although there are by most measures more lawyers in this country than farmers,[53] the great compromise that in 1898 protected farmers from being forced into bankruptcy remains intact. Indeed, the compromise was broadened by the Code; under the act, farmer really meant farmer: an individual who worked the land.[54] Under section 101(20), the term includes any person that receives more than 80 percent of its gross income from farming operations.[55] "Person" includes partnerships and corporations.[56] The

---

[46] See Paul M. Black & Michael J. Herbert, *Bankcard's Revenge: A Critique of the 1984 Consumer Credit Amendments to the Bankruptcy Code*, 19 U. Rich. L. Rev. 845, 850 n. 22 (1985).

[47] Bankruptcy Code § 109(b).

[48] Bankruptcy Code § 303(a).

[49] Bankruptcy Code §§ 109(d), 303(a).

[50] Bankruptcy Code §§ 109(b), (d); 303(a).

[51] Bankruptcy Code §§ 109(d), 303(a).

[52] Bankruptcy Code § 303(a). For a discussion of the term "family farmer," see § 6.02 of this chapter.

[53] Not to mention that according to some statistics, there are more employees of the Department of Agriculture than farms. To most people, it is a matter of considerable rejoicing that neither lawyers nor government bureaucrats are likely to be given similar advantages in bankruptcy.

[54] Bankruptcy Act § 1(7): "Farmer shall mean an individual personally engaged in farming or tillage of the soil . . ."

[55] Bankruptcy Code § 101(20).

[56] Bankruptcy Code § 101(41).

"farmer" sheltered by a kindly Congress from being crushed by cruel top-hatted bankers may well be a multi-million dollar limited partnership, run by accountants from air-conditioned offices on behalf of the doctors who have tax-sheltered their income in it.

[D]—Technical Requirements for Involuntary Petition

[1]—Who May File

In most cases, an involuntary petition must be filed by at least three creditors. Each of the creditors must have a claim that is non-contingent and that is not the subject of a bona fide dispute. At least $10,000 worth of the claims must be unsecured.[57] The petition must be against only one debtor; there are no joint involuntary cases.[58] Of course, if there is a related group of debtors who all owe money to the same creditors, those creditors might file separate petitions against each of the companies; however, each of the petitions must comply with all of the requirements set out in the Code.

This requirement of multiple petitioners is a fundamental part of the compromise that opened the door to involuntary bankruptcy in the 1898 Act and subsequently the Code. Judge Friendly discussed this compromise in a 1961 case:

> [T]he entire process that resulted in the enactment of the Act of 1898 was a pitched battle between those who wanted to give the creditor an effective remedy to assure equal distribution of a bankrupt's assets and those who were determined to protect the debtor from the harassment of ill-considered or oppressive involuntary petitions, including those by a single creditor interest. The requirement of three creditors was one of many provisions reflecting a compromise between the two opposing positions.[59]

In recognition that it is difficult and sometimes impossible to find three petitioners for a debtor with few debts, there is a further rule. If the debtor has fewer than 12 creditors with non-contingent, undisputed claims, then the petition may be filed by a single creditor who is owed at least $10,000 of unsecured debt. In determining the number of creditors, all employees and insiders of the debtor are excluded, as are creditors who have received various types of avoidable transfers.[60] Thus, the actual number of creditors may be well in excess of 12.

---

[57] Bankruptcy Code § 303(b)(1). Prior to the 1994 Amendments, this amount was only $5,000. The amount will continue to be increased, at three-year intervals, in accordance with any rise in the consumer price index. Bankruptcy Code § 104(b)(1).

[58] In re Western Land Bank, Inc., 116 Bankr. 721, 724 (Bankr. C.D. Cal. 1990).

[59] In re Gibraltor Amusements, 291 F.2d 22, 28 (2d. Cir. 1961), (Friendly, J., dissenting), cert. denied, 368 U.S. 925 (1961).

[60] Bankruptcy Code § 303(b)(2). Prior to the 1994 Amendments, this amount was only $5,000. The amount will continue to be increased, at three-year intervals, in accordance with any rise in the consumer price index. Bankruptcy Code § 104(b)(1).

To be eligible as a petitioner, the creditor must have a claim at the time the petition is filed. The creditor may be a transferee of the claim; if so, the claimant must attach the documents evidencing the transfer to the petition.[61] However, the claim will not be counted toward the minimum if it was transferred or split for the purpose of filing an involuntary petition.[62] For example, suppose that River Bank wished to file an involuntary petition against D'Arcy, but was unable to persuade two other creditors to join in the petition. River Bank splits its claim into three parts, and assigns two parts to wholly owned subsidiaries. If River and its subsidiaries petition for involuntary bankruptcy, the petition will be denied because the three petitioners will count as one rather than three.

The rule against multiplying creditors by splitting claims is designed to protect the policy underlying the three-creditor requirement. The rule is designed to protect most debtors from being put into risk of bankruptcy by a single creditor whose motivations may include personal animus or simple refusal to deal reasonably with a debt. This policy, however is not always followed rigorously; closely affiliated creditors which both have claims against the debtor have been counted as two petitioners, so long as each claim arose separately.[63]

There are some special additional rules for partnership debtors. First, an involuntary petition against a partnership may also be filed by "fewer than all of the general partners." (Note that if all the general partners file the petition, the petition is perfectly valid; however, a petition filed by all the partners is a voluntary petition, not an involuntary petition). Second, if all of the general partners are in bankruptcy, an involuntary petition against the partnership itself may be filed by any general partner, by the trustee of any general partner, or by any creditor of the partnership. In this case there is no requirement that any set number of creditors file the petition, or that there be any particular amount of debt owed to the filing creditor.[64] These rules are in addition to the rules stated in the two previous paragraphs; an involuntary petition that meets all the usual requirements is also valid against a partnership debtor.

There is also a special rule that deals with debtors who are already the subject of a foreign bankruptcy. An involuntary petition may be filed by a foreign representative of the estate in a foreign proceeding concerning the debtor.[65] For example, suppose that InterGalactic Trading Corp., a multinational company, is in receivership in England. InterGalactic owns an office building and cosiderable equipment and inventory in New Jersey. The English receiver may file an involuntary bankruptcy petition against InterGalactic in the proper New Jersey district. The American bankruptcy will deal with the property in America, while the English receivership deals with the property in England. Although the American proceeding

[61] Bankruptcy Rule 1003(a).

[62] In re McMeekin & Shoreman, 16 Bankr. 805, 808-09 (Bankr. D. Mass. 1982).

[63] In re Gibraltor Amusements, 291 F.2d 22 (2d. Cir. 1961), cert. denied, 368 U.S. 925 (1961).

[64] Bankruptcy Code § 303(b)(3).

[65] Bankruptcy Code § 303(b)(4).

will be technically seperate from the English proceeding, and will operate under American rules rather than English rules, the English receiver is at least given the opportunity to initiate the American proceeding. An involuntary bankruptcy initiated by a foreign representative functions as an alternative to an ancillary proceeding under section 304, an issue discussed in Chapter 21.[66] The main difference is that an ancillary proceeding effectively places the property in the United States under the power of the foreign court.

Other creditors may join the petition after it is filed. To do so, a creditor must hold a non-contingent, unsecured claim.[67] There is no requirement that the claim be of any particular amount.

The filing may under some circumstances be dismissed without a determination of its merits. There are three grounds for dismissal. The court may dismiss a petition on the motion of any petitioner, or with the consent of all petitioners and the debtor, or for lack of prosecution by the petitioners—but only after notice to all creditors and an opportunity for a hearing.[68] This is to give other creditors, who may want the bankruptcy to go forward, an opportunity to join in the petition or otherwise intervene in the proceedings.

[2]—Contents of Involuntary Petition

The involuntary petition is a fairly simple document; the Official Form is little more than a checklist. Its most significant elements include:

1. Information about the debtor, including information that shows the debtor is a person against whom an order for relief may be entered;
2. Information about the petitioners that shows they meet the requirements for filing a petition, both in terms of the number of petitioners and the amount of unsecured debt they are owed;
3. A statement regarding venue—specifically, a statement that the debtor has been located within the district for the 180 days immediately proceeding the petition (or has been located in the district for more of that period than in any other district);
4. An allegation that at least one of the substantive bases for granting the petition exists (for example, that the debtor is generally not paying its debts as they become due); the petitioners may add a supplement containing the facts supporting the allegation.[69]

[E]—Substantive Bases for Granting Involuntary Petition

The primary basis for granting an involuntary petition is that the debtor is generally not paying its debts as they come due[70] —in other words, that the debtor

[66] See § 21.02.

[67] Bankruptcy Code § 303(c).

[68] Bankruptcy Code § 303(j).

[69] Official Form 5.

[70] Bankruptcy Code § 303(h)(1).

is equitably insolvent. If the petition is not controverted, this need not be proven; the petition will be granted and the case will continue. However, if the debtor does resist the petition in a timely fashion, the court must try the matter and make its determination as quickly as possible.[71]

Broadly speaking, the statutory standard is met if the debtor is substantially overdue on its significant debts.[72] Ordinarily, the failure to pay a single creditor is insufficient,[73] even if there is only one creditor. The courts have recognized an exception to this in "exceptional circumstances," a phrase that generally connotes an absence of any effective non-bankruptcy remedy.[74] The general reluctance to approve a one-creditor involuntary bankruptcy reflects a broader concern about the appropriateness of bankruptcy to resolve disputes that involve only two parties.[75]

There is also a concern about the possibility of creditors using the threat of an involuntary petition as a tool in negotiations. Consequently, those debts that are subject to a bona fide dispute are not counted when the court determines whether the debtor is failing to meet its obligations.[76] This prevents one party to a dispute from attempting to coerce another with threats of forced bankruptcy.

Section 303(h)(2) gives a second, rarely used, basis on which the court may grant a controverted petition, and in doing so preserves a last vestige of the old "acts of bankruptcy." Whether or not the debtor is equitably insolvent, the court must grant the petition if a "custodian" (such as a receiver, trustee, or assignee for benefit of creditors) was appointed or took possession of the debtor's property within the 120 days before the petition was filed.[77] Note that there is an exception to this if the custodian was appointed to take charge of "less than substantially all" the debtor's property for the purpose of enforcing a lien—for example, if a sheriff seizes a portion of the debtor's property to foreclose, that is not a sufficient basis to grant a controverted involuntary petition.[78] Note too that when the court grants an involuntary petition on this basis, it is in effect removing and converting the case—removing the matter from state court and converting it from a state insolvency proceeding to a bankruptcy proceeding. The fundamental rationale for this is that the federal bankruptcy courts are the better forum, with the better law; and if either the debtor or the creditors wish the insolvency to be adjudicated there, then that is where it will be adjudicated.

---

[71] Bankruptcy Rule 1013(a).

[72] For a discussion of the specific cases, see Collier on Bankruptcy ¶ 303.12[4].

[73] See In re 7H Land & Cattle Co., 6 Bankr. 29, 31 (Bankr. Nev. 1980).

[74] See In re H.I.J.R. Properties Denver, 115 Bankr. 275, 278 (D. Colo. 1990).

[75] For another aspect of this problem, see § 22.04 of this book regarding so-called single-asset bankruptcies.

[76] Bankruptcy Code § 303(h)(1).

[77] Bankruptcy Code § 303(h)(2).

[78] Bankruptcy Code § 303(h)(2).

[F]—Penalties for Unsubstantiated Petition

A final protection is provided to potential involuntary bankrupts by section 303(i). If the court dismisses the petition on the merits, the court may grant judgment against all of the petitioners for the debtor's costs and attorney's fees.[79] Moreover, if the court determines that any petitioner acted in bad faith, the court may award additional damages against that petitioner, including any damages proximately caused by the filing, and even punitive damages.[80] The damages awarded for "bad faith" filing are not necessarily awarded against all petitioners. Some may have legitimately, if erroneously, believed that the filing was justified; they may be liable for costs and attorney's fees but not for other damages. Only the petitioners who had no legitimate grounds for joining in the petition are subject to the broader measure of damages.

[G]—Gap Period

An order for relief against the debtor does not immediately follow the filing of an involuntary petition.[81] The debtor has the opportunity to controvert the petition; and, if it does, there must be a hearing. At that hearing the relief might or might not be granted. In consequence, for some weeks the bankruptcy status of the debtor may remain in doubt. This period of time—between the petition and the order, if any—is colloquially known as the "gap period" or the "involuntary gap."

There are several special rules that apply during the gap period. First, the automatic stay does apply, because it is triggered by the petition, not the order for relief.[82] Second, a bankruptcy estate is created, because the estate is created by the "commencement of the case," and an involuntary case is commenced by the petition.[83] However, unless the court orders otherwise, the debtor may continue to operate its business (if any) and may continue to use, acquire, or dispose of property as if no case had been commenced.[84] Moreover, there is no automatic appointment of a trustee; the court may, on request of a party of interest, and after notice to the

[79] Bankruptcy Code § 303(i)(1). Although the wording of the provision is somewhat ambiguous—it states that the court may grant judgment for costs "or" attorney's fees—it is reasonably clear that this means that the court may award one or the other or both or neither. It does not mean that the court may award only one or the other. See Collier on Bankruptcy ¶ 303.39 and Kenneth N. Klee, *Legislative History of the New Bankruptcy Code*, 54 Am. Bankruptcy L. J. 275, 297 (1980); see also Bankruptcy Code § 102(5) (" 'or' is not exclusive").

[80] Bankruptcy Code § 303(i)(2).

[81] In an involuntary proceeding, the filing of the petition is the commencement of the case but not the order for relief. Bankruptcy Code §§ 303(b), 303(h). This contrasts from a voluntary case, in which the filing is both. An order for relief is not entered in an involuntary case until the time has passed for controverting the petition or, if controverted, the court has found the petition justified. Bankruptcy Code § 303(h).

[82] Bankruptcy Code § 362(a).

[83] Bankruptcy Code §§ 541(a), 303(b).

[84] Bankruptcy Code § 303(f).

debtor plus an opportunity for a hearing, appoint an interim trustee. This appointment is to be made only if it is "necessary to preserve the property of the estate or to prevent loss to the estate."[85]

There are two special provisions that deal with transactions during the gap period. Under Section 549, any transfer that is made by the debtor after the filing of the involuntary petition but before the order for relief has limited validity against the trustee. To the extent that the transferee gave value, including services, after the commencement of the case and in exchange for the transfer, the transaction is valid. Otherwise, the transaction is avoidable.[86] For example, suppose that, during the gap period, the debtor sold one thousand widgets for their fair market value ($5,000) and received in exchange $5,000 in cash. The transaction is valid; the trustee cannot avoid it. This is true even if the transferee knew that an involuntary petition was pending.[87] Similarly, wages that are paid by the debtor during the gap period for work done during the gap period may be retained by the employee. However, transfers made to satisfy or secure a pre-petition debt are avoidable. For example, suppose that, during the gap period, the debtor granted a security interest in its inventory to secure a loan that had been made prior to the filing of the petition. That security interest is avoidable if an order for relief is ultimately entered.[88] This is true even if the secured party had no notice that an involuntary petition was pending.

Section 549 also provides very limited protection to real estate transactions that are completed during the gap period. For example, suppose that, during the gap period, Paula completed the purchase of real property from the debtor. Paula may retain this property if the following conditions are met:

1. Paula must be a good faith purchaser, and
2. Paula must have concluded the transaction without knowledge of the fact that an involuntary petition was pending, and
3. Paula must have paid present fair equivalent value for the property, and
4. Generally, the deed must have been recorded prior to the time a copy or notice of the petition was filed in the real estate records.[89]

Note that the value paid for the property must not only be "fair equivalent value" but must also be "present value." Thus, a transfer of real property by the debtor in satisfaction of a pre-existing debt owed to Paula would not fit within the protections of Section 549(c). The transaction in that case would be avoided.

A purchaser who does not meet all the requirements of Section 549(c) may still have some protection. In the example given, suppose that Paula paid only $40,000 for the property, while is in fact worth $120,000. Paula cannot keep the property, because she has not paid fair equivalent value for it. However, she will be given

[85] Bankruptcy Code § 303(g).

[86] Bankruptcy Code § 549(a), (b).

[87] Bankruptcy Code § 549(b).

[88] Bankruptcy Code § 549(a), (b).

[89] Bankruptcy Code § 549(c).

a lien on the property for the $40,000 she did pay (and thus, effectively, a secured claim in the bankruptcy) if the following requirements are met:

1. Paula acted in good faith, and
2. Paula did not know that the petition had been filed, and
3. The $40,000 she paid was present value (that is, the property was not transferred because of a previous payment made by Paula or a debt owed to Paula), and
4. The deed was recorded prior to the time a copy or notice of the petition was filed in the real estate records.[90]

The other protection given to gap creditors is found in Section 504, which deals with priority unsecured claims.[91] Section 507(a)(2) states that unsecured claims allowed under Section 502(f) are given the second highest priority.[92] Section 502(f) claims are claims arising in the ordinary course of the debtor's business or financial affairs after the commencement of an involuntary case but before the appointment of a trustee for the order for relief (whichever occurs first).[93] Although claims are given a very high priority, this is not necessarily very helpful to creditors. In many cases, even first priority claims (administrative expenses) are left unpaid.[94] Thus, as a practical matter, once creditors learn of an involuntary petition, they are unlikely to deal with the debtor on anything but a C.O.D. basis. The risk of nonpayment, even with a second priority claim, is simply too high.

This in turn helps to explain why there are restrictions on involuntary petitions. The mere filing of an involuntary petition has a devastating effect on a debtor's ability to get credit. Thus, the mere fact that a petition has been filed may in fact drive a basically sound company into insolvency.

§ 6.04 Venue—Where to File the Petition

There are two sets of venue provisions under the Code. One deals with the venue for matters that arise during the case; these are dealt with in Chapter 5.[95] The other deals with the petition and thus with the case itself. The latter is designed to dovetail with substantive rules, most notably, those involving the applicable state law. For example, the relevant state law is significant with regard to the exemptions that an

---

[90] Bankruptcy Code § 549(c).

[91] For a fuller discussion of priority claims, see § 10.04[B], [C] of this book.

[92] Bankruptcy Code § 507(a)(2).

[93] Bankruptcy Code § 502(f).

[94] In a typical Chapter 7 case, no assets are distributed to creditors at all. See Michael J. Herbert and Dominic E. Pacitti, *Down and Out in Richmond, Virginia: The Distribution of Assets in Chapter 7 Bankruptcy Proceedings Closed During 1984-87*, 22 U. Rich L. Rev. 303 (1988). Note, however, that most involuntary cases involve businesses, and it is possible that the chance for a distribution on priority claims may be higher than usual in those cases.

[95] See § 5.06.

individual debtor may claim. A Texas bankrupt may claim Texas exemptions—which one (correctly) supposes are bigger than those in most other states.[96] Technically, the rules determining the state of the debtor's exemptions and the rules determining venue are independent of each other; however, they are virtually word-for-word identical, so that the venue for the case will normally be in a district in the state whose exemption laws will apply. This simplifies the necessary choice of law decision; in nearly all cases, a court will be applying the law of the state in which the court sits. Presumably the judge will be familiar with those rules.

The venue for the case itself is governed by section 1408 of U.S.C. Title 28. In most cases, a bankruptcy petition may be filed in the district where the debtor's "domicile, residence, principal place of business in the United States, or principal assets in the United States" has been located during the proceeding 180 days "or for a longer portion of such one-hundred-and-eighty-day period" than any other domicile, residence, principal place of business or principal place of assets in the U.S.[97] Note that this means, in most cases, that there will be only one possible venue. Note further that the venue provisions make it clear there is no requirement that a debtor be a U.S. citizen.

A simple application of the basic venue rule: Sam files bankruptcy on July 4, 1997. During 120 of the proceeding 180 days, he has resided in Houston, Texas; during the remaining 60 days, he has resided in Phoenix, Arizona. Sam has no place of business; his few assets are all in Houston. Sam must file in the Southern District of Texas.

There are three additional venue rules of significance. First, if there is a pending case involving the debtor's affiliate,[98] general partner, or partnership, the debtor may file in the district where that case is pending. In the example given, if Sam was a partner in Sam, Pam & Ram, Attorneys at Law, and the partnership was already in a bankruptcy proceeding in the Southern District of Ohio, Sam could file his personal bankruptcy in that district, rather than the Southern District of Texas. Note that this provision is not mandatory; Sam could file in whichever district he preferred.

The second rule is one of forum non conveniens. Under section 1412 of Title 28, the court has the power to transfer a case to another district, even though it was filed in the proper district. This can be done "in the interest of justice or for the convenience of the parties."[99] This power to transfer is rarely exercised and there is little case law interpreting it.

Finally, there is a rule to deal with a case filed in the wrong venue. As is true in modern procedural systems generally, the federal system in particular, venue is not viewed as jurisdictional. The normal remedy for a misfiling is transfer, not

---

[96] For a discussion of exemptions, see Chapter 11 of this book.

[97] 28 U.S.C. § 1408.

[98] "Affiliate" is defined in Bankruptcy Code § 101(2); broadly speaking, it means a business that is closely tied to the debtor.

[99] 28 U.S.C. § 1412. For a more extended treatment of this provision, see Collier on Bankruptcy ¶ 3.02[4].

dismissal; the bankruptcy court has broad power to transfer a misfiled case to the proper court.[100]

---

[100] 28 U.S.C. § 1477(a).

CHAPTER 7

Property of the Estate

§ 7.01 Introduction

A bankruptcy petition creates an "estate";[1] that is, a new legal entity separate and apart from the debtor who filed the petition (or, in an involuntary case, the debtor against whom the petition was filed). Unless the bankruptcy is a pure no-asset case, the estate has property. It is the property of the estate that is administered in the proceeding. That property is defined very broadly, to encompass virtually every property right the debtor has at the time of the petition. Whether post-petition property is included in the estate depends in part on the nature of the property and in part on whether the proceeding is under Chapter 7 or one of the reorganization Chapters. Sections 7.05 through 7.07 of this chapter discuss different rules used in the various forms of bankruptcy.

Under the old Bankruptcy Act, the rules regarding property of the estate were made somewhat complicated by the fact that property which would not ultimately be administered in the case (such as exempt property) never became part of the estate. The Code's approach is different. Virtually everything goes into the estate; it is then divided up between the debtor and the various creditors. Thus, exempt property begins as property of the estate, even though it will eventually be handed over to the debtor. Similarly, the debtor's encumbered property is property of estate, even if in all likelihood it will shortly be surrendered to the lienholder. This approach avoids preliminary squabbles over what is or is not subject to bankruptcy administration, leaving for later and presumably more orderly determination who takes what from the pot.

§ 7.02 General Rules Regarding Property of the Estate

The primary rule governing property of the estate is section 541(a). Under that provision, the estate is comprised of all the following property, regardless of where it is located or who is in possession:

> 1. **Pre-Petition Property** With very limited exceptions, all legal or equitable interests of the debtor in property as of the commencement of the case.[2]
>
> 2. **Community Property** All interests of the debtor and the debtor's spouse in community property as of the commencement of the case *if*

---

[1] Bankruptcy Code § 541(a).

[2] Bankruptcy Code § 541(a)(1). For a full discussion of the various exceptions to this rule, see § 7.04 of this chapter.

either (i) the property is under the sole, equal, or joint management and control of the debtor or (ii) the property is "liable" for an allowable claim against the debtor or the debtor and the debtor's spouse.[3] Thus, property that is entirely controlled by the spouse and not subject to any of the debtor's debts is excluded.

3. **Property Recovered During the Case**Property recovered by the trustee from third parties.[4] For example, property recovered from a third party by the trustee/DIP because the transfer to that third party was a preference or a fraudulent transfer is property of the estate.

4. **Property Rights Preserved For the Estate**During the bankruptcy, certain property interests may be avoided; if they are, they may also be preserved for the benefit of the estate (this issue is discussed in § 13.06 of this book). For example, a security interest in the debtor's factory machines may be avoided because it was obtained through a preferential transfer. That security interest, however, is effectively transferred to the trustee/DIP, who may use it to obtain priority against other lienholders and thus further augment the estate. The security interest— a property interest preserved for the benefit of the estate—is part of the property of the estate.[5]

5. **Certain Post-Petition Property "Windfalls"** Generally speaking, in a Chapter 7 (liquidation) proceeding, property acquired by the debtor post-petition does not become part of the estate. This is a key part of the "fresh start" policy that partially underlies bankruptcy law;[6] the liquidating debtor generally begins anew when the petition is filed and generally gets to keep all the property acquired thereafter.

There are a few exceptions to this rule contained in section 541(a)(5). In three situations, post-petition property will become part of the estate, if the property would have been part of the estate had the debtor had it when the case began and the debtor in fact acquires it or becomes entitled to it within 180 days after the petition. These three situations are: (i) property received by bequest, devise, or inheritance; (ii) property received as a result of a property settlement or divorce decree, and (iii) property received as beneficiary of a life insurance policy or a death benefit plan.[7] For example, suppose that Dora files bankruptcy on July 1, 1997, and inherits $1,000,000 from her mother on July 8. Although that property was received post-petition, it becomes part of the bankruptcy estate and is available to pay Dora's creditors through the

[3] Bankruptcy Code § 541(a)(2). Note that in the latter case, the property is property of the estate only to the extent that it is liable for claims against the debtor or the debtor and spouse.

[4] Bankruptcy Code § 541(a)(3).

[5] Bankruptcy Code § 541(a)(4).

[6] For a discussion of the fresh start, see § 1.01[B] of this book.

[7] Bankruptcy Code § 541(a)(5).

bankruptcy distribution process. Similarly, if Dora's mother had died on July 8, and Dora was the beneficiary of her mother's $250,000 life insurance policy, the $250,000 received post-petition would be part of Dora's bankruptcy estate. The usual reason given for these exceptions is that an impecunious debtor foreseeing the imminence of any of these events might rush into bankruptcy to prevent the assets from becoming available to creditors.

6. **Post-Petition Proceeds of Property of the Estate and Post-Petition Earnings** After the petition is filed, both the debtor and the property of the estate may continue to generate income. The debtor most typically generates income by earning wages—put simply, the debtor works, the employer pays. The property of the estate may generate income because it is sold, invested or otherwise producing income. For example, a rental property that was owned by the debtor when the petition was filed becomes property of the estate; it remains however a rental property and the tenant continues to pay each month for the right to remain in possession. Section 541(a)(6), in setting the boundaries of the estate, distinguishes between income that is attributable to the debtor's wages for post-petition services and income that is attributable to property of the estate. The former does not become property of the estate; the latter does.

Specifically, proceeds, products, offspring, rents, or profits of or from property of the estate are property of the estate; earnings from services performed by an individual debtor post-petition are not property of the estate.[8] For example, money received when property of the estate is sold ("proceeds") is property of the estate. The rent received on leased property of the estate is also property of the estate. If the estate includes a cow, the cow's post-petition calf is property of the estate.

However, an individual debtor's own personal wages are not property of the estate, to the extent they were earned after the petition was filed.[9] For example, suppose that Fred Mertz, a janitor, files Chapter 7 bankruptcy on June 30, 1996. On July 31, 1996, Mertz receives a paycheck from his employer for the janitorial services he performed from July 1 through July 31. That check is not property of the estate. Mertz' filing is treated as a financial "death" that occurred on June 30. July 1 marks his financial rebirth, and his earnings on and after that date are treated as part of his fresh start.

Problems with the application of this rule can arise when the debtor becomes entitled to payment for work performed partially before and

[8] Bankruptcy Code § 541(a)(6): "Such estate is comprised of all of the following property . . . Proceeds, product, offspring, rents, or profits of or from property of the estate . . ."

[9] Bankruptcy Code § 541(a)(6): "Such estate is comprised of all the following property . . . except such as are earnings from services performed by an individual debtor after the commencement of the case."

partially after the petition. The court must allocate the payment between the pre-petition and the post-petition work; the former is property of the estate; the latter belongs to the debtor.[10] This problems can be especially acute if the earnings involve bonuses or similar compensation related to or calculated on the basis of the debtor's work over an extended period of time.

For example, suppose that Bob Cratchit is an assistant sales manager of Scrooge & Marley Enterprises, Inc. Cratchit receives a base salary of $36,000 per year, plus a year-end bonus of up to $6,000 per year depending on his personal full-year sales results, plus a year-end "profit-share" bonus that depends upon over-all company results; this profit-share bonus is not of a set amount, and may even be omitted if the year was bad. On September 1, 1997, Cratchit files Chapter 7 Bankruptcy; on December 31, 1997, Cratchit is awarded a $3,000 personal results bonus and a $1,200 profit-share bonus. How much of this is attributable to post-petition services and how much to pre-petition services? Cratchit may well argue that at least 33.33% of the bonuses was attributable to his post-petition work (representing the four months from September through December). Indeed, he might even argue that the percentage should be higher, if most of his results and/or most of the company's profits were earned during those last four months. The trustee will try to claim all of the $1,200 profit-share bonus, arguing that since it was based on the results for the entire company, the part attributable to Cratchit's post-petition work is negligible. There is very little guidance in the case law to determine which argument, if either, is correct. There is no simple rule to apply in situations of this sort; the cases are quite fact specific.

7. **Post-Petition Property Acquired by the Estate** As noted, the Code distinguishes between the estate and the debtor. One part of this is that property acquired post-petition by the estate, not by the debtor, is property of the estate.[11] This provision is essentially an extension of subsection (a)(6), discussed in the previous paragraph; it makes clear that even if the property acquired by the estate is not "proceeds, product, offspring, rents, or profits" arising from property of the estate, if the property was acquired by the estate and not by the debtor, the property is part of the estate and is not part of the property of the debtor. For example, suppose that ABC, Inc., a company that designs software, is in bankruptcy. The business continues to operate during the bankruptcy, and the company successfully develops and markets a popular computer game, "Escape from the Trustee's Clutches." This game, and more importantly the money received for licensing it to eager teenagers, is arguably not a proceed or profit of the estate's property; even so, the game and the money are property of the estate since each is property acquired by the estate.

---

[10] See Rav v. Ryerson (In re Ryerson), 739 F.2d 1423 (9th Cir. 1984).

[11] Bankruptcy Code § 541(a)(7).

§ 7.03 Restrictions on Transfer

Sometimes property is owned subject to restrictions on its transfer to another. For example, when property is used as collateral for a loan, the loan agreement often limits the borrowers ability to transfer it. What effect does this have on the debtor's bankruptcy estate? In most cases, none.

As a general rule, it does not matter that the debtor's property interest is subject to restrictions on transfer. With the exception of certain beneficial interests in trusts—namely, those that are subject to enforceable non-bankruptcy restrictions on transfer[12] —an interest of the debtor in property becomes property of the estate "notwithstanding any provision . . . that restricts or conditions transfer of [the] interest by the debtor . . ."[13] For example, suppose that Doug owns property subject to a security interest held by River Bank. Under the security agreement, Doug may not sell or otherwise transfer title to the collateral without the prior written permission of River Bank. This provision does not prevent the collateral from becoming part of Doug's bankruptcy estate.[14] In ignoring virtually all restrictions on transfer, the Code deviates sharply from the old Bankruptcy act.

§ 7.04 Property Excluded from the Estate

Although the basic policy of the Code is to include everything in the estate, and then remove from it property distributed, abandoned, or exempted, there are a few absolute exclusions. These exclusions are drawn narrowly. The majority of them deal with interests arising from trusts or similar divisions of property into legal and equitable interests.

The first of these deals with a power of the debtor that may be exercised solely for the benefit of another person.[15] The most obvious example of this is a power of appointment under a trust that the trustee cannot exercise in his or her own favor. For example, a trust might be created that empowers Theodore to assign the principal to either Ahmad or Boris, but not to himself. Theodore goes into bankruptcy. This power does not become part of the property of the estate, and thus cannot be exercised by the trustee. The reason for this is to preserve the ability of the settlor of the trust (the person who created the trust) to determine both who would benefit and who would decide who would benefit from the trust. Since Theodore's creditors cannot directly gain anything from Theodore's exercise of the power, the Code

---

[12] For a full discussion of these beneficial interests, and their significance in bankruptcy, see § 7.04 of this chapter.

[13] Bankruptcy Code § 541(c)(1).

[14] Note that this does not mean that River Bank will necessarily lose its lien. In general, properly created liens survive not only the bankruptcy filing but the bankruptcy itself. See § 12.01. By placing the encumbered property into the estate, however, the trustee/DIP is given the power to administer it, and the lienholder is obliged to seek either the property or its monetary equivalent from the court. See Chapter 8 regarding the automatic stay and the right to adequate protection.

[15] Bankruptcy Code § 541(b)(1)

presumes there no sound reason to subvert the settlor's intention by handing the power of appointment over to the trustee/DIP.

The second exclusion is of broader significance. In 1984, BAFJA[16] added section 541(b)(2) to the Code. Under that provision, the estate does not include any interest the debtor has as lessee of nonresidential real property once the stated term of the lease expires. If the lease expires prior to the bankruptcy, the leasehold interest is never part of the estate; if it expires during the bankruptcy, the leasehold interest ceases to be part of the estate.[17] For example, suppose that Dottie Lane, Inc. is the lessee of a warehouse; the lease, by its own terms, expires on July 1, 1997. If Dottie Lane files bankruptcy on August 1, 1997, Dottie Lane's now-expired leasehold interest is not property of the estate. If Dottie Lane files on June 1, 1997, Dottie Lane's leasehold interest will initially be part of the estate, but when the lease expires on July 1, that interest will cease to be part of the estate. Two points are worth stressing. First, this provision must be read in conjunction with the automatic stay; the landlord's right to evict the debtor is still governed by section 362.[18] Second, it applies only to leases that expire as scheduled. Suppose that, under a lease contract, any default in payment by the lessee automatically terminates the lease. If the lessee defaults and then files bankruptcy, the mere fact that this automatic termination clause has been triggered does not mean that the lessee's interest in the property is excluded from the estate. To the contrary; the leasehold interest is part of the estate, and the enforceability of the automatic termination provision is governed by section 365, which is discussed in Chapter 9 of this book.

The third exclusion, added in 1990, is of very limited significance. The right of a debtor to participate in certain educational programs is not property of the estate. In addition, the debtor's accreditation or licensing as an educational institution is not property of the estate.[19] Thus, should Harvard go bankrupt, the trustee cannot sell its accreditation to Yale.

The fourth exclusion is also rather narrow. Property of the estate does not include certain interests in liquid or gaseous hydrocarbons that had been transferred or are subject to an agreement to transfer them.[20] This was designed to deal with specific problems created for the energy industry by the scope of the Bankruptcy Code's rules regarding the scope of the estate.

The 1994 Amendments added a fifth narrow exclusion. Property of the estate does not include the debtor's interest in certain proceeds of a sale by the debtor of a money order. These proceeds are excluded if the sale of the money order was made during the fourteen days prior to the filing of the petition and under an agreement that prohibits the comingling of the proceeds with other property of the debtor.[21]

---

[16] The Bankruptcy Amendments and Federal Judgeship Act of 1984—see § 3.04 for a discussion of these amendments.

[17] Bankruptcy Code § 541(b)(2).

[18] For a discussion of the automatic stay, see Chapter 8 of this book.

[19] Bankruptcy Code § 541(b)(3).

[20] Bankruptcy Code § 541(b)(4).

[21] Bankruptcy Code § 541(b)(5)(1994 Amendments). Note that it does not matter whether the proceeds were comingled or not; the key question is whether the agreement prohibited comingling.

The sixth exclusion is probably the most significant. It deals with non-assignable beneficial interests in trusts. In any trust relationship, there are at least three roles, usually involving at least three persons. The settlor creates the trust; the trustee administers it; and the beneficiary gets the loot, as and when the trust document and (in some cases) the trustee determine. The trustee holds legal title; the beneficiary, the equitable (a/k/a/ beneficial) interest in the trust corpus.[22] If the trust permits the beneficiary to assign the beneficial interest in the trust to a third party, the beneficiary's interest in the trust is property of the estate and is distributed to creditors. However, many trusts prohibit the beneficiary from assigning the beneficial interest. In many circumstances, these restrictions are enforceable under non-bankruptcy law.

Implicit in the enforceability of restrictions on transfer of the beneficial interest is that creditors of the beneficiary cannot seize the corpus of the trust. No matter how much the beneficiary of such a trust owes, no matter how delinquent on debts, creditors may only latch on to property when, if and as it is distributed to the beneficiary. They may not reach the property while it is still held in trust.[23]

Restrictions on transfer of beneficial interests in trusts have sometimes been used to ensure a continued income for the feckless offspring of the very rich. A wealthy parent or grandparent, dismayed by the inability of Junior to avoid squandering money on snipe ranches and pearl mines, may set up a trust that pays out $10,000 per month for bare maintenance expenses and prohibits the transfer of Junior's interest to anybody else. This has led to the somewhat dismissive sobriquet "spendthrift trust." To what extent are these restrictions on transfer valid once Junior has declared bankruptcy?

There is probably nothing in the Constitution that forces Congress to recognize spendthrift trusts in bankruptcy, and it is arguable that such recognition is unfair to those debtors whose ancestors had neither the wealth nor the wit to provide for their prodigal offspring.[24] However, section 541(c)(2) continues a long tradition of giving effect to this particular restriction on transfer. "A restriction on the transfer of a beneficial interest of the debtor in a trust that is enforceable under applicable nonbankrutpcy law is enforceable in a case under this title."[25] Thus, if Bertie Wooster's aunts have had the good sense to restrict his ability to transfer his

[22] The trust corpus is the property that is administered; it is usually investments, such as stocks, bonds, or other securities, but may be tangible property or virtually anything else.

[23] See generally, Restatement of Trusts 2d § 152 (1959).

[24] Note, however, that recognition of spendthrift trusts is in line with one theory of bankruptcy, namely that is should be transparent to state property and creditor's rights law, neither broadening nor narrowing the substantive rights of creditors but only enforcing them more efficiently. See § 1.02[B] of this book.

[25] Bankruptcy Code § 541(c)(2). The court will look closely at the terms of the trust to determine whether it is in fact a true spendthrift trust or merely a sham. See, for example, Pitrat v. Garlikov, 947 F.2d 419, 425 (9th Cir. 1991) (pension plan in which trustee and beneficiary are the same individual can qualify as spendthrift trust, but the beneficiary's access to the trust funds must be even more restrictive than usual).

beneficial interest in the Wooster family trust, his future prosperity is secure from the bankruptcy trustee.[26]

In sober fact, however, this provision, although certainly protective of the classic spendthrift trust, and the classic twit who needs a spendthrift trust, is far more democratic. It has its greatest impact in an arena far removed from the foibles of the idle rich: pension funds. It has long been clear that restrictions on the transfer of pension funds held in trust, if recognized or required by state law, fit within the exclusion. In a notable decision, the Supreme Court held that federal law restrictions are equally effective, and in doing so further effectively broadened the scope of this exception beyond what had traditionally been assumed. *Patterson v. Shumate*,[27] relying on the plain language of the Code, held that federal law making employee interests in certain pension funds inalienable fit within section 541(c)(2); thus, the employee's rights were not property of the estate.[28] This ruling resolved a long dispute in the lower courts over whether the phrase "applicable nonbankruptcy law" in section 541(c)(2) meant any law or only state law. More importantly for debtors, it gave substantial protection to pension rights. Indeed, it is undoubtedly true that the so-called spendthrift trust exclusion protects far more financially unfortunate middle-class employees than muddled and befuddled million-heirs

The final blanket exception largely excludes from the estate property in which the debtor holds only legal title and not an equitable interest. All that does pass into the estate is the bare legal title;[29] the real value of the property—the equitable interest—does not do so. For example, suppose that the debtor is trustee of Bertie Wooster's spendthrift trust. As trustee, he holds bare legal title. He is not entitled to take money out of the trust (indeed, to do so would not only violate his fiduciary duty but also create a debt that would be non-dischargeable under the bankruptcy Code).[30] The property in the trust is not "his" property; it is not normally subject to the claims of his creditors outside of bankruptcy. It is thus not subject to the claims of his creditors in bankruptcy.

§ 7.05 Special Rules—Chapter 11 Reorganization

There is no special rule in Chapter 11 regarding property of the estate. However, in the typical Chapter 11, much post-petition property will be property of the estate under section 541(a)(6) and (7). Under those provisions, the estate includes "proceeds, product, offspring, rents or profits of or from property of the estate,"[31] or property acquired by the estate,[32] which will encompass most of what a Chapter

---

[26] See generally, Pelham G. Wodehouse, The World of Jeeves (1967).

[27] 504 U.S. 753 (1992).

[28] See also Matter of Childs, 129 Bankr. 14 (Bankr. D. Conn. 1991) (state law restrictions on state employee's right to alienate pension funds held in trust prevented the employee's interest from becoming property of the estate).

[29] Bankruptcy Code § 541(d).

[30] See Bankruptcy Code § 523(a)(4).

[31] Bankruptcy Code § 541(a)(6)

[32] Bankruptcy Code § 547(a)(7).

11 debtor normally receives after the petition. Moreover, the concept of property of the estate is of somewhat less significance in Chapter 11 than in Chapter 7, because the debtor must nearly always use property acquired post-petition to fund the plan of reorganization, whether or not that property is part of the estate.

§ 7.06 Special Rules—Chapter 12 Family Farmer Reorganization

Since Chapter 12 deals with reorganization of the estate, and thus involves post-petition property, the scope of the estate is wider than it is in Chapter 7. Indeed, this is necessary to effectuate the reorganization. Section 1207, which defines property of the estate in context of Chapter 12, encompasses

> 1. All the property included in section 541 (basically, all property owned prior to bankruptcy plus very limited property acquired post-petition),[33] and
>
> 2. All property "of the kind specified" in section 541 that the debtor acquires after the commencement of the case, but before the case is closed, dismissed, or converted to a Chapter 7 case,[34] and
>
> 3. All earnings from services that the debtor performs after the commencement of the case, but before the case is closed, dismissed, or converted to Chapter 7.[35]

For example, the income that the debtor earns from the operation of the farm during the pendency of the proceeding is property of the estate. Generally speaking, this would not be true in a Chapter 7 proceeding; in Chapter 7 only the income that was attributable to the property of the estate or received by the estate would be included.

§ 7.07 Special Rules—Chapter 13 Individual Debtor with Regular Income Reorganization

Like Chapters 11 and 12, Chapter 13 involves a reorganization; it thus deals with post-petition property that the debtor acquires. Indeed, this is necessary to effectuate the plan of reorganization. In Chapter 13, property of the estate includes everything included in Chapter 7[36] (basically, all pre-petition and only some post-petition property of the debtor).[37] In addition, it includes:

---

[33] Bankruptcy Code § 1207(a)(1). For a more complete discussion of property of the estate under Bankruptcy Code § 541, see § 7.02 of this chapter.

[34] Bankruptcy Code § 1207(a)(1). This includes virtually every type of property that the debtor might acquire.

[35] Bankruptcy Code § 1207(a)(2).

[36] Bankruptcy Code § 1306(a).

[37] See § 7.02 of this chapter.

1. All property "of the kind specified" in Section 541 that the debtor acquires after the commencement of the case but before the case is either closed, dismissed, or converted to Chapter 7, 11 or 12,[38] and

2. All earnings from services that the debtor performs after the commencement of the case but before the case is closed, dismissed, or converted to Chapter 7, 11, or 12.[39]

For example, the debtor's wages earned post-petition are property of the estate. This is not true in a Chapter 7 proceeding, in which post-petition wages are specifically excluded.[40]

[38] Bankruptcy Code § 1306(a)(1).

[39] Bankruptcy Code § 1306(a)(2).

[40] See § 7.02 of this chapter.

CHAPTER 8

The Automatic Stay

§ 8.01 Introduction

This Chapter deals with one of the most significant aspects of a bankruptcy proceeding—the automatic stay of virtually all civil actions involving the debtor, the debtor's property, or property of the estate. One of the goals of bankruptcy is an orderly liquidation, or an orderly reorganization, of the debtor's property or property of the estate under bankruptcy court supervision. To achieve the goal of orderly administration, other judicial and non-judicial proceedings are stayed. This gives a breathing space both to the liquidating trustee and the reorganizing debtor in possession. Although important in any bankruptcy, this breathing space is of particular significance in Chapter 11. It gives the debtor in possession a realistic opportunity to negotiate with creditors and propose a plan. The automatic stay is also the focus of much bankruptcy litigation, particularly in Chapter 11, and especially between the debtor and its lien creditors and lessors.

As a general rule, a creditor who has a security interest in, or other lien on, the debtor's property would rather get the property, sell it, and forget the bankruptcy proceeding; similarly, a lessor of real or personal property often wants to retake possession and re-lease. Under some circumstances, a lien creditor or lessor can get the court to lift the stay and permit it to do what it wishes with the property. Requests to lift the stay are, for obvious reasons, usually resisted by the debtor.

Remember, however, that bankruptcy law is generally protective of property rights, such as liens. The automatic stay rules craft a balance between the debtor's desire to keep the property and the claimant's wish to seize it. If the debtor has no valuable property interest in the property, and does not need it, the court is supposed to lift the stay; so too if the debtor cannot protect the value of the claimant's interest in the property.

The stay itself is relatively uncontroversial; virtually all commentators, whatever their philosophy of bankruptcy, agree that a stay is necessary to make the proceeding feasible. There are, however, a number of criticisms of the stay as applied, particularly of the apparent unwillingness of many courts to lift or modify the stay in protracted Chapter 11 reorganizations. It is frequently argued that the refusal to lift the stay in hopeless proceedings—and thus to terminate those proceedings—results in unnecessary loss to creditors, especially undersecured creditors who are not entitled to interest on their claims during the period between the filing and the confirmation of a plan.[1] It may also, by continuing the debtor in business, lead to

---

[1] For a full discussion of the rules regarding pendency interest, and the effect that the Bankruptcy Code's denial of pendency interest has on the real value of undersecured obligations, see § 10.02[D] of this book.

the useless accumulation of yet more unpayable debt. Worse still, it may even cause damage to other companies forced to deal with a competitor that does not have to pay its bills.[2] To a large degree, these criticisms are part of the broader critique of Chapter 11 bankruptcy, discussed in Chapter 17.[3]

More recently, there has been great concern in some parts of the country about allegedly abusive consumer filings. There has been a pattern, especially in Los Angeles, of filings to prevent eviction of a tenant from an apartment. In the view of some, these filings, made when there is no real intent to liquidate or reorganize, but only to stall an inevitable eviction, are abusive. To others, they represent a crude but legitimate method of trying to hold onto one's home during times of severe financial distress. The 1994 Amendments address this problem indirectly by imposing regulations on so-called "bankruptcy mills" that are in the business of churning out petitions for cases of this type.[4]

This discussion of the automatic stay must be read in conjunction with Chapter 9, which deals with the right of the trustee/DIP to use, sell, or lease property. The same issues regarding the balance between the debtor's and the claimant's interest in the property arise in determining the former's right to use or dispose of property to which each has a claim. Similar issues also arise in context of the assumption of contractual and lease obligations by the trustee/DIP; those matters are also discussed in Chapter 9.

§ 8.02 Actions Stayed

Under section 362, the filing of the bankruptcy petition operates as a stay of nearly all non-criminal actions against the debtor, the debtor's property or property of the estate.[5] When reading the rules, carefully note that they apply variously to the debtor, the estate, property of the debtor, or property of the estate. Not all of these are equally protected, or protected in the same way.

The scope of the stay is extremely broad, including, though not limited, to the following:

Judicial/Administrative Actions

The automatic stay blocks the commencement or continuation of any judicial or administrative action against the debtor that was or could have been commenced before the commencement of the case. It also bars judicial and administrative actions against the debtor to recover a pre-petition claim.[6] For example, if the petition was

---

[2] In the view of some, the ability of airlines to continue in business during protracted Chapter 11 proceedings has seriously impaired the viability of those airlines that do not have bankruptcy protection.

[3] See § 17.01.

[4] See Bankruptcy Code § 110(1994 Amendments).

[5] Bankruptcy Code § 362(a).

[6] Bankruptcy Code § 362(a)(1).

filed on January 1, 1997, a case that either was pending or could have been filed before that date, or that derives from a claim that arose before that date, is stayed. If the debtor had negligently injured Alice on May 1, 1996, Alice's tort action is stayed; if the debtor had breached a contract with Belinda on July 1, 1996, her action is likewise stayed. Even if the pending litigation is in its final stages, the stay applies; even if the jury is just about to rule, the case must stop. In a perhaps unnecessary additional provision, the stay rules also specifically block the commencement or continuation of a proceeding before the United States Tax Court concerning the debtor.[7]

Enforcement of Judgments

The automatic stay also forbids actions to enforce a judgment obtained before the commencement of the case. For example, if Belinda has reduced her contract claim against the debtor to judgment on July 1, 1996, and the debtor files bankruptcy on January 1, 1997, Belinda is stayed from taking action to collect her judgment. The stay itself encompasses actions against the debtor and against property of the estate, but not against property of the debtor.[8] Note, however, that virtually all property of the debtor is subject to other protections. At the beginning of the case, the debtor will likely have no property, because virtually all of any debtor's property goes into the estate.[9] When the debtor exempts property, that property will come out of the estate but will be protected against creditor action by the exemption laws.[10] Property that is subject to a pre-petition lien and is abandoned or otherwise returned to the debtor is protected from foreclosure during the case by another provision of § 362, namely § 362(a)(5), which is discussed below. It is thus rare that there will be much property of the debtor that can be seized during the pendency of the bankruptcy.

Note that quite often it is during (and because of) enforcement proceedings that the debtor files its bankruptcy petition. The pressure of an enforcement action is one of the strongest motivations for filing, precisely because filings stop the enforcement proceeding. So long as the enforcement process is incomplete, the stay applies. For example, if the Sheriff is in the midst of selling foreclosed property, but the hammer has not fallen and the sale has not been completed, the stay prevents the sale from going forward.

Acts to Obtain Possession/Control of Property

The stay prohibits any act to obtain possession of property of the estate, to obtain possession of property from the estate, or to exercise control over property of the estate.[11] Note that this provision is broad enough to encompass property that is simply in custody of the estate. In addition, the stay prohibits any act to collect, assess, or recover any pre-petition claim against the debtor.[12] Note that these

---

[7] Bankruptcy Code § 362(a)(8).

[8] Bankruptcy Code § 362(a)(2).

[9] See § 7.02 of this book.

[10] See Chapter 11 of this book for a discussion of the effect of exemption laws.

[11] Bankruptcy Code § 362(a)(3).

[12] Bankruptcy Code § 362(a)(6).

provisions do not apply to property of the debtor; however, as noted in the preceding paragraph, there are exemption laws and other provisions in and out of the Bankruptcy Code that effectively protect much of the debtor's property from seizure.

These provisions extend the stay beyond any formal judicial or administrative proceeding; they are, for example, clearly broad enough to prohibit self-help repossession.[13] They also restrict virtually all other forms of collection action. For example, in one case, the creditor (a hotel) tried to coerce payment from the debtor (the restaurant in the hotel) by refusing to allow restaurant patrons to order from the hotel bar and by posting signs that encouraged hotel guests not to use the restaurant. This violated the stay.[14] The language is potentially broad enough to include even routine attempts to collect the debt, such as sending an ordinary demand letter or dunning by telephone; however, it is unlikely that, even if it found a technical violation of the stay, a court would impose any sanction on a creditor that inadvertently sent such a letter, e.g., because it forgot to instruct its computer not to do so.

Many courts draw a line between actions that indicate an effort to collect and those that merely inform the debtor of the obligation or of the creditor's refusal to do business:

> The case law supports a distinction between communications between the creditor and debtor that contain threats or harassment and those that merely set forth the fact that money is owing. Thus, courts have held the automatic stay violated by letters giving notice of intent to terminate a lease . . . by a college that refused to give transcripts to the debtor to force payment, and by a creditor who made repeated visits and telephone calls to the debtor. On the other hand . . . we have treated other communications that merely set forth the fact of the debt [as not violating] the automatic stay.[15]

Liens. Section 362(a) stays any act to create, perfect, or enforce any lien against property of the estate,[16] and similarly stays any act to create, perfect, or enforce a lien against property of the debtor to the extent that the lien secures a pre-petition claim.[17] Note that the protection given to property of the estate is rather broader than that given to property of the debtor, since the former is protected against all liens and the latter only against liens securing pre-petition obligations. This part of the stay has created particular problems for lien creditors whose perfection was in process at the time of the petition; those problems have been ameliorated by an exception to the stay discussed in § 8.03[B][2] of this chapter.

Setoff. The stay prohibits the exercise of any right of setoff if the claim owed to the debtor by the offsetting creditor arose pre-petition.[18] For example, if the debt

---

[13] See In re Holman, 92 Bankr. 764 (Bankr. S.D. Ohio 1988).

[14] In re Sechuan City, Inc., 96 Bankr. 37, 40-42 (Bankr. E. D. Pa. 1989).

[15] Morgan Guaranty Trust Co. v. American Savings and Loan Association, 804 F.2d 1487, 1491 n.4 (9th Cir. 1986), cert denied, 482 U.S. 929 (1987).

[16] Bankruptcy Code § 362(a)(4).

[17] Bankruptcy Code § 362(a)(5)

[18] Bankruptcy Code § 362(a)(7).

owed by the creditor to the debtor arose on May 1, and the petition was filed on May 15, section 362 stays the creditor from setting off the debt it owes to the debtor against any debt the debtor owes to it. The right of setoff is discussed in more detail in Chapter 10.[19]

Note that the stay does not destroy any underlying rights; neither the debts nor the interests securing debts are avoided. The judgment holder retains its judgment; the lienholder its lien; the mutual obligor its right of setoff.[20] The stay merely prevents the exercise of those rights unless and until certain conditions are met. Moreover, as will be discussed in § 8.06[B] [2], any creditor who has a property right affected by the stay is entitled to have the value of that property right protected for so long as the stay remains in effect. This does not mean that the substantive rights are untouched; a right delayed is a right diminished. It means however that, except in the most unusual case, the right will remain fundamentally intact:

> [W]hile the automatic stay may adversely impact on the substantive rights of creditors, the purpose of the automatic stay is not substantive, but procedural. The automatic stay is intended as a form of procedural protection under which the debtor in a reorganization case can prepare and present a proposed plan free from unauthorized creditor pressure. The purpose of the automatic stay is not to ultimately determine the substantive rights of any party, nor to ultimately prevent the exercise of the available rights of any party.[21]

Note as well that these rules *only* deal with the debtor, the debtor's property, and/or property of the estate. With very limited exceptions, third parties who have direct or secondary liability on the same obligations are unprotected by the statute. Even if the third party is an affiliate of the debtor, such as a co-principal, surety, or related company, the automatic stay generally does not apply.[22] Except in unusual circumstances, the creditor may pursue its rights against the other obligor. Thus, for example, if an obligation of the debtor is guaranteed by another, the stay does not normally prevent the creditor from pursuing the guarantor. The exceptions to this rule are discussed in §§ 8.04 and 8.05 of this chapter.

§ 8.03 Exceptions to the Automatic Stay

[A]—Introduction

There are many limitations on the automatic stay; not least of which is the bankruptcy itself. Once the case is over, or property abandoned (and thus no longer

---

[19] See § 10.09.

[20] Of course, in some cases these rights will be avoided under other provisions of the Bankruptcy Code.

[21] In re Hughes-Bechtol, Inc., 117 Bankr. 890, 905-06 (Bankr. S. D. Ohio 1990).

[22] See In re Sowers, 164 Bankr. 256 (Bankr. E.D. Va. 1994) (action against debtor's employer for failure to honor pre-petition garnishment order not barred by the automatic stay, since it was not a disguised effort to collect from the debtor).

administered in the case), the stay ends. There are also actions that are never subject to the stay at all; some of these deal with the rights of owners and encumbrancers (private rights) and others with the power of government (public rights).

[B]—Private Rights Excepted From the Stay

Congress has enacted a great many exceptions to the automatic stay. Many of these exceptions are extremely narrow, designed to deal with rare (or even unique) cases.[23] However, there are several important exceptions dealing broadly with private rights, and several dealing broadly with governmental powers. Only these major exceptions are covered in this discussion.

When reading these exceptions, it is important to remember that the court's general power to enjoin actions under section 105 is unaffected. Where appropriate, a bankruptcy court might block an action otherwise permitted by the section 362 exceptions. Of course, in light of the fact that Congress has broadly validated those actions, it is only in rare and extreme cases that a section 105 injunction would be appropriate.

[1]—Alimony, Maintenance, Support, and Paternity

The first of the major private rights exceptions deals with alimony, maintenance, and support. The Bankruptcy Code in general is quite solicitous of rights arising from marital or parental obligations. One aspect of this is that the automatic stay does not apply to the collection of alimony, maintenance, or support from property that is not property of the estate.[24] The stay does protect property of the estate; but other property (such as a Chapter 7 debtor's post-petition earnings) may be seized without bankruptcy court permission.

The 1994 Amendments broadened this exception to the stay. Under the provision as amended, the automatic stay does not apply to the commencement or continuation of any action or proceeding regarding (1) the establishment of paternity, (2) the establishment or modification of an order for alimony, maintenance, or support.[25] Thus, the stay not only permits the collection of alimony, maintenance or support already ordered but also the establishment or modification of such an order. It also permits paternity suits to go forward despite the bankruptcy.

[2]—Perfection of Certain Interests

The second major private exception gives limited relief to persons who acquire interests in the debtor's property just before bankruptcy, and who have not yet had time to perfect those interests. This provision primarily protects last-minute lienholders who extended credit during the final days before the petition. The

---

[23] For an example of these rarities, see the second subsection (14) to Bankruptcy Code § 362(b), under which the stay does not affect the ability of an accrediting agency to revoke the accreditation of an educational institution. (This provision is scheduled to expire on October 1, 1996, perhaps much to the relief of a few shaky schools).

[24] Bankruptcy Code § 362(b)(2)[B].

[25] Bankruptcy Code § 362(b)(2)(A)(1994 Amendments).

exception is narrowly tailored to protect the interests of lienholders who would otherwise not be allowed the same amount of time to perfect as those who happened to have obtained their liens earlier.

Broadly speaking, if a lien is created or perfected during the preference period (which is usually 90 days before the filing of the bankruptcy petition[26] the lien must be perfected within 10 days of attachment to be effective against the trustee/DIP. (In addition, the lien must have attached at approximately the same time the extension of credit was made.)[27] Code section 362(b)(3) ensures that, if the debtor files bankruptcy within that 10 day grace period, the lienholder may still go ahead and complete the perfection of its lien, despite the automatic stay.[28]

For example, suppose that River Bank and Duchess Manufacturing Corp. entered into a loan agreement on June 1. Pursuant to the loan agreement, River Bank lent $100,000 to Duchess, and Duchess executed a security agreement covering Duchess's equipment on June 1. The Bankruptcy Code allows River Bank 10 days to perfect its security interest in Duchess's equipment. Duchess files bankruptcy on June 5. The automatic stay does not prevent River Bank from taking the necessary step to perfect its security interest (that step is the filing of a U.C.C. Article 9 financing statement) so long as River Bank does so within the 10 day period, that is, by June 11.

[3]—Commercial Real Estate Leases

Section 362(a)(10) provides an exception to the stay that protects lessors of nonresidential realty. If the lease has terminated because its stated term has expired, the lessor may retake possession of the property.[29] This exception applies regardless of when the lease expired; that is, regardless of whether it expired prior to the petition or during the case. For example, suppose that the debtor was leasing commercial real property under a lease that expired on June 1, 1997. The fact that the automatic stay was in force because the debtor filed bankruptcy on May 15, 1997 would not prevent the lessor from taking possession of the property on or after June 1.

[4]—Negotiable Instruments

The last important private rights exception is rooted in the requirements of U.C.C. article 3for enforcement of a negotiable instrument. The exception permits the creditor to present a negotiable instrument, to give notice of its dishonor, and to protest its dishonor.[30] The reason for this exception is somewhat complex. Under Article 3, in some circumstances, a holder of a negotiable instrument[31] cannot

---

[26] See § 14.02[F] of this book.

[27] For a fuller discussion of this, see Chapter 14 of this book.

[28] Bankruptcy Code § 362(b)(3). Note that the 1994 Amendments slightly changed this provision to permit the creditor not only to perfect the security interest initially, but also to maintain or continue the perfection of the security interest.

[29] Bankruptcy Code § 362(b)(10).

[30] Bankruptcy Code § 362(b)(11).

[31] In the context of this discussion, the holder is the creditor.

proceed against some of the parties to the instrument unless three things have happened. First, the holder must present[32] the instrument; second, the instrument must be dishonored.[33] third, the person whom the holder wishes to sue must be given notice of the dishonor.[34] In some circumstances, the presentation must be made and the notice must be given within a short period of time; otherwise, the obligation of the person who was entitled to the notice is discharged.[35] All of this means that in some situations, a co-obligor could be discharged from its obligation because the stay prevented the creditor from presenting or giving the required notice. Because of this, the stay does not prevent presentation or notice.

Similarly, the stay does not prevent "protest." The reasons for this are similar to the reasons for allowing presentment and notice of dishonor, although because of amendments to U.C.C. Article 3 that are now in force in most states, those reasons are less compelling. "Protest" refers to a process that is used when a dishonored check was either drawn or made payable outside the United States. Under prior law, protest was mandatory; under the 1990 version of Article 3, it is merely a way of creating evidence of dishonor, and is not a precondition to anyone's liability.[36] The Bankruptcy Code, however, preceded this change and so still permits protest, despite the stay, even though protest is no longer necessary under U.S. law.[37]

[C]—Exceptions for Governmental Police and Regulatory Powers

There are a number of exceptions that limit the effect of the stay on governmental actions. Criminal actions against the debtor are not stayed at all.[38] Bankruptcy thus does not provide even a temporary haven for those accused of criminal misconduct. Similarly, the stay does not apply to government actions to enforce its police or regulatory power, or to enforce non-money judgments obtained in police or regulatory actions.[39] For example, an action to force a polluter to desist from contaminating air, water, or land is not stayed when the polluter files bankruptcy.[40]

---

[32] Roughly speaking, presentation is a demand for payment from the person who is supposed to pay the instrument.

[33] Dishonor usually means that the person to whom the instrument was presented refused to pay it.

[34] U.C.C. § 3-503(a).

[35] U.C.C. §§ 3-405(c), 3-414(d), 3-414(f), 3-415(c), 3-415(e). For fuller discussions of presentment, dishonor, notice of dishonor, and protest, see Thomas D. Crandall, Michael J. Herbert, and Lary Lawrence, Uniform Commercial Code §§ 15.15 -15.21(1993) and Barry L. Zaretsky, Gerald T. McLaughlin & Neil B. Cohen, Commercial Law & Practice Guide ¶ 14.06 (1991). Note that the specifics of all these rules were changed somewhat in the 1990 version of the Uniform Commercial Code; the discussion in this book derives from the 1990 version.

[36] U.C.C. § 3-505(b) and official comment.

[37] Note, however, that protest might still be required by the law of the foreign country. U.C.C. § 3-305 official comment. There is thus at least some reason to continue the exception to the stay.

[38] Bankruptcy Code § 362(b)(1).

[39] Bankruptcy Code § 362(b)(4), (5).

[40] See Penn Terra Ltd. v. Department of Environmental Resources, 733 F.2d 267 (3d Cir. 1984).

Note that the police powers exception deals only with government actions that are essentially to protect "public interests" rather than the pecuniary interests of the government. Many governments engage in what are to all intents and purposes commercial activities. A city for example may run a municipal utility. Its customers may have overdue bills. Some of its customers with overdue bills may file bankruptcy. An action by the utility to collect those bills post petition is stayed; the utility's pecuniary interest it getting payment is not transformed into a police or regulatory power just because it happens to belong to a government. Similarly, the exercise of a government power for the purpose of vindicating a private pecuniary right, rather than a general public interest, is subject to the stay.[41]

The usual interpretation of these provisions distinguishes between the proceeding itself and an actual seizure of property pursuant to a money judgment. The former is covered by the exception; the latter is not. Thus, the stay does not stop the government from enjoining acts that pollute.[42] Neither does the stay prevent the government from obtaining a money judgment against the a wrongdoer, such as a polluter.[43] However, the stay does prevent the government from actually enforcing a money judgment.[44] The government, in advancing its police and regulatory powers may thus do everything but collect money from the debtor; to get the money, it must first get the court to lift the stay.

Note that the police power/regulatory power exceptions even permit the seizure of property if the seizure is related to the government's police powers and does not involve the collection of a money judgment. For example, a civil forfeiture proceeding is not stayed.[45] Neither is an action by a state bar to revoke a license to practice law.[46]

There are some extremely limited stay exceptions that protect a governmental pecuniary interest. Under section 362(b)(8), the stay does not prevent the commencement of any action by the Secretary of Housing and Urban Development to foreclose a mortgage or deed of trust if the mortgage or deed of trust is or was insured under the National Housing Act and covers property or properties consisting of five or

[41] See In re Kuck, 116 Bankr. 821 (Bankr. S. D. Ala. 1990). In that case, the state was stayed from suspending driver's licenses and automobile tags for failure to file an accident report, because the requirement was to facilitate the collection of private claims for money damages.

[42] According to Collier's:

> By far the greatest amount of judicial activity under section 362(b)(4) has to do with the enforcement of environmental laws. Most courts have concluded that section 362(b)(4) will permit a governmental unit to fix civil liability and to enforce present compliance with environmental laws, even where an expenditure of funds may be necessary as long as no attempt is made to collect on a judgment based upon past violations.

Collier on Bankruptcy ¶ 362.05[4] (citations omitted).

[43] United States v. Nicolet, 857 F.2d 202 (3rd Cir. 1988).

[44] United States v. Nicolet, 857 F.2d 202 (3rd Cir. 1988); see also, Thomas Solvent Co. v. Kelley, 44 Bankr. 83 (Bankr. W.D. Mich. 1984).

[45] In re James, 940 F.2d 46 (3d. Cir. 1991).

[46] In re Wade, 948 F.2d 1122 (9th Cir. 1991).

more living units.[47] Note that this exception only permits the commencement of the foreclosure proceeding, not the actual sale of the property. There are also two provisions that effectively limit the duration of the stay to 90 days with regard to certain interests held by the government in ships that have been financed under certain government programs.[48]

Finally, section 362(b)(9) permits a government to do such things as issue a notice of tax deficiency, conduct an audit, and demand tax returns.[49] It does not, however, permit further steps, such as the commencement or continuation of a United States Tax Court proceeding.[50] The function of this provision is rather limited; it merely allows taxing authorities to take steps to investigate or establish the taxpayer's liability.

§ 8.04 Automatic Co-debtor Stay—Chapters 12 and 13

In proceedings under most Chapters of the Code, the automatic stay applies only to actions involving the debtor or the estate. It does not prevent a creditor from pursuing remedies against other persons or property. Most significantly for a creditor, the stay does not affect its rights to go after co-obligors, such as co-signers or guarantors.

A slightly different rule applies in Chapters 12 and 13. Under both of those Chapters, there is a limited automatic stay against certain co-obligors of the debtor. For the stay to apply, two primary conditions must be met. First, the debt involved must be a consumer debt.[51] Second, the co-obligor must be an individual, not an organization such as a corporation or partnership.[52] In addition, if the co-obligor is a professional surety—more precisely, if he or she became liable on the debt, or secured the debt, in the ordinary course of his or her business, the stay does not apply.[53]

The legislative history confirms what is obvious from the text; this limited stay is designed to protect co-obligors who incurred obligations because of a family relationship to, or friendship for, the debtor.[54] By doing so, the Code protects the debtor from the demands of the codebtor. At least, that is the hope.

Although it is possible to imagine other situations in which the stay could apply, as a practical matter it is virtually limited to circumstances such as a parent, spouse, or friend co-signing a note. Congress was concerned that because of the underlying relationship, the debtor would feel inordinate pressure to pay the obligation unless

---

[47] Bankruptcy Code § 362(b)(8).

[48] Bankruptcy Code § 362(b)(12), (13).

[49] Bankruptcy Code § 362(b)(9).

[50] Indeed, Bankruptcy Code § 362(a)(8) specifically stays Tax Court proceedings.

[51] Bankruptcy Code §§ 1201(a), 1301(a).

[52] Bankruptcy Code §§ 1201(a), 1301(a).

[53] Bankruptcy Code §§ 1201(a), 1301(a).

[54] H. R. Rep. No. 595, 95th Cong., 1st Sess 121-22 (1978).

action against the co-obligor was protected, at least temporarily, by an automatic stay. This in turn would disrupt the Chapter 12/Chapter 13 reorganization process. Congress may have been naive about the degree to which the stay actually relieves pressure on the debtor; after all, the stay does not discharge the co-obligor's obligation, but merely delays the enforcement of that obligation.[55] Thus, the stay may not in fact be sufficient to shield the debtor from pressure from the co-obligor.

These provisions are often referred to as the co-signer provisions. The term "co-signer" is a trifle misleading. It does not refer only to co-makers of an obligation; rather it encompasses all sureties. Indeed, although the word "co-signer" is used colloquially, the actual statutory provisions refer to any person who is liable on the debt with the debtor.

There is only one statutory exception to the co-debtor stay; it is rooted in the requirements of U.C.C. Article 3 for enforcement of a negotiable instrument .[56] The exception permits the creditor to present a negotiable instrument and to give notice of its dishonor. The reason for this exception is somewhat complex. Under Article 3, in some circumstances, a holder of a negotiable instrument.[57] cannot proceed against some of the parties to the instrument unless three things have happened. First, the holder must present[58] the instrument; second, the instrument must be dishonored.[59] third, the person whom the holder wishes to sue must be given notice of the dishonor. In some circumstances, the presentation must be made and the notice must be given within a short period of time; otherwise, the obligation of the person who was entitled to the notice is discharged. All of this means that in some (rather unusual) situations, a co-obligor could be discharged from its obligation because the stay prevented the creditor from presenting or giving the required notice. Because of this, the stay does not prevent presentation or notice.[60] This exception is exactly the same as one of the exceptions to the automatic stay regarding the debtor.

Because the co-debtor stay is designed to protect the Chapter 12/Chapter 13 process, it does not apply in other situations. Thus, if the case is closed, dismissed, or converted to Chapter 7 or Chapter 11, the stay automatically terminates.[61] The stay may also be terminated by the court; this issue is discussed in § 8.06[B] of this chapter.

---

[55] H. R. Rep. No. 595, 95th Cong., 1st Sess, 123 (1978).

[56] This issue is also discussed, in slightly more detail, in § 8.03[B][4] of this chapter.

[57] In the context of this discussion, the holder is the creditor.

[58] Roughly speaking, "presentation" is a demand for payment from the person who is supposed to pay the instrument.

[59] "Dishonor" usually means that the person to whom the instrument was presented refused to pay it.

[60] Note that presentment, dishonor, and notice are required only for some types of suretyship contracts; this is not a necessary or even a usual part of the contract. See generally, U.C.C. §§ 3-419 and 3-412 through 3-415.

[61] Bankruptcy Code §§ 1201(a)(2), 1301(a)(2).

§ 8.05 Discretionary Stays

The automatic stay is not the only power the court has to impose limits on creditor action. It is reasonably well established that the court may impose other stays under section 105. That provision empowers the court to issue any order that is "necessary or appropriate" to carry out the provisions of the Code.[62] On occasion, courts have used this power to impose stays on actions against persons other than the debtor.

Generally, a discretionary stay is imposed only when the non-debtor would otherwise face irreparable injury[63] or where the case itself would be seriously disrupted. For example, the debtor may be an indispensable party to litigation involving another. If the litigation goes forward, the non-debtor would be severely impaired in protecting its interests because of the absence of the debtor. The bankruptcy court has but two choices—lift the stay on actions against the debtor, which would protect the non-debtor but might disrupt the bankruptcy, or impose a stay on the proceedings against the non-debtor. Although neither choice is wholly attractive, a number of courts have held that the latter is better than the former in at least some cases. Similarly, it is sometimes true that a third-party action would inevitably distract the debtor's management from the case. A good example of this occurred in the A.H. Robins reorganization, a case discussed in Chapter 17.[64] In that case, the manufacturer of the Dalkon Shield intrauterine contraceptive device went into bankruptcy in an effort to deal with the products liability claims arising from problems with that device. Its liability insurer, Aetna, was involved in related litigation. The court enjoined the actions against Aetna, despite the plaintiff's promise to leave the Robins company alone as much as possible:

> Inevitably, Aetna must involve Robins in this litigation. Aetna's primary defence logically will be that Robins—not Aetna—is responsible for the injuries suffered by these plaintiffs . . . Despite the plaintiffs' good intentions, Robins will inexorably be drawn into this litigation. Because this involvement will put a substantial burden on Robins, it will detract from the reorganization process.[65]

It is broadly true, however, that bankruptcy courts are extremely sparing in their exercise of power over non-bankruptcy proceedings concerning non-debtors. Only in the absence of any alternative is a court likely to enter such a discretionary stay. Moreover, the court is not likely to make the stay broader or longer than is absolutely necessary.

---

[62] See Bankruptcy Code § 105(a).

[63] See, e.g., United States v. Seitles, 106 Bankr. 36 (S.D.N.Y. 1989), vacated after settlement, 742 F. Supp. 1275 (S.D.N.Y. 1990).

[64] See §§ 17.04 and 17.06.

[65] In re A.H. Robins Co., Inc., 828 F.2d 1023, 1026 (4th Cir. 1986), cert. denied, Oberg v. Aetna Casualty & Surety Co., 485 U.S. 969 (1988).

§ 8.06 Duration of the Automatic Stay; Termination

[A]—Automatic Termination of the Stay

The automatic stay is intended to serve only the limited purpose of giving the debtor in possession or trustee the opportunity to deal effectively with the property of the estate and the demands of creditors. Thus, the stay automatically terminates when that purpose is no longer served. The automatic stay terminates upon the occurrence of any of several events. The stay of any act against property of the estate (but not the stay of an act against the debtor) terminates when the property is no longer part of the estate.[66] For example, when the trustee abandons property, the stay terminates and a claimant to the property may proceed against it.[67] The stay of all other actions (including actions against the debtor) terminates at the time the case is closed or dismissed, or at the time a discharge is granted or denied.[68] For example, if a case is dismissed under section 707(b) of the Code as an abuse of the bankruptcy system, the debtor and the debtor's property are no longer protected by the automatic stay.[69]

The fact that the stay terminates upon closure of the case or the grant of a discharge does not necessarily mean that the debtor is once again vulnerable to its creditors. As is discussed in Chapter 12, other provisions of the Code prevent creditors from taking action on discharged debt.[70] However, liens on property are not discharged in bankruptcy; thus, the lifting of the automatic stay can result in the seizure of encumbered property. To retain such property after the case is closed or the discharge granted, the debtor must have come to some accommodation with the creditor. This can be done through the bankruptcy proceeding itself—for example, through reaffirmation of the debt or the confirmation of a reorganization plan—or outside the bankruptcy, through formal or informal agreement with the creditor.

The stay may also be lifted or modified in whole or in part at an earlier stage of the proceeding. This is done to protect the interests of lienholders, co-owners, and other claimants. The governing rules are discussed in the next subsection.

[B]—Terminating or Modifying the Stay Upon Request of a Party

[1]—Introduction

As noted above, the automatic stay is designed to affect "remedies" but not "rights." More precisely, the stay postpones but does not permanently bar the establishment or enforcement of rights against the debtor, the debtor's property, or

---

[66] Bankruptcy Code § 362(c)(1).

[67] Note, however, that there may be other Code or non-Code bodies of law, such as exemption law, that effectively protect the property from actual seizure by a creditor. See Chapter 11 of this book.

[68] Bankruptcy Code § 362(c)(2).

[69] See § 16.03[B] of this book for a discussion of dismissal under Bankruptcy Code § 707(b).

[70] See § 12.10.

the estate's property. Section 362 does not in and of itself terminate any claim (unlike, for example, section 544, the "strong arm" clause, discussed in Chapter 13).[71] However, postponement of a right is a diminution of a right; and, under some circumstances, that diminution may indeed be total. For example, suppose that Chaste Bank has a security interest in $100,000 worth of equipment that is property of Jamal Construction, Inc., Debtor-in-Possession. The stay prevents Chaste from repossessing then reselling its collateral, an action it would have taken on July 1 if it could have. Suppose further that on July 15 insurance on the collateral lapses because the DIP has not paid the insurer, and that on July 17 the equipment is destroyed by a fire that occurred due to the DIP's negligence. In this case, delay has become destruction; Chaste had $100,000 of property and now has nothing, a loss that was, to some degree at least, caused by the stay.

There are many less dramatic examples. Even properly maintained equipment depreciates in value over time. If the DIP is not maintaining payments, the amount of the debt increases; this may result in unpaid debt, debt that would never had been incurred had the stay been lifted and the collateral liquidated. Shifts in market interest rates may mean that the lender is involuntarily locked into a transaction that is less profitable than a new one might be. In short, it is more than a little disingenuous to pretend that the stay of a "remedy" has no effect on a "right."

The drafters of the Code were not unaware of this problem. Moreover, they were largely in agreement with the traditional bankruptcy policy of treating "property" interests with greater deference than other interests. Consequently, section 362 provides a person who has a claim to property protected by the stay with an opportunity to seek relief from the stay.

Keep a few basics in mind while considering this material. First, stay litigation is almost always about property.[72] With very few exceptions, only a person who has a property right, such as a co-owner or a lienholder, has standing to seek relief from the stay. Unsecured creditors, who have no property rights, ordinarily do not have standing to ask for the stay to be lifted or modified. Second, stay litigation is not necessarily all or nothing; the court may and often does give limited or conditional relief.[73] Third, it is possible to have more than one action for relief from the stay; one decision is not necessarily res judicata with regard to another; it is only determinative of the situation at the time of the decision. If circumstances change, the court's ruling might also change. For example, the judge might reasonably decide early on in the case that the debtor is providing adequate protection, and thus not terminate the stay; at a later point, when the debtor's financial situation has deteriorated further, and there is no sign of a feasible reorganization plan in sight, the court might just as reasonably rule that adequate protection is no longer being provided and allow the claimant to seize the property.

Section 362(d) sets out the rules for relief from the stay. That provision states in part:

---

[71] See § 13.02.

[72] The primary area in which non-property issues are involved in stay litigation is the "more appropriate forum" cases, discussed in § 8.06[B][3] of this chapter.

[73] See § 8.06[B][6] of this chapter.

> On request of a party in interest and after notice and a hearing, the court shall grant relief from thc stay . . . such as by terminating, annulling, modifying, or conditioning such stay—
>
> (1) for cause, including the lack of adequate protection of an interest in property of such party in interest; or
>
> (2) with respect to a stay of an act against property . . . if—
>
> (A) the debtor does not have an equity in such property; and
>
> (B) such property is not necessary to an effective reorganization.[74]

The two primary substantive grounds—for cause and no equity/not necessary for reorganization—are taken up in order.[75]

[2]—For Cause—Lack of Adequate Protection

Most of the automatic stay litigation involves section 362(d)(1), which requires the court to grant relief from the stay "for cause, including the lack of adequate protection of an interest in property."[76] Although the phrase "for cause" encompasses a number of other matters,[77] nearly all of the disputes under section 362(d)(1) deal with adequate protection. The claimant insists that its interest is not adequately protected, and demands relief; the debtor responds that it has provided adequate protection and is therefore entitled to have the stay continued. The goal of the adequate protection rules is to give the claimant a high degree of certainty that it will eventually obtain at least the nominal value of its claim, while at the same time not crippling the debtor, especially in its efforts to reorganize.

Two questions predominate. What is adequate protection? What interests are entitled to adequate protection?

The concept of adequate protection is deeply rooted in the traditional respect given to property rights in bankruptcy. Although such respect is probably not constitutionally required, it undoubtedly derives from the same concern for property rights that underlies the 5th and 14th Amendments.[78]

The legislative history regarding adequate protection reflects its quasi-constitutional origin:

> The concept is derived from the 5th Amendment protection of property interest. It is not intended to be confined strictly to the Constitutional protection required, however. This section, and the concept of adequate protection, is based as much on policy grounds as on Constitutional

[74] Bankruptcy Code § 362(d).

[75] Note that the 1994 Amendments added a further basis for relief with regard to so-called single asset real estate cases. This is discussed in § 8.06[B][5] of this chapter and § 22.04 of Chapter 22.

[76] Bankruptcy Code § 362(d)(1).

[77] See § 8.06[B][3] of this chapter.

[78] For this reason, adequate protection is irrelevant where unsecured creditors are concerned. See In re Tellier, 125 Bankr. 348 (Bankr. D.R. I. 1991).

> grounds. Secured creditors should not be deprived of the benefit of their bargain. There may be situations in bankruptcy where giving a secured creditor an absolute right to his bargain may be impossible, or seriously detrimental to the bankruptcy laws. Thus, this section recognizes the availability of alternate means of protecting a secured creditor's interest. Though the creditor might not receive his bargain in kind, the purpose of the section is to insure that the secured creditor receives in value essentially what he bargained for.[79]

The earliest formulations of the doctrine long predate the Code.[80] Indeed, section 361, which sets out the standards for adequate protection, is essentially a mere codification of prior law. Some of its key language is taken directly from older cases.

The section describes two specific methods of giving adequate protection, and sets a standard by which other methods are to be measured. First, adequate protection may be given by making a payment or payments to the claimant.[81] This is probably the most common form of adequate protection, at least where there is no "equity cushion"—that is, no excess of collateral over the amount of the debt. The adequate protection payments are supposed to offset any decrease in the value of the claimant's interest in the property. For example, suppose that River Bank's collateral is depreciating at the rate of $300 per month. To protect River Bank's interest—and thus to avoid modification of the automatic stay—the debtor may agree to pay River Bank $300 per month during the period after the filing of the petition and before confirmation of the plan.[82]

Section 361(2) gives an alternative. It states that the debtor may provide adequate protection by providing the claimant with an additional or replacement lien.[83] For example, if River Bank's collateral is depreciating at the rate of $300 per month, the debtor, rather than making a $300 per month payment might instead give River Bank additional collateral. Similarly, if River Bank's collateral is inventory that is being sold by the debtor, the debtor might protect River Bank's interest by giving it a security interest in new inventory that it acquires.[84] This alternative is valuable to debtors that have tight cash flow but significant unencumbered assets. Since such debtors are rare, this is probably the least common means of providing adequate protection.

Often, additional actions will be necessary to give adequate protection; in addition, the debtor will attempt to provide adequate protection in ways other than

---

[79] H.R. Rep. No. 95-595, 95th Cong. 1st Sess. 339 (1977).

[80] See In re Murel Holding Corp., 75 F.2d 941 (2d Cir. 1935).

[81] Bankruptcy Code § 361(1).

[82] Note that a somewhat different approach to adequate protection applies during the plan period. For a discussion of this, see § 17.11 of this book.

[83] Bankruptcy Code § 361(2).

[84] Note that the debtor will only need to do this to the extent that River Bank is not adequately protected by the fact that the proceeds of its collateral (e.g., cash or accounts received by the debtor in exchange for the inventory) will normally remain subject to its security interest. For a discussion of the continuation of a security interest in proceeds, see § 10.03 of this book.

payments or additional liens. An example of the first is insurance; it is routine for the court to require that the property be covered by adequate casualty insurance. Thus, if the property is destroyed, the insurance proceeds will provide an adequate substitute.

Insofar as alternative forms of adequate protection are concerned, section 361(3), borrowing a phrase from Judge Benjamin Cardozo, states that the debtor must provide the claimant something that will "result in the realization" by the claimant "of the indubitable equivalent" of the claimant's interest in the property.[85] The phrase "indubitable equivalent" comes from Cardozo's opinion in *In re Murel Holding Corp.*,[86] a case that long predated the Code but greatly influenced its drafting. That case provided more than a catchphrase; it provided an attitude toward adequate protection; an attitude of skepticism toward anything but cash or other tangible property as an equivalent for a property interest. *In re Murel Holding* involved a plan that in effect substituted only a doubtfully secured and speculative promise of future payment for an immediate realization on a property interest. Cardozo found this inadequate and even suggested that permitting such a substitution might be unconstitutional. In his own words:

> [W]e are to remember not only the underlying purposes of the section, but the constitutional limitations to which it must conform. It is plain that "adequate protection" must be completely compensatory; and that payment ten years hence is not generally the equivalent of payment now. Interest is indeed the common measure of the difference, but a creditor who fears the safety of his principal will scarcely be content with that; he wishes to get his money or at least the property. We see no reason to suppose that the statute was intended to deprive him of that in the interest of junior holders, unless by a substitute of the most indubitable equivalence.[87]

We are given very little guidance in the statute for what constitutes an indubitable equivalent; the one thing we are told is that it is not sufficient to give the creditor an administrative priority claim.[88] The protection must be something more tangible and certain than that. The legislative history provides some suggestions, but emphasizes flexibility:

> The [indubitable equivalent] method gives the parties and the courts flexibility by allowing such other relief as will result in the realization by the protected entity of the value of its interest in the property involved . . . For example, another form of adequate protection might be the guarantee by a third party outside the judicial process of compensation for any loss incurred in the case . . .

---

[85] Bankruptcy Code § 361(3).

[86] 75 F.2d 941 (2d Cir. 1935).

[87] 75 F.2d at 942.

[88] Bankruptcy Code § 361(3).

> The paragraph also defines, more clearly than the others, the general concept of adequate protection, by requiring such relief as will result in the realization of value. It is the general category, and as such, is defined by the concept involved rather than any particular method of adequate protection.[89]

A very common form of adequate protection may well fall under this catchall category, although it is sometimes thought of as a non-statutory exception to section 361. This is the "equity cushion." Suppose that the debtor has a substantial equity in the property, far in excess of the present or likely value of the claim. The mere existence of this "equity cushion" may be sufficient to provide adequate protection (especially if there is sufficient insurance to protect against casualty loss.) For example, if the property is reasonably valued at $100,000, and River Bank's lien secures only a $20,000 debt, a court is very likely to say that, because of the $80,000 equity cushion, no additional protection is required. It is extremely unlikely that, even with interest added or[90] and the property depreciating at a normal rate, the debt will ever exceed the value of the collateral. Courts have routinely so ruled in cases with far smaller equity cushions than that given in the hypothetical—according to one court, courts will generally find adequate protection when the equity cushion is 20% or more of the debt secured; routinely require additional protection if the equity cushion is under 11%, and are divided if the equity cushion is in between those two figures.[91]

When adequate protection is based on an equity cushion, the creditor may again seek relief later in the case. As time passes the cushion shrinks; as the amount of the debt increases and the value of the collateral decreases, the degree of protection provided is reduced. At some point in time, therefore, the court might hold that additional protection must be provided.[92]

What happens when adequate protection proves to be inadequate? On occasion, alas, the courts err. When they do, there is no realistic way of providing the claimant with the true full equivalent of its claim. There will almost certainly be little or nothing in the estate. The Code does the best it can; it provides the claimant with a "super-priority" unsecured claim, prior to all other unsecured claims, including administrative claims.[93] For example, suppose the River Bank has a $500,000 secured claim, and the court decides that the claim is adequately protected. As things turn out, when the collateral is finally liquidated, it yields only $475,000. River Bank is entitled to a super-priority unsecured claim for the $25,000 deficiency. Of course, the value of that claim is far more speculative than the value of a secured claim, because there may not be any money left in the estate after the secured claims are paid and thus no money even for a super-priority unsecured claim.

---

[89] H. Rep. No. 95-595 (1977).

[90] Remember that since this is an oversecured claim, the creditor is entitled to pendency interest. See § 10.03[C][3] of this book.

[91] In re Kost, 102 Bankr. 829, 831-32 (D. Wyo. 1989).

[92] This is an issue of particular significance in a protracted reorganization case.

[93] Bankruptcy Code § 507(b).

Just as fundamental to adequate protection analysis as the form the protection must take is the entitlement to that protection. Not every claim must be protected. Unsecured claims are entitled to nothing, because they do not represent an interest in specific property.[94] Even secured claims may be entitled to only limited protection. This is of particular significance in reorganization proceedings.

As is discussed in Chapter 10,[95] during the period between the filing of the petition and the payment of claims or confirmation of the plan, interest is added to some, but not all, secured claims. If the amount of the claim is less than the value of the property securing it, interest will accrue on the claim—but only to the extent of the surplus value.[96] For example, if River Bank's claim is for $45,000 and the collateral is worth $50,000, up to $5,000 in interest may be added to it during the petition-to-confirmation period. By contrast, if Chaste Bank's claim is $45,000, and the property is worth only $40,000, Chaste Bank has a $40,000 secured claim, a $5,000 unsecured claim, and, prior to confirmation, is entitled to interest on neither.[97] Similarly, if Chaste Bank's collateral is worth $45,000, it has a $45,000 secured claim but no right to any interest.[98]

These rules carry over to adequate protection. Only the nominal value of the secured claim is entitled to adequate protection. The oversecured creditor is entitled to protection of the principal plus allowed interest—in the example given, River Bank is entitled to adequate protection of up to $50,000, depending on how much interest actually accrues. The undersecured creditor or the exactly secured creditor is not so lucky. If Chaste Bank's secured claim is not entitled to interest, it is not entitled to obtain adequate protection for more than the original dollar value of its claim—in the example given, $40,000 or $45,000.

This is true even though the real value of Chaste Bank's claim is diminishing. Since Chaste is prevented by the stay from obtaining and disposing of its collateral, Chaste is suffering lost opportunity costs. Suppose that if Chaste could repossess and sell its collateral, it could invest the proceeds of the sale at 10% per annum interest. If its collateral and thus the claim is worth $40,000, and the period between petition and confirmation lasts for one year, Chaste is effectively losing $4,000 because of the stay. Many commentators argued that this loss should be paid for—that Chaste should be given that $4,000 as the price of maintaining the stay.[99] Whatever the merits of this argument, it has been wholly unsuccessful. The Supreme Court, relying on what it saw as the plain meaning of the Code, unequivocally rejected it.[100] The undersecured creditor is entitled to nothing for its lost

[94] In re Tellier, 125 Bankr. 348, 349 (Bankr. R.I. 1991).

[95] See § 10.03[C][3].

[96] Bankruptcy Code § 506(b).

[97] Bankruptcy Code § 502(b)(2).

[98] Bankruptcy Code § 506(b).

[99] See Douglas G. Baird & Thomas H. Jackson, *Corporate Reorganizations and the Treatment of Diverse Ownership Interests: A Comment on Adequate Protection of Secured Creditors in Bankruptcy*, 51 U. Chi. L. Rev. 97 (1984).

[100] United Savings Association of Texas v. Timers of Inwood Forest Associates, Ltd., 484 U.S. 365 (1988).

opportunity.[101] It is thus not true that adequate protection results in full recompense for lost property rights; rather, it provides only partial protection for those whose collateral is worth the amount of the debt or less than the amount of the debt.[102] The usual policy justification for this is that bankruptcy is a common disaster, causing losses that ought to be shared out in some reasonable way among those affected; given the relatively good treatment afforded secured claimants, occasional opportunity costs represent little enough contribution from them for the greater good.

Another point about litigation over adequate protection is often overlooked in law school discussions of the matter. Most of the time, adequate protection issues are not resolved through litigation but through negotiation. Most often, the only reason the claimant files a request for relief is to force the debtor to deal reasonably. Because of the powerful position secured creditors have in most bankruptcies, the debtor is usually willing to come up with a reasonable method of providing protection, thereby avoiding both the cost and the risk of stay litigation. Given the relatively clear rules regarding what is normally required to pass muster before the court, the negotiated protection usually is identical to the protection a judge would order. The debtor commits to the maintenance of insurance and periodic payments equal to the depreciation of the property (plus, in some cases, the interest accruing). This does not mean that secured creditors are satisfied with what they can obtain—most of the time they are not—but rather that the courts have evolved fairly good guidelines as to what the debtor must give and the creditor can get.

[3]—For Cause—Better Forum/Matters Tangential to the Bankruptcy

A less litigated situation in which relief from the stay is sought and granted involves disputes over peripheral issues. A number of courts have been willing to lift the stay when there is a more appropriate forum to hear the matter, especially if the matter is only minimally or tangentially connected with the bankruptcy case. The most common situation relates to ongoing domestic relations matters in state courts. Generally speaking, bankruptcy judges will lift the stay with regard to these matters.[103] However, actions to collect or enforce claims are generally left subject to the stay.[104] The reason for this is that the substantive determinations are a central function of state family courts, not of bankruptcy courts. However, once the determination has been made, the enforcement of a judgment, particularly if it involves property of the estate, directly involves the bankruptcy court's central function of distributing available property to creditors under the Bankruptcy Code's

---

[101] 484 U.S. at 382. Although not explicit, the case clearly indicates that the "exactly secured" creditor—whose collateral equals but does not exceed the amount of the debt—is likewise not entitled to pendency interest.

[102] Even the oversecured creditor may lose out, if it is not sufficiently oversecured; for example, if the collateral is worth only $1,000 more than the debt, the creditor is entitled to obtain, and thus entitled to have protection with regard to, only $1,000 in interest.

[103] See, for example, In re El-Amin, 126 Bankr. 855 (Bankr. E.D. Va. 1991); In re Murray, 31 Bankr. 499 (Bankr. E.D. Pa. 1983). Note that the stay only applies to some aspects of domestic relations litigation. See § 8.03[B][1] of this chapter.

[104] See, for example, In re El-Amin, 126 Bankr. 855 (Bankr. E.D. Va. 1991).

distributional structure. "Once [a spouse's] interests are determined in the divorce court she can pursue her monetary claims as a creditor in this debtor's estate . . ."[105]

Other examples are given in the legislative history:

> A probate proceeding in which the debtor is the executor or administrator of another's estate usually will not be related to the bankruptcy case, and should not be stayed. Generally, proceedings in which the debtor is a fiduciary, or involving post-petition activities of the debtor, need not be stayed because they bear no relationship to the purpose of the automatic stay, which is debtor protection from his creditors. The facts of each request will determine whether relief is appropriate under the circumstances.[106]

[4]—No Equity/Not Necessary for Reorganization

If the debtor has no stake in and no use for property, there is no good reason to prevent other claimants from exercising their rights to it. For this reason, the court will lift the stay of actions against property if the debtor has no equity in the property and it is not necessary for an effective reorganization.[107] Note that both of these requirements must be met. Note further that this provision is of primary significance in Chapter 11, 12, and 13; since Chapter 7 bankruptcy does not involve reorganization, the second part of the rule ("not necessary to an effective reorganization") is irrelevant in those proceedings.

If the debtor has an equity in the property, then there may still be a good reason to permit the automatic stay to continue, even though the property may be liquidated. The DIP or trustee may be in the best position to obtain a good price for it. By contrast, if there is no equity in the property, then only the claimant has any stake in the property.

In addition, the debtor must have no important use for the property. Even property in which the debtor has no equity can be vital to the operation of the debtor; if it does, it may be appropriate to leave the stay in place. For example, WorldWide RoadRunner Transport, Ltd., Debtor-in-Possession, obviously needs its tractor-trailers to continue in business and thus to have any chance of reorganization. Even if the tractor-trailers are subject to liens securing debt far in excess of their value, the stay will not be lifted under section 362(d)(2)(although it may be lifted on other grounds).

In effect, this rule protects two values the goods have to the debtor. It protects the value of the property as property; that is, as a financial asset. It also protects the use value of the property; that is, as a necessary component of the debtor's going concern value. Only if the property has neither asset value nor use value to the estate will the stay be lifted under this provision.

---

[105] In re Fisher, 67 Bankr. 666, 670 (Bankr. D. Colo. 1986).

[106] H.R. Rep. No. 595, 95th Cong., 1st Sess. 343-44 (1977), see also, S. Rep. No. 989, 95th Cong., 2nd Sess. 52 (1978).

[107] Bankruptcy Code § 362(d)(2).

In general, courts have been fairly pro-debtor in their interpretation of this provision, especially with regard to the "necessary for reorganization" requirement. While it is clear that retention of the property must be more than merely convenient to the estate, there is no requirement that the property be absolutely indispensable.[108] The determination is always fact specific; what is necessary in one reorganization might not be necessary in another.

Implicit in the "necessary for effective reorganization" requirement is that there be some realistic possibility of a reorganization. In the words of the Supreme Court:

> Once the movement under Section 362(d)(2) establishes that he is an undersecured creditor, it is the burden of the *debtor* to establish that collateral at issue is "necessary to an effective reorganization." What this requires is not merely a showing that if there is conceivably to be an effective reorganization, this property will be needed for it; but that the property is essential for an effective reorganization *that is in prospect.* This means, as many lower courts, including the en banc court in this case, have properly said, that there must be a "reasonable possibility of a successful reorganization within a reasonable time."[109]

The usual textual justification for this reading of the rule is rooted in the fact that the statute refers to an "effective" reorganization.[110]

Note that, in effect, this is a feasibility test. One of the points at which creditors may make an attack on the entire reorganization is at the point they are attempting to lift the stay. If the debtor has no equity in the property, and there is no reasonable prospect for reorganization, then the stay will be lifted. Lifting the stay will, in many cases, precipitate liquidation. The same issue arises when the debtor proposes the plan; one of the requirements for confirmation is that the plan be feasible.[111] However, at the automatic stay stage, the feasibility test should be applied somewhat more lightly. This is particularly true if the stay litigation occurs early in the proceeding. For example, assume that a creditor seeks to lift the stay under section 362(d)(2) only thirty days after the petition is filed; assume further that the court holds the final hearing just thirty days later. At this point, we are only sixty days past the petition, and only half-way through the 120-day "exclusivity" period during which the debtor has the sole right to file a plan of reorganization. In many cases, the debtor will simply not have had enough time to prepare and present a confirmable plan. The fact that it has not yet done so should not translate into an automatic lifting of the stay on the basis of infeasibility. While the debtor certainly must be able to present the court with more than "unsubstantiated hopes for a successful reorganization,"[112] it should not ordinarily be necessary to have an actual, finished plan in hand.

---

[108] In re Fields, 127 Bankr. 150 (Bankr. W.D.Tex. 1991).

[109] United Savings Association of Texas v. Timbers of Innwood Forest Associates, Ltd., 484 U.S. 365, 375-76 (1988).

[110] See In re 8th Street Village Limited Partnership, 94 Bankr. 993, 996 (N.D. Ill. 1988).

[111] See § 17.15[C] of this book.

[112] In re Canal Place Limited Partnership, 921 F.2d 569, 577 (5th. Cir. 1991).

There are, of course, some cases in which the debtor's situation is so obviously hopeless that lifting of the stay (or, for that matter, conversion or dismissal) is appropriate even at the very beginning of the proceeding. The debtor with a severely negative cash flow, no reasonable prospects for additional income or refinancing, and deteriorating property should be forced into liquidation, or at least out of reorganization, at the earliest possible opportunity. Stay litigation provides the courts with a vehicle for doing this.

Moreover, as time goes by and the proceeding drags on, the court's attitude towards feasibility should (and in many courts does) change. If a debtor cannot show a strong prospect for reorganization six months or a year after the petition is filed, the court should move the case towards its almost inevitable climax. If, after that length of time, the debtor cannot show a strong probability that it will quickly be able to get and have confirmed a feasible plan, the court should find that the property is not necessary for an effective reorganization and lift the stay.

[5]—Single Asset Case

The 1994 Amendments include provisions to deal with so-called single asset real estate bankruptcies. Under one of these provisions, the stay may be lifted 90 days after the petition if the debtor fails to file a plan that has a reasonable possibility of confirmation and is not making monthly payments.[113] This, and other issues relating to single asset bankruptcy, is further discussed in Chapter 22.[114]

[6]—Form of Relief

Although most lawyers think of stay litigation as an effort to lift the stay completely, and most cases deal with that issue, the court actually has considerable flexibility in crafting more limited remedies. The court may terminate, annul, modify or place conditions the continuation of the stay.[115] At one extreme, the court may annul the stay *ab initio* and thereby validate prior actions that violated it. More commonly, a court may well decide that lifting the stay entirely is too draconian a sanction, especially if the debtor's failure to provide adequate protection is easily cured. For example, a creditor has good grounds to ask for relief when the debtor fails to pay casualty insurance. Rather than lift the stay immediately, however, the court may simply require the debtor to obtain and maintain adequate insurance in the future. An order of this type can be self-executing; in other words, the court may order that the stay automatically and immediately terminates if there is another lapse in the insurance coverage. This type of order avoids the need for further stay litigation. The court may also lift the stay for some purposes but not for others; for example, the stay may be lifted to permit a state court to determine liability and assess damages, but kept in place with regard to collection efforts.[116]

It is also worth noting that relief may be given to one claimant but not to another. For example, if two creditors have liens on the same property, and only one requests

[113] Bankruptcy Code § 362(d)(3)(1994 Amendments).

[114] See § 22.04.

[115] Bankruptcy Code § 362(d).

[116] See In re Revco D.S., Inc., 99 Bankr. 768, 777 (N.D. Ohio 1989).

insurance as a condition of maintaining the stay, the court could order the debtor to maintain only enough insurance to protect the interest of the requesting creditor. This issue rarely arises because in most cases there is only one creditor with a lien, or a least a significant lien, on any given piece of property.

[7]—Procedures

Congress hoped to provide not only direct substantive protection to claimants' rights but also procedural protection. Accordingly, it set out rules designed to expedite stay litigation. In the view of many, this effort has not been successful, and further tightening of the rules is a consistent demand of creditor groups. In the 1994 Amendments, a further attempt was made to satisfy this demand.

Under section 362(e), the court must take action on a request for relief from the stay within 30 days after the request is made. If it does not do so, the stay is automatically terminated.[117] Alas, what the Code gives, the Code takes away. The court does not have to take any final action within that 30-day period. Upon notice and with opportunity for a hearing, the court may—and often does—continue the stay pending a final determination of the claimant's request.[118]

Prior to the 1994 Amendments, the court was only required to commence the final hearing within 30 days of the conclusion of any preliminary hearing.[119] This requirement often proved illusory. There was no time limit on the conclusion of the final hearing or the court's entry of judgment after the final hearing. Further, there was no practical way of forcing the judge to make timely rulings on adequate protection. This meant that a judge who did not want to be rushed could not be rushed.

The 1994 Amendments attempt to change this, although whether they will do so is still dependent upon the willingness of bankruptcy judges to comply. Under the amended version of section 362(e), the final hearing must be *concluded* within 30 days after the conclusion of the preliminary hearing.[120] However, Congress could not quite bring itself to make this absolutely mandatory. The 30-day period may be extended with the consent of the parties in interest or for a specific time that the court finds is required by *compelling circumstances.*[121] A bankruptcy judge who is bound and determined not to permit a lifting of the stay can still stall off the final hearing; all that is required is that the catch-phrase "compelling circumstances" be used. It is to be hoped, however, that bankruptcy courts will finally accept the congressional judgment that automatic stay litigation should be prompt and thus will be much less likely to permit extensions than they have been in the past.

In any event, that is a hope shared by nearly all secured creditors. They have long expressed concern about the reluctance of bankruptcy judges to lift the automatic

---

[117] Bankruptcy Code § 362(e).

[118] Bankruptcy Code § 362(e).

[119] Bankruptcy Code § 362(e)(amended 1994).

[120] Bankruptcy Code § 362(e)(1994 Amendments).

[121] Bankruptcy Code § 362(e)(1994 Amendments).

stay. They view many bankruptcy judges as being, on this issue at least, rather pro-debtor. They are especially concerned that some bankruptcy judges seem to view a Chapter 11 case as a success only if a plan is confirmed, and as a failure if the debtor lands in liquidation. This perception that reorganization is always desirable and liquidation always undesirable may lead judges to accept a far too optimistic assessment of the adequacy of protection given to claimants. That in turn may simply delay, and make worse, the inevitable liquidation of the debtor. Whether this creditor perception is entirely true is debatable; certainly, few bankruptcy judges perceive themselves as being biased toward debtors. Whatever the truth of the matter, there is widespread dissatisfaction with the application of adequate protection law.

The Code also provides rarely used procedures for emergency ex parte relief from the stay. This is available only if two conditions are met. First, the action must be necessary to prevent irreparable damage to the claimant's property interest. Second, the damage must be immanent—if there is time for notice and hearing, the court may not act without them.[122]

Finally, the Code codifies the basic rules regarding the burden of proof. The party requesting the relief carries the burden of proof as to the debtor's equity in the property.[123] Thus, if River Bank is requesting relief because the debtor has no equity and the property is not necessary for reorganization, River Bank must prove debtor's lack of equity. As to all other issues, the trustee/DIP carries the burden of proof.[124] In the example given, if River Bank proves that the debtor has no equity in the property, the debtor must prove that the property is necessary for reorganization; if it fails to do so, the stay will be lifted.

Although not explicitly stated in the Code, it is reasonably clear that "burden of proof" means the burden of persuasion. The party that carries the burden of proof must not only put on evidence supporting its position, it must convince the judge that its position is correct. The standard for carrying the burden of proof is the ordinary one in civil litigation—preponderance of the evidence.

[8]—Adequate Protection of Leasehold Interest

The interest of a lessor under a "true" lease of real or personal property is also entitled to adequate protection. The automatic stay/adequate protection issue is, however, somewhat complicated by the rules that permit a trustee/DIP to assume or reject the lease.[125] Particularly in a reorganization proceeding, the trustee or debtor in possession is likely to seek to assume any valuable lease. However, a final decision on assumption or rejection may take weeks or even months. Often, the lease will be in default during this period; either the rent payments stopped before bankruptcy or were stopped post-petition. The lessor generally wants to get the property back. The courts disagree as to whether the stay can be lifted for a lack of adequate protection prior to the time that the trustee/DIP makes its

[122] Bankruptcy Code § 362(f), Bankruptcy Rule 4001(a)(2).

[123] Bankruptcy Code § 362(g)(1).

[124] Bankruptcy Code § 362(g)(2).

[125] For a discussion of the right to assume or reject leases, see § 9.04 of this book.

assumption/rejection decision.[126] In essence, this debate is over whether a leasehold interest is entitled to adequate protection only under § 365, governing the assumption of leases.[127] or whether it is also entitled to adequate protection under the rules in § 362.

§ 8.07 Enforcement of the Stay

[A]—Actions Void

The great majority of courts have held that actions in violation of the automatic stay are entirely void, even if the person taking the action had no notice of the stay.[128] Even actions taken by the government, such as a foreclosure sale[129] are entirely without legal effect. The fact that the action taken may have been entirely innocent and in good faith is a defense against sanctions, but does not protect the action itself.

[B]—Contempt

Prior to BAFJA in 1984, there was no explicit set of sanctions for violation of the stay. Most courts held that the appropriate enforcement mechanism was civil contempt. The automatic stay operates a court order; as is true with any court order, the stay may be enforced by contempt proceedings. Since BAFJA, which added specific sanctions, the courts have been divided over whether a contempt action is still available; some hold that it is while others have held that the BAFJA rules are exclusive and preempt a contempt action.[130]

A predicate to any contempt proceeding, however, is knowledge of the court's order. If a creditor takes action in ignorance of the automatic stay, it is not guilty of contempt. For example, if Friendly Finance repossesses Dora Debtor's car after she has filed bankruptcy but before it has been notified of the bankruptcy, Friendly is in violation of the stay (and the action is therefore void[131] but is not in contempt,

---

[126] In re Reice, 88 Bankr. 676 (Bankr. E.D. Pa. 1988)(plain meaning of § 362(d)(1) permits free assumption motion for lifting the stay) and In re Sweetwater, 40 Bankr. 733 (Bankr. D. Utah 1984) (structure of Bankruptcy Code indicates that adequate protection under § 362 was designed for liens and security interests and that § 365, dealing with the assumption of leases, is the properly applicable rule).

[127] See § 9.04 of this book.

[128] See, e.g., In re Smith, 876 F.2d 524 (6th Cir. 1989).

[129] Anglemyer v. United States, 115 Bankr. 510 (D. Md. 1990).

[130] Although the Code contains sanctions for some violations of the stay in Bankruptcy Code § 362(h), it is assumed by a majority of courts that these do not affect the courts' power to impose other sanctions, which are apparently viewed as aspects of the courts' contempt power. See, for example, In re Skinner, 917 F.2d 444 (10th Cir. 1990). There is a substantial minority of cases that disagrees. See, for example, University Medical Center v. Sullivan, 122 Bankr. 919, 932 (E.D. Pa. 1990) (Bankruptcy Code § 362(h) supplants the courts' contempt power).

[131] As noted above, the generally accepted rule is that any action in violation of the stay is void. See In re Schwartz, 954 F.2d 569 (9th Cir. 1992).

or at least is not subject to sanctions.[132] As soon as Friendly is notified of the stay, however, it must promptly return the car; failure to do so is contemptuous and may result in sanctions against it.[133]

In most cases, creditors learn of the filing and thus of the stay by the court; assuming that a creditor has been properly scheduled by the debtor, the creditor should receive prompt notification of the filing from the clerk's office. However, this is not the only way in which the creditor can learn of the bankruptcy and (more importantly) of the stay. Oral notification by the debtor or the debtor's lawyer may be sufficient; a creditor who ignores such notice and proceeds with its action may be in contempt.

Even after the creditor learns of the filing, the court might not impose sanctions if the violation is inadvertent.[134] For example, if the violation occurs because of a clerical error, or the failure to clear a computer file, the creditor might escape contempt sanctions. Even in that case, however, the creditor may be required to compensate the debtor for damages.[135]

[C]—Statutory Sanctions

The Bankruptcy Code itself only partially codifies the sanctions that may be imposed upon a creditor that violates the stay. Section 362(h), which on its face deals only with injury to individuals caused by willful violations, specifically empowers the court to grant relief. The relief shall include the individual actual damages, costs, and attorney's fees.[136] In "appropriate circumstances" it may include punitive damages.[137] Since the violations must be willful, it is generally assumed that, as with contempt sanctions, section 362(h) sanctions are inappropriate for an inadvertent violation, or one taken without notice of the stay.

For example, suppose that River Bank repossessed Doug Debtor's car, and, despite the fact that it received formal notice of the bankruptcy from the court, refused to return the car to Doug. Doug was forced to rent another car to get to work and to do his shopping. The cost of the rental car was $175 per week for a total of 6 weeks. Doug also had to pay his lawyer $300 to make a (successful) motion in the bankruptcy court to force return of the car and to establish damages for the violation of the stay. Doug is entitled to recover not only the car but also the rental cost (6 x $175, a total of $1,050) plus his attorney's fees ($300); his monetary recovery will be $1,350.[138] Note that, in this case, the debtor obtains the recovery rather than the trustee, since the costs were born by Doug and not by the estate.

---

[132] See, for example, Commercial Credit Corp. v. Reed, 154 Bankr. 471 (E.D. Tex. 1993).

[133] 154 Bankr. at 476.

[134] In re Conti, 42 Bankr. 122 (Bankr. E.D. Va. 1984).

[135] 42 Bankr. at 128.

[136] Bankruptcy Code § 362(h).

[137] Bankruptcy Code § 362(h).

[138] This is in addition to the fact that the creditor might face other sanctions for its violation of the automatic stay.

Under some circumstances, Doug will also be able to recover punitive damages from River Bank. Generally speaking, courts are reluctant to grant punitive damages, because compensatory damages are usually sufficient both to recompense the debtor (or the estate) and to deter the creditor.[139] However, if the creditor's action is sufficiently egregious—or, more precisely, if the judge views the creditor's action as sufficiently outrageous—punitive damages may be awarded. For example, under at least one case, if Doug's employer, after learning of the stay, continued to dock his paycheck to obtain payment on a pre-petition debt, punitive damages would be appropriate.[140]

These Code created sanctions may not be exclusive. As noted above, many courts believe that contempt sanctions are still permissible. Moreover, the courts have consistently asserted the power to impose equivalent sanctions for violation of the stay, even when the debtor is a business entity rather than an individual,[141] or where the estate rather than the debtor is injured. There is a considerable dispute about the source of this power; although some courts have simply applied section 362(h).[142] others have refused to because of the plain language of the statute.[143] However, even if there is no power to sanction misconduct involving a corporate debtor under section 362, there surely is under section 105, the Bankruptcy Code's blanket grant of authority to issue appropriate orders.[144]

[D]—Sovereign Immunity

Traditionally, there was one large hole in the Code's enforcement scheme for the automatic stay: sovereign immunity. Although governmental action in violation of the stay was treated as void, the government was not liable to pay damages.[145] Participation in the bankruptcy proceedings, however, was generally deemed to be a waiver of sovereign immunity, and governmental units that did such things as filing a proof of claim often subjected themselves to liability. This whole area has been clarified by the 1994 Amendments, under which the consent exception to sovereign immunity is spelled out in detail. Broadly speaking, a governmental unit that files a proof of claim has waived sovereign immunity with regard to most matters that arose out of the same transaction or occurance reflected in the proof of claim.[146]

---

139 Some courts have said that punitive damages are appropriate only if the creditor's conduct was not only wilful but also malicious or in bad faith. See In re Crysen/Montenay Energy Co., 902 F.2d 1098, 1105 (2d Cir. 1990); In re Hooker Investments, Co., 116 Bankr. 375 (Bankr. S.D.N.Y. 1990).

140 See In re Everett, 127 Bankr. 781, 784 (Bankr. E.D.N.C. 1991).

141 See In re Atlantic Business and Community Corporation, 901 F.2d 325, 329 (3d Cir. 1990); Budget Service Co. v. Better Homes of Virginia, Inc., 804 F.2d 289, 299 (4th Cir. 1986).

142 See In re Atlantic Business and Community Corporation, 901 F.2d 325 (3d Cir. 1990); Budget Service Co. v. Better Homes of Virginia, Inc., 804 F.2d 289 (4th Cir. 1986).

143 See In re Prairie Trunk Railway, 1112 Bankr. 924 (Bankr. N.D. Ill. 1991).

144 Bankruptcy Code § 105.

145 See United States v. Nordic Village, Inc., 112 S. Ct. 1011 (1992), and Hoffman v. Connecticut Department of Income Maintenance, 492 U.S. 96 (1989).

146 Bankruptcy Code § 106(1994 Amendments).

CHAPTER 9

Operating the Debtor

§ 9.01 Introduction

The reorganizing debtor, and even to a lesser extent some liquidating debtors, is not a static entity. Its financial affairs do not cease with the filing of the petition. This is particularly true if the debtor is or has a business. A business must obtain supplies, sell property or services, meet payrolls, use equipment, obtain credit. Each of these activities must be conducted by the trustee or debtor in possession. Each of them may be opposed by creditors, especially lien creditors, who believe that surrender of property and/or prompt liquidation would better serve their interests. By the same token, the debtor's continuing operation may be supported by other creditors, most likely general unsecured creditors, whose only hope for recovery of any part of their claims rests in the success of the debtor's ongoing business. Needless to say, the owners and managers of the debtor usually push for continued reorganization efforts, because only the debtor's success can possibly save their jobs.

The Bankruptcy Code balances the interests of those who support continued operation of the debtor and those who oppose it. The fulcrum of this balance is "adequate protection," a concept already explored in conjunction with the automatic stay.[1] The issues are slightly different, but the focus is the same: to what extent is it proper to subject unwilling creditors to the additional risks involved in continued operation of the debtor? Whether the existing rules strike the proper balance is a matter of no little debate.[2]

Preliminarily, note that the rules regarding operation of the debtor broadly apply to all Chapters. Even a Chapter 7 trustee may continue to operate the debtor for a time, if that is the most reasonable means of conducting its liquidation.[3] However, most of the time these rules become important only in the reorganization Chapters, and most particularly in Chapter 11. Only in Chapter 11 is the operation of the debtor likely to be prolonged, and thus to create any serious problem with regard to protecting the interest of claimants.

§ 9.02 Supervisory Authority of the Court

At the core of the Code's rules about operating the debtor is the fact that the Chapter 11 debtor's operations is that the debtor is not the entity that filed. When ABC, Inc., becomes ABC, Inc., Debtor-in-Possession, a new legal entity with new

---

[1] See § 8.06[B][2] of this book.

[2] This is essentially the same issue as the desirability of Chapter 11 proceedings, a matter discussed in § 17.01 of this book.

[3] Bankruptcy Code § 721.

responsibilities is created. The buildings may be the same; the same unreliable widgets may be shipped by the same disgruntled work force; the same angry bankers are still trying to extract their collateral—but the entity itself is new.

This fact has many implications, major and minor. Too often overlooked by management is the fact that they are no longer running the company they used to run. They are running a new and legally distinct company; moreover, they are running it under court supervision and with fiduciary duties to creditors.

It is extremely important for the debtor's attorneys to make these facts clear to managers who are not used to, and are generally resentful of, outside oversight. Failure to accept the limitations on their power, however, can create a dangerous and even fatal situation for the debtor (not to mention civil and even criminal liability for themselves). To take only one example: in one very large, well-publicized bankruptcy, the managers of the debtor in possession thought nothing of paying themselves huge bonuses without court permission. Those bonuses had to be returned, and moreover very nearly led to the appointment of a trustee.[4] Had the court decided that the managers acted fraudulently, rather than just stupidly, far more severe sanctions would undoubtedly have been applied.

§ 9.03 Use, Sale or Lease of Property

[A]—Introduction

As noted in Chapter 8, section 362 of the code stays actions against the debtor and property of both the debtor and the estate. Section 363 goes further; it authorizes the trustee or DIP to use, sell or lease property of the estate, subject to certain controls. This provision is central to liquidation and even more so to reorganization bankruptcy. This section details both the general rules and the primary exceptions to and limitations on them.

[B]—Cash Collateral

Great concern was expressed during the drafting of the Code about the adequacy of protection given to what was referred to as "soft" collateral.[5] Roughly speaking, "soft" collateral was collateral that was either cash or near-cash; collateral that could easily be misappropriated or dissipated by a dishonest or incompetent debtor.[6] After a number of proposals for dealing with this problem were rejected, Congress adopted the scheme embodied in subsections 363(a). (c)(2), (c)(3) and (c)(4).

The first of those subsections defines what is now known as "cash" collateral. The definition is not entirely self evident. It includes not only cash but also "negotiable instruments, documents of title, securities, deposit accounts, . . . other cash equivalents . . .and . . . proceeds, products, offspring, rents or profits of

[4] Ronald J. Bacigal, The Limits of Litigation: The Dalkon Sheild Controversy 64-71 (1990).

[5] This phrase appeared in the House version of the Code but was subsequently deleted.

[6] Initially, "soft collateral" was defined rather more broadly than "cash collateral" is; it included inventory, accounts, contract rights, general intangibles, and chattel paper.

property subject to a security interest"; since the 1994 Amendments, it also includes hotel and motel receipts.[7] This definition creates some amusing if not particularly significant anomalies; for example, suppose that Friendly Finance has a security interest in the debtor's cow, Elsie. Elsie is not cash collateral; her "proceed, product [or] offspring," Charlie the Calf, apparently is.

Cash collateral is given considerable protection. The trustee/DIP may not use, sell, or lease it unless either the creditor consents or the court, after notice and a hearing, authorizes it.[8] Moreover, the trustee/DIP must segregate and separately account for cash collateral unless either the creditor consents to other treatment or the court, in its order permitting use of cash collateral, relieves the trustee/DIP of these obligations.[9] In effect, this provision places the burden on the debtor to raise adequate protection issues (in most circumstances, this is up to the creditor). Indeed, in some cases, the court will simultaneously hear the debtor's request to use cash collateral with a creditor's demand for adequate protection of its interest in the property.[10]

There are practical problems of timing. The trustee/DIP frequently needs immediate access to cash collateral, because the business will immediately collapse if it does not get it. The court is required to act "promptly." The court may hold a preliminary hearing on the request, and may give temporary permission—but only if there is a "reasonable likelihood" that the trustee/DIP will prevail at the final hearing.[11]

Rule 4001(b) gives more detailed guidance for the conduct of hearings on use of cash collateral. The final hearing must be at least 15 days after service of the trustee/DIP's motion for authorization. If the movant so requests, the court may conduct an earlier preliminary hearing. However, at the preliminary hearing, the court may only authorize the use of "that amount of cash collateral as is necessary to avoid immediate and irreparable harm to the estate pending a final hearing."[12] Obvious examples include an immediately due payroll or a vital shipment that is arriving C.O.D.

Even the rule, however, does not fully deal with the most difficult situation—one in which the need for cash collateral is so great and immediate that the ordinary forms of notice and hearing are not available. It is generally assumed that, if the emergency is sufficiently grave, the notice may be nothing more than telephoning those creditors who can be reached; the hearing may be nothing more than a conference call.[13] Procedures of this sort, which are not rare, appear to be reasonably satisfactory to all concerned; at least, there is very little litigation over them.

---

[7] Bankruptcy Code § 363(a).

[8] Bankruptcy Code § 363(c)(2).

[9] Bankruptcy Code § 363(c)(4).

[10] This is specifically permitted by Bankruptcy Code § 363(c)(3).

[11] Bankruptcy Code § 363(c)(3).

[12] Bankruptcy Rule 4001(b)(2).

[13] See Collier on Bankruptcy ¶ 363.04.

[C]—Other Property

[1]—Ordinary Course of Business Transactions

The trustee/DIP is given much greater discretion to deal with property that is *not* cash collateral, even property that is collateral, but *non-cash* collateral. There are special rules for co-owners and for those claiming an interest arising from marital rights; but even these do not give an absolute right to block the trustee/DIP's action. The reason for this is simple. Whether liquidating or reorganizing a business, the trustee/DIP must be given substantial leeway to make appropriate bargains for the disposition or acquisition of property. "Appropriate" in this context essentially means "most profitable." Deference to the wishes of other claimants can impede profitable bargains. As is so often the case, the Code does not entirely ignore the interests of those claimants, but to some degree subordinates them to the goal of achieving a reasonably quick, reasonably successful liquidation or reorganization. It is assumed that achievement of this goal will produce benefits to creditors as a group that will outweigh any infringement on the interests of particular claimants.

In consequence, under section 363(c)(1), whenever operation of the debtor is authorized under the relevant provisions of Chapters 7, 11, 12 or 13, the trustee or DIP has the general right to deal with property. Unless the court orders otherwise, the trustee/DIP "may enter into transactions, including the sale or lease of property of the estate, in the ordinary course of business . . . and may use property of the estate in the ordinary course of business."[14] There is no requirement that there be any notice to others, or any hearing.[15]

For example, suppose that DuBois Corp., Debtor-in-Possession, is a ranch in the wombat trade. DuBois raises, fattens and slaughters wombats, then sells their meat to packers. After the filing of DuBois's Chapter 11 bankruptcy, DuBois's managers may continue to enter into the usual contracts to buy feed, employ ranch hands, sell and ship meat without any prior notice to creditors or approval from the court.[16] The reason is obvious; the business could not possibly function if it needed approval for every transaction, and there would be no hope of reorganization.

Note that the court may, by an appropriate order, restrict the ability of DuBois's managers to conduct business.[17] For example, if the court decided that the managers were entering into foolish or improper supply contracts it might require any of those contracts to receive prior approval by the court. This is rarely done, and usually only as an alternative to displacing management altogether.

[2]—Non-Ordinary Course Transactions

In contrast to ordinary course of business transactions, non-ordinary course transactions are subject to prior court scrutiny. Under section 363(b), a non-ordinary

[14] Bankruptcy Code § 363(c)(1).

[15] Bankruptcy Code § 363(c)(1).

[16] This assumes that none of the wombats are cash collateral; however, as noted in § 9.03[B], the offspring of collateral may be classified as cash collateral.

[17] Bankruptcy Code § 363(c)(1).

course use, sale, or lease of property must be preceded by notice and an opportunity for a hearing.[18] This provision deals with two rather different situations. The first is a bankruptcy in which the trustee is not authorized to conduct the business of the debtor—the typical Chapter 7 case. The second is one in which the trustee/DIP is authorized to conduct the debtor's business, but wishes to enter into a transaction that is outside the ordinary scope of that business.

For example, suppose that DuBois Unlimited is a Chapter 11 Debtor-in-Possession that has two businesses: tobacco products and food processing. DuBois's management decides that the business can best reorganize if it sells off the tobacco business and concentrates all its efforts on the food business.[19] That sale is outside the ordinary course of business, because DuBois is in the business of selling tobacco, not tobacco companies. It cannot be done without notice and an opportunity for a hearing.

[D]—Adequate Protection

The requirement of adequate protection, discussed previously in conjunction with the automatic stay, applies with equal force under section 363. Anyone who has a property interest in property of the estate is entitled to adequate protection of that interest. The court must ensure that adequate protection is provided.

Under section 363(e), adequate protection is made an integral part of the rules regarding the debtor's use, sale, or lease of property. On request of a person who has an interest in any property that is being used, sold, or leased, or any property that the trustee/DIP proposes to use, sell or lease, the court must prohibit or condition the use, sale, or lease to the extent necessary to provide adequate protection.[20] This provision protects lienholders, lessors, lessees, and co-owners; for example the holder of a mortgage on real estate, the lessor of realty or personalty, and a joint tenant would all be entitled to adequate protection of their interests.

The nature of the interest protected, and the means of providing protection, are essentially the same under section 363 as they are under section 362 (automatic stay). These are fully discussed in § 8.06[B] [2] of this book. Indeed, the claimant seeking adequate protection will very often be asking, in the alternative, for conditions on the use, sale, or lease of the property and for relief from the automatic stay. Broadly speaking, the claimant with the interest in the property is entitled to have the value of that interest protected from diminution. This can be done either by giving that person the property in question or other property (including money) to offset the diminution. The only real difference is that the use, sale, or lease of the property may make the adequate protection issue more urgent; use accelerates depreciation in value while sale or lease may make it difficult for the claimant to seize the property (and in some circumstances may even terminate its rights to the property).

[18] Bankruptcy Code § 363(b)(1).

[19] Note that this could be done either during the proceeding or as part of the plan. For purposes of this discussion, we are assuming that management wishes to sell the business prior to submitting the plan.

[20] Bankruptcy Code § 363(e).

Section 363(d) coordinates the section 362 rules regarding termination, limitation, or conditioning the stay with the use, sale, or lease rules. The trustee/DIP may not use, sell, or lease property if that is inconsistent with relief granted from the stay.[21] For example, suppose Carlotta has a security interest in some light trucks owned by Delta. Carlotta sought and obtained an order from the court section 362(d)(1) which imposed a condition on the continuation of the automatic stay. The condition prohibited the DIP from using the trucks to haul more than the maximum load recommended by the manufacturer. That same limitation applies to the DIP's right to use the collateral under section 363.

[E]—Continuation of Liens on the Property and Other Interests in the Property

If property that is subject to a lien or other third-party interest is sold by the trustee/DIP, an obvious question arises: does the buyer take free of or subject to the interest of the third party? This issue is dealt with at length in section 363.

The primary rules are set out in subsection (f), under which the trustee/DIP may sell property free and clear of third party interests only if at least one of the following applies:

1. Applicable nonbankruptcy law permits sale of the property free and clear of the interest.[22] For example, suppose that the debtor's inventory of widgets is collateral for a loan. If the debtor is in the business of selling widgets, and the buyer buys the goods in good faith and without knowledge that the purchase violates the security agreement, then the buyer takes free of any security interest created by the debtor under the provisions of Article 9 of the Uniform Commercial Code.[23]

2. The holder of the interest consents to selling the interest free and clear of the interest.[24]

3. The interest is a lien, and the price at which the encumbered property to be sold is greater than the aggregate value of all the liens on the property.[25] For example, suppose that the property is subject to mortgages securing a total of $363,000. Provided that the sales price is over $363,000, the trustee may sell it free and clear of the mortgages.

4. The interest is the subject of a bona fide dispute.[26] For example, suppose that River Bank claims to have a perfected security interest in equipment that the DIP wishes to sell free and clear. The DIP asserts that the security agreement inadequately described the collateral, and is therefore invalid

---

[21] Bankruptcy Code § 363(d).

[22] Bankruptcy Code § 363(f)(1).

[23] U.C.C. § 9-307(1). For a fuller discussion of this rule, see Thomas D. Crandall, Michael J. Herbert & Lary Lawrence, Uniform Commercial Code § 26.16.3 (1993).

[24] Bankruptcy Code § 363(f)(2).

[25] Bankruptcy Code § 363(f)(3).

[26] Bankruptcy Code § 363(f)(4).

under the rules of U.C.C. Article 9.[27] The assertion is legitimate; there are bona fide reasons to believe that the security agreement may indeed be fatally flawed. The property may be sold free and clear.

5. The holder of the interest could be compelled, in a legal or equitable proceeding, to accept a money satisfaction of the interest.[28] This may deal with situations in which the claimant does not have a specific right to the property, but rather a right to the property in lieu of payment. Most liens are of interests of this type; the lien creditor's right to the property is simply a method of obtaining payment; if payment is forthcoming, the creditor cannot keep the property. There has been some confusion about the apparent breadth of this provision, which, since it could apply to nearly all liens, seems to render the first four largely redundant.[29]

Note that these provisions do not have anything directly to do with the claimant's right to adequate protection. While in some circumstances the property can be sold free and clear of the interest, the interest still must be protected. This can be accomplished by paying the claimant from the proceeds of the sale or by giving the claimant other property of the estate in substitution for the property sold.

There are a number of additional rules dealing with special situations. The first deals with dower or curtesy. Regardless of whether the subsection 363(f) rules laid out above apply, the trustee/DIP may sell any property free and clear of either vested or contingent dower/curtesy rights.[30] In addition to other forms of adequate protection, the spouse who has the dower/curtesy interest is given a right of first refusal. He or she may purchase the property at the price agreed upon between the trustee/DIP and the purchaser.[31] In addition, when the property is sold, the trustee must distribute to the spouse the portion of the net sale proceeds corresponding to the dower/curtesy interest.[32]

Subsection (h) deals with the sale of property owned by the debtor and one or more other persons as tenants in common, joint tenants, or tenants by the entirety. This provision is designed to protect not only the joint owner's interest in the value of the property but also the joint owner's interest in the property itself. To the extent feasible, the bankruptcy court is supposed to distribute the property in kind or to sell the debtor's interest in the whole rather than sell the entire property (including the co-owner's interest) and distribute to the co-owner its portion of the proceeds of sale.

If it is feasible to split the property up between the debtor and the co-owner(s) the court must do so. For example, suppose that D and C are equal joint tenants of

[27] Article 9 requires that the security agreement include a description of the collateral. U.C.C. § 9-203(1)(a). See Thomas D. Crandall, Michael J. Herbert & Lary Lawrence, Uniform Commercial Code § 24.5 (1993).

[28] Bankruptcy Code § 363(f)(5).

[29] See In re Stroud Wholesale, Inc., 47 Bankr. 999 (E.D.N.C. 1985).

[30] Bankruptcy Code § 363(g).

[31] Bankruptcy Code § 363(i).

[32] Bankruptcy Code § 363(j).

100 virtually indistinguishable acres of farmland. Suppose further that these acres could readily be divided into two equal, compact halves, each half with adequate access, drainage, and water; each half composed of equally tillable soil. Partition in kind is practicable; the court may not sell the farmland as a whole. If the parcel is partitioned, the debtor's fifty acres will be sold and the co-owner's fifty acres left untouched. An alternative to partition is the sale of the debtor's undivided interest in the whole. In other words, one option is to sell D's interest in the property, leaving C's interest alone, so that the buyer will become C's co-owner. If this form of sale would result in substantially the same amount for the estate as would a sale of the whole, then the trustee/DIP may not sell the property as a whole.

However, distribution in kind or sale of the debtor's interest alone is appropriate only where that would not impair the success of the bankruptcy proceeding. Under the relevant provision, the court is to sell the property as a whole, including the interest of the co-owner(s), if all four of the following conditions are met.[33]

1. Partition in kind between the estate and the co-owners is impracticable.[34]
2. Sale of the estate's undivided interest in the property would realize significantly less for the estate than sale of the property free of the co-owner(s) interest.[35]
3. The benefit to the estate outweighs the detriment to the co-owners, and,[36]
4. The property is not used in the production, transmission, or distribution for sale of electric energy or of natural or synthetic gas for heat, light, or power.[37]

The constitutionality of selling the entire property, including the interest of a co-owner, has been challenged but upheld.[38]

[F]—Ipso Facto Clauses

The Code generally limits the effect of so-called "ipso facto" clauses. These are provisions that place a borrower or lessee in default whenever it is in financial trouble or files bankruptcy. Full recognition of these provisions would seriously impair the ability of the debtor to be liquidated or reorganized, since they would deprive the debtor of needed property. Section 363 contains one such limitation. The ability of the trustee/DIP to use, sell, or lease property, or for a plan of reorganization to provide for use, sale, or lease of property, is generally unaffected by any ipso facto clause that appears in the loan or lease agreement.[39]

---

[33] These requirements are cumulative, not alternative; all of them must be met to permit a sale of both the debtor's and the co-owner(s)' interest. See In re Haley, 100 Bankr. 13 (Bankr. N.D. Cal. 1989).

[34] Bankruptcy Code § 363(h)(1).

[35] Bankruptcy Code § 363(h)(2).

[36] Bankruptcy Code § 363(h)(3).

[37] Bankruptcy Code § 363(h)(4).

[38] In re Tsunis, 39 Bankr. 977 (E.D.N.Y. 1983), affirmed, 733 F.2d 27 (2d Cir. 1984).

[39] Bankruptcy Code § 363(l).

[G]—Rigged Sales

A facially proper sale may be avoided by the trustee/DIP if the price was rigged—that is, controlled by an agreement among potential bidders at the sale.[40] In the alternative, the trustee/DIP may enforce the sale but increase the price. It may "recover from a party to [the] agreement any amount by which the value of the property sold exceeds the price at which [the] sale was consummated."[41] Note that this damage remedy may be recovered against anyone who was a party to the collusive sale, not just the actual buyer.

Whichever alternative (avoidance or increased price) is chosen, the trustee/DIP is also entitled to the costs, attorneys' fees, and expenses incurred. (Although the Code is not explicit on the point, it appears that these expenses may also be recovered from anyone who was involved in the bid rigging.) In addition, the court has the discretion to award punitive damages against any of the bid-riggers who entered into the agreement "in willful disregard" of the applicable subsection of the Code.[42] It appears from the wording of this provision that the requirement of "willful disregard" of section 363(n) may require some knowledge or at least notice of the Code's prohibition on bid-rigging.

[H]—Procedural Burdens

Whenever there is a dispute over the right to use, sell, or lease property, section 363(o) regulates the burden of proof. The trustee or DIP bears the burden of proof on the issue of adequate protection. The party asserting an interest in the property bears the burden of proof on the validity, priority, and extent of its interest.[43]

[I]—Appeals

The ability to effectively appeal the judge's decision to permit sale or lease of property is somewhat limited. To preserve rights against bona fide purchasers, the appellant must obtain a stay of the sale or lease pending the appeal. Otherwise, reversal or modification of the decision does not affect the validity of the sale or lease if the buyer or lessee acquired the property in good faith.[44] For example, if the court has approved the non-ordinary course sale of property free of River Bank's security interest to a BFP, and the court is later reversed, the sale to the BFP is still valid and River Bank can only seek redress, if any, against the trustee or DIP.

---

[40] Bankruptcy Code § 363(n).

[41] Bankruptcy Code § 363(n).

[42] Bankruptcy Code § 363(n).

[43] Bankruptcy Code § 363(o)(1), (2).

[44] Bankruptcy Code § 363(m).

§ 9.04 Executory Contracts and Unexpired Leases

[A]—Introduction

One of the most significant powers of the trustee or debtor in possession is the power to assume or reject pre-petition executory contracts and unexpired leases, and to assign the benefits of those contracts and leases to third parties.[45] While there is occasionally some dismay about giving the trustee/DIP this power, at least two reasons are offered in justification. First, the power to reject a contract or lease or to assign its benefits is not unique to bankruptcy. With rare exception, any contract (including, today, most contracts to lease real property) may be breached at any time by any party. It has long been commonplace that contracting parties are not legally bound to perform their contracts. Except for a few cases in which specific performance will be ordered, parties to a contract are free to perform or not to perform, just as they wish. The only difference is that a person who does not perform is legally obligated to pay whatever damages non-performance may have caused. Similarly, it is generally true that contract and lease rights may be assigned to third parties. The Uniform Commercial Code codifies much of this law in Articles 2, 2A, and 9.[46]

The second reason harkens back to the common disaster model of bankruptcy. If a debtor was not allowed to reject contracts and leases, there would be two undesirable effects. The debtor could be saddled with crippling obligations. Worse, those claimants whose rights were based on incomplete contracts and leases would be put in a better position than those whose claims were based on completed transactions. Consider the following example:

> ABC Co., prior to its bankruptcy, entered into two contracts for the purchase of widgets. Each contract was for the same amount ($10,000) and had the same terms. Contract 1, with DEF Inc. was executory at the time of ABC's bankruptcy filing. Contract 2, with GHE Ltd had been performed by GHE; conforming widgets were properly delivered but had not been paid for when ABC filed.

If ABC could not reject the DEF contract, the DEF would in effect be given a preferred position; its widgets would have to be paid for in full. There is no obvious reason why a claimant on an unperformed contract should be given more than a claimant on a performed contract. The even-handed treatment implicit in the executory contract rules becomes more obvious when it is understood that rejection of a contract or lease is treated as a breach of the contract or lease, breach that occurred upon the petition. A contract or lease rejected during the bankruptcy is treated as if it were a contract or lease breached as the bankruptcy was filed.

Since the rejection of an executory contract or unexpired lease is treated as a breach that creates a claim in the bankruptcy, another question arises. The aggrieved

---

[45] Note that these rules apply to leases under which the debtor is either lessor or lessee, although most of the issues arise with regard to debtors who are lessees.

[46] See U.C.C. §§ 2-210, 2A-303, 9-318; see Thomas D. Crandall, Michael J. Herbert & Lary Lawrence, Uniform Commercial Code §§ 3.6, 11.2-11.4 (1993).

party is entitled to damages, in most cases damages equal to what it would get outside of bankruptcy. Why then does the debtor reject? What does the debtor gain?

The key to this is the difference between the amount of the claim and the amount actually paid on the claim. While the amount of the claim is measured according to the usual rules of contract law, the amount actually paid is determined by the distributional rules of the Bankruptcy Code. The claim created by rejection is just another general unsecured claim, of which only a fraction is paid. Thus, the usual incentive to back out of an unprofitable (or insufficiently profitable) deal is multiplied considerably.

For example, suppose that ABC Company has a contract with DEF under which ABC is to supply DEF with 10,000 widgets at $10 apiece. Because of changes in the market price of widgets, ABC could now sell the same widgets for $12 each. If ABC breaches the contract so that it can sell to another company at the higher price, it will have to pay DEF damages; in most cases, the damages would be $2 per widget—$20,000—and would entirely cancel out the gain to ABC from breach. Suppose further that ABC is in Chapter 11 bankruptcy, and contemplates a 25% payout on general unsecured claims. Breach now becomes profitable. The gain to ABC—$20,000—is unaffected. However, the real cost of breach is reduced by 75%. While it is true that DEF will have a claim for $20,000, only 25% of that claim will actually be paid. Thus, at a cost of $5,000 ABC has secured a gain of $20,000, for a net increase in its assets of $15,000. This gain can be used to finance the debtor's operations or the debtor's plan of reorganization.

The rules regarding assumption, rejection, and assignment are among the most complex and most frequently revised provisions of the Code. Section 365 is stuffed with intricate rules that deal with particular types of contracts and leases, including those regarding commercial real estate leases, shopping center leases, and aircraft gates. Only the most important of these are discussed in this section.

[B]—Definition of "Executory Contract"

Section 365 permits the rejection of executory contracts, not all contracts. What is an "executory contract" for bankruptcy purposes? For a number of years, the courts have overwhelmingly accepted the definition of Professor Vern Countryman. A contract is executory only if it is executory on both sides—only if both the debtor and the other party have material unperformed duties.[47] For example, suppose that prior to the bankruptcy the debtor entered into a contract to purchase 100,000 widgets for $50,000. All of the widgets were delivered in good order; the seller had fully performed its obligations. Debtor then files its bankruptcy petition. Under the generally accepted rule, the contract could not be rejected by the debtor.

[C]—Effect of Assumption and Rejection; Timing

It is well established that assumption is all or nothing. If the debtor assumes the contract or lease, the debtor assumes all the obligations under the contract or lease. The debtor cannot unilaterally choose the favorable terms and reject the unfavorable

---

[47] See Collier on Bankruptcy ¶ 365.2.

terms, although, of course, the other contracting party might agree to modification of the contract or lease. The obligations created by the assumption, if not met by the debtor, create administrative expenses with an administrative priority.[48] As noted above, rejection is deemed to be a breach of the contract or lease, creating a claim that ordinarily will be a general unsecured claim.[49]

There is no single date by which the trustee/DIP must assume or reject. Generally, in a Chapter 7 case, the decision must be made within 60 days of the order for relief (unless the court extends this period).[50] In a Chapter 9, 11, 12, or 13 case, the confirmation of the plan is usually the date by which the decision must be made, although the court can change this for cause.[51]

[D]—Ipso Facto Clauses

As noted above, there is a general policy in the Bankruptcy Code against the enforcement of ipso facto clauses.[52] A common ipso facto clause is a provision that says the contract or lease is breached merely because of bankruptcy, insolvency, or the like. The problem Congress saw with these clauses is that, if enforced, they would seriously impair the ability of many debtors to reorganize in bankruptcy. Section 365 contains several provisions that limit the effect of these clauses. They do not generally prevent assumption of a lease or contract, or its assignment,[53] and they do not generally permit termination of the lease or contract during the bankruptcy proceeding.[54] Similarly, an ipso facto clause that terminates the lease or contract upon assignment is not generally enforceable.[55]

[E]—Cure/Adequate Assurance of Performance

Generally speaking, assumption of a contract or lease requires the cure of any existing default. Under section 365(b)(1), the trustee/DIP must (i) either cure the default or provide adequate assurance that it will cure the default, and (ii) compensate, or provide adequate assurance of prompt compensation, for any actual pecuniary loss caused by the default and (iii) provide adequate assurance of future performance.[56] For example, suppose that the debtor, prior to the bankruptcy, was leasing equipment from LeaseWorld. The debtor failed to pay two installments of the rent. Each installment was for $10,000. In addition, the debtor had failed to pay for insurance on the equipment. If the Debtor in Possession wants to assume the lease, it must pay the back installments of rent, reinstate the insurance, and provide some method of assuring that future performance will be forthcoming. This might

---

[48] In re Norwegian Health Spa, Inc., 79 Bankr. 507 (Bankr. N.D. Ga. 1987).

[49] See Bankruptcy Code § 502(g).

[50] Bankruptcy Code § 365(d)(1).

[51] Bankruptcy Code § 365(d)(2).

[52] See § 9.03[F] of this chapter.

[53] Bankruptcy Code § 365(b)(2).

[54] Bankruptcy Code § 365(e)(1).

[55] Bankruptcy Code § 365(f)(3).

[56] Bankruptcy Code § 365(b)(1).

require more than a mere promise; for example, the DIP might be required to escrow money for the rent and insurance payments. There are special rules regarding adequate protection for shopping center leases that are discussed in § 9.05[D] of this chapter.

Some defaults do not have to be cured. If the default is under a so-called ipso facto clause, the trustee/DIP may ignore it. If the contract or lease makes the debtor's financial condition or filing of bankruptcy an act of default, this default need not be cured.[57] These provisions create defaults that (i) are not necessarily harmful to the other party and (ii) are generally incurable. If it is a default to file bankruptcy, and a contract or lease may not be assumed if there is a default, then a debtor who has filed bankruptcy cannot assume that contract or lease, no matter how important it may be to the debtor's prospects of reorganization. In consequence, the trustee/DIP does not have to cure a default under a provision that relates to (i) the insolvency or financial condition of the debtor, (ii) the commencement of a bankruptcy case, (iii) the appointment of a trustee or other custodian for the debtor's property, (iv) the fact that a trustee or other custodian has taken possession of the debtor's property, or (v) the satisfaction of any penalty rate or provision arising from a failure to perform a non-monetary obligation.[58]

The same rules effectively apply with regard to the assignment of the contract or lease. To be assigned, the contract or lease must first be properly assumed.[59] This means that defaults, other than those under ipso facto clauses, must be cured. Moreover, whether or not there are defaults, the debtor must provide adequate assurance of future performance by the assignee of the lease or contract.[60]

§ 9.05 Special Limitations on Assumption or Rejection and Assignment

[A]—Introduction

Although the power to assume or reject has in general been read very broadly, there are some limitations. One set of limitations of special interest to labor lawyers, namely those that deal with collective bargaining contracts and retirement benefits, are covered separately in § 22.03 of this book.

[B]—Real Estate Leases

Section 365(d) contains a number of special protections for real estate leases and contracts. The first few relate to timing. As noted above, there are various rules for determining the time for assumption or rejection.[61] In Chapter 7, the trustee must

---

[57] Bankruptcy Code § 365(b)(2); see § 9.04[D] of this chapter.

[58] Bankruptcy Code § 365(b)(2). The last of these five defaults that do not have to be cured was added by the 1994 Amendments.

[59] Bankruptcy Code § 365(f)(2)(A).

[60] Bankruptcy Code § 365(f)(2)(B).

[61] See § 9.04[C] of this chapter.

ordinarily assume or reject a lease or contract, including a lease of residential real estate within 60 days of the order for relief.[62] In chapters 9, 11, 12, or 13, the trustee/DIP must assume or reject a lease or contract, including a lease of residential real property by the confirmation of the plan unless the court sets a different time.[63] More significantly for some lessors, regardless of the chapter under which the case is filed, the trustee/DIP must assume or reject a lease of non-residential real property within 60 days of the order for relief, unless the court extends the time.[64]

In addition, the lessor of non-residential real property is given rights that are arguably greater than those given by the general adequate protection rules. Unless and until the lease is rejected, the trustee/DIP must timely perform all of the debtor's obligations under the lease (except for those contained in ipso facto clauses).[65] This means, for example, that the rent must be paid in full and on time, and that other obligations (such as maintenance of the property) must also be complied with. The court, for cause, may slightly alter this, by permitting obligations to be met late, so long as they are met within 60 days after the order for relief.[66] For example, if the petition is filed on July 1, the court may order that the July 1 rent payment be paid on July 15; but it may not postpone the payment to August 30. This provision prevents the debtor from getting a free ride under the lease for the period between the filing of the case and the decision to assume or reject.

There are also other special rules dealing with real estate leases. This include protection of the rights of the debtor's lessee and of the lessor of a lease assigned by the debtor. If the debtor is the lessor, and the debtor rejects the lease, the existing tenant may either vacate the premises and treat the rejection as a breach or may remain on the premises for the balance of the lease term and any renewal term.[67] If the debtor is the lessee, and assigns the property to a new tenant, the lessor may demand a new security deposit from the new tenant.[68]

[C]—Personal Property Leases

A provision was added by the 1994 Amendments to provide limited protection for some personal property lessors against the trustee/DIP's delay in assuming or rejecting the lease. Personal property lessors have long complained about these delays, during which they neither receive rent from the trustee/DIP nor have the right

[62] Bankruptcy Code § 365(d)(1). During that 60-day period, the court may extend the time. Failure to assume within the time period set is deemed to be rejection. Id.

[63] Bankruptcy Code § 365(d)(2).

[64] Bankruptcy Code § 365(d)(4).

[65] Bankruptcy Code § 365(d)(3).

[66] Bankruptcy Code § 365(d)(3).

[67] Bankruptcy Code § 365(h)(1). Prior to the 1994 Amendments, the language of this provision suggested that only a lessee in possession was protected; under the provision as amended it is clear that the lessee is protected so long as the lease has commenced, whether or not the lessee is already in possession of the property.

[68] Bankruptcy Code § 365(l). The deposit must be on substantially the same terms that the landlord would have offered similar tenants. Id.

to retrieve the goods and re-lease them to someone else. As noted in the prior subsection of this chapter, commercial real estate lessors are given considerable protection against delay. The amendment provides far less to commercial personal property lessors.

Under section 365(d)(10), the trustee/DIP has a limited obligation to make interim rental payments during the period before it assumes or rejects the lease. This obligation only arises in a Chapter 11 case. It only applies to rental payments (and other obligations) that arise "from and after" sixty days after the order for relief. It applies only to commercial leases—not to those for personal, family, or household purposes. Moreover, it is not absolutely mandatory; the court, after notice and an opportunity for a hearing, may relieve the trustee/DIP of the obligation to make the interim payments, depending upon "the equities of the case."[69]

[D]—Shopping Center Leases

Shopping center leases are provided with even more protection than other real estate leases. These are designed to protect the full value of the shopping center, not merely the value of the lease to the debtor. Among the many goals of those operating shopping centers is to have the right mix of stores. The classic shopping center has one or more "anchor" stores (usually large all-purpose realtors) and a variety of specialized shops. Certain kinds of stores may be prohibited entirely; for example, many shopping malls prohibit liquor stores and adult bookstores on the theory that these detract from the family atmosphere they are trying to create. Other considerations include common opening and closing times, and avoiding empty space. Nothing horrifies a mall manager more than the possibility of closed and shuttered shops.[70]

Section 365(b)(3) protects shopping centers[71] with regard to these concerns. Under that section, the trustee or DIP must provide the lessor with adequate assurance of the following:

1. **Payment of Rent/Performance of Lease** The trustee/DIP must provide adequate assurance that there will be a sufficient source of the rent and other consideration due under the lease. If the lease is assigned, the trustee/DIP must provide adequate assurance that the financial condition and the operating performance of the assignee is similar to the financial condition and the operating performance that the debtor had when the debtor and the lessor entered into the lease.[72] This means that the assignee must have about the same ability to pay, and about the same likelihood of performance as the debtor did originally—the measure is how sound the debtor

---

[69] Bankruptcy Code § 365(d)(10) (1994 Amendments). Note that the court also has the power to make the interim payment requirements more stringent.

[70] This is why vacant space, when it does exist, is usually hidden behind a facade.

[71] The term "shopping center" is not defined. It encompasses more than an enclosed mall or a single building, however; it may include a cluster of reasonably contiguous buildings operated as a whole. See In re Joshua Slocum, Ltd., 922 F.2d 1081 (3d Cir. 1990).

[72] Bankruptcy Code § 365(b)(3)(A).

was when it signed the lease, not how sound it is when the assignment is made.

2. **Percentage Rent** Shopping center leases often use percentage rents—that is, part or all of the rent will be based on a percentage of the store's sales. If the lessee's business falters, that rent will fall. The trustee/DIP is required to give adequate assurance that the percentage rent will not decline "substantially."[73] This is an indirect method of policing the adequacy of the debtor's efforts to keep the business running.

3. **Assumption/Assignment Subject to all Terms of Lease** If the lease is assumed or assigned, the trustee/DIP must give adequate assurance that the assumption or assignment is subject to all the provisions of the lease, "including (but not limited to)" provisions that deal with matters such as "radius, location, use, or exclusivity."[74] Moreover, the trustee/DIP must give adequate assurance that there will be no breach of any such provision contained in any other lease relating to the shopping center, any financing agreement relating to the shopping center, or any master agreement relating to the shopping center.[75] Although this subsection may be unnecessary (given the general rules about the effect of assumption or assignment) it makes clear that the duty of the lessee-debtor or its assignee goes beyond merely paying rent. All of the applicable rules regarding such things as opening or closing hours, signs, displays, and so forth must be complied with.

4. **Preserving the Mix** Finally, the trustee/DIP must give adequate assurance that assumption or assignment of the lease will not disrupt any tenant mix or balance in the shopping center.[76] For example, if the debtor has been selling books, it may be prohibited from suddenly converting itself into a sweatshirt store because that would disturb the desired mix.

Note that these requirements are in addition to all of the other requirements imposed on an assuming or assigning trustee/DIP, including the other requirements that relate generally to leases of real property.

§ 9.06 Non-Delegable Duties/Non-Assignable Benefits

[A]—Introduction

For many years, the general trend in contract law has been to broaden the ability of contracting parties to assign their benefits or delegate their duties. This is reflected in the Bankruptcy Code's limitations on ipso facto clauses. There are, however, still some limitations and these limitations are reflected in section 365.

---

[73] Bankruptcy Code § 365(b)(3)(B).

[74] Bankruptcy Code § 365(b)(3)(C).

[75] Bankruptcy Code § 365(b)(3)(C).

[76] Bankruptcy Code § 365(b)(3)(D).

It is a staple of contract law that some duties cannot be delegated because they are fundamental to the underlying bargain. These duties are often misleadingly referred to as "personal services." This is not quite accurate. Many personal services can be delegated and some non-delegable duties are not personal services. The real issue is whether performance by a particular person or organization is a fundamental part of the bargain. Personal services only come into it because it is easiest to find illustrations in certain types of personal service contracts. For example, if Alice enters into a contract to have her portrait painted by William Constable, he cannot delegate his duty to Jackson Pollock. The identity of the artist and the style of the painting are fundamental parts of the bargain.

Even rarer than non-delegable duties are non-assignable benefits. There are now very few circumstances under which a party to a contract is prohibited from assigning the benefit of its bargain to another. Many of the few restrictions that still exist are in fact round-about ways of restricting delegation.

The few restrictions that do exist survive bankruptcy. Under section 365(c)(1), the trustee/DIP cannot assume or assign any contract or lease if applicable law[77] excuses the other party from accepting performance from (or rendering performance to) any person who does not consent to the assumption or assignment.[78] This applies whether or not there is any contractual limitation on assignment or delegation.[79]

[B]—Contracts to Extend Credit/Issue Securities.

There is a long tradition in the law of classifying contracts to make loans as "personal" and therefore non-assignable contracts. As is true generally in this area of law, use of the term "personal" is unhelpful and misleading. Contracts to extend credit are more precisely characterized as contracts in which (traditionally at least) the identity (and creditworthiness) of the borrower is a fundamental part of the bargain.[80] This issue applies with special force when the borrower has gone bankrupt. In consequence, the trustee/DIP may not assume or assign a contract to make a loan, extend other forms of debt financing or financial accommodation, or to issue a security (such as a stock or bond) of the debtor.[81] This limitation applies regardless of whether there is a limitation in the contract itself.[82] Moreover, as there is no provision in this subsection regarding consent, the prohibition applies regardless of the consent of the other party.[83] Of course, this does not prevent the lender and the debtor from entering into a new, post-petition credit agreement; that agreement, however, would nearly always require court approval.[84]

---

[77] This encompasses all law applicable to the particular contract, whether state or federal.

[78] Bankruptcy Code § 365(e)(2)(A).

[79] In re Pioneer Ford Sales, Inc., 729 F.2d 27 (1st Cir. 1984).

[80] It is an interesting question whether this logic entirely applies to modern mass-marketed credit cards; however, the Bankruptcy Code draws no distinction between them and other extensions of credit.

[81] Bankruptcy Code § 365(e)(2)(B).

[82] Bankruptcy Code § 365(e)(2)(B).

[83] In re Sun Runner Marne, Inc., 945 F.2d 1089 (9th Cir. 1991).

[84] For a discussion of post-petition credit extensions, see § 9.08 of this chapter.

The limitation has been fairly narrowly construed. It applies only when the focus of the contract is an extension of credit. For example, many contracts for the sale of goods or services, and virtually all leases, involve an extension of credit, because the buyer or lessee is not obligated to pay for the property or services immediately. The mere fact that a contract for sale of widgets provides for 30 days' unsecured open account credit does not mean that the contract is non-assumable or non-assignable.[85]

§ 9.07 Utility Service

Section 366 sets out a series of special rules to deal with the problem of utility service. In most cases, utilities are monopoly providers; it is usually impracticable or impossible for a debtor to obtain service from any alternate source. In consequence, utilities are in an extraordinarily powerful position vis a vis the debtor. A refusal by a utility to deal with a debtor virtually forces liquidation. For this reason, there are restrictions on a utility's ability to refuse or terminate service. In exchange, the utility is usually entitled to a special form of adequate protection—a deposit.

Under section 366(a), utilities are prohibited from altering, refusing, or discontinuing service to the trustee/DIP or the debtor merely because a bankruptcy case has been filed or pre-petition utility bills are unpaid.[86] Neither may they discriminate against the trustee, DIP or debtor on those bases; that is, a utility cannot charge higher rates to bankrupts. This provision is rather more expansive than the automatic stay; the stay does not prohibit a creditor from refusing to deal so long as that refusal is not used as a tool for coercing payment of a pre-petition debt.[87] Under section 366(a), the motivation of the utility is irrelevant.

The utility is entitled to adequate protection; and, unlike others so entitled has to be protected within a short period of time. The utility is to be given "adequate assurance of payment [for post-petition services], in the form of a deposit or other security" within 20 days after the date of the order for relief.[88] The utility does not have to ask for this protection; it is supposed to be offered by the debtor/trustee/DIP. If it is not, the utility may then alter, refuse, or discontinue service.[89] Note that even a failure to give adequate assurance does not permit discrimination—thus it is probably true that the utility may cut off or reduce service, but may not charge extra. If the parties cannot come to an agreement regarding the assurance of payment, the court may, upon notice and opportunity for a hearing, determine what is required.[90]

Although the statute refers to a deposit, this is not the only way that adequate assurance may be provided. In at least some cases, the mere fact that the utility is

[85] See In re Cole Bros., Inc., 154 Bankr. 689 (Bankr. W.D. Mich. 1992). This issue was explicitly discussed in the legislative history. See 124 Cong. Rec. H11,093 (Sept. 28, 1978).

[86] Bankruptcy Code § 366(a).

[87] For a full discussion of this issue, see § 8.02 of this book.

[88] Bankruptcy Code § 366(b).

[89] Bankruptcy Code § 366(b). See In re Hanratty, 907 F.2d 1418 (3d Cir. 1990).

[90] Bankruptcy Code § 366(b).

entitled to an administrative priority may be sufficient. For example, if the debtor has sufficient unencumbered assets to ensure, or at least virtually ensure, that all administrative claims will be paid, a deposit may be unnecessary.[91]

§ 9.08 Obtaining Credit

Generally, when the trustee/DIP is operating the debtor's business, it is necessary to obtain credit. Most commonly, this will be short-term, unsecured credit, such as the 30 days' open account credit given by most suppliers to their buyers. Other times the credit will be long-term, structural credit. A reorganizing debtor generally has to reorganize its entire financial structure, including its long-term institutional debt. For example, When ABC Enterprises reorganizes, it may well have to get rid of an existing mortgage debt by selling off some property to reduce the debt and refinancing the rest at a lower monthly payment.

Section 364 deals with the ability of the trustee and the debtor in possession to obtain credit during the proceeding. It is structured much like section 363, which deals with use, sale, or lease of property. At its core are two distinctions: ordinary course debt vs. non-ordinary course debt and secured debt vs. unsecured debt. The degree of court control over the debtor is slightest when the debt is ordinary course unsecured and greatest when the debt is secured. The reason for this is that the risks to other creditors are generally greatest when the debtor is giving security for an extension of credit; the secured claim is entitled to full payment, and that payment effectively comes out of the assets that would otherwise be distributed on unsecured claims. Thus, the court should not permit the debtor to secure an obligation unless it is reasonably certain that the overall result of the transaction will benefit creditors generally.

Under section 364(a), if the trustee/DIP is authorized to operate the debtor's business, then (unless the court orders otherwise) the trustee/DIP may obtain unsecured credit and incur unsecured debt in the ordinary course of business. No notice, hearing, or order is required for any particular transaction. This debt is allowed as an administrative expense (and thus given an administrative priority).[92] The reason for this very loose rule is obvious; it would be pointlessly time-consuming and expensive for the trustee/DIP to run to the court for every little credit transaction. In a single day even a modest business might enter into a dozen small contracts with suppliers, each of which involves a brief extension of credit. Requiring approval of each would effectively kill the debtor. If the court is concerned that there is abuse of this power, it may enter an order imposing more stringent control (however, such an order would probably be a prelude to dismissing the trustee, converting the case, or displacing the DIP with a trustee).

---

[91] In re Penn Jersey Corp., 72 Bankr. 981 (Bankr. E.D. Pa. 1987).

[92] Bankruptcy Code § 364(a). For a discussion of administrative expenses and administrative priority, see § 10.04[B] of this book.

If the transaction involves unsecured, non-ordinary course debt, however, there must be prior notice and opportunity for a hearing.[93] For example, suppose that Dummey Corporation, Debtor-In-Possession, wishes to obtain an unsecured $50,000 line of credit to help it meet its payroll as it comes due. Assume further that Dummey has never had this type of credit facility in the past, and that it is not usual in Dummey's industry. This is almost certainly a non-ordinary course transaction (at least, a cautious attorney for the lender will make that assumption) and will require notice and an opportunity to be heard. The usual price of failing to comply with the notice/hearing requirement is that the debt will be treated as a general unsecured claim rather than a priority administrative claim (although on rare occasion courts have retroactively validated the transaction and given the loan priority status).[94]

There is another form of non-ordinary course unsecured debt regulated by section 364—"superpriority" debt. If the trustee/DIP cannot obtain unsecured debt because the administrative priority is not sufficiently attractive to a potential creditor, the court may, after notice and an opportunity for a hearing, permit the trustee/DIP to offer a priority that is even higher.[95] Note that this order is to be granted only if the normal administrative priority is insufficient to get the extension of credit.

In many cases, the rules on non-ordinary course unsecured debt are of no significance, for the simple reason that a bankrupt has great difficulty obtaining substantial unsecured credit. Many creditors are unwilling to deal with reorganizing debtors under any circumstances; those that are willing usually want every possible personal guarantee and scrap of collateral that is available. As noted, the court should be cautious (perhaps more cautious than many courts are) in permitting secured debt. If the extension of credit will generate benefits over and above the cost of encumbering property, well and good; however, if the net effect of permitting the grant of the lien is to reduce the ultimate payout to existing creditors, then it was a mistake.

In any event, if the debtor cannot otherwise get credit, the court, after notice and opportunity for a hearing, may permit the trustee/DIP to obtain credit secured by property that is unencumbered or that is secured by a junior lien on property already encumbered.[96] Sometimes even this is not enough. There may be no unencumbered property, and the creditor may refuse to accept a lien that is junior to an existing lien. The final and most drastic possibility is to permit the trustee/DIP to grant a lien that is equal to or senior to existing liens.

At this point we see one of the clearest conflicts between the Code's general policy of protecting existing property interests and the desire to find some means of reorganizing a debtor. Suppose, for example, that River Bank has encumbered virtually all the assets of Dummey Corporation, DIP. River refuses to extend any more credit to Dummey, and in fact is actively trying to get the stay lifted and so

---

[93] Bankruptcy Code § 364(b). Note that this subsection also applies to situations in which a trustee who is not authorized to conduct the debtor's business seeks to obtain credit.

[94] For a fuller discussion of this, see Collier on Bankruptcy ¶ 364.03.

[95] Bankruptcy Code § 364(c)(1).

[96] Bankruptcy Code § 364(c)(2), (3).

terminate the Chapter 11 proceeding. Sharque Investments has offered to lend Dummey $2,000,000—but is demanding (in addition to a very high interest rate) first priority liens on Dummey's real and personal property. No other potential lender is even willing to talk to Dummey. Dummey is completely out of cash and cannot meet its payroll unless it gets the loan. Failure to meet the payroll will certainly mean the end of the reorganization efforts; Dummey will have to convert to Chapter 7 and liquidate. If Dummey does get the loan, it will likely be able to survive for at least six more months; by then, Dummey hopes, market conditions will have improved and it will be possible to put forward an acceptable plan of reorganization. On the one hand, the Code repeatedly tells us to protect the interest of the existing lienholder, River Bank. If Sharque is given priority over them, River may lose the benefit of its lien. On the other hand, the Code encourages us to find ways to reorganize rather than to liquidate a going business. If Sharque cannot be given priority, Dummey will collapse immediately.

Section 364(d) attempts to balance those interests by permitting but restricting the grant of equal or priority liens. The adequacy of the balance is largely dependant on one's view of the effectiveness of the reorganization chapters. To the extent that one believes reorganization in general, Chapter 11 in particular, is largely futile, the balance favors the debtor far too much. To the extent one believes that reorganization can preserve value for creditors and jobs for workers, the balance is about right.

Equal or priority liens may be authorized, but only after notice and an opportunity for a hearing if and only if: (i) the trustee/DIP cannot obtain the credit in any other way, and (ii) the interest of the existing lienholder is adequately protected.[97] The trustee/DIP has the burden of proving adequate protection.[98] To continue with the hypothetical, suppose that the court determines that (1) the total value of Dummey's assets is $7,000,000; (2) the amount of River Bank's secured claim is $4,500,000, so that even after the Sharque lien attaches, River Bank will be fully secured with an equity cushion of $500,000; (3) Dummey's assets are fully insured against casualty loss and (4) the payments Dummey proposes to make on the River Bank debt will be enough to cover allowable interest and offset depreciation. Assuming all those things are true, River Bank is adequately protected; the odds are overwhelming that its demotion from senior to junior creditor will not affect its ultimate recovery of its claim.

From the standpoint of River Bank, however, there is still a slight fly in the ointment. The judge can be wrong. Indeed, if the judge's calculations were self-evidently correct, Sharque would not be insisting that it get a first priority lien. There would be no need for the additional protection if it really were certain that both River and Sharque would be paid in full no matter what happened. Sharque is asking for priority because there is uncertainty. By giving Sharque the priority it asks, we place the burden of that uncertainty on River. This is the point at which the Code tilts from protecting property to facilitating reorganization.

---

[97] Bankruptcy Code § 364(d)(1). For a full discussion of the concept of adequate protection, see § 8.06[B][2] of this book.

[98] Bankruptcy Code § 364(d)(2).

It should also be stressed that the risk placed on River Bank in this hypothetical is not different in kind from the risk placed on River Bank throughout the rules regarding operation of the debtor. Depending on the circumstances, the debtor may retain, use, sell, lease, or encumber property subject to liens; it may where permitted encumber that property with junior, equal, or superior liens. At all times and in each of these circumstances the creditor is entitled only to "adequate" (not absolute) protection. Loss of property because the court miscalculated when permitting a senior lien to attach is not different in kind from loss of property because the court miscalculated when it allowed the debtor to use the collateral.

An order authorizing the debtor to obtain non-ordinary course unsecured debt or secured debt may be appealed. However, the appeal may well be a futile gesture, unless the transaction is stayed pending the appeal. A reversal or modification of the authorization or a grant of a priority or lien, does not affect the validity of the debt or the lien, or the priority of the lien, if the creditor extended credit in good faith.[99] To return to the hypothetical, suppose the River Bank appeals the bankruptcy court's grant of a senior lien to Sharque. River was unable to obtain a stay of the loan, so Sharque lent the money and obtained the lien. On appeal, the court rules that the bankruptcy judge erred in his adequate protection calculation and should not have given Sharque priority over River. However, if Sharque acted in good faith when making the loan (and the mere fact that Sharque knew the issue was on appeal does not mean that it acted in bad faith)[100] the loan is good, the lien is good, and Sharque keeps its priority over River.

The most difficult problems arise when the debtor is seeking emergency funding. For example, suppose that the debtor filed Chapter 11 bankruptcy on May 1. The following day, it expects a shipment of vital inventory for which it must pay C.O.D.; but there is no cash available to pay. Infinity Bank is willing to lend enough money to pay for the inventory, but only if it gets a first priority security interest in the inventory and other property of the debtor. If the debtor does not obtain the financing to pay for the inventory, it may have to shut down for a week or two, and this might seriously diminish its chances of reorganization. The debtor asks for immediate permission from the court to enter into the loan agreement; and there is simply no time to have a full-scale hearing.

Even an emergency situation cannot entirely excuse the lack of notice or some opportunity to be heard. This is certainly clear under the language of the Code itself, and may even be required by the Constitution.[101] Some type of notice and some type of opportunity must be given, even if it is only a telephone conference with the most significant creditors.[102] Note that failure to provide notice or an opportunity to be heard is a more serious problem for the creditor than are errors of judgment by the court. An attack on the adequacy of the notice and hearing is not protected

---

[99] Bankruptcy Code § 364(e).

[100] Bankruptcy Code § 364(e).

[101] Credit Alliance Corp. v. Dunning-Ray Ins. Agency, Inc. (In re Blumer), 66 Bankr. 109 (9th Cir. Bankr. App. Panel 1986), aff'd, 826 F.2d 1069 (9th Cir. 1987).

[102] See In re Ellingsen MacLean Oil Co., 65 Bankr. 358 (W.D. Mich. 1986), aff'd, 834 F.2d 599 (6th Cir. 1987), cert. denied, 488 U.S. 817 (1988).

by the rule that immunizes good faith transactions. Even though the creditor may have acted in good faith, that will not necessarily be sufficient to preserve its rights under the credit agreement if the court failed to provide due process when issuing the order.[103]

Another potential barrier to the debtor obtaining necessary cash is the securities laws. Both federal and state law regulates the issuance of certain kinds of credit instruments. For example, a company issuing a bond that is to be publicly traded must generally comply with complex and burdensome state and federal "registration" laws that are designed to give information about the bond to the investing public.[104] These laws are not only expensive to comply with; they are to some degree redundant in banrkuptcy because the information disclosed in the registration process is generally available through the bankruptcy court, the creditor's committee, or (in a Chapter 11 case) the disclosure statement that must be made when soliciting approval of the plan.[105] There is, in consequence, a limited exemption from these laws under section 364(f). Unless the debtor is a securities underwriter,[106] section 364(f) preempts all state and federal registration laws with regard to the offer or sale under section 364 "of a security that is not an equity security."[107] Thus, a debtor who wishes to raise cash by issuing a debt security (such as a bond or commercial paper), whether for its operations or to fund its reorganization plan, may do so without registering the security. Note, however, that this exemption does not include equity securities, such as common or preferred stock. Note too that it only exempts the debtor from compliance with registration laws. There are other securities laws, most notably, those that prohibit fraud in securities transactions. They continue to apply.

§ 9.09 Abandonment of Property

Section 554 authorizes the trustee/DIP to abandon property of the estate. This Code section means exactly what it suggests; abandoned property is simply dropped from the estate and taken by either the debtor or another interest holder. While this provision is of primary importance in Chapter 7 liquidation, it applies across the board. The purpose of abandonment is to permit the trustee to shed property that is unduly difficult or expensive to retain, or is of such minimal value that it is not worth administering.

Section 554(a) deals with a request by the trustee/DIP to abandon property. Under that provision, the trustee may abandon property that is burdensome to the estate

---

[103] Id.

[104] For a general discussion of registration in the federal securities law context, see 1 Louis Loss & Joel Seligman, Securities Regulation ch. 2 (3d ed. 1989).

[105] For a discussion of the Chapter 11 disclosure statement, see § 17.14[B] of this book.

[106] Broadly speaking, an underwriter is a person who is distributing a security to others, rather than holding it for investment. See 2 Louis Loss & Joel Seligman, Securities Regulation 1108-1110 (3d ed. 1989).

[107] Bankruptcy Code § 364(f).

or that is of inconsequential value and benefit to the estate.[108] Similarly, section 554(b) permits any other party in interest to seek a court order to force the trustee to abandon burdensome or minimally valuable property.[109] In either case, there must be notice and an opportunity for a hearing.[110] If, as is typically the case, there is no objection made to the abandonment after the notice is given, the court may dispense with a hearing; however, a hearing is required if there is an objection.[111]

Note that there are two somewhat different substantive bases for abandonment. The first is that the property is burdensome; the second is that it is of inconsequential value and benefit. Although in many cases both bases will be present, the statute only requires one. A good example of property that may be abandoned, arguably on both bases, is property that is subject to a lien securing a debt that is greater than the value of the property, and that requires maintenance. For example, suppose that the debtor owns a herd of cows worth $500,000. The cows are subject to a valid, unavoidable security interest securing a $750,000 loan. Moreover, the cows are consuming thousands of dollars worth of feed and producing a minuscule amount of milk. The cows are burdensome to the estate (because the cost of maintaining them exceeds the income from their milk) and are of little or no value because there is no equity. Retaining the cows, in fact, would be detrimental to the interests of the creditors. The trustee therefore should abandon the cows to the secured creditor.

A pure issue of excessive burden to the estate might arise if there was a small equity in the cows—say, $3,000—but the net cost of maintaining them (that is, the excess of feed over milk) was so high that it was likely to exceed the $3,000 equity before the cows could be sold. A converse situation—one involving trivial value but no particular burden—would exist if the property was not cows but rather unimproved realty subject to a mortgage securing a debt greater than the value of the property.

The propriety of the abandonment may depend upon the nature of the proceeding or the point the proceedings have reached at the time the issue arises. For example, while it is ordinarily appropriate in a liquidation to abandon property when there is no equity, this is not necessarily true in a reorganization. If the property is needed for an effective reorganization, then it does have value and benefit to the estate, even though the lien on it is "under water." Similarly, it may be inappropriate to abandon property at the beginning of the proceeding, before it is clear whether the property does or does not have value. For this reason, it has long been established by the case law that the trustee may wait a reasonable time before deciding whether to abandon property.[112] Indeed, it may well be the trustee's duty to wait, especially if there

[108] Bankruptcy Code § 554(a).

[109] Bankruptcy Code § 554(b).

[110] Bankruptcy Code § 554(a), (b).

[111] Bankruptcy Rule 6007(a).

[112] Stanolind Oil & Gas Co. v. Logan, 92 F.2d 28 (5th Cir. 1937), cert. denied, 302 U.S. 763 (1938). Even astonishly long periods of time may be permissible under rare circumstances. See In re Aldrich's Estate, 35 Cal.2d 20, 215 P.2d 724 (1950) (25 years). Cf. Sparhawk v. Yerkes, 142 U.S. 1 (1891) (majority held that 12 years was too long; two justices dissented, holding that the delay merely exhibited wise judgment).

is a reasonable possibility that the market price of the property will rise in the foreseeable future.

Under the Bankruptcy Act, it was often unclear whether abandonment had occurred, because it was not always necessary for the trustee to take any formal action to abandon. The Code appears to cure this problem (at least in a properly conducted proceeding) by requiring notice and, where applicable, a hearing to effectuate abandonment. Subsections 554(c) and (d) also help to clarify the issue.

Subsection 554(c) specifies that, unless the court orders otherwise, all property that is scheduled but not otherwise administered by the time the case is closed is abandoned to the debtor.[113] This rule does not add a substantive basis for abandonment. It is always improper for the trustee to abandon property that is valuable and not burdensome. Rather, section 554(c) is designed to deal with a situation in which property that could properly have been abandoned by the trustee is not in fact either administered or abandoned.

Apart from the situation covered by subsection (c), however, formal abandonment is normally required. Subsection 554(d) states that "[u]nless the court orders otherwise, property of the estate that is not abandoned under this section and that is not administered in the case remains property of the estate."[114] This provision deals primarily with property that was not scheduled, whether the failure to schedule was fraudulent or merely an honest error. That property remains a part of the estate, and, where appropriate, the case can be reopened to permit distribution of that property to the creditors.[115]

---

[113] Bankruptcy Code § 554(c).

[114] Bankruptcy Code § 554(d).

[115] In re Medley, 29 Bankr. 84 (Bankr. M.D. Tenn. 1983).

CHAPTER 10

Claims and Interests

§ 10.01 General Principles and Rules of Priority

The rights of those other than the debtor in the estate and in the property of the estate are essentially divided into two basic classes: claims and interests. Broadly speaking, the term "claim" refers either to (i) a debt owed or potentially owed or (ii) a right against the debtor to an equitable remedy that arises from the breach of a contract.[1] Similarly, the term interest has two meanings; these differ significantly.[2] Sometimes, "interest" means a right to specific property of the estate. For example, the mortgage lien that secures repayment of a debt is an "interest" in the encumbered property. Similarly, the joint tenant of property co-owned with the debtor has an "interest." At other times, the term "interest" means a right to the residue of the estate after all claims are satisfied. When used this way, the term is a synonym for "equity." For example, the rights of stockholders in a bankrupt corporation is an interest; if there is still property in the corporation after all the creditors' claims have been satisfied, the stockholders are entitled to it. These two quite different meanings of the word "interest" must not be confused. The former refers to a property right in things owned by the estate; it involves divided ownership of identifiable property. The latter refers to the right to obtain whatever is left over.

Claims are further divided into at least two more categories. A claim may be a "secured claim" or an "unsecured claim". The former means that the claimant is (i) owed a debt and (ii) has collateral to secure the debt. In bankruptcy, a secured claim is a claim coupled with an interest, using the term "interest" to mean a right in the debtor's property. By contrast, an unsecured claim is simply a debt; the creditor has no interest in any particular property of the debtor that it may look to if the debt is not paid.

The distinctions between secured debt, unsecured debt and equity are not created by the Bankruptcy Code. It is a distinction that comes from, and indeed is fundamental to, the Anglo-American law of Creditor's Rights. The Code largely, but not entirely, preserves the traditional common-law priority structure, which has at its root the basic principle that debt always precedes equity, and that secured debt precedes unsecured debt. This priority structure ranks rights in roughly the following order, from top to bottom:

---

[1] Bankruptcy Code § 101(5).

[2] It may be useful to note yet a third meaning of the term "interest"—that is, payment for a loan or other extension of credit. Borrowers, including some bankruptcy debtors, pay interest for loans; yet this interest is neither an interest in particular property nor a right to obtain the residue of the debtor's property when all debts are paid.

Secured Debt

Unsecured Debt

Subordinated Debt

Equity

These categories are not comprehensive, for each may have many sub-categories; for example, there may be different levels of subordination among classes of subordinated debt. Similarly, there may be different classes of equity; stock that has a liquidation preference ranks higher than common stock, even though both are equity. In addition, the Bankruptcy Code to some extent stratifies the unsecured debt category by giving some unsecured claims priority over others. There are a number of classes of priority claims, not all of which are likely to exist in any particular bankruptcy. Note too that in bankruptcy parlance, "debts" are usually referred to as "claims." In a very slightly complex corporate bankruptcy, therefore, the actual categories might look something like this.

Secured Claims

Priority 1 Unsecured Claims

Priority 3 Unsecured Claims

Priority 7 Unsecured Claims

Priority 8 Unsecured Claims

General (Non-Priority) Unsecured Claims

Subordinated Unsecured Claims

Preferred Stock A

Preferred Stock B

Common Stock

Even this list may not be complete; in a reorganization proceeding, the debtor has the power to subdivide still further the general unsecured claims into classes, each of which may be treated differently.[3]

Roughly speaking, unless otherwise agreed by individual holders of claims or interests (or, in Chapter 11, by a class of claims or interests), each category is entitled to full satisfaction before any junior category is entitled to anything. For example, unless the Administrative Expense claims (the Priority 1 claims) are paid in full, the Priority Wage claims (Priority 3) are paid nothing. Unless all the claims are paid in full, nothing is paid on the Preferred Stock A. Any individual claim holder or interest holder may voluntarily sacrifice the right to payment; but this is exceedingly rare.

The rule that claims and interests are paid according to a predetermined order (which, in the bankruptcy context, is set by Congress through the Code) is called the "absolute priority rule." Absolute priority governs the distribution of the estate's property under Chapters 7, 12, 13 and sometimes 11. As suggested, one

---

[3] This power is broadest under Chapter 11, but also exists under Chapters 12 and 13—see §§ 17.11[D], 19.07[B], and 18.07[E] of this book, respectively.

distinguishing feature of Chapter 11 is that the absolute priority rule may be partially disregarded if enough claimants agree; this issue is studied further in Chapter 17.[4]

§ 10.02 Claims

[A]—Introduction

Roughly speaking, the term "claim" is synonymous with debt; obligations owed by the debtor create claims. However, "claim" is a term of art and should be used rather than "debt." "Debt" is often used to mean obligations that are fixed and definite; claim, as used in the Code, has no such limitation.

In the bankruptcy hierarchy of distribution, claims come first. As noted, this merely reflects a long-standing general rule that debt precedes equity. Indeed, this rule is virtually definitional, since equity is generally thought of as the residual claim against assets—that is, by definition, equity is the right to whatever is left over after all debts are satisfied in full.

[B]—Definition of Claim

The Code has an exceptionally broad definition of the term "claim"; virtually any kind of obligation potentially owed by the debtor to another is a claim. The term includes any "right to payment, whether or not [it] is reduced to judgment, liquidated, unliquidated, fixed, contingent, matured, unmatured, disputed, undisputed, legal, equitable, secured, or unsecured."[5] The word also encompasses any "right to an equitable remedy for breach of performance if [it] gives rise to a right to payment," also without regard to whether the right to the equitable remedy "is reduced to judgment, fixed, contingent, matured, unmatured, disputed, undisputed, secured, or unsecured."[6] Note especially that even speculative or uncertain rights are encompassed within the definition; thus, even a claimant who may not in fact be able to prove that it has rights still has a claim until there is some determination made about whether those rights exist or not, and whether they have value or not. This is a distinct change from the old Bankruptcy Act[7] and was designed as part of Congress' effort to enable the bankruptcy proceeding to deal comprehensively with the debtor's financial affairs.[8]

It is common among lawyers and judges to speak of the holders of claims as "creditors," "unsecured creditors," "priority creditors," "secured creditors" and the like. To be absolutely precise, however, the Code does not generally deal with

---

[4] See § 17.15[D].

[5] Bankruptcy Code § 101(5)(A).

[6] Bankruptcy Code § 101(5)(B).

[7] Under the old Bankruptcy Act, the term "claim" was defined only as a function of whether the claim was provable, and thus would be dealt with in the bankruptcy proceeding; essentially, it was used to limit the scope of the bankruptcy.

[8] Collier on Bankruptcy ¶ 101.5.

"creditors"; it deals with "claims" and "holders of claims."[9] This seemingly nitpicking nomenclature serves the useful purpose of clarifying that a creditor's status in the bankruptcy is based on its claim or claims, and not directly on the underlying obligation. For example, as is discussed in § 10.03 [C] of this chapter, a creditor holding an undersecured debt has two claims in the bankruptcy, one secured and one unsecured. The creditor has separate rights regarding each of the claims.

[C]—Allowance of Claims

The extremely broad definition of "claim" in section 101 is somewhat narrowed by section 502. Generally speaking, for a claim to be given status in the bankruptcy, and for its holder to exercise rights based on the claim, the claim must be "allowed." In most cases, claims are allowed perfunctorily. They are "deemed allowed" if a proof of claim is filed[10] unless a party in interest (such as the debtor, the trustee, or another creditor) objects.[11] If there is an objection, the court, after notice and an opportunity for a hearing, determines the amount of the claim (if any) in "lawful currency of the United States as of the date of the filing of the petition . . ."[12]

As noted, contingent and unliquidated rights to payment are claims. Sometimes, the contingency will be removed or the claim liquidated before the bankruptcy proceeding is completed. For example, assume that Sara is a surety of Dora, the debtor, on a $1,000 loan. Sara has not been required to pay the loan when the bankruptcy is filed; her claim for reimbursement from Dora is thus contingent and unliquidated at the time of the petition. During the course of the bankruptcy, however, Sara is forced to pay the entire amount of the loan to the creditor. Her claim has now become non-contingent and liquidated; it is the amount that she paid the creditor, $1,000.

More often, however, it is necessary to determine a value for contingent/unliquidated claims during the bankruptcy. Sometimes this is accomplished by lifting the automatic stay and conducting or permitting another court to conduct a full trial on the merits. In other cases, this is not practical, either because of the time involved or because there is no adequate way of measuring the claim through normal litigation.

In these circumstances, the bankruptcy court may estimate the amount of the claim and allow it for that estimated amount. The court may estimate whenever fixing or liquidating the claim would unduly delay administration of the case.[13] It may also make an estimate of the claim when it is a right to payment arising from a right

---

[9] Indeed, the term "creditor" is defined in terms of claims—a creditor is an "entity" that has a claim. See Bankruptcy Code § 101(10).

[10] Generally speaking, a proof of claim must be filed for the claim to be allowed. Bankruptcy Rule 3002(a). However, in a Chapter 11 or Chapter 9 case, if the claim is scheduled by the debtor the filing of a proof of claim is permitted but not required. Bankruptcy Rule 3003(c).

[11] Bankruptcy Code § 502(a).

[12] Bankruptcy Code § 502(b).

[13] Bankruptcy Code § 502(c)(1).

to an equitable remedy for breach of performance of a contract.[14] This last rule reflects the fact that bankruptcy is designed to deal only with money and property. A key goal of any bankruptcy proceeding is to turn all claims into exact dollar amounts, so that a distribution of money may be made either by the trustee or by the debtor-in-possession.

There are some specific limitations on allowance of claims.[15] Some of these are rooted in the underlying non-bankruptcy substantive law, while others are Code-imposed caps. The latter type of limitation is designed to deal with at least two problems. First, some claims are so large that their allowance might deprive other claimants of any meaningful share in the meager proceeds of the estate; in a few (though only a very few) instances, the Code restricts the amount of such claims. Second, some claims may be unusually large because the claim is not subject to mitigation; the claimant is allowed to ask for damages without regard to whether those damages could have been avoided. The classic, though not the only, example of a Code-capped claim is the claim of a real property lessor. This cannot exceed the sum of (1) past due rent plus (2) the greater of one year's rent or 15% of the remaining rent on the lease (and in no event to exceed three years' rent).[16] Suppose that at the time of the bankruptcy the debtor was lessee under a real estate lease that had 25 years to run. If the lessor were able to make a claim for all of the unpaid future rent, the amount of the claim might well reduce all the other claims to insignificance. The lessor is protected, since it is allowed to make a claim for up to three years' future rent, by which time the property probably will have been re-leased. While traditional common law rules did not require the lessor to seek a new tenant, this has been changing; and, in any event, Congress saw no reason not to include mitigation in the bankruptcy context, where other creditors are also seeking some relief from the very limited pot of assets.

Other Code-imposed limitations on the amount of the claim include the following:

1. Claims for unmatured interest (interest that accrues after the petition was filed) are generally not allowed.[17] This issue is discussed at greater length in § 10.02[D] of this chapter.

2. Taxes assessed against property are allowed only to the extent of the value of the estate's interest in the property.[18] For example, if real property worth $40,000 has been assessed with real estate taxes of $50,000, only $40,000 of the claim will be allowed. In essence, this provision treats property taxes as non-recourse claims, collectable only against the property subject to the tax.

---

[14] Bankruptcy Code § 502(c)(2).

[15] Note that all of these limitations only apply if an objection is made. In the absence of an objection, a claim is equal to the amount stated in the proof of claim. Bankruptcy Code § 502(a).

[16] Bankruptcy Code § 502(b)(6).

[17] Bankruptcy Code § 502(b)(2).

[18] Bankruptcy Code § 502(b)(3).

3. A claim made for services rendered by an "insider"[19] or an attorney for the debtor may only be allowed to the extent that the claim equals the reasonable value of those services.[20]

4. Claims by an employee for damages resulting from termination of employment are limited to compensation unpaid at the time of the firing plus one year's future compensation.[21]

[D]—Interest on Claims

If the obligation was one on which interest accrued, either by contract or rule of law, the allowed claim includes pre-petition interest.[22] Note, however, that post-petition interest is not allowed on unsecured claims (although in some cases it is on secured claims).[23] The general disallowance of post-petition interest is sometimes criticized as illogical,[24] however, it has been defended as a means by which a more even distribution of the debtor's limited assets is made possible.[25] In truth, the rule rarely has much significance; in most cases the distribution on unsecured claims is either non-existent or so tiny that the addition of interest would make little difference to the claimants.

Note too that in a reorganization case the rule disallowing post-petition interest applies during only during a part of the proceeding. Interest does not accrue during the "pendency period"—that is, the period of time from the commencement of the case to the confirmation of the plan. During the plan period, however, payments on all types of claims must include compensation for the claimant's loss of use of the money. Although not necessarily designated as interest, this compensation serves an essentially equivalent function. A fuller discussion of this issue is found in the various chapters of this book that discuss reorganization bankruptcy.[26]

---

[19] "Insiders" are close relatives and other close affiliates of the debtor. See Bankruptcy Code § 101(31).

[20] Bankrutpcy Code § 502(b)(4). Some lawyers may view this as a most regrettable provision.

[21] Bankruptcy Code § 502(7).

[22] See Bankruptcy Code § 502(b)(2), which lists unmatured interest as an exception to the allowance of a claim for interest, thus at least implicitly validating claims for pre-petition interest.

[23] Bankruptcy Code § 506(b). There is a nugatory exception to this rule in Chapter 7. If the debtor turns out to be solvent, then post petition interest is paid on all claims; this interest is at the statutory "legal rate" rather than at any agreed-to contract rate. Bankruptcy Code § 726(a)(5).

[24] See John C. McCoid, II, *Pendency Interest In Bankruptcy*, 68 Am. Bankr. L. J. 1 (1994). Professor McCoid's article includes both an interesting analysis of the issue and a concise history of the rule reaching back to the 1700's.

[25] The usual concern is that some forms of debt, such as bank loans, carry interest while other forms do not; if interest accrued pre-petition, interest-bearing debts would become relatively larger and thus receive a greater share of the distribution.

[26] See §§ 17.12, 19.07, and 18.08 for the treatment of this issue in Chapters 11, 12, and 13, respectively.

§ 10.03 Secured Claims

[A]—Types of Secured Claims

A secured claim is simply a claim that is coupled with some form of interest in property. Under our law, the mere fact that Alonzo has lent money money to Bette does not give Alonzo the right to any of Bette's property. Indeed, even the fact that Bette is in default under the loan does not in and of itself give Alonzo the right to Bette's property. Even if the debt is liquidated—even if the default and the amount due have been determined by a final court judgment—it remains a claim against Bette, not against any particular property of Bette. For Alonzo to seize Bette's property, Alonzo must obtain a further right against that property. This right is sometimes referred to as a "lien."[27] A lien may arise involuntarily or voluntarily. For example, a judgment lien that attaches to Bette's property after Alonzo dockets her judgment against his[28] is one type of involuntary lien; a mortgage given by Bette to secure repayment is one type of voluntary lien.[29]

The Bankruptcy Code does not, in general, distinguish between voluntary and involuntary liens. With minor exceptions, all give rise to secured claims, and each of those claims has the priority given to it by the non-bankruptcy law that created the lien. What all of these lien claims have in common is that the holder has not merely a claim for money but also a right to seize particular property.

[B]—Effect of Filing on Secured Claims; Post-Petition Property

Secured claims, although in many ways protected in bankruptcy, are not unaffected by the filing. At the very least, they are subject to the automatic stay of actions against the debtor and the property; the lien cannot be foreclosed upon unless and until the court so permits.[30] The proceeding also limits the rights of the secured claim holder in a number of other ways. One of these is the limitation on the degree to which a pre-petition lien can encumber property that the debtor acquires post-petition.

Some liens extend not only to the property originally encumbered, but also to after-acquired property—that is, property that the debtor obtains after the lien is originally created. The right to after-acquired property may be rather narrow, limited to property that relates directly to the encumbered property; or it may be broad, encompassing almost any kind of property the debtor subsequently obtains. An

---

[27] The term "lien" should be used with caution. It is sometimes used broadly, to refer to any property interest that gives rights in property to enforce an obligation, whether voluntary or involuntary—for example, Bankruptcy Code § 101(37) says that " 'lien' means charge against or interest in property to secure payment of a debt or performance of an obligation." At other times, "lien" refers only to involuntarily created rights, such as a mechanics' lien or a judgment lien.

[28] For a discussion of judicial and other involuntary liens, see §§ 2.03-2.05 of this book.

[29] See § 2.02 of this book for a discussion of mortgages and other voluntary liens.

[30] See § 8.02 of this book for a full discussion of the impact of the automatic stay on secured claims.

example of the former is the right found in many mortgages to rents obtained from the real estate. If the mortgagor of the real estate rents it to a third party, the mortgagee obtains a lien on the rents that the lessee pays.[31] Another type of after-acquired property, familiar to students of the Uniform Commercial Code's Article on Secured Transactions, is "proceeds." Proceeds consist of money or other property obtained by the debtor when the encumbered property is sold or otherwise disposed of. For example, suppose that Doug has given an Article 9 security interest in his car to River Bank. If Doug sells his car to Beauregard for $2,000, that $2,000 is proceeds, and is automatically subject to the security interest.[32]

Some liens may extend much more broadly to after-acquired property. For example, an Article 9 security interest in a commercial transaction can encompass broad categories of collateral, both now owned and subsequently acquired by the debtor, if the parties so agree.[33] A business may grant a security interest in "all inventory, now owned or hereafter acquired." The security interest immediately attaches to existing inventory, and will automatically attach to new inventory when and as it is acquired by the debtor.[34]

Bankruptcy significantly curtails the lien creditor's right to after-acquired property. A pre-petition lien may encumber any property acquired up to the commencement of the case. However, unless the court orders otherwise, property acquired by the debtor after the commencement of the case will be subject to the lien if but only if:

1. The property is proceeds, product, offspring, rents, or profits of property that was subject to a security agreement[35] prior to the commencement of the case; and

2. The security agreement provides that the lien will extend to that after-acquired property; and

3. The provision in the security agreement that provides for inclusion of the after-acquired property is enforceable under the non-bankruptcy law

[31] Note that, at least in those states following the "lien theory" of mortgages, any right to rents prior to foreclosure must be based on the contract between mortgagor and mortgagee; it is not an automatic incident of the mortgage itself. See Grant S. Nelson & Dale A. Whitman, Real Estate Finance Law § 4.23 (3d ed. 1993).

[32] See U.C.C. § 9-306.

[33] See Thomas D. Crandall, Michael J. Herbert, and Lary Lawrence, Uniform Commercial Code § 24.15 (1993). There are many limitations on the ability to use after-acquired property clauses in consumer transactions—see for example U.C.C. § 9-204(2) and Federal Trade Commission's Unfair Credit Practices Regulations, 16 C.F.R. § 444.2(a)(4) (1994).

[34] See Thomas D. Crandall, Michael J. Herbert, and Lary Lawrence, Uniform Commercial Code § 24.15 (1993).

[35] Note that in bankruptcy the term "security agreement" extends to all consensual liens, not just to Article 9 security interests (Bankruptcy Code § 101(50)); thus, it includes such things as mortgages and deeds of trust but excludes such things as judicial or mechanics' liens.

that applicable to the security agreement.[36]

The court may alter the scope of after-acquired property subject to the lien, but only after notice and an opportunity for a hearing, and only if it is appropriate, "based on the equities of the case."[37] Collier's gives the following example, which suggests that the court should not permit the pre-petition lien to give the secured creditor the benefit of work done after the petition was filed:

> Under the equity exception in section 552(b), the secured party should not receive a windfall benefit when the trustee uses assets of the estate, for example, to finish uncompleted inventory (which is proceeds of collateral acquired by the debtor pre-petition) subject to a pre-petition security interest.[38]

There are also circumstances in which the pre-petition secured creditor will get more after-acquired property than is encompassed by section 552(b). A reorganizing debtor often has to cut special deals with its secured creditors to permit the case to continue. It is quite appropriate (with court permission) to give a secured creditor a lien on post-petition property in exchange for a promise to lend additional money[39] or in settlement of a dispute over adequate protection of the secured claim.[40]

[C]—Bifurcation; Pendency Interest

[1]—Introduction

One of the most important set of rules regarding claims in bankruptcy is that contained in section 506 regarding the classification of a claim as secured. A secured claim almost always has real value; an unsecured claim usually does not. With very rare exceptions, the holder of a secured claim will receive either its collateral or a distribution equal to the amount of the claim. The holder of an unsecured claim is lucky if it receives even a tiny percentage of the amount of its claim.

Section 506 deals with two issues regarding the allowance of a secured claim. The first is the treatment of an undersecured debt. The second is the degree to which post-petition interest on the claim is allowed.

[2]—Allowance of Secured Claim

A secured claim generally cannot be for more than the value of the property securing the debt.[41] For example, suppose that Friendly Finance is owed $100,000

---

[36] Bankruptcy Code § 552(b)(1), (2). The 1994 Amendments slightly revised this section to encompass "the fees, charges, accounts, or other payments for the use or occupancy of rooms and other public facilities in hotels, motels, or other lodging properties . . ."

[37] Bankruptcy Code § 552(b)(1), (2).

[38] Collier on Bankruptcy ¶ 552.02.

[39] For the rules governing post-petition extensions of credit, see § 9.08 of this book.

[40] See § 8.06[B][2] of this book for a discussion of adequate protection.

[41] Bankruptcy Code § 506(a).

by the debtor, and that this debt is secured by the debtor's equipment. Assuming that Friendly's security interest was properly created and cannot be avoided by the trustee/DIP, Friendly has a secured claim. The amount of that secured claim depends on the value of Friendly's interest in the estate's interest in the equipment. Assuming that the debtor was the sole owner of the equipment, and that the equipment is now wholly the property of the estate, Friendly's secured claim will be equal to the lesser of the debt owed or the equipment's value. If the equipment is worth $120,000, Friendly's allowed secured claim is $100,000. If the equipment is worth only $80,000, Friendly's allowed secured claim is $80,000. In the latter case, Friendly also gets a separate, allowed general unsecured claim for the remaining $20,000. When this bifurcation of an obligation occurs, the creditor has separate rights on each of its two claims.

Value is to be determined "in light of the purpose of the valuation and of the proposed disposition or use" of the property.[42] Broadly speaking, the value of the collateral is likely to be set higher in a reorganization than in a liquidation. Most litigation over the value of collateral occurs in the context of adequate protection and the automatic stay, not the allowance of the claim itself.

[3]—Post-Petition Interest on Secured Claims

What about interest on the secured claim? Most debt that is wholly or partially secured was originally incurred under an agreement that requires the debtor to pay interest on the unpaid portion of the obligation. Is that interest added to the creditor's claim?

As discussed in § 10.02[D], post-petition interest is not allowed on unsecured claims during the pendency period (after commencement of the case and before a plan of reorganization, if applicable, is confirmed). Pendency period interest is, however, allowed on some secured claims. If the debt is oversecured—if the collateral is worth more than the amount of the obligation—then interest is allowed, and added to the secured claim, up to the full amount of the surplus.[43] Thus, if the debt owed to Friendly Finance is $50,000, and the collateral is worth $60,000, Friendly will be allowed up to $10,000 in pendency interest, and the amount of its allowed secured claim may over time rise to as much as $60,000. Once the surplus has been exhausted, however, the creditor will not be allowed either a secured or an unsecured claim for any further interest.

Note that the secured claim may also be increased not only by the interest that accrues on the loan, but also by "any reasonable fees, costs, or charges provided for under the agreement under which such claim arose."[44] This means that late fees, attorney's fees, and the like may be added on. However, the total of all principal, interest, fees, costs, and charges is limited by the value of the collateral; in the example given, $60,000.

---

[42] Bankruptcy Code § 506(a).

[43] Bankruptcy Code § 506(b).

[44] Bankruptcy Code § 506(b).

The rule that the partially secured debt is not entitled to pendency interest has been attacked for providing many secured claims with less than full payment during the pendency period. Since the secured creditor loses the use of its property during that period, it does not in fact receive the full value of the property if it is not compensated for lost use. If, for example, River Bank has only $1,000 of collateral securing its $1,000 debt, it is entitled to no interest. This is in spite of the fact that, but for the automatic stay, River Bank could have seized its collateral, sold it, and re-invested the proceeds. Although it is indeed true that River Bank should eventually receive $1,000 through the bankruptcy proceeding, this in fact is less than the value its interest would have had outside of bankruptcy because of its inability to foreclose and reinvest. It may be considerably less if the proceeding is a protracted Chapter 11 reorganization. In the view of some, this improperly forces a secured creditor, who is unlikely to benefit from the reorganization[45] to subsidize the reorganization for the benefit of the unsecured creditors, who may get a better payout if the reorganization succeeds.[46] On the other hand, the no-interest rule has been defended as a recognition that bankruptcy is a common disaster—like a shipwreck—in which the burden of loss should be shared among all stakeholders.[47] It is at least a crude means of helping to provide some payment on unsecured claims; virtually all of most debtors' non-exempt property already goes to pay secured claims[48] and allowing interest on those claims that are not oversecured would simply exacerbate this problem.

In any event, any doubt about the proper interpretation of the Code was resolved by the Supreme Court. It ruled in 1988 that the plain language of the Code mandated the denial of any pendency interest on debts that are not oversecured.[49] As it is unlikely that Congress will address the issue, this ruling has probably laid the matter to rest.

---

[45] Since the value of a secured claim is fixed by the value of the collateral, it is unlikely that even a successful reorganization will result in improved payment on secured claims.

[46] Thomas H. Jackson, The Logic and Limits of Bankruptcy Law 189-90 (1986).

[47] See McCoid, *Pendency Interest in Bankruptcy*, 68 Am. Bankr. L. J. 1, (1994). (I note that this is not Professor McCoid's own position.) The shipwreck model of bankruptcy dates back at least to the Eighteenth Century; Professor McCoid quotes a 1743 case, Ex parte Bennet: "[I]t is a dead fund, and in such a shipwreck, if there is salvage of part to each person, in this general loss, it is as much as can be expected."

[48] For a discussion about the percentage of the debtor's assets that are distributed on secured claims, see Michael J. Herbert & Dominic E. Pacitti, *Down and Out in Richmond, Virginia: The Distribution of Assets in Chapter 7 Bankruptcy Proceedings Closed During 1984-87*, 22 U. Rich. L. Rev. 303. (1988)

[49] United Savings Association of Texas v. Timbers of Inwood Forest Associates, Ltd., 484 U.S. 365 (1988).

§ 10.04 Unsecured Claims

[A]—Introduction

All unsecured claims rank below each and every secured claim. This however does not mean that all unsecured claims rank equally. Some are given priority. The priority claims themselves are ranked from highest (usually, administrative claims) to lowest priority. These priorities are established by the Bankruptcy Code, not by state law. This is one area of bankruptcy law that is not entirely "transparent" to other bodies of law; indeed, the Code-created priorities represent one of the most obvious ways in which Congress has used its bankruptcy power to create substantive debtor-creditor law.[50] Moreover, although some priorities have remained virtually unchanged for decades, others have been added as Congress reacts to particular real and perceived problems. The most recent changes were made in the 1994 Amendments.

[B]—Administrative Expenses

Administrative expenses are nearly always given the highest priority among the unsecured claims, and thus the best chance of payment.[51] (There are exceptions; for example, on rare occasions, a super-priority is given to claims that arise from errors by the court in determining that a secured claim has adequate protection. This issue is discussed elsewhere in this book.)

Administrative expenses are those that arise from the expenses involved in the bankruptcy proceeding itself. Section 503 sets out the various administrative expenses; these include, among others,

> Costs of Preserving the Estate—The actual, necessary costs of preserving the estate, including compensation for services rendered post-petition, and taxes incurred by the estate.[52]
>
> Compensation of Trustee and Others—The pay and expenses awarded to the trustee, any examiner, any other "professional person" and the debtor's attorney.[53]
>
> Reimbursement of Expenses/Compensation of Professionals—Under some circumstances, creditors may be reimbursed for their expenses in taking actions that benefit the estate[54] and the attorneys or accountants they

---

[50] As to the advisability of this use of bankruptcy law, see § 1.02[B] of this book.

[51] Note that, although administrative expenses seem to fit within the broad definition of claims stated in Bankruptcy Code § 101(5), they are given very slightly different status in the Code. See Bankruptcy Code § 507(a), which distinguishes "expenses" and "claims."

[52] Bankruptcy Code § 503(b)(1).

[53] Bankruptcy Code §§ 503(b)(2), 330(a). For a discussion of the rules governing the award of compensation and reimbursement, see § 20.03 of this book.

[54] Bankruptcy Code § 503(b)(3).

used in taking these actions may be awarded compensation for their services.[55]

[C]—Other Priority Claims

Following the administrative priority are eight other priorities. Whenever the absolute priority rules applies (which is to say, in all cases except some Chapter 11 cases) each claim in each priority class is entitled to payment in full before any payment is made on any claim in a lower priority class. When there is not enough to pay fully each claim in a particular class, all the claims in that class are paid pro-rata, and no payment is made with regard to claims in a lower priority class. These priorities, the second through ninth, are discussed in this subparagraph.

The second priority is given to claims allowed under section 502(f).[56] These are claims that arise in the ordinary course of an involuntary debtor's business or financial affairs after the commencement of the case but before the earlier of the entry of the order for relief or the appointment of a trustee.[57] They are sometimes known as "gap" claims, because they arise during the gap between the involuntary petition and the order for relief. The gap claims are discussed in Chapter 6.[58]

The third priority is given to certain wage claims. These claims must have been earned within 90 days before the filing of the petition (or the date on which the debtor stopped during business, whichever occurred first). Under the 1994 Amendments, this priority is also available, under some circumstances, for sales commissions that are earned either by an individual, or by a corporation with only one employee, acting as an independent contractor regarding the sale of goods or services for the debtor. The priority may not exceed $4,000 for each claimant.[59] Thus, if a particular claim is for $5,000, the claimant will have a $4,000 priority claim and a $1,000 general unsecured claim. This priority is intended to provide some protection for employees, because of Congress' assumption that most employees have great need for, and little ability to obtain, protection against their employer's bankruptcy.

Priority four is related to priority three; it is for certain contributions to employee benefit plans. The priority relates only to those contributions that arise from services rendered within the earlier of 180 days before the filing of the petition or 180 days before the debtor ceased business. The amount of the priority for each employee benefit plan is capped. It may not exceed:

---

[55] Bankruptcy Code § 503(b)(4).

[56] Bankruptcy Code § 507(a)(2).

[57] Bankruptcy Code § 502(f).

[58] See § 6.03[G].

[59] Bankruptcy Code § 507(a)(3). Under the 1994 Amendments, this amount was increased from $2,000 to $4,000; the amount has also been indexed to the Consumer Price Index and will periodically rise in the future.

The number of employees covered by the plan times $4,000, minus
The amounts paid to the covered employees under the wage priority and the amount paid by the estate on behalf of such employees under any other employee benefit plan.[60]

For example, suppose that 100 employees had, during the 180-day period, earned the right to a $700,000 benefit plan contribution to benefit plan A, and that the debtor had failed to pay this contribution before bankruptcy. Those employees had also established aggregate wage priority claims in the amount of $160,000, and the estate has already paid $34,000 into benefit plan B. Benefit plan A has a priority claim in the amount of $206,000 ((100 x $4,000) = $400,000 -$160,000 -$34,000).

The fifth priority—more accurately, the fifth priorities, since there are two of them—deal with the special problems of farmers and fishermen who have handed over their grain or fish bankruptcy grain elevators and fish storage facilities. Each is given a priority claim for their produce or its proceeds. The priority is capped at $4,000.[61]

The sixth priority gives limited protection to individual buyers who have made a down payment or layaway deposit to a now-bankrupt seller. The payment may be for the purchase, lease, or rental of property, or for the purchase of services. The property or services must be consumer in nature; that is, acquired for personal, family, or household use. The priority is capped at $1800 per individual claimant.[62]

The 1994 Amendments added a priority, put in the seventh position, and thus demoting two existing priorities. This new priority covers allowed claims for debts to a spouse, former spouse, or child of the debtor for alimony, maintenance, or support. The claim must be in connection with a separation agreement, divorce decree, or other order of a court of record. It does not apply to the extent that the obligation is assigned to another entity (either voluntarily or involuntarily). Moreover, the claim must actually be for alimony, maintenance, or support; it is not sufficient that it be designated as such.[63]

The eighth, and most complex of the priority provisions deals with various taxes, customs duties, and penalties.[64] There are no dollar caps on any of the tax priorities; however, most of them have various time limits. For example, the priority for income taxes encompasses roughly three years' worth of taxes.[65] By contrast, the property tax priority may include about one year's taxes.[66] It is important to remember that

---

[60] Bankruptcy Code § 507(a)(4). Under the 1994 Amendments, this amount was increased from $2,000 to $4,000; the amount has also been indexed to the Consumer Price Index and will periodically rise in the future.

[61] Bankruptcy Code § 507(a)(5). Under the 1994 Amendments, this amount was increased from $2,000 to $4,000; the amount has also been indexed to the Consumer Price Index and will periodically rise in the future.

[62] Bankruptcy Code § 507(a)(6) (1994 Amendments).

[63] Bankruptcy Code § 507(a)(7) (1994 Amendments).

[64] Bankruptcy Code § 507(a)(8).

[65] Bankruptcy Code § 507(a)(8)(A)(i).

[66] Bankruptcy Code § 547(a)(8)(B).

many tax claims will actually be secured claims. A non-avoidable allowed secured claim arising from a valid tax lien has the samc status as any other secured claim, and will be given priority above all unsecured claims. The priority thus deals only with unsecured tax claims.

The ninth priority had its genesis in the troubles of the financial world during the 1980's. It creates a priority claim for unkept commitments of the debtor to maintain the capital of an insured depository institution. This priority is uncapped.[67]

The 1994 Amendments also provide for indexing the capped priorities. In the future, the amount of the cap will automaticaly change every three years to adjust for changes in the Consumer Price Index.[68]

[D]—General Unsecured Claims

"General unsecured claims" is the name given to the great residual pot into which claims not otherwise classified are dropped. In consumer cases, these tend to consist of debts to retailers, small loans, and credit card obligations.[69] In business cases, trade debt is usually the main component, although unsecured bank loans are not uncommon. In a business case there may also be unsecured debt that is represented by investment securities. Long term debt of this sort is generally represented by a bond; short term debt, by commercial paper. Some or all of this type of unsecured debt may be publicly traded in the securities markets. (Note, however, that neither a bond nor commercial paper necessarily represents unsecured debt; either may be secured by collateral, in which case the debt it represents is a secured claim.)

Tort obligations (other than those represented by a non-avoidable judgment lien) are general unsecured claims. Unlike those whose claims are based in contract, tort claimants have little or no opportunity to evaluate or take precautions against the risk involved in dealing with the debtor. This may be inappropriate. Widgets, Inc., a supplier, can evaluate the risk of selling on open account to Dummey Corporation, and choose to do so. The innocent bystander run down by one of Dummey's trucks had little or no way of knowing its risks and did not choose to encounter them. Despite this, both are lumped together when the all-too-limited assets of Dummey are shared out in bankruptcy. Whether justified or not, this treatment may be inevitable; it would be difficult to create any bankruptcy system that provided reasonable assurance of payment for tort claims without making it unduly difficult for business entities to obtain financing. Giving a tort claim priority would often be futile (since even priority claims are seldom paid);[70] placing tort claims above secured claims would make many forms of business financing exceedingly difficult to obtain.

---

[67] Bankruptcy Code § 507(a)(9).

[68] Bankruptcy Code § 104(b) (1994 Amendments).

[69] See Teresa A. Sullivan, Elizabeth Warren & Jay Lawrence Westbrook, As We Forgive Our Debtors 275-76 (1989).

[70] Note, however, that this is not entirely true in the type of bankruptcy most likely to generate substantial tort claims—business bankruptcy. Even in liquidation, many business produce enough to pay all their priority claims, and a part of their general unsecured claims.

In liquidation bankruptcy, the general unsecured claims are unlikely to be paid, even in part.[71] By contrast, a successful reorganization may provide for substantial payment; even, in very rare cases, for full payment. In liquidation, all general unsecured claims are treated equally; whatever assets remain when the superior claims are paid in full are divided pro rata. In reorganization, especially (although not exclusively) in Chapter 11 reorganization, the general unsecured claims may be further subdivided by the plan into classes. So long as the classifications are justified, and so long as the plan provides for payment of the liquidation value of each claim in each class, the plan may treat some classes more favorably than others.[72]

§ 10.05 Subordinated Claims

[A]—Introduction

Some claims may rank even below general unsecured claims. These subordinated claims are still debt; they rank above equity. However, since they are the lowest rank of debt, the chance of payment in all but a few cases is exceedingly remote. Section 510 partially codifies the rules regarding claim subordination. The two primary aspects of section 510 are discussed in this section.

[B]—Subordination by Agreement

Some claims are subordinated by agreement of the claim holder. The Code states laconically that "[a] subordination agreement is enforceable in a case under this title to the same extent that such agreement is enforceable under applicable nonbankruptcy law."[73] Any debt may be subordinated because the creditor is willing to accept additional risk for additional reward or in some cases because the creditor wishes to make a quasi-equity investment. For example, the president of a closely-held corporation may loan money to it, and agree to accept a subordinated obligation, so as to infuse capital without making it harder for the corporation to obtain non-subordinated loans from outsiders. There is even a good deal of publicly traded subordinated debt—often referred to as debentures—which predictably offers a higher rate of interest than ordinary bonds to offset the higher risk of non-payment.

[C]—Equitable Subordination

Long before the enactment of the Bankruptcy Code, the courts recognized that in some cases a claim could be forcibly subordinated because of circumstances that rendered it inappropriate to treat the claim on a par with other unsecured claims. "Equitable subordination," as this forced subordination came to be known, is

---

[71] See Dominic E. Pacitti & Michael J. Herbert, *Down and Out in Richmond, Virginia: The Distribution of Assets in Chapter 7 Bankruptcy Proceedings Closed During 1984-87*, 22 U. Rich. L. Rev. 303 (1988).

[72] For more detailed discussion about claim classification in Chapter 11 reorganization proceedings, see § 17.11[D] of this book.

[73] Bankruptcy Code § 510(a).

expressly recognized in section 510(c). Although rarely sought or granted, the possibility that a claim might be forcibly subordinated to other claims can be a powerful tool in negotiations.

As one might expect when the word "equitable" appears, there is no rigid test for application of this doctrine. Broadly speaking, equitable subordination is a tool used by the courts to change the nominal status for one of two reasons. The first is that the claim is substantively something other than it appears to be; for example, a right named a claim might in economic substance really be an equity interest. The second is punitive; bad behavior by the claimant, nearly always an insider claimant, that injured other claimants may result in the wrongdoer's demotion to a lower priority level. These two reasons are not always separate; in a number of cases the court subordinates in part because of the economic function of the right and in part because the mischaracterization of the right as a claim rather than equity was part of a pattern of misbehavior.

The first situation is easily illustrated. Suppose that Close Corp., a small company with only five shareholders, is set up with an initial capital of $100,000. On the books of the company, $1,000 of that initial capital is listed as common stock and $99,000 as loans made by the shareholders. This is a "highly leveraged" company in which nearly all of its capital comes from loans—it is leveraged at 99:1, that is 99% debt and 1% equity. Assume further that, under the loan agreement between the company and its shareholders, interest on the loan accrues at a "minimum rate" of 10% per annum, but neither interest nor principal need be paid unless the company makes at least $20,000 in profits during a fiscal year. Moreover, if the company makes less than $20,000, interest for the proceeding year is forgiven. If the company makes at least that amount of profit, then the company must pay all accrued interest for the preceding year plus $9,900 in principal. If the company makes more than $50,000 profit in a fiscal year, then it must pay the minimum interest rate (10%) plus a "bonus rate" of 25% additional interest, plus $9,900 in profit. If the company makes more than $100,000 profit, the bonus rate jumps to 55%.

The "loans" made by the shareholders will probably be recast as equity, and subordinated to the claims of outside creditors. The fact that the company is highly leveraged, although a factor in the view of many courts[74] is not necessarily dispositive. Of greatest importance in the example given is that the debt was treated as if it were a stock investment. If the company does poorly, the investors recover little or nothing on their investment. If the company does extraordinarily well, the "lenders" receive an extraordinarily large return (as much as 65%). The usual mark of debt is that the debtor is obligated to pay regardless of financial condition (and, conversely, that if it does better than expected it need only pay an amount set or at least pegged to an external standard such as a prime rate). Equity on the other hand rises or falls with the enterprise.[75]

Equitable subordination is also used to penalize certain creditors, usually but not always insiders, for actions that inappropriately subjected other creditors to undue and unanticipated risks. One commonly used formulation sets out a three part test:

---

[74] See Collier on Bankruptcy ¶ 510.05[4] [a] for a general discussion of the significance of undercapitalization in equitable subordination.

[75] See In re Carolee's Combine, Inc., 3 Bankr. 324 (N.D. Ga. 1980).

(i) The claimant must have engaged in some type of inequitable conduct.

(ii) The misconduct must have resulted in injury to the creditors of the bankruptcy or conferred an unfair advantage on the claimant.

(iii) Equitable subordination must not be inconsistent with the provisions of the Bankruptcy [Code].[76]

According to one commentator, "the courts have generally restricted equitable subordination in the bankruptcy context to three categories of cases:

"(1) those in which a fiduciary of the debtor misuses his position to the disadvantage of other creditors;

(2) those in which a third party in effect, controls the debtor to the disadvantage of others; and

(3) those in which a third party defrauds other creditors."[77]

The concept is somewhat similar to that underlying estoppel and detrimental reliance—the claimant has done something that caused other creditors to act in a way that was damaging to their interests. Outright fraud is the most obvious example.[78] However, the mere fact that insiders have used their power over the debtor to better their position at the expense of outside creditors (e.g., by raising their own salaries while not paying creditors) can be sufficient;[79] so can conduct that inappropriately benefits the creditor at the expense of the debtor (and thus indirectly at the expense of the debtor's creditors).[80]

§ 10.06 Interests

[A]—Introduction

The term "interest" has two primary meanings in the Code. When referring to specific property, the word refers to some form of co-ownership or lien. Thus, a secured creditor has an interest in property of the debtor or property of the estate. This type of interest is discussed throughout this book in the context of the treatment of liens and other divided property interests.

---

[76] Benjamin v. Diamond (In re Mobile Steel Co.), 563 F.2d 692 (5th Cir. 1977); see also Speco, Inc. v. Valley State Bank (In re Sepco, Inc.), 36 Bankr. 279 (D.S.D. 1984), aff'd, United States v. Arlon Industries, Inc., 750 F.2d 51 (8th Cir. 1984).

[77] Steven A. Karg, *A Bankruptcy Trap for the Unwary Creditor: Equitable Subordination Resulting from Excess Creditor Control*, 15 Seton Hall Legis. J. 434, (1991) (footnotes omitted).

[78] See Pepper v. Litton, 308 U.S. 295 (1939).

[79] See In re Lemco Gypsum, Inc., 911 F.2d 1553 (11th Cir. 1990), reh.den., 930 F.2d 925 (11th Cir. 1991).

[80] See In re Aluminum Mills Corp., 132 Bankr. 869 (Bankr. N.D. Ill. 1991).

The other meaning refers to interests in the debtor itself (and thus obviously has meaning only if the debtor is a corporation, partnership, or other artificial entity). Interests of this type—roughly speaking, equity in the debtor—represent ownership not of particular property, but of the value of the entity over and above all claims. This is the residual interest after all debt is paid. If the debtor is insolvent, there is no equity.

In liquidation, interests (in the latter sense of the term) are nearly always ignored, because there is hardly ever any residual value. Even in reorganization, interests in the debtor may be insignificant, because the debtor is still likely to be insolvent. However, in Chapter 11 it is possible for interests to participate in the distribution under the plan, even if claims are not paid in full—so long as the claimants agree to this.[81] Claimants may in fact agree to this as a way of facilitating the implementation of the plan.

[B]—Allowance of interests

The procedure for allowing an interest is virtually identical to the procedure for allowing a claim. Ordinarily, a proof of interest must be filed. If no objection is made, the interest is deemed allowed. Objection can be made by any party in interest, including a creditor of a general partner in a partnership that is a debtor under Chapter 7.[82] As is true with claims, however, there is no requirement that a claim of interest be filed in a Chapter 11 proceeding, so long as the interest is scheduled by the debtor.[83] Neither the Code nor the rules contain any detail concerning the adjudication of a contested interest. This is in contrast to the adjudication of contested claims. The reason for this lack of detail is undoubtedly that interests, which are nearly always worthless, are rarely contested.

[C]—Priority Interests

Just as there can be priority claims, so too there can be priority interests. These priorities, however, are not created by the Bankruptcy Code; rather, they are the result of the contract underlying the interest. The most familiar example of a priority interest is stock with a liquidation preference. For example, ABC Inc. may have issued a class of stock, Preferred Stock A, which has a $100 liquidation preference. This means that, upon liquidation of the company, whether in bankruptcy or out, a payment of up to $100 per share will be paid to the holders of this stock before anything is paid on common stock. Thus, once all debt of every kind is paid, whatever is left will be applied first to this liquidation preference; if there is not enough to pay the full $100 on each share, whatever remains will be distributed pro rata. Of course, as a practical matter it is highly unlikely that liquidation will produce anything for preferred stock.

---

[81] For a discussion of this issue see § 17.15[D] of this book.

[82] Bankruptcy Code § 502(a).

[83] Bankruptcy Code § 1111(a), Bankruptcy Rule 3003(b)(1), (c)(2).

[D]—General Interests

Although not a term of art under the Code, the term "general interests" is useful to describe the "ordinary" equity interest in a company. An obvious example of a general interest is common stock—that is, stock with no liquidation preference. Similarly, the ownership rights of general and limited partners are normally general interests in the debtor. There may be more than one class of general interest; for example, a corporation might issue two types of common stock. One type has voting rights; the other does not. Neither has a liquidation preference. Both rank equally in bankruptcy. Ranking as it does even below preferred interests, general interests are unlikely to receive any distribution except in a successful reorganization.

[E]—Subordinated interests

At the very, very bottom of the Bankruptcy pyramid are subordinated interests—interests that are even lower than typical common stock in a corporation. An interest may be subordinated in either of two ways. First, it may be subordinated by agreement. This agreement may have been entered into when the legal entity was created; it is certainly lawful to create a class of stock that is subordinated to common stock. A subordination agreement may also have been entered into after the stock was initially issued. The Bankruptcy Code makes subordination agreements enforceable to the extent they are enforceable under applicable non-bankruptcy law.[84]

In addition, an interest may be equitably subordinated by the court. Although equitable subordination is usually thought of in context of claims, the statutory provision that recognize equitable subordination applies to interest as well. Section 510(c) states, in part, that, "after notice and [an opportunity for] a hearing, the court may under principles of equitable subordination, subordinate for purposes of distribution . . . all or part of an allowed interest to all or part of another allowed interest."[85] The considerations discussed with equitable subordination of claims would also control for equitable subordination of an interest.[86] However, given the fact that virtually all interests are worthless, the chance that anyone would bother to seek equitable subordination of an interest is only very slightly more than zero.

§ 10.07 Co-Ownership

[A]—Introduction

In a number of cases, the property rights of the estate will co-exist with the property rights of another. In one sense, all secured claims involve co-ownership; the claimant has a property interest (the lien) and the debtor. However, this paragraph is concerned with property rights that are not linked to a claim. For example, the

[84] Bankruptcy Code § 510(a).

[85] Bankruptcy Code § 510(c)(1).

[86] See § 10.05[C] for a discussion of equitable subordination of claims.

debtor may be a joint tenant or a tenant in common of real property.[87] The co-owner in that type of situation has neither a claim against the estate[88] nor an interest in the debtor. Moreover, the co-ownership right is normally not an interest in property of the estate, because, with a limited exception for community property, the co-owner's interest does not become property of the estate.[89] Ideally, a co-owner ought to be left unaffected by the bankruptcy. However, this is sometimes impossible. On occasion, it becomes necessary either to partition the property and sell the debtor's portion or to sell both the interest of the estate and the co-owner. The rules governing this eventuality are contained in § 363 of the Code, and discussed at length in § 9.03[E] of this book.

[B]—Leases

Leases, whether of real property or personal property, have some of the features of liens. Indeed, some personal property transactions that are called leases are, in fact, substantively the credit sale of property subject to a security interest.[90] Those "leases" are not treated as leases at all; rather they are treated as Article 9 security interests and, if they comply with the requirements of Article 9, they will create secured claims.[91]

The true lease, however, is somewhat different, regardless of whether it is a lease of personal or real property. It is a form of divided ownership, but unlike a lien, the interest of the lessor exists for purposes other than insuring payment. At the end of the lease, the property will be returned to the lessor who may re-lease it, sell it, or use it. The assumption of both parties is that the lessor will get the property back, which is what differentiates it from a credit sale. The lease also differs from other forms of joint ownership, such as joint tenancy, because the interest of one owner (the lessee) is limited in time and contingent upon the lessee making rent payments to the lessor.

Insofar as bankruptcy is concerned, the interest of a lessor of real or personal property is dealt with in a manner that recognizes its hybrid character. The lessor has a claim for rent. The lessor also has an interest in property of the estate (the debtor's leasehold interest). Finally, the lessor has a property interest that is not part of the estate. The lessor's right to get the property at the end of the lease term is a right that never belonged to the debtor, and thus does not become part of the estate.

---

[87] I do not discuss tenancy by the entireties at this point, because that form of ownership insulates both the rights of the debtor and the debtor's spouse if the debt incurred by the debtor was not a mutual debt of both.

[88] The term "claims" encompasses right to payment and rights to equitable remedy for breach of performance. In a typical co-ownership case, neither of these would exist. See Bankruptcy Code § 101(5) and § 10.02 of this chapter.

[89] Bankruptcy Code § 541. The limited exception for community property is contained in § 541(a)(2); that exception and all the rules concerning property of the estate are discussed in detail in Chapter 7 of this book.

[90] See U.C.C. § 1-201(37).

[91] See Thomas D. Crandall, Michael J. Herbert, and Lary Lawrence, Uniform Commercial Code §§ 2.2.8, 9.3.3 and 23.5 (1993).

The complexity of lease rights has generated difficult and complex rules. The most important of these are contained in § 365 of the Code, and are discussed in depth in § 9.05 of this book.

§ 10.08 Anomalous Rights

On occasion, it is extremely difficult to classify a particular right as a claim or an interest. As the discussion in the previous sections suggest, debt and equity are not two different species. They are simply shorthand ways of defining rights, and they exist on a continuum from the purest type of debt (a precisely defined right not in any way conditioned on the obligor's financial status) to the purest form of equity (a variable right wholly conditioned on the obligor's financial condition). A right to collect $10,000 whether or not the debtor can pay is clearly a claim. A right to participate in the obligor's profits, whatever they are and if there are any at all, is clearly an interest. What about a right to collect $10,000, subject to a one-year postponement of the due date if the debtor is insolvent? Or a right to collect $10,000 which can at any time be converted into common stock? Or common stock that can at any time be converted into debt at the rate of $100 per share tendered?

As a general principle, the classification of anomalous rights is done functionally. If a particular right has the substance of equity, it will be treated as equity.[92] However, this is sometimes entangled in the court's analysis of the propriety of the action that created the right. If it appears to the court that a particular right has odd features because it was used to cheat other claimants, the court is likely to treat the right as one subordinate to those claimants.

§ 10.09 Setoff

As noted in Chapter 2, the right to offset one mutual debt against another is well established in the law.[93] This right has received broad protection in bankruptcy since the Act of 1800. The Bankruptcy Code only slightly restricted setoff rights from what had previously been allowed.

Broadly speaking, a right of setoff is treated by the Bankruptcy Code as if it were a secured claim. Like a secured claim, the right of setoff is treated as a property interest, entitling the claimant to both payment and adequate protection; like a secured claim, exercise of the rights created by the law of setoff are subject to the automatic stay.

Section 553 largely codifies the right of setoff in bankruptcy, although it must be read in conjunction with the provisions on the automatic stay. Subsection (a) begins with the broad statement that "except as otherwise provided" in sections 553, 362, and 363, the Code "does not affect any right of a creditor to offset a mutual

---

[92] See § 10.05[C] for a discussion of this in the context of equitable subordination of claims.

[93] See § 2.06.

debt . . .that arose before the commencement of the case."[94] Then follow the exceptions.

One exception, or rather limitation, is implicit in the opening language. The debt must be one that can be offset under the common law; this is contained in the term "mutual debt." As is true with liens, the Code does not create any right of offset; it merely gives effect to a right otherwise created. The right to setoff depends upon there being an appropriate relationship between the debts; this is discussed in Chapter 2.[95]

The first real exception to the rule preserving setoff rights is that the creditor's claim against the debtor not be disallowed; a disallowed claim may not be set off.[96] This is to prevent a creditor who does not have a claim cognizable in bankruptcy from effectively reviving that claim as a right of setoff. There is one limitation on this: if the claim was disallowed under section 502(b)(3) (a claim for taxes assessed against property to the extent that it exceeds the value of the property assessed for those taxes) the claim may still create a right of setoff recognized in bankruptcy. For example, suppose that $10,000 of taxes are assessed against property worth only $8,000. The tax claim is disallowed to the extent that it exceeds the property's value (that is, $2,000). Suppose further, however, that the government imposing the tax owes the debtor $12,000. The government's right to setoff the taxes against the debt is unimpaired; although the government has only an $8,000 tax claim, it has a $10,000 right of setoff.

The second exception to the preservation of setoff rights deals with transferred claims, and is a kind of quasi-preference provision. If the creditor's claim against the debtor was transferred to the creditor, by someone other than the debtor, either

(1) post-petition or

(2) during the 90 days prior to the petition, and while the debtor was insolvent,

the setoff right is effectively voided.[97] For example, suppose that on June 1, Chang owed Danuta $20,000 while Danuta owed Taissa $15,000. On August 1, Chang purchased Taissa's claim against Danuta; thus on that date, Chang owed Danuta $20,000 and Danuta owed Chang $15,000. Further assume that Danuta was insolvent at the time. On October 1, Danuta filed bankruptcy. Ordinarily, Chang would have a right to offset the two debts, leaving a net obligation of $5,000 owing to Danuta. However, since Chang obtained the offsetting debt within the 90 days before Danuta's filing, and because Danuta was insolvent at the time, Chang does not have

[94] Bankruptcy Code § 553(a).

[95] See § 2.06.

[96] Bankruptcy Code § 553(a)(1). Note that the technical requirement is that the claim not be disallowed, rather than it actually be allowed. In re Davidovich, 901 F.2d 1533 (10th Cir. 1990).

[97] Bankruptcy Code § 553(a)(2) Note that the debtor is presumed to have been insolvent during the 90 day period. Bankruptcy Code § 553(c). This presumption may be rebutted by the creditor asserting the right of setoff.

a right of setoff. Chang still has a $15,000 claim against Danuta, but this claim is merely a general unsecured claim. The purpose of this provision is to prohibit trafficking in setoff rights. Whether this trafficking is truly offensive or not is debateable. In some cases, the mere fact that a claim has been transferred from one creditor to another has no real impact on other creditors. For example, suppose that Alice has a claim against Danuta for $10,000, which offsets Danuta's claim against Alice for $15,000. Alice sells this claim to Bert, who can then offset it against Danuta's claim against it for $17,000. Alice has lost a $10,000 offset right; Bert has gained it. The effect on other creditors is zero; both before and after the transfer, the offset reduced the assets available to them by exactly the same amount, $10,000. Where a true preference is concerned, this type of situation generally leads the courts to say that the transfer is not avoidable because it has not diminished the estate.[98] However, there is no similar rule under section 553(a)(2); the setoff right is voided without regard to whether creditors were injured by the transfer.

Section 553(a)(3) is similar, but it deals with the debt owed to the debtor rather than the claim against the debtor. If the debt owed to the debtor was incurred within 90 days before the filing, while the debtor was insolvent, for the purpose of obtaining a right of setoff, the creditor will not have that right in bankruptcy.[99] For example, suppose that on June 1, Danuta owes $20,000 to River Bank. On July 1 River Bank requires Danuta to deposit $20,000 in its account at River Bank, and to keep that money in the account as a condition of the loan. That deposit is often referred to as an offsetting balance—it is required as a method of ensuring payment. A bank "deposit" is in fact a debt of the bank to the depositor—it thus creates a debt that can be set off against the debt owed by the depositor to the bank. Assuming that Danuta was insolvent on July 1, and filed bankruptcy within 90 days, River Bank will have no right of setoff in Danuta's bankruptcy. This provision is more justifiable than section 553(a)(2), because it fits more neatly into the concerns underlying preference law. The setoff in these circumstances is really no different from a security interest; River Bank is forcing Danuta to make the deposit for exactly the same reasons, and with exactly the same effect, as if it had forced Danuta to give it a security interest in $20,000 worth of equipment.

Finally, section 553(b) also creates an exception for a right of setoff exercised pre-petition. It is a "true" preference rule. For this reason, it is discussed in the chapter on preferences.[100]

---

[98] See § 14.03 [J] of this book regarding the general preference treatment of this type of transaction. There are of course situations in which other creditors will be worse off. For example, suppose that in the hypothetical Alice had both a $10,000 right of setoff and a perfected security interest in $10,000 of Danuta's property. Danuta's debt to Alice would be paid in full regardless of whether Alice had a right of setoff. Thus, Alice's transfer of its setoff right to Bert would effectively diminish the assets available to other creditors, because Bert would also be paid in full. In that situation, it is easy to see why Bert should not have a right of setoff.

[99] Bankruptcy Code § 553(a)(3). Note that the debtor is presumed to have been insolvent during the 90 day period. Bankruptcy Code § 553(c). This presumption may be rebutted by the creditor asserting the right of setoff.

[100] See § 14.06 of this book.

As indicated, the right of setoff exists independently of the exercise of the right. The former generally survives the filing of the petition and is entitled to adequate protection. The latter, however, is blocked by the automatic stay. If there were any doubt about this, it is resolved by section 362(a)(7) which explicitly extends the stay to "the setoff of any debt owing to the debtor that arose before the commencement of the case . . . against any claim against the debtor."[101] To exercise its right, the creditor must obtain an order from the court lifting or modifying the stay.[102]

The creditor with a setoff right is, however, entitled to adequate protection, however. This means that the value of the setoff must be protected, just like the value of a secured claim. That protection can be provided by cash payments, by a substitute right (such as a lien on other property) or by any other "indubitable equivalent."[103]

---

[101] Bankruptcy Code § 362(a)(7).

[102] For a detailed discussion about this, see § 8.06 of this book.

[103] See § 8.06[B][2] for a detailed discussion of adequate protection.

CHAPTER 11

Exemptions and Redemption

§ 11.01 Introduction

In this chapter, we take a look at two sets of rules that allow the debtor to retrieve some assets from the estate. Some property is "exempt," meaning that it is not subject to seizure by unsecured creditors, and is thus not liquidated by the trustee. Other property is subject to "redemption," meaning that the debtor has the right to purchase it for a lump sum from lienholders.

Both of these are but parts of a larger picture. From the debtor's standpoint, a key issue in bankruptcy is retaining as much property as possible. Exemption laws help. Redemption laws are occasionally useful (but only if the debtor has some immediate source of funds, because redemption requires a single payment in full.) There are other strategies, however.

Insofar as the Bankruptcy Code is concerned, the chief alternative strategy is reorganization. Indeed, the most significant difference between bankruptcy reorganization and bankruptcy liquidation is that in reorganization the debtor is usually able to keep more assets (at the cost of making payments out of future income). Thus, a debtor who wishes to retain more property than the exemptions allow might be attracted to Chapter 11, 12, or 13.

There are also what amount to quasi-reorganization strategies. Even in a Chapter 7 proceeding, particular debts can be reorganized rather than liquidated. One method of doing this is reaffirmation of a partially secured obligation. In exchange for a binding promise by the debtor to pay the entire debt despite the discharge, the secured creditor may allow the debtor to keep the encumbered property and pay the debt over time (rather than in a lump sum as redemption requires). The mechanics of reaffirmation, and the strict procedural rules that must be followed, are discussed in Chapter 12.[1]

In addition, there are many situations in which debtor and creditor merely enter into an informal arrangement regarding encumbered property. There is no requirement that there be a formal reaffirmation agreement; and sometimes there is no express agreement at all. In many cases, the debtor merely continues to make payments and the creditor refrains from foreclosing on its lien. There is anecdotal evidence that arrangements of this type may be used far more frequently than any or perhaps all of the formal methods of protecting non-exempt property.

Finally, it must be emphasized that there may well be two parties with whom the debtor must come to terms if it wishes to retain property. If the value of the property exceeds both the exemption, if any, and the amount of any lien, the debtor must deal with both the lien holder and the trustee. In effect, property of this type has

[1] See § 12.09.

three owners—the debtor, through his or her exemption, the creditor, through its lien, and the trustee, as administrator of the estate's property. The debtor must acquire all three interests to become the sole owner of the property.

§ 11.02 Background

Exemptions have been an integral part of debtor creditor law for centuries. The underlying policy is simple. It is generally accepted that, no matter how bad an individual's financial troubles, he or she should not be utterly deprived of the basic necessities of life. For this reason, creditors have long been prohibited from seizing such things as clothing, cooking and eating utensils, beds and other basic furnishings. It is also generally true that items of great sentimental but (usually) little monetary value, such as family Bibles and wedding rings, have been exempted. For many years, there was little amendment of exemption laws, so that many of them preserved in legal amber a picture of 19th century rural American life—exempting a cow, a couple of pigs, a spinning wheel, and the like. In recent years, most states have updated their exemption laws to reflect more usefully the necessities of life in an urban industrial society.

In this country, exemption law has traditionally been the province of state governments. Although most states have roughly similar exemption rules, there are some that stand out as notably pro-creditor or pro-debtor. Florida and Texas are often pointed to by critics as virtual havens for deadbeats, permitting some debtors to exempt literally millions of dollars' worth of property. In most states, however, exemptions are relatively modest.

There has been much debate over whether exemption levels matter very much. Theoretically, generous exemptions should encourage bankruptcy, because they permit a debtor to discharge debt "cheaply;" that is, without the surrender of much property. However, there is surprisingly little evidence to support that contention; to the contrary, the evidence indicates that exemption levels have little or no impact on the frequency of bankruptcy.[2] This does not mean that there are no bankruptcies in which the debtor exploits generous exemptions; merely that the number of such bankruptcies is so small as to be statistically invisible.

There are two plausible explanations for this. The first is that there are other factors involved in the decision to file bankruptcy, and these factors make bankruptcy undesirable for persons with substantial unencumbered assets. Those factors may include, at least, whatever residual stigma attaches to bankruptcy as well as the damage bankruptcy does to one's later ability to obtain credit. The second is the ease with which creditors can obtain property as collateral. With limited exceptions, exemptions do not affect liens; encumbered property goes to creditors even if it is exempt. Thus, generous exemptions are of assistance only to those who have substantial debts and substantial unencumbered exempt assets. Lenders are generally chary of loaning large sums without collateral; generous exemption laws make them more so, because they cannot rely on being able to seize property after

---

[2] See § 1.02[C] of this book for a further discussion of this issue.

a judgment is rendered. Thus, the main effect of generous exemption laws may simply be to give creditors yet another incentive to get collateral.

Since the 1898 Act, federal bankruptcy law has largely left exemptions to individual states. The Bankruptcy Act borrowed the applicable state rules to determine what the debtor could retain against the trustee. This had the advantage of transparency to state law (and thus limited forum shopping between state and federal courts). It had the disadvantage of limiting national uniformity, since exemptions differed from state to state. It also had the effect of preserving exemption rules that were increasingly obsolete; until recently, few states had amended their rules to take account of the vast 20th-Century migration of Americans from farms with mules to suburban tract houses with garages.

The drafters of the Bankruptcy Code were concerned that state exemption laws were too varied, too out of date, and too limited. There was some support for federalizing exemption law entirely; but this was considered politically impossible. A compromise was ultimately reached; the Bankruptcy Code contains a set of federal exemptions, but authorizes individual states to "opt out," limiting their residents to state exemptions. Somewhat to the dismay of the supporters of federal exemptions, the great majority of states have opted out.[3] Exemption law thus remains largely a state preserve.

In the opt-out states, debtors may only use the state exemptions (plus the so-called alternative federal exemptions, discussed below). In the states that have not opted out, each debtor may choose either the state or the federal exemptions. The choice is all or nothing; a debtor may not "mix and match" exemptions, choosing the most favorable state and the most favorable federal rules.[4] Moreover, if the case is a joint husband-and-wife bankruptcy, both must choose the same set of exemptions; if they cannot agree, then both will be "deemed" to have chosen the federal exemptions.[5]

The federal exemptions have had an impact even in many of the opt-out states. During the 1980's, many states updated their own exemptions, often using parts of the federal exemptions as a model. Thus, although the goals of the exemption federalizers were not achieved, exemptions today are at least somewhat more modern, and perhaps a bit more uniform, than they were prior to the Code.

Moreover, it is important to stress that the opt-out affects only the list of exempt property. It does not affect other provisions of section 522. For example, even in an opt-out state the Bankruptcy Code rules avoiding certain liens on exempt property still apply.[6] In addition, it may be possible to double the effective amount of state exemptions. Under section 522(m), each individual debtor in a joint case is entitled to exemptions. For example, suppose that Bob and Carol, who are married, file a joint Chapter 7. Under state law, $5,000 of their homestead is exempt. In a state

[3] At last count, thirty-five states have opted out. Collier on Bankruptcy ¶ 522.02 n. 4a.

[4] See Collier on Bankruptcy ¶ 522.02.

[5] Bankruptcy Code § 522(b). This provision was added by BAFJA to curb the then-existing practice of "stacking" exemptions—that is, each spouse choosing a different set to get the largest overall number and value of exemptions.

[6] See § 11.09 of this chapter for a discussion of lien avoidance.

law proceeding, only one exemption could be claimed, even though both Bob and Carol are defendants. However, some but not all courts have held that in a bankruptcy proceeding each may exempt $5,000 assuming that each contributed to the maintenance of the home; this effectively doubles the exemption to $10,000.[7]

§ 11.03 State Exemptions

As noted in Chapter 2, state exemptions vary significantly, and in some cases substantially, from state to state. This has led to occasional argument, to date always rejected, that incorporation of state exemptions violates the Constitutional requirement that Bankruptcy laws be uniform nationwide.[8] These differences do create some problems with regard to forum shopping—that is, debtors choosing the state in which to go bankrupt. This problem is somewhat alleviated by a combination of the venue rules, which require the debtor to file in the district in which the debtor has been located for the preceding 180 days,[9] and section 522(b)(2)(A) which permits the debtor to elect the state exemptions applicable "at the place in which the debtor's domicile has been located for the 180 days immediately preceding the date of the filing . . .or for a longer portion of such 180 day period than in any other place."[10] Although forum shopping is much discussed, there appear to be only a few cases in which an individual debtor clearly moved from one state to another to enjoy greater exemptions.[11] This no doubt is in large part because only a few debtors are able to use the exemptions they already have.[12]

State exemptions are usually divided into two categories, the homestead exemption and the specific exemptions. In Chapter 2, typical state exemptions are described.[13] Because of their variety, they are not further discussed in this Chapter, which instead uses the federal exemptions as a model.

---

[7] See John T. Mather Memorial Hospital v. Pearl, 723 F.2d 193 (2d Cir. 1983), Cheeseman v. Nachman (In re Cheeseman), 656 F.2d 60 (4th Cir. 1981). For the contrary view, see In re Talmadge, 832 F.2d 1120 (9th Cir. 1987), and First National Bank v. Norris, 701 F.2d 902 (11th Cir. 1983).

[8] See Hanover National Bank v. Moyses, 186 U.S. 181 (1902); In re Sullivan, 680 F.2d 1131 (7th Cir. 1982), cert. denied, 459 U.S. 992 (1982).

[9] See § 6.04 of this book regarding the venue requirements.

[10] Bankruptcy Code § 522(b)(2)(A).

[11] Note, however, that there is evidence that large, publically held companies engage frequently in forum shopping; however, since they do not enjoy exemptions, this is for other reasons, including the court's amenability to extending the period during which the debtor alone may propose a Chapter 11 reorganization plan and to the payment of large attorney's fees. See Lynn M. LoPucki & William C. Shifford, *Venue Choice and Forum Shopping in the Bankruptcy Reorganization of Large, Publicly Held Companies*, 1991 Wis. L. Rev. 11.

[12] Michael J. Herbert & Domenic E. Pacitti, *Down and Out in Richmond, Virginia: The Distribution of Assets in Chapter 7 Bankruptcy Proceedings Closed During 1984-1987*, 22 U. Rich. L. Rev. 303, 318-19 (1988)

[13] See § 2.09 of this book.

§ 11.04 Alternative Federal Exemptions

Although most discussion of exemptions concentrates on the state vs. federal exemption distinction, there are actually three potential groups of exemptions available to the debtor. Bankruptcy Code § 522(b)(2) also permits a debtor to exempt property that is protected under non-bankruptcy Federal law.[14] This is an alternative to the Code's federal exemptions but not the state exemptions; indeed, the alternative federal exemptions are elected in conjunction with state exemptions; and, unlike the Code's federal exemptions, states are not empowered to "opt out." Any person who chooses the state exemptions or who is limited to the state exemptions is also entitled to the alternative federal exemptions. Most of these alternative federal exemptions involve retirement and death benefits.[15] Since many of these exemptions also appear in the state exemptions anyway.[16] this provision is of relatively little significance.

§ 11.05 Tenancy by Entireties

Another group of state laws indirectly affect the rights of creditors to seize property. These are the rules that, in many states, protect property held as tenants by the entireties and (in some cases) by joint tenancy. Broadly speaking, certain forms of joint property ownership function as exemptions insofar as creditors are concerned. The most common example is tenancy by the entireties. A tenancy by the entireties (which is a form of joint ownership available only to a married couple) is an interest that cannot be transferred or encumbered (whether voluntarily or involuntarily) by the unilateral action of one spouse. A deed or mortgage executed solely by the husband or the wife has no effect. Similarly, if a judgment is rendered on a debt incurred solely by the wife, no judicial lien arising from that judgment can attach to the property. The property can be transferred or encumbered by both spouses acting jointly; it can also be subject to a judicial lien arising from a jointly incurred obligation. For example, suppose that Homer and Marge own their home as tenants by the entireties. If Homer mortgages the property to Burns Bank, that mortgage is unenforceable. If Marge incurs an individual credit card debt, then a judgment lien based on that debt cannot be imposed on the home. Only by acting jointly in incurring an obligation can Homer and Marge subject the property to any voluntary or involuntary lien.[17]

In the bankruptcy context, this means that only joint creditors have any rights in the home. If there are no joint creditors, then Homer and Marge may keep the property—all of the property, not just the homestead exemption. Thus, their mode of ownership acts as if it were an exemption, insofar as individual debts are

[14] Bankruptcy Code § 522(b)(2)(A).

[15] For a partial list, see Collier on Bankruptcy ¶ 522.02.

[16] And, for that matter, the federal exemptions.

[17] See generally, Roger A. Cunningham, William B. Stoebuck & Dale A. Whitman, The Law of Property 205-06 (2d Ed. 1993). Note that these rules do not apply in all states. Note as well that, although tenency by the entireties originated as an estate in land, it is generally true today that personal property may also be owned as entireties property. Id. at 208.

concerned. Note, however, that the property is subject to their joint obligations. If both signed the mortgage, or if both are liable on the credit card, then they can only protect it against those creditors to the extent of their ordinary homestead and wildcard exemptions.[18]

§ 11.06 Federal Exemptions—§ 522(d)

In the minority of states that have not opted out, the individual debtor is free to choose the federal exemptions rather than the state exemptions. The attractiveness of the federal exemptions diminished over time, largely because many of the exemptions were subject to "caps" that did not increase with inflation. Exemptions that to many creditors seemed absurdly generous in 1978 were, by 1994, on the stingy side. Because of this the 1994 Amendments made two important changes. First, the existing caps were doubled. Second, the caps are now subject to an escalator clause, under which they will be adjusted upward every three years in accordance with the increase in the Consumer Price Index.[19] This discussion uses the new caps created by the 1994 Amendments. In consequence, they are twice as large as the caps referred to in the existing case law.

The structure of the federal exemptions is similar to that of most state exemptions; there is a "homestead" exemption (which, despite its name, does not have to be used to protect the debtor's home), a "wildcard" exemption that may be used for anything, and a variety of specific exemptions that may be used only for specific types of property. The homestead, wildcard, and some of the specific exemptions have dollar caps. A few of the specific exemptions have no cap. As is true with all exemption schemes, the Bankruptcy Code's represents an attempt to preserve from creditors the minimum basics of life.

[A]—Homestead Exemption

The Code's homestead exemption is now $15,000.[20] The debtor may exempt up to that amount of its equity in qualifying property. Various kinds of residential property qualify; they are:

1. Real property that the debtor or a dependant of the debtor uses as a residence,

2. Personal property that the debtor or a dependant of the debtor uses as residence (for example, a mobile home),

3. An interest in a cooperative that the debtor or a dependant of the debtor uses as a residence,

4. A burial plot for the debtor or a dependant of the debtor. (There is no requirement that the burial plot be currently used as a residence.)[21]

---

[18] Id. at 206-07.

[19] Bankruptcy Reform Act of 1994, Pub. Law 103-394, § 108(d),(e).

[20] Bankruptcy Code § 522(d)(1) (1994 Amendments).

[21] Bankruptcy Code § 522(d)(1).

The debtor is not required to use the homestead exemption for a homestead, nor is the value of the exemption entirely lost if the debtor has no homestead. In this respect the Code differs from many state exemption laws; traditionally the state required (i) that there be a homestead; (ii) that the person claiming the homestead be the head of a family (in the traditional sense of the term); and (iii) that the exemption be used only for the homestead. Not so under the Bankruptcy Code. The debtor may use up to $7,500 of the homestead exemption as a "wildcard;" that is, to exempt any unencumbered property whatsoever.[22] For example, suppose that Dora chooses to apply only $7,500 of her homestead exemption to her home. She may then use the remaining $7,500 to keep her collection of signed first editions of Matthew Bender's "Understanding" series.

Note that the homestead exemption does not give the debtor any guarantee of keeping the home. Indeed, in most cases, it will not. The debtor must still deal with the mortgage debt, if any, and must also purchase any excess equity above the exemption. That excess equity "belongs" to the trustee.

For example, suppose that the debtor's home is worth $100,000. It is subject to a $75,000 mortgage. There is thus $25,000 equity in the house. The debtor may exempt only up to $15,000 of that equity.

The debtor must make some deal with the mortgage holder, so that it will not foreclose. This could be done through refinancing or redemption; it might also be done by reaffirmation or simply by informal, out-of-bankruptcy agreement. The debtor must also acquire the $10,000 in equity over and above the exemption. That excess is part of the property available to the debtor's unsecured creditors. If the debtor can raise the money, the debtor may be able to "purchase" this excess equity from the trustee. Anecdotal evidence indicates that trustees are generally willing to sell the excess to the debtor, so long as the debtor is willing to pay the full value of that excess; but if the excess is large, it may be impossible for the debtor to raise enough money to purchase it.

[B]—Wildcard Exemption

The debtor is given a wildcard exemption in the amount of at least $800; this amount may be increased to as much as $8,300, since up to $7,500 of the homestead exemption may be shifted to the wildcard.[23] As the name indicates, the wildcard may be used for anything. The debtor may use it to increase the cap on any of the specific exemptions, or may use it to keep property that is otherwise not exempted at all.[24] Thus, for example, a debtor who wishes to keep his collection of Mickey Mantle baseball cards may use this exemption to do so.

[C]—Specific Exemptions

In addition to the homestead and wildcard exemptions, there are a number of specific exemptions. These exemptions protect particular kinds of property. Like the

---

[22] Bankruptcy Code § 522(d)(5).

[23] Bankruptcy Code § 522(d)(5).

[24] See In re Smith, 640 F.2d 888 (7th Cir. 1981).

homestead exemption, many of these have caps; the debtor may or may not be able to keep the property. The exemption is not of an object, but of an object up to a stated value. If the property is worth more than the cap, and the debtor cannot raise the money to buy the excess, the property will be sold and the debtor will only receive that portion of the sales proceeds that equals the amount of the exemption. These specific exemptions are as follows:

1. Motor Vehicle. Section 522(d)(2) provides a specific exemption of up to $2,400 in value for one motor vehicle.[25] Suppose that the debtor owns a car worth $8,000, subject to a security interest securing $3,500. The debtor may exempt $2,400 of the equity. To keep the car, the debtor must in addition make a deal with the secured creditor and purchase the remaining $2,100 value from the trustee.

This provision draws no distinction based on the use of the vehicle; thus it covers both vehicles used for personal purposes and vehicles used for business purposes. In the latter case, the vehicle might also qualify as a "tool of the trade" and thus be eligible for both the $2,400 vehicle exemption and the $1,500 tools of the trade exemption discussed below.

2. Consumer Goods. Section 522(d)(3) exempts "household furnishings, household goods, wearing apparel, appliances, books, animals, crops, or musical instruments" if these are held primarily for the personal, family, or household use of the debtor or a dependent of the debtor.[26] This exemption is subject to two caps. There is a $400 cap for any particular item, and an $8,000 aggregate cap. Thus, the debtor may exempt only $400 of the value of a $1,000 refrigerator. Similarly, if the debtor has 22 items of furniture, each worth exactly $400 dollars, the debtor may only keep 20 of them under this exemption.

3. Jewelry. Under section 522(d)(4), the debtor may exempt up to $1,000 worth of jewelry held primarily for the personal, family or household use of the debtor or a dependent.[27] Note that jewelry could also qualify as wearing apparel under the previous exemption; the reason for creating the separate exemption was to permit a debtor to keep a more valuable piece of jewelry; section (d)(4), unlike section (d)(3) does not impose a $400 cap on individual items but only the $1,000 aggregate cap.

4. Wildcard. Section 522(d)(5) is the wildcard exemption, discussed above. Remember that the wildcard may be applied to anything; thus, it can be used to exempt property that would otherwise have to be sold or purchased by the debtor because of a cap.

5. Tools of the Trade. Section 522(d)(6) gives the debtor a $1,500 exemption for "implements, professional books, or tools, of the trade."[28] These "tools of the trade" may be exempted if they are used either by the debtor or by a dependent of the debtor. The key issue that arises (apart from valuation) is the use to which the goods

[25] Bankruptcy Code § 522(d)(2).

[26] Bankruptcy Code § 522(d)(3).

[27] Bankruptcy Code § 522(d)(4).

[28] Bankruptcy Code § 522(d)(6).

are actually put by the debtor. It is not unusual for a debtor to have dual use property. A good example is a home computer used both to write books about bankruptcy and play computer games. The court should focus on the primary use of the debtor at the time the petition is filed.[29]

6. Unmatured Life Insurance Contracts. There is in section 522(d)(7) an uncapped exemption for any unmatured life insurance contract owned by the debtor, except for a credit life insurance contract.[30] This exemption applies to the contract itself, and not to any related rights such as the right to borrow the loan value of the contract (a matter dealt with in the next exemption).

7. Cash Values of Life Insurance Contracts. Section 522(d)(8) creates a capped exemption for the debtors interest in any accrued dividend under, accrued interest under, or loan value of certain unmatured life insurance contracts. To be covered the contract must be owned by the debtor; in addition the insured must be either:

> The debtor, or
>
> A person of whom the debtor is a dependant (for example, a parent who is providing the debtor's support and maintenance).[31]

Note that this exemption does not cover an insurance policy under which a dependent of the debtor is the insured. Note too that, unlike the section (d)(7) exemption, there is no exclusion of credit life contracts—a minor point, however, since credit life contracts are ordinarily "term life" contracts which have no dividends, interest, or loan value.

The exemption is capped at $8,000.[32] This cap may be reduced if the insurance company has been required under the policy to apply part of the loan value to make premium payments post-petition.[33] For example, if the policy has a loan value of $10,000, and the insurance company was required to draw on that loan value to pay a post-petition $400 premium that the debtor failed to pay, the debtor may only exempt $7,600 of the loan value, not $8,000.

8. Health Aids. In section 522(d)(9) there is an uncapped exemption for professionally prescribed health aids for the debtor or a dependant.[34] The key to this exemption is the requirement that there be a professional prescription. Certain health aids—such as a specially designed bed or a "hearing enhancer"—might be purchased with or without doctor's orders. Only in the former case is the health aid exempt under this subsection (of course, it might be otherwise exempt under section 522(d)(3) as a household furnishing).

9. Earnings Substitutes. Section 522(d)(10) is of great importance to many debtors. It exempts the debtor's right to receive a variety of earnings substitutes, including such things as:

---

[29] See In re Currie, 34 Bankr. 745 (Bankr. Kan. 1983).

[30] Bankruptcy Code § 522(d)(7).

[31] Bankruptcy Code § 522(d)(8).

[32] Bankruptcy Code § 522(d)(8).

[33] Bankruptcy Code § 522(d)(8); see also Bankruptcy Code § 542(d).

[34] Bankruptcy Code § 522(d)(9).

A. Social security benefits,

B. Unemployment compensation,

C. Local public assistance benefits,

D. Veterans' benefits

E. Disability, illness, or unemployment benefits provided by an employer,

F. Alimony, support, or maintenance, to the extent reasonably necessary for the support of the debtor and the debtor's dependents,

G. In most cases, payments under a pension or profit sharing plan provided by an employer, to the extent reasonably necessary for the support of the debtor and the debtor's defendants .[35]

Note that there is no cap at all on most of these benefits, and no absolute dollar cap on any of them. The basic rationale for all of these exemptions is twofold. First, they are all forms of post-petition income, and are thus the financial underpinning of the debtor's fresh start. Second, in most cases they represent the only income available to the debtor, who would otherwise be reduced to utter destitution. Many debtors who have property that qualifies for this exemption are too old, too ill, or too injured to earn wages. If the bankruptcy proceeding absorbed this source of income, some debtors would literally starve to death.

10. Compensation for Losses. Similar reasoning to that discussed regarding earnings substitutes underlies the exemption in section 522(d)(11), which encompasses varies forms of compensation for actual loss. The debtor may exempt its right to receive:

1. An award under a crime victim's reparation law;

2. Payment based on the wrongful death of a person of whom the debtor was a dependent, to the extent reasonably necessary for the support of the debtor and the debtor's dependents;

3. Payment of benefits under a life insurance contract that insured an individual of whom the debtor was a dependent, to the extent reasonably necessary for the support of the debtor and the debtor's dependents;

4. Payment, not to exceed $15,000, on account of personal bodily injury suffered by the debtor or an individual of whom the debtor is a dependant (Note that this part of the exemption does not cover an award for either pain and suffering or actual pecuniary loss. It is designed to cover the loss directly caused by the injury itself (for example, the loss of a leg), not the secondary costs (such as medical expenses). The medical expenses recovered will thus be included in that part of the estate distributed to creditors (including, no doubt, the doctor and hospital that are owed those expenses);

5. Payment compensating for lost future earnings of the debtor or an individual of whom the debtor is a dependent, to the extent reasonably necessary for the support of the debtor and the debtor's dependents.[36]

---

[35] Bankruptcy Code § 522(d)(10).

[36] Bankruptcy Code § 522(d)(11).

This cluster of exemptions is, like the (d)(10) cluster, designed to protect a source of funds that is in most cases the only source that the debtor has.

§ 11.07 Loss of Exemptions

[A]—Waiver of Exemptions

Under the old Bankruptcy Act, and in many states today, the benefit of the exemption laws can be waived by agreement. This is not true now in bankruptcy. Section 522(e) makes unenforceable any exemption waiver executed in favor of a creditor who holds an unsecured claim.[37] Moreover, a wavier of the debtor's power to avoid certain liens on exempt property is also unenforceable.[38] This implicitly validates waivers regarding other secured claims; but the fact that secured claims, unless avoidable, always have priority over exemptions makes such a wavier meaningless.

The purpose for this provision was pure consumer protection. Congress was concerned that many exemption waivers were made without full understanding of the consequences. This provision is also in line with other state and federal enactments restricting or prohibiting exemption waivers.[39]

Note, however, that there is another way in which liens can be at least implicitly waived—failure to take the necessary action to claim an exemption. Section 522(l) requires the debtor to list assets claimed as exempt; if the debtor fails to do so, a dependant of the debtor may file the list.[40] If no one ever files the list, the exemptions may be lost.[41]

[B]—Liens on Exempt Property

In most cases, a voluntary lien (such as a mortgage or a security interest) on otherwise exempt property destroys the effect of the exemption. An exemption is valid against the claims of unsecured creditors seeking judicial liens—not against the claims of creditors to whom the debtor has agreed to give a property interest.[42] Thus, if the debtor owns a home worth $75,000, and it is subject to a mortgage securing $100,000, the debtor may not claim the homestead exemption. Similarly, if the debtor has a car worth $4,000 subject to a security interest securing $5,000, the debtor cannot exempt the car. This rule is often expressed as follows: exemptions may only be claimed in the debtor's equity in property.

---

[37] Bankruptcy Code § 522(e).

[38] Bankruptcy Code § 522(e); for a discussion of the power to avoid certain liens on exempt property, see § 11.09 of this chapter.

[39] See, for example, Federal Trade Commission Unfair Credit Practices Regulations 16 C.F.R. § 444.2(a)(2) (1994).

[40] Bankruptcy Code § 522(l).

[41] This appears to be rather a remote contingency, however, since even if the debtor misses the deadline for listing exemptions, amendments are rather freely allowed. See Collier on Bankruptcy ¶ 522.26.

[42] See § 2.09 of this book.

There are exceptions to this. The Code provides that some (but by no means all) voluntary liens on some exempt property are avoidable, permitting the debtor to claim exemptions in spite of the fact that the property was used as collateral.[43] A fair number of states have followed suit in their own exemption laws.[44]

[C]—Misconduct and Miscellaneous

The debtor may be deprived of the benefit of exemptions because of fraud or similar misconduct in the proceeding. The power of the Court to strip the debtor of exemptions may arise from any of several sources. First and most obvious, exemptions created by state law are subject to state law restrictions (except where those restrictions are superseded by the Code). Thus, if the debtor's misconduct would deprive it of the exemption under state statutory or case law, the same result ordinarily will apply in bankruptcy.[45]

Second, under section 522(g), the debtor's ability to exempt property recovered by the trustee from a third party is limited. The debtor may not exempt that property unless:

1. The transfer was involuntary and the debtor did not conceal the property or

2. The debtor could have avoided the transfer under the rules regarding avoidance of non-purchase-money security interests in household property, tools of the trade, and health aids.[46]

Thus, as a general rule, voluntarily transferred property recovered by the trustee under rules such as those that avoid preferences or fraudulent transfers may not be exempted by the debtor. Section 522(g) does not require a showing of fraud or other specific misconduct; rather, it requires only a showing that the avoided transfer was made voluntarily. However, this provision is grouped with those directly involving misconduct because its purpose is partially prophylactic; some of the time the debtor will have been engaged in misconduct when the property was transferred.

A third potential problem arises if the debtor converted many of its non-exempt assets to exempt assets just before bankruptcy. There is no per se prohibition on this so-called "exemption planning;[47] indeed, there is no statutory provision that directly

---

[43] See § 11.09 of this chapter.

[44] See, for example, Va. Code Ann § 34-28 (1990 Repl. Volume), which provides for the avoidance of non-purchase money liens on exempt property.

[45] See Collier on Bankruptcy ¶ 522.08[2].

[46] Bankruptcy Code § 522(g). For a discussion of the debtor's ability to avoid non-purchase-money security interests in certain exempt goods, see § 11.09 of this chapter.

[47] The legislative history, if anyone still reads legislative history, is quite specific on this point:

> As under current law, the debtor will be permitted to convert nonexempt property into exempt property before filing a bankruptcy petition. See Hearings, pt. 3, at 1355-58. The practice is not fraudulent as to creditors and permits the debtor to make full use of the exemptions to which he is entitled under the law.

H. Rep. 95-595 (1977); See also S. Rep. No. 95-989 (1978).

deals with it. Attacks on last-second conversion are thus made indirectly—either under the rules on fraudulent conveyances or under the rules regulating discharge. Broadly speaking, the most important factor appears to be the amount involved and the type of property involved. Courts tend to permit exemption planning if the amounts involved are relatively small, if the non-exempt property sold was sold for fair value, and if the exempt property purchased was covered by an exemption that was "capped."[48]

§ 11.08 Procedures

[A]—What to File; Who May File; When to File

Exemptions are not automatically given to the debtor; except in rare circumstances, the debtor must personally claim them. This is simply done, however, by filing a list with the bankruptcy court. That list may then be examined by parties in interest who may then file objections. Since exemptions are personal, they may generally be claimed only by the debtor; however, if the debtor fails to file the list, a dependant of the debtor may do so.[49] The list of exemptions is supposed to be filed with the debtor's schedule of assets.[50] If the debtor does not file, a dependant has 30 days from the time required for filing the schedules (usually 15 days after the petition[51] to file the list.[52]

[B]—Objections

Objections ordinarily must be filed within 30 days of the creditors' meeting or the filing of any amendment to the list of exempt property.[53] They may be filed by the case trustee or any creditor.[54] The burden of proof that an item of property is not exempt is on the objecting party.[55]

---

[48] See, for example, Hanson v. First Nat'l. Bank (In re Hanson), 848 F.2d 866 (8th Cir. 1988) (debtor converted about $34,000 of non-exempt property to $31,000 of exempt property, consisting of a $20,000 insurance policy (the amount of the state exemption for insurance) and an $11,000 payment on the mortgage).

[49] Bankruptcy Code § 522(l).

[50] Bankruptcy Rule 4003(a).

[51] Bankruptcy Rule 1007(c).

[52] Bankruptcy Rule 4003(a).

[53] Bankruptcy Rule 4003(b). The court may extend this if a request for extension is made before the 30 day period expires.

[54] Bankruptcy Rule 4003(b).

[55] Bankruptcy Rule 4003(c).

§ 11.09 Preservation of Certain Exemptions Against Certain Liens

[A]—Introduction

As noted above, liens generally trump exemptions.[56] There are, however, some exceptions. Section 522(f) affects the validity of judgment liens and some security interests to the extent they interfere with exemptions. These rules are not generally subject to the states' opt-out power. This can be very important in some cases. For example, if state law creates a homestead exemption but prohibits a debtor from asserting it against a judgment lienholder, the federal rule that avoids such liens when they impair exemptions supersedes, and the exemption may be claimed.[57] Similarly, attempts by several states to restrict the effect of the bankruptcy rule avoiding some security interests on exempt property have been held unconstitutional violations of the Supremacy Clause.[58] As noted below, however, the 1994 Amendments have slightly altered this rule and given the states a limited power to supercede the debtor's right to avoid a security interest in implements, professional books, tools of the trade, farm animals, or crops.[59]

[B]—Judgment Liens

Section 522(f)(1) provides the debtor with a rather obvious protection for its exempt property: it allows the debtor to avoid the "fixing" of most judicial liens to the extent the lien impairs an exemption.[60] This applies to all exempt property (unlike the limitations on security interests discussed in the next subsection). Unlike most avoiding powers, it does not destroy the lien entirely. The lien remains valid to the extent that the property is not exempt. For example, suppose that under relevant state law, the debtor was entitled to a $25,000 homestead exemption. The debtor's home is worth $100,000, is subject to a $40,000 mortgage and a $60,000 judgment lien. When the debtor uses its $25,000 exemption, the debtor avoids only $25,000 of the judgment lien; if the house is sold, the mortgage holder will get $40,000, the debtor will get $25,000, and the judgment lienholder will get the remainder ($35,000, assuming no costs of sale).

The Supreme Court has found considerable significance in the fact that this provision refers not to the lien itself but rather to the "fixing" of the lien. In *Farrey v. Sanderfoot*,[61] the Court held that this means the debtor's property interest must exist before the lien attaches to it. That case involved a divorce decree under which the debtor was granted sole title to the couple's home, previously held in joint tenancy, and the wife was simultaneously given a lien against the property to secure

---

[56] See § 11.07[B] of this chapter.

[57] Owen v. Owen, 500 U.S. 305 (1991).

[58] See, for example, In re Pelter, 64 Bankr. 492 (Bankr. W. D. Okla. 1986); In re Vaughn, 67 Bankr 140 (Bankr. C.D. Ill. 1986); In re Strain, 16 Bankr. 797 (Bankr. Id. 1982).

[59] See § 11.09[C] of this chapter.

[60] Bankruptcy Code § 522(f)(1). Liens regarding alimony, maintenance and support are not affected (1994 Amendments).

[61] 500 U.S. 291 (1991).

his obligation to pay her half the value of the house. Since the interest was created simultaneously with the creation of his right to the property, it was not a lien that had "fixed" to his property but rather an encumbrance that the debtor took along with the real estate, "as if he had purchased an already encumbered [property]."[62]

[C]—Security Interests

Section 522(f)(2) contains a limitation on the validity of some security interests against some exempt property. This provision was controversial when first enacted. That controversy has abated, not least because other law has left most of this provision meaningless.

The debtor may avoid the fixing of a lien to the extent it impairs an exemption if the lien is a non-possessory, non-purchase-money security interest and the property is either

> 1. Household furnishings, household goods, clothing, appliances, books, animals, crops, musical instruments or jewelry held primarily for the personal, family or household use of the debtor or a dependent, or
>
> 2. Implements, professional books, or tools, of the debtor's trade or a dependent's trade, or
>
> 3. Professionally prescribed health aids for the debtor or a dependent.[63]
>
> Note that this rule is narrow in several respects. It does not encompass all exempt property, but only a few kinds. It does not avoid all security interests, but only those that are "non-possessory" (for example, it does not affect pawned goods) and "non-purchase-money" (it does not affect security interests that secure the repayment of the purchase price of the goods).

The 1994 Amendments have slightly changed these rules. The 1994 Amendment applies if (1) the debor is claiming state exemptions, and (2) state law permits the debtor either to waive the right to claim federal exemptions or prohibits the debtor from claiming federal exemptions, and (3) state law either permits the debtor to claim exemptions without limitation and amount, but subject to consensual liens, or prohibits avoidance of consensual liens on otherwise exempt property. If these three conditions are met, the debtor may not avoid the fixing of a non-possessory, non-purchase money security interest in implements, professional books, tools of the trade, farm animals, or crops to the extent that the value of this property exceeds $5,000.[64] For example, suppose that the debtor resides in an opt-out state that prohibits avoidance of consensual liens on exempt property. The debtor is given a non-possessory, non-purchase money security interest in a bull worth $12,000. The debtor may avoid the security interest to the extent of $5,000 but the bull remains subject to it with regard to the remaining $7,000.

---

[62] Id. at 300.

[63] Bankruptcy Code § 522(f)(2).

[64] Bankruptcy Code § 522(f)(3) (1994 Amendments).

The primary impetus for the section 522(f) avoidance power was Congress' concern about what is often referred to as an "HHG" security interest. Traditionally, it was common for consumer lenders making personal loans to retain a security interest in all of the debtor's HouseHold Goods (thus, "HHG.") This had little to do with the value of those goods, which were for the most part scarcely worth selling. However, the HHG had a considerable in terrorem effect. A room full of used furniture, plus old pots and pans, is of little market value; but is extremely difficult for a debtor of modest income to replace. Consumer creditors believed, with some justification, that a debtor faced with repossession of these goods would make extraordinary efforts to pay the debt.[65] It was thus not the value of the property lost but the pressure imposed by the possibility of repossession that concerned Congress. It was also the fact that the HHG is non-purchase-money—that is, that it did not permit the debtor to acquire the goods—that was offensive; thus, Congress did not impair the ability of a purchase-money creditor to seize its collateral, even if it is of the type described in section 522(f)(2).

A classic example of a purchase money transaction is the typical purchase of new furniture. Most people do not pay in full in cash. They make a down payment, and raise the rest of the purchase price either by getting an extension of credit from the furniture store or by borrowing money from a bank or other financial institution. In either case, the credit extension or loan is almost certainly going to be secured by a security interest in the furniture purchased. Section 522(f) has no effect whatsoever on that security interest, provided it covers only the furniture that was bought on credit or with the loan. The basic rationale for this is simple. Most consumers need, or at least want, access to purchase money financing. Access to purchase money financing would be severely restricted if purchase money security interests were unenforceable; many stores and lenders would be unwilling to deal with certain buyers if they could not get collateral.

Since the enactment of the Code in 1978, the HHG issue has largely been dealt with by other bodies of law. Some states restrict the use of non-purchase money security interests in consumer transactions.[66] More significantly, perhaps, is the fact that since 1985 it has been an unfair trade practice for "non-purchase-money" consumer lenders to take an HHG security interest.[67] Since by statute in some states and by rule nationwide lenders have largely been prevented from obtaining non-purchase-money security interests in most of the types of collateral listed in section 522(f)(2), that provision is of greatly diminished significance.

This does not mean that it has no significance at all. It covers some types of property that are not protected by the Federal Trade Commission's rule, such as tools

[65] See Michael J. Herbert, *Straining the Gnat: A Critique of the 1984 Federal Trade Commission Consumer Credit Regulations*, 38 S.C. L. Rev. 329, 352 (1987).

[66] See, for example, Unif. Cons. Credit Code § 3.301 (1974).

[67] For distinctly contrasting discussions of this rule, promulgated by the Federal Trade Commission, see Michael J. Herbert, *Straining the Gant: A Critique of the 1984 Federal Trade Commission Consumer Credit Regulations*, 38 S.C. L. Rev. 329, 352 (1987) (once described to its author by a supporter of the rule as "unduly negative and unnecessarily sarcastic") and Jean Braucher, *Defining Unfairness: Empathy and Economic Analysis at the Federal Trade Commission*, 68 B. U. L. Rev. 349 (1988).

of the trade.[68] It also encompasses a wider range of creditors. For example, the FTC's declaration that HHG's are an unfair trade practice applies only to professional consumer creditors, and not to other lenders.[69] However, the diminished significance of the rule is evidenced by the fact that it was once among the most litigated sections of the Code and now arises only occasionally (at least insofar as the reported case law is concerned).

Section 522(f)(2) also touched off two other important disputes. Cases under it have largely been responsible for the precise delineation of the difference between a purchase-money and a non-purchase-money security interest.[70] More importantly for this discussion, section 522(f)(2) led to considerable litigation over the Constitutional limits of the bankruptcy power.

It takes no great thought to realize that section 522(f)(2) raises a potential conflict between Congress' power to enact uniform bankruptcy laws and the Fifth Amendment's prohibition on seizing property without due process or (where applicable) just compensation. Creditors, outraged by the realization that much of their collateral may have become unavailable to them, asserted that the section was an unconstitutional taking of property. This issue, fascinating as it is, was largely brushed aside by most courts examining it; in general, they picked their way around the constitutional issue by holding that section 522(f)(2) applied only to security interests that arose after the Code, thus shifting the issue from a question of whether property had been taken to a question of whether Congress might lawfully limit the effect of contracts not yet made.[71] This latter question could rather easily be answered in the affirmative. When the issue finally reached the Supreme Court, in *United States v. Security Industrial Bank*,[72] the Court essentially reached this result, although expressing itself in a slightly different fashion. The case made three basic points. First, the retroactive destruction of a property right might violate the Fifth Amendment. Second, as a rule of statutory construction, laws should not be interpreted in a way that creates a constitutional issue unless such construction is unavoidable. Third, bankruptcy laws should not be construed to eliminate pre-existing property rights unless Congress explicitly so states.

It is clear that there is some boundary to what Congress can do with existing "property" rights. *Security Industrial Bank* to a limited extent reaffirmed the older cases, discussed in Chapter 1, which distinguished between the undoubted power to eliminate "contract" rights (that is, personal liability of the debtor) and the doubtful power to eliminate "property" rights (that is, claims to things owned by the debtor).[73] Where that boundary lies remains unclear, precisely because the distinction drawn is in some respects artificial.

---

[68] The rule only prohibits non-PMSI's in household goods, which is defined in an essentially common-sense manner. See 16 C.F.R. §§ 444.2(a)(4), 444.1(i) (1994).

[69] 16 C.F.R. §§ 444.2(a), 444.1(a) (1994).

[70] See Thomas D. Crandall, Michael J. Herbert & Lary Lawrence, Uniform Commercial Code § 25.3 (1993).

[71] See Collier on Bankruptcy ¶ 522.29[2].

[72] 459 U.S. 70 (1982).

[73] See § 1.04 of this book.

§ 11.10 Exemption Strategies

One important role a lawyer may play in counseling an individual debtor is helping the debtor to get the maximum benefit of exemptions. This is not only a question of dollar amount; it also involves the debtor's personal preferences and the possibility that there are other strategies available to protect some property. In a state that has not opted out, the first decision is between the state and the federal exemptions. This can create an immediate problem in a joint case because, as noted, both spouses must choose the same set.[74] It may well be that one spouse would benefit more from the federal exemptions while the other would benefit more from the state exemptions. The diligent lawyer should be alert to this possible conflict of interest, to the ethical requirement that both clients be fully informed about the conflict,[75] and to the possible desirability of separate filings.

Using the federal exemptions as a model, consider the following illustrations of ways in which the exemptions (and other rules) can be used to protect property that is particularly valuable to the debtor:

1. Jessica Fletcher, a modestly successful mystery writer, went bankrupt because of foolish speculation in cattle futures. She owns, free and clear of any lien, computer equipment and software worth $3,000 which she uses both for word processing and to do research on the Internet. For both personal and professional reasons, this is a piece of property that she especially wants to retain. She can do so by combining the Tools of the Trade Exemption ($1,500), the Wildcard Exemption ($800), plus $700 of her Homestead Exemption. The price of this is that she will have to give up other property, and may have a particularly difficult time keeping her home since the Homestead Exemption will now be significantly reduced.

2. Axel Grease, a slightly aging bankrupt biker, wants more than anything else in the world to hang on to his Hawg motorcycle. It is worth $10,000 and is unencumbered. Axel can use half of his Homestead Exemption ($7,500), his Motor Vehicle Exemption ($2,400), and $100.00 of his Wildcard Exemption to keep the bike.

3. Same basic facts as Example 2, but suppose the bike is worth $13,000. Axel uses half his Homestead Exemption, his Motor Vehicle Exemption, and his full $800 Wildcard Exemption. This still leaves him $2,300 short. Axel may be able to get the trustee to agree to sell him the remaining $2,300 worth of the motorcycle. Assume he does so, and raises the cash by selling all of his other exempt assets, thus stripping his house bare.

4. Same basic facts as Examples 2 and 3, but suppose the bike is worth $15,000 and is subject to a $1,200 security interest. Axel proceeds to use

---

[74] See § 11.02 of this chapter.

[75] Model Code of Professional Responsibility EC 5-16; Model Rules of Professional Conduct Rule 1.7(b)(2).

half his Homestead Exemption, his Motor Vehicle Exemption, his Wildcard Exemption, the cash he raises from selling all his other exempt property, and finally reaffirms the secured debt to keep the bike.

As Examples 3 and 4 suggest, an occasional debtor may make decisions that can be troublesome to the lawyer involved. The trouble may be particularly acute if the debtor has dependents. Suppose that Axel has three dependent minor children. Axel's lawyer might well be concerned that his desire to keep the Hawg is causing him to make decisions in the bankruptcy proceeding that are inappropriate. This problem becomes a direct ethical difficulty if a reaffirmation is involved. As noted in Chapter 12, the debtor's lawyer has to file a statement that the reaffirmation will not be unduly burdensome on the debtor's dependents.[76]

§ 11.11 Redemption

[A]—Right of Redemption

Under some circumstances, the debtor has the right to "redeem" property from a lienholder. Redemption simply means that the debtor may buy out the lien and thus become the owner of the property. Many state law include rights of redemption; some of these are discussed in Chapter 2.[77] These rights are not disturbed by the bankruptcy. However, the Code goes beyond the traditional recognition of state-created redemption rights; it includes an additional right of redemption, limited to individual Chapter 7 debtors seeking to retain encumbered but exempt or abandoned personal property.

The main problem with the typical state law redemption right is that to redeem, the debtor must pay the underlying obligation in full. This often is impossible. Insofar as personal property is concerned, the key provision is section 9-506 of the Uniform Commercial Code, which requires full payment for redemption.[78] By contrast, the Bankruptcy Code permits the Chapter 7 debtor to redeem for the lesser of (i) the obligation or (ii) the value of the property redeemed.

Under section 722 of the Bankruptcy Code, an individual debtor may redeem from a lien certain tangible personal property intended primarily for personal, family, or household use. This right applies even if there has been a wavier of redemption rights. To be eligible for redemption, the property must either be exempt under section 522 or must have been abandoned by the trustee to the lienholder. (Other property is not subject to redemption because of the interest that unsecured creditors have in its liquidation and the distribution of liquidation proceeds.) In addition, the

---

[76] See § 12.09.

[77] See § 2.07.

[78] U.C.C. § 9-506. In this context, full payment includes not only the principal and interest but also other contractual obligations, such as late fees and lawyer's fees. It also includes "the expenses reasonably incurred by the secured party in retaking, holding and preparing the collateral for in arranging for the sale . . ." See Thomas D. Crandall, Michael J. Herbert & Lary Lawrence, Uniform Commercial Code § 27.10 (1993).

debt secured by the lien must be a dischargeable consumer debt. The key benefit for the debtor is that full payment of the obligation is not necessarily required. The debtor need only pay the lienholder the amount of the allowed secured claim.[79] Since a secured claim cannot be for more than the value of the collateral securing the claim,[80] if the obligation is greater than the value of the property, the debtor need only pay the latter, not the former.

For example, suppose that Douglas owed River Bank $10,000, which represented the amount River Bank had advanced Douglas to purchase a car. The car secures the debt. The car is worth only $7,000; since the lien is underwater, the trustee has abandoned it to River Bank.[81] Under the Uniform Commercial Code, Douglas would have to pay at least $10,000 to redeem. If the agreement provided for other costs, such as River Bank's attorney's fees, Douglas would also have to pay them to redeem. However, under the Bankruptcy Code, Douglas would have to pay only $7,000. Because the car is worth only $7,000, that is the amount of the allowed secured claim.[82] By cutting the potential cost of redemption, section 722 provides some help to those debtors who are trying to keep property, at least those who are trying to keep property that is worth less than the debt it secures.

In most cases, this help is not enough. In the example given, it may be just as difficult to raise $7,000 as $10,000; indeed, in most cases it will be impossible to raise either sum. What the typical debtor really needs is the ability to pay the obligation over time. The redemption provision does not give that right to the debtor; the prevailing view in the courts is that Congress did not intend the debtor to have the right to redeem in installments.[83] In consequence, many consumer debtors who wish to retain more property than section 522's exemptions allow must file for reorganization under Chapter 11 or Chapter 13; a plan of reorganization under either Chapter may be used to make payments over time.[84] As an alternative, the debtor may be able to renegotiate the loan with the creditor; in exchange for the debtor's reaffirmation of the debt, the creditor may be willing to accept payment over time. The problem with the reaffirmation alternative is that the creditor must agree to it.[85] By contrast with reaffirmation, a Chapter 13 plan, and in some cases a Chapter 11 plan, each allowing installment payments, may be forced on the creditor against its will.

---

[79] Bankruptcy Code § 722.

[80] Bankruptcy Code § 506(b); see § 10.03[C] of this book for a full discussion of this issue.

[81] Note that even if it had not been abandoned, there would be a right to redeem since the property is subject to an exemption; it does not matter that the exemption is only partial. See In re Fitzgerald, 20 Bankr. 27 (Bankr. N.D.N.Y. 1982).

[82] Bankruptcy Code § 506(b).

[83] Although there are a few bankruptcy court cases to the contrary, this is the overwhelming majority rule. See In re Edwards, 901 F.2d 1383 (7th Cir. 1990); In re Bell, 700 F.2d 1053 (6th Cir. 1983); In re Horne, 132 Bankr. 661 (Bankr. N.D. Ga. 1991).

[84] There is a technical statutory argument that Bankruptcy Code § 521(2)(B), which gives the court discretion to give the debtor additional time to take certain actions, including redemption, that the debtor has stated an intention to perform, may permit a limited form of installment redemption.

[85] See § 12.09 of this book.

[B]—Procedures

One of the debtor's duties under section 521 is to file notice, ordinarily within 30 days after filing the petition, of its intention to redeem property. Unless the court orders otherwise, the redemption is supposed to occur within 45 days after the notice is filed.[86] In some cases, the debtor and the creditor will agree on the value of the property, no other party will object, and no court hearing will be required. If there is a dispute, the court, after notice and a hearing, may determine the appropriate price and authorize the redemption.[87] As is true so often throughout the Code, the issue of valuation is the most difficult and certainly the most important, since it determines how much actually has to be paid by the debtor.

§ 11.12 Retention of Encumbered Property Without Redemption or Reaffirmation

As noted elsewhere in this book, there are many informal arrangements for the retention of property by the debtor. If property is encumbered, and the value of the property is less than the amount of the debt (or less than the amount of the debt plus the debtor's exemption in the property) the trustee has no interest in the property. The debtor must, of course, deal with the interest of the secured creditor through some means. The Code formally recognizes four: reorganization, redemption, reaffirmation or surrender. Is there a fifth? Assume that the debtor has never gone into default on the underlying obligation. May the debtor simply maintain the scheduled payments and keep the property? Such arrangements are, in point of fact, fairly common; the creditor will frequently be delighted to continue receiving each payment in full and on time. There is no barrier to a creditor acquiescing in such payments. The real question is whether the debtor has the right to retain the property—if the secured creditor wants to foreclose, may it?

The Code is silent on the issue. There have, however, been quite a number of cases and a bit of scholarly comment. There is at present a split among the Circuit Courts that may soon lead to a Supreme Court resolution.[88]

The strongest argument for the debtor is that if there is no default, there is no state law right to seize the property; there should thus be no right to force the debtor to take any formal action to retain possession. For example, under Article 9 of the Uniform Commercial Code, it is the debtor's default on its obligations that triggers the secured party's right to repossess and sell collateral.[89] Prior to default, the debtor

[86] Bankruptcy Code § 521(2)(A), (B).

[87] Bankruptcy Rule 6008.

[88] For a couple of recent articles, see Oliver B. Pollak, *Reaffirmation and Retention in Bankruptcy: Conflict in the Circuits Over Protecting the Secured Creditor*, 111 Bank. L. J. 302 (1994) and Arnold B. Cohen, *Chapter 7 Debtors Who Are Current in Secured Debt Obligations May Retain Collateral Without Reaffirmation, or Use of Chapter 13*, 2 Bankr. L. & Prac. 323 (1993).

[89] Uniform Commercial Code §§ 9-503, 9-501(1). For a fuller discussion of the secured party's rights upon default, see Thomas D. Crandall, Michael J. Herbert & Lary Lawrence, Uniform Commercial Code §§ 27.6-27.9 (1993).

retains possession (unless otherwise agreed). Why, it is argued, should a creditor have more rights in bankruptcy than it has outside bankruptcy?

Because, retort the secured creditors, bankruptcy has changed the nature of our bargain. Prior to bankruptcy, the secured creditor not only had collateral; it also had the personal obligation of the debtor. If the collateral was insufficient to cover the loan, the debtor was still liable and other property of the debtor could be subjected to judicial liens. Only in those rare cases in which the creditor agrees to lend on a non-recourse basis is the creditor limited to recovery from collateral.[90] But because of the bankruptcy discharge, the debtor is no longer personally liable. If the debtor does eventually default on the loan, the creditor may look to nothing except its collateral. In effect, bankruptcy transforms what was a recourse obligation into a non-recourse obligation.

In effect, the creditors are arguing for a quid-pro-quo. If the debtor wants to keep the collateral, the creditors want something in exchange. Reorganization means greater payment on any unsecured portion of the obligation. Redemption means immediate payment. Reaffirmation means that the debt will not be discharged; there is thus no conversion of the obligation from recourse to non-recourse. In the rhetorical flourish of one court, retention without a quid-pro-quo is not a "fresh start" but a "head start."[91]

The policy question underlying this issue is a close and complex one. It may be that retention of property without personal obligation on the underlying debt creates an unfair and unbargained for risk for secured claimants. The statutory construction issue is less close, at least if one uses a narrow textual analysis; there is virtually nothing in the words of the Code to support the creditors' position.

---

[90] For a discussion of non-recourse lending, see § 17.10[C] of this book.

[91] In re Taylor, 3 F.3d 1512, 1516 (11th Cir. 1993).

CHAPTER 12

Discharge and Reaffirmation

§ 12.01 Introduction

The main bankruptcy goal of nearly all debtors is discharge. Discharge is also the primary distinguishing feature of bankruptcy; it is what most clearly separates bankruptcy proceedings from state insolvency proceedings. Discharge means quite simply that those obligationss not satisfied through or in conjunction with the bankruptcy proceeding cease to be binding on the debtor. The creditor may take no action to collect discharged debts from the debtor; the debtor may feel a moral, but has no legal, obligation.

The Code contains a number of discharge rules. The availability and scope of discharge depends on the Chapter under which the proceeding was conducted and in some cases on whether the debtor is a natural person or an organization. In rare cases, discharge may be denied entirely to an eligible debtor because of the debtor's misconduct. Some particular debts are non-dischargeable, either in whole or in part. Some debts are dischargeable in one bankruptcy chapter but not in others. Still other debts may or may not be dischargeable, depending on the debtor's particular circumstances. The debtor may also exchange its right to discharge for something else—usually the right to retain encumbered property—by reaffirming the debt. All of these issues are discussed in this chapter.

Discharge is individual, given to a particular debtor. If there are other persons liable on the obligation, they remain liable during and after the bankruptcy. For example, if the debtor is a co-principal who has signed a promissory note, the discharge of the debtor in bankruptcy does not affect the liability of the other signer. Similarly, the obligations of a surety on a debt is not affected by the fact that the principal has been discharged. Indeed, the primary reason for having a surety is to provide protection against the principal's insolvency or bankruptcy.

A final preliminary point is worth emphasis. Discharge affects debts, not liens. The property interest of a mortgagee, secured party, or other lienholder in property of the estate or of the debtor is unaffected by the discharge. Only the right to proceed personally against the debtor is lost. Courts have over and over again reiterated the rule that "liens survive discharge."[1]

For example, suppose that D'Arcy owed $100,000 to Friendly Finance, secured by a mortgage on D'Arcy's home. D'Arcy filed bankruptcy; the court found that the value of the home was $80,000; Friendly thus had an $80,000 secured claim and a $20,000 unsecured claim. Suppose further that there was a 5% distribution

[1] The two most recent Supreme Court cases to reiterate this principal are Nobelman v. American Savings Bank, 113 S. Ct. 2106 (1993), and Dewsnup v. Timm, 112 S. Ct. 773 (1992). These cases severely restricted so-called lien-stripping.

on the unsecured claims and that the house was not sold by either the trustee or Friendly during the bankruptcy, so that when D'Arcy emerges from the bankruptcy, she still has possession of, and title to, the house.

Friendly receives $1,000 on its unsecured claim. It may not sue D'Arcy personally for either the $19,000 still unpaid on the unsecured claim or for the $80,000 value of the house. It may however foreclose its mortgage. This means that Friendly may seize the house, sell it, and apply the proceeds to the debt. It may not obtain a judgment for, or recover, any deficiency from D'Arcy or D'Arcy's other assets. The bankruptcy has effectively converted the debt to a non-recourse obligation, payable only from the property that secures the debt.

This means that a lien creditor who does not get paid through the bankruptcy proceeding can actually wind up with less than the amount of its secured claim. Suppose that the net proceeds of Friendly's foreclosure sale are only $65,000. Friendly is entitled only to $65,000, even though its secured claim was $80,000 and even though secured claims are ordinarily paid in full. To put it another way, the lien creditor who realizes on its lien rather than obtaining a cash payment takes the risk that the value of the property was initially miscalculated or that other factors (such as a poorly conducted sale or unexpected depreciation) resulted in a lower than expected price.

What if the opposite is true? What if the value placed on the property was based on an unduly pessimistic estimate of its ultimate sale price? If the sale of the property nets $99,000 or more, does Friendly get to keep $99,000 (the unpaid debt) or only $80,000 (the amount of the secured claim)? This is another way of asking whether the debtor can lien-strip.[2] Lien stripping is not permitted in Chapter 7. If the debt is secured solely by the debtor's homestead, it is not permitted in Chapter 13, or Chapter 11 cases either. Thus, if the D'Arcy had been either a Chapter 7, Chapter 13, or Chapter 11 debtor, Friendly Finance would be entitled to all the proceeds of the sale, up to $99,000, even though the unpaid debt had been discharged and even though the creditor would have no right to collect that amount from any other assets of the debtor.

In other words, what survives the bankruptcy is the lien, not the secured claim. Although the amount of the secured claim is based on the value of the lien at the time the amount of the secured claim was determined, the secured claim is not itself the lien nor is its amount determinative of the value of the lien at another point in time. Post-bankruptcy, the lien may be worth more, less, or the same as the amount of the secured claim. At any given point in time, the lien is worth the lesser of the entire obligation secured by the lien or the value of the property to which the lien attaches.

The discharge provisions have been the battleground for much of the debate over bankruptcy policy. To many critics of the Code, discharge is much too easy and much too cheap. According to them, discharge is granted without sufficient inquiry into the debtor's ability to pay, and thus provides an incentive to resort to bankruptcy

---

[2] For a discussions of lien-stripping under the various Chapters, see Chapters 17, 18 and 19 of this book.

unnecessarily and wastefully.[3] This in turn burdens the entire economy, perhaps especially those whose economic situations force them to seek high-risk credit. Discharge risk may make such credit unavailable or very expensive. These criticisms led to BAFJA's modest limitations on the availability of discharge; those limitations are discussed in Chapter 3.[4]

In the view of those who defend the Code, the discharge rules have engendered little abuse, especially by consumers.[5] In their view, except for rare cases, discharge merely confirms what is all too palpably the case—the debtor cannot pay or at least cannot pay without enduring undue hardship or imposing unconscionable difficulties on dependents. According to them, bankruptcy discharge merely imposes an official end on an already fruitless collection effort. Any serious attempt to impose a higher cost on discharge will be either futile or cruel. These views were without doubt the reason why BAFJA's limitations on discharge were, in the end, so modest.

As is so often true in debates over bankruptcy policy, one's viewpoint largely depends on the interpretation one gives to rather spotty data. While it has been said that over a billion dollars a year is needlessly discharged, that figure was based on how much money could be extracted from debtors if they were forced to turn over to their creditors all of their income in excess of the federal poverty line.[6] The late Senator Everett Dirksen, a hard-shell conservative Republican, used to quip that "a billion here, a billion there, pretty soon it adds up to real money." True enough; but looked at another way, its data may be viewed as saying that bankruptcy is a remarkably successful welfare program, as it allows tens of thousands of families to escape poverty at a cost of only $1 billion a year, a cost spread very thinly among tens of millions of borrowers. Almost the only comments one can safely make about this debate are that the data are woefully inadequate, and usually inconclusive, and that the values brought by the observer to analysis of those data inevitably shape the conclusions drawn.

§ 12.02 Denial of Discharge

[A]—Introduction

Under some circumstances, the debtor's discharge may be entirely denied. A denial means that none of the debtor's debts are discharged; contrast this with the rules discussed in the next section, which make certain specific obligations non-dischargeable. The reasons for denying discharge are somewhat varied; most, but

[3] The best elaboration of this argument is found in the Purdue Study, which argued that $1,100,000,000 of debt was unnecessarily discharged each year. Credit Research Center, Krannert School of Management, Purdue University Monograph No. 23, Consumer Bankruptcy Study, vol. 1 at 88-91 (1982).

[4] See § 3.04.

[5] Teresa A. Sullivan, Elizabeth Warren & Jay Lawrence Westbrook, As We Forgive Our Debtors: Bankruptcy and Consumer Credit in America 219-24 (1989).

[6] Credit Research Center, Krannert School of Management, Purdue University Monograph No. 23, Consumer Bankruptcy Study 45, 90 (1982).

not all, are rooted in misconduct by the debtor. The primary provision is section 727(a). This section, part of Chapter 7, has only limited applicability to other proceedings. Generally, in the reorganization chapters, the issue of discharge is dealt with in context of the confirmation of the plan; misconduct is punished by the court's refusal to confirm. Since discharge occurs upon confirmation in Chapter 11, and upon completion of a confirmed plan in Chapters 12 and 13, denial of confirmation has roughly the same effect as denial of discharge does in Chapter 7. This section deals with the denial of discharge under the various chapters.

[B]—Denial of Discharge Under Chapter 7

Section 727 lists a number of situations in which discharge is denied. These include the following:

1. **Eligibility.** Only individuals are eligible for a Chapter 7 discharge.[7] A corporation, partnership, or other legal entity may not be discharged.
2. **Fraudulent Transfer/Destruction/Concealment of Property.** If the debtor, intending to hinder, delay, or defraud a creditor or the trustee has transferred, removed, destroyed, mutilated or concealed certain property, or has permitted any of these things to occur, discharge is denied.[8] This is a denial for a particular kind of misconduct; that is, the attempt to evade the Chapter 7 bargain, which is essentially a swap of current assets for discharge of current obligations.
3. **Failure to Maintain Records.** If the debtor has concealed, destroyed, falsified or failed to preserve relevant records, discharge is denied unless the debtor's act or failure was justified.[9] This provision is partly punitive, because the failure to maintain records is often indicative of an attempt to defraud creditors. However, there is no requirement that there be a bad motivation underlying the debtor's lack of records. Thus, this provision is also designed to protect creditors against the negligence or incompetence of the only party who is likely to have the necessary information—that is, the debtor.

The level of records required is not the same for all debtors. Roughly speaking, it is a question of what is reasonable under the debtor's particular circumstances. According to the leading case decided under the old Bankruptcy Act: "The law is not unqualified in imposing a requirement to keep books or records, and it does not require that if they are kept they shall be kept in any special form . . . It is a question in each instance of reasonableness in the particular circumstances."[10]

The obligation of some debtors to keep records may be satisfied by something pretty sketchy, especially if minimal records are normal in the

[7] Bankruptcy Code § 727(a)(1).

[8] Bankruptcy Code § 727(a)(2).

[9] Bankruptcy Code § 727(a)(3).

[10] In re Underhill, 82 F.2d 258, 259-60 (1936).

debtor's line of work. Courts have in general required little of those debtors whose financial activities are simple, such as ordinary wage earners.[11] However, regardless of the simplicity of the debtor's financial activities, it is expected that some records ought to be kept. For example, even a very small business is ordinarily expected to have reasonable records of its financial activities; failure to produce such records justifies denial of discharge.[12] Only if the business is so tiny that records would not ordinarily be kept will their absence be excused.[13] If the trustee or the objecting creditor demonstrates that the records are inadequate, it is up to the debtor to justify that inadequacy.[14]

4. **Misconduct in the Current Proceeding.** Discharge may be denied for serious misconduct by the debtor in the proceedings itself, such a perjury, bribery, withholding relevant records, failure to account for missing assets, refusal to obey court orders and the like.[15] Discharge will not be denied, however, if there is a sufficient justification for the debtor's conduct. For example, the debtor cannot be forced to surrender its right against self-incrimination.[16] By the same token, however, if the debtor is granted immunity and still refuses to testify, discharge will be denied.[17]

5. **Repeat Filings/Time Limits.** There are time limits on the frequency with which bankruptcy discharge may be obtained. A debtor may not obtain a Chapter 7 discharge within 6 years of a prior Chapter 7 or Chapter 11 discharge.[18] The six year period is measured from the filing of the petition in the first case to the filing of the petition in the second case—it is thus filing to filing, not discharge to discharge. Thus, if Douglas filed a Chapter 7 or Chapter 11 petition on June 30, 1994, and was discharged in that proceeding, he cannot obtain another Chapter 7 discharge in any proceeding filed before July 1, 2000. Note that technically, this does not prohibit a premature filing; it only prohibits discharge in a second case that is prematurely filed.

The time bar is more flexible if the earlier discharge was obtained in a Chapter 12 or a Chapter 13 proceeding. The six year limit does not bar discharge if either of the following two circumstances apply:

a. The payments under the Chapter 12 or Chapter 13 plan totaled at least 100 percent of the allowed unsecured claims.[19] There is some ambiguity in

---

[11] In re Weismann, 1 F. Supp. 723 (S.D.N.Y. 1932).

[12] Meridian Bank v. Alten, 958 F.2d 1226, 1232 (3d Cir. 1992).

[13] In re Ridley, 115 Bankr. 731, 735 (Bankr. D. Mass. 1990).

[14] Meridian Bank v. Alten, 958 F.2d 1226, 1230-31 (3d Cir. 1992).

[15] Bankruptcy Code § 727(a)(4) -(6).

[16] Bankruptcy Code § 727(a)(6)(B).

[17] *Id.*

[18] Bankruptcy Code § 727(a)(8).

[19] Bankruptcy Code § 727(a)(9)(A).

the language about whether the plan payments must actually equal the real value of the claims. The Code says that the payments must equal the allowed unsecured claims—not the value of the amount of the allowed unsecured claims. It is not clear whether this means that the payments, when reduced to present value, must equal the amount of the claims. If they do not, then the payments need only equal the nominal amount of the claims. For example, if the allowed unsecured claims total $100,000, and the Chapter 12/Chapter 13 debtor pays out $100,000 on them, the requirement is satisfied, even though the payment was made over a three-to-five year period and its actual value, measured as of the commencement of the plan, was thus less than $100,000.

b. The payment under the Chapter 12 or Chapter 13 plan totaled at least 70 percent of the allowed unsecured claims, the plan was proposed in good faith, and the plan was the debtor's best effort to make payment.[20] "Best efforts" is a rather open-ended standard; the legislative history describes what the court should evaluate as follows:

> The court should balance the debtor's assets, including family income, health insurance, retirement benefits, and other wealth, a sum which is generally determinable, against the foreseeable necessary living expenses of the debtor and the debtor's dependents, which unfortunately is rarely quantifiable. In determining the expenses of the debtor and the debtor's dependents, the court should consider the stability of the debtor's employment, if any, the age of the debtor, the number of the debtor's dependents and their ages, the condition of equipment and tools necessary to the debtor's employment or to the operation of his business, and other foreseeable expenses that the debtor will be required to pay during the period of the plan, other than payments to be made to creditors under the plan.[21]

In all other circumstances, the usual six-year bar applies. Thus, if Douglas filed a Chapter 13 petition on June 30, 1994, and received a discharge upon the completion of a plan that provided for a 50% payout on unsecured claims, Douglas cannot obtain a Chapter 7 discharge in any proceeding filed before July 1, 2000.

6. **Misconduct in Prior or Concurrent Proceedings.** Discharge can be denied not only because of misconduct in the present case but because of misconduct in an earlier case. If, during the previous year, the debtor has done such things as make a fraudulent transfer, concealed or destroyed records, lied in conjunction with the case, committed perjury—or indeed committed any of the acts specified in section 727(a)(2) -(6), discharge may be denied. Discharge may also be denied if, during the case, the debtor

[20] Bankruptcy Code § 727(a)(9)(B). Again, it is unclear if payments are reduced to present value.

[21] 124 Cong. Rec. H32,401 (Sept. 28, 1978); S34,001 (Oct 5, 1978).

has done any of these things in another case that concerns an "insider" of the debtor.[22]

7. **Waiver of Discharge.** Finally, the debtor is not discharged if the debtor makes an effective waiver of the discharge. To be effective, the waiver must be in writing; it must be executed by the debtor after the order for relief (i.e., in a voluntary case, after the filing of the petition), and it must be approved by the court.[23]

Parties in interest have the right to challenge the debtor's discharge. The trustee, every creditor, and the U.S. Trustee all have standing to object to discharge.[24] On request of any party in interest, the court may order the trustee to examine the debtor's actions and conduct to determine whether there is a basis for denying discharge.[25]

[C]—Denial of Discharge Under Chapter 11

In nearly all circumstances, a Chapter 11 debtor is discharged if the Chapter 11 plan is confirmed. This does not mean that important issues such as misconduct by the debtor are irrelevant. Rather, it means that they arise in context of plan confirmation, rather than in a separate discharge proceeding. To put it another way, the court may refuse confirmation—and thus effectively deny discharge—for many of the same reasons that it would directly rule on discharge in a Chapter 7 case.[26] Moreover, debtor misconduct in Chapter 11 may cause creditors to reject the plan, and thus make confirmation difficult or impossible. The requirements for confirmation under Chapter 11 are discussed in Chapter 17.[27]

There is one exception to this. A Chapter 11 plan may provide for the liquidation, rather than the reorganization of the debtor. Such a plan may be virtually indistinguishable from a Chapter 7 proceeding. In consequence, Chapter 7 rules for discharge are applied to some liquidation Chapter 11s. Under section 1141(d)(3), confirmation of the plan does not discharge the debtor if:

1. The plan provides for the liquidation of all, or substantially all, the property of the estate, and
2. The debtor does not engage in business after consummation of the plan, and
3. If the case had been under Chapter 7, discharge would have been denied under section 727(a).[28]

---

[22] Bankruptcy Code § 727(a)(7). "Insiders" are close affiliates of the debtor, such as relatives or related legal entities. See Bankruptcy Code § 101(31).

[23] Bankruptcy Code § 727(a)(10).

[24] Bankruptcy Code § 727(c)(1).

[25] Bankruptcy Code § 727(c)(2).

[26] The most obvious difference is that there is no general time bar for discharge in a Chapter 11 proceeding; the debtor need not wait the six years required by Chapter 7.

[27] See § 17.15.

[28] Bankruptcy Code § 1141(d)(3).

Note that this does not mean necessarily that there is no discharge in a liquidating Chapter 11; it merely means that in some such proceedings the non-discharge rules of Chapter 7 apply. The reason for this provision is to prevent a debtor from doing an end-run around Chapter 7's limitations on discharge by filing a purely nominal Chapter 11 proceeding that was in all key respects substantively identical to a Chapter 7 proceeding.

Finally, as in Chapter 7, a Chapter 11 discharge can be waived. There are procedural requirements that must be met. To be effective, the waiver must be in writing; it must be executed by the debtor after the order for relief (i.e., in a voluntary case, after the filing of the petition), and it must be approved by the court.[29]

[D]—Denial of Discharge Under Chapters 12 and 13

Ordinarily, discharge is granted under Chapters 12 and 13 only upon completion of the plan payments. As is true with Chapter 11, the court must confirm the plan, and it is nearly always in the process of confirmation that issues of debtor misconduct arise. The court may refuse confirmation—and thus effectively preclude discharge, which generally requires completion of a confirmed plan—for many of the same reasons that it would directly rule on discharge in a Chapter 7 case.[30] The requirements for confirmation under Chapters 12 and 13 are discussed in §§ 19.08 and 18.08 of this book. Under limited circumstances, a discharge can be given even though the plan has not been completed; the only difference between this type of discharge and regular discharge is that the scope is narrower. These issues are also discussed more fully in §§ 12.05[C][3] and 12.07 of this chapter.

A Chapter 12 or a Chapter 13 discharge can be waived. There are procedural requirements that must be met. To be effective, the waiver must be in writing; it must be executed by the debtor after the order for relief (i.e., after the filing of the petition), and it must be approved by the court.[31]

§ 12.03 Non-Dischargeable Debts

Section 523 lists a number of debts that are not discharged in most bankruptcies. These non-dischargeable debts have little in common beyond the obvious fact that Congress has found them to be unworthy of discharge, usually because the debtor's failure to pay them is considered to be in some sense unjustifiable. Whether these debts actually will be paid is of course speculative; what little data there are suggest that non-dischargeable debts are seldom recovered, either because the debtor seldom acquires enough money to pay them or because the cost of monitoring the debtor to determine whether the debtor has the ability to pay is unduly great.

---

[29] Bankruptcy Code § 1141(d)(4).

[30] The most obvious difference is that there is no general time bar for discharge in a Chapter 12 or 13 proceeding; the debtor need not wait the six years required by Chapter 7 to obtain a second discharge.

[31] Bankruptcy Code §§ 1228(a), 1328(a).

There is a long tradition of interpreting the exceptions to discharge narrowly. Many cases have held that, to be non-dischargeable, the debt must fit clearly within one of the exceptions.[32] Over the years, Congress has made many changes to the list of non-dischargeable debts, reflecting different balances between the debtor's interest in discharge and the interests of creditors or the public at large in attempting to collect certain types of debts. Two of the most recent changes—the limitations on discharge for debts arising from driving while intoxicated and from the savings and loan bailouts of the 1980's and 90's—clearly reflect the impact of hot political issues on the bankruptcy discharge rules.

Whether a particular debt is non-dischargeable depends to some extent on the Chapter under which the debtor has filed. Congress, as part of its effort to make Chapter 13 more attractive to consumer debtors than Chapter 7, broadened the scope of potential discharge. Thus, some of the obligations listed in this paragraph may in fact be discharged if the debtor successfully completes a Chapter 13 plan of reorganization. This broader discharge is one of the main attractions of a Chapter 13 bankruptcy, at least for some debtors.

At present, there are more than a dozen types of debt that are classified non-dischargeable under section 523. The major ones are as follows:

> **Taxes.** A number of tax obligations are non-dischargeable, including those given priority under section 507,[33] some of those for which a return was filed late or not at all, and those for which the debtor filed a fraudulent return or otherwise evaded.[34] In addition, if the debtor borrows money to pay a non-dischargeable tax obligation it owes to the United States, the debtor's obligation on the loan is itself non-dischargeable.[35]
>
> **Fraud.** Generally, debts arising from fraudulent actions by the debtor to obtain property, money, services, or credit are non-dischargeable. The same is true with regard to fraudulent actions to obtain an extension, renewal, or refinancing of credit; thus, the debt may be non-dischargeable either because it was initially obtained by fraud or because the lender was induced to extend the due date by fraud. The statutory provision is written broadly, to encompass many actions that have been labeled "fraud." These include false pretenses, false representations, and actual fraud. In addition, the debt will be non-dischargeable if the debtor used a written statement that contains a materially false representation of the debtor's financial condition or an insider's financial condition if (1) the creditor reasonably relied on it and (2) the debtor "caused to be made or published with intent to deceive."[36] This last provision is often used to block

---

[32] See Collier on Bankruptcy ¶ 523.05A.

[33] For a discussion of tax priorities, see § 10.04[C] of this book.

[34] Bankruptcy Code § 523(a)(1).

[35] Bankruptcy Code § 523(a)(14). This was added by the 1994 Amendments.

[36] Bankruptcy Code § 523(a)(2).

discharge of a loan made in reliance on a false financial statement; the most litigated aspect of the exception is that the statement must be materially false. Minor errors not clearly relevant to the decision to lend are not enough.[37]

BAFJA added a subsection to this provision that created a presumption of fraud in two circumstances; this subsection has since been amended, most recently in 1994. As now written, the first circumstance relates to consumer debts owed to one creditor for luxury goods or services incurred within sixty days before the order for relief and totaling more than $1,000. The second is for consumer credit advances of more than $1,000 under an open end credit plan (the most common example of an open end credit plan is a credit card) obtained within sixty days before the order for relief.[38] For example, suppose that Dora, a consumer debtor, took a $1,200 cash advance on her MonsterCard one week before she filed bankruptcy. That advance is presumed to have been obtained by fraud, and thus to be non-dischargeable.[39] The rule only creates a presumption; it can be rebutted by evidence that the debtor had a legitimate reason for obtaining the extension of credit.

Unscheduled Debts. Under some circumstances, debts not scheduled by the debtor are not discharged. Broadly speaking, this applies only if the creditor did not have timely notice of the proceeding; if it did, and failed to file a proof of claim, the debt owed to it is discharged.[40]

Fraud by a Fiduciary. Debts arising from the debtor's fraud or defalcation while acting in a fiduciary capacity, as well as debts arising from the debtor's embezzlement or larceny, are not dischargeable.[41] For example, if the debtor was a lawyer who had stolen client funds, the debt to the client is a non-dischargeable debt. There has been a fair amount of case law, most of it old, over the meaning of "fiduciary capacity." Although there has been a tendency to read the term somewhat narrowly, there is no doubt that it applies to persons such as lawyers, guardians, executors, key employees, and the like.[42] Note, however, that the

---

[37] Collier on Bankruptcy ¶ 523.09[2].

[38] Bankruptcy Code § 523(a)(2). "Luxury goods or services" is defined as those that are not reasonably acquired for the support or maintenance of the debtor or the debtor's dependents. What they may entail, and whether they are measured by an objective or a subjective standard, is not fully resolved. For a skeptical review of this provision, see Paul M. Black & Michael J. Herbert, *Bankcard's Revenge: A Critique of the 1984 Consumer Credit Amendments to the Bankruptcy Code*, 19 U. Rich. L. Rev. 845, 870-74 (1985). The amounts are now indexed to the CPI. Bankruptcy Code § 104.

[39] This rule was imposed by Congress in response to creditor grumbles that many consumers were indulging themselves in a last minute binge before bankruptcy. The evidence supporting this complaint is largely anecdotal.

[40] Bankruptcy Code § 523(a)(3).

[41] Bankruptcy Code § 523(a)(4).

[42] Collier on Bankruptcy ¶ 523.14.

"fiduciary capacity" language only debts arising from fraud or defalcation; debts arising from embezzlement and larceny are non-dischargeable regardless of the capacity of the debtor at the time of the wrongful acts. Thus, a debt arising from the theft of the creditor's property is non-dischargeable, even though the thieving debtor never was in a fiduciary relationship with the claimant.

Alimony, Maintenance and Support; Other Related Obligations. Generally speaking, obligations of the debtor to provide alimony, maintenance, or support of a spouse, former spouse, or child are non-dischargeable.[43] This provision reflects a general policy of preventing bankruptcy from becoming a haven for those who are unwilling to provide for their present or prior families, and who thereby increase the support burdens placed on the taxpayer. To be non-dischargeable, these obligations must arise in connection with a separation agreement, divorce decree, or other order of a court of record.[44]

In most circumstances, however, if the obligation has been assigned to a third party, whether the assignment was voluntarily or involuntary, the obligation will be dischargeable.[45] There is an exception to this exception if the assignment was to the federal or a state government.[46] As a general rule, the characterization of the obligation as alimony, maintenance or support by the court entering the order will control; however, that characterization is not dispositive. If the obligation is not "actually in the nature of" alimony, maintenance or support, it will be dischargeable. For example, a court order directing one spouse to pay debt on property awarded to the other spouse is not alimony and is therefore dischargeable.[47]

The 1994 Amendments somewhat broadened the protection given to obligations arising out of a marital breakdown. It added a new exception to discharge for obligations that do not fit within the existing exception for alimony, maintenance and support, but which do arise in the course of a divorce or separation, or in connection with a separation agreement or divorce degree. These obligations are not dischargeable unless either the debtor does not have the ability to pay the obligation from its disposable income or discharge of the debt would benefit the debtor more than it would harm the spouse, former spouse, or child who benefits from the obligation.[48]

---

[43] Bankruptcy Code § 523(a)(5).

[44] Bankruptcy Code § 523(a)(5).

[45] Bankruptcy Code § 523(a)(5)(A).

[46] Bankruptcy Code § 523(a)(5)(A).

[47] Fife v. Fife, 1 Utah 2d 281, 265 P.2d 642 (1954).

[48] Bankruptcy Code § 523(a)(15) (1994 Amendments).

Intentional Torts. A debt arising from a "willful and malicious injury" by the debtor is non-dischargeable.[49] This provision has been read rather broadly to encompass generally any obligation arising from an intentional tort.[50] This term may, however, exclude what might be called a "technical" intentional tort. The clearest example is inadvertent conversion of property. Although conversion is usually classified as an intentional tort, some conversions occur without any conscious wrongdoing on the part of a converter—e.g., a good faith purchase of goods from a thief. There is case law for holding that the debt is dischargeable.[51] Although there was some confusion under pre-code law as to whether "reckless" conduct or "gross" negligence was willful and malicious, it now appears clear that they are not.[52]

Fines, Penalties, and Forfeitures. Most fines, penalties, and forfeitures owed to governmental units are non-dischargeable. Those fines that are compensation for pecuniary loss, and certain tax penalties, are excluded from this rule and are thus dischargeable unless made non-dischargeable under another provision.[53]

Educational Loans. An outcry about alleged bankruptcy abuse by students who had received government-backed student loans led to the enactment of what is now section 523(a)(8). That section restricts, although it does not entirely prohibit, the bankruptcy discharge of student loans made, insured, or guaranteed by the government. These loans are not dischargeable unless (1) the loan first became due more than seven years before the bankruptcy or (2) excepting the loan from discharge would impose undue hardship on the debtor and the debtor's dependents.[54]

The undue hardship exception to non-dischargeability has generated a mass of litigation, most of it quite fact specific. Courts are most likely to find undue hardship if the debtor's income is at or near the federal poverty line,[55] especially if there are other circumstances, such as health problems.[56] Some courts have gone so far as to say that even poverty-level income is not enough to demonstrate undue hardship if the debtor has the capacity to make more money but is refusing to do so. Other courts have been more lenient, requiring only that the debtor need only

[49] Bankruptcy Code § 523(a)(6).

[50] Collier on Bankruptcy ¶ 523.16[1].

[51] See Davis v. Aetna Acceptance Co., 293 U.S. 328 (1934).

[52] Collier on Bankruptcy ¶ 523.16[1].

[53] Bankruptcy Code § 523(a)(7).

[54] Bankruptcy Code § 523(a)(8).

[55] See In re Bryant, 72 Bankr. 913 (Bankr. E.D. Pa. 1987).

[56] See Cheesman v. Tennessee Student Assistance Corp. (In re Cheesman), 25 F.3d 356 (6th Cir. 1994).

demonstrate "modest" income an a "no-frills" budget.[57] At least two circuit courts have used the following three part test:

> "[U]ndue hardship" requir [es] a three-part showing (1) that the debtor cannot maintain, based on current income and expenses, a "minimal" standard of living for [himself] and [his] dependants if forced to repay the loans; (2) that additional circumstances exist indicating that this state of affairs is likely to persist for a significant portion of the repayment period of the student loans; and (3) that the debtor has made good faith efforts to repay the loans.[58]

The non-discharge rules regarding student loans represent one of the most obvious reactions to the problem of "high roller" bankruptcy. Like section 707(b), which restricts access to Chapter 7 liquidation,[59] they are based on an image of widespread abuse by debtors who, having gained advantages not available to many people, ungratefully refuse to pay for those advantages. The image often adduced was that of a doctor whose education, heavily subsidized, was about to be turned into a high six-figure income but who first wished to shed debt. However, there is reason to believe that in practice the rules mainly burden those whose incomes are modest. It may well be those whose educations have not in fact enabled them to rise into the upper middle class who bear the brunt of the limitation on discharge.

It is also interesting to note that, unusual among the non-dischargeable debts, educational loans may in fact be discharged if non-dischargeability would impose undue hardship. It is difficult to see how payment an educational loan imposes more hardship on the debtor and the debtor's family than payment of an obligation arising out of unpaid taxes, embezzlement, or drunk driving. Perhaps the most plausible explanation for this lies in the image that gave birth to the non-dischargeability provision—the image of the rich ungrateful graduate. It may well be that Congress was offended mostly by the ingratitude, not the fact that the obligation was a student loan. A rich graduate, who ought to be grateful, is therefore not given a discharge. A poor graduate—who has little to be grateful for, since education has not in fact improved income prospects—may be discharged.

DUI Debts. Politics also played a significant role in the enactment of section 523(a)(9). It makes non-dischargeable any obligation for death or personal injury that is caused by the debtor's operation of a motor vehicle while unlawfully intoxicated on alcohol, drugs, or "another

[57] For discussions of this provision from various perspectives, see Arthur Ryman, *Contract Obligation: A Discussion of Morality, Bankruptcy, and Student Debt,* 42 Drake L. Rev. 205 (1993); Oliver B. Pollak & David B. Hicks, *Student Loans, Chapter 13, Classification of Debt, Unfair Discrimination and the Fresh Start After the Student Loan Default Prevention Initiative Act of 1990,* 1993 Det. Coll. of Law Rev. 1617 (1993); and Janice E. Kosel, *Running the Gauntlet of "Undue Hardship"—the Discharge of Student Loans in Bankruptcy,* 11 Golden Gate L. Rev. 457 (1981).

[58] In re Roberson, 999 F.2d 1132, 1135 (7th Cir. 1993), quoting Brunner v. New York State Higher Education Services Corp., 831 F.2d 395, 396 (2d Cir. 1987).

[59] For a discussion of Bankruptcy Code § 707(b), see § 16.03[B] of this book.

substance."[60] Perhaps surprisingly, this provision has engendered little litigation.

Debts Undischarged in Prior Proceedings. Under section 523(a)(10), a debtor may not obtain discharge for an obligation that either was or could have been scheduled in a prior bankruptcy proceeding, if the debtor either waived discharge or (with a few exceptions) was denied discharge.[61] The primary effect of this provision is to prevent a debtor who was denied discharge because of misconduct in one proceeding from obtaining discharge in a subsequent proceeding.

Fraud on Depository Institutions. As part of its reaction to the collapse of a large part of the American financial industry in the late 1980's, Congress added two non-dischargeable obligations. The first of these relates to certain obligations arising out of any act of fraud or defalcation while acting in a fiduciary capacity with respect to any depository institution or insured credit union.[62] This provision appears to be wholly redundant to section 523(a)(4), which more generally makes debts arising from fraud by a fiduciary non-dischargeable.[63]

Failure to Maintain Capital Requirements. The second addition to section 523 that arose from the collapse of banks and thrift institutions is section 523(a)(12), which applies to debtors for "malicious or reckless" failure by the debtor to fulfill its commitment to a Federal depository institution regulatory agency (such as the F.D.I.C. to maintain the capital of a financial institution).[64]

Finally, the 1994 Amendments added certain cxriminal restitution orders and post-petition condo fees.[65]

§ 12.04 Chapter 7 Discharge

[A]—Introduction

Most bankruptcies are filed, and still more are closed, under Chapter 7. Discharge is thus primarily an issue under that Chapter. Moreover, in most cases, discharge

[60] Bankruptcy Code § 523(a)(9).

[61] Bankruptcy Code § 523(a)(10).

[62] Bankruptcy Code § 523(a)(11).

[63] Of more real significance is Bankruptcy Code § 523(e), which broadens or at least clarifies who is classified as a fiduciary of a depository institution or insured credit union. It extends fiduciary duties to every "institution-affiliated party," a term which is defined in the Federal Deposit Insurance Act and the Federal Credit Union Act. See Bankruptcy Code § 101(33).

[64] Bankruptcy Code § 523(a)(12).

[65] Bankruptcy Code § 523(a)(13), (16).

is the only real function of Chapter 7, because there are no assets to be liquidated by or distributed by the trustee.[66]

[B]—Persons Eligible

Only natural persons—human beings—are eligible for Chapter 7 discharge.[67] A corporation or other business entity does not obtain discharge of its debts. The reason for this is rooted in the fact that, from time to time, federal tax laws are framed in such a way that tax advantages can be gained from the purchase of "shell" entities. Roughly, when the tax laws permit a profitable company to acquire and use the net operating loss of a defunct company, the acquiring company is able to reduce its federal income tax. The drafters of the Bankruptcy Code thought that this was bad tax policy. Consequently, they impose a price on any such acquisition. A profitable company may acquire a post-Chapter 7 shell; it may, if the Internal Revenue Code permits, use the net operating loss. However, it may have to pay a steep price. If, to obtain the tax benefits, the acquiring entity must merge with the shell, the acquiring entity thereby becomes liable for the shell's remaining debts because those debts have not been discharged.

As is true throughout the Code, any particular debtor may be denied discharge because of misconduct. This is discussed in § 12.02 of this chapter.

[C]—Timing of Discharge

The Chapter 7 discharge is supposed to be granted promptly. Under Rule 4004, once the time set for filing objections to discharge and motions to dismiss for substantial abuse, the court is to grant the discharge "forthwith."[68] This need not be done if there is a pending objection to discharge or to dismiss for substantial abuse. Moreover, the court may sui sponte delay entry of the order of discharge for 30 days; and if there is a motion made within that 30 day period, to a further date certain.[69]

[D]—Scope of Discharge

The full list of non-dischargeable debts set out in Section 523 of the Code and discussed in § 12.03 of this chapter is applicable in Chapter 7. This means that under some circumstances, Chapter 7 is a poor choice for the debtor. For example, if the debtor owes large tax obligations, or has committed fraud or some other intentional tort, it may be better for the debtor to file under Chapter 13 and obtain its more expansive discharge.

---

[66] See Michael J. Herbert & Domenic E. Pacitti, *Down and Out in Richmond, Virginia: The Distribution of Assets in Chapter 7 Bankruptcy Proceedings Closed During 1984-87,* 22 U. Rich. L. Rev. 303, 311 (1988) (92.3% of Chapter 7 cases are no-asset cases). See also, General Accounting Office, Report to the Chairman, Committee on the Judiciary of the House of Representatives, Bankruptcy Reform Act of 1978—A Before and After Look 56-57 (1983) (97% of Chapter 7 cases are no-asset cases).

[67] Bankruptcy Code § 727(a)(1).

[68] Bankruptcy Rule 4004(c).

[69] Bankruptcy Rule 4004(c).

Apart from the section 523 debts, Chapter 7 discharge extends to all debts that arose before the order for relief (i.e., in a voluntary case, all pre-petition debts).[70] Note that as a general rule, post-petition debts are not discharged. This is part and parcel of the structure of Chapter 7, which is designed to deal almost exclusively with pre-petition debt and pre-petition property. Some post petition debts are encompassed in the discharge—namely, those that are treated "as if" they were incurred pre-petition. These include an number of claims, for example, the claims of involuntary gap creditors (those who extended credit after an involuntary petition and before the order for relief), the claims of those from whom property was recovered by the trustee, and claims arising from the rejection of executory contracts and unexpired leases.[71]

§ 12.05 Chapter 13 Discharge

[A]—Persons Eligible

Chapter 13 by its terms is available only to individual debtors.[72] In consequence, there is no need for any additional limitation on those eligible for discharge. Since business entities cannot use Chapter 13, there are no concerns about the sale of shell companies emerging from it. As is true throughout the Code, any particular debtor may be denied discharge because of misconduct. This is discussed in § 12.02 of this chapter.

[B]—Timing of Discharge

Ordinarily, a Chapter 13 discharge is granted only upon completion of the plan of reorganization (which means upon completion of either the initial plan or if the plan has been modified, of the modified plan). The court is to grant the discharge "as soon as practicable" after the debtor makes the last plan payment.[73] An earlier, hardship discharge may be requested under some circumstances.[74]

[C]—Scope of Discharge

[1]—Introduction

The scope of discharge under Chapter 13 depends on whether the debtor successfully completes his or her plan. Successful completion—either of the original plan or of a modified plan—entitles the debtor to a broader discharge than is available under other Chapters. The debtor may under some circumstances obtain a

---

[70] Bankruptcy Code § 727(b).

[71] See Bankruptcy Code §§ 727(b) and 502.

[72] Bankruptcy Code § 109(e).

[73] Bankruptcy Code § 1328(a).

[74] For a discussion of hardship discharge, see § 12.05[C][3] of this chapter.

narrower hardship discharge. The discharge encompasses only those debts that were provided for under the plan and those that were disallowed under section 502.[75]

[2]—Discharge Upon Completion of Plan

As is discussed in depth in Chapter 18, the core of the Chapter 13 proceeding is the debtor's plan for repayment of all or (more commonly) a portion of his or her debts over a three to five year period.[76] As one of the incentives given to debtors to choose this route, Congress provided a broad discharge provision for those who complete their plans. Under section 1328, all plan obligations and all section 502 disallowed obligations are discharged except for the following:

> "Long term" obligations; more precisely, claims on which the last payment is due after the due date of the final payment under the plan.[77]
>
> Alimony, maintenance and support obligations that are non-dischargeable under section 523(a)(5).[78]
>
> Educational loans that are non-dischargeable under section 523(a)(8).[79]
>
> Driving while intoxicated obligations that are non-dischargeable under section 523(a)(9).[80]
>
> Restitution obligations included in a sentence imposed upon the debtor's conviction of a crime.[81]
>
> Criminal fines.[82]

This means of course that some debtors may gain considerably from a Chapter 13 filing. For example, a debtor with considerable tax liabilities, or who has committed an intentional tort, may in Chapter 13 obtain discharge of those debts. This discharge is not, however, cost-free. Chapter 13 usually requires a greater total payment from the debtor than Chapter 7. In addition, when evaluating the adequacy of payments proposed by the Chapter 13 debtor, many courts have considered how much the debtor proposes to pay with regard to debts that would not be dischargeable under

---

[75] Bankruptcy Code § 1305(a) has the effect of permitting the discharge of certain post-petition obligations, namely, those for taxes and for consumer obligations arising from property or services necessary for the debtor's performance under the plan.

[76] See § 18.01.

[77] Bankruptcy Code § 1328(a)(1), 1322(a)(5).

[78] Bankruptcy Code § 1328(a)(2). For a fuller discussion of non-dischargeable alimony, maintenance, and support obligations, see § 12.03 of this chapter.

[79] Bankruptcy Code § 1328(a)(2). For a fuller discussion of non-dischargeable educational loans, see § 12.03 of this chapter.

[80] Bankruptcy Code § 1328(a)(2). For a fuller discussion of non-dischargeable DUI obligations, see § 12.03 of this chapter.

[81] Bankruptcy Code § 1328(a).

[82] Bankruptcy Code § 1328(a). This was added by the 1994 Amendments.

Chapter 7; such courts may require the debtor to pay even more than would otherwise be the case in Chapter 13.[83]

Congress itself has shown ambivalence about the breadth of Chapter 13 discharge. The scope of the Chapter 13 regular discharge has gradually been narrowing since the original Code. Nothing could better illustrate the difficulties presented by any effort to strike a reasonable balance between competing interests in bankruptcy. Congress at first sought to draw debtors into Chapter 13 by offering a generous discharge; then, seemingly appalled by the fact that people actually took advantage of that offer, turned more and more restrictive.

[3]—Hardship Discharge

In many cases, the Chapter 13 debtor cannot complete the plan. The debtor has a broad right to modify the plan; if the modified plan is confirmed and the debtor completes it, the debtor is still given the full Chapter 13 discharge.[84] However, modification is often impractical.[85] The Chapter 13 debtor may then choose to convert the case to Chapter 7, and obtain a Chapter 7 discharge. In the alternative, the debtor may request a Chapter 13 "hardship discharge." The court may grant the discharge only if

1. The debtor's failure to complete the plan payments is due to circumstances for which the debtor should not justly be held accountable.
2. The creditors have received at least the Chapter 7 liquidation value of their unsecured claims. In calculating this, the payments actually made are reduced to present value as of the effective date of the plan. For example, suppose that if the case had been a Chapter 7 case, rather than a Chapter 13 case, $10,000 would have been distributed on the unsecured claims. If, when reduced to present value as of the effective date of the plan, the payments actually made are at least equal to $10,000, this requirement is met.
3. Modification of the plan is not practicable.[86] The hardship discharge, however, is no broader than a Chapter 7 discharge;[87] indeed, it may be narrower since, as is generally true in Chapter 13, certain long-term obligations are not discharged.[88] The real value of the hardship discharge is simply that it avoids the additional cost and time that might be involved in converting the case to Chapter 7.

---

[83] See § 18.08[A][2] of this book.

[84] For a full discussion of Chapter 13 modification, see § 18.09 of this book.

[85] For a particularly striking example, see In re Bond, 36 Bankr. 49 (Bankr. E.D.N.C. 1984) (Chapter 13 debtor could neither complete nor modify the plan because she was dead).

[86] Bankruptcy Code § 1328(b).

[87] Bankruptcy Code § 1328(c)(2).

[88] Bankruptcy Code § 1328(c)(1).

§ 12.06 Chapter 11 Discharge

[A]—Persons Eligible

As discussed in Chapter 6, Chapter 11 is broadly available to nearly every person.[89] Everyone who is eligible to file Chapter 11 is eligible for a Chapter 11 discharge. Unlike Chapter 7, discharge is available to corporations, partnerships, and other artificial entities in Chapter 11.

[B]—Timing of Discharge

Unlike Chapters 12 and 13, Chapter 11 discharge is normally granted when the plan is confirmed; indeed, it is the fact of confirmation itself that ordinarily discharges the debtor.[90] Either the plan or the order of confirmation can provide for a postponement of discharge, but this is very rare.

[C]—Scope of Discharge

The scope rules of Chapter 11's discharge provision are rather simple. Essentially, the obligations under the Chapter 11 plan substitute for the debtor's pre-confirmation obligations. Insofar as corporations and other artificial entities are concerned, virtually all existing debt is discharged, and the sole remaining obligations are those undertaken in the plan.[91] The situation of the individual Chapter 11 debtor is more complicated, since he or she remains obligated on all the debts listed in section 523 as non-dischargeable.[92]

§ 12.07 Chapter 12 Discharge

[A]—Persons Eligible

The Chapter 12 discharge is available to anyone who may be a Chapter 12 debtor. Eligibility for Chapter 12 is limited to "family farmers," a term which can include some closely held family corporations and partnerships.[93]

[B]—Timing of Discharge

Ordinarily, a Chapter 12 discharge is granted only upon completion of the plan of reorganization (which means upon completion of either the initial plan or if the plan has been modified, of the modified plan). The court is to grant the discharge "as soon as practicable" after the debtor makes the last plan payment (other than

---

[89] See § 6.02[B].

[90] Bankruptcy Code § 1141(d)(1)(A).

[91] Bankruptcy Code § 1141(d)(1)(A).

[92] Bankruptcy Code § 1141(d)(2). For a discussion of those debts, see § 12.03 of this chapter.

[93] For a definition of "family farmer," see § 6.02[B] of this book.

certain payments permitted on long-term debt).[94] An earlier hardship discharge may be requested under some circumstances.[95]

[C]—Scope of Discharge

The discharge encompasses those debts that were provided for under the plan, administrative expenses, and claims that were disallowed under section 502.[96] Unlike a Chapter 13 discharge, a Chapter 12 discharge does not encompass otherwise non-dischargeable debts. The Chapter 12 debtor thus remains obligated, even after the discharge is granted, on the full list of section 523 debts.[97] In addition, the Chapter 12 debtor remains obligated on long-term debts that extend beyond the completion of the plan.[98]

Like Chapter 13, Chapter 12 does provide for an early hardship discharge. The scope of the hardship discharge is exactly the same as the scope of the regular Chapter 12 discharge[99] (in this respect, Chapter 12 differs from Chapter 13). A hardship discharge may be granted if the debtor's failure to complete the plan is excusable, and creditors have received at least the liquidation value of their claims, and modification of the plan is not practicable.[100]

§ 12.08 Revocation of Discharge

[A]—Introduction

Under very limited circumstances, a discharge previously granted may be revoked. Revocation always involves serious misconduct by the debtor. In addition, revocation may only be requested within a relatively short time after the discharge was granted. Even when the debtor has committed a seriously wrongful act, the need for finality and closure militates for an early statute of repose. Because this need for finality is considered to be greater in a reorganization proceeding that in a liquidation proceeding, the requirements for revoking confirmation under Chapters 11, 12 and 13 are even more restrictive than the requirements under Chapter 7.

[B]—Revocation Under Chapter 7

Under Chapter 7, discharge may only be revoked in three circumstances. These are as follows:

1. The discharge was obtained by the debtor's fraud, and the person who is requesting that discharge be revoked did not know of the fraud until after the discharge was granted.[101]

---

[94] Bankruptcy Code § 1228(a).

[95] For a discussion of hardship discharge, see § 12.06[C] of this chapter.

[96] Bankruptcy Code § 1228(a).

[97] For a discussion of section 523 debts, see § 12.03 of this chapter.

[98] Bankruptcy Code § 1228(a)(1).

[99] Bankruptcy Code § 1228(c).

[100] Bankruptcy Code § 1228(b).

[101] Bankruptcy Code § 727(d)(1).

2. The debtor acquired property of the estate, or became entitled to acquire property that would be property of the estate, and both knowingly and fraudulently failed to report this, or to deliver or surrender the property to the trustee.[102] For example, if the debtor receives an inheritance within 180 days of the filing of the petition, that property is property of the estate;[103] failure to report its receipt or to hand it over to the trustee is grounds for revocation of discharge.
3. The debtor engaged in certain types of misconduct during the case.[104] These are unjustified refusal to testify or refusal to obey other lawful orders of the court.

The trustee, any creditor, and the United States Trustee all have standing to assert any of these grounds for revocation.[105] The court may not revoke the discharge without notice and an opportunity for a hearing.[106] There are tight time limitations placed on raising any of these objections. Fraud may be raised only within one year after the discharge is granted.[107] Failure to report/surrender property and misconduct may only be raised within the later of one year after the discharge is granted and the date the case is closed.[108]

[C]—Revocation Under Chapter 11

Because under Chapter 11 confirmation is nearly always the point at which the debtor obtains discharge, revocation of the discharge is dealt with in conjunction with revocation of the former. Section 1144 contains a detailed discussion of revocation of confirmation. In brief, any party in interest may move for revocation of the confirmation order, but only within 180 days after the order was entered.[109] The only basis on which the court may revoke confirmation is if it was procured by fraud.[110] If the confirmation is revoked, the court must, among other things, revoke the debtor's discharge.[111]

[D]—Revocation Under Chapters 12 and 13

Chapters 12 and 13 have identical revocation provisions. Note that unlike Chapter 11, Chapters 12 and 13 separate confirmation from discharge; thus a revocation of an order of confirmation is unrelated to an order revoking discharge.[112] It is

---

[102] Bankruptcy Code § 727(d)(2).

[103] See § 7.02 of this book.

[104] Bankruptcy Code § 727(d)(3), (a)(6).

[105] Bankruptcy Code § 727(d).

[106] Bankruptcy Code § 727(d).

[107] Bankruptcy Code § 727(e)(1).

[108] Bankruptcy Code § 727(e)(2).

[109] Bankruptcy Code § 1144.

[110] This is made very clear in the statute—"the court may revoke such order if and only if such order was procured by fraud." Bankruptcy Code § 1144.

[111] Bankruptcy Code § 1144(2).

[112] For a discussion of revocation of confirmation under Chapters 12 and 13, see §§ 19.10 and 18.10, respectively.

virtually impossible for a discharge to be granted during the time in which the confirmation could still be revoked.

Any party in interest may move for revocation of the discharge. The motion must be made within one year the discharge was granted. The discharge may be revoked if and only if (i) the discharge was obtained by fraud and (ii) the moving party did not know of the fraud until after the discharge was granted.[113] Prior to any revocation of the discharge, the court must provide notice and an opportunity for a hearing.

§ 12.09 Reaffirmation

Reaffirmation of discharged debts has a long and controversial history. Many debtors, prompted by conscience or by creditor pressure, are willing to sacrifice at least some of the benefits of bankruptcy by reaffirming one or more discharged debts. Nearly every state has held that, insofar as contract law is concerned, those reaffirmed debts are binding, even though the creditor gave no new consideration for the debtor's promise to pay.[114] Reaffirmation has long been classified as a situation where "moral consideration" will support a contract—or, perhaps more candidly, as a situation in which consideration is unnecessary.[115]

Congress became concerned about what it saw as an excessive number of reaffirmations. There is at least anecdotal evidence that, under the Bankruptcy Act, a significant number of debtors were virtually undoing their bankruptcies by reaffirming all their discharged obligations. Congress was particularly troubled by the assertion that in many cases the reaffirmations were procured under duress, or that the debtor was poorly advised and not acting in his or her own best interests.

The Bankruptcy Code considerably changed the process of reaffirmation. In the original version of the Code, reaffirmation agreements required the approval of the judge. Neither creditors nor busy bankruptcy judges were entirely happy about this, so BAFJA largely shifted the burden of evaluating the appropriateness of reaffirmation agreements to the debtor's attorney, and the 1994 Amendments tinkered further with the rules. The judge now makes the determination only in cases where the debtor is not represented by counsel. This structure too has its critics; there are concerns that imposing the burden of evaluating reaffirmations on counsel can create conflicts of interest that may not be adequately addressed by the lawyers involved.

At present, the following requirements must be met for a reaffirmation agreement to be binding:

1. The agreement must be enforceable under applicable non-bankruptcy law.[116] This pretty clearly means that a state may further restrict or prohibit reaffirmations by making judicial or legislative changes in their own contract law.

---

113 Bankruptcy Code §§ 1228(d), 1328(e).

114 E. Allan Farnsworth, Contracts § 2.8 (1990).

115 Id.

116 Bankruptcy Code § 524(c).

2. The agreement must be made before the discharge is granted.[117] Among other things, this requirement ensures that the agreement is made while the case is still pending and the debtor's and creditor's actions are still readily subject to court control.

3. The debtor has the right to rescind the agreement. The agreement may be rescinded up to the later of (i) the discharge or (ii) sixty days after the agreement is filed with the court. All that the debtor need do to rescind is give notice of rescission to the holder of the claim. There is no requirement that this notice be in any particular form.[118] The purpose of this rescission right is to allow a cooling off period; many debtors, in an unwarranted burst of optimism, may make promises of repayment that on calm reflection are impracticable.

4. The agreement must contain a clear and conspicuous statement of the debtor's rescission rights.[119] It must also contain a clear and conspicuous statement that the debtor is not required to enter into the agreement.[120]

5. The agreement must be filed with the court.[121]

6. If the debtor was represented by counsel during the negotiation of the agreement, the attorney must file a declaration or affidavit containing the attorney's approval of the agreement. Specifically, the attorney must state that (i) the agreement represents a fully informed and voluntary agreement by the debtor, (ii) the agreement does not impose an undue hardship on the debtor or a dependent of the debtor, and (iii) the attorney has fully advised the debtor of the legal effect and consequences of the agreement and of any default under the agreement.[122]

7. If the debtor is an individual, and was not represented by a lawyer in the negotiation of the agreement, the court has additional obligations. The court must hold a hearing at which the debtor appears in person. At the hearing, the court must inform the debtor that the agreement is not required, and of its legal effect and consequences, as well as the consequences of default. Moreover, the court may approve the agreement only if (i) it does not impose an undue hardship on the debtor or a dependent of the debtor, and (ii) it is in the best interests of the debtor. Normally, the agreement is enforceable only if the court approves it.[123] However, court approval is not required if the debt is a consumer debt secured by real property.[124]

---

[117] Bankruptcy Code § 524(c)(1).

[118] Bankruptcy Code § 524(c)(2). Bankruptcy Code § 524(c)(4) states, rather obviously, that the agreement is not enforceable if the debtor exercises its right to rescind.

[119] Bankruptcy Code § 524(c)(2)(A).

[120] Bankruptcy Code § 524(c)(2)(B).

[121] Bankruptcy Code § 524(c)(3).

[122] Bankruptcy Code § 523(c)(3). The last requirement was added by the 1994 Amendments.

[123] Bankruptcy Code §§ 524 (c)(6)(A), (d).

[124] Bankruptcy Code §§ 524(c)(6)(B), (d)(2).

The lawyer's obligation can create problems. For example, suppose that Doug, who has three dependent children and a net monthly income of $1,400, wishes to reaffirm his $350 per month obligation to Easy Rider Motors, so that he can keep his motorcycle. Doug uses this motorcycle only for personal recreation. Doug's lawyer is forced to evaluate not only the client's wish to keep the motorcycle, but also the impact that the monthly payments will have on the kids. This presents at least some conflict of interest. Unfortunately, there is little in the case law or the literature to assist lawyers in dealing with problems of this type.

It is generally believed that reaffirmations are rarely appropriate for anything other than secured debt. Seldom will the debtor receive benefits from paying an unsecured claim that are in any way equivalent to the cost of the payments. It thus appears that reaffirmation agreements are used almost exclusively as a way of allowing the debtor to keep encumbered property that would otherwise be lost to the creditors. It is a more flexible device than redemption, because redemption requires a lump-sum payment and reaffirmation permits payment over time. Indeed, to some degree reaffirmation agreements turn Chapter 7 proceedings into quasi-reorganizations; as in a reorganization, the reaffirming debtor gets to keep more of its present assets in exchange for its future income. Unlike a regular reorganization, however, the reaffirming debtor need not deal with all of its creditors. It may in effect prefer some creditors over others.

Finally, it is important to stress that a reaffirmation is a contract. The creditor must agree to the reaffirmation. Even if the debtor proposes to pay the obligation in full and as scheduled, the creditor may refuse the offer. (In this respect, reaffirmation is less flexible than redemption or reorganization, since creditors must accept proper redemption payments and, generally speaking, cannot prevent reorganization.)

Similarly, reaffirmation does not require the parties to agree to the exact terms of the original obligation; as is true with any contract, a contract underlying a reaffirmed debt can be modified. Within broad limits, the creditor may be given more favorable terms under the reaffirmation agreement than it had under the original agreement. For example, courts have found that it may be permissible to include in the reaffirmation agreement payment by the debtor of the creditor's costs of entering into the agreement, even though no such provision appeared in the original agreement.[125] Of course, at some point the additional terms might make the agreement unduly burdensome or not in the best interests of the debtor; it is even possible that an unduly one-sided reaffirmation agreement might be attacked, post-bankruptcy, as unconscionable. The reaffirmation agreement may also modify the original contract in ways that are favorable to the debtor. A creditor who is reasonably confident of the debtor's ability to pay might well agree to a longer payment schedule with lower monthly payments.

As a final, and probably unnecessary, sop to creditors, BAFJA added section 524(f), which states the obvious: the reaffirmation rules do not prevent a debtor from voluntarily repaying any debt. Discharge merely removes any legal significance from an obligation. It does not prevent anyone who either feels a moral obligation

[125] See In re Sholos, 11 Bankr. 782 (Bankr. W.D. Pa. 1981).

to pay from paying; nor does it prohibit payment by a debtor who hopes thereby to gain a material advantage. This section is not quite the forlorn hope that cynics assume: there is anecdotal evidence that a small but not negligible amount of discharged debt is voluntarily repaid.

§ 12.10 Effect of Discharge

Discharge has a number of direct and indirect effects on the debtor and the debtor's obligations. The discharge voids any judgment based on the debtor's personal liability for a discharged debt.[126] It operates as an injunction against any action to collect, recover, or offset any discharged debt as a personal liability of the debtor.[127] There are also special rules that deal with the effect of the discharge on community property.[128] All of these rules apply even if the discharge of the underlying debt is waived.

Note that most of these rules apply only to the debtor's personal liability. This is but one expression of the basic bankruptcy policy, discussed earlier in this Chapter,[129] that liens survive the bankruptcy. The avoidance of judgments, and the injunction against actions, does not apply to judgments or actions in rem—that is, judgments or actions that relate solely to property and do not impose any personal obligation on the debtor. For example, discharge does not prevent a mortgage holder from foreclosing on the mortgaged property.

The Code also contains limited protections against discrimination against bankrupts. These limits apply primarily but not exclusively to governmental agencies. Except with regard to employment, and in some cases student loans, private parties are not prohibited from anti-debtor discrimination; and, indeed, such discrimination is assumed to be part of the hidden cost of bankruptcy.

With a few limited exceptions that are rarely relevant, a governmental unit is prohibited from discriminating against debtors with regard to licenses, permits, charters, franchises, or employment.[130] The term "governmental unit" encompasses federal, state, local, commonwealth, and territorial governments and their agencies.[131] The purpose of this anti-discrimination provision is to prevent the government from frustrating the fresh start goal by impeding the ability of the debtor to make a living.

When it comes to the question of determining what conduct constitutes unfair discrimination, the prohibition has been read somewhat narrowly. The statute only prohibits discrimination that is based solely on the bankruptcy or the effects of the bankruptcy. It does not prohibit discrimination based on factors that may be related

---

[126] Bankruptcy Code § 524(a)(1).

[127] Bankruptcy Code § 524(a)(2).

[128] Bankruptcy Code § 524(a)(3), (b), (e).

[129] See § 12.01.

[130] Bankruptcy Code § 525(a).

[131] Bankruptcy Code § 101(27).

to the bankruptcy, such as the debtor's financial condition and financial responsibility.[132] The key question is whether the government is applying a test that is facially neutral—a test that applies equally to all. For example, a reasonably based rule that every person who wishes to obtain a business license must either have a minimum level of unencumbered assets or obtain a minimum level of insurance is normally permissible, even though this will have the effect of disqualifying a disproportionate number of former bankrupts. To put it in language familiar to civil rights attorneys, section 525(a) does not include a disparate impact test.

Most courts have been somewhat more flexible in their interpretation of the matters encompassed by the anti-discrimination prohibition. The language "license, permit, charter, franchise, or other similar grant" has been read to encompass a wide variety of government benefits. Not only are obvious things, such as business licenses, covered; certain entitlements, such as the right to remain in public housing and thus receive an indirect subsidy from the government, have been held to be protected.[133] On the other hand, if the government benefit involves an extension of credit, courts are likely to find that the government is not prohibited from discriminating, because that form of discrimination is not prohibited by section 525.

Section 525(b) imposes a more limited prohibition on discrimination by private parties. Private employers may not terminate or otherwise discriminate against former bankrupts merely because of the bankruptcy, the debtor's pre-discharge insolvency, or the fact that discharged debts are unpaid.[134] There is practically no reported litigation under this provision; what little there is suggests that the employer's duty is no greater than that of a governmental entity. The employer may not discriminate per se against the former bankrupt. It may, however, take into account financial responsibility; if it does so according to facially neutral criteria, there will be no prohibited discrimination.

The 1994 Amendments added a further limitation that applies both to governmental and private creditors. Under section 525(c), neither a governmental unit nor certain private lenders are permitted to discriminate with regard to student loans. The prohibition applies to the grant of a loan, a loan guarantee, or loan insurance.[135] This provision was apparently added in the belief that refusal of student loans to former bankrupts would, by restricting their access to further education, unduly increase the possibility of future financial trouble. It stands in curious contrast to the provision that generally denies discharge to student loans, however.

---

[132] Collier on Bankruptcy ¶ 525.02.

[133] In re Sudler, 71 Bankr. 780 (Bankr. E.D. Pa. 1987).

[134] Bankruptcy Code § 525(b).

[135] Bankruptcy Code § 525(c) (1994 Amendment).

CHAPTER 13

General Avoiding Powers; General Limitations on Avoiding Powers

§ 13.01 Introduction

In this and subsequent chapters, we explore the so-called avoiding powers of the trustee and the Debtor-in-Possession. The trustee/DIP is given authority to set aside various transactions because they are considered improper. In some cases, the impropriety is fairly obvious, such as the fraudulent transfer of assets on which creditors relied in making the decision to extend credit. In other cases, the powers are more controversial: some transactions that cannot be set aside outside of bankruptcy, and do not normally hurt any third party, may be set aside in bankruptcy without any showing that anyone has been injured by the transaction. Some of the avoiding powers are directly borrowed from state law. Others depend in part on state law rules. Still others are entirely or almost entirely federal rules. None, however, can be preempted by state laws.

These powers are powers of avoidance; the Code does not make the transaction void but merely gives the trustee/DIP the right to avoid them.[1] In most cases, of course, the duty of the trustee/DIP to creditors requires that the power to avoid be exercised. However, in some cases, it may be reasonable to leave the transaction alone. For example, if the transfer is small, or its voidability uncertain, it may be unduly expensive to attempt avoidance. In addition, it may be reasonable to refrain from avoiding a transaction as a way of reaching agreement with the transferee on other matters. It may be sensible—and permissible—for a DIP to drop a preference action against a creditor in exchange for the creditor agreeing to provide new financing at reasonable rates that makes it possible to fund a reorganization plan.

This Chapter discusses a number of general avoiding powers that, while important, do not require extensive discussion. There are many other avoiding powers discussed in detail elsewhere in this book. These include preferences,[2] fraudulent transactions avoidable under section 548 of the Code,[3] and certain non-possessory, non-purchase money security interests.[4]

There are also limitations on the avoidance powers. Some of these limitations are specific to the power; for example, there are specific limitations on the ability of the trustee/DIP to avoid a preference. The specific limitations are discussed in

[1] By contrast, actions in violation of the automatic stay are generally viewed as void ab initio—see § 8.07[A] of this book.

[2] See Chapter 14 of this book.

[3] See Chapter 15 of this book.

[4] See § 11.09 of this book.

conjunction with the specific discussion of the avoiding power.[5] Others are of broader application; these general limitations are discussed in this Chapter.

A final note. Avoidance powers are exercised by the trustee in a Chapter 7 case. They are exercised by the debtor-in-possession in a Chapter 11 or 12 case, unless a trustee is appointed. There is some confusion about who exercises the avoidance rights in a Chapter 13 case, because the Chapter 13 DIP is not explicitly given the broad powers provided to the Chapter 11 and Chapter 12 DIP. The courts are divided over whether the Chapter 13 DIP may avoid transactions; many have held that only the Chapter 13 trustee may exercize the avoidance powers.

§ 13.02 Strong-Arm Clause

Section 544(a), often known as the strong-arm clause, is the single most significant of the trustee/DIP's avoiding powers. This section primarily affects transfers that were incomplete on the date of the bankruptcy. It gives the trustee the status of a person whose rights are interposed between the transferor and the transferee, and who thus is unaffected by the transfer. There are three subsections, each of which is taken up in turn.

Section 544(a)(1) gives the trustee/DIP the status of a hypothetical lien holder—more specifically, the rights of a person who obtained, as of the commencement of the case, "a judicial lien on all property on which a creditor on a simple contract could have obtained . . . a judicial lien."[6] Note that this status arises whether or not there actually is such a creditor. The single most significant impact of this rule is on unperfected Article 9 security interests (although it is by no means the only interest affected). As noted in Chapter 2, in nearly every case (the exceptions are not relevant in the bankruptcy context) only a perfected security interest has priority over a judicial lien.[7] Thus, an unperfected security interest is subject to the rights of the trustee/DIP; it is therefore worthless in bankruptcy.

This result also suggests one of the objections to section 544(a). Outside of bankruptcy, if there were no judicial lien, the fact that the security interest was unperfected would not matter. The perfection rules of Article 9 are designed to protect lienholders, buyers, and other secured creditors. They do not protect general unsecured creditors. As between a general unsecured creditor and the holder of an unperfected security interest, the holder of the unperfected security interest has priority.[8] Why, then, should there be a different outcome in bankruptcy? If there is no buyer, no secured creditor, and no actual lienholder, why should the trustee, and thus the unsecured creditors get what they would not have gotten otherwise?

A number of justifications have been offered for this. The strongest is that section 544(a) is a prophylactic measure that polices against the possibility of fraud and

---

[5] For example, see § 14.03, in which the limitations on preference avoidance are discussed.

[6] Bankruptcy Code § 544(a)(1).

[7] See § 2.02[C][1].

[8] See Thomas D. Crandall, Michael J. Herbert & Lary Lawrence, Uniform Commercial Code § 26.5 (1993).

injury to third parties. For example, given the ease with which an Article 9 security interest can be perfected, imposing a bankruptcy penalty for non-perfection may be justifiable to prevent even the chance that the failure to perfect has misled others. Critics, however, are unconvinced, and there have been proposals to rewrite section 544(a) so as to protect only those creditors who are protected under state law.

Second, section 544(a)(2) endows the trustee/DIP with the rights of a hypothetical creditor that extends credit to the debtor at the time the case was commenced and simultaneously obtains execution against the debtor that is returned unsatisfied.[9] This strong-arm power is relatively insignificant. It is not further discussed in this book.

Finally, the trustee/DIP has the rights of a bona fide purchaser of realty (other than fixtures.[10] Again, it does not matter whether there actually is a BFP of realty, or indeed anyone who has been injured by the failure to record the deed. This provision permits the avoidance of incomplete real estate transfers made by the debtor. For example, suppose that Dora executed a deed transferring Blancmange Acre to Bette on July 1, 1997. The deed was never recorded and, under state law, at least some BFP's take free of unrecorded deeds. Dora filed bankruptcy on July 7, 1998. The trustee, as a hypothetical BFP, can avoid the transfer to Bette, thus pulling Blancmange Acre into the estate.

Note that under state law the ability of a BFP to avoid an unrecorded deed is generally limited. If the BFP has or should have notice of the buyer's rights, the BFP usually takes subject to those rights. For example, it is generally true that, if the buyer is in possession of the property, the BFP cannot avoid the purchase. In the prior hypothetical, if Bette had been in possession of Blancmange Acre, her rights might have been superior to those of an actual BFP, even though the deed was unrecorded.[11] This type of limitation, however, does not necessarily affect the rights of the trustee/DIP under section 544(a)(3). The bankruptcy question is not whether all BFPs take free of the purchaser's interest, but rather whether any BFP takes free. Thus, so long as some type or class of BFP would be able to avoid the transfer from debtor to the purchaser, the trustee/DIP can avoid the transfer.[12] In the Dora-Bette example, if, under state law, Bette's possession protected her interest against all BFPs, regardless of whether they had knowledge or notice of it, then the trustee/DIP could not avoid Bette's interest. However, if Bette's possession protected her interest only against those BFP's who knew or should have known that she was in possession, then the trustee/DIP could avoid it.

---

[9] Bankruptcy Code § 544(a)(2).

[10] Bankruptcy Code § 544(a)(3).

[11] See Roger A. Cunningham, William B. Stoebuck & Dale A. Whitman, The Law of Property 838 (2d ed. 1993).

[12] "The trustee shall have, as of the commencement of the case, *and without regard to any knowledge of the trustee or of any creditor* the rights and powers of . . . (3) a bona fide purchaser of real property . . ." Bankruptcy Code § 544(a) (emphasis added).

§ 13.03 Power to Exercise Avoiding Powers of Actual Unsecured Creditors

Section 544(b) enables the trustee/DIP to avoid transactions that are avoidable by actual general unsecured creditors under non-bankruptcy law.[13] Although this generally means state law, it does encompass other federal laws as well. Unlike section 544(a), which is similarly based on non-bankruptcy law, section 544(b) does not create a set of hypothetical rights. Rather, it merely provides for the enforcement by the trustee/DIP of rights that the actual unsecured creditors of the debtor already have.[14] There must really be a creditor who could avoid the transaction outside the bankruptcy.

Note, however, that while the power of avoidance is derivative of the power given to a real creditor or creditors, it is exercised for the benefit of all the creditors. Outside bankruptcy, the avoidance might only be used to benefit the particular creditor who seeks avoidance; for example, the complaining creditor's claim might be satisfied by avoiding only $7,000 of a $30,000 transfer; the remainder might be left intact. Inside bankruptcy, there is no such limitation. The transfer is avoided not just to the extent necessary to obtain payment for an individual creditor, but rather to the extent necessary to provide payment of all of the unsecured claims.[15] Since full satisfaction of all unsecured claims is highly improbable, for all practical purposes this means that the transaction is entirely avoided.

Technically, avoidance under section 544(b) is avoidance under federal bankruptcy law; however, the section is entirely transparent to the underlying state or federal law. In other words, the trustee/DIP can under this section avoid if, but only if, the transaction is avoidable under other law. Broadly speaking, under this provision, transactions that can be avoided outside of bankruptcy can be avoided inside brankruptcy; and transactions that cannot be avoided ouside bankruptcy cannot be avoided inside bankruptcy. The rights and limitations of the non-bankruptcy law apply, and except as specifically provided in the Bankruptcy Code, the rights created and limitations imposed by the Code do not.[16] For example, if a creditor with an allowable claim could under applicable state law challenge a fraudulent transfer that occurred three years previously, the trustee/DIP may make the same challenge under section 544(b). This is so even though the Bankruptcy Code's fraudulent transfer provision only permits challenges against transfers that occur within one year.[17]

---

[13] Bankruptcy Code § 544(b).

[14] Specifically, those creditors who have claims allowable under section 502 or disallowed only because of section 502(e) (disallowed claimes for reimbursement or contribution). Bankruptcy Code § 544(b). Note that this provision does not permit the trustee/DIP to assert the rights of a secured creditor. See Collier on Bankruptcy ¶ 544.03.

[15] For the classic articulation of this rule, see Moore v. Bay (In re Estate of Sassard & Kimball), 284 U.S. 4 (1931).

[16] See Havee v. Belk, 775 F.2d 1209, 1218-19 (4th Cir. 1985).

[17] See Chapter 15 of this book.

The transparency of section 544(b) to the actual rights of actual creditors can either expand or limit the ability of the trustee/DIP to avoid a transaction. For example, an avoidance right can be extinguished by pre-petition actions of the creditor from whom the trustee/DIP's right is derived. Until the case is filed, the avoidance power belongs to creditors; they may waive it, be estopped from enforcing it, fail to act within the statute of limitations, or compromise it. A pre-filing waiver, estoppel, failure to act timely, or settlement generally has been held to extinguish the trustee/DIP's power to avoid under section 544(b).[18] In short, the trustee/DIP cannot avoid the transaction because the right to avoid ceased to exist prior to the time that the rights of existing creditors passed from them to the trustee/DIP.

§ 13.04 Avoidance of Statutory Liens

By and large, liens on the debtor's property that are created by statute are enforceable in bankruptcy and give the lienholder a secured claim. There are, however, some exceptions to this. Section 545 permits the trustee/DIP to avoid "the fixing of a statutory lien" on certain "property of the debtor."[19]

A statutory lien is defined by section 101 of the Code; the definition excludes both consensual liens and judicial liens. However, the term "statutory" is a bit misleading. The phrase includes a lien of distress for rent, whether or not that lien arises from a statute. It also excludes all security interests and judicial liens, even if they are created by a statute.[20] The liens avoided fall into three groups.

The first group consists of liens that Congress views as attempts to circumvent the bankruptcy distribution system by giving liens, and thus secured claims, to certain favored creditors who would otherwise be unsecured. These are liens that are pegged to the debtor's financial failure. Included, among others, are statutory liens that first become effective when bankruptcy is filed, when the debtor becomes insolvent, or when the debtor's financial condition fails to meet a specified standard.[21]

The second group of avoided statutory liens are those that are not "perfected or enforceable" when the case is commenced against a hypothetical bona fide purchaser that purchases the property subject to the lien at that time.[22] The lien is avoided only to the extent that it is not perfected or enforceable against the BFP.[23] As is true with the strong arm clause provisions of section 544, there is no requirement that there be an actual BFP of the encumbered property. The third group of avoided

[18] See Harris v. Huff (In re Huff), 160 Bankr. 256, 261 (Bankr. M.D. Ga. 1993) (pre-petition agreement not to contest fraudulent transfer estopped Chapter 7 trustee from challenging it); see also, Hays & Co. v. Merrill Lynch, Pierce, Fenner & Smith, Inc., 885 F.2d 1149 (3d Cir. 1989) (pre-petition arbitration agreement binding on trustee).

[19] Bankruptcy Code § 545.

[20] Bankruptcy Code § 101(53).

[21] Bankruptcy Code § 545(a)(1) (A), (D)-(E).

[22] Bankruptcy Code § 545(2).

[23] Bankruptcy Code § 545(2).

liens is for rent and distress for rent.[24] As noted, the latter lien need not in fact be created by a statute to be avoidable.

§ 13.05 Post-Petition Transfers of Estate Property

[A]—Unauthorized Transactions

As a general rule, the Trustee/DIP may avoid any transfer of property of the estate that (1) occurs after the commencement of the case and (2) is not authorized either by the Bankruptcy Code or by the Court.[25] For example, suppose that, after the petition, the debtor continues to make payments from the estate for pre-petition debt. Further assume that the court has not authorized these payments to be made (and generally speaking, the court will not so authorize). The trustee can force the creditor who received those payments to pay them back. A limited protection against avoidance is provided for post-petition real estate transactions. A transferee of real estate may keep the real estate transfer if the following conditions are met:

1. The transferee must be a good-faith purchaser, and
2. The transferee must not have known that the case had been commenced, and
3. The transferee must have paid the present fair equivalent value for the property, and
4. Generally, the deed must have been recorded prior to the time a copy or notice of the petition was filed in the real estate records.[26]

If the real estate transferee met all of the requirements except the requirement that fair equivalent value be paid, the transferee will have a lien on the property for whatever present value was paid.[27]

There is a limited period during which post-petition transfers may be avoided. An action or proceeding must be commenced before the earlier of (1) two years after the date of the transfer, or (2) the time the case is closed or dismissed.[28]

[B]—Gap Transfers

In an involuntary case, there can be a gap between the filing of the petition and the court's determination as to whether the petition is justified. Transfers of property by the estate may occur during this period. The treatment of those transfers, which are given somewhat more protection than other post-petition transfers, is discussed at length in Chapter 6.[29]

---

[24] Bankruptcy Code § 545(3), (4). Note that the legislative history incorrectly states that a common-law lien for rent is avoidable. S. Rep. No. 95-989 (1978).

[25] Bankruptcy Code § 549(a)(1), (2) (B).

[26] Bankruptcy Code § 549(c).

[27] Bankruptcy Code § 549(c). For a somewhat more detailed discussion of this provision in context of the protection of "gap transferees" see § 6.03[G] of this book.

[28] Bankruptcy Code § 549(d).

[29] See § 6.03[G].

§ 13.06 Preservation of Avoided Transfers for the Benefit of the Estate

Section 551 provides that any transfer avoided under sections 522 (Exempt Property), 544 (Strong-arm Clause), 545 (Statutory Liens), 547 (Preferences) 548 (Fraudulent Transfers), 549 (Post-petition Transfers), or 724(a) (Liens Securing Noncompensatory Damages), and any lien that is void under section 506(d) (Undersecured Creditors), is preserved for the benefit of the estate with respect to property of the estate.[30] Translated to simpler English, once the trustee/DIP has avoided a lien, or the lien of an undersecured creditor has been reduced to the value of the collateral, the transfer or lien automatically belongs to the trustee/DIP. For example, suppose that a security interest in a widget-making machine is avoided as a preferential transfer under section 547. The creditor loses its security interest. The trustee/DIP now, in effect, owns that security interest. In most cases, this is of no significance to the actual distribution of the estate's assets. The widget machines are property of the estate and the avoidance of the security interest means that their value will be distributed to the holders of unsecured claims in accordance with the Code's distributional structure. However, the preservation rule has an important effect if there is more than one lien on the property, and the senior lien is avoided.[31]

In the example given, assume that the widgets are worth $1,000,000, and that they are subject to two security interests. The senior security interest secures a debt of $800,000. The junior, subordinate, security interest, secures $600,000. Had the bankruptcy never occurred, and had both creditors foreclosed their liens, the net proceeds of the sale would have been split between the creditors according to their priorities. Assuming that the net proceeds were $1,000,000, the senior creditor would have received $800,000, the entire amount of the debt owed to it. The junior creditor would have received the remaining $200,000, and had a $400,000 deficiency.

Further assume that, because of the bankruptcy, the senior security interest has been avoided. It was a preference because there was a 12-day gap between the creation of the security interest and the filing of the financing statement.[32] On the other hand, the junior security interest was not a preference. The net result of this is that because a bankruptcy was filed, there is only one creditor who still has a lien on the property — the junior creditor. If section 551 did not exist, the junior creditor would move into the senior position. The junior creditor could look to the entire $1,000,000 of collateral as security for its $600,000 loan. It would be in a better position in bankruptcy than it was outside of bankruptcy.

Because of section 551, the trustee inherits the rights that the senior creditor had outside of bankruptcy. The trustee, in effect, has a senior lien securing $800,000 on the property. This means that the holder of the junior lien is in exactly the same

---

[30] Bankruptcy Code § 551.

[31] According to the legislative history, the purpose of § 551 is to prevent "junior lienors from improving their position at the expense of the estate when a senior lien is avoided." H.R. Rep. 595, 95th Cong., 1st Sess. 376 (1977), S. Rep. No. 989, 95th Cong., 2d Sess. 91 (1978).

[32] For a discussion about this preference rule, see Chapter 14.

position it was before the bankruptcy. It has the remaining $200,000 worth of widget machines to secure the $600,000 obligation. This translates into a $200,000 secured claim and a $400,000 unsecured claim.

Fundamentally, section 551 creates a right of subrogation. As is true with other subrogation rights, it puts the trustee/DIP in exactly the same position as the holder of the avoided transfer or the void lien, neither better nor worse. It represents a decision by Congress that the benefit of the avoidance should go to the unsecured creditors, and not to the holder of the junior interest in the property involved. It is, however, an incomplete subordination. The trustee/DIP does not obtain all the rights held by the person who had rights avoided; rather, the trustee/DIP only inherits the rights that were in fact avoided. Other rights that the transferee obtained in the transaction, but that were not avoided, are not given to the trustee/DIP.[33]

§ 13.07 Recovery of Avoided Transfers

The various avoidance powers are not self-executing. If property has been transferred, and that transfer is avoidable, there has to be a mechanism for getting the property back. Even a court ruling that avoids a transfer requires further action to recover the property transferred (unless the transferee surrenders it). The rules governing the actual recovery of the property are found in section 550. Section 550(a) states the general rule that, to the extent a transfer is avoided under section 544 (Strong-arm Clause), section 545 (Statutory Liens), section 547 (Preferences), section 548 (Fraudulent Transfers), section 549 (Post-petition Transfers), section 553(b) (Set-off Preferences), or section 724(a) (certain liens securing noncompensatory damages), the trustee may recover either the property transferred or, if the court so orders, the value of the property.[34]

Note that section 550 only comes into play if there has been some form of actual transfer. The avoidance of a lien on the property generally does not require any further action because the previously encumbered property is in the custody of the trustee/DIP and there is no way in which the creditor can exercise any power over the property. However, if tangible property has been physically transferred, or if money has been credited to the transferee's account, then the property must be physically recaptured or the transfer reversed on the books of the various banks involved.

Note as well that the trustee/DIP may recover the property or its value. This is of significance if the property transferred was not money. Although court approval is required to obtain the value of the property, rather than the property itself, courts routinely grant such permission. Particularly in a liquidation case, the trustee will often prefer to have the value (money) rather than the property (which the trustee would just then have to turn around and sell anyway. Moreover, the property may

[33] Robinson v. Howard Bank (In re Kors, Inc.), 819 F.2d 19 (2d Cir. 1987) (trustee did not, under § 551, obtain the subordination rights held by the holder of an avoided security interest, because the subordination rights were not avoided).

[34] Bankruptcy Code § 550(a).

have been damaged or destroyed; or it may have simply depreciated in value.) It is well established that the value the trustee can recover is the value it had when it was transferred, not the value it has when it is recovered.[35] Interestingly, though, if the property has appreciated in value, the trustee/DIP probably cannot be forced to accept the value of the property at the date of transfer. The trustee/DIP apparently may still recover the property itself.[36] and, in that case, will obviously want to do so.

In most cases, the property, or its value, may be recovered either from (1) the initial transferee or the entity for whose benefit the transfer was made, or (2) any immediate or mediate transferee of the initial transferee.[37] This means that the trustee/DIP can pursue a recovery not only from the person who got the property, but also anyone who was the beneficiary of the transfer and any subsequent transferee. For example, suppose that, shortly before the bankruptcy, Dora Debtor fraudulently transferred her car to her husband, Doug Debtor. Doug then fraudulently transferred the car to his cousin, Sam Debtor. Dora's trustee can recover the value of the car from Doug (the trustee cannot recover the car itself from Doug because he does not have it), or can recover either the car or its value from Sam. Of course, if the trustee does recover the value of the car from Doug, the trustee cannot also recover from Sam.[38]

§ 13.08 General Limitations on Avoiding Powers.

[A]—Introduction

There are a number of limitations on the avoiding powers of the trustee/DIP. Some of these are discussed in context of the specific avoiding power, for example, the exceptions to the preference avoidance rules under section 547.[39] Others are of such narrow applicability that they are not discussed further in this work.[40] The most important of the general limitations are discussed in the following subparagraphs.

---

[35] Drewes v. FM Da-Sota Elevator Co. (In re Da-Sota Elevator Co.), 939 F.2d 654 (8th Cir. 1991); Gennrich v. Montana Sport U.S.A., Ltd. (In re International Ski Service, Inc.), 119 Bankr. 654 (Bankr. W.D. Wis. 1990); Pritchard v. Brown (In re Brown), 118 Bankr. 57 (Bankr. N.D. Tex. 1990). There is at least one case that fixed the date of the petition, rather than the date of the transfer, as the proper date for measuring value. Hall v. Arthur Young & Co. (In re Computer Universe, Inc.), 58 Bankr. 28 (Bankr. M.D. Fla. 1986). See also Collier on Bankruptcy ¶ 550.02.

[36] This at least fits the plain language of Bankruptcy Code § 550(a).

[37] Bankruptcy Code § 550(a)(1), (2).

[38] Bankruptcy Code § 550(c): "The trustee is entitled to only a single satisfaction under sub-section (a) of this section."

[39] See § 14.03 of this book.

[40] For an example, see § 546(e)-(g), which limits avoidance of margin payments and transfers under swap agreements.

[B]—Timing

There are a number of time-based limitations on the avoidance of a transaction in bankruptcy. Some of these relate to the filing of the petition; for example, most preferential transfers that occur more than 90 days before the petition are unavoidable.[41] Others relate to non-bankruptcy statutes of limitation; if a non-bankruptcy avoidance power exercised by the trustee/DIP under section 544(b) lapses prior to the bankruptcy, the trustee/DIP may not use that avoiding power.[42] In addition, section 546 sets time limits for the avoidance of transactions under sections 544 (Strong Arm Clause), 545 (Statutory Liens), 547 (Preferences), 548 (Fraudulent Transfers) and 553 (Setoff).[43] In most cases, the avoidance action must be commenced by the earlier of (i) two years after the entry of the order for relief, or (ii) the closing or dismissal of the case. However, if a trustee is first appointed or elected in the case more than one year but less than two years after the entry of the order for relief, then the avoidance aciton must be commenced by the earlier of (i) one year after the appointment or election of the trustee, or (ii) the closing or dismissal of the case.[44] This is designed to give a trustee who is appointed late in the day a reasonable opportunity to investigate avoidable transfers. For example, suppose that a case is filed under Chapter 11. The debtor is initially a debtor in possession; however, twenty-two months after the case was filed a trustee is appointed. Rather than force the trustee to make a hasty investigation of transfers that might be avoided, the limitations period is extended beyond the normal two-year limit to give the trustee a full year.

Section 549 (Postpetition Transactions) has its own limitations period; an action to avoid a postpetition transfer must be commenced by the earlier of (1) two years after the transfer was avoided or (2) the closing or dismissal of the case.[45] Section 550, which deals with the actual recovery of property after its transfer is avoided, imposes another limitation. An action to recover the property transferred, or its value, must be commenced by the earlier of (1) one year after the transfer was avoided or (2) the time the case is closed or dismissed.[46] For example, suppose that Dubois was appointed trustee in ABC Industries' Chapter 11 was filed on May 1, 1996. The DIP wishes to avoid a preference paid by the company just before its filing. The DIP must commence the action to avoid the preference before the case is closed or dismissed, and in any event before May 1, 1998. Suppose further that, after a hearing, the court rules that the challenged transaction is indeed a preference and enters an order avoiding it on March 1, 1998. If the creditor does not pay the preference back, the DIP will have to take further action to recover it under section 550 before the case is closed or dismissed and in any event before March 1, 1999.

---

[41] See § 14.02[F] of this book.

[42] See § 13.03 of this chapter.

[43] Note that only a few setoffs are avoidable. See § 10.09 of this book.

[44] Bankruptcy Code § 546(a)(1). This provision was changed to its present form by the 1994 Amendments.

[45] Bankruptcy Code § 549(d).

[46] Bankruptcy Code § 550(e).

[C]—Rights to Perfect

The right of the trustee to avoid a transfer under section 544 (Strong-Arm Clause), section 545 (Statutory Liens) and section 549 (Postpetition Transfer) is subject to any "generally applicable law" that permits perfection of an interest in property to be effective against an entity that acquired rights in the property before perfection.[47] This primarily protects two-step transactions that are incomplete at the time of bankruptcy.[48] A simple example of this is contained in Article 9 of the Uniform Commercial Code. Article 9 security interests are two-step transactions; the first step is attachment, which makes grants the security interest to the secured party while the second step is perfection (usually done by the filing of a "financing statement" in the public records), which establishes priority against third parties.[49] Generally, an interest in the property that arises between attachment and perfection will have priority over the security interest. However, there are exceptions; the most important relates to a "purchase money security interest" (a PMSI), which is created in conjunction with the debtor's acquisition of the property used as collateral.[50] There is a grace period of 10 to 20 days during which the PMSI may be perfected and still be effective against interests that arose during the grace period.[51] Section 546(b) protects the creation against some of the trustee/DIP's avoidance powers on the basis that bankruptcy should not strip away a right of delayed perfection given by state law:

> The purpose of the subsection is to protect, in spite of the surprise intervention of a bankruptcy petition, those whom State law protects by allowing them to perfect their liens or interests as of an effective date that is earlier than the date of the perfection.[52]

In short, this provision simply provides limited protection to existing state law grace periods.

[D]—Reclamation Rights

Another limitation on avoidance powers that protects a state-created creditor right relates to reclamation. One of the traditional rights given to credit sellers of goods is the ability to reclaim those goods after delivery if the seller discovers (after delivery) that the buyer is insolvent.[53] This right is codified in the Uniform

---

[47] Bankruptcy Code § 546(b). Note that this limitation does not apply to other avoiding powers, such as those involving preferences or fraudulent transfers. This provision was slightly expanded by the 1994 Amendments to protect not only the initial perfection of the interest but also its maintenance or continuation.

[48] For discussion of two-step transfers, see § 14.02[B] of this book.

[49] For a fuller discussion of this, see § 2.02[C][1] of this book.

[50] See § 11.09[C] of this book.

[51] U.C.C. § 9-301(2); see generally, Thomas D. Crandall, Michael J. Herbert & Lary Lawrence, Uniform Commercial Code § 26.7.3 (1993).

[52] S. Rep. No. 989, 95th Cong., 2d Sess. 86 (1978).

[53] For a fuller discussion of reclamation, see § 2.13 of this book.

Commercial Code[54] and recognized, although with limitations, by the Bankruptcy Code. The trustee's power to avoid a reclamation under section 544(a) (Strong-arm Clause), 545 (Statutory Liens), 547 (Preferences), and 549 (Postpetition Transactions) is limited by section 546(c).[55] Under that provision, a right of reclamation is protected if the right exists under non-bankruptcy statutory or case law, and if the seller made a written demand for reclamation, which usually must be made within 10 days after the buyer received the goods.[56] Even if the seller has the right to reclaim, and made the necessary demand, the court may refuse reclamation in kind and give the seller either a lien on property of the estate for the value of the goods or classify the seller's claim for payment as an administrative expense.[57]

[E]—Protection of Remote Good Faith Transferees

Some protection against avoidance is given to remote good faith transferees. The rule is strikingly similar to the rules regarding holders in due course of negotiable instruments and good faith purchasers of investment securities. Under section 550(b)(1), the trustee may not recover from a subsequent transferee if the transferee "takes for value, including satisfaction or securing of present or antecedent debt, in good faith, and without knowledge of the voidability of the transfer avoided."[58] Moreover, any transferee of the property after a protected remote transferee who takes the property in "good faith" is also protected from liability under section 550(b)(2).[59]

For example:

> Shortly before her bankruptcy, Dora Debtor fraudulently conveyed her car to her sister, Dottie Deficit. Dottie sold the car for fair value to Reliable Motors. Reliable Motors had no knowledge of the fact that Dottie had received the car in a fraudulent transfer. Reliable Motors sold the car to Bonita Buyer, who purchased it in good faith.

Dora's trustee can recover the value of the car from Dottie. It cannot recover the value of the car from Reliable Motors, nor can it recover either the car or the value of the car from Bonita. Reliable Motors met all the requirements under section 550(b)(1), and thus is protected. Bonita, who purchased in good faith, meets the requirement of section 550(b)(2), and is also protected from liability. Note that these

---

[54] U.C.C. § 2-702(2); for a full discussion of this provision, see Thomas D. Crandall, Michael J. Herbert & Lary Lawrence, Uniform Commercial Code § 8.13.3 (1993).

[55] Note that the other avoidance powers of the trustee/DIP, such as those arising from fraudulent transfers or the state law avoidance rights of actual creditors, are not affected by this limitation. Note too Bankruptcy Code § 546(d), which contains a somewhat different reclamation right for grain farmers and fishermen; that provision is not discussed in this book.

[56] Bankruptcy Code § 546(c)(1). The 1994 Amendments provided that, if the ten-day period expired after the commencement of the case, the seller would have 20 days after the receipt of the goods by the debtor to make the demand for reclamation.

[57] Bankruptcy Code § 546(c)(2).

[58] Bankruptcy Code § 550(b)(1).

[59] Bankruptcy Code § 550(b)(2).

protections apply only to transferees *after* the first transferee. Even if Dottie had acted in good faith and without knowledge that the transfer was a fraudulent transfer, she would not be protected; the trustees could still recover from her.

[F]—Protection of Good Faith Transferees Who Improve Property

Much more limited protection is given to those transferees, whether immediate or subsequent, from whom the trustee/DIP may recover. If a transferee has made improvements on the property transferred, the transferee may be entitled to a lien on the property. Under section 550(d)(1), a good faith transferee from whom the trustee may recover has a lien on the property recovered to secure the lesser of (a) the cost to the transferee of any improvement made after the transfer, less the amount of any profit realized by or accruing to the transferee from the property, and (b) any increase in the value of the property as a result of the improvement.[60] For example, suppose that, shortly before her bankruptcy, Dottie Debtor transferred a piece of real property to Bob Chong in satisfaction of the $35,000 debt she owed to Chong. Although the transfer was a preference, Chong acted in good faith. After obtaining possession of the property, Chong spent $50,000 to build a new house on it. The value of the property increased by $40,000 because of the improvement. Chong did not sell the property or rent it to anyone else. When the trustee recovers the property, Chong is entitled to a $40,000 lien on it; in bankruptcy, this translates to a $40,000 secured claim. (Note that Chong is not entitled to $50,000, the cost of his improvements, because the increase in value was less than the cost of the improvement).

The lien exists only if improvements are made on the property, and only if those improvements increase the value of the property. If the property increases in value on its own, and not because of any improvements made by the transferee, the transferee has no lien at all. The term "improvement" encompasses physical additions or changes to the property, repairs to the property, payment of tax on the property, payment of any debt secured by a lien that is superior to or equal to the rights of the trustee, and preservation of the property.[61]

---

[60] Bankruptcy Code § 550(d)(1).

[61] Bankruptcy Code § 550(d)(2).

CHAPTER 14

Preferences

§ 14.01 Introduction

This Chapter deals with one of the more controversial avoidance powers given in the Bankruptcy Code—the power of the trustee (or debtor in possession) to avoid certain pre-petition transactions as "preferences." Preferences differ from fraudulent transfers in two important ways. First, preferences are not generally avoidable under state law; fraudulent transfers are:[1] Second, preferences are usually bona fide payments on bona fide obligations; fraudulent transfers are not.[2] The preference rules contained in the Bankruptcy Code thus often result in distributing the debtor's assets in a way that is different from the way they would have been distributed under state law.[3]

Broadly speaking, a preference occurs whenever a debtor favors one creditor over another in paying out its limited resources. For example, if Donna owes $1000 to Chuck and $500 to Carla, but has only $500 in available assets, Donna may decide to pay the entire $500 to Carla. She has thereby "preferred" one creditor (Carla) over another creditor (Chuck). Since both obligations are legitimate, and the payment to Carla was not intended to defraud Chuck, state law does not generally interfere with Donna's choice.

In bankruptcy, some, but not all, preferences may be avoided. Avoidance means that the transferee is forced to return the transferred property or its value.[4] In the above example, if the payment to Carla is a preference as that term is defined under the Bankruptcy Code, and is not subject to any exception, Carla will have to return the $500 payment to the bankruptcy estate. In return, Carla will receive a $500 claim against the estate.[5] Of course, Carla's $500 claim is worth far less than $500, because the dividend from the estate is unlikely to be more than a small percentage of the face value of the claim. The difference between the $500 returned and the actual, bankruptcy value of Carla's $500 claim is the gain to the estate; to the extent this gain exceeds the cost of obtaining it, it increases the amount paid to creditors other than Carla. Assume that it cost $200 to recover the preference; the gain to creditors generally is $300. If the claims of all creditors equals $500,000, and none

---

[1] Collier on Bankruptcy ¶ 547.01; see also Kapela v. Newman, 649 F.2d 887 (1st Cir. 1981). This distinction can be overstated; preferences are recoverable in some states' insolvency proceedings.

[2] For a general discussion of fraudulent transfer law under state law and the Bankruptcy Code, see Chapter 15 of this book.

[3] For a discussion of why this is controversial and perhaps undesirable, see § 1.02[B] of this book.

[4] Bankruptcy Code § 550.

[5] Bankruptcy Code § 502(h).

of the claims has any priority over the others, then an additional .06% will be distributed on each claim.

The avoidance of preferences is not self-evidently beneficial to creditors as a whole. The preferee loses the benefit of the preference by having to return it; and, although the property will then be re-transferred to creditors generally, this is not without cost. The recovery of a preference usually involves an expenditure by the estate (for attorney's fees, if nothing else); this means that the net gain to the estate is less than the amount of the preference. This further means that although some creditors will receive more than they would have done if the preference had not been avoided, the total amount that all creditors receive will be less than if the preference had been preserved. In our example, the cost of recovering the $500 paid to Carla is assumed to be $200. If so, the net gain to the estate is only $300; the total amount of money received by all of Donna's creditors (including Carla) will be $200 less than it would have been otherwise. Carla loses $500; the other creditors gain only $300. Insofar as the creditors are concerned, the remaining $200 is lost.

Is preference avoidance good policy? There has been much recent discussion of this issue.[6] Many justifications for preference law have been put forward. The two most widely cited are "preservation of the estate" and "equality of distribution."[7]

The former justification is based on the not-unreasonable assumption that creditors as a whole are likely to receive a greater payout if the debtor's assets remain intact until bankruptcy. If they do, the trustee can conduct an orderly liquidation or the debtor in possession will have a greater chance of reorganizing. Orderly liquidation tends to produce more money than piecemeal dismemberment; reorganizations are likely to produce more money than any form of liquidation. In theory, preference law, by forcing the return of property transferred to creditors, preserves the estate. If creditors must return what they have obtained from the debtor by individual actions, they have no incentive to pick off the debtor's assets one by one; thus, the debtor's assets will remain intact to be administered as a whole through the bankruptcy proceeding. The most sophisticated version of this theory is rooted in the Creditor's Bargain theory of bankruptcy law, discussed in Chapter 7 of this book. In brief, it assumes that creditors would generally prefer to receive equal treatment in a larger asset pool than unequal treatment in a smaller, even though they might sometimes benefit from taking a disproportionate share of the smaller pool.[8]

There are many problems with this theory, not least of which is that preference law probably does not accomplish the goal of discouraging individual creditor actions. A creditor—more precisely, a credit manager—wrangling with a troubled

[6] For a couple of good examples, see Charles Jordan Tabb, *Rethinking Preferences*, 43 S.C. L. Rev. 981 (1992) and John C. McCoid, *Bankruptcy, Preferences & Efficiency: An Expression of Doubt*, 67 Va. L. Rev. 249 (1981). For a personal favorite, see Michael J. Herbert, *The Trustee versus the Trade Creditor*, 17 U. Rich. L. Rev. 667 (1983).

[7] Collier on Bankruptcy ¶ 547.01.

[8] See generally Bruce R. Krause, Note, *Preferential Transfers and the Value of The Insolvent Firm*, 87 Yale L. J. 1449, 1450 (1978); Thomas H. Jackson, The Logic and Limits of Bankruptcy Law 124 (1986).

debtor is unlikely to worry much about preference law or to ponder the subtleties of the Creditors' Bargain. The creditor rarely knows in advance whether bankruptcy will be filed, let alone when it will be filed. In most cases, the preference rules apply only to transfers made during the 90 days before the bankruptcy.[9] A creditor may well take a transfer from the debtor hoping that bankruptcy will be held off for at least 90 more days, in which case the creditor gets to keep the property. Even if the creditor gets caught, and has to pay back the preference, the creditor is only obligated to hand back the property or the value of the property transferred; there is no penalty or interest charged.[10] Thus, even a preferee has gained the use of the transferred property for a substantial period of time—probably months or years, since the preference does not have to be paid back unless and until the trustee/DIP discovers it and takes action to avoid it. Although there has not been any rigorous empirical study of the matter, most of the anecdotal evidence indicates that the risk of avoidance under the preference rules has little or no impact on individual creditor efforts to collect from troubled debtors.

In addition, there is a much more effective method of preventing dismemberment of the debtor: the bankruptcy petition itself. As was discussed in Chapter 8, the filing of the petition triggers the automatic stay of virtually every action that would affect the debtor's property.[11] At the very most, preference rules marginally discourage creditor action. By contrast, the automatic stay forces creditors to leave the debtor's assets alone. It is thus a far more powerful tool than preference law could possibly be.

The second traditional rationale, preserving equality of distribution, has an equal surface appeal but upon analysis appears just as questionable. The idea is that preference law protects the Bankruptcy Code's policy of equal distribution among creditors by forcing those who have received unequal distributions to return the excess they received. The problem with this is that there is no policy of equal distribution. As we studied in Chapter 10, bankruptcy law creates a distinct hierarchy of claims. Rather than equal distribution, the Code mandates radically unequal distribution of the debtor's assets among the creditors.

A more subtle version of this rationale, however, provides the most logical defense of preference law. The preference rules are a means of effectuating the system of distribution mandated by Congress in the Bankruptcy Code. Bankruptcy is the last opportunity for most creditors to obtain any payment from the debtor, and it is virtually certain that there will not be enough in the estate to go around. Given these facts, Congress has established a set of priorities that identify those debts it thinks should be given the best chance of payment. Congress has ranked debts in order of perceived importance and has further mandated pro rata payment of claims within each rank, so that each creditor in the rank bears only a proportionate share of the loss. Preferences disturb this statutory distribution system by allowing the preferred creditor to obtain more than the Code would give it. Preferences are thus avoided to increase the number and amount of claims, and the value of the assets,

---

[9] Bankruptcy Code § 547(b)(4).

[10] Bankruptcy Code § 550.

[11] Bankruptcy Code § 362.

dealt with under the Code's system. In short, a creditor who "ought to have" received $10,000, but who in fact received $20,000 because of a preference must pay back the preference and be given instead the $10,000 that Congress says it deserved.[12] Whether this is a sufficient justification for the costs involved is debateable; however, the preference rules are so deeply ingrained in bankruptcy law and bankruptcy thinking that any radical change is unlikely.

§ 14.02 Preferences Defined — Section 547(b)

[A]—Introduction

The Code's primary preference provision is section 547. "Preferences" are defined in section 547(b), which sets out 6 elements. A preference is a transfer (i) of a property, (ii) to or for the benefit of a creditor, (iii) on an antecedent debt, (iv) made while the debtor was insolvent, (v) made during the preference period (usually the 90 days before the bankruptcy, but 1 full year for insiders of the debtor), and (vi) that enables to creditor to receive more than it would get in a Chapter 7 liquidation of the debtor.[13] Each of these 6 elements requires careful analysis of the statute and the very extensive case law.

[B]—Transfer of Property/Date of Transfer

A preference involves a transfer of the debtors property; to be precise "any transfer of an interest of the debtor in property."[14] The transfer may be voluntary or involuntary. For example, a voluntary payment of a debt may be a preference; but so may the involuntary imposition of a judicial lien or a tax lien on the debtor's property. The transfer may be of all rights in the property or only a partial interest in the property. For example, the grant of a security interest in the property, which gives the secured party only limited rights, is a transfer that may be a preference.

It is often important to determine the date on which the transfer occurs. The date may determine whether the transfer was within the preference period or was on an antecedent debt; it may also determine whether an exception to the avoidance rule applies. In a number of cases, the date of the transfer is not self-evident.

Most of the difficulty regarding the date of transfer involves two-step transfers. A number of transfers require more than one act to complete the transaction. The first step makes the transaction effective between the original parties to the transaction. A second step is required to establish the transferee's rights against third parties. For example, a conveyance of real property generally requires both the execution of a deed and the recording of the deed.[15] Step one—execution—makes

[12] See generally Charles Jordan Tabb, *Rethinking Preferences*, 43 S.C. L. Rev. 981 (1992); Vern Countryman, *The Concept of a Voidable Preference in Bankruptcy*, 38 Vand. L. Rev. 713 (1985).

[13] Bankruptcy Code § 547(b).

[14] Bankruptcy Code § 547(b).

[15] See, for example, In re Lewis W. Shurtleff, Inc., 778 F.2d 1416 (9th Cir. 1985); In re Freedlander, Inc., 107 Bankr. 88 (Bankr. E.D. Va. 1989).

the transaction effective between the seller and the buyer. Step two—recording—is required to establish the buyer's rights against certain third parties, such as subsequent bona fide purchasers of the realty. Similarly, an Article 9 secured transaction often requires two steps. Step one is attachment, which establishes the rights and obligations of the debtor and the secured party.[16] Step two is an additional act to perfect the security interest, which establishes the secured party's rights in the collateral as against other claimant to the same collateral, such as the holder of a subsequent judgment lien the property.[17] Similar rules apply to other personal property security transactions, such as preferred ship mortgages.[18] At which point—step one or step two—is the transfer made for preference purposes?

This issue is addressed by section 547(e). It sets out rules to determine the time at which a transfer is complete. These rules deal with transfers of both real property and personal property, and with one-step and two-step transfers.

Section 547(e)(2) sets out the basic rules for determining when a transfer is made. It distinguishes between the time at which the transfer is effective between the parties and the time at which it is "perfected." There are four situations dealt with by the rules. The first two deal with situations in which the transfer was perfected prior to the commencement of the bankruptcy case; the second two with situations in which perfection occurred after the commencement of the case:

1. If the transfer is perfected at the time it becomes effective between the parties, or within 10 days thereafter, the transfer occurs on the date it becomes effective. For example, suppose the transfer became effective between debtor and creditor on January 1, 1996, and was perfected on January 5, 1996. The transfer is deemed to have occurred on January 1.[19]

2. If the transfer is perfected more than 10 days after the time it becomes effective, the transfer occurs on the date it was perfected. If the transfer became effective on January 1, but was not perfected until January 15, the transfer is deemed to have occurred on January 15.[20]

3. If the transfer was not perfected by the later of the date of commencement of the case or 10 days after the transfer became effective, the

[16] U.C.C. § 9-203. For a general discussion of attachment, see Thomas D. Crandall, Michael J. Herbert & Lary Lawrence, Uniform Commercial Code, Chapter 24 (1993); Barry L. Zaretsky, Gerald T. McLaughlin & Neil B. Cohen, Commercial Law & Practice Guide Chapter 29 (1991).

[17] U.C.C. §§ 9-301 to -305. For a general discussion of perfection, see Thomas D. Crandall, Michael J. Herbert & Lary Lawrence, Uniform Commercial Code, Chapter 25 (1993); Barry L. Zaretsky, Gerald T. McLaughlin & Neil B. Cohen, Commercial Law & Practice Guide Chapter 30 (1991).

[18] In re Gottschalk, 46 Bankr. 49 (Bankr. M.D. Fla. 1985).

[19] Bankruptcy Code § 547(e)(2)(A). Note that this provision protects one-step transfers that become effective against third parties at the same time they become effective against the original parties.

[20] Bankruptcy Code § 547(e)(2)(B).

transfer occurs immediately before the date of the filing of the petition. For example, suppose that the transfer became effective on January 1, the bankruptcy was filed on January 7, and the transfer was perfected on January 15. The transfer is deemed to have occurred immediately before January 7 (which apparently means that it is deemed to have occurred on January 6).[21]

4. If the transfer was not perfected on the date of commencement of the case, but was perfected within 10 days after it became effective, the transfer occurs on the date it became effective. If the transfer became effective on January 1, the bankruptcy was filed on January 5, and the transfer was perfected on January 7, the transfer is deemed to have occurred on January 1.[22]

The key problems are determining what is necessary to make the transfer effective between the parties and what is necessary to perfect the transfer. The Code does not deal with the first issue, which is consequently left to other law. Nor does the Code state what acts are necessary to perfect the transfer; this too is a question resolved outside the Code.[23] However, the Code does define what legal status constitutes perfection. In other words, the Code does not tell you how to perfect (this is determined by relevant non-Code law) but it does tell you what legal result your actions must have for the transfer to be perfected under section 547.

If the property transferred is realty (other than fixtures), the transfer is perfected only when a bona fide purchaser of that property from the debtor cannot acquire an interest that is superior to the right of the transferee.[24] This does not mean that there is such a purchaser, nor does it make the trustee a bona fide purchaser.[25] Neither does it mean that every bona fide purchaser would have a superior interest. For example, it is generally true that a bona fide purchaser who has notice of an existing interest takes subject to it. This is irrelevant in determining the date of perfection under section 547(e); the question is not whether a BFP would have a superior right but rather whether a BFP *could* have a superior right. Broadly speaking, a BFP can obtain rights superior to those of the holder of an unrecorded interest in the realty.[26] Thus, as a general principle, an interest in realty is not perfected until it is properly noted in the real estate records.[27]

For example, suppose that on August 1 Alice executes and delivers to Bette a mortgage on her home. Under relevant state law, a BFP without notice does not take

---

[21] Bankruptcy Code § 547(e)(2)(C).

[22] Bankruptcy Code § 547(e)(2)(A), (C).

[23] Collier on Bankruptcy ¶ 547.16[2].

[24] Bankruptcy Code § 547(e)(1)(A).

[25] Collier on Bankruptcy ¶ 547.18.

[26] See, for example, In re Lewis W. Shurtleff, Inc., 778 F.2d 1416 (9th Cir. 1985).

[27] This remains a matter of state law, however; if in the relevant state a BFP takes subject to an unrecorded deed, then the transfer is complete when the deed is executed and delivered. See Collier on Bankruptcy ¶ 547.17.

subject to an unrecorded mortgage. Bette records the mortgage on August 8. The transfer became effective between Alice and Bette on August 1 and was perfected on August 8; because this was within the 10 day grace period given by section 547(e)(2)(A), the transfer is deemed to have occurred on August 1. If Bette had not recorded until August 12, the transfer would be deemed to have occurred on August 12.

With regard to personal property and fixtures, the rule is somewhat different. A transfer is perfected when a creditor on a simple contract cannot acquire a judicial lien that is superior to the interest of the transferee.[28] There does not have to be such a creditor; nor must all such creditors have rights superior to the transferee. All that is required is that a creditor of that type could obtain a lien that has priority over the rights of the transferee.

This rule is of primary importance with regard to security interests under Article 9 of the Uniform Commercial Code; indeed the Bankruptcy Code rule was designed to mesh with the related U.C.C. rules. Most but not all security interests in personalty and fixtures are governed by Article 9. Like the Bankruptcy Code, Article 9 uses the word "perfection" to describe the status and priority of security interests. Article 9 security interests may either be perfected or unperfected. Under Article 9, a judicial lien generally has priority over a security interest that is not perfected under the Article 9 perfection rules.[29] By contrast, a security interest that is perfected under Article 9 has priority over a subsequent judicial lien.[30]

This means that, for all practical purposes, perfection under Article 9 is also perfection under the Bankruptcy Code. Except with regard to purchase money security interests in consumer goods, Article 9 perfection generally requires that a public record of the security interest be made.[31] For most transactions, this record is a document called a financing statement.[32] which (depending on the type of transaction and the relevant state) is filed either "centrally" in the state capital or "locally" at the county courthouse or register of deeds.[33] There are other forms of recording for other types of property. For example, if the property is a titled motor vehicle, the record is a notation on the certificate of title.[34]

Suppose that on June 1 Sam Paul lends money to Danuta, and Danuta executes a security agreement giving Sam Paul rights in her business equipment as collateral.

---

[28] Bankruptcy Code § 547(e)(1)(B).

[29] U.C.C. § 9-301(1)(b).

[30] This is not directly stated in the U.C.C., but derives from § 9-201, which states that the security interest is effective against third parties except as otherwise stated in Article 9. Note that a perfected security interest can be subordinate to a judicial lien with regard to certain advances of credit made to the debtor after the lien attaches. U.C.C. § 9-301(4). It does not appear that this limited subordination to judicial liens affects the Article 9 secured party's rights under Bankruptcy Code § 547.

[31] U.C.C. § 9-302.

[32] U.C.C. 9-302(1). The proper form for an Article 9 financing statement is set out in U.C.C. § 9-402.

[33] U.C.C. § 9-401.

[34] U.C.C. § 9-302(3)(b).

Sam Paul files the necessary financing statement on June 5. The transaction became effective between the parties on June 1, and was perfected on June 5. The transfer is deemed to have occurred on June 1, since perfection was within the 10 day grace period.

A final aspect of the date of transfer rules is of special significance to certain types of Article 9 security interests. For section 547 purposes, no transfer can occur until the debtor has rights in the property transferred.[35] Under Article 9, the debtor and secured party may agree that the security interest will attach to "after acquired property," that is, property that the debtor does not have at the time the security agreement is entered into.[36] When the debtor does acquire the property, the security interest will automatically attach without any further action by the parties.[37] If a proper financing statement has been filed, that security interest will also be perfected.[38] These rules are carried over into Section 547; the transfer of the after acquired property from the debtor to the secured party will not occur until the debtor acquires rights in it. For example, if on January 1, D'Arcy and Shaka enter into a security agreement that covers all of D'Arcy's inventory, including after-acquired inventory, and D'Arcy acquires new inventory on June 1, the transfer of the security interest in the new inventory occurs on June 1, not January 1. The significance of this rule is further explored in § 14.03[F] of this chapter.

[C]—To or For the Benefit of a Creditor

The preference may either be direct or indirect; that is, the property may either be transferred *to* a creditor (direct preference) or *for the benefit* of a creditor (indirect preference).[39] In most cases, this element is self-evident. However, it has created problems in one situation: the treatment of indirect preferences that benefit creditors who are also "insiders" (close affiliates) of the debtor. This issue is explored in § 14.04 of this chapter.

[D]—Antecedent Debt

A preference is a transfer made regarding an antecedent debt—an obligation of the debtor that arose before the transfer was made.[40] A contemporaneous exchange is not a preference (although if inadequate value is received by the debtor, it may be a fraudulent transfer).[41] For example, if Doug pays $18,000 in cash to buy a new car during the preference period, his transfer of cash to the seller is not a preference.The antecedent debt requirement derives from the notion that preference

---

[35] Bankruptcy Code § 547(e)(3).

[36] U.C.C. § 9-204(1), (2).

[37] U.C.C. § 9-204 comment 1.

[38] U.C.C. § 9-402 comment 2; see Thomas D. Crandall, Michael J. Herbert & Lary Lawrence, Uniform Commercial Code, § 25.15.10 (1993)

[39] Bankruptcy Code § 547(b)(1).

[40] Bankruptcy Code § 547(b)(2).

[41] Bankruptcy Code § 548(a)(2). For a general discussion of fraudulent transfers under the Code, see Chapter 15 of this book.

law deals with transfers that deplete the estate—more precisely, transfers that reduce the amount available for distribution under the Code's rules. The exchange of one asset for another—of $18,000 cash for an $18,000 car—does not diminish the amount available to creditors.[42]

Courts have generally found that the antecedent debt requirement is met if there is any appreciable time lag between the creation of the obligation and the transfer.[43] Even a gap of a day or even less is sufficient.[44] The strict reading of antecedent debt creates a number of practical problems, because it is often impossible for an exchange to be absolutely contemporaneous. To take the example given above, Doug is much more likely to pay for his new car by giving the dealer a check than $18,000 in greenbacks; yet payment by check is not technically a contemporaneous transfer.[45] These problems have been ameliorated in part by the ten-day grace period given by § 547(e) for two-step transfers and in part by various exceptions to the avoidance rules set out in § 547(c). For example, suppose that a debt was incurred on January 1, and was secured by a mortgage executed and delivered the same day. The mortgage was not filed until January 5. There is no antecedent debt problem because the mortgage transfer was perfected within 10 days of the date it became effective between the parties; thus, the transfer is deemed to have occurred on the January 1, contemporaneously with the creation of the obligation.[46] Similarly, § 547(c)(1) ordinarily protects payments by check.[47]

[E]—Insolvency

The debtor must be insolvent at the time of the transfer.[48] This requirement is rooted in the assumption that creditors are not hurt when a solvent debtor prefers one creditor over another, because there are still enough assets available for all creditors to be paid in full. Insolvency under § 547(b) is so-called "balance sheet insolvency"; that is, a debtor is insolvent when its assets are worth less than the amount of its debts.[49] There may be difficulties in valuing the assets and the debts, so the issue of insolvency can present considerable evidentiary problems. The trustee/DIP is aided by a statutory presumption that the debtor was insolvent during

---

[42] See Collier on Bankruptcy ¶ 547.05. Note, however, that if the goods transferred are non-exempt, while the goods received are exempt, the amount of assets available to creditors is diminished. This issue, however, is dealt with under fraudulent transfer law rather than preference law.

[43] See Collier on Bankruptcy ¶ 547.05.

[44] For an extreme example, see National City Bank of New York v. Hotchkiss, 231 U.S. 50 (1913) (holding that a lapse of several hours between making loan and obtaining collateral meant that transfer of collateral was on an antecedent debt).

[45] See H.R. Rep. No. 95-595, 95th Cong. 2d Sess. (1977) 373 ("Strictly speaking [a payment by check] may be a credit transaction because the seller does not receive payment until the check is cleared through the debtor's bank.")

[46] Bankruptcy Code § 547(e)(2)(A).

[47] See § 14.03[B] of this chapter.

[48] Bankruptcy Code § 547(b)(3).

[49] Bankruptcy Code § 101(32).

the 90 days immediately preceding the filing of the petition.[50] This presumption shifts only the burden of going forward with the evidence, not the burden of persuasion; if the transferee adduces any significant evidence that the debtor was solvent at the time of the transfer, the presumption is rebutted.[51] If there is no evidence either way, however, the trustee/DIP has carried its burden of proving insolvency by virtue of the presumption.

[F]—Preference Period

Section 547 does not avoid all transfers that prefer one creditor over another. Transfers that are relatively remote from the filing of the bankruptcy have traditionally been left untouched; only those proximate to filing are avoided. Under the current version of the Code, the preference period generally extends back only 90 days.[52] Thus, if Deng pays Czyz the $10,000 he owes her on January 1, but does not file bankruptcy until May 1, Czyz has not received a preference.

There is an exception to this. If Czyz is an insider of Deng, then the preference period is one year.[53] This longer preference period is based on the plausible theory that insiders have special knowledge of the debtor's financial state, special ability to coerce payment from the debtor, and often some level of control over whether and when to file bankruptcy. They thus have a great advantage over other creditors based on their relationships to the debtor; some of this advantage is taken away by subjecting them to greater preference risk.

"Insider" is defined in section 101(31). If the debtor is an individual, "insider" includes certain of the debtor's relatives, the debtor's business partners, and business entities of which the debtor is a general partner, officer, director, or control person.[54] If the debtor is a business organization, "insider" includes persons who are partners, officers, directors, or control persons, as well as business affiliates (such as subsidiary or parent corporations).[55]

Finally, it is important to keep in mind the significance of the 10 day grace period for two-step transfers. If the second step occurred during the preference period, but within 10 days of the first step, the transfer is deemed to have occurred when the first step was taken. If that was outside the preference period, there is no preference.

[G]—Improvement in Position

The final requirement focuses on whether the transfer allows the transferee to obtain more than it would under the Code's basic distributional structure. That

---

50 Bankruptcy Code § 547(f).

51 WJM, Inc. v. Mass. Dept. of Pub. Welfare, 840 F.2d 996 (1st Cir. 1988); Clay v. Traders Bank, 708 F.2d 1347 (8th Cir. 1983).

52 Bankruptcy Code § 547(b)(4)(A).

53 Bankruptcy Code § 547(b)(4)(B).

54 Bankruptcy Code § 101(31)(A).

55 The relevant definition of "insider" appears at Bankruptcy Code § 101(31)(b)-(c), (e)-(f); the definition of "affiliate" is at Bankruptcy Code § 101(2).

structure, which is rigidly enforced in Chapter 7 (liquidation) bankruptcy becomes the yardstick by which the transferee's position is measured. The law compares the actual, post-transfer position of the creditor with the position it would have been in if there had been no transfer and the claim had been dealt with under Chapter 7. (Note that treatment in a hypothetical Chapter 7 is always the base line for betterment in position, even if the actual bankruptcy is under one of the other chapters). If the creditor, as a result of the transfer, is in a better position than it would have been in under Chapter 7, the requirement is met.[56]

For example, suppose that Clara holds a general unsecured claim in the amount of $500. During the preference period, Clara received a $100 payment on that claim, reducing it to $400. Suppose further that Clara would have received 6% of her $500 claim ($30) if her debtor had gone into Chapter 7 and no transfer had been made. The transfer has enabled her to receive more than the $30 she would have got in the hypothetical Chapter 7. She has already received $100 and still has a $400 claim against the debtor. If her debtor is in an actual Chapter 7 proceeding, Clara will still receive about 6% on her remaining claim ($24 on her $400 claim); thus, the transfer has enabled her to receive $124 instead of $30. Her position has thus been improved by the transfer. Even if Clara had received only a $30 transfer during the preference period, she still would have improved her position; she would have not only the $30 she would have received in Chapter 7, but also her remaining $470 claim, worth about $28.20 in the bankruptcy.

The requirement that the transfer enable the creditor to better its position is nearly always met if the debt is unsecured. Almost by definition, any payment on an unsecured debt by an insolvent debtor betters the creditor's position, because there will not be enough money to pay all the creditors in full. The only significant exception is payment on a priority unsecured debt. If there would have been enough money in a Chapter 7 proceeding to pay in full all debts with the same priority, then there is no preference. For example, suppose that during the preference period the debtor paid $500 in back wages to its employees. Suppose further that these wages would have been entitled to priority under the rules of section 507(a)(3)[57] and that in a hypothetical Chapter 7 liquidation of the debtor, there would have been enough money to pay all of the priority wage claims. There is no preference, because the claim would have been paid in full anyway.

By contrast with payments on unsecured claims, payments on secured claims are usually protected against preference avoidance precisely because of the betterment in possession rule. Broadly speaking, secured claims have the highest priority in the bankruptcy distribution structure. In Chapter 7 (and indeed in every Chapter) secured claims must almost always be paid in full.[58] Thus, payments on secured claims during the preference period do not improve the creditor's position and are not preferences.[59]

---

[56] Bankruptcy Code § 547(b)(5).

[57] Bankruptcy Code § 507(a)(3).

[58] See § 10.03 of this book.

[59] Collier on Bankruptcy ¶ 547.08.

However, it is important to note a limitation on the protection of secured claims. If an obligation is only partially secured, the Bankruptcy Code treats that obligation as generating two claims: a secured claim and an unsecured claim.[60] The secured claim is equal to the value of the collateral. The unsecured claim is equal to the excess of the obligation over the value of the collateral. If $80,000 of collateral secured $100,000 of debt, the creditor has an $80,000 secured claim and a $20,000 unsecured claim.

This creates a preference problem for payments on an undersecured obligation. To the extent the payment is credited to the unsecured claim, there is a betterment in position; to the extent the payment is credited to the secured claim, there is no betterment in position. Generally, courts have treated payments on undersecured obligations as applying first to the unsecured claim. In the example given ($80,000 collateral and $100,000 debt), if $15,000 in payments were made during the preference period, all of the payments would be subject to avoidance.[61] If $30,000 in payments were made, only the first $20,000 would be subject to avoidance; the remainder would be payments on the secured claim, payments that did not better the creditor's position.

§ 14.03 Exceptions to Avoidance

[A]—Introduction

Not all transfers that meet the requirements of section 547(b) are actually avoided. Sometimes the trustee/DIP will not bother to attempt recovery of the preference because the amount is too small to warrant the costs of recovery. The trustee/DIP also faces sovereign immunity problems if the transferee was a government or a governmental agency.[62] Of greater significance for the lawyer, however, are the statutory exceptions set out in section 547(c). That subsection immunizes certain transactions from avoidance even though those transaction meet all of the requirements for avoidance in section 547(b).

There is no cohesive rationale linking all of the eight statutory exceptions, although most are designed to identify transactions that Congress considers so important that they should not be subject to avoidance risk. Many of the exceptions are ambiguous; this, coupled with the monetary significance of the exceptions, has

---

[60] Bankruptcy Code § 506(a). For a fuller discussion of the Bankruptcy Code's treatment of undersecured obligations, see § 10.03[C] of this book.

[61] Collier on Bankruptcy ¶ 547.08. Note that if the creditor were to release an equivalent value of collateral, the payment on the unsecured portion of the debt would not be avoidable. Vern Countryman, *The Concept of a Voidable Preference in Bankruptcy*, 38 Vand. L. Rev. 713, 744 (1985); see also Bankruptcy Code § 547(c)(1).

[62] Hoffman v. State of Connecticut (In re Willington Convalescent Home), 850 F.2d 50 (2d Cir. 1988), aff'd 492 U.S. 96 (1989). For a broader discussion of the ability of a trustee/DIP to recover a transfer from the government, see § 8.07[D] of this book. See also, Steven M. Richman, *More Equal Than Others: State Sovereign Immunity Under the Bankruptcy Code*, 21 Rutgers L. J. 603 (1990).

generated a vast body of case law. Some exceptions have antecedents in prior law; others are new to the Code. Finally, several of the exceptions can overlap; some parts of a transaction may fit into one exception while other parts fit into another exception. Also note that the section 547(c) exceptions only affect the trustee/DIP's power to avoid a transfer under section 547. If the transfer runs afoul of another avoidance power, such as the power to avoid fraudulent transfers, section 547(c) will not preserve it.

[B]—Substantially Contemporaneous Exchange for New Value

The first exception protects transfers to the extent they were intended by the debtor and the creditor to be a contemporaneous exchange for new value and were in fact substantially contemporaneous.[63] Most of the litigation has concerned two issues. What is the scope of this exception? What is a substantially contemporaneous exchange?

The legislative history of section 547(c)(1) indicates that Congress had in mind the technical preference problem created when the debtor pays by check. A payment by check is not complete until the check is paid by the bank on which it is drawn. Suppose Diaz purchases widgets on January 1, and gives Shiraz a check to pay for those widgets at the same time. The check clears Diaz' bank on January 4. Technically, the payment was made on January 4, and was consequently on an antecedent debt. However, according to the legislative history, this is normally a transaction intended to be contemporaneous and which was in fact substantially contemporaneous; thus, even if it fits within section 547(b), it is not avoidable.[64]

What if the check was post-dated to January 15? In that case, the parties would not have intended a contemporaneous transfer, but rather a credit transaction in which payment was delayed for 14 days. It would thus not fall under the exception. Similarly, if the seller failed to deposit the check within a reasonable period of time, it would not be a substantially contemporaneous exchange.[65] Finally, if the check is dishonored, it is not a substantially contemporaneous exchange.[66]

Does this exception apply to anything other than payment by check? As discussed in Chapter 1, the Supreme Court has generally supported a textualist "plain meaning" approach to Bankruptcy Code interpretation.[67] Under that approach, it is clear that the substantially contemporaneous exception should not be limited to check payment. There is nothing in the statutory text that so limits the exception. Although the courts have not been particularly expansive in their reading of the exception,

---

[63] Bankruptcy Code § 547(c)(1).

[64] H.R. Rep. No. 595, 95th Cong. 2d Sess. 373 (1977), S. Rep. No. 989, 95th Cong., 2d Sess. 88 (1978).

[65] Michael J. Herbert, *The Trustee versus the Trade Creditor: A Critique of Section 547(c)(1), (2) & (4) of the Bankruptcy Code*, 17 U. Rich. L. Rev. 667, 673 n. 23 (1983).

[66] Goger v. Cudahy Foods Co. (In re Standard Food Servs., Inc.), 723 F.2d 820 (11th Cir. 1984).

[67] See § 1.03.

it has certainly been used to protect things other than check payments.[68] However, much of the litigation over the exception has involved attempts to bootstrap the contemporaneous exchange exception onto other exceptions and grace periods, such as the 10 or 20 days given by sections 547(e) and 547(c)(3) to perfect interests in two-step transfers. Courts have been particularly unwilling to permit such bootstrapping.[69]

The other major interpretive difficulty is created by the phrase "substantially contemporaneous." What exactly does it mean? The legislative history suggests that a time lapse of thirty days or more between the debt and the payment might still be substantially contemporaneous.[70] The courts have not always been so generous.[71] Probably the best rule of thumb is that a transfer is substantially contemporaneous if the time lag is caused by the normal processing of documents necessary to complete the transfer.

[C]—Ordinary Course of Business Transfers

The second exception is for certain transactions that are in the ordinary course of business for the debtor and the transferee. Specifically, a transfer is not avoidable to the extent that the transfer meets three requirements.[72]

1. The transfer is in payment of a debt that was incurred in the ordinary course of the debtor's business or financial affairs and in the ordinary course of the transferee's business or financial affairs.[73]

2. The transfer itself was made in the ordinary course of business or financial affairs of the debtor and of the transferee.[74]

3. The transfer was made according to ordinary business terms.[75]

In evaluating whether this exception applies, courts have debated over whether "ordinary course" refers to general practice in the industry or to prior conduct between the parties. For example, suppose debtor is a buyer of widgets who has

---

[68] See, for example, Drabkin v. A.I. Credit Corp., 800 F.2d 1153 (D.C. Cir. 1986) (holding that release of security interest can constitute substantially contemporaneous exchange for new value under section 547(c)(1) exception).

[69] Union Bank & Trust Co. v. Baker (In re Tressler), 771 F.2d 791 (3d Cir. 1985); Gower v. Ford Motor Credit Co. (In re Davis), 734 F.2d 604 (11th Cir. 1984).

[70] Michael J. Herbert, *The Trustee versus the Trade Creditor: A Critique of Section 547(c)(1), (2) &(4) of the Bankruptcy Code*, 17 U. Rich. L. Rev. 667, 673 n. 23 (1983).

[71] See In re Coco, 67 Bankr. 365 (S.D.N.Y. 1986) (7 days not too long; 34 days too long); In re Arctic Air Conditioning, Inc., 35 Bankr. 107 (Bankr. E.D. Tenn. 1983) (30 days too long); Cf. In re Quade, 108 Bankr. 681 (Bankr. N.D. Iowa 1989) (6 days not too long).

[72] Note that prior to the 1984 Amendments, there was a fourth requirement that the transfer be made within 45 days after the debt was incurred.

[73] Bankruptcy Code § 547(c)(2)(A).

[74] Bankruptcy Code § 547(c)(2)(B).

[75] Bankruptcy Code § 547(c)(2)(C).

consistently paid its supplier 30 days late, even though most widget buyers pay on time. Is this "ordinary course" or not? It appears that most courts look most heavily to the ongoing payment practices of the parties, although the industry norm is sometimes significant.[76] Even quite long time lags between the due date of the obligation and its payment may be excused, if this truly reflects an established practice between the parties[77] sporadic and irregular payments may indeed be ordinary course if they are consistent with the parties' mode of dealing.[78] Also of great significance are the actions of the creditor. If the creditor put pressure on the debtor to make payments, most courts say the payments are not in ordinary course.[79]

Prior to 1991, it was unclear whether this exception could apply to payments on long term indebtedness. Courts were split between the plain language of the text on the one hand and policy arguments, linked to the legislative history and the purpose of preference law, on the other.[80] In *Union Bank v. Wolas*[81] the Supreme Court ruled in favor of the plain language of the statutory text and held that payments of long term debt could be protected by the ordinary course exception. This rule has, to say the least been controversial; in the view of some, it profoundly undercuts the whole purpose of preference law.[82]

[D]—Grace Period for Late Perfection of Purchase Money Interests

Section 547(b)(3) protects from preference avoidance certain purchase money security interests that were not perfected in a timely fashion.[83] This exception is exceedingly narrow in scope and has been almost indistinguishable from the grace period for perfection provided by § 547(e). It applies only to certain security interests

---

76 See In re Ajayem Lumber Corp, 145 Bankr. 813 (S.D.N.Y. 1992) (delay of 34 days within range of parties' prior practice and industry norm); In re Steel Improvement Co., 79 Bankr. 681 (Bankr. E.D. Mich. 1987); Collier on Bankruptcy ¶ 547.10. Cf. In re Xonics Imaging, Inc., 837 F.2d 763 (7th Cir. 1988) (transferee must show a pattern of late payments for such payments to constitute ordinary course transfers).

77 In re Gardiner Matthews Plantation Co., 118 Bankr. 384 (Bankr. S.C. 1989) (payments protected under ordinary course of business exception even though time lag between delivery and payment ranged from 108 to 191 days).

78 In re National Office Products, Inc., 119 Bankr 896 (D.R.I. 1990).

79 Xtra, Inc. v. Seawinds, Ltd. (In re Seawinds), 888 F.2d 640 (9th Cir. 1989); Marathon Oil Co. v. Flatau (In re Craig Oil), 785 F.2d 1563 (11th Cir. 1986) (whenever the debtor's "normal" payments are the result of unusual collection activity by the creditor, the exception does not apply).

80 For an extended critique of the issue, see Lissa L. Broome, *Payments on Long-Term Debt as Voidable Preferences: The Impact of the 1984 Bankruptcy Amendments*, 1987 Duke L. J. 78. See also, Michael J. Herbert, *The Trustee versus the Trade Creditor II: The 1984 Amendment to Section 547(c)(2) of the Bankruptcy Code*, 2 Bankr. Dev. J. 201 (1985).

81 502 U.S. 151 (1991).

82 For a good discussion of this, see Charles Jordan Tabb, *Rethinking Preferences*, 43 S.C. L. Rev. 981 (1992).

83 Bankruptcy Code § 547(c)(3). Note that this provision applies to interests in both real estate and personalty; the term "security interest" is defined as any "lien created by agreement." Bankruptcy Code § 101(51).

that are given to enable the debtor to acquire the property that is used to secure the debt, and that are in fact so used. A typical example is a security interest in a car given to secure a loan made to acquire the car. Further, to qualify for protection under this exception, the security interest must be perfected within twenty days after the debtor receives possession of the property.

In many cases in which the § 547(c)(3) exception applies, the § 547(e)(2)(B) grace period also applies, and there is thus no preference in the first place. However, the grace period given under the two sections differs in three respects, two slight and one significant. The grace period under § 547(e)(2)(B) runs from the time the transfer is effective between the parties to perfection; the § 547(c)(3) grace period runs from possession to perfection. In addition, the § 547(e)(2)(B) grace period merely establishes the date of the transfer, while the § 547(c)(3) exception protects the transfer regardless of its date. This is occasionally important if the debt was incurred prior to the date that the debtor obtained possession. Suppose that on January 1, the debtor enters into a contract to purchase a farm tractor. The purchase is on credit; the seller retains a security interest in the tractor to secure repayment. The tractor is delivered on January 5, and the financing statement is filed on January 7. Under section 547(e)(2)(b), the transfer of the security interest in the tractor occurred on January 5, because under Article 9 the transfer became effective between the parties on January 5 and was perfected within ten days thereafter. This, however, does not cure the creditor's preference problem; the obligation was incurred on January 1, so the transfer of the security interest on January 5 was a transfer on account of an antecedent debt. However, the transfer is protected from avoidance because of section 547(c)(3). The extension of credit enabled to debtor to acquire the tractor and was perfected within 20 days after the debtor got the tractor. The exception in effect excuses the delay between the creation of the debt and the transfer of the security interest.

A more significant difference between sections 547(e) and section 547(c)(3), was created by the 1994 Amendments. Prior to the Amendments, the 547(c)(3) grace period was only ten days — the same as section 547(3). This was because, at the time the Bankruptcy Code was originally drafted, Article 9 of the U.C.C. contained a similar ten-day grace period for the perfection of purchase money security interest.[84]

However, most states lengthened that grace period, typically to twenty days.[85] This created a problem if the purchase money interest was perfected more than ten but less than twenty days after the property was acquired by the debtor. The courts universally held that the ten-day period contained in section 547(c)(3) controlled; thus, the purchase money interest would not be protected. The 1994 Amendments changed this by conforming the time period in section 547(c)(3) to that actually used by most of the states. In turn, this means that the grace period allowed by the

[84] U.C.C. §§ 9-312(4), 9-313(4)(a).

[85] Thomas D. Crandall, Michael J. Herbert & Lary Lawrence, Uniform Commercial Code, § 26.9.2 (1993); Barry L. Zaretsky, Gerald T. McLaughlin & Neil B. Cohen, Commercial Law & Practice Guide § 31.04[2][b][iii] n. 25 (1991).

purchase money exception is longer than the grace period permitted to all two-step tranfers by section 547(e).

[E]—Advance of New Value Subsequent to Preference

Section 547(c)(4) provides what amounts to a setoff of post-preference advances of credit against previous preferences.[86] The theory underlying the subsequent advance exception is that the transferee has "replenished" the estate by adding new value to it.[87] It is sometimes erroneously referred to as the "net result rule," which it is not; unlike the section 547(c)(5) exception it does not net out all transactions during the preference period but merely permits later advances of new value to reduce earlier preferences.[88] To qualify, the subsequent advance must:

Either be

1. Unsecured, or

2. Secured by an avoidable security interest, and

Either be

1. Not paid by the debtor, or

2. Paid by the debtor, but the payment itself is avoidable.[89]

For example, suppose that Pushkin received a $3000 preference on January 1 and made a subsequent $2000 advance of credit to DuBois on February 1. If the February 1 advance was unsecured, and was not subsequently repaid by the debtor, the amount of the preference is reduced to $1000. If the February 1 advance was fully secured by collateral, and that security interest is not itself avoidable, then the preference is not reduced at all. If the February 1 advance was repaid, but $500 of that repayment is avoided by the trustee/DIP, then the preference is reduced to $2500.

The key thing to keep in mind about this exception is that the preference and the advance of credit must occur in a particular order: the advance must follow the

[86] Bankruptcy Code § 547(c)(4).

[87] Richard B. Levin, *An Introduction to the Trustee's Avoiding Powers*, 53 Am. Bankr. L. J. 173, 187 (1979).

[88] It is generally assumed that the non-statutory, pre-Code net result rule does not survive the enactment of the Code. In re Fulgham Constr. Corp., 706 F.2d 171 (6th Cir. 1983). Indeed, according to one authority, the net result rule should not have been applied after 1903, when an amendment to the Bankruptcy Act made it obsolete. Michael J. Herbert, *The Trustee versus the Trade Creditor: A Critique of Section 547(c)(1), (2) & (4) of the Bankruptcy Code*, 17 U. Rich. L. Rev. 667, 674-675 & n.29 (1983).

[89] Bankruptcy Code § 547(c)(4). According to at least some courts, if the debt is paid by someone other than the debtor, and the payment has no effect on the debtor's property, the fact that the debt was paid does not preclude the application of this exception. In re Formed Tubes, Inc., 46 Bankr. 645 (Bankr. E.D. Mich. 1985). This reading of the statute certainly fits the plain meaning of its language; it also focuses appropriately on the gain to the estate rather than the loss to the creditor.

preference.[90] For example, suppose that during the preference period the following transactions occurred:

January 1	Advance of $5000 by Pushkin to DuBois
February 1	Preference of $3500 paid by DuBois to Pushkin
February 15	Advance of $4000 by Pushkin to DuBois
February 20	Preference of $5500 paid by DuBois to Pushkin

The January 1 advance of new value may not be set off against either of the preferences, because it occurred before both of them. The February 15 advance of new value may be set off only against the prior preference, the February 1 preference. Thus, Pushkin still has a preference liability of $5,500. This is true even though the total of the two advances equals the total of the two preferences.

[F]—Floating Liens/Net Result Rule

Section 547(c)(5) creates an exception for certain Article 9 floating liens. A floating lien is simply a security interest in a generic pool of collateral rather than specific items of collateral. For example, River Bank might have a security interest in all the inventory and accounts receivable of National Ethanol. As National Ethanol sells its inventory, it generates accounts receivable; as it collects its receivables it obtains cash; it uses the cash to pay River Bank, which then advances it more money to buy more inventory. The collateral is an ever-changing pool of inventory and receivables on which the security interest floats.

Prior to the 1970's, floating liens were subject to substantial preference risk, because each time the debtor obtained new collateral for the pool a new transfer of property to the secured creditor was made. A series of cases largely eliminated the risk,[91] and the addition ofsection 547(c)(5) when the Code was enacted codified one particular method of dealing with the problem. That section gives broad though incomplete protection to the most common forms of the floating liens.

The exception applies to perfected security interests in inventory, receivables, and their proceeds.[92] It does not apply to floating liens on other types of collateral; but floating liens on things other than inventory or receivables are rare. The inventory or receivables floating lien security interest is broadly protected from avoidance, but there is an important exception. To the extent that the obligation secured by the floating lien is less undersecured on the date of the petition than it was at the beginning of the preference period (or on the date the lender first gave new value, if that date was later than the beginning of the preference period) there is a preference.[93]

---

[90] In re Wingspread Corp., 120 Bankr. 8 (Bankr. S.D.N.Y. 1990); In re Excel Enterprises, Inc., 83 Bankr. 427 (Bankr. W.D. La. 1988).

[91] Richard F. Duncan, *Preferential Transfers, The Floating Lien, and Section 547(c)(5) of the Bankruptcy Reform Act of 1978*, 36 Ark. L. Rev. 1 (1982).

[92] Bankruptcy Code § 547(c)(5)

[93] Bankruptcy Code § 547(c)(5)(A).

For example, on July 1 River Bank had a security interest in the inventory of Reliable Motors. The obligation secured was $100,000; the inventory was worth $80,000; since River Bank was an outsider, the preference period was 90 days. Ninety days later, on September 30, Reliable Motors filed its petition. At that time, the obligation secured was $60,000 and the inventory was worth $55,000. River Bank was $20,000 undersecured at the beginning of the preference period and $5,000 undersecured at the time of filing the petition. River Bank must repay $15,000 to the estate.

There are several things to note about this exception. First, it is a true net result rule; the court does not look at the individual transactions that occurred during the preference period, but only the net result.[94] In the example given, there may have been a dozen or more payments by Reliable Motors and advances of credit by River Bank; these are all ignored. The court merely snapshots the beginning and the end of the 90 day or (in the case of an insider) one year period.

Second, the key to the provision is the value of the collateral on the two snapshot dates. As elsewhere under the Code, valuation can be a tricky business. Should the court use wholesale value? retail value? liquidation value? going concern value? The cases indicate that value should be pegged to the actual situation of the debtor.[95] Thus, if the debtor is a wholesaler in liquidation, a liquidation wholesale value is appropriate. If, by contrast, the debtor is a retailer with a reasonable chance of reorganization, a going concern retail value would normally be appropriate.

Third, it is reasonably clear that if the creditor was fully secured or over secured at the beginning of the preference period, it does not matter at all what the creditor's position was at the end.[96] The exception, by its terms, preserves the lien to the extent it does not reduce a deficiency. If there is no deficiency to start with, there is no avoidance. Thus, a fully secured creditor who becomes even more secured apparently retains all of its collateral.[97]

Fourth, the rule deals with increases of value that relate to transfers made during the preference period. An increase in value due solely to an increase in market price does not raise a preference issue, let alone the application of the floating lien exception.[98] For example, if River Bank has a floating lien on an inventory of 100 $20 U.S. "Double Eagle" gold coins, and the market value of those 100 coins rises from $675 each to $750 each during the preference period, that $75,000 increase in value is not a preference. No new property was acquired; no transfer occurred; thus neither section 547(b) nor section 547(c)(5) apply. (This has also been justified on the language of the exception, which refers to an improvement in position that

---

[94] Collier on Bankruptcy ¶ 547.13.

[95] In re Ebbler Furniture and Appliances, Inc., 804 F.2d 87, (7th Cir. 1986); In re Lackow Brothers, Inc., 752 F.2d 1529 ((11th Cir. 1985).

[96] In re Southwest Equip. Rental, Inc., 137 Bankr. 263 (Bankr. E.D. Tenn. 1992).

[97] This appears to be so even though there is a potential betterment in position; the more oversecured a creditor is, the more interest it can potentially obtain on the debt during the pendency period. See § 10.03[C] of this book regarding pendency interest.

[98] See, for example, In re Nivens, 22 Bankr. 287 (Bankr. N.D. Tex. 1982).

is "to the prejudice of other creditors holding unsecured claims"[99]). It is clear, however, that if any measurable part of the increase in value was due to property incorporated into the inventory, there has been a transfer and thus may be a preference. For example, suppose the inventory became more valuable because it was completed by the addition of parts that were not previously inventory. The necessary transfer would occur; if the other requirements of sections 547(b) and (c)(5) were met, the transfer would be voidable.[100]

[G]—Statutory Liens

The sixth exception protects statutory liens, such as mechanic's liens and repair liens, that are not avoidable under section 545.[101] As discussed in Chapter 2, there are a variety of liens created by state and federal laws that give the lienholder the right to claim property as security for an unpaid obligation. If the lien is triggered by the obligor's insolvency or bankruptcy, is unprotected from bona fide purchasers of the property, or is related to a rental obligation, the lien is avoided.[102] The section 547(c)(6) exception applies to those liens that are *not* avoidable under section 545 and protects them from avoidance under section 547.

A simple illustration: On February 1, D'Annunzio takes her car to Garibaldi for repairs. The repairs are performed that day, giving rise to D'Annunzio's obligation to pay Garibaldi, and Garibaldi gives D'Annunzio an itemized bill. Under local state law, Garibaldi is given a lien on the car if D'Annunzio does not pay within 3 days of being given an itemized bill, and this lien is good against a bona fide purchaser. D'Annunzio fails to pay, so the lien "fixes" on February 4. A few days later, D'Annunzio goes into bankruptcy. Since the lien attached to the car several days after the debt was incurred, there was a transfer on an antecedent debt and most likely a section 547(b) preference. However, since Garibaldi's lien is not avoidable under section 545, it is not avoidable under section 547 either.

[H]—Alimony, Maintenance, Support

The 1994 Amendments, following a long-standing bankruptcy policy of favoring alimony, maintenance and support claims, added a new limitation on the trustees' avoiding powers under section 547. The new provision precludes the avoidance of many such payments. To qualify for this exception, the transfer must be a bona fide payment to a spouse, former spouse, or child for alimony, maintenance, or support. Further, the payment must be in connection with a separation agreement, divorce decree, other order of a court of record, or property settlement agreement. The exception does not apply if the debt has been assigned voluntarily or involuntarily. Moreover, the fact that the liability underlying the payment is designated in the order

---

[99] Collier on Bankruptcy ¶ 547.13.

[100] It is less clear whether this is true if the increase in value was due to the debtor's labor rather than the addition of new property. The increase in value due to labor is not an increase that merely relates to market fluctuation; however, it is not a transfer of property, either.

[101] Bankruptcy Code § 547(c)(6).

[102] Bankruptcy Code § 545.

or agreement as alimony, maintenance, or support is not dispositive; the liability must actually be in the nature of alimony, maintenance, or support.[103] Thus, a payment made purusuant to some other obligation, such as the division of the marital property, cannot be protected from preference avoidance by this exception.

[I]—Consumer Debtors

Section 547(c)(8) provides a limited exception for relatively small payments made by consumer debtors. It applies if the debtor is an individual whose debts are primarily consumer debts,[104] (a definition that fits the great majority of bankrupts). It is not, however, limited to consumer debts, and thus apparently can protect the payment of a business debt by a consumer debtor. The transfer must be rather small; the exception applies only if the aggregate value of all property that constitutes or is affected by the transfer is less than $600.[105] The usual reason given for this exception is that such small transfers have little effect on the actual distribution of the estate and are often unduly expensive to recover.

There is considerable ambiguity in the wording of the exception. Two perplexities stand out. First, if there is a transfer of more than $600, does the exception permit the transferee to keep $599.99 or must the entire transfer be returned? The very limited case law suggests that the latter reading is correct.[106] Second, the statute oddly links the phrases "aggregate value" and "such transfer." Does the aggregate value language mean that we aggregate the value of all transfers made to the same creditor on the same debt to determine whether we are within the $600 limit—or does the phrase "such transfer" mean that we aggregate only the amounts of property transferred at the same time? For example, suppose that a consumer debtor paid $500 on the first of each month on the same unsecured debt during the preference period. If the three payments are aggregated, the $600 ceiling is breached and the entire $1500 must be repaid. If each is viewed separately, all three are within the ceiling and are protected. The very few cases that are squarely on point have supported the view that payments to the same creditor within the preference period are to be aggregated; if together they equal $600 or more, all are avoidable.[107]

While it might be better policy to aggregate all of the payments, the statutory language seems clear that only payments made at the same time as part of the same transfer should be aggregated. If this is the correct reading, then, in the example given, all three payments should be protected. By contrast, if the debtor had made two of the $500 payments at the same time (for example, by simultaneously giving the creditor $500 in cash and a security interest in $500 of collateral) they should be aggregated.

---

[103] Bankruptcy Code § 547(c)(7) (1994 Amendments).

[104] Bankruptcy Code § 547(c)(8).

[105] Bankruptcy Code § 547(c)(8).

[106] In re Via, 107 Bankr. 91 (Bankr. W.D. Va. 1989); In re Vickery, 63 Bankr. 222 (Bankr. E.D. Tenn. 1986).

[107] In re Bunner, 145 Bankr. 266 (Bankr. C.D. Ill. 1992); In re Lewis, 116 Bankr. 54 (Bankr. Md. 1990). There is dicta to the contrary in In re Vickery, 63 Bankr. 222 (Bankr. E.D. Tenn. 1986).

[J]—Substitution of Creditors

A final exception to the preference rules appears nowhere in the Code. Rather, it has been carved out by case law, both pre-code and post-Code. It is, or at least arguably is, present in the policies underlying section 547. Whether it would find favor with the present Supreme Court, with its insistence on the staututory text, is uncertain.

This exception relates to what are often referred to as "earmarked" loans—that is, loans earmarked for the repayment of an existing loan. Suppose that Danuta owes River Bank $100,000. Danuta refinances this loan by borrowing $100,000 from Sam with the specific purpose, agreed to by both parties, of repaying the loan to River Bank; and the funds are applied to that debt. However, the repayment is made within the preference period, and all of the other requirements of section 547(b) appear to be met.

On the face of it, River Bank has received a preference. However, a long line of cases has ruled otherwise. The rationale is that there has been no diminution of the estate—the financial situation of Danuta, and the liquidation shares of its creditors, are exactly the same as they were before the transaction. All that has changed is the identity of one of those creditors: Sam is now a creditor, River Bank is not. The courts have generally tried to fit this rationale into the structure of the preference rule by saying that the proceeds of the second loan never really became part of the debtor's assets; thus, there was no transfer by the debtor. Since a transfer by the debtor is an element of a preference, there is no preference.[108]

The reasoning is somewhat disingenuous. The rule applies not only where the payment is made directly by the new creditor to the old but also where the payment is made through the borrower. In the former situation, it is at least plausible to argue that the borrower never "owned" the money newly lent; in the latter it is not. However, in the latter situation there must be a specific agreement that the new loan be for repayment of the old; where the payment is made directly, no such specific agreement is required.[109]

§ 14.04 Indirect Preferences

Preferences can either be direct or indirect—either "to" a creditor or "for the benefit" of a creditor. A series of cases utilized this rule to create a somewhat strange result when an insider received an indirect benefit during the preference period. The following discussion, which is somewhat complicated, may be skipped by those who have little interest in this issue. The reason is that the 1994 Amendments overturned the cases discussed. I include the discussion, however, in part because the cases will continue to be of interest for some time to come and because they perhaps illustrate

---

[108] See, for example, Grubb v. General Contract Purchase Corp, 18 F. Supp. 680 (S.D.N.Y. 1937), aff'd, 94 F.2d 70 (2d Cir. 1938); In re Sun Railings, Inc., 5 Bankr. 538 (Bankr. S.D. Fla. 1980).

[109] In re Bohlen Enterprises, Ltd., 859 F.2d 561 (8th Cir. 1988).

that an excessive reliance on the "plain language" of a statute may indeed reach results that were not at all contemplated by those who wrote the statute. To understand this issue, it is first necessary to examine a bit of suretyship law and how it interacts with bankruptcy law.

Suppose that the president of Dummy Corporation guarantees an obligation of Dummy to River Bank. The president, as a guarantor (a form of surety), owes a contingent obligation to River Bank (if Dummy doesn't pay, the president must).[110] In addition, as a surety, the president has a right of reimbursement against Dummy—if he has to pay any of the debt Dummy owes to River Bank, he is entitled to recover an equal amount from Dummy.[111] Thus, the president has a contingent claim against Dummy for any money paid to River Bank under the guarantee. The contingent claim against Dummy makes the president a creditor of Dummy, at least for bankruptcy purposes.[112] And, since every payment made by Dummy reduces the president's possible obligation to River Bank, the president indirectly benefits from those payments. Thus, each payment by Dummy on the loan is a payment that is both directly to one of its creditors (River Bank) and is indirectly for the benefit of another (the president). Finally, the president of Dummy Corporation is an insider of Dummy Corporation.

All of this has created a problem for lenders, because a number of cases have held that this dual benefit means that the payments to the lender (River Bank) fall under the one year insider preference period rather than the normal 90 day preference period. In syllogistic form:

> Dummy's president is an insider creditor of Dummy.
>
> Dummy's payments to River Bank are for the benefit of Dummy's president.
>
> Therefore, Dummy's payments to River Bank are for the benefit of an insider creditor.
>
> The preference period for a payment that is for the benefit of an insider creditor is one year.
>
> Therefore, the preference period for Dummy's payments to River Bank is one year.

Therefore, River Bank has to disgorge the payments it received during the year prior to bankruptcy.[113] This was true even though the payments were made to River Bank, an outsider, rather than the president.

This approach was criticized for various reasons. In the view of some, it represented an excessive reliance on a literal reading of several complex statutory

---

[110] Laurence P. Simpson, Handbook on the Law of Suretyship § 50 (1950).

[111] Laurence P. Simpson, Handbook on the Law of Suretyship §§ 47-48 (1950).

[112] Bankruptcy Code §§ 101(5), (10).

[113] This syllogism encapsulates the core of the leading case, Levit v. Ingersoll Rand Financial Corp. (In re Deprizio), 874 F.2d 1186 (7th Cir. 1989).

texts, thereby reaching an end result that Congress surely never had in mind. Others complained that it unduly increased the risk to creditors by reducing the value of suretyship rights.[114] A few commentators were supportive, although even tended to suggest that a more sophisticated analysis was in order.[115]

It was widely expected that, if Congress did manage to pass bankruptcy reform legislation, the so-called *Deprizio* rule would go. Go it did. Congress specifically overturned*Deprizio*, although in a slightly unusual fashion. Rather than address this issue in section 547, Congress amended section 550, which deals with the actual recovery of avoided transfers. Under the new provision, if a transfer is made between 90 days and one year before the filing of the petition, and is avoided under section 547(b), and was for the benefit of a creditor who was an insider at the time of the transfer, the trustee may not recover from a transferee that is not an insider.[116] The reason for putting this provision in section 550 is that Congress intended to protect the third party creditor who received the payment, not the insider who benefitted from it. Thus, in the example given, the payment made by Dummy to River Bank can be recovered from Dummy's president (the insider creditor) but not from River Bank (the outsider creditor). In essence, the new provision puts the outside creditor who obtains an insider guarantee in exactly the same position as the outside creditor who does not obtain such a guarantee. Either is at risk for payments made during the 90-day period; neither is at risk for payments made during the 91-day to one-year period. However, the basic principle, that an indirect beneficiary may be forced to disgorge a preference, remains largely intact. The insider guarantor (in our example, Dummy's president) who indirectly benefitted from the debtor's preferential transfers (in our example, the payments made by Dummy Corporation) may still be forced to disgorge the benefit it received to the estate.

§ 14.05 Procedural Issues/Effect of Avoidance

Preference law is not self-executing; the trustee/DIP must take action to recover the transfer. This is normally done by adversary proceeding in the bankruptcy court.[117] If the creditor has submitted itself to the jurisdiction of the bankruptcy court (as, for example, by filing a proof of claim) there is no right to a jury trial.[118] The trustee/DIP carries the burden of persuasion as to all elements of the preference; however, there is a rebuttable presumption that the debtor was insolvent during the

---

[114] See Donald W. Baker, *Repayments of Loan Guaranteed by Insiders as Avoidable Preferences in Bankruptcy: Deprizio and Its Aftermath*, 23 U.C.C. L. J. 115 (1990); Robert F. Higgins & David E. Peterson, *Is There a One-Year Preference Period for Non-Insiders?*, 64 Am. Bankr. L. J. 383 (1990).

[115] Jay Lawrence Westbrook, *Two Thoughts About Insider Preferences*, 76 Minn. L. Rev. 73 (1991).

[116] Bankruptcy Code § 550(c) (1994 Amendments).

[117] In re McCombs Properties, VI, Ltd., 88 Bankr. 261 (Bankr. C.D. Cal. 1988); In re Magic Circle Energy Corp., 64 Bankr. 269 (Bankr. W.D. Okl. 1986)

[118] Lagencamp v. Culp, 498 U.S. 42 (1990).

90 days prior to the filing of the petition.[119] The creditor carries the burden of persuasion as to the applicability of any exception to the avoidance rules.[120]

Occasionally a trustee or debtor in possession has refused or neglected to pursue a preference. Sometimes this decision is legitimate—for example, it might be unduly expensive to the estate to attempt recovery of a small preference or a preference made to a person not subject to service of process in the United States. Other times, however, the failure to recover a preference is based on neglect or even bad faith—for example, a debtor in possession might be reluctant to recover insider preferences made to its managers. This is clearly a breach of the fiduciary duty owed to the creditors. Less clear is the appropriate remedy. Some cases have held that a Chapter 11 creditor's committee has the implicit right to pursue a preference if the trustee or debtor in possession improperly fails to do so.[121] An individual creditor, however, has no such right. It may be possible to have the DIP replaced with a trustee, or have the trustee replaced; it should be possible to obtain an order from the court under section 105 to force the trustee/DIP to take appropriate action.[122]

The effect of avoidance varies with the nature of the transfer. If the transfer was merely of a lien on property still in possession of the debtor, the lien simply ceases to exist and the creditor is left with a general unsecured claim. If the transfer was of money or other property physically transferred to the creditor, the trustee may recover the property or (if the court so orders) the value of the property.[123] The trustee ordinarily seeks recovery against the preferee. However, the trustee may often recover from a subsequent transferee.[124] Subsequent transferees are given some protection by bona fide purchaser rules, which are discussed in Chapter 13 of this book. Similarly, creditors who have improved property that is subsequently recovered by the estate are provided with some protection for the value of their improvements (this is also discussed in Chapter 13). The creditor who is forced to return property is given a general unsecured claim equal to the value of the property.[125] This may create practical problems for a Chapter 11 debtor if the resulting claim is large, because the preferee is likely to be a particularly hostile creditor, unwilling to cooperate in the formulation or confirmation of the plan.

---

[119] Bankruptcy Code § 547(f), (g).

[120] Bankruptcy Code § 547(g).

[121] In re STN Enterprises, 779 F.2d 901 (2d Cir. 1985); cf. Unsecured Noteholders' Committee v. First National Bank & Trust Co. (In re Amarex, Inc.), 36 Bankr. 59 (Bankr. W.D. Okla. 1984) (Creditor's committee may seek permission to sue for recover of preference in the name of the trustee in extraordinary circumstances).

[122] Bankrutpcy Code § 105(a) permits the court to enter any "necessary or appropriate" orders.

[123] Bankruptcy Code § 550(a).

[124] Bankruptcy Code § 550(a)(2).

[125] Bankruptcy Code § 502(h).

§ 14.06 Setoff Preferences

Not all preference rules are contained in section 547. Section 553(b) contains a preference provision that in key respects resembles the net result rule applied to floating liens in the section 547(c)(5) exception. The section 553 provision permits the trustee/DIP to recover certain pre-petition setoffs as preferences.[126]

With certain limited exceptions, a setoff exercised within 90 days prior to the filing of the petition can be avoided to the extent there was a reduction in the insufficiency. "Insufficiency" means the amount by which the debt owed by the offsetting creditor to the debtor was larger than the debt owed by the debtor to the offsetting creditor.[127] The amount of the insufficiency is measured at two points—(1) the date of the setoff and (2) the later of (a) 90 days before the filing of the petition and (b) the first date during that 90 days on which there was an insufficiency.[128]

Suppose that on June 1, which is 90 days before the filing of the petition, Debussy owes Chopin $10,000 and Chopin owes Debussy $12,000. On August 15, Debussy owes Chopin $11,000 and Chopin owes Debussy $11,500. On August 15, Chopin offsets the two obligations, leaving a net obligation of $500 owed by Chopin to Debussy. At the beginning of the 90 day period, the insufficiency was $2000 ($12,000 -$10,000). At the time the debts were offset, the insufficiency was $500 ($11,500 -$11,000). Thus, a setoff preference of $1,500 occurred and that amount may be recovered.

Note that the setoff preference rule is much simpler than the section 547 preference rules. There are no elaborate requirements; most notably, there is no requirement that the debtor be insolvent. Similarly, there are no exceptions to the rule.

Two other quasi-preference rules appear in section 553(a)(2) and (3). These are structured as provisions dealing with the basic right of setoff, rather than as provisions avoiding setoffs already made. For this reason, they are discussed in the general material on setoffs, in Chapter 10.[129]

---

[126] For a general discussion of setoff, see § 2.06 of this book.

[127] Bankruptcy Code § 553(b)(2).

[128] Bankruptcy Code § 553(b)(1).

[129] See § 10.09.

CHAPTER 15

Fraudulent Transfers and Fraudulent Obligations

§ 15.01 Introduction

Among the avoidance powers given to the trustee/DIP is the power to avoid fraudulent transfers and fraudulent obligations. Broadly speaking, a fraudulent transfer is either (i) a transfer made with the intention of defrauding creditors or (ii) a transfer made by an insolvent for grossly inadequate consideration. Many of the classic fraudulent transfers met both criteria—for example, a person who, on the eve of suffering a $10,000,000 judgment, transfers all her assets to a spouse or a relative for $1. Needless to say, there is a strong tradition, both inside and outside bankruptcy, of avoiding such transfers. The usual justification for this is that these transfers impose an unfair, unbargained-for risk on creditors. Those who extend credit normally assume that the borrower will conduct financial affairs normally, and that it will not squander or hide assets when collection time comes. The willingness to extend credit is based at least in part on this assumption; it is, to all intents and purposes, an implied term of the deal. Fraudulent transfer law is the vehicle for enforcing this implied term.

Parallel to the fraudulent transfer is the fraudulent obligation, which is also prohibited. An example of a fraudulent obligation is a debt that exists without any legal basis. For example, A might execute a promissory note to pay B $100,000—even though A has not obtained a loan, or purchased anything, from B. The motivation for the fraudulent obligation is much the same as the motivation for the fraudulent transfer; the difference is that the former involves a creation of a claim while the latter involves the transfer of property.

A fraudulent transfer differs in significant ways from a preference (not least in the fact that fraudulent transfers and obligations, unlike preferences, are prohibited both in bankruptcy and outside of bankruptcy). Although these two avoidance powers may have had a common origin, and still to a limited degree overlap, they have in practice diverged very materially. Modern preference law is almost entirely indifferent to the motivation of transferor and transferee,[1] and applies whether or not the transaction was wholly bona fide. Fraudulent transfer law, by contrast, is often concerned with the motivation underlying the transaction, and always with the commercial legitimacy of the debtor's action. A great many preferences are received by creditors who are not even aware of the fact that the payments are preferential, and who did nothing to cause the preference to be made.[2] By contrast, in nearly

---

[1] For an argument that preference law unwisely retains some vestiges of motivation, see Lawrence Ponoroff, *Evil Intentions and an Irresolute Endorsement for Scientific Realism: Bankruptcy Preferences One More Time,* 1993 Wis. L. Rev. 1439.

[2] See Chapter 14 of this book.

all cases, the beneficiary of a fraudulent transfer or obligation had at least some notice that the transaction was flawed; in a good many of cases, the recipient knew perfectly well that the transferor was trying to cheat creditors. Preference law protects some creditors, but it does so at the expense of others; it enforces the Bankruptcy Code's scheme of distribution by recovering property from those who have received more than their allocated share.[3] Fraudulent transfer law protects creditors as a group from the misconduct of the debtor. Admittedly, these are differences of degree, not kind, and there are undoubtedly some preferences that are also fraudulent transfers.

Many reasons have been advanced for avoiding fraudulent transfers. Some of these are simple moral statements. Others focus on the creditors' expectations; as indicated, the most commonly stated reason is that the debtor is violating an implied term of the agreement, and even implicitly misrepresenting its intentions regarding its assets and intentions. This latter argument is not entirely convincing, for three reasons. First, a creditor who truly depends on the debtor's assets in making a decision to lend is likely to obtain a mortgage on or security interest in them. Liens give much greater protection than any fraudulent conveyance law possibly could. Second, the theory does not explain why creditors who have not in any tangible sense relied on the debtor's assets or financial honesty should be allowed to avoid a fraudulent transfer. For example, someone who has been injured by another's reckless driving has not relied upon the driver's wealth, does not expect that the driver will be worth $30,000,000, and never considered whether the driver would retain, conceal, or dissipate that fortune. Yet that creditor has the same right as a contract creditor to avoid the driver's fraudulent transfers. This right today may be justified on a rather different basis: recovery of the transfer places the costs of the driver's actions on the driver rather than on taxpayers or purchasers of insurance. Third, the theory simply cannot explain why, under some fraudulent transaction statutes, people who were not even creditors at the time of the transaction are protected. It is thus impossible to separate fraudulent transfer law entirely from the moral consideration that one who has done an injury must to the extent possible pay for that injury; and if payment is not volunteered it will be coerced. It is also conceivable that the enforcement of this moral principle through fraudulent transfer law may marginally increase the care that the rich and reckless take, since they should know they cannot lawfully hide their assets.

In any event, the Bankruptcy Code provides two primary bases on which the trustee/DIP may avoid a fraudulent transfer or obligation.[4] Section 548 is the Code's own version of fraudulent transfer law; it is remarkable only in that it reaches back just one year. In addition, the trustee/DIP may avoid transfers using applicable state law; this can be of particular importance if the challenged transfer occurred more than one year before the petition. These two powers are discussed in sequence.

---

[3] To the extent that preference law encourages orderly liquidation or facilitates reorganization, it may also benefit creditors as a whole; but there is strong reason to doubt that preference law has this effect. See § 14.01 of this book.

[4] Note that some of the other avoidance powers, although not usually thought of as fraudulent transfer provisions, can also be used in some cases to avoid the types of transactions avoidable under section 548.

§ 15.02 Fraudulent Transfers Under Bankruptcy Code Section 548

[A]—Introduction

Section 548, which is derived from prior uniform legislation on fraudulent transfers, defines two primary types of fraudulent transfers and obligations. The first type involves "actual fraud;" that is, it requires the actual intent to cheat creditors. The second type deals with situations in which the transfer or obligation was in exchange for grossly inadequate consideration and was made by a person who is unable to pay debts. This type grew out of the so-called "badges of fraud," that is, evidence that created an inference or even a presumption of actual fraud. In traditional language, this is "constructive fraud," a term not today encouraged because it is rooted in an unnecessary legal fiction. As it stands today, the second type of fraudulent transfer has nothing to do with fraud in the traditional sense of the term; it is the acts of the transferor, not the intention underlying those acts, that matters.

Although the two types of transfers are distinct, there is often a degree of confusion about the distinction. In large part, this is because many of the same facts will be used to establish both. For example, gross inadequacy of consideration is an element of the second type of fraudulent transaction. Grossly inadequate consideration is also evidence of the first type—evidence of actual fraud.

[B]—Actual Fraud

Under section 548(a)(1), the trustee/DIP may avoid any transfer of the debtor's property, and any obligation incurred by the debtor if

1. The transfer was made or the obligation incurred within one year[5] prior to the date of the filing of the petition, and

2. The transfer was made or the obligation incurred with actual intent to "hinder, delay, or defraud" any "entity"[6] to which the debtor either was indebted at the time or the transfer or to which the debtor subsequently became indebted.[7]

Note that this applies equally to voluntary and involuntary transfers[8] although it is unusual for an involuntary transfer to be made with actual fraudulent intent.

The predicate intent to establish actual fraud can be difficult to prove. Indeed, it is very rare than any transferor will be so foolish as to declare openly an intention to injure creditors. For this reason, intent must ordinarily be established by inference from the circumstances of the transaction. Long dubbed "badges of fraud," a number of rather common-sense factors have been identified by the courts to help in the

---

[5] Note that in this respect, Bankruptcy Code § 548 differs from the typical state law fraudulent transfer statute, which either has no limitation or a longer limitation period.

[6] This term includes both human beings and organizations. Bankruptcy Code § 101(15).

[7] Bankruptcy Code § 548(a)(1).

[8] Bankruptcy Code § 548(a)(1).

search for the necessary intent. Among the many circumstances that indicate fraud are a retention of ownership, use or possessory rights in the transferred property[9] transfer in payment of a forgiven debt[10] transfer to a newly-created, closely-held corporation[11] and transfer to a close relative.[12] Contrary to what is sometimes said, however, it is not per se fraudulent to make a transfer to a spouse, sibling or parent; while this is strong evidence of fraudulent intent, especially if adequate consideration is lacking, it is not dispositive.[13]

Indeed, none of the badges of fraud is dispositive. Generally, they are only guidelines, creating inferences that the trier of fact may or may not draw in any particular case. The Uniform Fraudulent Transfer Act (the "U.F.T.A.") includes a list of the traditional badges of fraud; this list is frequently cited in section 548 litigation. This list is contained in § 4(b), which lists as factors for determining actual intent the following:

1. The fact that the transfer was made to or the obligation is in favor of an insider of the transferor.[14] This is the familiar transfer to spouse or friend.

2. The fact that the debtor retained possession or control of the property transferred after the transfer.[15] This suggests that the transfer is merely to shift legal title to another, thus keeping it from creditors, while continuing to enjoy all the benefits of ownership.

3. The fact that the transfer or the obligation was disclosed or concealed.[16] If it was disclosed, this tends to negate fraud; if it was concealed, this tends to evidence fraud. The logic is that people with legitimate purposes are unlikely to hide their actions.

---

[9] In re Nemeroff, 74 Bankr. 30 (E.D. La. 1987).

[10] In re Colwell, 93 F.2d 946 (7th Cir. 1937).

[11] Chorost v. Grand Rapids Factory Show Rooms, Inc., 77 F. Supp. 276 (D.N.J. 1948), aff'd, 172 F.2d 327 (3d Cir. 1949).

[12] McWilliams v. Edmonson, 162 F.2d 454 (5th Cir. 1947), cert. denied, 332 U.S. 835 (1947) (sister); Levy v. Bukes, 65 F. Supp. 494 (W.D. Pa. 1946) (spouse).

[13] Chichester v. Golden, 204 F. Supp. 634 (S.D. Cal. 1962).

[14] U.F.T.A. § 4(b)(1). "Insider" as used in the Uniform Fraudulent Transfer Act has much the same definition as it has under the Bankruptcy Code. It encompasses close relatives and close business affiliates. See U.F.T.A. § 1(7).

[15] U.F.T.A. § 4(b)(2). Note that, under modern secured transactions law, the fact that a debtor remains in physical possession of property subject to a security interest is not a fraudulent transfer (nor does it create a badge of fraud), provided that the security interest has been properly perfected by the filing of a financing statement or other notice-giving device. Prior to the late 19th Century development of laws that provided for public notice, however, such security interests were often struck down as fraudulent transfers. For a discussion of the current rules regarding perfection of a security interest, see § 2.02[C] of this book.

[16] U.F.T.A. § 4(b)(3).

4. Before the transfer was made or the obligation was incurred, the debtor had been sued or threatened with suit.[17] A classic example is the person who transfers all of her property to her spouse when sued for $10,000,000; it is reasonable to infer that this was done to shield the property from the plaintiff.

5. The transfer was of substantially all the debtor's assets.[18] This action suggests that the debtor was trying to make itself judgment-proof.

6. The debtor absconded.[19] "Absconded" means that the debtor attempted to conceal himself or herself, particularly if the debtor attempted to move beyond the reach of service of process.[20]

7. The debtor removed or concealed assets.[21] Again, this refers to an attempt to hide assets from creditors or to remove them from the reach of service of process. Openly moving assets from one known location within a jurisdiction to another known location within a jurisdiction would not normally evidence fraud.

8. The value of the consideration received by the debtor was (or was not) reasonably equivalent to the value of the asset transferred or the amount of the obligation incurred.[22] For example, this indicia of fraud would be present if the debtor sold a car worth $25,000 for $25. Note that this badge of fraud dovetails with the key elements of "constructive" fraud — that is, adequacy or inadequacy of consideration.[23] It differs in that inadequacy of consideration is not a necessary element of actual fraud, nor does adequacy of consideration necessarily suffice to prove the absence of fraud.

9. The debtor was insolvent or became insolvent shortly after the transfer was made or the obligation was incurred.[24] Once again, this badge of fraud is quite similar to one of the elements of "constructive" fraud, that is insolvency.[25] However, as is true with adequacy of consideration, solvency is merely an element; the fact that the debtor was solvent does not necessarily disprove actual fraud nor does the fact that the debtor was insolvent necessarily prove it.

---

[17] U.F.T.A. § 4(b)(4).

[18] U.F.T.A. § 4(b)(5).

[19] U.F.T.A. § 4(a)(6).

[20] Note too that the modern extension of long-arm jurisdiction, permitting the service of process across state lines, has reduced the significance of this badge of fraud.

[21] U.F.T.A. § 4(b)(7).

[22] U.F.T.A. § 4(b)(8).

[23] See U.F.T.A. § 5 and Bankruptcy Code § 548(a)(2)(A).

[24] U.F.T.A. § 4(b)(9).

[25] See U.F.T.A. § 5 and Bankruptcy Code § 548(a)(2)(B)(i).

10. The transfer occurred shortly before or shortly after a substantial debt was incurred.[26] This badge of fraud also dovetails with an element of "constructive" fraud — inability to meet actual or prospective obligations.[27]

11. The debtor transferred the essential assets of its business to a lienholder who then retransferred the assets to an insider of the debtor.[28]

The "actual intent" branch of fraudulent conveyance law has greatly diminished in significance over the years. This is due to the development of the rules avoiding transfers by an insolvent. There are very few cases covered by the actual intent rules that are not also covered by the insolvent transferor rules; and the latter ground is usually easier to prove, because there is no intent requirement.

[C]—Insolvent Transferor / Inadequacy of Consideration ("Constructive Fraud")

[1]—General Requirements

The second basis for avoidance under section 548 is spelled out in subsection (a)(2). It requires two conditions. The first is that the debtor received, in exchange for the transfer or the obligation, less than "reasonably equivalent value."[29] The second is that the debtor be unable to pay debts; more precisely, either

1. The debtor was insolvent on the date the transfer was made or the obligation incurred, or

2. The debtor became insolvent as a result of the transfer or obligation, or

3. The debtor was engaged in a business or transaction for which its remaining property was an unreasonably small capital, or

4. The debtor was about to engage in a business or transaction for which its remaining property was an unreasonably small capital, or

5. The debtor intended to incur debts that would be beyond its ability to pay as they came due, or

6. The debtor believed that it would incur debts that would be beyond its ability to pay as they came due.[30]

The transfer involved may be either a voluntary or an involuntary one.[31]

---

[26] U.F.T.A. § 4(b)(10).

[27] Bankruptcy Code § 548(a)(2)(B)(iii).

[28] U.F.T.A. § 4(b)(11).

[29] Bankruptcy Code § 548(a)(2)(A).

[30] Bankruptcy Code § 548(a)(2)(B).

[31] Bankruptcy Code § 548(a).

In the context of this provision, "insolvent" refers to balance-sheet insolvency; that is, fewer assets than debts.[32] For example, if the fair value of the debtor's property is $500,000, and the total of its debts is $750,000, the debtor is insolvent. "Value" means (i) property, (ii) the satisfaction of a debt, or (iii) the securing of a debt.[33] Thus, if the transferor receives property in exchange for the transfer, it receives value; if it obtains discharge of an obligation for the transfer, it receives value; if the transferor provides collateral for an existing loan owed by the transferor, the transferor receives value.[34] Remember, however, that the standard is not whether value was received, but whether the value was reasonably equivalent to what was surrendered. If the property received in exchange is of trivial value in comparison with what was given up, the transfer was not for reasonably equivalent value. Finally, value specifically does not include an executory promise to furnish support to the debtor or to a relative of the debtor.[35] This is to prevent a debtor from shielding a transfer by claiming that the transferor has made an unperformed promise to take care of him or her—for example, a promise by the sister who has received all of the debtor's property to take care of the debtor for the rest of her life.

The intent of the transferor is generally irrelevant. Only in the fifth example, a transfer made by a person who intended to incur debts that could not be paid, does the transferor's motivation matter. Even then, the intent does not relate to the transfer; rather it relates to the transferor's future financial activity. Thus, the person challenging the transfer on this basis does not have to prove, directly or by inference, that the transferor meant to cheat creditors; and evidence of good intention should be inadmissible.

There are still a number of difficult questions that must be addressed. The most heavily litigated is the meaning of "reasonably equivalent value." If the transfer was for reasonably equivalent value, it does not matter what the transferor's financial state was. The classic cases, in which no consideration or purely nominal consideration is given, are easy. More difficult are those in which the transferee is getting a good deal but not an incredible one. For example, suppose that Reliable Motors, an insolvent car dealership, attempts to work its way out of its financial straits by holding a sale. It sells cars at $50 over factory invoice—hundreds of dollars less than other dealers are offering. When Reliable finally does go bankrupt, the trustee might try to undo the sales, arguing that the purchase price was abnormally low and that Reliable thus made little or no profit. The buyers, in turn, might argue that in context the price was reasonable. Reliable was trying to clear old model cars off its lot to make room for newer cars; in addition, Reliable (which like most car dealers purchased its inventory on credit from the manufacturer) was trying to raise cash

---

[32] Bankruptcy Code § 101(32).

[33] Bankruptcy Code § 548(d)(2)(A).

[34] An example of the last would be a transfer of a security interest in the debtor's inventory to secure a debt it already owes to River Bank. Note, however, that if this transaction occurs shortly before the bankruptcy it might be avoided as a preference. See Chapter 14 of this book.

[35] Bankruptcy Code § 548(d)(2)(A). The definition of "relative" appears in Bankruptcy Code § 101(45), and includes blood and blood and marriage relationships within the third degree as defined by the common law.

to pay down its debt and reduce its interest payments. On these facts, the buyers should probably prevail.

One issue has attracted considerable notice in recent years—whether it is ever appropriate for a bankruptcy court to evaluate the propriety of the price paid at a foreclosure sale. That question, with the Supreme Court's recent answer ("no!") is explored in § 15.02[C] [3] of this chapter. Another hot topic, now somewhat fading in significance, is the ability of creditors to attach some leveraged buyouts as being or including fraudulent transfers. It is discussed in § 15.04 of this chapter.

It is clear that reasonably equivalent value does not mean dollar for dollar equivalence.[36] Whether sufficient value was received depends on the "totality of the circumstances," (a rather unhelpful phrase).[37] There are many reasons why a bargain price transaction should not necessarily be avoided. It may be difficult to determine what the "real" value of the property was when it was sold. Indeed, economists tell us that there is no "real" value except the price a willing buyer will exchange with a willing seller. Financially troubled debtors often have to sell at low prices because (i) they need money immediately and (ii) their buyers are taking the added risk that the seller will be unable to pay for claims that warranty terms or other parts of the bargain were breached. There is also the obvious problem of determining what the value was at the time of the transaction, because subsequent events may, in hindsight, alter the perception of the deal.[38]

These problems are particularly acute if the value is not entirely tangible. It is pretty easy to determine the value of fungible goods regularly sold in an established market. It is far more difficult to determine the value of an investment in an uncertain business venture. For example, *In re Fairchild Aircraft Corp.*[39] involved payments made by Fairchild for aviation fuel purchased by its affiliate, Air Kentucky. Air Kentucky was a struggling commuter airline that Fairchild hoped to prop up[40] so that it could purchase Fairchild planes. The court held that the indirect benefits that Fairchild reasonably hoped it would gain were value in determining whether its fuel payments were for reasonably equivalent value.[41]

Indeed, rather vague concepts of value, such as "synergy," have been used to find that a transfer was not fraudulent. Synergy was a vogue notion a few years back, used to justify conglomerates. It expressed the supposition that a combination of the right businesses would add value to the whole because of the links that would grow between them. It is the theory that a business that publishes books, makes movies, and records compact disks will be more valuable than three separate businesses, because creativity will flow from one segment to another. Similarly, it

---

[36] See In re Fairchild Aircraft Corp., 6 F.3d 1119 (5th Cir. 1993).

[37] In re Besing, 981 F.2d 1488, 1495-96 (5th Cir. 1993).

[38] It is well accepted that the reasonable equivalence of the value is to be determined as of the time the value is given. See In re Morris Communications NC, Inc., 914 F.2d 458 (4th Cir. 1990).

[39] 6 F.3d 1119 (5th Cir. 1993).

[40] No pun intended.

[41] In re Fairchild Aircraft Corp., 6 F.3d at 1126.

has been supposed that it is beneficial for the same company to manufacture automobiles and aircraft. Although synergy is now out of vogue (indeed, it is about three vogues back), and its benefits doubtful (recently, many conglomerates have been unbundling into smaller and smaller more specialized businesses), it has been accepted as a value for fraudulent transfer purposes in some cases.[42]

One plausible justification for the acceptance of indeterminate values as reasonably equivalent value is the generally hands-off approach that courts have long taken toward business decisions. In the corporate law arena, this is called the business judgment rule—which broadly means that boards of directors are free to take actions that are not palpably absurd or adverse to shareholder interests. If courts were too narrow in their review of intangible sources of value, then fraudulent transfer law would significantly inhibit business decision making. That is generally assumed to be undesirable, usually on the basis that courts lack the experience necessary to make business judgments. A notable exception to this hands-off approach is the courts' quite routine application of fraudulent transfer law to leveraged buy-outs.[43]

[2]—Sureties

One problem that arises from time to time is whether an obligation incurred by, or a payment made by, an insolvent surety is fraudulent. For example, consider the situation of an insolvent corporate president who guarantees a loan to the corporation. The argument is that in many cases, a surety receives no benefit for its promise or payment, because the benefit of the underlying transaction went to the principal, not the surety. In the example given, the money went to the corporation, a different legal entity from its president. Thus, it has been argued, if the other requirements for establishing a fraudulent transfer are met, the obligation of or payment by the surety should be avoided.

In some cases this argument is successful. In others it is not. The reason why it often fails is that sureties generally receive indirect benefits that provide substantially equivalent value. For example, suppose that, in the example given, the guarantor is not only the president but also the sole stockholder of the borrowing corporation. As the sole owner of the company, the stockholder's investment will increase to the extent that the loan is beneficial to the corporation. For example, if the loan enables the corporation to make $20,000 in profits, the value of the ownership of the corporation will rise correspondingly.[44] Since the guarantor benefits indirectly from the loan, it does receive value for its guarantee. So long as this benefit can reasonably be measured as equivalent to the cost of the guarantee, the requirement that reasonably equivalent value be received is met.[45]

---

[42] See Mellon Bank, N.A. v. Metro Communications, Inc., 945 F.2d 635 (3d Cir. 1991).

[43] See § 15.04 of this chapter.

[44] For purposes of this example, I ignore the fact that taxation and transaction costs involved in realizing on this increased value may mean that the gain to the shareholder is less than $20,000. Note too that even if the president was not the sole stockholder, or not a stockholder at all, the president might receive an indirect benefit—increased salary.

[45] See Rubin v. Manufacturers Hanover Trust, 661 F.2d 979 (2d Cir. 1981). Like *Rubin*, most of the actual reported cases have involved inter-corporate guarantees, that is, guarantees

In addition, there is also a question about how the guarantee should be priced. In the example given, suppose that the guarantor stood surety for a $200,000 obligation of the corporation. Does this mean that the indirect benefit must be roughly equal to $200,000? The better reasoned view is no. When one guarantees a $200,000 debt, one does not owe $200,000; one merely has created the possibility that, sometime in the future, one may become liable for $200,000. If the principal—in the example given, the corporation—pays the debt, the surety owes nothing; if it pays $197,822 the surety owes only the remaining $2,178. Moreover, if the surety does pay, it is entitled to recover all that it pays from the principal; if the principal has unencumbered assets, the surety will recover at least a part of what it paid out.

To work through this, consider a matter that puzzled me greatly as a child. For the life of me, I could not understand how bail bondsmen made money. For some reason or other, I frequently passed by a sign that advertised bail bonds for 10% of the amount required; that is, for $200 the bondsman would post a $2,000 bail bond with the court and spring errant friends and relations. It seemed to me that the bondsman was acting with much generosity if little sense, and I understood why the sign looked so beat up and shabby. In fact I was receiving my first lesson in surety law. The bondsman made money because most defendants showed up in court and the bondsman did not have to pay on the bond. So too with our corporate guarantor.

This should be taken into account in deciding what value the surety exchanged. If, in the example given, the likelihood of payment, as measured at the time the guarantee was given, was high, then the real amount of the debt incurred by the guarantor is correspondingly low.[46] It is that amount, not the amount of the debt guaranteed, that should be compared with the value indirectely received. The indirect value should also be measured at the time of the guarantee; if the guarantee enables the corporation to obtain an opportunity that has direct value to it and indirect value to the guarantor when the guarantee was given, it should not matter that, due to subsequent misfortune, the opportunity in fact turned out to be worth less or even worthless.

[3]—Pre-Petition Foreclosure Sales

Foreclosure sales are usually concluded at bargain-basement prices. Often, the winning bid will be for far less than the supposed value of the property. Traditionally, however, it was assumed that fraudulent transfer law did not apply to properly conducted, non-collusive foreclosure sales.[47] The primary reason was the need for

---

between entities within a related group of companies. For a fuller discussion of these issues, see Scott F. Norberg, *Avoidability of Intercorporate Guarantees Under Sections 548(a)(2) and 544(b) of the Bankruptcy Code,* 64 N.C. L. Rev. 1099 (1986).

[46] For an excellent discussion of this issue, see Judge Posner's opinion in In re Xonics Photochemical, Inc., 841 F.2d 198 (7th Cir. 1988).

[47] Note that this is spelled out explicitly in the Uniform Fraudulent Transfer Act:

For the purposes of Sections 4(a)(2) and 5, a person gives a reasonble equivalent value if the person acquires an interest of the debtor in an asset pursuant to a regularly conducted,

finality; any uncertainty about the sale transaction would if anything inhibit the willingness of bidders to purchase and thus make the sale price even lower. There were also federalism concerns. Foreclosure law is overwhelmingly state law; states are presumably as competent as the federal government to protect creditor rights; and by long tradition this was an area of law left to them. Finally, the best indicator of the "real" value of the property is normally the price that it fetched at the auction (assuming the auction was conducted in a reasonable manner, and there was no collusion among bidders). There are many reasons why the price is low—uncertainties about the degree to which the property may have deteriorated in the hands of a failing owner, lack of recourse against the seller for problems, inability of the owner to wait for a particularly interested buyer, etc. None of these was generally thought to raise a fraudulent transfer issue.

This assumption was rudely and abruptly challenged when, in 1980, the Fifth Circuit Court of Appeals held that a non-judicial foreclosure sale could subsequently be challenged under section 548. This has since been known as the *Durrett* problem, after the name of the case, *Durrett v. Washington National Insurance Co.*[48] In a somewhat ambiguous opinion, the court held (at a minimum) that under the circumstances of the case a sale price equal to about 57% of the "value" of the foreclosed property was not substantially equivalent value and, at a maximum, that the sale price must always be at least 70% of the property's "value" to be substantially equivalent value. Other courts promptly divided into three camps, asserting, respectively, the following positions: (i) nonjudicial foreclosure sales were subject to fraudulent transfer challenge and 70% was the required minimum; (ii) nonjudicial foreclosure sales were subject to fraudulent transfer challenge, but there was no required minimum and (iii) nonjudicial foreclosure sales were subject to challenge only if they were collusive or conducted improperly under applicable foreclosure law. Many other possible rules were suggested.[49]

The difficulties spawned by the *Durrett* rule and the various interpretations of it have been put to rest by the Supreme Court in a delightfully named case, *BFP v Resolution Trust Corporation.*[50] BFP was a partnership formed for the purpose of purchasing a home. The home was purchased subject to a first deed of trust in favor of Imperial Savings Association. When the loan went into default, Imperial foreclosed; at the foreclosure sale the home was purchased by Paul Osborne for $433,000.00. Several months after the foreclosure sale, the partnership filed bankruptcy and sought to avoid the sale to Osborne under section 548. BFP alleged that the home was actually worth over $725,000 and thus the price paid was not reasonably equivalent value.

> noncollusive foreclosure sale or execution of a power of sale for the acquisition or disposition of the interest of the debtor upon default under a mortgage, deed of trust, or security agreement.

U.F.T.A. § 3(b).

[48] 621 F.2d 201 (5th Cir. 1980).

[49] For a good general discussion of the cases, see Helen J. Durham, *A Decade of Division Among the Circuits: Application of Section 548(a)(2) of the Bankruptcy Code to Foreclosure Sales,* 19 Mem. St. U. L. Rev. 381 (1989).

[50] 114 S. Ct. 1757 (1994).

In a 5 to 4 decision, in which both majority and dissent claimed to be following the plain meaning rule, the Supreme Court entirely swept away *Durrett*. Looking first to the statute, Justice Scalia, writing for the majority, noted that section 548 refers to "reasonably equivalent value" rather than the more common formulation "fair market value." In his view, this meant that the measure of adequacy for fraudulent transfer purposes is distinctly different from than that applicable when statute calls for a measure based on fair market value. Moreover, given the context of the normal foreclosure sale, this is justified:

> That suspicion [that Congress meant something different from "fair market value" when it said "reasonably equivalent value"] becomes a certitude when one considers that market value, as it is commonly understood, has no applicability in the forced-sale context; indeed, it is the very *antithesis* of forced-sale value . . . In short, "fair market value" presumes market conditions that, by definition, simply do not obtain in the context of a forced sale.[51]

Scalia also explored the history of fraudulent transfer law and its relationship to foreclosure law. He noted that while, in general, foreclosure law permits the setting aside of a sale when the price is unconscionably low, the power given to the bankruptcy court is a power to avoid fraudulent transfers, not to enforce state foreclosure statutes.[52] He also noted that, traditionally, fraudulent transfer law did not meddle with validly conducted foreclosures:

> Fraudulent transfer law and foreclosure law enjoyed over 400 years of peaceful coexistence in Anglo-American jurisprudence until the Fifth Circuit's unprecedented 1980 decision in *Durrett*. To our knowledge, no prior decision had ever applied the "grossly inadequate price" badge of fraud under fraudulent transfer law to set aside a foreclosure sale.[53]

In light of all this, the majority returned to the traditional rule. Having posed the question in the case as "whether the consideration received from a non-collusive, real estate mortgage foreclosure sale conducted in conformance with applicable state law conclusively satisfies the Bankruptcy Code's requirement that transfers of property by insolvent debtors . . . be in exchange for a 'reasonably equivalent value,"[54] the Court answered yes. Thus, after *BFP*, it is clear that, in bankruptcy, a prior foreclosure may only be attacked under section 548 if it was collusive or otherwise in violation of state procedural law.[55] Assuming that there is no fatal procedural defect in the mortgage foreclosure, the price paid, however small, is a reasonably equivalent value for § 548 purposes.

---

[51] 114 S. Ct. at 1761.

[52] 114 S. Ct. at 1763-64.

[53] 114 S. Ct. at 1764.

[54] 114 S. Ct at 1757-58.

[55] Note that *BFP* does not prevent an attack based on state fraudulent transfer law; however, traditionally, state fraudulent transfer law has followed the rule adopted in *BFP*.

[4]—Timing of the transaction

Only those transfers made within the year prior to the petition are avoidable under section 548. Because of this time limitation, it is necessary to determine when a transfer was made. Those made more than a year before the petition cannot be attacked under section 548 (although they may still be attacked under the relevant state fraudulent transfer law). Section 548(d)(1) states that a transfer occurs when the transfer "is so perfected that a bona fide purchaser . . . against whom applicable law permits such transfer to be perfected cannot acquire an interest . . . that is superior to [that of] the transferee."[56] Translated, this provision deals with the same two-step transfer problem discussed in other contexts, such as preference,[57] and the "strong-arm" clause.[58]

Some transfers require more than one step to become valid against third parties. For example, execution of a deed or mortgage on realty does not make the conveyance good against all third parties; recordation is required. In particular, a bona fide purchaser can take free of the interest represented by the unrecorded deed or mortgage. Until recordation occurs, therefore, the transaction has not occurred for section 548 purposes.

For example, suppose that on February 1, 1997, Vera executes a deed in favor of Park. The deed is not recorded until August 15, 1997. Vera files bankruptcy on July 1, 1998. The transfer from Vera to Park occurred on August 15, 1997; it is thus within the 1 year period. If, at the time of the transfer, Vera was insolvent, and if the price paid was grossly inadequate, the trustee/DIP may avoid the transfer under section 548. If the deed had been recorded on March 1, 1997, the transfer would have occurred on that date and the transaction would not be avoidable under section 548 (although it might still be under state law, which the trustee/DIP may also use). If the deed had never been recorded, the transfer would have occurred "immediately before the date of the filing of the petition,"[59] which presumably means on June 30, 1998.

[D]—Transfers to General Partners

Section 548(b) contains a special fraudulent transaction provision applicable only to bankrupt partnerships. The trustee/DIP may avoid any transfer of property, or any obligation incurred, if the transfer was made to, or the debt owed to, a general partner and if, in addition,

1. The transfer was made or the obligation incurred within one year before the filing, and

2. Either the partnership was insolvent or the partnership became insolvent as a result of the transfer or obligation.[60]

---

[56] Bankruptcy Code § 548(d)(1).

[57] For a discussion of this issue in the preference context, see § 14.02 of this book.

[58] See § 13.02 of this book.

[59] Bankruptcy Code § 548(d)(1).

[60] Bankruptcy Code § 548(b).

This rule is far more absolute than either of the rules contained in subsection (a); the issues of proof are quite minimal. Fraudulent intent is immaterial, and it is irrelevant whether the exchange was for a reasonably equivalent value.

In understanding this rule, it is important to stress that it only applies when the partnership, together with its general partners, has fewer assets than liabilities. A partnership is only insolvent when its assets, together with the excess of each partner's own properties over the partner's own debts, is less than the total debts of the partnership.[61] This is because partners are answerable for the debts of a partnership; thus, the excess of the partners' assets over and above the parners' personal debts are for all practical purposes assets of the partnership available to the partnership's creditors.[62]

For example, assume Arsenio and Bernice are partners. The partnership owns $50,000 in assets and has $70,000 in debts. Arsenio and Bernice each own $10,000 in nonpartnership property and each has $5,000 of nonpartnership debts. Arsenio's "excess" is $5,000; Bernice's excess is $5,000; the sum of Arsenio's excess plus Bernice's excess plus the partnership's property is $60,000, $10,000 less than the partnership's debts. The partnership is insolvent. Any transfer of property by the partnership to Bernice is fraudulent. Even if Bernice were to pay the partnership $5,000 for $5,000 worth of the partnership's property, the situation would be exactly the same. In either case, the creditors of the partnership would be able to reach only a total of $60,000. Thus, Bernice's purchase, although for a reasonably equivalent value, would be avoidable.

§ 15.03 Fraudulent Transfers Under State Law

As stressed throughout this Chapter, the power of the trustee/DIP to avoid a fraudulent transfer is not limited to section 548. Pursuant to section 544(b), a fraudulent transfer or fraudulent obligation may also be avoided if it is avoidable under relevant state law by someone who is actually a creditor in the bankruptcy proceeding.[63] The fact that state law is not likely to have a one-year limitation is what makes this power especially valuable; however, there may be limitations on who may sue.

There are also some circumstances under which state fraudulent transfer laws have a broader scope than does § 548. Some state laws include various preferences in their list of fraudulent transfers; this occasionally makes it possible to avoid a preference under § 544(b) when it cannot be avoided under § 547.[64] However, in other circumstances, the state fraudulent transfer law is narrower than § 548. One common example relates to the proper party plaintiff. Under some state fraudulent

[61] Bankruptcy Code § 101(32)(B).

[62] See § 1.05 of this book.

[63] Bankruptcy Code § 544(b) gives the trustee/DIP the power to "avoid any transfer of an interest of the debtor in property or any obligation incurred by the debtor that is voidable under applicable law by a creditor holding an unsecured claim that is allowable . . .".

[64] In re Purco, Inc., 76 Bankr. 523 (Bankr. W.D. Pa. 1987).

transfer laws, only a person who was a creditor at the time of the transfer has standing to attack it. Since the rights of the trustee/DIP under § 544(b) are entirely derivative of those of an actual creditor, if there is no actual creditor who has standing to avoid the transaction under state fraudulent conveyance law, the trustee/DIP has no standing either. This problem does not arise under § 548, which draws no distinction between types of creditors and in any event does not require that there be any actual creditor who is affected by the transfer.

§ 15.04 Leveraged Buy-Outs

During the 1980's, the so-called Leveraged Buy-Out (LBO) became a popular tool for changing the control of publicly held corporations. Briefly, the typical LBO involves a group of investors, often but not necessarily the top management of the company, who buy out the interests of the stockholders using borrowed money ("leverage"). The company so purchased is actually an obligor (sometimes the only obligor) on the loan. In effect, the buyers use the credit worthiness of the company they are acquiring to buy out the equity interests of the shareholders. LBOs can be used for many purposes, including the spin-off of an unwanted division or subsidiary. However, the most publicized have involved taking a company private. This means that the end result of the LBO is the conversion of a corporation with many stockholders and an actively traded stock to a corporation with few stockholders and stock that is rarely if ever traded. In place of the vanished stockholders is debt.

LBOs have been both praised and panned. The massive conversion of equity to debt creates risks for the company, because debt must be paid regardless of the success of the business while equity shares in fortune and misfortune alike. In its simplest terms, corporations must pay interest but do not have to declare dividends.[65] Certainly, many LBOs have ended in disaster, with sizable companies, overburdened by debt, making their way to the bankruptcy court. Nor is that disaster merely one for the management and the banks that lent the money; other creditors and the company's non-management work force also suffer. Defenders of LBOs, however, point out that burdensome debt can in fact be an advantage; it forces managers to concentrate on running the business in the most efficient manner possible by raising the stakes: success means riches and failure means bankruptcy. It is undeniably true that a number of LBOs have been successful, and have led to the reorganization of sleepy businesses into strong competitors.

LBOs popped up on the fraudulent transfer screen because the very structure of an LBO looks suspiciously like a transfer for inadequate consideration. There are massive transfers of property, either as collateral or as payments, from the corporation. The direct beneficiaries of those transfers, however, are not the corporation itself. Rather, they are the surviving group of stockholders, whose ownership is being paid for by those transfers. Assuming that the transfers make the

---

[65] For a fuller discussion of the differences between debt and equity, see § 1.05 of this book.

corporation insolvent or leave it with inadequate capital to continue its business (an assumption all too easy to make once the corporation has collapsed into bankruptcy because of the costs of the LBO) then where, exactly, is the reasonably equivalent value the corporation received in exchange? And if there is no reasonably equivalent value, are not the transfers fraudulent and thus avoidable?

As noted, the core basis for attacking a leveraged buyout as a fraudulent transfer is that in many LBO's, the company acquired provides the funding for its own acquisition. The following is a sketch of two major categories of LBOs:

> In the first category, selling shareholders financed the buyout by accepting the buyer's note for most or all of the purchase price of the shares. Simultaneously with the purchase, the buyers caused the corporation to endorse the note or guarantee its payment and grant the sellers a security interest in corporate assets. Corporate assets and earnings are expected to be the primary source for repaying the acquisition debt.
>
> Within the second category, buyouts financed by an independent lender, a further distinction should be made between two methods of outside financing. First, a lending institution may advance the funds required for the acquisition to the buyers. Typically, the buyers give the lender their own secured note. In a simultaneous transaction, the buyers acquire the shares, assume control, and cause the corporation to endorse or guarantee their note and to secure the obligations with a lien on corporate assets . . .
>
> Second, in an effort to reduce the risk of a challenge by creditors, the parties may structure the transaction so that the lender advances funds directly to the acquired corporation.[66]

For example, suppose that DCH Corporation is a widely-held company whose major stockholders and leading managers are George Dewey, Mary Cheatham, and Jeri Howe. Dewey, Cheatham & Howe borrow money from River Bank which they use to purchase all of the other stock of DCH. DCH then guarantees from River Bank, secures its guarantee with all of its assets, and makes all the payments on the note.

When DCH goes bankrupt, its other creditors complain that DCH's guarantee, security interest, and payments are all fraudulent transfers. The rationale is that DCH, the transferor, received nothing in exchange for its transfer. Assuming that DCH was insolvent when the transfer was made, became insolvent as a result of the transfer, had inadequate capital, or lacked ability to pay its debts, the basic requirements of § 548 appear to be met. Note that the creditors can attack various aspects of the transaction. They can attack the guarantee as a fraudulent obligation, they can attack the transfer of the security interest in their property as a fraudulent transaction, and they can attack any one or all of the payments made as fraudulent transactions. Depending upon whether the company met the other requirements for avoidance, they may be able to attack all or any of these steps in the LBO.

---

[66] David G. Carlson, *Leveraged Buyouts in Bankruptcy*, 20 Ga. L. Rev. 73, 80-83 (1985).

It is certainly clear that DCH did not receive any direct benefits from the transaction. All of the money went to stockholders. It did, however, arguably receive indirect benefits — Dewey, Cheatham & Howe presumably are especially hard-working managers now that they own the entire company. The problem, almost insurmountable, is to convince a skeptical bankruptcy court that the value is real, let alone reasonably equivalent.

There are many much more complicated variations on the basic fact pattern set out. Those who structure LBO's have worked very hard to try to skirt around the provisions of § 548 (and of state fraudulent conveyance law). To a large degree, these efforts have been unsuccessful, because of the difficulties involved in convincing a court that new or rejuvenated management constitutes a measurable, reasonably equivalent value.[67] The exact structure of the transaction has made very little difference: "Variations of the form of the transaction may make the fraudulent transfer problem less apparent, yet the transaction remains the same in substance."[68] While in some cases the structure of the transaction may affect who is liable — because of the protections given by § 548 and other fraudulent transfer laws to bona fide purchasers — it seems that there is little that can be done to insulate an LBO entirely.

Do not assume, however, that all leveraged buyouts involve fraudulent transfers. If the company never becomes insolvent, never lacks adequate capital, or never loses its ability to pay, and if there was not actual intent to defraud creditors, there is no fraudulent transfer. Broadly speaking, it can be said that a successful LBO (one that does not result in the company's default, insolvency, or bankruptcy) probably never involves a fraudulent transfer. In any event, no creditor would raise the issue. It is precisely when the LBO fails that the fraudulent transfer challenge arises. There is not much dissent from the proposition that some LBOs are fraudulent in every sense of the word. The concern is that existing fraudulent transfer law is a clumsy tool, ill-designed for the purpose of policing misconduct in the LBO setting.

With the decline in popularity of LBOs in recent years, the issue has dropped back from a boil to a simmer. However, LBOs are by no means extinct and may become popular again in the future. This is thus an issue that will not go away. It would probably be desirable to fashion a particular form of fraudulent transfer law to the special issues involved in LBOs. If one assumes, as many commentators do, that LBOs have at least some social utility, they should not be unduly discouraged by application of a fraudulent conveyance law that, arguably, was not designed for this type of transaction. Whether Congress will seriously attack this issue is doubtful. It is both complicated and, insofar as there is any political advantage, it is in leaving the law in place; leveraged buyouts have a bad name and legislation designed to facilitate them is unlikely to bring in many votes.

---

[67] See, for example, Moody v. Security Pacific Business Credit, Inc., 127 Bankr. 958 (W.D. Pa. 1991); Credit Managers Association v. Federal Co., 629 F. Supp. 175 (C.D. Cal. 1985).

[68] Keven J. Liss, *Fraudulent Conveyance Law and Leveraged Buyouts,* 87 Colum. L. Rev. 1491, 1499 (1987).

§ 15.05 Procedures; Liabilities; Protection of Bona Fide Purchasers

As discussed more fully in Chapter 13, the trustee/DIP may, as a general rule, recover an avoided transfer from either the immediate recipient of an the transferred property or from subsequent transferees. However, if a remote transferee is a bona fide purchaser, the trustee/DIP may not recover the property. Moreover, as a general rule, those who make valuable improvements to the transferred property are given a lien on the property — in effect, secured claim for the improvements made. Finally, the trustee/ DIP has the option of recovering the value of the property rather than the property itself.[69]

Section 548(c) also provides some protection to the immediate transferee. The protection is given only if three conditions are met. First, the transfer must not also be avoidable under sections 544, 545, or 547. Second, the transferee must have given value. Third, the value must have been given in good faith. If these conditions are met, the transferee will be given a lien on the transferred property for the amount of the value given. In some cases, the transferee may even be permitted to retain the transferred property.[70]

---

[69] See § 13.07 of this book for the complete discussion of these issues.

[70] Bankruptcy Code § 548(c).

CHAPTER 16

Liquidation Under Chapter 7

§ 16.01 Introduction

It is often the case that Chapter 7 liquidation is not studied separately from general bankruptcy law. The reason for this is that most bankruptcy law is predicated on the notion that liquidation under Chapter 7 is the norm and all other bankruptcy proceedings are variations on that norm. In consequence, most of what goes on in Chapter 7 is covered elsewhere in the Code. To an extent, this perception is true. Most bankruptcies are filed under Chapter 7, and an even greater number are closed under Chapter 7. Moreover, the result reached in a Chapter 7 bankruptcy is the baseline for the minimum result that much be reached outside of Chapter 7. The other Chapters impose the "best interest of creditors" test on plans of reorganization; this is but another way of saying that every creditor is entitled to at least the payment it would have received if the debtor had liquidated under Chapter 7. This Chapter is thus in many important respects the touchstone for every other.

There are, however, some important respects in which the Chapter 7 proceeding is distinctive. For example, the role of the Chapter 7 trustee is quite different from that of the Chapter 12 or Chapter 13 trustee. A number of the most important of these distinctive provisions are discussed in this Chapter.

§ 16.02 Chapter 7 and Liquidation

Chapter 7 is usually thought of as the "straight" bankruptcy or "liquidation" bankruptcy Chapter. Note, however, that although liquidation of the debtor is primarily the function of Chapter 7, liquidation may also occur under other chapters as well. A Chapter 11 plan may provide for partial or even complete liquidation of the debtor.[1] Moreover, Chapter 7 does not require an immediate "fire sale" of the debtor's assets; the Chapter 7 trustee may in appropriate circumstances opt for an extended, orderly liquidation and may even continue to run the debtor's business for a time.[2]

§ 16.03 Dismissal of a Chapter 7 Case

[A]—Dismissal "For Cause"— Section 707(a)

Section 707(a) provides that a Chapter 7 case may be dismissed for cause.[3] It

---

[1] Bankruptcy Code § 1123(b)(4); see § 17.11[J] of this book for a liquidating Chapter 11 plan.

[2] Bankruptcy Code § 721; see § 16.07 of this chapter.

[3] Bankruptcy Code § 707(a).

sets out three rather straightforward and non-controversial bases for dismissing a case; these are not exclusive. Neither the listed bases, nor any other, is particularly common. The three bases given by the statute are as follows:

1. Unreasonable delay by the debtor that is prejudicial to creditors.[4] Note that the statute sets out two requirements—unreasonable delay and prejudice to creditors. A good example is the failure to file schedules or to appear to meetings of creditors.[5]

2. Failure to pay required fees.[6] Traditionally, there has been no provision for filing bankruptcy in forma pauperis. This has changed slightly. As discussed in Chapter 6,[7] it is possible to pay in installments and there is a pilot project permitting in forma pauperis petitions in a few districts.

3. Failure to file the schedules and statement of financial affairs within the required time (usually 15 days).[8] Unlike the other bases for dismissal under section 707(a), only the United States Trustee may move for dismissal because of a failure to meet this 15 day deadline.[9] The section 707(a)(3) provision was added by BAFJA in 1984 in an effort to deter bad faith filings made strictly to obtain the benefits of the stay, with no intention actually to liquidate.[10]

There are some procedural requirements for dismissal; as one might expect, the usually loose rules regarding notice and the opportunity to be heard do not apply when the question is dismissal. There must be 20 days notice.[11] And, unlike many proceedings under the Bankruptcy Code, there must be an actual hearing on the motion to dismiss.[12]

[B]—Dismissal of Consumer Case That is a Substantial Abuse—Section 707(b)

One of the many responses made by BAFJA to creditor complaints about the supposed laxity of consumer bankruptcy rules was section 707(b), a somewhat peculiar provision that permits the dismissal of abusive filings.[13] It applies only in

[4] Bankruptcy Code § 707(a)(1).

[5] See In re Ladd, 82 Bankr. 476 (Bankr. N.D. Ind. 1988).

[6] Bankruptcy Code § 707(a)(2).

[7] See § 6.01.

[8] Bankruptcy Code § 707(a)(3).

[9] Bankruptcy Code § 707(a)(3).

[10] Collier on Bankruptcy ¶ 707.01.

[11] Bankruptcy Rule 2002(a).

[12] Bankruptcy Code § 707(a).

[13] For a general discussion of the original version of § 707(b), see Paul M. Black & Michael J. Herbert, *Bankcard's Revenge: A Critique of the 1984 Consumer Credit Amendments to the Bankruptcy Code*, 19 U. Rich. L. Rev. 845, 856-861 (1985). Section 707(b) was slightly amended in 1986.

Chapter 7 proceedings, and only if the debtor is an individual who has primarily consumer debts. The court may dismiss if it finds that granting relief would be a "substantial abuse" of the provisions of Chapter 7.[14] In effect, this power forces the debtor either to exit bankruptcy altogether or to refile under one of the reorganization chapters. It is but a tiny remnant of much more ambitious proposals made by creditors. Because of this, it is also one of the most confusing provisions in the entire Code; much of its incoherence derives from the fact that it was a patchwork political compromise.

There are many oddities in this section. First, the substantial abuse issue cannot be raised by any creditor or indeed by anybody who has a direct pecuniary interest in the matter. It may only be raised sua sponte by the court or by the United States Trustee, and "*not* at the request or suggestion of an party in interest."[15] Thus, the motion cannot be made by the very persons who are most likely to be interested in making it. Moreover, neither the judge nor the U.S. Trustee is supposed to act on any request by a creditor to make the motion.[16] Indeed, some courts have imposed an exclusionary rule that prohibits the judge and (less often) the U.S. Trustee from raising the issue if a creditor has asked him or her to do so.[17]

This procedure creates real problems for lawyers and judges. A creditor's lawyer who spots what appears to be substantial abuse may have to remain silent, because noting the issue to the judge or the U.S. Trustee may actually prevent it from being raised. Judges often feel awkward being put in the position of raising the matter sua sponte. Moreover, it is not necessarily easy to spot substantial abuse. Generally, the problem of finding files that evidence substantial abuse has been dealt with by the use of screening procedures that identify suspicious cases. This screening is based on a review of the debtor's own statement of income and expenses, which must be filed with the petition.[18]

The second major problem is substantive. Section 707(b) applies only if the debtor's obligations are "primarily consumer debts." What in the world does that phrase mean? There are two sub-questions—what is consumer debt and how do we determine whether a person's debts are primarily consumer. In most cases, the issue

[14] Bankruptcy Code § 707(b).

[15] Bankruptcy Code § 707(b) (emphasis added). Prior to the 1986 Amendments, even the U.S. Trustee was barred from raising the issue; the power to raise a substantial abuse question was granted when the U.S. Trustee program became (nearly) universal. See Michael J. Herbert, *Once More Unto the Breach, Dear Friends: The 1986 Reforms of the Reformed Bankruptcy Reform Act,* 16 Cap. U. L. Rev. 325, 331 (1987).

[16] An apparent corollary of this is that it may be ethically improper for a creditor to bring allegations of substantial abuse to be made by a creditor's lawyer to the judge or the U.S. Trustee.

[17] See In re Christian, 804 F.2d 46 (3d Cir. 1986). Some courts impose the prohibition only if the creditor's request was made "flagrantly, intentionally, or repeatedly." In re Hudson, 56 Bankr. 415, 420 (Bankr. N.D. Ohio 1985). There are also courts that apply the prohibition only if the request is made to the judge, not if it is made to the U.S. Trustee. See In re Clark, 927 F.2d 793 (4th Cir. 1991).

[18] See Collier on Bankruptcy ¶ 707.05.

is a simple one, because most individual debtors have no business debt at all and few have very much. There are however occasional borderline cases.

Section 101(8) of the Code defines consumer debt functionally; what was the purpose for which the debt was incurred? If it was incurred "primarily for a personal, family, or household purpose" it is a consumer debt. Thus, neither the source of the loan nor the collateral used to secure it nor the account from which the debt was paid matter. An individual who hocks her house to borrow money for buying investment property, and who pays the loan out of her personal checking account, is incurring business debt, not consumer debt. A sole proprietor who borrows money against her stocks and bonds for her kid's orthodontia,[19] and who pays the loan out of her business checking account, is incurring consumer debt.[20] Some courts use what is known as the "profit motive" test—if the debtor was seeking a profit with the proceeds of the loan, the obligation is not a consumer debt.[21]

Insofar as what "primarily" means, there are at least three possible interpretations—most of the number of debts, most of the amount of debts, or a blend of both. Under the first reading, a debtor has primarily consumer debts if 16 of the 31 debts it owes are consumer obligation—even though those 16 debts might total only a few hundred dollars and the remainder a few hundred thousand. Under the second, only the amount is important, and if the debtor had a single $250,000 business debt but 350 consumer debts totalling $249,999, section 707(b) would not apply. Under the final test, the court would somehow blend quantity and magnitude. The courts have not been consistent, and each of these approaches finds support.[22]

The third problem, like the first, is procedural; there is a "presumption" that the debtor is entitled to the relief sought.[23] How this presumption operates is unclear. The cases have not explicitly determined whether it merely states the fairly obvious point that the party seeking dismissal for substantial abuse carries the burden of proof, or whether it creates a higher standard of proof than preponderance of the evidence.[24]

By far the most significant issue, however, is the meaning of "substantial abuse." The cases have articulated a number of rules. These rules are not particularly reconcilable. The crucial underlying issue is the degree to which section 707(b) is properly used to force a debtor either to forgo bankruptcy relief or seek it in a reorganization proceeding. This is the crux of the conflict that led to the underlying compromise

---

[19] Note that if the debt is incurred to aid an adult offspring, some courts will not consider it a consumer debt. See In re Green, 70 Bankr. 164 (Bankr. W. D. Ark 1986).

[20] Note that a few cases, following an unfortunate and inaccurate comment made in the debate over the Bankruptcy Reform Act, have ruled that debt secured by real property is never consumer debt. "[A] consumer debt does not include a debt to any extent that the debt is secured by real property." 124 Cong. Rec. H11,909 (Sept. 28, 1978); S17,406 (Oct. 6, 1978). Most courts reject this reasoning. See In re Kelley, 841 F.2d 908 (9th Cir. 1988).

[21] See In re Booth, 858 F.2d 1051 (5th Cir. 1988).

[22] See Collier on Bankruptcy ¶ 707.06.

[23] Bankruptcy Code § 707(b).

[24] See In re Kelly, 841 F.2d 908 (9th Cir. 1988).

reflected in that section—a compromise between those who wanted to require many consumer bankrupts to reorganize and those who thought forced reorganization impractical or undesirable.

The most obvious way to flesh out substantial abuse it to say that if the debtor is making enough money to pay off a substantial amount of debt, Chapter 7 filing is improper. Generally, the courts have held that ability to pay is at least a factor in determining whether there is substantial abuse.[25] However, ability to pay standing alone may not be enough, especially in light of the fact that Congress has long resisted imposing mandatory reorganization on consumer debtors. Generally, the courts have looked for other factors as well, using an open-ended "totality of the circumstances" test. One formulation of this is as follows:

> The meaning of "substantial abuse" is ascertained from the totality of the circumstances such as whether the debtor is seeking an advantage over creditors; whether the debtor is honest in relationships with creditors; or whether the debtor is needy such that the financial predicament warrants discharge of debts in exchange for liquidation of assets. Substantial abuse can be predicated upon either lack of honesty or want of need.
>
> Debtor's honesty is ascertained by the good faith and candor exhibited in filing schedules and other documents; whether debtor engaged in any eve of bankruptcy purchases; and whether debtor has been forced into filing a Chapter 7 petition by unforeseen or catastrophic events. Debtor's honesty is measured by an ability to repay debts out of future earnings. Other relevant factors include whether debtor is eligible for adjustment under Chapter 13 of the Bankruptcy Code; whether there are state remedies available which may potentially ease debtor's financial predicament; whether debtor has relief available through private negotiations; and whether debtor's expenses can be significantly reduced without deprivation of food, clothing, shelter and other necessities.[26]

The courts are especially likely to find substantial abuse if the debtor's financial problems appear temporary; for example, a Harvard Medical School graduate who sought to discharge his debts at the beginning of this three-year residency was found to be substantially abusing Chapter 7 because of his excellent future income prospects.[27]

§ 16.04 Conversion of the Case

The debtor has the right, at any time, to convert the case to Chapter 11, 12, or 13, assuming that the debtor is eligible for the chapter selected and further that the

[25] Collier on Bankruptcy ¶ 707.07.

[26] In re Donald L. Sanseverino, 171 Bankr. 46, 48 (Bankr. N.D. Ohio 1994) (citations omitted).

[27] In re Dominguez, 166 Bankr. 66 (Bankr. E.D. N.C. 1994).

case was not previously converted from one of those chapters to Chapter 7.[28] Any waiver of the right to convert is unenforceable.[29] The case may not be involuntarily converted to Chapter 13[30] or Chapter 12[31] this is in line with the wholly voluntary nature of those Chapters. However, on request of a party in interest, and after notice and an opportunity for a hearing, the case may be converted to Chapter 11 at any time.[32]

§ 16.05 Selection of Trustee

The Chapter 7 trustee may be elected by the creditors (although in practice this rarely happens). Virtually every creditor who holds an allowable, undisputed, fixed, liquidated, unsecured claim may vote.[33] Creditors who have interests that are materially adverse to creditors generally, and creditors who are also insiders of the debtor, are not eligible to vote.[34] The concern is that they might not vote for the trustee best able to vindicate the rights of the creditors. The limitation to those with unsecured claims is based on a similar concern; the fundamental role of the Chapter 7 trustee is to protect the interests of unsecured creditors. Although the trustee is involved with secured claims, as a practical matter that function is a minor one because the collateral is usually just abandoned to the secured party.

An election must be requested by creditors who are eligible to vote. The requesting creditors must hold at least 20 percent (in amount) of the claims that may vote.[35] The election is held at the creditors' section 341 meeting.[36] At least 20 percent (in amount) of the eligible claims must vote; the trustee candidate wins upon a majority of the votes cast by the creditors. The vote is by creditor, not by claim.[37]

In all but a handful of cases, however, the trustee is actually appointed by the U.S. Trustee. The U.S. trustee is obligated to appoint a "disinterested" member of the panel of private trustees[38] to serve as interim trustee "promptly after the order for relief."[39] If another person is elected trustee, then the interim trustee is displaced by the elected trustee.[40] However, when no trustee is elected, the interim trustee becomes the trustee.[41]

---

[28] Bankruptcy Code § 706(a).

[29] Bankruptcy Code § 706(a).

[30] Bankruptcy Code § 706(c).

[31] Bankruptcy Code § 706(c).

[32] Bankruptcy Code § 706(b).

[33] Bankruptcy Code § 702(a).

[34] Bankruptcy Code § 702(a)(2), (3).

[35] Bankruptcy Code § 702(b).

[36] See § 4.09 of this book for a discussion of the section 341 meeting.

[37] Bankruptcy Code § 702(c).

[38] The U.S. Trustee is required to create a panel of private trustees from which the trustee for a particular case is ordinarily selected. See § 4.03 of this book.

[39] Bankruptcy Code § 701(a)(1).

[40] Bankruptcy Code § 701(b).

[41] Bankruptcy Code § 702(d).

§ 16.06 Duties of the Trustee

The duties of the Chapter 7 trustee are particularly extensive; much more so than the Chapter 12 or Chapter 13 trustee. The reason is that the Chapter 7 trustee administers the estate, while the Chapter 12 trustee (usually) and the Chapter 13 trustee (always) merely supervise the debtor-in-possession. In most Chapter 7 cases, the debtor does practically nothing after the petition and schedules are filed.

The trustee is required to:

1. Collect the property of the estate, reduce it to cash (unless it is entirely exempt or is surrendered), and close the estate expeditiously.[42] Expeditiously does not mean hastily; if the case is complicated, or if an orderly liquidation will better the position of creditors,[43] the trustee may and should take the time necessary. However, there appear to be more problems of undue delay than of unseemly haste. There have been problems in at least some districts with getting even simple Chapter 7 cases closed promptly.[44]

2. Be accountable for all property received.[45] This is a part of the trustee's fiduciary duty to the estate; the trustee is personally liable for property misappropriated or just mislaid.[46] It is also part of the reason why the trustee must post a bond securing proper performance of duties.[47]

3. Ensure that the debtor performs his or her intentions as specified in section 521(2)(b).[48] Under section 521, an individual consumer debtor must file a statement of intention with regard to retention, surrender, exemption, and redemption of property; section 521(2)(b) gives the debtor 45 days to act on that stated intention.[49]

4. Investigate the financial affairs of the debtor.[50] In most cases, this investigation is slight; in complex cases, it may be quite extensive and may involve hiring professionals, such as accountants hired to audit the debtor's books.

---

[42] Bankruptcy Code § 704(1).

[43] See Bankruptcy Code § 721 (Authorization to Operate Business).

[44] See Michael J. Herbert and Domenic E. Pacitti, *Down and Out in Richmond, Virginia: The Distribution of Assets in Chapter 7 Bankruptcy Proceedings Closed During 1984-87,* 22 U. Rich. L. Rev. 303, 317-318 (1988)

[45] Bankruptcy Code § 704(2).

[46] See Collier on Bankruptcy ¶ 704.04. Failure to comply with this duty is a basis for removal of the trustee. See Bankruptcy Code § 324(a).

[47] Bankruptcy Code § 322.

[48] Bankruptcy Code § 704(3).

[49] For a fuller discussion of the operation of Bankruptcy Code § 521, see § 6.02[C] of this book.

[50] Bankruptcy Code § 704(4).

5. "If a purpose would be served," examine the proofs of claim and object to the allowance of any improper claim.[51] The opening language of this provision merely recognizes the fact that in most Chapter 7 cases there is no reason to examine the proofs of claim; there will be no assets distributed to unsecured creditors and thus no reason to examine their proofs of claim.

6. "If advisable" oppose the debtor's discharge.[52] The grounds for denying discharge in Chapter 7 are discussed in Chapter 12.[53]

7. (Unless the court orders otherwise) supply to any party in interest any information requested about the estate and the estate's administration.[54]

8. (If the debtor has a business, and the operation of the business has been authorized) file with (i) the court, (ii) the U.S. Trustee, and (ii) any relevant governmental tax authority, periodic reports and summaries of the operation of the business. These reports and summaries must include a statement of receipts and disbursements, as well as any other information that the U.S. Trustee or the court requires.[55]

9. Make a final report and file a final account of the administration of the estate with both the court and the U. S. Trustee.[56]

§ 16.07 Authorization to do Business

The classic Chapter 7 case is a speedy liquidation of the debtor's meager assets. This, however, is not always required. If the debtor was or had a business, the trustee may, under some circumstances, continue to operate the business for a time, generally for the purpose of winding up profitable contracts. This is governed by section 721, which states: "[t]he court may authorize the trustee to operate the business of the debtor for a limited period, if such operation is in the best interest of the estate and consistent with the orderly liquidation of the estate."[57]

Unlike Chapter 11, Chapter 7 requires that the trustee get authorization from the court to continue the debtor's business. Note that operation of the business is not an end in itself; it is simply a means of liquidation. The trustee is not to rehabilitate the business, but only to facilitate the sale of its assets. The court may permit operation of the business if only and only if it is in the best interest of the estate. Moreover, the authorization may only be for a "limited period."[58] There is

[51] Bankruptcy Code § 704(5).

[52] Bankruptcy Code § 704(6).

[53] See § 12.02 of this book.

[54] Bankruptcy Code § 704(7).

[55] Bankruptcy Code § 704(8).

[56] Bankruptcy Code § 704(9).

[57] Bankruptcy Code § 721.

[58] Bankruptcy Code § 721.

practically no case law under section 721. This is not surprising; it is rare that a company enters Chapter 7 if there is any life at all left in it. Moreover, a creditor is unlikely to object to, or appeal, a request by the trustee to finish up work in progress; assuming that the contract is a profitable one, the benefits of completing it are almost always obvious to all concerned.

§ 16.08 Redemption

An individual Chapter 7 debtor has a limited, Bankruptcy Code-created right to "redeem" personal property that is subject to a lien. This is essentially a right to buy out the lien from the lien holder. It is discussed in detail in Chapter 11.[59]

§ 16.09 Creditors' Committee

The creditors in a Chapter 7 proceeding have a rarely exercised right to elect a creditors' committee. They may do so at a section 341 hearing; every creditor who has the right to vote on a trustee has the right to vote for a creditors' committee.[60] The committee must be composed of not fewer than three and not more than eleven creditors; each of the creditors must hold an allowed unsecured claim entitled to distribution in the proceeding.[61]

The powers of the Chapter 7 creditors' committee are rather circumscribed. The committee may consult with the trustee and the United States trustee regarding the administration of the estate. It may make recommendations about the trustee's performance (in plain English, it may complain about the trustee's performance). It may also submit either to the court or to the U.S. Trustee any question "affecting" the administration of the estate.[62] In sum, the committee acts in an advisory capacity; it is expected to do so in the interests of all creditors, and not merely in the interests of its members.[63]

The key function of the committee is to make noise; its chief right is to be heard by the court. It is likely that it has an absolute right to be heard on any matter materially affecting the liquidation. This would certainly include the proposed sale of property, the trustee's method of dealing with claims, and the discharge. The committee may take positions contrary to those of the trustee, and in some circumstances may even have the right to appeal decisions of the bankruptcy court.[64]

---

[59] See § 11.11.

[60] For a discussion of the right to vote for the trustee, see § 16.05 of this chapter.

[61] Bankruptcy Code § 705(a).

[62] Bankruptcy Code § 705(b).

[63] In re Kenney Co., 136 F. 451 (D. Ind. 1905).

[64] Securities and Exchange Commission v. U.S. Realty & Improvement Co., 310 U.S. 434 (1940).

§ 16.10 Partnership Liquidation

As noted in Chapter 1, a partnership has some, but not all, of the attributes of a legal entity.[65] A partnership can own property in its own name; can enter contracts in its own name; can sue or be sued in its own name. In this respect, it is like a corporation. However, unlike the shareholders of a corporation, the general partners of a partnership are personally liable for all of the partnership's debts. Their liability, however, is secondary; a creditor of the partnership cannot reach the assets of a general partner unless and until the assets of the partnership are exhausted.

This same basic pattern is preserved in bankruptcy. One of the provisions that reflects this is § 723, which deals with the rights of a partnership trustee against general partners. Basically, the trustee of the partnership, as representative of the partnership's creditors, is given the right to do whaι the creditors themselves would do outside of bankruptcy—to recover unpaid claims from the partners.

There are two somewhat different situations dealt with in § 723. The first is an action by the trustee against a general partner who is not in bankruptcy. The second deals with a claim by the trustee against a general partner who is in bankruptcy.

The first case is illustrated by the following hypothetical:

> Sam Spade and Miles Archer are general partners in the firm of Spade & Archer. Spade & Archer has filed bankruptcy under Chapter 7. However, neither Sam Spade nor Miles Archer has filed any form of bankruptcy. The total assets of Spade & Archer amount to $150,000. The total obligations of Spade & Archer amount to $500,000. All of these obligations are allowed unsecured claims in the bankruptcy.

Because the property of the estate is insufficient to pay all of the allowed claims, and because under state law both Sam Spade and Miles Archer are personally liable for the unpaid claims, the trustee of Spade & Archer has a claim against each partner to the extent that, under applicable non-bankruptcy law, the general partner is personally liable. Normally, this personal liability would be for the entire amount of the deficiency ($350,000).[66] The trustee may recover from either Sam Spade or Miles Archer, or both; of course, the total recovery from both of them cannot exceed $350,000. Note one implication of this — assuming that at least one of the partners has sufficient assets, the creditors of the partnership will be paid in full.

Of course, in many cases, the financial failure of a partnership also means the financial failure of the partners. It is thus quite common for one or more of the general partners to be in bankruptcy as well. Assume that, in the hypothetical given, Sam Spade is not in bankruptcy but Miles Archer is. To the extent practicable, the trustee is required to seek recovery of the deficiency from a general partner who is not in bankruptcy.[67] Thus, the trustee normally will be required to seek recovery

---

[65] See § 1.05.

[66] Bankruptcy Code § 723(a). The wording of this provision was slightly changed by the 1994 Amendments.

[67] Bankruptcy Code § 723(b).

of the $350,000 deficiency first from Sam Spade. If he cannot pay the entire amount of the deficiency, or if for some reason the trustee cannot find either Sam or Sam's assets, then the trustee goes after Miles Archer.

There is an obvious problem created when the trustee pursues the bankrupt Miles Archer. Miles Archer has personal creditors whom he has not paid. These personal creditors would prefer not to share his scanty assets with the creditors of the partnership. Consider the following example:

> As in the prior hypothetical, Spade & Archer is in Chapter 7 bankruptcy; the allowed claims are $350,000. Sam Spade is not in bankruptcy; he is in Rio de Janeiro and the trustee cannot reach him. Miles Archer is also in Chapter 7 bankruptcy; his assets total $100,000; the personal claims against him total $200,000, all unsecured. All of the claims are allowed.

In this example, Archer's personal creditors will receive a fifty percent distribution if left alone. However, if the claim of the trustee of Spade & Archer can make a $350,000 claim against Miles Archer's estate, then the total amount of the claims against Miles Archer will be $550,000 and the distribution less than twenty percent. Unfortunately for Miles Archer's personal creditors, this is exactly what happens. With a very limited exception, all of the claims against the partnership are bundled together into the trustee's claim against the partner.[68]

§ 16.11 Distribution of Property of the Estate

Although it is generally true that Chapter 7 liquidations do not result in the distribution of property to creditors,[69] there is a fairly elaborate set of rules for those cases that do. Secured claims are dealt with only indirectly, because encumbered property is either abandoned by the trustee to the lienholder or, if the property is worth more than the lien, sold, and the lienholder paid from the proceeds of the disposition.[70] The primary rule for the distribution of property with regard to unsecured claims is § 726(a). That section sets out six categories that are to be paid in order. These categories are:

> 1. First, the allowed priority claims in order of their priority.[71] The priorities, and the order of the priorities, are fully discussed in Chapter 10.

---

[68] Bankruptcy Code § 723(c). If this produces a surplus in the partnership bankruptcy, the surplus would be returned to Archer's estate. See Bankruptcy Code § 723(d).

[69] See § 1.01[C] of this book..

[70] Cf. Bankruptcy Code § 725, which requires that, prior to final distribution of the property of the estate, the trustee after notice and an opportunity for a hearing must dispose of any property in which an entity other than the estate has an interest, such as a lien.

[71] Bankruptcy Code § 726(a)(1). The 1994 Amendments added a requirement to this section that the proof of claim either have been filed on time or, although tardy, before the date on which the trustee commenced distribution.

2. Second in line for payment are the allowed general unsecured claims (other than certain claims that were filed late and certain claims for fines, penalties, and punitive damages). To be included in this group, the claimant must have either filed a timely proof of claim or whose proof of claim was late, but excusably late.[72]

3. The third group consists of those claims that, although they were filed late and the late filing was not excused, have still been allowed.[73]

4. The fourth group consists of those allowed claims, whether secured or unsecured, that represent any fine, penalty, or forfeiture; or represent multiple, exemplary, or punitive damages arising before the earlier of the order for relief or the appointment of a trustee, to the extent that the fine, penalty, forfeiture, or damages do not represent compensation for actual pecuniary loss suffered by the holder of such claim.[74] For example, if a claimant has obtained a judgment for both compensatory damages and punitive damages arising out of a battery committed by the debtor, the compensatory damages would be in category 2, and the punitive damages would in this category.

5. Interest on all of the claims in the first four categories, charged at the legal rate from the date of the filing of the petition to the date of payment.[75] As noted elsewhere in this book,[76] interest does not accrue on unsecured claims, and accrues on secured claims only to the extent that the value of the collateral exceeds the amount of the debt. However, in the very, very rare case in which there is property left in the estate after claims have been paid, a further payment of interest on those claims will also be made. Note that this further payment is at the "legal rate" which means the rate set by statute and not the rate established by the parties' contract.

6. Finally, if after the payment of all the claims, and interest on the claims, there is still money in the estate, this is paid to the debtor.[77] Cases of this type are almost nonexistent.

---

[72] Bankruptcy Code § 726(a)(2).

[73] Bankruptcy Code § 726(a)(3).

[74] Bankruptcy Code § 726(a)(4).

[75] Bankruptcy Code § 726(a)(5).

[76] See § 10.02[D].

[77] Bankruptcy Code § 726(a)(6).

CHAPTER **17**

Reorganization Under Chapter 11

§ 17.01 Introduction

As noted throughout this book, there is a longstanding and continuing belief that reorganization captures, or at least can capture, the "going concern value" of the estate. By doing so, it benefits creditors, who obtain a greater distribution on their claims; equity holders, who have a better chance of obtaining something from their investments; and other "stakeholders" such as employees (who keep their jobs), suppliers (who keep their customers) and governments (who keep their taxes). These goals are of greatest significance in Chapter 11 proceedings, since those are most likely to involve businesses with many creditors, owners, employees, and so on.

The earliest attempts to reorganize businesses through insolvency law generally involved railroads, which, through bad luck, mismanagement, or fraud, collapsed with depressing frequency in the 19th Century. Bankruptcy law moved into the railroad reorganization arena with old section 77, and into corporate reorganization with section 77B. Reorganization was embraced more broadly in 1938 by the Chandler Act, which provided four chapters (X through XIII) encompassing most types of debtors.

Chapter 11 of the Bankruptcy Code is the successor to Chapters X, XI, and XII of the Bankruptcy Act. Those were the business reorganization chapters, each theoretically designed for a different type of reorganization. Chapter XI, which was by far the most used of the three, is the primary antecedent of Chapter 11, although bits of the other two Bankruptcy Act chapters survived, and a number of new provisions were added.

Under the Act, considerable confusion and difficulty were created by the fact that the two primary business reorganization Chapters, X and XI, had substantially different requirements and procedures. Most notably, in Chapter X, which was designed for large companies with publicly traded stocks and bonds, existing management was replaced and the Securities and Exchange Commission played a major role. By contrast, in Chapter XI (designed for smaller, closely held companies) existing management generally stayed in place and the SEC was not involved. The rationale for these differences was that a Chapter X reorganization involved the interests of the investing public (and thus needed the scrutiny of their watchdog, the SEC); by contrast, a Chapter XI case only involved a few owners who did not need any government protection of their interests. In practice, however, the distinction led to protracted and largely unproductive struggles over which Chapter was the appropriate one.[1]

---

[1] See Collier on Bankruptcy ¶ 1100.01. Note that Chapter XII, which was hardly ever used, was not implicated in this struggle between the two primary reorganization chapters.

In consequence, Congress devised Chapter 11 as a "one size fits all" proceeding. Except for Subchapter IV, which imposes a series of special rules on railroad reorganization, and a handful of "small business" provisions added in 1994, Chapter 11 makes few formal distinctions between different types of debtor. Chapter 11 draws most heavily on old Chapter XI, most notably in the dominant role it gives to the existing management of the debtor, who nearly always controls the Debtor-in-Possession throughout the proceeding. Similarly, the SEC, which had so prominent a role under old Chapter X, plays virtually no part in Chapter 11.[2]

Although primarily a business reorganization Chapter, it is now well-established that the Chapter 11 debtor need not have any business activities. After years of conflict in the lower courts, the Supreme Court in 1991 flatly stated that Chapter 11 is available even to purely consumer debtors.[3] Whether it is in fact advisable for consumers to use Chapter 11 is debatable; in the view of some commentators, Chapter 11 availability is an invitation to abuse by creditors and (perhaps more worrisomely) debtor's attorneys, for whom Chapter 11 is a potential source of greater fees than Chapters 7 and 13.[4] In any event, it appears that consumer Chapter 11 proceedings remain rare, due to the considerable expense involved.

Chapter 11 itself has become controversial in recent years. In the view of some commentators, Congress went much too far in giving control of the Chapter 11 debtor to the debtor in possession, and indeed of the whole Chapter 11 process to the debtor's pre-bankruptcy management.[5] The debtor's managers may be unduly optimistic about the prospects of reorganization. Worse still is the problem of "moral hazard." This phrase refers to the effects that protection against loss has on risk-taking. The owners and managers of a debtor will have neither equity nor jobs if the debtor is liquidated; if it is reorganized, they may salvage both. Given the fact that the company is probably insolvent, they have nothing to lose and much to gain; the managers at least may keep their salaries a little longer if the company's demise can be postponed. In this situation, management is tempted to take wild chances in the hope that some miracle might yet save the company. This problem arises even before bankruptcy but may be exacerbated by it.[6]

By contrast, creditors, who still have some stake in the enterprise are, in the view of these critics, given too little power. Worse still, there is a perception that the bankruptcy system is stacked in favor of the Chapter 11 debtor; reorganization is

[2] See § 17.07 of this chapter for a discussion of the SEC's current role.

[3] Toibb v. Radloff, 501 U.S. 157 (1991). The Court relied primarily on the plain meaning of Bankruptcy Code § 109(e), not to mention the careful explication of the statute and the underlying policy set out in Michael J. Herbert, *Consumer Chapter 11 Proceedings: Abuse or Alternative?*, 91 Com. L. J. 234 (1986).

[4] For a particularly strong and sustained critique, see Cheri L. Cohen, *Chapter 11 for Individual Consumer Debtors: Fresh Start or False Start?*, 13 N. Ill. U. L. Rev. 401 (1993).

[5] For an early and widely cited critique, see Lynn M. LoPucki, *The Debtor in Full Control—Systems Failure Under Chapter 11 of the Bankruptcy Code, Parts 1 & 2*, 57 Am. Bankr. L. J. 99, 247 (1983).

[6] See Joseph E. Stiglitz, *Some Aspects of the Pure Theory of Corporate Finance: Bankruptcies and Take-overs*, 3 Bell J. Econ. & Mgmt. Sci. 458 (1972).

viewed as "success" while liquidation is viewed as "failure." In fact, some say, success should be measured by the swift and cheap redistribution of the debtor's assets to those who can use them profitably.[7]

To sum up this concern:

> [I]n the ordinary case, a Chapter 11 filing transforms a corporate debtor into "debtor-in-possession" and leaves existing management in control of the firm's resources. Congress apparently believed that a management team already familiar with the company's business would be more likely to reorganize a troubled firm successfully than would a newly appointed trustee . . . .
>
> This presumption favoring management's continued control, when combined with other provisions of Chapter 11 . . . effectively gave managers powerful incentives to pursue bankruptcy reorganization. Managers are more likely to keep their jobs by reorganizing rather than liquidating their firm, and during reorganization they can operate without the constraints ordinarily imposed by creditors.[8]

The most extreme statement of the case against Chapter 11 has been made by the authors of the preceding quotation, Professor Michael Bradley and Mr. Michael Rosenzweig, who have assembled empirical data that they say proves that Chapter 11 often subtracts value, rather than adds value, to the debtor's assets.[9] Their data come from a narrow base—Chapter 11 debtors with publicly traded securities—so it may or may not reflect problems that reach beyond that base to the vast majority of Chapter 11 cases. In any event, their solution is broader than their sample; they would abolish Chapter 11, at least for corporations.[10]

The Bradley & Rosenzweig proposal has sparked a lively exchange. Their work has been attacked for its methodology, data, and conclusions.[11] As is true with so many such debates, the data are not so conclusive that either side is bereft of ammunition; however, those opposed to Bradley & Rosenzweig at least seem to have the edge in numbers. The view of the critics can easily be summarized by the following quotation:

> A recent well-publicized paper by Michael Bradley and Michael Rosenzweig purports to conduct a thorough econometric investigation of

[7] For a sampler of these views, see Michael Bradley & Michael Rosenzweig, *The Untenable Case for Chapter 11,* 101 Yale L. J. 1043, 1045 n. 11 (1992).

[8] Michael Bradley & Michael Rosenzweig, *The Untenable Case for Chapter 11,* 101 Yale L. J. 1043, 1044-45 (1992).

[9] Michael Bradley & Michael Rosenzweig, *The Untenable Case for Chapter 11,* 101 Yale L. J. 1043 (1992).

[10] Id. at 1049.

[11] For just a couple of examples, see Elizabeth Warren, *The Untenable Case for Repeal of Chapter 11,* 102 Yale L. J. 437 (1992), and Donald R. Korobkin, *The Unwarranted Case Against Corporate Reorganization: A Reply to Bradley and Rosenzweig,* 78 Iowa L. Rev. 669 (1993).

> corporate bankruptcy and concludes, based on a variety of empirical "findings," that under the Bankruptcy Code has become increasingly "endogenous" and has resulted in such increased costs or losses that the Code should be repealed. The Bradley & Rosenzweig article has generated considerable debate both in the popular press and in academia, but mainly on practical grounds.
>
> In this article we critically examine the econometric evidence marshalled by Bradley & Rosenzweig. Our examination of their evidence, in addition to our own work, reveals that their evidence is vacuous, and that the conclusions they reach are not compelled by their empirical analysis. Accordingly, further research in this area seems warranted.[12]

Other critics of Chapter 11 make more modest proposals. They call for relatively minor reforms that would shift greater power to both the creditors and the court. For example, many critics have recommended tighter time limits on the proceeding, to force either a plan or a liquidation within a year or so; some of these proposals found their way into the 1994 Amendments. Still other discuss the possibility of prohibiting some particular types of Chapter 11 proceedings, such as so-called single-asset cases in which there is only one significant creditor. This issue is discussed in depth in Chapter 22 of this book.[13]

Another notable change of direction has occurred since the 1978 Bankruptcy Reform Act. There has also been a gradual move from the Code's goal of a unified reorganization Chapter. Even under the original Code, special provisions were included in Chapter 11 for railroad reorganizations;[14] in addition, Chapter 13 has always been available for small proprietorship cases.[15] In 1986, Congress added Chapter 12 to deal with family farm reorganizations. At present, there are proposals to add a new Chapter 10, quite unlike old Chapter X, to deal with small businesses. A few scraps of these proposals was included in the 1994 Amendments.

It is unlikely that Chapter 11 will be abolished. Rightly or wrongly, the belief that it saves companies and jobs is too well ingrained to be destroyed by any but the most unequivocal evidence that it does not. It is, however, probable that some future reform proposals will be adopted. It is also possible that Congress will continue its gradual return to something resembling the old Bankruptcy Act system, in which different types of business reorganizations will be placed under different Chapters.

---

[12] Jagdeep S. Bhandari & Lawrence A. Weiss, *The Untenable Case for Chapter 11: A Review of the Evidence,* 67 Am. Bankr. L. J. 131 (1993).

[13] See § 22.04.

[14] For a short discussion of the railroad provisions, see § 17.19 of this chapter.

[15] See § 18.06 of this book for a discussion of Chapter 13 proprietorship reorganizations.

§ 17.02 Goals of Reorganization; Going Concern Value

The main difference between liquidation and reorganization is that in liquidation present assets are surrendered and debts paid, if at all, from them; in reorganization, present assets are retained and debts paid from future income. The distinction is not absolute; most successful reorganizations require partial liquidation; assets the reorganizing company cannot use profitably are sold to raise cash for operations and for the plan of reorganization.

In theory, keeping the debtor's assets intact allows it to retain its going concern value, which should be greater than its liquidation value. Going concern value is a highly refined concept, but its gist can be explained rather simply. Imagine if you will a building, 10 widget making machines, 100,000 unassembled widget parts, 2 computers, a room full of office equipment, six trucks, 3 forklifts, 50 skilled widget production workers and 7 competent managers. Which is more valuable—an unconnected collection of these objects and persons, or a functioning widget company?

A widget company, with its equipment, supplies, and personnel brought together and already functioning should be more valuable than the separate items that go into it. The machines are in place. The workers have experience working with the machines and with each other. The company has name recognition, a credit rating, customers, suppliers, and lenders willing to do business with it. Under normal circumstances, a buyer should be willing to pay more for the whole than for a collection of unconnected component parts. This is the going concern value that Chapter 11 seeks to preserve. If it succeeds in doing so, there will be more available to pay creditors; indeed, there may even be something left for the equity holders.

Of course, this model is not always descriptive of a financially troubled company. Sometimes there is no going concern value; sometimes indeed a company is actually subtracting value from its assets. Suppose that Wally Widgets, Inc. has name recognition precisely because its widgets are so bad that they sell for less money than it costs to make them. Other companies could use Wally's assets to make good widgets that would sell at a profit, and are willing to pay a price for those assets that reflects those expected profits. Wally's is actually more valuable in liquidation than it is as an existing enterprise. Either it should be broken up and sold—or if kept together, should be sold to someone who can run it profitably. Either way, Wally's existing management (and perhaps its work force) should be got rid of. One of the chief criticisms of Chapter 11 is that it deals poorly with situations of this sort.

§ 17.03 Role of Existing Management

One of the basic differences between liquidation and reorganization bankruptcy is that in the latter the debtor is largely kept intact and under current management. The Chapter 11 debtor usually operates as a debtor in possession. This in turn generally means that those who were in control of the debtor prior to bankruptcy remain in control throughout the bankruptcy. This raises some obvious concerns:

if the debtor is financially troubled because, at least in part, its management is incompetent or crooked, then retention of that management reduces the likelihood of successful reorganization. On the other hand, replacement of existing management imposes a potentially crippling cost on the debtor. At the very least, new management must learn about the business, and must do so at a time when the demands of both operation and the reorganization allow precious little time for OJT (on-the-job training). In addition, the appointment of new management may be perceived by suppliers, customers, and employees as a virtual admission that the company is in a hopeless situation and thus may further complicate efforts to convince them to continue dealing with it. Finally, there is no obvious source of better management for most companies. Management and entrepreneurial skills cannot be ordered in job lots from office supply companies. While there are indeed a limited number of turnaround artists—managers who specialize in salvaging troubled companies (for of course very high profits)—they usually appear, if at all, before the company has actually landed in bankruptcy.

Because of this, for better or worse, nearly every Chapter 11 debtor depends heavily on the skills of those who are already in place. However, their role is not exactly the same as it was before the bankruptcy. The managers are now not primarily responsible to the owners, let alone to themselves, but to the creditors. Their ability to act outside the ordinary course of business is constrained, as they must obtain court permission to do so.[16] And, needless to say, they are prohibited from wholly self-serving actions.

§ 17.04 Role of the Creditors' Committee(s)

Except for "small business" cases, there is normally supposed to be at least one Creditors' Committee, and in some cases there may be more than one. The basic function of the creditors' committee is to act as both advisor to and watchdog of the debtor. Ideally, the committee scrutinizes the debtor's actions, makes recommendations concerning such matters as the appointment of a trustee, and serves as the main forum for negotiating the plan. In practice, however, the Creditors' Committee is often a paper tiger. Indeed, in small Chapter 11 proceedings, it can be impossible to assemble a Creditors' Committee.[17]

The United States Trustee is charged with the responsibility of appointing the "official" Creditors' Committee, who are to be both holders of unsecured claims and representatives of all unsecured claimants.[18] Ordinarily, the committee is to consist of the holders of the seven largest unsecured claims.[19] This in itself can

[16] See § 9.03[C][2] of this book.

[17] In an effort to encourage participation on the Creditors' Committee, the 1994 Amendments permit the court to reimburse the committee member's out-of-pocket expenses. Bankruptcy Code § 503(b)(3)(F) (1994 Amendments). Prior to this change, the Code was silent on the issue and many courts held that reimbursement for expenses was not permitted.

[18] Bankruptcy Code § 1102(a)(1).

[19] Bankruptcy Code § 1102(b)(1).

create problems. There are some Chapter 11 cases in which there are fewer than seven unsecured claims. There are many in which only one or two unsecured claims are large enough to make it worth the creditor's while to serve on the committee. The U.S. Trustee has no power of conscription; only those who are "willing to serve" are to be appointed.[20]

There are also frequent conflict of interest problems. Not uncommonly, a major unsecured claimant is also a major secured claimant. For example, the holder of a $650,000 debt secured by $500,000 worth of collateral may well be the one of the largest unsecured creditors by reason of its $150,000 unsecured claim. Yet there is serious question about the propriety of a creditors with a large secured claim sitting on the Creditors' Committee. Because of its secured status, the creditor may well favor the immediate liquidation of the debtor. That, however, may not be in the best interests of unsecured creditors, whose only hope for substantial payment is a successful reorganization. It is generally accepted that the members of the Creditors' Committee owe a fiduciary duty to unsecured creditors;[21] the undersecured creditor's conflict of interest may prevent it from fulfilling that duty. Yet if that creditor is excluded, the likelihood that the committee will even exist, let alone do anything, is greatly reduced.

There have been a number of suggestions that the United States Trustee office ought to fill this gap. There are, however, institutional limitations on its ability to do so, not least limited personnel and budget. There have also been a number of proposals to delete Creditors' Committees and other forms of creditor participation from very small business reorganizations. This would follow the pattern of Chapters 12 and 13 regarding the operation of the debtor and the formulation of the plan, and thereby reduce both the discretion of the debtor and the need for creditor involvement. Enactment of yet another reorganization Chapter would however move the Code still further from the 1978 effort to achieve greater uniformity. In the 1994 Amendments, only a few bits of the small business reorganization scheme were adopted.

In occasional cases, there are additional Creditors' Committees. On request of a party in interest, the court may order the United States Trustee to appoint one or more special Creditors' Committees if this is necessary to assure adequate protection of some group of creditors.[22] For example, in some of the mass tort bankruptcies, the tort victims have been given a separate Creditors' Committee to represent their special interests.[23] The appointment of an additional committee generally

---

[20] Bankruptcy Code § 1102(b)(1).

[21] In the words of one case, a member of a creditors' committee must be "honest, loyal, trustworthy and without conflicting interests, and with undivided loyalty and allegiance to their constituents . . . Conflicts of interest on the part of representative persons or committees are thus not [to] be tolerated." Johns-Manville Sales Corp. v. Doan (In re Johns-Manville Corp.), 26 Bankr. 919, 925 (1983).

[22] Bankruptcy Code § 1102(a)(2).

[23] For an example, see Ronald J. Bacigal, The Limits of Litigation: The Dalkon Shield Controversy 59-61 (1990). In that case, the first tort claimants' committee disintegrated and was replaced by a second committee.

complicates the case, and may make it more difficult to put together a plan. Consequently, the court should only do so if there are such severe conflicts of interest that the official creditors' committee either cannot function or is running roughshod over the interests of a definable group of creditors. There are inevitably conflicts between creditors; but the mere presence of conflicts is not ordinarily enough to trigger the appointment of an additional committee. There is no set number of members for these additional committees, although experience suggests that they should not be too large; excessive membership breeds excessive conflict.[24]

§ 17.05 Role of Equity Holders

By and large, equity holders (or in the Code's parlance, interest holders) have little or no function *as such* in Chapter 11 cases. Of course, if the debtor is a partnership or closely held corporation, the equity holders are also likely to be the managers. As managers, they have an important role to play; but as owners they are largely irrelevant unless they are able to convince the creditors to permit them a stake in the reorganized entity. If, as is often the case, they are given nothing by the reorganization plan, they are deemed to have rejected the plan and do not even vote.[25]

In a medium-to-large reorganization, where the company's stock is publicly traded, the existing equity holders are sometimes displaced wholly or in part as owners by creditors. For example, a plan might provide that the reorganized company would be owned 98% by pre-petition creditors (who would in effect be trading part of their debt for equity in the new company) and 2% by pre-petition stockholders. In smaller cases, the assets are more likely than the business to be reorganized. Reorganization of a small business generally involves the purchase of its assets by one or more investors. Under some circumstances, those investors may in fact be the old owners.

In rare cases, there is a committee, similar in structure and purpose to a Creditors' Committee, to represent equity. On request of a party in interest, the court may order the U.S. Trustee to appoint a committee of equity security holders. This is done only if necessary to assure adequate representation of the equity holders.[26] Normally, this committee consists of the seven largest holders of the debtor's equity securities.[27]

There is some uncertainty about the degree to which equity holders can exercise power over the management of the debtor. This divides into two issues. First, what rights do the equity holders have as parties in interest in the bankruptcy? Second, what powers do the equity holders have as equity holders?

---

[24] In the Dalkon Shield case, the first committee of 38 members fell to pieces and was replaced with a five-member committee. Id. at 60-61.

[25] Bankruptcy Code § 1126(g).

[26] Bankruptcy Code § 1102(a)(2).

[27] Bankruptcy Code § 1102(b)(2).

The Bankruptcy Code gives all parties in interest, including equity holders, the right to be heard in matters that affect them. The equity holders also have the power to seek the displacement of current management and the appointment of a trustee.[28] However, it is unusual for equity holders to have any interest in exercising these powers because will probably receive nothing under the plan.

A more difficult question arises in the occasional case where shareholders attempt to enforce their rights as shareholders. Outside of bankruptcy, it is broadly true that the function of corporate management is to create the maximum return for shareholders on their investment. While there are many limitations and modifications of this doctrine, it remains largely true that the job of corporate management is to enrich corporate owners. All of this changes in bankruptcy.

The function of the debtor in possession (or, more precisely, those persons that are actually managing the debtor in possession) is to act on behalf of the entire bankruptcy estate.[29] This creates a diffuse and sometimes contradictory set of fiduciary duties to all stakeholders in the reorganizing entity.[30] As a practical matter, the DIP's efforts normally will be aimed at maximum return for creditors, because in nearly all Chapter 11 cases the entity is hopelessly insolvent and the equity interests are completely under water. Where, exactly, does this leave the equity holders? Do they still retain the rights they would have outside of bankruptcy? There is very little guidance in the case law.

One of the specific questions that has arisen in a few cases is whether the shareholders of a Chapter 11 debtor still retain their state law right to replace the board of trustees. Generally speaking, the courts have allowed shareholders to elect a board, provided that this will not interfere with the bankruptcy proceeding.[31] However, the ability to elect a board is rather hollow. The board cannot unilaterally exercise its most important power—that is, to replace the management—at least before the confirmation of the plan.[32]

Equity holders want not only a role in the proceeding; they also want a stake in the outcome. The role of equity holders in the reorganized entity has recently spawned a great deal of discussion. This discussion has arisen from so-called single asset bankruptcies, in which there is only one significant creditor who is trying to block reorganization. This issue is discussed in depth in Chapter 22.[33]

---

[28] See § 17.06 of this chapter.

[29] See, for example, In re Pacific Forest Industries, Inc., 95 Bankr. 740 (Bankr. C.D. Cal. 1989).

[30] Raymond T. Nimmer and Richard B. Feinberg, *Chapter 11 Business Governance: Fiduciary Duties, Business Judgment, Trustees and Exclusivity,* 6 Bankr. Dev. J. 1 (1989).

[31] In re Johns' Manville Corp., 801 F.2d 60 (2d Cir. 1986); Saxon Industries, Inc. v. NKFW Partners (In re Saxon Industries, Inc.), 39 Bankr. 49 (Bankr. S.D.N.Y. 1984).

[32] In re Lifeguard Industries, 37 Bankr. 3 (Bankr. S.D. Ohio 1983).

[33] See § 22.04.

§ 17.06 Appointment of Trustee or Examiner

Despite the great costs involved in displacing current management, and the likelihood that such displacement is merely a prelude to liquidation, there are times that there is no practical alternative. Management may be so incompetent, or so corrupt, that the impact of replacing them, however bad, is less awful than keeping them in place. The court is thus empowered to displace current management by the appointment of a trustee.

At any time after commencement of the case and before confirmation of the plan, any party in interest (and the United States Trustee) may request the appointment of a trustee to displace management.[34] After notice and an opportunity for a hearing, the court "shall" appoint a trustee on either of the following bases:

> FOR CAUSE. A trustee may be appointed "for cause," which includes but is not limited to "fraud, dishonesty, incompetence, or gross mismanagement . . . either before or after the commencement of the case."[35]
>
> INTEREST OF CREDITORS/OWNERS. A trustee may be appointed if it is in the interests of creditors, equity security holders, or others having interests in the estate.[36]

In practice, these two bases tend to be interchangeable; appointment of a trustee is likely to be in the interests of creditors or owners because the management of the DIP is dishonest or incompetent.

Like so many bankruptcy rules, those regarding the appointment of a trustee are intended to be flexible and to give the bankruptcy judge considerable leeway to deal with the precise facts of a specific case. Although the statute says that the court "shall" appoint a trustee if the required criteria are met, the courts in fact have considerable discretion. The appointment of a trustee seldom improves matters and often constitutes a recognition of the awful truth that Chapter 11 so often evades: there simply is no hope for reorganization. In consequence, bankruptcy courts often tolerate a considerable amount of incompetence and even misbehavior without calling in a trustee. For example, in the A.H. Robins bankruptcy, it was discovered that over $7,000,000 of grossly improper payments had been made by the debtor in possession, including $5,500,000 diverted through non-bankruptcy subsidiaries and $1,750,000 in deferred bonuses paid to Robins' corporate executives and retirees. These payments had been made contrary to the repeated advice of Robins' own lawyers and its director of employee benefits.[37] Although the judge was incensed,

---

[34] Bankruptcy Code § 1104(a). Prior to the 1994 Amendments, the trustee was appointed by the United States Trustee after consulation with parties in interest. The 1994 Amendments gave the creditors the right to elect a trustee; if they do not do so, the trustee will be selected as before. Bankruptcy Code § 1104(b), (d) (1994 Amendments).

[35] Bankruptcy Code § 1104(a)(1).

[36] Bankruptcy Code § 1104(a)(2). Note that the statute merely states that the appointment must be in the "interests of" creditors or owners; it does not state that the appointment must be "in the best interests of." Omission of the word "best" is probably meaningless.

[37] Ronald J. Bacigal, The Limits of Litigation: The Dalkon Shield Controversy 64-65 (1990).

and imposed considerable sanctions, he refused to appoint a trustee,[38] in large part because he doubted a trustee could run the company as profitably:

> Judge Merhige was reluctant to appoint a trustee in light of the fact that Robins's current management continued to be profitable while in Chapter Eleven reorganization. When the Dalkon Shield committee's lawyer joint in the call for appointment of a trustee, the judge pointed out that A. H. Robins had generated more than $100 million in annual profits while in bankruptcy proceedings. The judge asked counsel whether he could guarantee that under a trustee, the company could continue to report a 30% gain in profits next quarter.[39]

Broadly speaking, the duties of the Chapter 11 trustee are the same as those of the Chapter 7 trustee, although there are some modest differences.[40] Chief among these are that the Chapter 11 trustee has a somewhat broader duty to investigate the debtor and must make a written report on the investigation.[41] Moreover, if it is still possible to go forward in Chapter 11, the trustee is to prepare and file a reorganization plan; if Chapter 11 is not feasible, the trustee is to recommend either a conversion of the case to another chapter or a dismissal.[42]

The trustee may be discharged, and the DIP restored, an act even rarer than the initial displacement of the DIP. At any time prior to confirmation, upon the request of a party in interest (or the United States trustee) the court may terminate the trustee's appointment and restore the debtor to possession and management of the property and business.[43] Note, however, that this does not necessarily mean that the pre-trustee management is restored; the debtor-in-possession may well be managed by somebody else.

The court has a less drastic alternative if it does not appoint a trustee: appointment of an examiner.[44] On motion of a party in interest (including the United States Trustee) the court "shall" appoint an examiner to investigate the debtor if

> 1. The appointment is in the interests of creditors, equity security holders, or others with an interest in the estate,[45] or
>
> 2. The debtor's fixed, unliquidated unsecured debts (excluding (i) debts for goods, services or taxes and (2) debts owed to an insider) exceed $5,000,000.[46]

---

[38] Id. at 69-71.

[39] Id. at 69.

[40] Bankruptcy Code § 1106(a).

[41] Bankruptcy Code § 1106(a) (3), (4).

[42] Bankruptcy Code § 1106(a)(5).

[43] Bankruptcy Code § 1105.

[44] Bankruptcy Code § 1104(c).

[45] Bankruptcy Code § 1104(c)(1).

[46] Bankruptcy Code § 1104(c)(2).

Note that the court's discretion is considerably more restrained; if the debtor exceeds the $5,000,000 debt limit, and a motion is made, the court must make the appointment.[47] Appointment is not mandatory, however, if no motion is made. This requirement is one of the last vestiges of the old distinction drawn in the Bankruptcy Act between "big" reorganizations (Chapter X) and little ones.

In cases where appointment is not mandatory, the courts exercise considerable discretion, just as they do with appointment of trustees. The appointment of the examiner is far less disruptive to the debtor than the appointment of the trustee; thus, the considerations that underlie the reluctance to appoint the latter do not apply in full force. However, appointment should not be routine. Examiners can be expensive and can slow down the proceeding. Moreover, much of what the examiner does can be done by the Creditors' Committee—assuming that it has the resources and that the debtor is cooperative.

The examiner's job is implicit in the title: to investigate "fraud, dishonesty, incompetence, misconduct, mismanagement or irregularity . . . by current or former management of the debtor."[48] The examiner is then to report to the court and the creditors' committee on its investigation.[49] The report may include recommendations for further action, such as the appointment of a trustee.

§ 17.07 Role of the Securities and Exchange Commission

As noted previously, under the Bankruptcy Act, the Securities and Exchange Commission (SEC) played a crucial role in Chapter X proceedings. Moreover, because of the uncertain line between Chapter X and Chapter XI, the SEC also had considerable influence in large Chapter XI proceedings as well (even though it had no formal role).[50] The SEC has not quite been banned from Chapter 11 cases. Under section 1109(a), it may raise, appear, and be heard on any issue in a Chapter 11 case.[51] It may not, however, appeal from any judgment, order or decree entered by the court.[52] In practice, the SEC has virtually disappeared from the bankruptcy courts, and there is virtually no call from creditors, stockholders, or others for its return. It thus appears that this is one change made by the Bankruptcy Code that has been accepted universally.

---

[47] Collier on Bankruptcy ¶ 1104.03[4][a]; see also, In re Revco D.S., Inc., 898 F.2d 498 (6th Cir. 1990 (plain language of the code requires appointment of examiner if unsecured debt exceeds $5,000,000 and U.S. Trustee so moves).

[48] Bankruptcy Code §§ 1104(c), 1106(a)(3).

[49] Bankruptcy Code § 1106(a)(4).

[50] The SEC often engaged in negotiations with borderline Chapter X/Chapter XI debtors to determine the conditions under which the debtor would be, in effect, allowed by the SEC to use the latter chapter.

[51] Bankruptcy Code § 1109(a).

[52] Bankruptcy Code § 1109(a).

§ 17.08 Conversion and Dismissal

In most circumstances, the Chapter 11 debtor enjoys the absolute right to give up on its efforts to reorganize and convert the case to Chapter 7.[53] This rule does no more than pragmatically recognize the fact that involuntary reorganization is very rarely successful or even sensible. However, there are circumstances where involuntary continuation is appropriate, either because the debtor is no longer directly involved in the case or because the proceeding was involuntary from the start. The debtor does *not* have an automatic, unilateral right to convert if (i) the debtor is not a debtor-in-possession (that is, if a trustee has been appointed to administer the estate and the business) or (ii) the case began as an involuntary Chapter 11 or (iii) the case was converted to Chapter 11 on the motion of someone other than the debtor.[54]

The flip side is involuntary conversion or dismissal; it is more restricted. Any of the parties in interest, and the U.S. Trustee, have the right to seek an involuntary conversion or dismissal. After notice and an opportunity for a hearing, the court may convert to Chapter 7, or may dismiss, "for cause." Cause includes:

1. Continuation of loss to or diminution of the estate plus absence of a reasonable likelihood of rehabilitation.[55] If the Chapter 11 debtor is continuing to lose money, especially if it is continuing to lose money on its current operations (without taking into account its obligations on prior debt) and there is no real hope of reorganization, the court may dismiss or convert.[56] In a case of this sort, conversion is more likely than dismissal, because a liquidation is both inevitable and immiinent.

2. Inability to effectuate a plan.[57]

3. Unreasonable delay by the debtor that is prejudicial to creditors.[58] If there is any provision of Chapter 11 that creditors wish were more firmly enforced, this is surely it. In the view of many creditors, extension follows extension, delay follows delay; yet the court does nothing. Of course, in the view of many debtors, creditors are consistently pressing for disastrous liquidation when a mutual beneficial plan of reorganization is just around the corner.

4. Failure to propose a plan within the time fixed.[59] This is another rule that creditors wish were imposed more strictly. It is rarely possible to get

---

[53] Bankruptcy Code § 1112(a).

[54] Bankruptcy Code § 1112(a) (1) -(3).

[55] Bankruptcy Code § 1112(b)(1).

[56] In the blunt words of an old § 77B case, "[h]owever honest in its efforts the debtor may be, and however sincere its motives, the District Court is not bound to clog its docket with visionary or impracticable schemes for resuscitation." Tennessee Publishing Co. v. American National Bank, 299 U.S. 18, 22 (1936).

[57] Bankruptcy Code § 1112(b)(2).

[58] Bankruptcy Code § 1112(b)(3).

[59] Bankruptcy Code § 1112(b)(4).

a dismissal on this basis, because of many courts' propensity to grant extensions of the period during which a plan may be proposed.[60] It is often asserted that stricter enforcement of time limits for proposing a plan would cure most of the perceived problems with Chapter 11. There are recent indications that courts are becoming more strict. Also the 1994 Amendments impose special time limits for "Single Asset Real Estate" bankruptcies; these time limits are discussed in § 22.04 of this book.

5. Denial of confirmation of every proposed plan and of a request made for additional time to file a new or modified plan.[61]

6. Revocation of confirmation and denial of confirmation of another plan or a modified plan.[62] This provision deals with misconduct by the debtor, since revocation of confirmation is permissible only when the confirmation was obtained by fraud.[63]

7. Inability to effect substantial consummation of the plan.[64] "Substantial consummation" is defined by the Code; it means (i) transfer of all or substantially all the property that the plan proposes be transferred, and (ii) assumption by the debtor or its successor of the business or of the management of all/substantially all the property dealt with by the plan and (iii) commencement of distributions under the plan.[65] In plain English, the debtor's inability to comply with the plan is a basis for conversion or dismissal.[66]

8. Material default by the debtor under the plan.[67] For example, the continued failure to make plan payments in full or as scheduled may lead to conversion or dismissal.

9. Termination of the plan by its own terms.[68]

10. Failure to pay required fees and charges.[69]

---

[60] For a discussion of the "exclusivity period" during which only the debtor may propose a plan, see § 17.11[C] of this chapter.

[61] Bankruptcy Code § 1112(b)(5).

[62] Bankruptcy Code § 1112(b)(6).

[63] Bankruptcy Code § 1144. For a discussion of revocation of confirmation, see § 17.17[B] of this chapter.

[64] Bankruptcy Code § 1112(b)(7).

[65] Bankruptcy Code § 1101(2).

[66] Note, however, that the plan can be modified either before or after its confirmation; and, if the modified plan is confirmed it becomes the plan that must be substantially consummated. See § 17.16 of this chapter for a discussion of plan modification.

[67] Bankruptcy Code § 1112(b)(8).

[68] Bankruptcy Code § 1112(b)(9).

[69] Bankruptcy Code § 1112(b)(10). This protection of the bankruptcy fisc is perhaps the basis for dismissal taken most seriously by the courts.

Conversion is subject to some limitations. First, a debtor cannot convert or be forced to convert to a Chapter for which the debtor is ineligible.[70] For example, a corporation cannot convert from Chapter 11 to Chapter 13 because corporations cannot file under Chapter 13;[71] neither could a railroad's creditors convert its Chapter 11 case to Chapter 7 or Chapter 12, because a railroad cannot file under those chapters.[72]

Second, conversion cannot be used to get around the limitations on involuntary filings. For example, farmers may not be put into involuntary bankruptcy. Thus, if the debtor is a farmer, its Chapter 11 case cannot be involuntarily converted to a Chapter 7 case.[73] Similarly, no one who is a Chapter 11 debtor can be forced into Chapter 13 because that chapter is purely voluntary.[74]

Finally, there are some special limitations on voluntary conversion to Chapters 12 and 13. The debtor may not convert to either chapter if it has received a Chapter 11 discharge.[75] Since a Chapter 11 discharge is normally granted when the plan is confirmed,[76] this virtually prevents voluntary post-confirmation conversion from Chapter 11 to Chapter 12 or 13. In addition, the debtor may not convert to Chapter 12 unless the conversion is "equitable,"[77] a term left undefined.

Along with the various statutory bases for dismissal, there is a widely recognized court created authority to dismiss a filing that is not made in good faith. Despite the lack of any statutory support, the basic concept is well established. Its applicability to particular situations, however, remains both uncertain and controversial. The courts do not even agree whether good faith should be measured by a subjective test focusing on the debtor's intention[78] or an objective test focusing on ability to reorganize.[79]

The bad faith issue has often arisen in context of new and specialized types of proceedings that deviate from the traditional pattern of Chapter 11. For example, good faith challenges have been made to the use of bankruptcy as a means of dealing with products liability litigation.[80] Bad faith has also become the primary rubric under which courts dismiss so-called single asset Chapter 11 cases. These cases, which involve a debtor who is attempting to reorganize a business that has only one

---

[70] Bankruptcy Code § 1112(f).

[71] Bankruptcy Code § 109(e); see § 6.02[B] of this book.

[72] Railroads are among the few debtors excluded from Chapter 7 liquidation (Bankruptcy Code § 109(b)); only a family farmer can file under Chapter 12 (Bankruptcy Code § 109(f)). See § 6.02[B] of this book.

[73] Bankruptcy Code § 1112(c).

[74] Bankruptcy Code § 1112(d).

[75] Bankruptcy Code § 1112(d)(2).

[76] Bankruptcy Code § 1141(d).

[77] Bankruptcy Code § 1112(d)(3).

[78] See In re Phoenix Piccadilly, Ltd., 849 F.2d 1393 (11th Cir. 1988).

[79] See Carolin Corp. v. Miller, 886 F.2d 693 (4th Cir. 1989).

[80] See In re Johns-Manville, 36 Bankr. 727 (Bankr. S.D.N.Y. 1984), app. den., 39 Bankr. 234 (S.D.N.Y. 1984), re-argument denied, 39 Bankr. 998 (S.D.N.Y. 1984).

substantial asset and only one substantial creditor have been rather freely dismissed as bad faith filings. This issue is discussed in greater detail in Chapter 20.[81]

§ 17.09 Operating the Debtor

Since Chapter 11 generally involves an ongoing business, there is no requirement that the trustee/DIP be given specific court permission to operate that business. To the contrary, authorization is automatic and may only be revoked on request of a party in interest, after notice and an opportunity for a hearing.[82] As it true generally, this constitutes authority to operate in the ordinary course of business only; court permission must be obtained for non-ordinary course transactions (and for incurring secured debt).[83]

There are no distinctive rules that pertain to Chapter 11 proceedings generally. However, many of the issues discussed in Chapter 8 (Automatic Stay) and Chapter 9 (Operating the Debtor) apply primarily in Chapter 11, because it is in Chapter 11 that the debtor's use, and the creditor's loss of repossession rights, become most significant. There are as well a few rules that apply to specific issues, and an entire subchapter that deals with railroads. Two other rules of significance are found in sections 1113 and 1114, which deal with the rejection of collective bargaining agreements and the payment of retirement benefits. Section 1113 is discussed in Chapter 22 as an example of a specialized use of bankruptcy.[84] Finally, there are some special rules regarding collateral and leasehold in ships and planes that require the Chapter 11 trustee/DIP to cure defaults and assume the contract obligations within 60 days of the order for relief; these modify the normal rules regarding the automatic stay and the use, sale, or lease of property.[85]

§ 17.10 Claims and Interests

[A]—In General

The status of the various claims and interests in Chapter 11 is generally the same as it is in other Bankruptcy chapters. The usual hierarchy, discussed at length in Chapter 10—secured claims, priority unsecured claims, general unsecured claims, subordinated unsecured claims, and equity—is followed.[86] The plan may alter this list to a degree. The Chapter 11 debtor has a fairly broad right to classify general unsecured claims, and to pay differing percentages to each class.[87] If the plan is

---

[81] See § 22.04.

[82] Bankruptcy Code § 1108.

[83] See Chapter 9 of this book for detailed discussions of the requirements that non-ordinary course debt and secured debt be approved by the court.

[84] See § 22.03.

[85] Bankruptcy Code § 1110.

[86] See § 10.01.

[87] See § 17.11[D] of this chapter.

approved by a sufficient number of creditors, it need not follow the "absolute priority rule;" in other words, a lower ranked class may get a distribution even though a higher rank is not paid in full.[88] This is based on the assumption that the plan produces a going-concern surplus which need not be as rigidly divided up as the basic liquidation value.

As is true generally throughout the Code, undersecured obligations are divided into two claims, a secured claim for the value of the collateral and an unsecured claim for the remainder. There is an complex exception to this rule that is unique to Chapter 11. As is discussed in § 17.10[C], below, the holder of undersecured debt can elect to have a secured claim for the full amount of the debt.

[B]—Proof of Claim or Interest

Although it is probably better practice to file a proof of claim or interest in Chapter 11, it is not always necessary. If the claim (or interest) is scheduled by the debtor, a proof of claim is "deemed" to have been filed, unless the claim or interest is scheduled as disputed, contingent or unliquidated.[89] As is true throughout the Code, the filing of the proof of claim or interest establishes the claim or interest unless the proof is disputed.[90]

[C]—Recourse/Nonrecourse Debt; Undersecured Debt (§ 1111(b))

First, an anecdote. Some years ago, when the Code was new to the world and I to the practice of law, I attended a seminar on bankruptcy that explored the just-enacted Bankruptcy Reform Act and the changes its Bankruptcy Code would make to lawyers. One entire session of this three-day seminar was spent on section 1111(b). In a room of two hundred anxious and intelligent lawyers there was, I think, by the end of that session a tiny band of five or six who thought they understood it. I was not among them. If this discussion seems inordinately long, given the fact that the rule in question is rarely used, it is perhaps reflective of the fact that I hope to be a bit more successful than were the speakers on that cold November afternoon.

Section 1111(b) actually contains two related sets of rules. The first involves the treatment of nonrecourse debt. The second involves the treatment of undersecured debt, whether recourse debt or non-recourse debt.

Nonrecourse debt is debt that is enforceable only against the property securing the debt. For example, suppose that D'Arcy borrows $100,000,000, plus change, from River Bank secured by D'Arcy's new office building. Under the loan agreement, D'Arcy has no personal obligation for the debt. If payments are not made, River Bank may foreclose on the building and sell it. However, whether or not the foreclosure sale yields enough to cover the debt, River Bank cannot pursue D'Arcy or any of D'Arcy's other assets.

Under section 1111(b), nonrecourse creditors, such as River Bank, are treated as if they were recourse creditors. In other words, for Chapter 11 purposes, they are

---

[88] See § 17.15[D] of this chapter.

[89] Bankruptcy Code § 1111(a).

[90] See §§ 10.02[C] and 10.06[B], respectively, of this book.

treated as if they had a right of recourse against the debtor, even though for other purposes they do not. The practical significance of this is that the undersecured, nonrecourse debtor is given an unsecured claim for the amount of the deficiency. In the example given, if the D'Arcy building was worth only $80,000,000, for Chapter 11 purposes only River Bank is given an $80,000,000 secured claim and a $20,000,000 (plus change) unsecured claim, even though River Bank does not have any rights outside of Chapter 11 to seize D'Arcy's other assets.[91]

There are two exceptions to this rule. First, River Bank can make the so-called 1111(b)(2) election, which is discussed further below; this will give River Bank what amounts to a non-recourse claim for the entire $100,000,000 (plus change). Second, if the D'Arcy office building is sold under section 363[92] or is to be sold under the plan, River Bank receives only what it is entitled to through the sale and does not receive the additional unsecured "deficiency" claim.[93] Thus, if the building actually sells for $83,000,000 (net of sale costs), that is all River Bank will get. The theory behind this latter exception is that the creditor is receiving exactly what it bargained for when it made a non-recourse loan — the proceeds from the sale of the encumbered property.

The rest of § 1111(b) deals with all undersecured claims, whether or not the claimant has recourse against the debtor. As a general rule, each claimant can elect to have the claim treated as if it were a non-recourse claim.[94] In other words, suppose that River Bank has a claim for $2,000,000 secured by property valued in the bankruptcy at $1,500,000. Regardless of whether River Bank's claim is a recourse claim or a nonrecourse claim, River Bank can elect to have it treated in Chapter 11 as a nonrecourse claim. There are only two exceptions to this. First, if the claimant's interest in the property is of inconsequential value, the election may not be made.[95] If River Bank's interest in the collateral was only worth $10.00, River Bank could not make the 1111(b) election. Second, if the claim is in fact a recourse claim, and the property is sold under § 363 or is to be sold under the plan, the election cannot be made.[96]

If the election is made, then the claim is a secured claim to the full extent that it is an allowed claim. In other words, if River Bank has a $10,000,000 claim secured by $8,000,000 of assets, and validly makes the 1111(b) election, River Bank will have a $10,000,000 secured claim. This is in contrast to the normal treatment of River Bank's claim; ordinarily, it would have an $8,000,000 secured claim and a

---

[91] Bankruptcy Code § 1111(b)(1)(A)

[92] For a discussion of sales under § 363 of the Bankruptcy Code, see § 9.03 of this book.

[93] Bankruptcy Code § 1111(b)(1)(A)(ii).

[94] Technically, the provision states that the election must be made by the class of which the claim is a part, and that the election must be by at least two-thirds an amount more than half in number. Bankruptcy Code § 1111(b)(1)(A)(i). However, as a general rule, each secured claim is in its own class and this election is thus ordinarily made by individual claims. See § 17.11[D] of this chapter for a discussion of the classification of secured claims.

[95] Bankruptcy Code § 1111(b)(1)(B)(i).

[96] Bankruptcy Code § 1111(b)(1)(B)(ii).

$2,000,000 unsecured claim.[97] Note, however, that unlike most secured claims, River Bank's claim need not be paid in full; only the value of the collateral must actually be paid.[98]

If you consider closely the effect of making the election, you can see the purpose of the election. It is to provide protection against lien-stripping.[99] Suppose that, in the example just given, the property is presently worth $8,000,000 only because of a temporary slump in the property market. There is reason to believe that it will soon be worth more than $10,000,000. In the normal circumstance, where River Bank's claim is bifurcated between a secured and an unsecured claim, the debtor can effectively lien-strip by paying the $8,000,000 secured claim in full and only a portion of the $2,000,000 unsecured claim. When the value of the property subsequently rises, the debtor will capture that increased value. By allowing River Bank to elect to have a $10,000,000 secured claim, we allow River Bank to avoid this effect.

Or so it seems on the surface. In fact, section 1111(b) provides very little real protection for undersecured creditors. This is because the requirements for plan confirmation do not actually force the debtor to pay the secured debt in full. In the River Bank example, the debtor does not have to provide for plan payments that have a present value of $10,000,000. It only has to provide plan payments that have a nominal value of $10,000,000 and a present value of $8,000,000. This factor, which is discussed further in § 17.12[D][4] of this chapter, greatly undercuts the real significance of 1111(b), and explains both why it is not often used and seldom understood. Indeed, a creditor can be worse off making the 1111(b) election because it loses its right to whatever dividend is paid on unsecured debt.

§ 17.11 The Plan

[A]—Introduction

As is true with any reorganization proceeding, the goal of Chapter 11 is the confirmation and successful completion of a plan of reorganization. The distinguishing feature of Chapter 11 is that the plan is, or at least is supposed to be, the fruit of a process of negotiation among the debtor, the creditors, and (in some cases) the interest holders. Nearly all creditors vote on the plan; and it is difficult to get the plan confirmed unless the required majority of creditors approve.

Chapter 11 thus stands at the midpoint between a common-law composition on the one hand and Chapters 12 and 13 on the other. In a composition, no creditor who dissents can be bound by the plan. In Chapters 12 and 13 most creditors do not even get to vote; if certain statutory requirements are met, all creditors, whatever their views, are bound. In Chapter 11, creditors vote under a modified form of

---

[97] See § 10.03[C] of this book for a discussion of the bifurcation of undersecured obligations.

[98] See § 17.12[D][4] of this chapter.

[99] For a discussion of lien-stripping, see § 17.12[D][3].

majority rule. If the requisite majority is obtained, then all creditors are bound. Only in limited circumstances may the plan be confirmed over the creditors' rejection.

Chapter 11 plans are often much more complicated than Chapter 12 or 13 plans. In part, this is because even a small Chapter 11 proceeding is likely to involve considerably more property and debt than even a large Chapter 12 or 13. In addition, it is broadly true that the Chapter 11 debtor has more flexibility in formulating its plan than do debtors under the other chapters. The usual justification for this greater flexibility is precisely the fact that the Chapter 11 creditors do have a much greater degree of input. If the requisite majority agrees to the debtor's proposal, there is less reason for a court to interfere than there is where no vote is taken at all.

As noted elsewhere, a Chapter 13 plan is usually filed with the petition.[100] By contrast, Chapter 11 usually involves post-filing negotiation, and a plan is often not ready for months or even years. However, in some circumstances a plan is actually put together before the filing. These "pre-packaged" Chapter 11 plans have drawn much attention in recent years,[101] and are explicitly permitted (and indeed somewhat facilitated) by the Code.[102] The reason for filing after the plan has been agreed to is to accomplish what cannot be accomplished outside bankruptcy—that is, to ensure the plan is binding on all creditors.

[B]—Process of Negotiation

There is very little law that governs the process of preparing and negotiating the Chapter 11 plan; indeed, the only explicit limitations on the process, bad faith and fraud, derive from the general law of contracts. Insofar as the plan itself is concerned, there are certain minimum standards that must ultimately be met; these are discussed in the following subsections. However, from the standpoint of the negotiating parties, those minimum payout standards are merely a baseline from which the negotiations begin.[103] The goal of most creditors is to get as much more than that minimum as possible; the goal of most debtors is to give as little extra as it can without so souring the creditors that they will not vote for the plan.

As noted, the plan has sometimes been partially or fully negotiated even before the Chapter 11 has been filed. Whether or not there has been pre-filing negotiation, the model for a Chapter 11 is the common-law composition. Ideally, all parties in interest are to hammer out a mutually satisfactory deal; the only reasons for doing

---

[100] See § 18.07[A] of this book.

[101] For a fuller discussion of pre-packaged plans, and the various considerations that have made them especially popular, see Marc S. Kirschner, Dan A. Kusnetz, Laurence Y. Colarsh & Craig S. Gatarz, *Prepackaged Bankruptcy Plans: The Deleveraging Tool of the '90s in the Wake of OID and Tax Concerns,* 21 Seton Hall L. Rev. 643 (1991).

[102] Bankruptcy Code § 1126(b) provides for voting on the plan of reorganization even before the case has been filed.

[103] Caveat: at times there is genuine uncertainty about the amount that must be paid to meet the minimum requirements; if so, that may be an explicit subject of discussion. However, since no dissenter can be forced to accept less than the minimum, no matter what is agreed to in the negotiations, it is technically impossible to determine the lowest payout required through the negotiating process.

this in bankruptcy are to take advantage of the automatic stay and to force dissenters into the plan.

This ideal is not always met. There are both practical and structural reasons for this. The practical problems are rooted in the fact that creditors, especially creditors with secured claims, are often uninterested in bargaining. A creditor with plenty of collateral may well want nothing more than a quick dismissal, conversion, or lifting of the automatic stay. Secured creditors are rarely benefitted by reorganization; and even unsecured creditors, who might hope for a better payout if the reorganization succeeds, may be so skeptical about the debtor's chances, and so disillusioned with the debtor's management, that they would just as soon take what they can in liquidation and go home.

The structural problems arise most frequently in small Chapter 11s. Creditors are not likely to waste time in negotiations if their stake is small. Even a creditor who is owed, say, $100,000 in unsecured debt is unlikely to spend much time dealing with the debtor if the best case scenario is a 25% payout over 5 years. Yet, in a great many Chapter 11 cases, that creditor may hold what is by far the largest unsecured claim against the debtor. Many observers have expressed concern about the fact that the typical Chapter 11 involves only small debtors and small creditors who have little interest in engaging in meaningful negotiations. This has led to a variety of proposals; among them, a new chapter for small business reorganizations and a more active role for the U.S. Trustee.[104]

[C]—When Plan May be Filed/The Exclusivity Period

The debtor may file a plan with the petition or at any other time during the case.[105] However, while Chapter 13 plans are usually filed with the petition, Chapter 11 plans seldom are. This is because Chapter 11, unlike Chapter 13, envisions negotiation over the plan, and the process of negotiation is generally not complete when the case is filed.

In most cases, the debtor has 120 days from the order for relief during which only it may file a plan.[106] (There are somewhat different rules that apply in "small business" and "single asset real estate" cases; these are discussed elsewhere.[107]) This "exclusivity period" is one of the most controversial provisions in Chapter 11. It is designed to give the debtor a chance to negotiate and prepare its own plan for reorganizing and escaping its financial troubles. At the end of that period, creditors are supposed to have their opportunity to do the same. There is little concern about the initial 120 day period. However, as will be discussed further below, the court has the power to extend that period, and this power has been routinely exercised. It is these extensions that are roundly criticized by creditors, and some courts have recently become less willing to grant extensions.

---

[104] For an overview of some currently pending proposals, see Walter A. Effross, *Bankruptcy Reform, Circa 1994,* 13-Mar Am. Bankr. Inst. J. 1 (1994).

[105] Bankruptcy Code § 1121(a).

[106] Bankruptcy Code § 1121(b).

[107] See § 17.18 of this chapter and § 22.04 of Chapter 22, respectively.

As indicated, others may file plans as well. Any party in interest (which includes the trustee, if any; a creditors' or equity security holders' committee; any creditor or equity security holder; or an indenture trustee) may file a plan under the following circumstances:

1. A trustee is appointed,[108] or

2. The debtor has not filed a plan within the exclusivity period,[109] or

3. The debtor has not filed a plan that has been accepted within the time set by the Code or the court.[110] In theory, this time period is 180 days after the order for relief; however, the time period is often extended.

On the face of it, these rules require the Chapter 11 debtor to proceed expeditiously. A plan is to be filed within 120 days and accepted within 180; if it is not, creditors can come in with their own ideas (which will often be swift liquidation). This, however, is one of those cases in which the statute bears no necessary resemblance to reality. The 120/180 day time limits have sometimes had no significance, because Congress has provided a loophole that has, in the hands of some courts, almost entirely swallowed the rule.

Section 1121(d), the bane of Chapter 11 creditors, states, in full: "On request of a party in interest made within the respective periods specified in subsections (b) and (c) of this section and after notice and a hearing, the court may for cause reduce or increase the 120-day period or the 180-day period referred to in this section."[111] In the view of many creditors, if you omit the word "reduce" and the phrase "for cause;" change "party in interest" to "debtor" and "may" almost to "shall;" you will have a good sense for the real content of this provision. In the view of many creditors, except in the most clearly abusive cases, courts routinely grant substantial extensions of both deadlines.[112]

This is a good point at which to consider again the problems created by the differing perceptions of the participants in a Chapter 11. The debtor is confident that somehow it will pull out of its current mess. The judge is inclined to think of reorganization as success and liquidation as failure. Creditors are apt to be divided, with general unsecured creditors willing to gamble on the off-chance that the reorganization might work and secured creditors disgusted, frustrated, and astounded at the naivete of everybody else. In some cases, extension follows extension, administrative priority debts mount, and liquidation draws slowly and inexorably nearer. Why, then, extend?

Most of the proposals for reform of Chapter 11 include stricter limitations on the exclusivity period. Indeed, it has been suggested that this is practically the only

---

[108] Bankruptcy Code § 1121(c)(1).

[109] Bankruptcy Code § 1121(c)(2).

[110] Bankruptcy Code § 1121(c)(3).

[111] Bankruptcy Code § 1121(d).

[112] For an example of these concerns, see Gerald Buccino, et al., *American Bankruptcy Institute Roundtable: Bankruptcy Reform'94*, 13-Mar Am. Bankr. Inst. J. 20A (1994).

reform necessary to deal with perceived abuse. Force the debtor to put its cards on the table earlier, the reasoning goes, and this will effectively weed out the few cases with prospects for success from the many doomed to failure. Indeed, some courts have already done this on their own.

The fundamental problem, however, is that it is extremely difficult to articulate a standard that does not arbitrarily exclude some debtors who still have prospects for reorganization. Most judges, and many lawyers, believe that each case should be evaluated on its own merits. One's evaluation of this issue, as of so many other Chapter 11 issues, depend on whether one believes that the benefits of successful proceedings outweigh the costs of the more numerous unsuccessful ones.

[D]—Classification

"Classification" of claims and interests means that the debtor subdivides the existing Code categories into narrower ones. For example, the Code treats all general unsecured debts alike. Under Chapter 7, all are paid pro-rata if anything is left over from the secured and priority claims. In Chapter 11, the debtor may split the general unsecured claims into various classes—for example, Class A for all claims of $500 or more and Class B for all claims under $500. Class A claims are paid fifty cents on the dollar; Class B claims are paid in full.

The Chapter 11 debtor has a broad right to classify, provided that the creditors approve the plan and that each claim is paid at least its liquidation value. The Code itself says remarkably little about classification. The following are the only explicit requirements:

> 1. Substantial Similarity. All claims or interests within a class must be substantially similar to each other.[113] This does not mean that they have to be identical; for example, it is possible to lump together claims arising from accounts payable with claims arising from unsecured operating loans. The key is that claims within the class must have broadly the same stake in the proceeding and goals for the reorganization.[114] For example, suppose that ABC's plan of reorganization lumps together tort claimants and contract claimants. The contract claimants are willing to accept a long, slow, and relatively protracted payout because they expect to recoup some of their losses by entering into new, profitable contracts with the reorganized entity. By contrast, the tort claimants want as much as possible immediately. The contract claimant's primary benefit from reorganization is the new business generated; the tort claimant's only benefit from reorganization is quick, maximum payout of the prior debt. It may be inappropriate to put both in the same class, especially if the tort claims are much smaller and fewer; if the tort claims can easily be outvoted by the contract claims, the tort claimants' interests will not be adequately taken into account in formulating the plan.

---

[113] Bankruptcy Code § 1122(a).

[114] See Collier on Bankruptcy ¶ 1122.04.

Note that the negative of this rule is nowhere stated in the Code—there is no requirement that substantially similar claims cannot be *separated* into classes. Indeed, this is the essence of classification. The debtor often seeks to separate apparently similar claims, for reasons that are sometimes clearly *bona fide* and at other times quite dubious.

2. Administrative Convenience. The one basis for classification explicitly recognized is administrative convenience: a plan may designate a class or classes consisting of every unsecured claim that is less than or reduced to an amount that the court approves as reasonably and necessary for administrative convenience.[115] It is common for the plan to include a class of small claims that will be paid in full, and thus unimpaired. By making this class unimpaired, the debtor saves the cost and effort involved in soliciting approval from a class that is often rather large but uninterested in the proceedings because their stake in it is so slight.

3. Designation and Disclosure. The plan must designate the classes,[116] and specify the treatment of each class.[117] This is to ensure that every creditor knows not only what it is getting but also what other creditors are getting.

4. Equality Within Classes. Although the plan can provide unequal treatment between classes, it must provide equal treatment within a class. Every claim or interest in a particular class must receive the same treatment—unless the holder of a particular claim or interest agrees to less.[118] This is essentially an anti-gerrymandering provision. It prevents a plan from lumping together in the same class creditors who get favorable treatment with those who get unfavorable treatment, in the hope that the former will vote "yes" in a sufficient majority to override the "no" votes of the latter.

[E]—Gerrymandering/Bad Faith

There is an ill-defined outer limit to classification. At some point, the classification becomes gerrymandering—the bankruptcy equivalent of the strange geographical boundaries drawn by political parties to ensure victory for their candidates. While broad latitude is allowed, there must be some reason other than the desire to win creditor approval for creating a class of claims. There is "one clear rule that emerges from the otherwise muddled case law on § 1122 claims classification: thou shalt not classify similar claims differently in order to gerrymander an affirmative vote on a reorganization plan."[119]

---

[115] Bankruptcy Code § 1122(b).

[116] Bankruptcy Code § 1123(a)(1). Note that the plan need not designate all of the Code-created classes. Id.

[117] Bankruptcy Code § 1123(3).

[118] Bankruptcy Code § 1123(a)(4).

[119] In re Greystone III Joint Venture, 948 F.2d F.2d 134, 139 (5th Cir. 1991), cert denied, 113 S. Ct. 72 (1992).

The gerrymandering issue arises most frequently in cramdown cases, especially "single asset" cases. It is always necessary to get at least one impaired class of claims to accept the Chapter 11 plan. It is sometimes impossible to do this without extremely agile manipulation of the classes. This issue is discussed in depth in Chapter 22.[120]

[F]—Impaired and Unimpaired Classes

Every class of claims and interests is either impaired or unimpaired. This distinction plays a crucial role, because it is the impaired classes that vote, not the unimpaired classes. The Code's definition is written from the practical standpoint that classes of claims or interests are nearly always impaired; thus, section 1124 says that (with one minor exclusion) a class of claims or interests is impaired *unless* the plan either:

> 1. Leaves the legal. equitable, and contractual rights of the holder of claim or interest holder unaltered, or
>
> 2. Cures defaults (other than ipso facto clause defaults), de-accelerates the obligation, compensates the holder of the claim or interest for damages, and does not otherwise alter the legal, equitable, or contractual rights of the holder.[121]

An example of the first: The debtor is obligated on a fully secured mortgage debt. The debtor makes all payments in full when due. The plan provides that all payments will be made in full when due. No provision of the mortgage or loan agreement is changed. No provision of the mortgage or loan agreement is violated. This is an unimpaired debt and (because ordinarily each secured claim is a class in and of itself) an unimpaired class.

An example of the second: The debtor is obligated on a fully secured equipment loan. The loan agreement calls for equal monthly payments of $1,000, with the entire obligation accelerated (made due and payable) if there is any default. The debtor missed one payment before bankruptcy and the DIP missed one payment after bankruptcy. The loan agreement also contains an ipso facto clause that makes filing bankruptcy an act of default. Under the plan, the missed payments are made immediately and in full (including penalties and interest) and the original maturity reinstated; all future payments will be made on time and as scheduled. No other changes of any kind are made. Since the violation of the ipso facto clause does not have to be cured,[122] and all other defaults have been cured, this claim is unimpaired and its class is unimpaired.

---

[120] See § 22.04.

[121] Bankruptcy Code § 1124. This provision was changed by the 1994 Amendments; prior to the Amendments, a class of claims or interests was unimpaired if the plan provided for full payment of the value of the claims or interests.

[122] Bankruptcy Code §§ 1124(a)(2)(A), 365(b)(2).

[G]—Contents of the Plan—Generally

The hallmark of Chapter 11 is flexibility. Unlike Chapters 12 and 13, where creditor participation is minimal, Chapter 11 provides at least the opportunity for substantial creditor involvement at all stages. Given this, and given the fact that the Chapter 11 plan is supposed to be accepted by most of the creditors, the courts see rather less need to supervise its contents than in the other chapters, in which the plan is always crammed down.

[H]—Contents of the Plan—Mandatory Provisions

Section 1123(a) contains a number of mandatory provisions—things that must appear in the plan (in this regard, see § 1129 which sets out the minimum requirements for confirmation, which includes things additional to the mandatory provisions of the plan). These are sketched out in this subsection; most are discussed in more detail elsewhere. The seven required provisions are:

1. Designation of classes of claims and interests.[123] (See § 17.11[D]).

2. Specification of any unimpaired classes.[124]

3. Specification of treatment of impaired claims and interests.[125] (See § 17.11[F])

4. Equal treatment of claims and interests within a class.[126] (See § 17.11[D])

5. Provision of adequate means for the plans implementation.[127] (See § 17.11[I])

6. If the debtor is a corporation, provision for including in the debtor's charter certain provisions about equity securities.[128]

7. Any provision in the plan that deals with the manner of selection of any officer, director, or trustee must be consistent with the interests of creditors, equity security holders, and public policy.[129]

[I]—Contents of the Plan—Adequate Means for Implementation

The plan must provide adequate means for its implementation. What those means are will vary with the plan itself. In a simple plan, the means may include nothing more than necessary adjustments to debt (such as curing defaults and de-accelerating

---

[123] Bankruptcy Code § 1123(a)(1).

[124] Bankruptcy Code § 1123(a)(2).

[125] Bankruptcy Code § 1123(a)(3).

[126] Bankruptcy Code § 1123(a)(4).

[127] Bankruptcy Code § 1123(a)(5).

[128] Bankruptcy Code § 1123(a)(6).

[129] Bankruptcy Code § 1123(a)(7).

debt, reducing the amount of unsecured claims and extending the maturity of secured claims). In other cases, the reorganization will be more profound, including the partial liquidation of the debtor and the merger of the remainder with another, healthy company. A corporate debtor may also have to rewrite its charter as part of its restructuring; and many larger debtors have to issue securities to raise capital. New stock or bonds may be issued to new investors; or, in some cases, new stock may be issued in partial satisfaction of existing debt. Section 1123 gives a partial list of the types of things that may be needed to make the plan work; it includes all of the matters just mentioned.[130] The list is not intended to be exhaustive.

[J]—Contents of the Plan—Optional Provisions

As noted, flexibility is the order of the day in Chapter 11. Many plans go far beyond the requirements of the statute to include other provisions that may be of assistance to the reorganization. Section 1123(b) gives blanket authorization to this. The debtor has broad authority to include in the plan various optional provisions. The plan may:

1. Impair, or leave unimpaired, any class of secured claims, unsecured claims, or interests.[131]

2. Provide for the assumption, rejection, or assignment of any executory contract or unexpired lease of the debtor, unless it has previously been rejected.[132]

3. Provide for the settlement or adjustment of any claim or interest that belongs to the debtor or the estate; or, in the alternative, for the retention and enforcement by the debtor, the trustee (if any), or a representative of the estate of any claim or interest that belongs to the debtor or the estate.[133]

4. Provide for the sale of all or substantially all of the property of the estate, and distribution of the proceeds of the sale among holders of claims or interests;[134] and

5. Modify the rights of holders of secured and unsecured claims. There is an exception to this. The plan may not modify the rights of a holder of a claim secured only by a security interest in real property that is the

---

[130] Bankruptcy Code § 1123(a)(5).

[131] Bankruptcy Code § 1123(b)(1). See § 17.11[F] of this chapter for a discussion of impairment.

[132] Bankruptcy Code § 1123(b)(2). The assumption, rejection, or assignment of contracts and leases is discussed in Chapter 9 of this book.

[133] Bankruptcy Code § 1123(b)(3). For example, if the estate has a claim for damages against a third party, this may be compromised or otherwise dealt with in the plan.

[134] Bankruptcy Code § 1123(b)(4). This is the provision that permits a so-called "liquidation plan," under which Chapter 11 becomes a substitute for Chapter 7.

debtor's principal residence.[135] The prohibition on modifying a homestead mortgage was added in 1994 to mesh Chapter 11 with Chapter 13. The scope and effect of this prohibition is discussed more fully in Chapter 18 of this book.[136]

6. Include any other "appropriate provision not inconsistent with the applicable provisions of this title."[137]

The last of these provisions is the most important; the plan may include almost anything that does not contradict the Code or frustrate its purposes.

§ 17.12 Confirmation Requirements That Affect the Contents of the Plan

[A]—Introduction

Section 1123 does not contain all of the mandatory provisions of the plan. The plan must also be formulated with an eye to the requirements for confirmation, which, in effect, impose a number of other requirements. The key other provisions are those relating to the treatment of claims and interests. These are set out in this paragraph.

[B]—Treatment of General Unsecured Debt

[1]—Mandatory Provisions

As noted, the plan must set out all classes of unsecured debt, specify whether the class is impaired or unimpaired, state the treatment of each class under the plan, and provide for equal treatment of all claims within a class.[138] The requirements for confirmation add a further requirement: the plan must meet the best interests of creditors test.[139] This means that any creditor who does not accept the plan must "receive or retain . . . property of a value, as of the effective date of the plan, that is not less than the amount [it] would . . . receive or retain if the debtor were liquidated under Chapter 7 . . . on such date."[140] As always in bankruptcy, the creditor's entitlement is its the Chapter 7 liquidation value of its claim. Since the Chapter 11 plan normally provides for payments over a period of time, the payments

---

[135] Bankruptcy Code § 1123(b)(5). This provision was added by the 1994 Amendments.

[136] See § 18.08[B][2].

[137] Bankruptcy Code § 1123(b)(6).

[138] Bankruptcy Code § 1123(a)(1) -(4). For a fuller discussion of classification under Chapter 11, see § 17.11[D] of this chapter.

[139] Note that despite its familiar name, this test applies to both claims and interests—interests are also entitled to liquidation value. However, in virtually every case, the Chapter 7 value of an interest is zero, so the "best interest of interest holders" test is of virtually no significance.

[140] Bankruptcy Code § 1129(a)(7)(A). Note that this rule is subject to an exception if the creditor has made the 1111(b) election, discussed in § 17.12[D][4] of this chapter.

actually proposed must be reduced to present value; it is that present value of the future claims that must at least equal what the creditor would get in Chapter 7. Thus, if the liquidation value of River Bank's unsecured claim is $10,000, and the debtor proposes to pay off that claim in five $2,000 annual installments, the plan cannot be confirmed if River Bank votes against it. River Bank would indeed be receiving a nominal payout of $10,000, but it would not be receiving payments that were worth $10,000 on the effective date of the plan.

This entitlement runs to each and every creditor. Even though the plan has been accepted by the requisite majority of the class, it cannot be confirmed if there is any dissenter who is not receiving this minimum. Of course, it is extremely rare that creditors as a whole will vote for a plan that gives them less than the statutory minimum, because in that case creditors are in effect agreeing to accept less than they already have. It is thus unusual for a plan to be accepted by the requisite majority and still fail the best interest of creditors test. It is more common that a plan being "crammed down" without the approval of creditors will flunk this requirement.[141]

[2]—Optional Provisions

So long as the debtor does not resort to cramdown, and so long as the plan meets the best interest of creditor's test, the debtor may propose almost anything. The debtor's ability to classify general unsecured debt is discussed in § 17.11 [D] of this chapter; note that while the debtor must meet certain requirements if it does choose to classify, the debtor is never required to classify in the first place. What the debtor may offer to its creditors, whether in a single class or separate classes, is limited almost solely by the imagination.

[C]—Treatment of Priority Unsecured Debt

Priority claims are given favored treatment under Chapter 11. Section 1129(a)(9), which sets out the confirmation requirements for priority debt, divides the priorities into three groups. The first group consists of priority 1 (administrative claims) and priority 2 (involuntary "gap" claims). The second consists of priority 3 (wages), priority 4 (employee benefits), priority 5 (grain elevators and fish processing facilities), priority 6 (layaway deposits), and priority 7 (alimony, maintenance, support). The third group contains only those tax claims that are given priority 8. There is no special treatment at all of priority 9 (bank bailout) claims.

The first group (priorities 1 and 2) is given the most favored status in the plan. Each claim is entitled to immediate full payment—payment, in cash and in the full amount of the allowed claim, on the effective date of the plan. The only exception to this is that the holder of a claim may agree to less favorable treatment.[142] The class itself, however, cannot bind any particular claimant; the right to full immediate payment is specific to each claim. Thus, even if the statutory majority of claims in the priority 1 or priority 2 class approves a plan under which the debtor does not

---

[141] For a fuller discussion of cramdown, see § 17.15[D] of this chapter.

[142] Bankruptcy Code § 1129(a)(9)(A).

make immediate full payment to them, the court cannot confirm the plan unless the vote was unanimous. Note that this requirement can be crippling to the debtor's efforts to effectuate the plan; it must often come up with a considerable amount of up-front money to get the plan confirmed.

The second group (priorities 3 through 7) is given slightly less favored status. Each claim is entitled to payment in full. Each class is entitled to immediate payment. This means that if a class does not accept the plan, the plan must provide for payment, in cash and in the full amount of the allowed claim, on the effective date of the plan.[143] However, if a class votes to accept the plan by the requisite dual majority, the plan does not have to provide for immediate payment (although it still must provide for full payment—payments that, when reduced to present value, equal the allowed amount of each claim).[144] Note the difference—in the first group, each claimant has the right to demand immediate full payment, regardless of how the class votes. In the second group, the class may vote to accept deferred payment in full, and this vote binds dissenters. Any individual holder of a claim may agree to accept less than full payment, but this binds no one else.

The third group (tax claims, priority 8) is given still less. Each claim is entitled to full payment, but neither claims nor class is entitled to immediate payment. The payments, when reduced to present value, must equal the allowed amount of each claim as of the effective date of the plan. However, the plan may provide for payments over a period of time—this period may not be more than six years after the date the tax on which the claim is based was assessed.[145] (Note that this may be a period of considerably less than six years from the effective date of the plan). Any individual claimant may accept a different treatment; but this does not bind other creditors.

[D]—Treatment of Secured Debt

[1]—Introduction

As is true throughout bankruptcy, secured debt is given highly favored treatment in Chapter 11. Although considerable changes in the rights of secured creditors are allowed—and indeed are usually necessary—the value of the secured claim is kept largely intact throughout the proceeding and the plan period. The holder of a secured claim is thus generally in a relatively powerful position, and many plans founder on the requirement that the secured claims be paid in full.

One minor point is worth noting. In general, each secured claim is in its own class. This is partly for the sake of convenience, partly because secured claimants generally want to negotiate individual deals, and partly because it is unusual for secured claims to be sufficiently similar to warrant their inclusion in the same class.

---

[143] Bankruptcy Code § 1129(a)(9)(B)(ii).

[144] Bankruptcy Code § 1129(a)(9)(B)(i).

[145] Bankruptcy Code § 1129(a)(9)(C); see 124 Cong Rec. H11,103 (Sept. 28, 1978), S17,320 (Oct 6, 1978).

[2]—Mandatory Provisions

The key mandatory provision regarding secured claims is contained in section 1129's requirements for confirmation. Specifically, the best interest of creditors test requires that each claimant receive over the course of the plan the full liquidation value of its claim.[146] For secured claims, this effectively means that the plan payments, when reduced to present value, must at least equal the lesser of (i) the amount of the debt or (ii) the value of the collateral securing the debt.[147] For example, if the debt is undersecured, and the property securing the debt is worth $100,000, then the payments under the plan must have a present value of $100,000, which means that they will be more than $100,000. How much more depends on the length of the payout period and the estimated interest rates for that period. In effect, this means that even if the debt is undersecured, the debtor must pay interest on it.

[3]—Lien Stripping

As was discussed elsewhere, lien stripping is a controversial area of bankruptcy law; the Supreme Court has curbed it in Chapter 7.[148] By contrast, it seems clear that lien stripping is broadly permitted in Chapter 11. The 1994 Amendments imposed one restriction on lien stripping: it is no longer possible to use Chapter 11 to lien strip a homestead mortgage.[149] The only other statutory limitation is contained in section 1111(b), discussed below.

[4]—Section 1111(b) Election

As noted above in § 17.10 [C] of this chapter, undersecured creditors generally have the right to have their claims treated as non-recourse secured claims for the entire nominal amount of the debt rather than as recourse claims that are bifurcated into secured claims and unsecured claims. If a creditor is owed $5,000,000 secured by $3,000,000 worth of property, that creditor generally has the option to be treated in the "normal" way — that is, to have a secured claim for $3,000,000 and an unsecured claim for $2,000,000 — or to make the § 1111(b)(2) election and have a secured claim for $5,000,000. As noted, on the face of it, the election is very attractive and a strong protection against lien-stripping by the debtor. However, this attraction and this protection are largely illusory. Section 1129(a)(7)(B) nearly guts § 1111(b)(2). This provision sets out the mandatory treatment of an 1111(b)(2) claim. It states that each holder of an 1111(b)(2) claim must receive or retain under the plan "property of a value, as of the effective date of the plan, that is not less than the value of such holder's interest in the estate's interest in the property that secures such claim."[150] This means that the best interest of creditors test does not

---

[146] Bankruptcy Code § 1129(a)(7)(A). Any individual creditor may agree to accept less, but this virtually never happens.

[147] For a fuller discussion of this, see § 10.03[C] of this book.

[148] See § 12.01 of this book.

[149] Bankruptcy Code § 1123(b)(5) (1994 Amendments).

[150] Bankruptcy Code § 1129(a)(7)(B).

require payment of the actual value of the claim, but only payment of the actual value of the collateral. Thus, in the example given, the best interest of creditors test is met if the sum of all payments made, when reduced to present value, equals $3,000,000. This means that the creditor will actually be worse off making the 1111(b) election than not making it, assuming that any dividend is paid on the unsecured claims. If it had *not* made the election, River Bank would have been entitled to payments whose present value is $3,000,000 on the secured claim plus at least the liquidation value of the $2,000,000 unsecured claim.

The same thing is true if the plan is confirmed through cramdown under the "fair and equitable" test—the absolute priority rule.[151] Under § 1129(b)(2)(A)(i)(II), the plan meets the fair and equitable test if each holder of a secured claim receives an account of the claim "deferred cash payments totaling at least the allowed amount of such claim, of a value, as of the effective date of the plan, of at least the value of such holder's interest in the estate's interest in such property."[152] Translated to plain English, this means that the holder of an 1111(b)(2) claim is entitled to payments that equal, in nominal terms, the entire amount of the claim but in actual terms only the value of the collateral. In the example given, River Bank would be entitled to plan payments equaling $5,000,000. However, when reduced to present value, these payments would only have to equal $3,000,000. If the debtor sufficiently extends the plan so that $5,000,000 nominal dollars paid over the life of the plan is worth only $3,000,000 in present value, the debtor will have met the requirement for confirmation under the fair and equitable test but will not in fact be paying River Bank anything more than the value of its collateral. Once again, River Bank will be worse off taking the election than not taking the election, because it will receive no dividend on the $2,000,000 that would otherwise have been the amount of its unsecured claim.

This does not always mean that the § 1111(b) election is a bad idea. For example, it may not be possible for the debtor to extend the plan for such a long period of time that it will meet both the requirement of paying the nominal amount of the claim and the actual value of the collateral. The property also might be sold in the future for more than it is presently worth; and under at least some circumstances, the § 1111(b) creditor will be able to collect the full amount of its claim from the sale proceeds. However, given the plan confirmation standards, the protection provided by § 1111(b) is so uncertain that the election is seldom made.

[5]—Optional Provisions

As is true with unsecured debt, so long as the debtor does not resort to cramdown, and so long as the plan meets the best interest of creditor's test, the debtor may propose almost anything. What the debtor may offer to its secured creditors is limited almost solely by the imagination. There are practical limits, however, because of the favored treatment of secured claims; creditors are unlikely, for example, to accept a debt-equity swap for a secured claim.

---

[151] For a discussion of both cramdown and the fair and equitable test, see § 17.15[D] of this chapter.

[152] Bankruptcy Code §1129(b)(2)(A)(i)(II).

§ 17.13 Securities Laws—Exemption from Registration

In some Chapter 11 plans, the debtor issues "securities" as a means of distributing the plan proceeds. For example, the debtor might propose to issue voting stock to the holders of its unsecured claims; say, one share for every $100 of claim. This type of plan, which is essentially a debt-for-equity swap, is rare but occasionally attractive. It creates, however, some potential problems with the securities laws. The issuance of stocks, bonds, and other securities is regulated by a number of state and federal laws; among the requirements is "registration" of the security with state and federal authorities. Compliance with the registration requirement is often time-consuming and expensive; imposition of them on a Chapter 11 debtor would create yet another barrier to effective reorganization.

Moreover, at least some of these regulations may be unnecessary. Federal regulation, and much state regulation, focuses on the information that the person acquiring the security has about the issuer of the security. The main function of registration is to provide information about the stock and the issuer that helps a potential investor evaluate opportunity and risk.[153] In Chapter 11, the disclosure statement serves a similar function; and, although less detailed than the information required by the registration process, arguably includes enough information for those who already know (or could know) a good deal about the debtor, such as its existing creditors and equity holders.

Because of this, there is a broad exemption from securities laws for most debtors who are issuing plan-related securities. Assuming that the debtor is not an "underwriter,"[154] then any securities it issues that are entirely or primarily in exchange for a claim, and interest, or an administrative claim are entirely exempt from federal, state, and local laws requiring registration.[155] Note that this exemption only applies to securities exchanged for existing debt or equity; it does not apply to securities issued to raise funds to finance the plan,[156] although the narrower registration exemption in section 364(f) can be used for that purpose.[157] Note as well that the exemption only relates to the registration requirements. There are other securities laws; most notably, those that prohibit fraud in securities transactions. They continue to apply.

---

[153] For a general discussion of registration in the federal securities law context, see 1&2 Louis Loss & Joel Seligman, Securities Regulation ch. 2 (3d ed. 1989).

[154] Broadly speaking, an underwriter is a person who is distributing a security to others, rather than holding it for investment. See 2 Louis Loss & Joel Seligman, Securities Regulation 1108-1110 (3d ed. 1989).

[155] Bankruptcy Code § 1145(a)(1).

[156] Collier on Bankruptcy ¶ 1145.01[e].

[157] See § 9.08 of this book for a discussion of § 364(f).

§ 17.14 Voting on the Plan

[A]—Introduction

The intended core of Chapter 11 is the agreement of the debtor and its creditors on a plan of reorganization. That agreement is meant to be an informed one. Thus, although the Code virtually banished the Securities and Exchange Commission from the reorganization process, one of the key ideas underlying securities law was retained. The debtor, who is in control of most of the information about its financial position and prospects, must provide that information to those who are to vote on its plan. Moreover, this information must be presented in a way that will enable the voter to make a reasoned decision, and it must be provided in a timely manner. This scheme, although simpler in structure, is very much in tune with the complex disclosure laws with which issuers of publicly traded stocks and bonds must comply.

[B]—Disclosure and Solicitation

Section 1125 deals with the process of providing information to the creditors and owners of the debtor. Subsection (b) prohibits anyone from soliciting the acceptance or rejection of a plan unless it simultaneously or has previously given the person solicited both (1) a copy of the plan or a summary of the plan and (2) a written disclosure statement approved by the court.[158] It is the disclosure statement that is crucial; for it is the means by which creditors and owners are given the information they need.

The disclosure statement may be approved by the court only after there has been both notice and an opportunity for a hearing.[159] The court may approve the disclosure statement only if the court determines that it contains "adequate information;" but it may do so without a valuation of the debtor or an appraisal of the debtor's assets.[160] "Adequate information" is a term of art. It means information that is sufficient to enable a hypothetical "reasonable investor typical of holders of claims or interests of the relevant class" to make an informed judgment about the proposed plan. It should be as detailed as is practicable given the "nature and history of the debtor and the condition of the debtor's books and records." It does not have to include information about other proposed or possible plans.[161] Thus, a small proprietorship with sketchy books may have a considerably lesser burden in preparing its disclosure statement than a large, publicly-traded corporation—both because the issues are less complex and because the records are (justifiably) less complete.

Note that the adequacy of the information is not measured against some absolute standard. Rather, it is measured from the perspective of the "typical investor" who is defined as an investor who has (1) a claim or interest of the relevant class; (2)

---

[158] Bankruptcy Code § 1125(b). Note the special rules for "small business" cases in § 17.18 of this chapter.

[159] Bankruptcy Code § 1125(b).

[160] Bankruptcy Code § 1125(b).

[161] Bankruptcy Code § 1125(a)(1).

the same type of relationship with the debtor as holders of claims or interests of that class generally have, and (3) the same ability to gather information about the debtor that holders of claims or interest of that class generally have.[162] The latter two requirements make it clear that information which would be adequate for, say, an insider would not necessarily be adequate information if most persons who held claims or interests of the same class were not insiders. The debtor does not have to send the same disclosure statement to everybody. Different classes may receive different disclosure statements; however, everyone within a particular class must receive the same disclosure statement.[163]

For creditors who are hostile to the debtor's plan, the hearing on the disclosure statement is one opportunity to block the reorganization. Many of the issues that are raised at other points in the proceeding can be raised here; the adequacy of protection, feasibility, good faith, and so on. A court is much more likely to be receptive to feasibility arguments at this point, because the debtor will have had sufficient time to demonstrate whether a plan can indeed work.

[C]—Voting; Statutory Majorities

Ordinarily, confirmation of the plan requires the approval of each impaired class of creditors and equity security holders.[164] Voting is by claim, not by claimant, and by class. Normally, every allowed claim has a vote; however, if a claim is held by an entity whose vote was in bad faith, or whose vote was solicited or procured in bad faith, the vote of that claim does not count.[165] In addition, unimpaired claims do not vote; and an unimpaired class is deemed to have accepted the plan.[166] Similarly, claims on which nothing will be paid do not vote; a class of claims that receives nothing is deemed to have rejected the plan.[167]

Approval does not require a unanimous vote; rather, it requires a dual majority. The first majority is of the number of claims; a class meets this majority if more than one-half in number votes to approve.[168] The second majority is of the amount of the claims; a class meets this majority if at least two-thirds of the amount of the claims vote to approve.[169] Note that in each case the majority is measured by the number or amount claims in the class, not by the number or amount of the claims that are voted. For example, suppose that a class consists of 30 claims totalling $180,000. If 16 claims totalling $120,000 vote to approve the plan, the class has approved the plan. If fewer than 16 claims vote to approve, than the class has rejected the plan. Even if 15 claims totalling $179,999.85 voted in favor, the class would

---

[162] Bankruptcy Code § 1125(a)(2).

[163] Bankruptcy Code § 1125(c).

[164] See § 17.11[F] of this chapter for a discussion of the difference between impaired and unimpaired claims.

[165] Bankruptcy Code § 1126(c), (e).

[166] Bankruptcy Code § 1126(f).

[167] Bankruptcy Code § 1126(g).

[168] Bankruptcy Code § 1126(c).

[169] Bankruptcy Code § 1126(c).

have rejected the plan, because both majorities must be achieved. Similarly, if 29 claims totalling $119,999.99 voted in favor, the class would have rejected the plan. This dual majority has the effect of preventing a plan from either being (1) accepted by a few large creditors over the objections of many small creditors, or (2) accepted by many small creditors over the objections of a few large creditors. The latter probably has more practical significance; in many Chapter 11 cases, a single creditor has a blocking vote because it holds more than one-third of the debt in a class.

[D]—Voting; Pre-packaged Plans

As noted above,[170] a fair number of Chapter 11 proceedings are "prepackaged;" that is, the plan is negotiated before the case is actually filed. Section 1126 facilitates the pre-packaged case by obviating the need in some cases for a second disclosure or vote. If the holder of a claim or interest either accepted or rejected the plan prior to the commencement of the case, that holder is "deemed" to have accepted or rejected the plan if either:

1. The solicitation of the acceptance or rejection was in compliance with any applicable nonbankrutpcy law, rule, or regulation,[171] or

2. If there is no applicable law, rule, or regulation, the solicitation followed disclosure of "adequate information" (as that phrase is defined in Chapter 11).[172] Thus, if there is no non-bankruptcy law that regulates the acceptance or rejection process, compliance with the disclosure and solicitation rules that would be applicable under Chapter 11 is sufficient to make the pre-filing vote binding on the creditor or interest holder.

[E]—Voting; Disqualification for Bad Faith

The court has the power, upon request of a party in interest and after notice and an opportunity for a hearing, to "designate any entity whose acceptance or rejection . . . was not in good faith, or was not solicited or procured in good faith or in accordance with the provisions of this title."[173] Although not explicitly stated, this is understood to be a power to disqualify the vote cast. This provision is triggered by some form of undisclosed special treatment for the claimant or interest holder—an undisclosed bribe. Voting for or against the plan because of the benefits in the plan itself could hardly ever be improper; indeed, the whole point of the proceeding is to give creditors the opportunity to jockey for the best possible payout.[174]

---

[170] See § 17.11[A] of this chapter.

[171] Bankruptcy Code § 1126(b)(1).

[172] Bankruptcy Code § 1126(b)(2).

[173] Bankruptcy Code § 1126(e).

[174] See Collier on Bankruptcy ¶ 1126.05.

§ 17.15 Confirmation of the Plan

[A]—Introduction

Confirmation of the plan is the court action that puts the plan into effect. Confirmation may occur only after notice and an actual hearing—not merely an opportunity for a hearing.[175] The confirmation may be granted only if a number of statutory requirements are met. Section 1129 contains a list of those requirements—but note that this provision cannot be read in isolation. Other sections, especially sections 1121 through 1126, are also directly relevant.

[B]—General Requirements for Confirmation

There are 13 basic requirements for confirmation set out in section 1129; however, compliance with many of these requirements involves compliance with other statutory provisions. In this section, we review those basic requirements, sometimes cross-referencing other sections in which the requirements are studied in greater detail.

These requirements are as follows:

1. The *plan* must comply with all of the applicable provisions of the Bankruptcy Code.[176] Note that this means, among many other things, that the plan must contain all of the mandatory provisions set out in section 1123.[177]

2. The *proponent of the plan* must comply with all applicable provisions of the Bankruptcy Code.[178]

3. The plan must have been proposed in good faith and not by any means prohibited by law.[179] This encompasses violations not only of bankruptcy law but also of other applicable federal and state law.[180] It probably does not include misconduct in the process of obtaining acceptances of the plan.[181]

4. The court must have approved payments made by the proponent, the debtor, and certain other parties, if those payments are for services, costs or expenses incident to the plan or to the case.[182] This is a part of the broader issue of court control of the costs of administration, which is more fully discussed in Chapters 10 and 20 of this book.[183]

---

175 Bankruptcy Code § 1128(a).

176 Bankruptcy Code § 1129(a)(1).

177 See § 17.11[H] of this chapter for those requirements.

178 Bankruptcy Code § 1129(a)(2).

179 Bankruptcy Code § 1129(a)(3).

180 In re Koelbl, 751 F.2d 137, 139 (2d Cir. 1984).

181 Collier on Bankruptcy ¶ 1129.02.

182 Bankruptcy Code § 1129(a)(4).

183 See §§ 10.04[B] and 20.03.

5. The proponent of the plan must disclose the identity and affiliations of (i) individuals who will be directors, officers or voting trustees of the reorganized debtor, (ii) any affiliate of the debtor who is participating with the debtor in a joint plan of reorganization, and any successor to the debtor under the plan.[184] The appointment or continuation of an individual as director, officer, or voting trustee must be consistent with the interests of (i) creditors, (ii) equity security holders and (iii) public policy.[185] In addition, the proponent of the plan must disclose the identity of any insider who will be retained or employed by the reorganized debtor, and the nature of the insider's compensation.[186]

6. If, after confirmation, the debtor will be (or will still be) in an industry whose rates are regulated by the government, and if the plan provides for a change in the debtor's rates, then either the debtor's regulating agency must have already approved the rate change, or the rate change is expressly conditioned upon the debtor obtaining the required approval.[187] An electric utility company is a good example of the type of debtor who must comply with this provision.

7. The "best interest of creditors" test must be met.[188] Under this test, each holder of a claim or interest is entitled to receive, under the plan, payments that, when reduced to present value, equal at least the Chapter 7 liquidation value of the claim or interest. The test is discussed in full in § 17.12 [D] (with regard to secured claims) and § 17.12[B] (with regard to unsecured claims). This provision also imposes requirements for those (rare) secured creditors who have made the "1111(b)" election to have their claims treated as non-recourse. The ins and outs of the 1111(b) election, and its effect on both the electing creditor and the debtor, are fully discussed in §§ 17.10[C] and 17.12[D][4].

8. Each class of claims or interests must either (i) accept the plan by the required statutory majority or (ii) be unimpaired under the plan.[189] CAUTION: although this is listed as a mandatory provision, it is not in fact mandatory. A plan can be confirmed even if this condition is not met—indeed, a good many plans are confirmed even though this condition was not met. Confirmation without sufficient creditor approval—Cramdown—is discussed in detail in § 17.15 of this chapter.

---

[184] Bankruptcy Code § 1129(a)(5)(A)(i).

[185] Bankruptcy Code § 1129(a)(5)(A)(ii).

[186] Bankruptcy Code § 1129(a)(5)(B).

[187] Bankruptcy Code § 1129(a)(6).

[188] Bankruptcy Code § 1129(a)(7). Note that the phrase "best interest of creditors test" does not appear in the Code; it comes from the Bankruptcy Act and is still widely used.

[189] Bankruptcy Code § 1129(a)(8). For the required majority in each class, see § 17.14[C] of this chapter.

9. Priority claims must generally be provided with full payment under the plan; some priority claims must be provided with full payment on the effective date of the plan.[190] This requirement is detailed in § 17.12[C] of this chapter.

10. If there are any impaired classes, at least one impaired class must accept the plan. In determining whether that class has accepted the plan, the approvals of insiders are not counted.[191] Thus, if the only class that accepted the plan has four creditors, and two of them are insiders, this requirement is not met, since more than half of the creditors must vote "yes" and the "yes" votes of the insiders do not count. Acceptance by at least one class, unlike acceptance by all classes, is mandatory. This rule is an important part of cramdown—see § 17.15[D][2] of this chapter.

11. The plan must be "feasible"—that is, there must be a realistic chance that it will work.[192] Feasibility is discussed further in § 17.15[C] of this chapter.

12. All required bankruptcy fees must either have been paid or are to be paid on the effective date of the plan.[193]

13. The plan must provide for the continuation of the retirement benefits (if any) established under the rules of section 1114.[194]

[C]—Feasibility

The court is not to confirm the plan unless it is "feasible"—more precisely, the court is not to confirm the plan unless the plan is not likely to be followed by the liquidation of the debtor or its successor, or even the need for further reorganization.[195] The only exception to this is found in the plan itself; if the plan calls for liquidation or a post-confirmation round of further reorganization, then that does not preclude confirmation.[196] The goal of this limitation is to curb repeated proceedings; the debtor is ordinarily expected to solve its financial problems once and for all. Given the high failure rate of confirmed plans, it is difficult to be entirely sanguine about the effectiveness of the feasibility requirement in weeding out no-hopers. Moreover, if the statutory majorities of creditors have voted for the plan, it is perhaps only rarely appropriate for the judge to second guess them on its prospects.

---

[190] Bankruptcy Code § 1129(a)(9).

[191] Bankruptcy Code § 1129(a)(10).

[192] Bankruptcy Code § 1129(a)(11).

[193] Bankruptcy Code § 1129(a)(12).

[194] Bankruptcy Code § 1129(a)(13).

[195] Bankruptcy Code § 1129(a)(11).

[196] Bankruptcy Code § 1129(a)(11).

[D]—Cramdown

[1]—Introduction

Ideally, a Chapter 11 plan will be approved by the requisite dual majority of creditors in each class. This is ideal in two senses: it facilitates confirmation and it reflects the considered opinion of those most interested in the case that the plan is reasonable and has fair prospects for success. Moreover, from the standpoint of equity holders, a creditor-approved plan may give even them some stake in the reorganized entity.

Sometimes this ideal is not achieved. One or more of the classes may vote the plan down. This does not entirely prevent the plan from being confirmed. The debtor may still seek confirmation. This type of confirmation—confirmation against the will of creditors—is known colorfully as cramdown (as in cram down their throats). This is codified in section 1129(b)(1), which states, in part:

> [I]f all of the applicable requirements of subsection (a) of this section other than paragraph (8) [acceptance by all classes] are met with respect to a plan, the court, on request of the proponent of the plan, shall confirm the plan notwithstanding the requirements of such paragraph if the plan does not discriminate unfairly, and is fair and equitable, with respect to each class of claims or interests that is impaired under, and has not accepted, the plan.[197]

The fact that Chapter 11 ever allows cramdown is controversial. Cramdown, to say the least, is in tension with the basic paradigm of Chapter 11: the composition. Composition requires all creditors; the "ordinary" Chapter 11 confirmation requires most creditors; cramdown requires hardly any creditors. It is at least theoretically possible to cram down a plan even though only one creditor votes "yes" and thousands vote "no."

The only rationale for this is that Chapter 11 evidences not only a goal of promoting debtor-creditor agreement but also a goal of obtaining reorganization. Cramdown deals with the situation in which those goals diverge. The creditors do not want the debtor to reorganize, or at least not on the terms proposed. This puts the two goals in conflict. Broadly speaking, the Code places the goal of obtaining reorganization above the goal of obtaining consensus. There is, however, a significant drawback to cramdown that make it unattractive to many debtors: the absolute priority rule.

[2]—Single Class Acceptance

One limitation on cramdown was added by BAFJA in 1984. No matter what, if there are any impaired claims,[198] at least one class of impaired claims must accept

---

[197] Bankruptcy Code § 1129(b)(1).

[198] Technically, the Code states that the minimum acceptance rule applies if there are any impaired classes of claims; but since impaired and unimpaired claims may not be put in the same class (they would not be substantially similiar), if there are any impaired claims there must be at least one impaired class of claims.

the plan.[199] It is thus not possible for a plan to be cramed down if every creditor votes "no." Moreover, in determining whether the necessary class has given its approval, the "yes" votes of insiders do not count.[200] This prevents the plan from in effect being approved by the existing owners over the dissent of all other claimants.

The requirement that one class accept has been one of the barriers to confirmation in a single-asset proceeding. In those proceedings, there is usually only one significant creditor, a financial institution that wants to shut the debtor down. Single-asset debtors have tried to work around this requirement by cobbling together a class of small claims that are technically impaired, but to so slight a degree that they are virtually certain to vote "yes" on the plan. Courts have generally looked with disfavor on this type of gerrymandering. (For a fuller discussion of single-asset cases, see Chapter 22.[201])

[3]—Absolute Priority Rule

The great disincentive to cramdown is the so-called absolute priority rule. The provision that permits cramdown, section 1129(b), also states that, if cramdown occurs, the plan must meet additional tests not imposed for ordinary confirmation. Specifically, the plan must "not discriminate unfairly" and must be "fair and equitable, with respect to each class of claims or interests that is impaired under, and has not accepted the plan."[202] It is the latter requirement that is of primary significance.

The phrase "fair and equitable" long predates the Code. Broadly speaking, it means that the plan must follow absolute, rather than relative priorities. As introduced in Chapter 10, the absolute priorities under the Bankruptcy Code range downward from secured debt through unsecured debt to equity; the residual rights of the owners are on the bottom. In a Chapter 7, this list is followed strictly; each rank is paid in full before the next rank is paid anything; when the money runs out, the last rank for which there is any money is paid pro rata. Chapter 11 usually permits the debtor to follow relative priority—each rank is entitled to its liquidation value, but the surplus realized through the reorganization's capture of going concern value may be distributed in almost any manner to which the debtor and creditors agree. In the absence of that agreement, however, the Code reimposes strict rank ordering. To put it another way, Chapter 11 permits relative priority in the distribution of the plan payments only if enough of the creditors are satisfied with that form of distribution; the debtor cannot impose relative priority on them.

Most importantly, the fair and equitable rule can make it virtually impossible for the owners to participate in the reorganized entity. Equity comes last. Only in the rarest Chapter 11 are all debts paid, and under absolute priority only if all debts are

---

[199] Bankruptcy Code § 1129(a)(10).

[200] Bankruptcy Code § 1129(a)(10). For the definition of insider, see Bankruptcy Code § 101(31).

[201] See § 22.04.

[202] Bankruptcy Code § 1129(b)(1).

paid may equity receive anything. Thus, it is very hard for the existing owners to retain any portion of the residual value of the company. Much, if not most, of the litigation over the absolute priority rule derives from owners' efforts to circumvent this problem.

Despite (or perhaps because of) its long antecedents, the drafters of the Code provided a detailed definition of "fair and equitable." Although the definition deals with secured claims, unsecured claims, and interests, only the first two parts are of much significance, because there is rarely any distribution to equity at all.[203] As regards each class of secured claims (remember that each secured claim is likely to be its own class), the plan must provide one of the three following alternatives:

1. *Retention of Lien and Full Payment.* Under this alternative, the creditor (A) retains the lien securing the claim (to the extent of the allowed amount of the claim), and (B) receives payments that when reduced to present value as of the effective date of the plan equal at least the value of the creditor's interest in the estate's interest in the property.[204] For example, suppose that River Bank holds a secured claim for $100,000; its collateral is $100,000 worth of real estate. The plan is fair and equitable as to River Bank if it keeps its mortgage and is given payments that, when discounted to present value, equal at least $100,000,

2. *Sale of Property and Attachment of Lien to Proceeds.* The second alternative permits the debtor, under the plan, to sell encumbered property. The plan is still fair and equitable as to the lienholder if the lien attaches to the proceeds of the sale, and the replacement lien is given the treatment provided for in the proceeding paragraph (retention and full payment) or the next paragraph (indubitable equivalent).[205]

3. *Indubitable Equivalent.* The third alternative is open ended; the plan will be fair and equitable as to a secured claim if it provides that the creditor receive the "indubitable equivalent" of its claim.[206] Indubitable equivalent is familiar to us from the rules on adequate protection.[207]

As a rule, there are relatively few problems meeting the absolute priority test with regard to secured debt, because the requirements are functionally almost identical to those that already apply under the best interest of creditors test; secured creditors

---

[203] Note, however, that the basic pattern applies to equity—preferred stock comes ahead of common stock. Bankruptcy Code § 1129(b)(2)(C).

[204] Bankruptcy Code § 1129(B)(2)(A)(i). Note the statute also requires that the payments must equal at least the allowed amount of the claim; but this is virtually redundant to the provision that the payments must have a value at least equal to that of the holder's interest of the estate's interest, because the latter is the allowed amount of the claim. See § 10.03 of this book.

[205] Bankruptcy Code § 1129(b)(2)(A)(ii).

[206] Bankruptcy Code § 1129(b)(2)(A)(iii).

[207] See § 8.06[B][2] of this book.

are entitled to the value of their property. The real problem arises with the treatment of unsecured claims. To be fair and equitable, the plan must either:

1. Provide that each holder of a claim receive or retain property with a value, as of the effective date of the plan, equal to the allowed amount of the claim, or

2. Provide that no holder of any junior claim or interest receive or retain any property under the plan on account of that claim or interest.[208]

For example, suppose that the general unsecured claims total $140,000. The plan must provide for payments that, discounted to present value, equal $140,000 or there must be no distribution to or retention of rights by equity holders. In its simplest terms, unless creditors are paid, the existing owners cannot continue to own the debtor based on their pre-bankruptcy ownership rights.

Note that the fair and equitable test may apply to only some classes. Only dissenting, impaired classes are entitled to absolute priority. Thus, it may still be possible for owners to retain rights in spite of the initial rejection of the plan by a class of creditors; if the plan can be modified to provide that class with full payment (and thus make it unimpaired), and the other classes do not change their votes from positive to negative, cramdown and the absolute priority rule can be avoided.

[4]—New Value Exception to the Absolute Priority Rule

As noted, much cramdown litigation relates to the owners' efforts to retain a stake in the company despite the fair and equitable requirement. In recent years, there has been a great deal of discussion about, and litigation over, the so-called "new value" exception to the absolute priority rule. In essence, this exception permits existing owners to participate in the ownership of the reorganized debtor, without the permission of the creditors, if the owners put "new value" into the debtor. For example, suppose that the plan calls for an infusion of $250,000 cash from the existing owners, in exchange for which they will own the post-reorganization company. If the creditors agree by the requisite statutory majorities, and the other requirements for confirmation are met, there is no problem with this proposal. However, if there is a dissenting class of creditors, and the plan can only be confirmed through cramdown, the question arises: does this proposal violate the absolute priority rule?

There is a great deal of confusion over this issue; indeed it is not even clear that the new value exception should be treated as an exception. In the view of some commentators, the infusion of new value is simply the purchase of the equity in the property. It is not an exception to anything; it is simply an offer to purchase the residual value of the debtor. As such, the focus of the court should simply be on the adequacy of the offer.

The exception, if that is what it is, predates the Code. In a number of Chapter X cases under the old Act, courts held that, despite the applicability of the fair and

[208] Bankruptcy Code § 1129(b)(2)(B).

equitable (absolute priority) test to Chapter X confirmation, the existing owners could keep an equity stake in the company if they made a necessary contribution of new value that was "money or money's worth, reasonably equivalent in view of all the circumstances, to the participation [in the plan's distribution] of the stockholder."[209] One of the uncertainties today is whether that old law still applies. In the view of some, the new value exception did not survive the adoption of the Code; others disagree. Although the issue divides both district and circuit courts, the Supreme Court has not yet resolved it.[210] In a particularly odd sequence of events, the Fifth Circuit first issued an opinion in which it held that the new value exception no longer existed—then withdrew that opinion and issued nearly the same opinion, except that it left out the discussion of the new value exception entirely.[211]

Although the Supreme Court has not directly ruled on the exception, it has dropped a tantalizing hint. It has said that, assuming the exception does apply, it requires a contribution of actual, valuable property. A promise by the owner to provide labor for the new entity (colorfully known as "sweat" equity) is insufficient to permit him to remain an owner of that entity in a cramdown case.[212] The Court in its opinion was careful not to accept or reject the basic notion of the new value exception.

If one assumes that the exception still exists, or that it is not an exception at all but merely a sale of residual value, an important issue remains. The sale of future ownership to existing owners carries with it the same risks that are involved in any insider transaction, such as insider trading of stocks and bonds. The present owners have access to information that may not be available to outsiders; worse still, they have the opportunity to change that information. In a worst case scenario, the owners might manipulate the books to make the company look worse off than it is, and thus to make their offer to purchase look better than it is. Moreover, that manipulation of information might discourage other bidders. The net result would be that the owners would be able to pick up the residual value for far less than it is worth. In addition, insiders who saw an opportunity to purchase valuable equity on the cheap would either fail to seek other potential buyers or would mislead those other buyers.[213]

On the other hand, this is not an insoluble problem. Even in the context of securities law, much insider trading is perfectly legal. More importantly, the risks

---

[209] Case v. Los Angeles Lumber Products Co., 308 U.S. 106, 122 (1939).

[210] See generally, Collier on Bankruptcy ¶ 1129.03 [i]. The Supreme Court recently took great pains to avoid addressing the new value exception — see U.S. Bancorp Mortgage Co. v. Bonner Mall Partnership, 115 S.Ct. 386 (1994).

[211] Phoenix Mutual Life Insurance Co. v. Greystone III Joint Venture (In re Greystone III Joint Venture), 948 F.2d 134 (1991), rehearing en banc denied, vacated, 948 F.2d 142 (1992), cert denied, 113 S.Ct. 72 (1992).

[212] Norwest Bank Worthington v. Ahlers, 485 U.S. 197 (1988). Remember, however, that if the creditors agree to accept sweat equity in return for the owner's participation in the reorganized entity, they may do so; the point of this case is that the owner may not force creditors to accept sweat equity.

[213] For a discussion of this issue from a somewhat different perspective, see Elizabeth Warren, *A Theory of Absolute Priority*, 1991 Ann. Surv. Am. L. Issue 1, 9.

underlying insider trading are considerably less in bankruptcy. The debtor's books and records are open for inspection. The debtor's managers may be interrogated under oath. The bankruptcy court should be able to determine the adequacy of the offer with a reasonable degree of certainty. There may thus be little need for a prophylactic prohibition on purchase of the equity by insiders.

There is a nagging question in all this. The issue arises because the creditors have rejected the plan. If the offer to purchase the equity by the existing owners is in fact an adequate one (and at least as good as any other likely offer) why are creditors opposed? There are possible reasons apart from concerns about the owners' offer. The most obvious is that creditors—or at least a class of creditors, since it takes only one dissenting class to trigger the problem—are unhappy with the distribution they are being offered. That distribution may be unsatisfactory, not because the price offered by the owners' is inadequate, but rather because too much is being distributed to other classes. In addition, there may also be such a breakdown of the business relationship between the debtor and creditors that nothing offered by the debtor would ever be enough. This may be the case in those bankruptcies in which the new value exception is most likely to be argued—single asset cases.

As perhaps suggested by the foregoing, I consider the best-reasoned approach to this problem is to treat the matter as a proposed purchase of the equity. Since the proposal comes from insiders, there is reason for the court to scrutinize it with special care, to be sure that information has not been manipulated and that the insiders have taken reasonable measures to market the equity to other possible purchasers. However, it seems foolish, even from the standpoint of creditors, to impose a total prohibition on purchase by those who in many cases will be the only potential purchasers. Whether this approach is within the present wording of the Bankruptcy Code, however, is a different question. There is little in the text to support the new value exception; thus, whether it is good policy or bad, it is possible that the Supreme Court will rule that it is not an available option.

§ 17.16 Modification

[A]—Introduction

Many Chapter 11 plans prove either unacceptable to creditors or, after it is confirmed but while it is ongoing, too ambitious. In the former case, the debtor may seek to modify it prior to the confirmation hearing. In the latter, the debtor must seek post-confirmation modification.

[B]—Pre-Confirmation

Prior to confirmation, the proponent of the plan may modify it at any time. The modification must comply with all of the requirements of sections 1122 and 1123. Once the modification is filed with the court, the modified plan becomes "the plan."[214] The proponent of the modification must comply with the disclosure and

[214] Bankruptcy Code § 1127(a).

solicitation requirements of section 1125.[215] Any holder of a claim or interest that has previously accepted or rejected a plan is deemed to have accepted or rejected the modified plan unless it changes its vote.[216]

[C]—Post-Confirmation

Post confirmation, a proposal to modify the plan may be made by either the proponent of the plan or by the reorganized debtor. The proposal must be made before the substantial consummation of the plan. The modified plan must comply with all of the requirements of sections 1122 and 1123. The plan becomes the plan only if circumstances warrant modification, and only if the court, after notice and an opportunity for a hearing, confirms the plan.[217] The proponent of the modified plan must comply with the disclosure and solicitation requirements of section 1125.[218] Any holder of a claim or interest that has previously accepted or rejected a plan is deemed to have accepted or rejected the modified plan unless it changes its vote.[219]

§ 17.17 Post-Confirmation Matters

[A]—Effect of Confirmation.

With very limited exceptions, the confirmation of the plan binds the debtor, its creditors, and its owners to the terms of the plan.[220] This is true whether or not the creditor or owner accepted the plan; this is the single greatest difference between the Chapter 11 plan and the common law composition. In addition, unless otherwise provided, confirmation re-vests the property of the estate in the debtor.[221] In effect, confirmation re-establishes the original entity and extinguishes the bankruptcy entity.

At least as important is the fact that confirmation is the point at which the discharge is granted.[222] In this respect, Chapter 11 differs from Chapters 12 and 13, under which discharge is normally granted when the plan is completed.[223] With limited exceptions, all of the claims and interests that existed prior to confirmation cease to exist,[224] and are replaced by the claims and interests created in the plan.

---

[215] Bankruptcy Code § 1127(c). For a discussion of the solicitation and disclosure requirements, see § 17.14[B] of this chapter.

[216] Bankruptcy Code § 1127(d).

[217] Bankruptcy Code § 1127(b).

[218] Bankruptcy Code § 1127(c). For a discussion of the solicitation and disclosure requirements, see § 17.14[B] of this chapter.

[219] Bankruptcy Code § 1127(d).

[220] Bankruptcy Code § 1141(a).

[221] Bankruptcy Code § 1141(b).

[222] Bankruptcy Code § 1141(d).

[223] See §§ 12.07 and 12.05 of this book, respectively.

[224] Bankruptcy Code § 1141(d)(1)(A), (B). Note that claims are extinguished whether or not the a proof of claim was filed or deemed filed; whether or not it was allowed; and whether

This is the Chapter 11 debtor's fresh start: a new debt and equity structure. Chapter 12 discusses more fully the effects of discharge.[225]

There are as noted limited exceptions to this fresh start. The individual Chapter 11 debtor, unlike the successful Chapter 13 debtor, is subject to the full list of non-dischargeable debts in section 523;[226] thus, the confirmation of a plan does not discharge an individual from those debts.[227] Moreover, a liquidating debtor who would be denied discharge in Chapter 7 is not entitled to any discharge.[228] The non-discharge rules are discussed more fully in Chapter 12.[229]

[B]—Revocation of Confirmation

As is true in the other reorganization chapters, an order confirming the plan may be revoked only in very limited circumstances. On request of a party in interest, made within 180 days of the entry of the confirmation order, the court, after notice and an opportunity for a hearing, may revoke the order "if and *only if*" it was procured by fraud.[230] The order revoking confirmation must contain provisions to protect any entity that acquired rights in good faith reliance on the confirmation.[231] It must also revoke the debtor's discharge.[232] The very limited time period, and the fact that fraud is the only basis for revocation, are imposed because the need for finality in the proceeding is so great. The debtor must be able to resume its normal business and financial affairs; those with whom it is dealing must have assurance that their transactions are valid.

[C]—Implementation of the Plan

Chapter 11 differs from Chapters 12 and 13 in that the implementation of the plan is largely in the hands of the debtor itself. Although the court retains the power to issue necessary orders for implementation,[233] it is the debtor (and any entity organized for the purpose of carrying out the plan) that is to carry out the plan.[234] Thus, for example, the plan payments come directly from the debtor (or in some cases, from a separate trust or similar entity created by the plan to service the plan payments). By contrast, in Chapters 12 and 13, the debtor makes payments to the standing trustee who distributes them to the creditors.[235]

---

or not the claimant voted to accept the plan. Bankruptcy Code § 1141(d)(1)(A). By contrast, interests are terminated only if the rights of holders of those interests are provided for by the plan. Bankruptcy Code § 1141(d)(1)(B).

[225] See § 12.06.

[226] For a discussion of the non-dischargeable debts, see § 12.03 of this book.

[227] Bankruptcy Code § 1141(d)(2).

[228] Bankruptcy Code § 1141(d)(3).

[229] See § 12.02[C].

[230] Bankruptcy Code § 1144 (emphasis added).

[231] Bankruptcy Code § 1144(1).

[232] Bankruptcy Code § 1144(2).

[233] Bankruptcy Code § 1142(b).

[234] Bankruptcy Code § 1142(a).

[235] See §§ 19.08 and 18.08[F] of this book, respectively.

§ 17.18 Small Business Chapter 11

Chapter 11 has been of little benefit to small businesses, largely because of its relatively elaborate procedures and consequent high costs. It was because of this that Congress, when it enacted the original Bankruptcy Reform Act in 1978, allowed small proprietorships to reorganize under Chapter 13. It also led to the enactment, in 1986, of Chapter 12 for family farmers. Pressure has been mounting for several years to enact a new small business reorganization Chapter. So far, this pressure has been largely resisted. However, in the 1994 Amendments, a few provisions were added to Chapter 11 to deal with small business.

The term "small business" is given a very restricted definition. Generally, it encompasses any person engaged in personal or business activities whose aggregate, non-contingent liquidated debts (both secured and unsecured) do not exceed $2,000,000 on the date of the petition.[236] However, it excludes any person whose primary activity is the business of owning or operating real estate.[237]

The procedures for a small business case are somewhat simpler than for other cases. A Creditors' Committee is not required; more precisely, on request of a party in interest and "for cause" the court may order that a Creditors' Committee not be appointed.[238] Two other simplifying provisions are optional; they apply only if the debtor is a small business and elects to be covered by these provisions.

The first of these optional provisions relates to the period for filing a plan. Under this provision, the exclusivity period (during which only the debtor may file a plan) is 100 days after the date of the order for relief; moreover, all plans must be filed within 160 days. These time periods may be changed on request of the party in interest, and after notice and an opportunity for hearing. Either time period may be reduced "for cause" and the debtor's exclusivity period may be increased if the debtor shows that the need for the increase "is caused by circumstances for which the debtor should not be held accountable."[239] Since there is no provision for extending the 160-day deadline, it appears that in any event the plan must be filed within that time period.

The other optional provision deals with the disclosure statement. If the debtor is a small business and has elected to be treated as a small business, the court may additionally approve a disclosure statement ex parte. This conditional approval is subject to final approval after notice and an opportunity for a hearing. Acceptance or rejection of the plan may be solicited based on the conditionally approved disclosure statement, if the debtor provides adequate information. Finally, the hearing on the disclosure statement may be combined with the hearing on confirmation.[240] This at least reduces the number of major hearings by one.

---

[236] Bankrupcty Code § 101(51C) (1994 Amendments).

[237] Id.

[238] Bankruptcy Code § 1102(a)(3).

[239] Bankruptcy Code § 1121(e).

[240] Bankruptcy Code § 1125(f).

Whether these minor changes will be found satisfactory is unclear. It is unlikely that creditors will regret the loss of the Creditors' Committee, since few ever bother to serve on the committee in a small case. Likewise, creditors are likely to applaud the 160-day cap on the filing of a plan. The compression of the approval process, and the combination of the hearing on the disclosure statement with the hearing on confirmation is also unlikely to cause objections; just as creditors do not want to undertake the expense of serving on the Creditors' Committee in small cases, so too they are not likely to miss the expense of two hearings. On the other hand, it remains to be seen whether debtors will elect to use the simplified procedures. Many debtors do not want to have a shortened deadline for the plan. An exclusivity period that may be as short as 100 days, and a total period for filing that apparently cannot exceed 160 days, may be unattractive to those debtors who are filing Chapter 11 precisely to gain an extended respite from the demands of their creditors.

§ 17.19 Railroad Reorganization

Subchapter IV of Chapter 11, which deals with railroad reorganizations, sets out rules for a narrow bankruptcy specialty which merits special treatment if for no other reason that it was the need to find a way to deal with defunct railways that led American bankruptcy law into the reorganization field. This section is only a sketch of the issues involved. However, it illustrates an approach to reorganization that is rather different from the rest of Chapter 11. Railroad reorganizations have many distinct features. This section only highlights a few of the most notable.

First, there is always a trustee. As soon as practical after the order for relief, the United States Secretary of Transportation submits a list of five qualified, disinterested persons who are willing to serve as the trustee. The United States Trustee appoints the case trustee from this list.[241]

Second, the regulatory structures remain largely in place. The Interstate Commerce Commission, the United States Department of Transportation, and state railroad regulatory bodies play the role that the SEC plays in other Chapter 11 proceedings. Like the SEC, these bodies may appear and be heard on any issue, but may not appeal.[242] Moreover, broadly speaking, federal, state, and local regulations that are applicable to railroads continue in force during the bankruptcy; and, with limited exceptions, the trustee is subject to the orders of any regulatory body.[243]

Third, there is a greater emphasis on "public interest" in railroad cases. Both the court and the trustee are explicitly required, when applying some (but not all) of the key provisions of Subchapter IV, to consider the public interest in addition to the interests of the debtor, creditors, and equity security holders.[244] At a minimum, this means that the ability of the public to have access to railroad transportation is

---

[241] Bankruptcy Code § 1163.

[242] Bankruptcy Code § 1164.

[243] Bankruptcy Code § 1166.

[244] Bankruptcy Code § 1165.

to be weighed along with the more conventional interests of the stakeholders in the railroad.[245]

Finally, there is an absolute time limit on the pendency period. If a plan has not been confirmed within five years after the date of the order for relief, the court "shall" order the trustee to cease operations and liquidate the estate.[246] The case is not converted to Chapter 7, however; the liquidation proceeds under Chapter 11, subchapter IV, but the liquidation is done "in the same manner *as if* the case were a case under Chapter 7 of this title."[247] This provision, which has been called "the most significant and radical section of subchapter IV,"[248] is designed to avoid interminable proceedings.

The rights of unions are also treated differently and more favorably in a railroad reorganization. Collective bargaining agreements are protected by section 1167. That provision states that neither the court nor the trustee may change the wages or working conditions of employees under a collective bargaining agreement that is subject to the Railway Labor Act except as provided in that act.[249] The provisions of section 1113, which deal with other collective bargaining agreements in Chapter 11, do not apply in a subchapter IV proceeding.[250] The Railway Labor Act requires much more elaborate procedures, and considerable government involvement, including the power to order cooling off periods.[251]

---

245 Note, however, that the court is not required to consider the public interest in all important matters; for example, it need not do so when making decisions under Bankuptcy Code § 363 (use, sale, and lease of property) or Bankruptcy Code § 364 (obtaining credit), even though these are among the most important decisions made. See Collier on Bankruptcy ¶ 1165.02.

246 Bankruptcy Code § 1174.

247 Bankruptcy Code § 1174 (emphasis added).

248 Collier on Bankruptcy ¶ 1174.01.

249 Bankruptcy Code § 1167.

250 Bankruptcy Code § 1113(a).

251 See generally, Railway Labor Act, 45 U.S.C. § 151 et. seq.

CHAPTER 18

Reorganization Under Chapter 13

§ 18.01 Introduction

Chapter 13 is the lineal descendent of Chapter XIII, the Bankruptcy Act's "Wage Earner Plan," which gave individuals an opportunity to obtain the advantages of reorganization bankruptcy. When drafting the Bankruptcy Code, Congress decided to broaden the old chapter and make it more attractive, in hopes that more debtors would use it, rather than Chapter 7, and thereby provide a greater recovery for creditors.

Congress broadened the chapter by making it available to persons other than wage earners. All this is required is that the debtor have a "regular income."[1] This requirement, discussed in more detail in § 6.02[B] of this book, means only that the debtor must have some source of income that is sufficiently regular to make it possible to fund a plan.[2]

Congress also simplified the structure of Chapter 13 reorganization. Old Chapter XIII had many of the same provisions for creditor participation that appear in Chapter 11.[3] These provisions were both burdensome to the debtor and in large measure irrelevant. Empirical evidence demonstrated that creditors had little interest in Chapter XIII proceedings and rarely took advantage of the procedural protections they were given.[4] Chapter 13 virtually eliminates those protections; it operates almost solely on the basis of cramdown. If the debtor's plan meets certain specified criteria, it will be confirmed; in most cases, this occurs without creditor action or input.

Chapter 13 debtors obtain advantages not available to Chapter 7 debtors. The most obvious is intrinsic to the nature of reorganization proceedings—the Chapter 13 debtor has a greater opportunity to retain its present assets by paying out their value from future income. In addition, the Chapter 13 debtor is usually given a broader discharge than the Chapter 7 debtor. This is explored more fully in Chapter 12.[5]

---

[1] Bankruptcy Code § 109(e).

[2] "[I]ndividual with regular income" means individual whose income is sufficiently stable and regular to enable such individual to make payments under a plan under chapter 13 of this title . . ." Bankruptcy Code § 101(30).

[3] Although there was no creditors' committee, there was a creditors' meeting and, more importantly, creditors did vote on the plan. Bankruptcy Act §§ 632, 633, 652, 653, 11 U.S.C. §§ 1032, 1033, 1052, 1053 (1976) (repealed 1979).

[4] See Marjorie Girth, *The Bankruptcy Reform Process: Maximizing Judicial Control in Wage Earners' Plans,* 11 U. Mich. J. L. Ref. 51 (1977) (creditors were almost entirely passive in Chapter XIII proceedings, treating it as a "low cost collection service").

[5] See § 12.05 of this book.

Finally, there is an additional automatic stay of actions against individual co-obligors on consumer debts; this is discussed in § 8.04 of this book.

Although both the number of Chapter 13 proceedings and the percentage of bankruptcy proceedings that were filed under Chapter 13 rose sharply after the effective date of the Code, Congress remained unsatisfied. Much of the debate over BAFJA was a debate over whether Chapter 13 should become mandatory for a substantial number of consumer debtors. Proposals that it should be were rejected, mainly because of a perception that mandatory consumer reorganization is impractical.[6] However, Congress did adopt several measures designed to further encourage the use of Chapter 13. Section 707(b), discussed in Chapter 16,[7] enables the court to dismiss abusive consumer Chapter 7 filings, and thus may push some debtors into Chapter 13. In addition, lawyers were required to certify that they had informed consumer debtors of the availability of Chapter 13.[8] The consumer debtor is similarly required to certify that he or she has been informed of that Chapter.[9]

Whether these additional provisions were either necessary or useful is less than clear; and to some degree they were counterbalanced by BAFJA's requirement that the debtor use three years' disposable income to fund the plan.[10] The number of Chapter 13 filings has risen sharply since BAFJA; but then, so has the total number of bankruptcies. The percentage of filings under Chapter 13 has been broadly stable, at about one-quarter of all filings.[11] This suggests that BAFJA, unlike the Code, has had little or no impact on the consumer debtor's choice between Chapter 7 and Chapter 13.

There are concerns that Chapter 13 is overused. Chapter 13 is in general more burdensome on the debtor and the debtor's family than is Chapter 7. And, while successful completion of a Chapter 13 carries with it considerable benefits, there is no guarantee that the plan will be successful. The non-completion rate is very high.[12] In part, this may be due to excessive optimism on the part of debtors; there

---

[6] There were also concerns that mandatory reorganization would unduly burden personal autonomy; indeed, it was argued that involuntary Chapter 13 proceedings could not operated without the imposition of involuntary servitude on the debtor. See H. R. Rep. No 595, 95th Cong., 1st Sess. 321 (1977).

[7] See § 16.03[B].

[8] This requirement is embodied in a statement included in Official Form 1, the voluntary petition.

[9] This statement is also included in Official Form 1.

[10] See § 18.08[A][2] of this chapter for a discussion of the disposable income requirement, which arguably raised the cost of Chapter 13 discharge.

[11] In the year ending June 30, 1986, the last year before BAFJA, there were 120,726 Chapter 13 cases filed; this was 25.26% of the 477,856 bankruptcies filed. In the year ending June 30, 1988, the first full year under BAFJA, there were 148,771 Chapter 13 filings, 25.02% of the 594,567 bankruptcy filings. In bankruptcy's peak fiscal year (so far), which ended June 30, 1992, the 267,121 Chapter 13 cases were 27.47% of the 972,490 total cases. Statistical Abstract of the United States table 865 (1993).

[12] For a particularly thorough discussion of the Chapter 13 failure rate, see Jean Braucher, *Lawyers and Consumer Bankruptcy: One Code, Many Cultures,* 67 Am. Bankr. L. J. 501

is a persistent impression that many debtors greatly overestimate their ability to pay. Of perhaps greater concern is the possibility, raised by some critics of Chapter 13 practice, that at least some lawyers may be advising their clients to file Chapter 13 for reasons unrelated to the clients' best interests. Some lawyers may be responding to the pressures of local legal culture—or, worse still, to a desire for the higher fees generated by Chapter 13 cases—rather than a sober appraisal of the client's financial ability and needs.[13] To the extent this is true, it raises a very serious question of professional responsibility that has perhaps not been fully considered by Congress and the courts.

Finally it is important to note a common phenomenon among bankruptcy judges. It is broadly true that the bench is partial toward Chapter 13, seeing it as a form of financial and social rehabilitation that is not only financially but morally superior to liquidation. In the words of one judge, "a person is just a better citizen if he will take advantage of Chapter 13 and file."[14] Whether this partiality is really appropriate is debateable, especially if Chapter 13 is inappropriate for some debtors. In addition, many judges are now struggling with what they view as abusive Chapter 13 filings.[15] The realization that Chapter 13 may be at least as subject to debtor abuse as Chapter 7 may cool the courts' enthusiasm.

Whatever the reason, it is clear that Chapter 13 has at last come into its own. Under the Act, Chapter XIII was a rather marginal form of bankruptcy, popular in only a few districts.[16] Today it is a major form of bankruptcy, in numerical terms at least second only to Chapter 7. This is perhaps the clearest sucess—or at least the clearest effect—of the reform effort that let to the Bankruptcy Code.

(1993). Professor Braucher's article includes considerable empirical data from four districts. According to her data, the non-completion rate for Chapter 13 plans ranges from a low of 35-40% in San Antonio (measured as a percentage of confirmed cases) to 80% in Austin (measured as a percentage of filed cases). Id. at 535. There are also other, somewhat older, data that suggest a completion rate of only about 30%. See Teresa A. Sullivan, Elizabeth Warren & Jay Lawrence Westbrook, As We Forgive Our Debtors 217 (1989).

[13] Jean Braucher, *Lawyers and Consumer Bankruptcy: One Code, Many Cultures,* 67 Am. Bankr. L. J. 501 (1993).

[14] *Bankruptcy Amendments Act of 1993: Hearings on S. 540 Before the Subcommittee on Courts and Administrative Practice,* 103d Cong., 1st Sess. 75 (1993) (statement of Hon. Ralph H. Kelley, Chief U.S. Bankruptcy Judge, Eastern District of Tennessee), *quoted in* Hon. Roger M. Whelan & Mandy S. Cohen, *Consumer Bankruptcy Reform: Balancing the Equities in Chapter 13,* 2 Am. Bankr. Inst. L. Rev. 165 (1994).

[15] For a fuller disucssion of this, see *Consumer Bankruptcy: Roundtable Discussion,* 2 Am. Bankr. Inst. L. Rev. 5 (1994).

[16] Marjorie Girth, *The Bankruptcy Reform Process: Maximizing Judicial Control in Wage Earners' Plans,* 11 U. Mich. J. L. Ref. 51 (1977).

§ 18.02 Filing, Conversion and Dismissal

A Chapter 13 bankruptcy may be filed by either an individual or an individual and spouse.[17] In most cases, the plan of reorganization is filed together with the plan. Incidentally, this practice of simultaneous filing—and the requirement that the plan must in nearly all cases be filed within 15 days after the petition—at times results in the plan payments beginning before the plan is confirmed, because unless the court orders otherwise, the payments begin 30 days after the plan is filed.[18]

§ 18.03 Property of the Estate

The definition of "property of the estate" in Chapter 13 is broader than it is in Chapter 7; it includes more post-petition property. For a full discussion of the scope of the Chapter 13 estate, see § 7.07 of this book.

§ 18.04 Role of the Trustee

The Chapter 13 trustee has a different role than the Chapter 7 trustee. There is no case trustee in Chapter 13; there is, however, a standing trustee appointed to supervise all cases in a district.[19] The standing trustee's duties are midway between those of a case trustee and the U.S. Trustee. The duties are primarily to supervise the debtor,[20] to appear and be heard on questions of valuation, confirmation, and modification,[21] to ensure that the debtor commences making payments in a timely fashion,[22] and to disburse payments made under the plan.[23]

There is evidence that the standing trustee can and in some districts does exercise considerable influence over the number of Chapter 13s filed and the structure of Chapter 13 plans. There is some question as to whether this is desirable, however. At a minimum, it creates considerable difference in treatment from district to district, even districts within the same state. Supporters of active standing trustees, however, insist that their work not only benefits creditors by increasing the amount of debt collected but also debtors by restoring their pride and self-esteem.

One recent study describes the effects that an activist standing trustee can have:

> The most aggressively influential chapter 13 standing trustee in the four cities studied is Marion "Al" Olson, who has held that position in San Antonio since 1976. From the effective date of the Bankruptcy Code in

[17] Bankruptcy Code §§ 109(e), 302. See § 6.02[D] of this book for a discussion of the rules regarding joint husband/wife bankruptcy cases.

[18] Bankruptcy Code § 1326(a)(1).

[19] Bankruptcy Code § 1302(a).

[20] Bankruptcy Code §1302(b)(1).

[21] Bankruptcy Code § 1302(b)(2).

[22] Bankruptcy Code § 1302(b)(5).

[23] Bankruptcy Code § 1326(c).

> 1979, he has striven toward two goals—to have as many debtors as possible to file in chapter 13, and to get them to file plans that pay 100% of general unsecured claims . . . He touts chapter 13 as a means to "self-reliance and self-worth and a feeling of accomplishment." . . . To promote more use of chapter 13, Olson uses moral suasion with lawyers and also financial incentives. He pays lawyers the first full payment under a chapter 13 plan toward attorneys' fees (less his own percentage fee) and has responded to pressure from the lawyers to speed up payment.[24]

§ 18.05 Role of the Debtor

All Chapter 13 estates are operated by a debtor in possession, who is always the debtor. The debtor has the rights and obligations of all debtors. In addition, the Chapter 13 debtor has many of the rights that a trustee would have regarding the use, sale and lease of property.[25] A debtor engaged in business has additional rights, discussed in the next section.

As a practical matter, the typical Chapter 13 debtor does virtually nothing except pay the lawyer and fund the plan. There usually is no business to manage; the estate is usually very small; the debtor simply continues to go to work and collect a paycheck. Few Chapter 13 cases involve any litigation, and what litigation does exist focuses mainly on whether the plan complies with the mandatory provisions of the Chapter.

§ 18.06 Debtor Engaged in Business

Chapter 13, unlike old Chapter XIII, is available to business debtors, provided that they conduct their business as individual proprietors (rather than as corporations, partnerships, or other legal entities) and fit within the general debt limitations. According to section 1304, a debtor that is self-employed and incurs trade credit in the production of income from the employment is "engaged in business."[26] There is no statutory requirement that this income provide the major part of the debtor's income or indeed any stated part of the income. Thus, a law professor who makes a few dollars writing student guides, and who gets the computers, disks, and paper necessary for that work on credit, is a debtor engaged in business for Chapter 13 purposes.

Since the Chapter 13 debtor is a debtor-in-possession, a debtor, not the standing trustee, has the automatic right to operate the business in ordinary course.[27] The

---

[24] Jean Braucher, *Lawyers and Consumer Bankruptcy: One Code, Many Cultures,* 67 Am. Bankr. L. J. 501, 557-58 (1993). Mr. Olson appears to have had some success with his efforts; both the Chapter 13 filing rate and the plan completion rate in San Antonio are high. Id. at 535 & 558.

[25] Bankruptcy Code § 1303. See In re Dodd, 73 Bankr. 67 (E.D. Cal. 1987).

[26] Bankruptcy Code § 1304(a).

[27] Bankruptcy Code § 1304(b) explicitly gives the debtor, not the trustee, the power to run the business. It does say that the court can order otherwise, but it is not entirely clear

debtor is subject to the usual limitations on the operation of a business imposed by sections 363 and 364 (see Chapters 8 and 9 of this book). Moreover, the court may impose additional limitations and conditions where appropriate.[28]

§ 18.07 The Plan

[A]—Introduction

At the core of Chapter 13 is the plan of reorganization. Unlike the Chapter 11 plan, the Chapter 13 plan is usually formulated without creditor participation; unsecured creditors especially are given practically no direct or even indirect role. In consequence, the contents of the plan are almost entirely set by the statutory requirements for confirmation.[29] Broadly speaking, these requirements adhere to the absolute priority rule; they also establish the standard by which the adequacy of the proposed payments is to be measured by the court. The requirements for confirmation under Chapter 13 are so well established that it is routine to file the plan with the petition.[30] Plans are so standardized that preparation often requires no more than filling in a computerized checklist and printing out the result.

[B]—Mandatory Provisions

There are only three mandatory provisions of the plan, the second and third of which are discussed elsewhere in this Chapter. However, these mandatory provisions must be read in light of the requirements for confirmation, which in effect add other mandatory provisions. The three provisions explicitly required in section 1322 are:

1. The plan must provide for the submission of a sufficient portion of the debtor's future income and earnings to the supervision and control of the trustee to fund the plan.[31]

2. The plan must provide for the full payment, in deferred cash payments, of all priority claims (unless the holder of a particular claim agrees to different treatment).[32]

---

whether this refers only to the imposition of limits on the debtor or permits the court to replace the debtor with the standing trustee. Collier's takes the position that the latter reading is correct. Collier on Bankruptcy ¶ 1304.01. In all but the rarest cases the issue is meaningless, since by definition the business must be a rather small proprietorship and it is nearly always impossible for such a business to be operated by anybody else over the objection of the proprietor.

[28] Bankruptcy Code § 1304(b).

[29] As indicated above, however, the Chapter 13 standing trustee may have a great deal of influence over what goes into the plan. See Jean Braucher, *Lawyers and Consumer Bankruptcy: One Code, Many Cultures,* 67 Am. Bankr. L. J. 501, 556-61 (1993).

[30] If the plan is not filed with the petition, it must normally be filed within fifteen days after the petition, although the court can extend this time "for cause shown and on notice as the court may direct." Bankruptcy Rule 3015(b).

[31] Bankruptcy Code § 1322(a)(1).

[32] Bankruptcy Code § 1322(a)(2).

3. If the plan classifies the claims, the plan must provide equal treatment of all claims in each class.[33] "Classification" is further discussed in § 18.07 of this chapter.

[C]—Optional Provisions

The Chapter 13 debtor may include a number of optional provisions in the plan, many of which are discussed in greater detail in other parts of this Chapter. The provisions that may be included are:

1. Classification of unsecured claims.[34] For a fuller discussion of classification, see § 18.07[E].

2. Modification of the rights of holders of secured claims, other than a claim secured only by a mortgage on the debtor's home.[35] This provision, one of the most controversial in Chapter 13, is discussed in § 18.08[B][2].

3. Provision for the curing or waiving of any default,[36] and, notwithstanding the limitation on modification of mortgage debt, the curing of defaults and maintenance of payments on secured or unsecured debt that extends beyond the end of the plan.[37] See § 18.08[B][2].

4. Payment of unsecured claims concurrently with other unsecured claims or secured claims.[38]

5. Payment of post-petition debts.[39]

6. Assumption, rejection, or assignment of executory contracts and unexpired leases.[40] For a detailed discussion of the issues raised by assumption, rejection, and assignment, see Chapter 9.

7. Payment of claims from the property of the estate or the property of the debtor (for example, partial liquidation of the estate's property).[41]

8. Vesting of the property of the estate in the debtor or another entity.[42]

9. Finally, a catch-all provision—the plan may include any other provision that is not inconsistent with the Bankruptcy Code.[43]

---

[33] Bankruptcy Code § 1322(a)(3).

[34] Bankruptcy Code § 1322(b(1).

[35] Bankruptcy Code § 1322(b)(2).

[36] Bankruptcy Code § 1322(b)(3).

[37] Bankruptcy Code § 1322(b)(5).

[38] Bankruptcy Code § 1322(b)(4).

[39] Bankruptcy Code § 1322(b)(6).

[40] Bankruptcy Code § 1322(b)(7).

[41] Bankruptcy Code § 1322(b)(8).

[42] Bankruptcy Code § 1322(b)(9).

[43] Bankruptcy Code § 1322(b)(10).

[D]—Duration of the plan

Ordinarily, the Chapter 13 plan lasts for three years. With court permission, the plan may last for as long as five years.[44] These time limits were imposed because of a concern that some Chapter XIII plans extended far longer and thus amounted to virtual peonage.[45]

Normally, an extension beyond three years is justified by the debtor's inability to deal with priority or secured debts in that amount of time. Some courts, however, have suggested that the debtor should extend the plan period when there is a substantial amount of debt that could not be discharged in any chapter other than chapter 13. The appropriateness of forcing a five year plan—rather than permitting it when volunteered by the debtor—is doubtful,[46] but the power to do so has not so far been curtailed by the Supreme Court.

[E]—Classification

The Chapter 13 debtor has a limited ability to classify general unsecured claims. By "classification" we mean that the debtor may create a class of claims that is in addition to those created by the Code. Insofar as the Code is concerned, all general unsecured claims are equal; classification by the debtor means that some are treated better than others.

Because there is so little creditor participation in Chapter 13—most particularly, because there is no vote on the plan—the general view has been that it is unfair to give the debtor substantial power to distinguish between types of general unsecured claims. Chapter 13 permits classification, but only if it does not unfairly discriminate against types of claims.

Unfair discrimination is not the clearest standard imaginable. All classifications discriminate; when does that discrimination become unfair? The Code does identify one type of permissible discrimination. If a debt is a consumer debt on which an individual other than the debtor is liable with the debtor, the plan may separately classify that debt and give it more favorable treatment.[47] This provision, added by BAFJA in 1984, was a simple bow to reality. In many cases, a consumer co-debtor is a family member or friend, and many debtors, feeling a strong moral obligation

---

[44] Bankruptcy Code § 1322(d). (Prior to the 1994 Amendments, this provision was § 1322(c)).

[45] Discussing the unlimited time period for Chapter XIII plans, the House Report on the Bankruptcy Code remarked: "Extensions on plans, new cases, and newly incurred debts put some debtors under court supervised repayment plans for seven to ten years. This has become the closest thing there is to involuntary servitude . . ." H. R. Rep. No. 595, 95th Cong., 1st Sess. 117 (1977).

[46] "[A] court considering confirmation of [a five-year plan] must ensure that the extension beyond three years is completely voluntary, and not imposed on the debtor by creditors or the chapter 13 trustee." Collier on Bankruptcy § 1322.15, citing In re Porter 102 Bankr. 773 (9th Cir. B.A.P 1989). See also, In re Taylor, 137 Bankr. 60 (Bankr. W. D. Okla. 1992) (debtor's desire to pay a student loan in full found to be insufficient cause to extend plan to more than 36 months).

[47] Bankruptcy Code § 1322(b)(1).

to protect the co-debtor, attempted to pay the debt outside of the plan. This in turn endangered the viability of the plan, since those extra payments came out of whatever the debtor had left after making the required plan payments. This risk to the plan, and the fact that many debtors would try to find some way to pay the debt regardless, led Congress to legitimize disparate treatment under the plan itself.[48]

In other cases, the boundaries of impermissible discrimination are less clear. One circuit has suggested a four-part test:

1. Is there a reasonable basis for the discrimination?

2. Can the debtor fulfill the plan without the discrimination?

3. Is the discrimination in good faith?

4. Is there a direct relationship between the degree of the discrimination and the rationale for the discrimination?[49]

Another formulation is that the classification must rationally further an articulated, legitimate interest of the debtor.[50]

A final note. Discrimination between claims or types of claims must be done through separate classifications. A debtor may not place differently treated claims in the same class; rather, each claim in any class must be treated the same.[51]

§ 18.08 Confirmation of the Plan

Confirmation of the plan requires more than that the plan contain the mandatory terms. At least six, and in nearly all cases seven, requirements must be met. These requirements are:

1. The plan must comply with all requirements of Chapter 13 and with other applicable requirements of the Code.[52]

2. All required fees and charges must be paid.[53]

3. The plan must be proposed in good faith and not by any means forbidden by law.[54] Historically, this requirement was viewed as a limitation

---

[48] "If, as a practical matter, the debtor is going to pay the codebtor claim, he should be permitted to separately classify it in Chapter 13." S. Rep. 65, 98th Cong. 1st Sess, 18 (1983).

[49] See In re Wolff, 22 Bankr. 510 (9th Cir. B.A.P. 1982).

[50] See In re Lawson, 93 Bankr. 979 (Bankr. N. D. Ill. 1988). Cf. In re Tucker, 150 Bankr. 203 (Bankr. N.D. Ohio 1992) (plan that provided for full payment of student loans and minimal payment of other obligations unfairly discriminated).

[51] Bankruptcy Code § 1322(a)(3).

[52] Bankruptcy Code § 1325(a)(1).

[53] Bankruptcy Code § 1325(a)(2).

[54] Bankruptcy Code § 1325(a)(3).

on the process of developing and obtaining approval of the plan—for example, bribing a creditor to vote for the plan would violate this requirement. In the Chapter 13 setting, however, this requirement has sometimes been held to affect the substance of the plan itself. For a discussion of this, see § 18.08[A][2].

4. The plan must meet the best interests of creditors test.[55] For a discussion of this, see § 18.08[A][1].

5. The secured creditors must vote for the plan, or retain their lien and get payments equal to the value of the claim, or get their collateral.[56] For a discussion of this, see § 18.08[B].

6. The debtor must be able to make all payments under the plan and otherwise comply with the plan.[57] This is sometimes known as the "feasibility requirement." It is not too scrupulously applied; the rule does not require certainty (as is obvious from the high failure rate of Chapter 13 plans) but only a reasonable possibility of success.[58]

7. In most cases, the plan will have to comply with the disposable income test.[59] For a discussion of disposable income, see § 18.08[A][2].

[A]—Treatment of General Unsecured Claims

Much of the litigation over Chapter 13, and much of the legislative tinkering with it, involves the treatment of general unsecured claims. The problem is reconciling the goals of Chapter 13. On the one hand, it is intended to increase the total recovery to the creditors. On the other, it is intended to give debtors an "honorable" way out of financial difficulties. Blood, however, is scarce in turnips and any increase in payments to creditors is at the cost of some hardship to the debtor (who in most cases is already strapped). A variety of tests have been used to strike the balance; at present, two statutory rules are of primary importance. The plan must meet the best interest of creditors test and in most cases must distribute the debtor's entire disposable income. A third test, good faith, was widely used prior to BAFJA and may still have significance today.

[1]—Best Interest of Creditors' Test

As is true throughout the Code, a creditor's bankruptcy entitlement is the liquidation value of the claim. This entitlement, still called by its Bankruptcy Act name, the "best interest of creditors test" (although that name appears nowhere in the Code), means that every creditor is entitled to get at least what it would have gotten in Chapter 7. Further, this is measured by the real value of the claim, not

---

[55] Bankruptcy Code § 1325(a)(4).

[56] Bankruptcy Code § 1325(a)(5).

[57] Bankruptcy Code § 1325(a)(6).

[58] For a discussion of the Chapter 13 failure rate, see § 18.01 of this chapter.

[59] Bankruptcy Code § 1325(b).

the nominal payments made over the plan period. Thus, the plan cannot be confirmed unless the value of the property to be distributed on each unsecured claim is at least equal to the amount that would have been paid on the claim had the estate been liquidated under Chapter 7 on the date that the plan became effective.[60] Because of the adjustment for present value, the payments made will be more than the the nominal amount of the claim's liquidation value. For example, if the liquidation value of a claim is $100, the payments made over the three year period would have to be significantly more than $100 to be worth $100 on the effective date of the plan.

[2]—The Disposable Income Test

One of the strongest objections to the original Code was that Chapter 13 only required the debtor to pay the Chapter 7 liquidation value of unsecured claims. It was correctly pointed out that this meant a debtor could get all the benefits of Chapter 13 (a broader discharge, retention of more assets, payments over time) for little real cost. In many cases, the debtor proposed to pay little or nothing on unsecured claims, even unsecured claims that would not have been dischargeable under Chapter 7, because the liquidation value of those claims was, in fact, zero. These zero-payment or nominal-payment plans came under harsh criticism. Many courts responded to this criticism by a rather strained reading of the requirement that the plan be proposed in good faith. Although, historically, this term referred only to procedural matters, a number of courts held that it meant that the Chapter 13 debtor had to make its best effort to pay as much under the plan as was practicable. Some courts held that this was especially true if a claim was dischargeable only under Chapter 13.[61]

BAFJA addressed this issue by adding section 1325(b) to the requirements for confirmation. Under that section, the court "may not" confirm a plan over the objection of either the trustee or the holder of any allowed secured claim unless the plan meets one of the two following requirements:

1. The claim of the objecting creditor is to be paid in full—that is, the actual, present value of the proposed payments must be at least equal to the amount of the claim,[62] or

2. The plan provides that all of the debtor's projected disposable income for the three years beginning with the first payment due under the plan will be applied to make payments under the plan.[63]

For practical reasons, the debtor nearly always chooses the second option. Moreover, since objection by the trustee or a creditor to a plan which does not provide for

[60] Bankruptcy Code § 1325(a)(4).

[61] See generally, Joseph P. Corish & Michael J. Herbert, *The Debtor's Dilemma: Disposable Income as the Code of Chapter 13 Discharge in Consumer Bankruptcy,* 47 La. L. Rev. 47 (1986).

[62] Bankruptcy Code § 1325(b)(1)(A).

[63] Bankruptcy Code § 1325(b)(1)(B). Note that even if the plan is for longer than five years, the debtor need only meet the disposable income requirement with regard to the first three years' income.

disbursement of disposable income is almost a foregone conclusion, it is routine to include such a provision in a plan without waiting for the objection actually to be made.

Disposable income has thus become the basic cost of Chapter 13 discharge. The Code defines this term only in part, and in the negative. Disposable income is that portion of the debtor's income that is *not* reasonably required (i) for the maintenance or support of the debtor or a dependent of the debtor, and (ii) if the debtor is engaged in businesses, for the continuation, preservation, and operation of the business.[64] Since most Chapter 13 debtors are not engaged in business, most of the case law interpreting this provision deals with whether a particular expenditure is reasonably necessary for the debtor and the debtor's dependents.

Recently, there has been a split in the Circuit Courts about the meaning of the phrase "projected disposable income." The Ninth Circuit has read this phrase in accordance with its ordinary meaning; the Chapter 13 debtor is required to make a reasoned estimate of future disposable income and provide for payment of that amount through the plan.[65] The Eighth Circuit, having perhaps a bit of trouble with the English language, disagrees; it reads the phrase to mean that the debtor must fund the plan with actual disposable income.[66]

The disposable income question generally arises in context of an objection to confirmation based on the alleged inadequacy of the debtor's funding of the plan. The court examines the debtor's projected income and proposed budget to determine whether, in the judge's opinion, the debtor is in fact surrendering all disposable income. To a large degree, the determination is an ad hoc one; however, there are at least some rules of thumb. These are sketched out in the following paragraphs.

The courts have not generally required the debtor to make a severe reduction in living standards. Contrary to a proposal made by creditors in the 1980's, Chapter 13 debtors are not required to turn over all income in excess of the federal poverty line.[67] This generally means that, despite occasional rhetoric in the cases to the

---

[64] Bankruptcy Code § 1325(b)(2).

[65] Anderson v. Satterlee (In re Anderson), 21 F.3d 355 (9th Cir. 1994). This issue arose in context of a rather high-handed attempt by the standing trustee to impose an additional requirement on confirmation—namely, the execution of a "best efforts certification" that gave the trustee the unilateral right to modify the debtor's payments, contrary to the modification provisions of the Code.

[66] Rowley v. Yarnall, 22 F.3d 190 (8th Cir. 1994). Note that this is a Chapter 12 cases; but Chapter 12 contains the same disposable income requirement as Chapter 13. See § 19.07[C] of this book.

[67] The chief basis for this proposal was the so-called "Purdue Study," more formally, Credit Research Center, Krannert School of Management, Purdue University, Monograph No. 23, Consumer Bankruptcy Study, Vol. I, Consumer's Right to Bankruptcy—Origins and Effects 88-91 (1982). The conclusions of this study were attacked by most commentators; for a sample of the debate, see Teresa A. Sullivan, Elizabeth Warren & Jay Lawrence Westbrook, *Limiting Access to Bankruptcy Discharge: An Analysis of the Creditors' Data,* 1983 Wis. L. Rev. 1091; A. Charlene Sullivan, *Reply: Limiting Access to Bankruptcy Discharge,* 1984 Wis. L. Rev. 1069; Teresa A. Sullivan, Elizabeth Warren & Jay Lawrence Westbrook, *Rejoinder: Limiting Access to Bankruptcy Discharge,* 1984 Wis. L. Rev. 1087.

contrary, middle class Chapter 13 debtors have generally been able to retain many of the benefits of their status,[68] this in turn means that a Chapter 13 plan may well bite harder on lower-middle class debtors, who have little to spare, than on those with larger incomes.[69] Some courts have explicitly stated that high income debtors should be able to retain more of their income, at least if they are making substantial payments to creditors.[70]

Collier's generalized description of the standard probably reflects the general attitude of most (though certainly not all) courts:

> [A] court determining the debtor's disposable income is not expected to, and should not, mandate drastic changes in the debtor's lifestyle to fit some preconceived norm for chapter 13 debtors. The debtor's expenses should be scrutinized only for luxuries which are not enjoyed by an average American family.
>
> . . .
>
> In short, the court cannot and should not order debtors to alter their lifestyles where there is no obvious indulgence in luxuries, even where one or more unsecured creditors demand such a change. To engage in such close judgments and supervision would be to contravene the intent of Congress. It would also place impossible burdens on the court in determining the absolute necessity of every expense in each debtor's budget.[71]

Some expenditures are clearly subject to close scrutiny and in many courts are not permitted at all. Charity, they say, "begins at home, but it ends with bankruptcy."[72] The debtor's budget may not generally include charitable contributions,[73] including, according to the great majority of courts, church tithes. The refusal to allow tithing has caused considerable comment,[74] but it probably does not raise any

---

[68] This is at least the conclusion of one early study; see Joseph P. Corish & Michael J. Herbert, *The Debtor's Dilemma: Disposable Income as the Code of Chapter 13 Discharge in Consumer Bankruptcy,* 47 La. L. Rev. 47, 73-74 (1986). At least one of the authors of this study, having reviewed more recent cases, sees no reason to change his initial view.

[69] Joseph P. Corish & Michael J. Herbert, *The Debtor's Dilemma: Disposable Income as the Code of Chapter 13 Discharge in Consumer Bankruptcy,* 47 La. L. Rev. 47, 73-74 (1986).

[70] See In re Anderson, 143 Bankr. 719 (Bankr. N.D. Neb. 1992).

[71] Collier on Bankruptcy ¶ 1325.08.

[72] Joseph P. Corish & Michael J. Herbert, *The Debtor's Dilemma: Disposable Income as the Cost of Chapter 13 Discharge in Consumer Bankruptcy,* 47 La. L. Rev. 47, 74 (1986).

[73] For an extreme case, see In re Red, 60 Bankr. 113 (Bankr. E.D. Tenn. 1986), partially overruled on other grounds by In re Minor, 1995 WL 66375, in which the court rejected a plan that included a $1.50 per week contribution to United Way. Some courts have been a bit more lenient, permitting charitable payments of a modest amount. See Collier on Bankruptcy ¶ 1325.08[4] [b]. See also In re Anderson, 143 Bankr. 719 (Bankr. N. D. Neb. 1992) (debtors with gross income of $3,144 per month limited to maximum $215 per month for combined recreational and charity expenses).

[74] See, for example, Carol Koenig, *To Tithe or Not to Tithe: The Constitutionality of Tithing in a Chapter 13 Bankruptcy Budget,* 32 Santa Clara L. Rev. 1231 (1992).

serious Constitutional issue, since the debtor could file under another Chapter (or not file at all) and thereby avoid the disposable income requirement.[75]

Many courts have been somewhat grudging in allowing recreational expenses, such as health club memberships.[76] Food and clothing budgets are expected to reflect at least a reasonable degree of austerity.[77] The case law, though, reflects a perhaps surprising degree of flexibility for mortgage payments; it appears that the courts are generally unwilling to force a debtor with a large mortgage to move to a cheaper home.[78] As is true with many items, however, the courts have been inconsistent; mortgage payments in the $1,000 per month range, which are hardly unusual, have been found both excessive[79] and reasonable.[80] A number of cases have also been rather grudging toward large monthly car payments, especially if the car in question provides something more than basic transportation. For example, a large monthly payment for a "fancy" car may be disallowed.[81]

In evaluating the needs of dependents, courts have also looked on anything remotely classified as a luxury with very jaundiced eyes. Those children who dread piano lessons might wish their parents into Chapter 13, because some courts might well say that the lessons are not necessary, and their cost is thus part of disposable income.[82] Private school tuition is almost certainly out of the question, at least where there are adequate public school alternatives.[83]

There has been much concern about the fact that the disposable income standard is enforced so inconsistently. In part, at least, those inconsistencies are an inevitable result of appointing a judge the "arbitrator and architect of the defendant's lifestyle."[84] The judge's personal views inevitably color the disposable income

---

[75] Note, however, that a debtor's insistence upon tithing may bar him or her from Chapter 7 relief; the filing may be classified as abusive and thus dismissed under § 707(b). See In re Faulkner, 165 Bankr. 644 (Bankr. W.D. Mo. 1994).

[76] See Daniel J. VonWeihe, *Necessary or Excessive: The Standard of "Reasonably Necessary" in Chapter 13 Bankruptcy,* 17 J. Corp. L. 639 (1992).

[77] See James Rodenberg, *Reasonably Necessary Expenses or Life of Riley?: The Disposable Income Test and a Chapter 13 Debtor's Lifestyle,* 56 Mo. L. Rev. 617 (1991).

[78] Id. at 636: "The bankruptcy courts very seldom refuse to confirm a plan because of the amount a debtor is expending for housing."

[79] See, for example, In re Kitson, 65 Bankr. 615 (Bankr. E.D. N.C. 1986) and In re Jones, 55 Bankr. 462 (Bankr. D.Minn. 1985).

[80] See In re Wood, 92 Bankr. 264, 266 (Bankr. S.D. Ohio 1988).

[81] In re Reyes, 106 Bankr. 155, 157 (Bankr. N.D. Ill. 1989). ("[A] Chevrolet Blazer is an obvious indulgence if ever there was one . . . purchased . . . simply because he wanted to drive an extravagant four wheel drive vehicle").

[82] See In re Anderson, 143 Bankr. 719 (Bankr. D. Neb. 1992), in which the court, while not prohibiting piano lessons, noted that they, together with other recreational expenses, must be reasonable.

[83] In re Jones, 55 Bankr. 462 (Bankr. D. Minn. 1985); Daniel J. Von Weihe, *Necessary or Excessive: The Standard of "Reasonably Necessary" in Chapter 13,* 17 J. Corp. L. 639, 651-52 (1992).

[84] Brian G. Smooke, Comment, *Section 1325(b) and Zero Payment Plans In Chapter 13,* 4 Bankr. Dev. J. 449 (1987).

decision to a degree greater than most other decisions, because the standard is so vague. In the words of one commentator, "[i]t is questionable whether courts should be making lifestyle judgments based on personal opinions without the guidance or instruction of legal standards."[85] The lack of a clearer legal standard, however, is the result of the compromise that underlay BAFJA's revision of Chapter 13. Creditor groups wanted a clear standard—the poverty line. Income in excess of the federally determined poverty line was to be distributed to creditors. Congress balked that proposal, and settled on the vague and thus inevitably somewhat arbitrary disposable income rule.

Given the statutory imposition of the disposable income requirement, what, if anything, remains of the judicially imposed good faith rule? Logically, it should have been eliminated except with regard to procedural misconduct. However, good faith as a substantive requirement persists in a number of cases. A good recent example is *In re Wilson*,[86] which reiterated a pre-BAFJA good faith test.[87] This test enumerates 11 factors, among them at least five that directly or indirectly overlap with the disposable income test. Those five are:

1. The amount of the debtor's income from all sources,

2. The living expenses of the debtor and his dependents,

3. The debtor's degree of effort,

4. The debtor's ability to earn and the likelihood of fluctuations in his earnings, and

5. Special circumstances, such as inordinate medical expenses.[88]

The other factors are the amount of attorney fees, the probable duration of the plan, the motivations of the debtor in seeking relief, the frequency with which the debtor has sought bankruptcy relief, the circumstances under which the debts were incurred, and the burden which plan administration would put on the trustee.[89] The propriety of these other six considerations is also questionable, especially because most of them are regulated by other specific provisions of the Code. The substantive good faith standard, however, remains attractive to some judges and standing trustees, especially who believe that it is their job, not Congress's, to determine who is eligible for relief, and who wish to make that determination based on their own views as to which debtors are deserving and which are deadbeats. This is not to say that their views are necessarily incorrect, but only to question whether they should be allowed to trump the explicit standards set out in the Code.

---

[85] Daniel J. Von Weihe, *Necessary or Excessive: The Standard of "Reasonably Necessary" in Chapter 13,* 17 J. Corp. L. 639, 653 (1992).

[86] 168 Bankr. 260 (Bankr. N.D. Fla. 1994).

[87] The test is derived from In re Kitchens, 702 F.2d 885 (11th Cir. 1983).

[88] In re Wilson, 168 Bankr. at 262.

[89] Id.

[3]—Treatment of Priority Unsecured Claims

Priority unsecured claims retain their priority under the Chapter 13 plan. This is effectuated by section 1322(a)(2), under which the plan must provide for full payment of section 507 priority claims unless the holder of any particular claim agrees otherwise.[90] With the exception of administrative claims,[91] this does not mean that the payment must occur immediately or before the payments are made on the general unsecured claims; payment may be made over the life of the plan. Indeed, there is no requirement that the payments be made from the beginning of the plan, or that they be made in equal installments.[92]

Note too that, although the term "full payment" is used, that term probably does not in this context mean that the debtor must pay the real value of the claims. There is no requirement in section 1322(a)(2) that the stream of payments be reduced to present value. Neither have the courts imposed such a requirement; the debtor need not pay any interest on the claims.[93] Of course, if the payments, when reduced to present value, do not equal their liquidation value, then the plan violates the best interest of creditors test and cannot be confirmed. For example, if a $10,000 priority claim would be paid in full on liquidation, then payment of $10,000 over three years, while it would meet the "payment in full" test would not meet the best interest of creditors test, because $10,000 over three years is worth less than $10,000 immediately. Thus, the real requirement is that the amount paid on priority claims equal (i) the full nominal amount of the claim and (ii) the full actual liquidation value of the claim.

The payment in full requirement also has an indirect impact on the scope of the Chapter 13 debtor's discharge. As noted in § 12.05 of this book, the Chapter 13 debtor generally enjoys a broader discharge than the Chapter 7, 11 or 12 debtor. However, some non-dischargeable debts are also priority debts—for example, certain taxes.[94] Although those debts will be dischargeable in Chapter 13, they still must be paid "in full" under the plan. Thus, the only real benefits given to the debtor with regard to those taxes is that (i) they may be paid over the three-to-five year plan period and (ii) only the liquidation value of the claim must be paid.

[B]—Treatment of Secured Claims

[1]—General Rules

Secured claims are, as in all bankruptcies, given favored treatment in Chapter 13. There are three methods of dealing with secured claims: payment, surrender, or creditor approval. Only the first two are widely used. The typical Chapter 13 debtor will decide to retain at least some encumbered property. If he or she does, the claim secured by the encumbrance is paid "in full" during (or in some cases, during and

---

[90] Bankruptcy Code § 1322(a)(2).

[91] See § 18.08[F] of this chapter for the treatment of administrative claims in Chapter 13.

[92] See In re Ferguson, 134 Bankr. 689 (Bankr. S.D. Fla. 1991).

[93] In re Hieb, 88 Bankr. 1019 (Bankr. S.D. 1988)

[94] See Bankruptcy Code §§ 507(a)(7) and 523(a)(1).

after) the plan.[95] In addition, the liens remain in place on the property until the payments are completed.[96]

The second option is surrender of the collateral. If the debtor does not want, or cannot afford to retain, encumbered property, the debtor may satisfy the secured claim by surrendering the property to the holder of the claim.[97] Since the secured claim cannot be greater than the value of the property securing it,[98] surrender of that property is considered the functional equivalent of full payment.

The third method, acceptance of the plan by the secured party,[99] is rare. More precisely, it is rare that the holder of a secured claim would accept anything less than full payment or surrender of the collateral. There is thus little purpose served in getting creditor approval for the plan, since full payment or surrender are equally sufficient to obtain confirmation.

As usual, however, these rules only protect the value of the secured claim, not the timing of payments. With the exception of the debtor's home mortgage (discussed in the next subsection), secured claims in Chapter 13 are subject to modification. The debtor may change the amount and time of payments, so long as this does not deprive the claimant of adequate protection.[100]

[2]—Special Rules Regarding Home Mortgages

Section 1322(b)(2) contains a controversial limitation on the ability of the Chapter 13 debtor to deal with secured obligations; a limitation that has been tightened up by recent Supreme Court decisions. Under that section, a plan may not modify the rights of the holder of a secured claim if that claim is secured only by "real property that is the debtor's principal residence."[101] This provision does not preclude the debtor and the lender from entering into an agreement to modify the mortgage debt; but it does prevent the debtor from forcing any modification through the plan.

This provision, put in to protect the interests of home lenders, seriously reduces the value of Chapter 13 to many debtors. It is generally true that home-owning bankrupts (and a bare majority of individual bankrupts are home-owners),[102] want very desperately to keep their homes. Yet the mortgage payment is usually the biggest item in the family budget, and if it cannot be reduced, the plan of

---

[95] Note that in this context, as is usually true in bankruptcy, the term "full payment" refers to the actual, present value of the payments, not the nominal dollar amount paid.

[96] Bankruptcy Code § 1325(a)(5)(B).

[97] Bankruptcy Code § 1325(a)(5)(C).

[98] Bankruptcy Code § 506(a). See § 10.03[C] of this book.

[99] Bankruptcy Code § 1325(a)(5)(A).

[100] Bankruptcy Code § 1322(a)(2). Although that section does not specifically reference adequate protection, various other provisions, especially those regarding the automatic stay, guarantee adequate protection for all secured claims.

[101] Bankruptcy Code § 1322(b)(2).

[102] See Teresa A. Sullivan, Elizabeth Warren & Jay Lawrence Westbrook, As We Forgive Our Debtors 129 (1989) (52% of bankrupts are home owners, as compared to 64% of the general population).

reorganization may fail. On the other hand, Congress did not want Chapter 13 to become a device by which homeowners could unilaterally rewrite their mortgage obligations. If the debtor can negotiate new terms with the lender, well and good; but the debtor cannot force the lender to accept new terms by redoing the mortgage through the plan.

For years, debtors' attorneys have tried to find ways around this limitation. One device of some utility was approved by many lower courts. Section 1322(b)(3) permits the plan to provide for the cure of any default.[103] Similarly, section 1322(b)(5) says that "notwithstanding paragraph (2) . . . [the plan may] provide for the curing of any default" on debts that extend beyond the three -to -five year period of the plan.[104] This interpretation, which received indirect approval from the Supreme Court, was codified by the 1994 Amendments. Under new section 1322(c), the debtor is explicitly given the right to cure defaults on its home mortgage up to the time the residence is sold at a foreclosure sale.[105] Suppose that, prior to bankruptcy, Dora has defaulted on her mortgage to River Bank, and River Bank, pursuant to the loan agreement, has accelerated the balance due. Because of the acceleration, the amount now due and payable on the mortgage is not the $750 monthly payment, but the entire $50,000 balance. Dora can pay the $750 per month, but has no hope of paying the $50,000. In her Chapter 13 plan, Dora may de-accelerate the mortgage by paying the missed installments, plus penalties, late charges, and additional interest; she may then resume the scheduled $750 per month payments.[106]

Other devices have fared less well. For a number of years, debtors sought to lien strip their mortgages in Chapter 13. They argued that § 1322(b)(2) protected only the amount of the secured claim. Thus, if the property was worth only $40,000, and was subject to a $50,000 mortgage, only $40,000 would be protected from modification. A number of lower courts accepted this reasoning.[107] The Supreme Court decisively rejected this argument, ruling, in *Nobelman v. American Savings Bank,*[108] that the dispositive language in the subsection was the phrase "rights of holders of secured claims;" in the Court's view, this meant that regardless of the value of the property, the entire amount of the mortgage debt was protected.[109] Put concretely, this means that unless the debtor pays off the entire amount of the mortgage, the secured creditor may still foreclose. This is true even though upon discharge, the debt will become non-recourse debt; that is, post-discharge the

---

[103] Bankruptcy Code § 1322(b)(3).

[104] Bankruptcy Code § 1322(b)(5); since the mortgage loan usually extends beyond the plan period, this is the section that is of primary importance in dealing with the cure of defaulted mortgages.

[105] Bankruptcy Code § 1322(c)(1) (1994 Amendments).

[106] Payment of the monthly installments under the plan is specifically permitted under §1332(c)(2) (1994 Amendments).

[107] See Daniel C. Fleming & Marianne McConnell, *The Treatment of Residential Mortgages in Chapter 13 After Nobelman,* 2 Am. Bankr. Inst. L. Rev. 147 (1994).

[108] 113 S. Ct. 2106 (1993).

[109] 113 S. Ct. at 2111.

creditor may only seize and sell the property; it may not obtain an in personam judgment against the debtor.[110]

Note that the *Nobelman* rule may or may not apply to junior mortgages. It is arguable that if the junior lien is entirely underwater (that is, if the property is not even valuable enough to cover the senior mortgage), the junior lienholder is not a holder of a secured claim and thus not within the limitation of section 1322(b)(2).[111]

Curiously, there appears until recently to have been little litigation over the applicability of section 1322(b)(2). Note that it applies only if the mortgage covers just the debtor's home. This clearly suggests that if the mortgage covers other property as well (which some mortgages do) that the limitation does not apply. This issue has only lately generated many court decisions, perhaps because of the widespread assumption, prior to *Nobelman*, that Chapter 13 already permitted lien stripping.

A number of courts have held that the section 1322(b)(2) limitation applies even though the mortgage encompasses other things, provided that those other things are directly related to the realty. Thus, the inclusion of fixtures, rents, royalties, improvements, oil and gas rights, trade fixtures, and the like has not generally taken the mortgage out of the category of a protected homestead mortgage.[112] However, a few cases have held to the contrary, ruling that the inclusion under the mortgage of anything other than the homestead, as defined in the narrowest possible way, removes the section 1322(b)(2) limitation and thus permits the Chapter 13 debtor to modify the mortgagee's claim to the same extent as any other secured claim.[113] The majority rule, permitting the inclusion of collateral directly related to the realty, is perhaps the more sensible; at least it is more in line with commercial reality. However, the minority rule is perhaps better supported by the plain language of the statute.

[C]—"Chapter 20"

A number of debtors have attempted to gain greater leverage over their home mortgages by filing, in succession, a Chapter 7 bankruptcy and a Chapter 13 bankruptcy. Since Chapter 13 does not require a six-year wait between discharges, it is possible to obtain, in quick succession, a Chapter 7 discharge and a Chapter 13 discharge. These serial cases have been nicknamed "Chapter 20" (7 plus 13).

The primary, although not the only, perceived advantage of the Chapter 20 is that it greatly reduces the difficulty of dealing with an under-secured home mortgage.

---

[110] For a fuller discussion of the transformation of lien obligations into non-recourse obligations upon discharge, see § 12.01 of this book.

[111] See, for example, In re Plouffe, 157 Bankr. 198 (Bankr. D. Conn. 1993).

[112] See, for example, In re Ireland, 137 Bankr. 65 (M.D. Fla. 1992) (improvements, easements, rights, appurtenances, rents, royalties; mineral, oil and gas rights; profits from water, water rights, and water stock; fixtures); In re Ross, 107 Bankr. 759 (Bankr. W.D. Okla. 1989) (insurance, rents, profits, buildings, and improvements).

[113] For a full, if rather partisan, discussion of this entire issue, see Daniel C. Fleming and Marianne McConnell, *The Treatment of Residential Mortgages in Chapter 13 After Nobleman,* 2 Am. Bankr. Inst. L. Rev. 147 (1994).

The Chapter 7 discharge eliminates the unsecured portion of a mortgage debt. The Chapter 13 plan cannot alter the mortgage debt, but the mortgage debt will have been reduced by the Chapter 7 discharge. Although the use of a Chapter 20 has been attacked, the Supreme Court, in *Johnson v. Home State Bank*, broadly validated its use while noting that in particular cases the Chapter 13 plan might be refused confirmation on the grounds of bad faith.[114]

The utility of a Chapter 20, however, has been called into doubt by other Supreme Court decisions. As noted elsewhere, the Supreme Court has rejected lien-stripping in Chapter 7[115] and the lien-stripping of home mortgages in Chapter 13.[116] At a minimum, it appears that, although the plan may not have to deal with the entire amount of the mortgage debt, the lien will not be discharged unless and until the entire amount of the mortgage debt is in fact paid. Thus, even if the mortgage debt is undersecured, the amount secured by the lien cannot be reduced either in Chapter 7 or under the home mortgage provisions of Chapter 13. Consequently, it does not appear that even a Chapter 20 can in fact discharge the lien for anything less than full payment of the debt, including the unsecured portion.

There are other possible reasons for filing a "Chapter 20." The discharge of unsecured debt in the Chapter 7 can make it possible for a debtor to fit within the dollar limitations of Chapter 13. Indeed, this was the case in *Johnson v. Home State Bank*. The debtors in that case had, prior to their Chapter 7 filing, too much debt to fit within Chapter 13's $100,000/$350,000 jurisdictional debt caps.[117] Another more dubious reason is to evade the Chapter 13 disposable income test. If, in the Chapter 7, all of the debtor's unsecured obligations are discharged, then the debtor will only have to deal in the Chapter 13 plan with its secured debt. Although secured creditors are entitled to the full value of their claims, they are not entitled to the debtor's disposable income. Whether sequential filings for the purpose of avoiding the disposable income requirement is in good faith is unclear.

[D]—Hearing on Confirmation

The court is required to hold a hearing on confirmation. Any party in interest may object to the confirmation.[118] Prior notice of the hearing is required.[119]

---

[114] 501 U.S. 78 (1991). For a detailed discussion of "Chapter 20" and this case, see Lex A. Coleman, *Individual Consumer "Chapter 20" Cases After Johnson: An Introduction to Non-Business Serial Filings Under Chapter 7 and Chapter 13 of the Bankruptcy Code*, 9 Bankr. Dev. J. 357 (1992).

[115] See § 12.01 of this book.

[116] Nobelman v. American Savings Bank, 113 S. Ct. 2106 (1993).

[117] 501 U.S. at 80. Note that these caps have been raised by the 1994 Amendments to $250,000 and 750,000. See § 6.02[B] of this book.

[118] Bankruptcy Code § 1324.

[119] See Bankruptcy Rules 3020 and 2002.

[E]—Effect of Confirmation

Confirmation of the Chapter 13 plan binds the debtor and every creditor, whether or not the creditor has been provided for by the plan and whether or not the creditor has accepted, objected to, or rejected the plan.[120] Confirmation also vests all property of the estate in the debtor, unless the order of confirmation provides otherwise.[121] What confirmation does not do is discharge the debtor; unlike the Chapter 11 debtor, the Chapter 13 debtor is discharged on completion of the plan (or upon a finding of hardship discharge). These rules are more fully discussed in Chapter 12.[122]

[F]—Plan Payments

The commencement of payment is ordinarily pegged to the filing of the plan, not its confirmation; unless the court orders otherwise, payments must begin within 30 days after filing.[123] Pre-confirmation payments are held by the trustee until the plan is either confirmed or not confirmed. If the plan is confirmed, the trustee distributes those payments in accordance with the plan. If the plan is not confirmed, the trustee returns the payments, minus any allowed administrative expenses, to the debtor.[124] Payments on any unpaid administrative priority debt and of any unpaid portion of the standing trustee's fee must occur prior to or at the same time as each payment to creditors under the plan.[125] Although nothing in the Code requires this, it is generally contemplated that the debtor's payments and the trustee's disbursements occur on a monthly basis.

§ 18.09 Modification of the Plan

[A]—Pre-Confirmation

The debtor has the right to modify the plan at any time prior to confirmation. The modified plan must comply with all of the mandatory requirements of section 1322.[126] After the debtor files the modified plan, it becomes "the plan."[127] Any secured creditor who accepted or rejected the original plan is deemed to have accepted or rejected the modified plan unless (i) the modification changes the creditor's rights

---

[120] Bankruptcy Code § 1327(a). As a general rule, of course, creditors neither accept nor reject a Chapter 13 plan, because they have no vote on it.

[121] Bankruptcy Code § 1327(b). Note that the property vests free and clear unless otherwise provided in the plan or the confirmation order. Bankruptcy Code § 1327(c).

[122] See § 12.05[B] of this book.

[123] Bankruptcy Code § 1326(a)(1).

[124] Bankruptcy Code § 1326(a)(2).

[125] Bankruptcy Code § 1326(b).

[126] Bankruptcy Code § 1323(a). For the required provisions of the plan, see § 18.07[B] of this chapter.

[127] Bankruptcy Code § 1323(b).

and (ii) the creditor changes its previous acceptance or rejection.[128] Since unsecured creditors do not vote on the plan, their view of the modified plan is irrelevant.

[B]—Post-Confirmation

The rules regarding modification of the plan after confirmation are interesting because they depart somewhat from the notion that Chapter 13 cases must be entirely voluntary. Chapter 13 cannot be commenced by a creditor, nor may a creditor file a plan; however, unsecured creditors (and the standing trustee) may propose modifications of the plan after confirmation. To this rather limited extent, a Chapter 13 debtor may be forced into a plan he or she does not want—or, more precisely, may be forced to chose between accepting an unwanted plan or converting to Chapter 7 or dismissing the case altogether.[129]

A modification may be proposed by the debtor, an unsecured creditor, or the trustee at any time after confirmation but before completion of payments. The modification may (i) increase or decrease payments, (ii) extend or reduce the time for payments, or (ii) alter the distribution to a creditor to the extent necessary to take account of payments made outside the plan.[130] The plan must comply with the usual requirements.[131] Any secured creditor who accepted or rejected the original plan is deemed to have accepted or rejected the modified plan unless (i) the modification changes the creditor's rights and (ii) the creditor changes its previous acceptance or rejection.[132] Since unsecured creditors do not vote on the plan, their view of the modified plan is irrelevant. The modified plan becomes "the plan" unless it is disapproved after notice and an opportunity for a hearing.[133]

The usual reasons for the debtor to propose modifications are a decrease in income or an unexpected rise in expenses. However, there is no requirement that either be shown; indeed, there is no requirement that the debtor show cause at all.[134] The only requirements for the modification are the requirements imposed on the original plan—for example, that it meet the best interests of creditors test and the disposable income test. The trustee may object to modification, as can any creditor whose rights under the plan are adversely affected. However, they cannot use the modification hearing to raise issues that could have been raised at the original confirmation hearing.[135]

---

[128] Bankruptcy Code § 1323(c).

[129] The debtor always has the right to convert to Chapter 7 and nearly always has the right to dismiss the case voluntarily. Bankruptcy Code § 1307(a), (b).

[130] Bankruptcy Code § 1329(a).

[131] Bankruptcy Code § 1329(b)(1), (c).

[132] Bankruptcy Code § 1323(c).

[133] Bankruptcy Code § 1329(b)(2).

[134] In re Davis, 34 Bankr. 319 (Bankr. E. D. Va. 1983).

[135] In re Stage, 79 Bankr. 487 (Bankr. S. D. Cal. 1987). However, note Rowley v. Yarnall, 22 F.3d 190 (8th Cir. 1994), a Chapter 12 case in which creditors were allowed to argue that the plan failed to meet the disposable income test through an objection to the debtors' motion for discharge.

There is no statutory requirement that the trustee or a creditor show cause for a proposed modification. However, some courts, looking to the essentially voluntary nature of Chapter 13, have required a showing that there was an unanticipated increase in the debtor's disposable income.[136] Although there are certainly good policy reasons why there should be a need to show cause for an involuntary modification, there is simply no statutory support for the rule. Under the prevailing "plain meaning" mode of interpreting bankruptcy law, the cases that impose the cause requirement are suspect.

§ 18.10 Revocation of Confirmation

The rules regarding revocation of an order of confirmation must inevitably balance the interest in fairness to creditors with the interest in finality. Thus, the timing and the substantive basis for revocation are both limited. On request of a party in interest, and after notice and an opportunity for a hearing, the court may revoke confirmation if it was procured by fraud. The request must be made within 180 days after the date the order of confirmation was entered.[137] If the order of confirmation is revoked, the court may either convert or dismiss the case under section 1307,[138] or, if the debtor submits a modified plan, that modified plan may be confirmed.[139] If so, the proceeding continues under the new plan.

---

[136] See In re Fitak, 92 Bankr. 243 (Bankr. S. D. Ohio 1988), aff'd, 121 Bankr 224 (S.D. Ohio 1990).

[137] Bankruptcy Code § 1330(a).

[138] Bankruptcy Code § 1330(b).

[139] Bankruptcy Code § 1330(b).

CHAPTER 19

Reorganization Under Chapter 12

§ 19.01 Goals of Reorganization

Chapter 12 was added to the Bankruptcy Code as part of the 1986 Amendments because of a perceived need for a new form of reorganization for so-called "family farmers." It is certainly true that few small farmers are able to reorganize successfully under Chapter 11.[1] Whether this is due to flaws with that chapter or the generally hopeless financial state of most Chapter 11 debtors is debatable.[2]

The rhetoric on both sides of the issue has been, at times, extreme. During the debates over Chapter 12, it was perhaps inevitable that there would be echoes of much earlier farm populist movements. In the words of one supporter of the legislation:

> You know, William Jennings Bryan in his famous speech, the Cross of Gold, almost 60[3] years ago, stated these words: "Destroy our cities and they will spring up again as if by magic; but destroy our farms, and the grass will grow in every city in our country." This legislation will hopefully stem the tide that we have seen so recently in the massive bankruptcies in the family farm area.[4]

From the opposition, a rather different opinion: "Congress was wrong to enact a law that redistributes wealth from existing mortgagees to existing mortgagors . . . [and will diminish] . . . the farm debtor's power to mortgage his land . . ."[5]

In any event, the traditional congressional interest in saving family farms led to the enactment of a "temporary" Chapter modeled largely on Chapter 13 rather than Chapter 11. Although Chapter 12 was supposed to expire in October 1993, Congress,

---

[1] Note as well that many farms, even small ones, cannot use Chapter 13 either because their debt level is too high or because they are organized in corporate or partnership form. For a discussion of Chapter 13 eligibility, see § 6.02[B] of this book.

[2] For one rather skeptical opinion, see Michael J. Herbert, *Once More Unto the Breach, Dear Friends: The 1986 Reforms of the Reformed Bankruptcy Reform Act,* 16 Cap. L. Rev. 325 (1987). For contrary views, more favorable to Chapter 12, see Carol Ann Eiden, *The Courts' Rule in Preserving the Family Farm During Bankruptcy Proceedings involving FMHA Loans,* 11 Law & Ineq. J. 417 (1993); William W. Horlock, Jr., *Chapter 12: Relief for the Family Farmer,* 5 Bankr. Dev. J. 229 (1987).

[3] Sic! In fact, when this speech in support of Chapter 12 was made, Bryan's Cross of Gold oration was already 90 years old.

[4] 132 Cong. Rec. H9001 (daily ed. Oct. 2, 1986) (remarks of Rep. Mike Synar).

[5] James J. White, *Taking From Farm Lenders and Farm Debtors: Chapter 12 of the Bankruptcy Code,* 13 J. Corp. L. 1, 2 (1987).

not surprisingly, extended it. This occurred despite the fact that there have not been many Chapter 12 filings.[6]

As indicated, Chapter 12 is limited and its goals fairly narrow: to provide a reorganization alternative to a single type of debtor, the family farmer.[7] It differs from Chapter 13 in that it always involves a business, while Chapter 13 usually involves only a consumer. It differs from at least the larger Chapter 11 cases in that it generally does not preserve the jobs and income of any but a few family members. Fundamentally, its justification must rest on the belief that there is a value to preserving family farming that merits special protection.

This chapter discusses the basic structure of Chapter 12, with special focus on provisions that are unique to it. It is relatively brief, because Chapter 12 is often given short shrift in bankruptcy courses, and because there has been relatively little litigation over even its the most controversial aspects. There is good reason to believe that this lack of litigation indicates that the worst fears of the Chapter 12 critics have by no means come to pass. This, at least, is the view of Professor Van Patten, who has strongly argued that debtors and creditors have managed to work quite well with Chapter 12.[8]

§ 19.02 Conversion and Dismissal

Chapter 12, like Chapter 13, is wholly voluntary; the debtor cannot be forced into it.[9] For the same reason, the debtor has an absolute right to convert a Chapter 12 case to a Chapter 7 case at any time. The right to convert cannot be waived.[10] This means that the Chapter 12 debtor who has come to the conclusion that the plan will not work or is too burdensome always has a ready exit. Any other party in interest (such as a creditor or the trustee) may request conversion of the case to Chapter 7, but only upon a showing that the debtor has committed fraud in connection with the case.[11]

---

[6] From the inception of Chapter 12 in 1986 through June 30, 1993, only about 15,000 Chapter 12 cases have been filed, and about half of those were filed before June 30, 1988. Since 1988, filings have held steady at about 1,400 -1,600 per year, even during the early 1990's when the overall rate of bankruptcy filings soared. This is only a tiny percentage of all bankruptcy filings. In the year ending June 30, 1992, for example, overall bankruptcy filings reached an all-time high of 972,490; of these only 1,634 (1.68%) were Chapter 12 filings. Ed Flynn, *Bankruptcy by the Numbers: Chapter 12 Filings Level Out,* 13 Am. Bankr. Inst. J. 7 (March 1994) Supporters of Chapter 12 have argued that, despite the low numbers, the Chapter has been a success. There is evidence that the success rate for Chapter 12 proceedings is high relative to Chapter 11 and 13 cases. See Jonathan K. Van Patten, *Chapter 12 in the Courts,* 38 S.D. L. Rev. 52, (1993) (indicating a confirmation rate of 60% and a confirmed plan completion rate of 90%).

[7] For a discussion of that term, and of all the eligibility requirements of Chapter 12, see § 6.02[B] of this book.

[8] Jonathan K. Van Patten, *Chapter 12 in the Courts,* 38 S.D. L. Rev. 52, (1993).

[9] See § 6.03 of this book for a discussion of involuntary bankruptcy.

[10] Bankruptcy Code § 1208(a).

[11] Bankruptcy Code § 1208(d).

Similarly, the debtor has a nearly absolute right to dismiss the case voluntarily; this right too cannot be waived.[12] There is one exception to the debtor's right to dismiss. If the debtor converted to Chapter 12 from either Chapter 7 or Chapter 11, the debtor may request but is not automatically entitled to dismissal.[13] Any party in interest may request involuntary dismissal for cause, including such things as mismanagement, failure to file a plan, failure to commence payments under the plan, or termination of the plan according to its own terms.[14] This gives creditors protection against the interminable prolongation of a no-hope proceeding.

§ 19.03 Role of the Trustee and the Debtor

Chapter 12, like Chapter 13, uses a standing trustee, that is, a trustee appointed to serve on all Chapter 12 cases.[15] The Chapter 12 trustee, however, plays a rather different, and somewhat hybrid, role. Like the Chapter 13 trustee, the Chapter 12 trustee is a party in interest, and as such is entitled to be heard on most matters, and carries out many of the same functions as a Chapter 7 trustee. In Chapter 12, however, the trustee is not empowered to advise or assist the debtor. The Chapter 12 trustee also has the broad investigatory powers given to the Chapter 11 trustee but not to the Chapter 13 trustee.[16] The most significant potential difference, however, lies in the fact that a Chapter 12 debtor in possession may under some circumstances be removed and replaced by the standing trustee. This cannot occur under Chapter 13.[17]

On request of a party in interest, and after notice and a hearing, the court may replace the debtor in possession with the standing trustee.[18] This may only be done "for cause," which includes fraud, dishonesty, incompetence, or gross mismanagement. Cause can be established on the basis of either pre-petition or post-petition actions of the debtor.[19] A takeover of the estate is not necessarily permanent; the debtor in possession may be subsequently reinstated by the court.[20]

§ 19.04 Property of the Estate

Under Chapter 12, the estate encompasses more post-petition property than under Chapter 7.[21] This is typical of the reorganization chapters. The details of this are discussed in Chapter 7 of this book.[22]

---

[12] Bankruptcy Code § 1208(b).

[13] Bankruptcy Code § 1208(b).

[14] Bankruptcy Code § 1208(c).

[15] Bankruptcy Code § 1202(a).

[16] Bankruptcy Code § 1202(b)(2).

[17] See § 18.04 of this book regarding the powers of the Chapter 13 trustee.

[18] Bankruptcy Code §§ 1204, 1202(b)(5).

[19] Bankruptcy Code § 1204(a).

[20] Bankruptcy Code § 1204(b).

[21] Bankruptcy Code § 1207.

[22] See § 7.06.

§ 19.05 Automatic Stay/Adequate Protection

There are several ways in which the Chapter 12 automatic stay/adequate protection rules differ from those that normally apply throughout the Code.[23] The first is a predicate to the second: Section 361, which provides the general definition of "adequate protection" for automatic stay and other purposes, does not apply in Chapter 12.[24] Instead, Chapter 12 contains its own, somewhat broader, definition. Under section 361, three types of protection are recognized: periodic payments, the grant of a lien on property, or any other means that provides the indubitable equivalent of the creditor's interest.[25] Section 1205 repeats those three method of giving protection,[26] and adds a fourth—payment of the rental value of the farm, or more precisely: "paying to such entity for the use of farmland the reasonable rent customary in the community where the property is located, based upon the rental value, net income, and earning capacity of the property."[27]

The lender may receive much less protection than it wants under this provision, because it in effect freezes in place a single use of the property and gives protection only for the value of that use. If the lender could seize the property, it might well be able to put the property to a more economically valuable use (for example, residential or commercial use).[28] This issue has not created much of a stir outside of law review articles, suggesting that it, like many of Chapter 12's perceived problems, has not caused much real world concern. In part this may be because farmland prices, which declined sharply in the early 1980's, have in more recent years been relatively stable; it is residential and especially commercial land values that have suffered the steepest declines. It also may be due to the fact that there are so few Chapter 12 cases, and not all of them generate adequate protection litigation. Indeed, to the extent land prices are stable, there is no need to provide anything in the way of adequate protection. While there is some ambiguity in the statute, the generally accepted view is that, like other forms of adequate protection, rent need

---

[23] For a discussion of those rules, see Chapters 8 and 9 of this book.

[24] Bankruptcy Code § 1205(a).

[25] Bankruptcy Code § 361.

[26] Bankruptcy Code § 1205(b)(1) -(4). Note two probably insignificant differences. Subsections (b)(1), (2), and (4) make it clear that co-owners, as well as creditors, are entitled to adequate protection; this is certainly true under § 361 as well. In addition, subsection (b)(4), the catchall provision, does not state that the relief granted must be the indubitable equivalent of the claimant's interest. Although this apparently permits somewhat broader forms of adequate protection than are allowed under § 361, there does not appear to be much practical significance to it.

[27] Bankruptcy Code § 1205(b)(3).

[28] In the view of one critic of Chapter 12, "[t]he borrower, by paying rent based on what may be a low economic value use of the property, would be able to keep the lender from foreclosing and converting it to what may be a higher economic value use." Michael J. Herbert, *Once More Unto the Breach, Dear Friends: The 1986 Reforms of the Reformed Bankruptcy Reform Act,* 16 Cap. U. L. Rev. 325, 345-46 (1987).

be paid when necessary to protect the creditor against a decline in the value of the property.[29] Thus, the issue may arise only rarely.

The final significant feature of the Chapter 12 automatic stay is borrowed from Chapter 13: the codebtor stay. Section 1201(a) provides for a stay of all civil actions to collect a consumer debt of the debtor from an individual who is also liable on the debt or who secured the debt;[30] this presumably protects the debtor from undue pressure to deal with that debt.[31] The scope of this codebtor stay is very limited. It does not apply if the debtor is a partnership or corporation, since a business entity has no consumer debts. It does not apply to the farm operations debt.[32] Finally, it does not apply if the codebtor became liable as a commercial surety.[33] The stay terminates when the case is closed, dismissed, or converted to Chapter 7.[34] The stay does not prevent the holder of a negotiable instrument signed by the codebtor from presenting it and giving notice to the codebtor of its dishonor.[35] which may be necessary to preserve the creditor's rights under Article 3 of the U.C.C.[36] The Chapter 12 codebtor stay provisions were copied almost verbatim from Chapter 13, and the discussion of the Chapter 13 version (which has been subject to far more court interpretation than the Chapter 12 version) is considerably more detailed.[37]

§ 19.06 Use, Sale and Lease of Property

The Chapter 12 debtor-in-possession or trustee has generally the same right to use, sell, or lease property as do trustees and debtors-in-possession under other chapters. The one significant difference is that the Chapter 12 DIP/trustee has a somewhat broader right to sell certain property free and clear of other interests. Under section 363(f), property may be sold free and clear only under limited circumstances.[38] Section 1206 gives a broader power to sell farmland and farm equipment free and clear of other interests, such as mortgages and security interests. The only requirement is that the proceeds of the sale be subject to the interest.[39]

---

[29] In re Anderson, 88 Bankr. 877 (Bankr. N.D. Ind. 1988); In re Turner, 82 Bankr. 465 (Bankr. W.D. Tenn. 1988). See Jonathan K. Van Patten, *Chapter 12 in the Courts,* 38 S.D. L. Rev. 52 (1993) ("only when the value of the land is declining is there even a need to consider adequate protection and, in such event, it will be met by the payment of reasonable rent").

[30] Bankruptcy Code § 1201(a).

[31] For a full discussion of the policy reasons underlying the codebtor stay, see § 8.04 of this book.

[32] In re SFW, Inc., 82 Bankr. 2d (Bankr S.D. Cal. 1988).

[33] Bankruptcy Code § 1201(a)(1).

[34] Bankruptcy Code § 1201(a)(2).

[35] Bankruptcy Code § 1201(b).

[36] See the discussion of this issue at § 8.04 of this book.

[37] See § 8.04 of this book.

[38] For a discussion of this, see § 9.03[E] of this book.

[39] Bankruptcy Code § 1206.

For example, the DIP can sell 40 acres of the farm free and clear of a mortgage provided that the mortgagee is given a lien on the money received from the sale.

§ 19.07 The Plan

[A]—Introduction

As is true with any reorganization proceeding, the key to Chapter 12 is the plan. The Chapter 12 plan rules are based very closely on the Chapter 13 plan rules. There is little creditor participation, and confirmation of the plan is based almost entirely on the debtor's ability to meet certain statutory mandates. Also, as in Chapter 13, there is a time limit on the plan; the Chapter 12 plan may not extend for more than three years without court permission, and in no event may extend for more than five years.[40]

[B]—Classification of Claims

As is true under Chapter 13, Chapter 12 allows little flexibility in adding classifications to those set out by the Code. The debtor in subdividing the general unsecured claims may not discriminate unfairly between classes.[41] The only type of claim that may clearly be separated from others is a consumer debt on which there is an individual who is liable along with the debtor (e.g., a car loan on which the debtor's mother cosigned).[42]

[C]—Treatment of Unsecured Claims

Unsecured claims are given essentially the same treatment in Chapter 12 as they are in Chapter 13. The debtor's plan is subject to two tests. The first, the "best interest of creditors" test, requires that the plan payments, when reduced to present value, must at least equal the Chapter 7 liquidation value of the unsecured claims.[43] For example, suppose that a $10,000 claim has a liquidation value of $300—that is, if this were a Chapter 7 proceeding, $300 would be distributed on this claim. Over the period of the plan, the payments made must, when reduced to present value, equal at least $300; the actual number of dollars paid will be more than that amount.[44]

---

[40] Bankruptcy Code § 1222(c). Note that there is a limited exception to this; payments on secured claims and certain long-term claims may be stretched beyond the three-to five-year period. Bankruptcy Code § 1222(c), (b)(5), (9). There is no requirement, however, that payments on secured claims be stretched beyond the plan period. Appeal of Freund (In re Fortney), 36 F.3d 701 (7th Cir. 1994).

[41] Bankruptcy Code § 1222(b)(1).

[42] Bankruptcy Code § 1222(b)(1).

[43] Bankruptcy Code § 1225(a)(4).

[44] For a discussion of present value and the means by which future payments are discounted to present value, see § 1.06 of this book.

The second test is the "disposable income" test. If the trustee or the holder of any allowed unsecured claim objects to confirmation, the court many not confirm the plan unless either:

1. The claim of the objector is to be paid in full; that is, the value of the property to be distributed on account of that claim is at least equal to the amount of the claim,[45] or

2. The plan provides that all of the debtor's disposable income for a period of at least three years from the date the first payment is due will be applied to making payments under the plan.[46]

As a practical matter, objection would automatically be made unless the plan is designed to provide either full payment or to meet the disposable income test. Full payment is usually infeasible, so virtually all Chapter 12 plans are designed to comply with the disposable income test. Under section 1225(b)(2), "disposable income" is defined as income not reasonably necessary for either (i) the maintenance and support of the debtor and the debtor's dependents or (ii) the continuation, preservation, and operation of the debtor's business. This is substantively identical to the Chapter 13 definition of disposable income. The meaning of the phrase is extensively discussed in § 18.08[A][2] of this book.

[D]—Treatment of Secured Claims

Secured claims are, as in all bankruptcies, given favored treatment in Chapter 12. As a practical matter, secured claims are paid in full during (or in some cases, during and after) the plan.[47] In addition, the liens remain in place on the property until the payments are completed. The only exceptions are those secured claims satisfied by surrender of the collateral. These are two of the three methods of dealing with secured claims that are permitted by the confirmation rules.[48] The third method, acceptance of the plan by the secured party,[49] is rare. More precisely, it is rare that the holder of a secured claim would accept anything less than full payment or surrender of the collateral.

§ 19.08 Confirmation

In addition to the basic requirements concerning payment of claims, the Chapter 12 plan must pass a number of other tests to be confirmed. These are set out in

---

[45] Bankruptcy Code § 1225(b)(1)(A).

[46] Bankruptcy Code § 1225(b)(1)(B). Note that this is slightly different from the Chapter 13 disposable income test, which only requires the debtor to commit its disposable income for three years. Under Chapter 12, the court may lengthen this period to the maximum period of the plan, five years.

[47] Remember that in this context, as throughout the Code, "full payment" refers to the actual, present value of the payments, not the nominal dollar amounts.

[48] Bankruptcy Code § 1225(a)(5)(B), (C).

[49] Bankruptcy Code § 1225(a)(5)(A).

sections 1222 (which sets mandatory requirements for the plan) and 1225 (which deals directly with confirmation). Among the more important are:

1. Surrender of Income. The plan must provide for the submission to the control of the trustee of that portion of the debtor's income necessary for execution of the plan.[50]

2. Treatment of Priority Claims. Unless a claimant otherwise agreed, the plan must provide for "full payment" of priority claims.[51]

3. Payment of Fees. The debtor must have paid all required fees and charges.[52]

4. Good Faith. The plan must be proposed in good faith and not by any means forbidden by law.[53]

5. Feasibility. The debtor must be able to make all plan payments and otherwise comply with the plan.[54]

Confirmation is binding upon virtually every party in interest, and revests the property of the estate in the debtor.[55] It does not, however, discharge the debtor; discharge occurs only later, usually on completion of the plan.[56] In this respect, Chapter 12 follows Chapter 13 rather than Chapter 11; in Chapter 11, confirmation and discharge occur simultaneously.

§ 19.09 Modification of the Plan

[A]—Prior to Confirmation

Occasionally, it becomes necessary to modify a proposed plan prior to confirmation (usually in response to the court's refusal to confirm). The debtor is given a virtually unlimited right to modify. The modification, of course, may not violate any of the requirements for a plan.[57] Once modified, the modified plan becomes "the plan";[58] in other words, for purposes of confirmation and other matters, it is the final version of the plan, not the original, that is controlling.

---

[50] Bankruptcy Code § 1222(a)(1). See also Bankruptcy Code § 1226(c), which sets out the trustee's basic obligation to distribute the plan proceeds.

[51] Bankruptcy Code § 1222(a)(2).

[52] Bankruptcy Code § 1225(a)(2).

[53] Bankruptcy Code § 1225(a)(3).

[54] Bankruptcy Code § 1225(a)(6). Obviously, this requirement really means that the debtor must appear able to make the payments.

[55] Bankruptcy Code § 1227.

[56] See § 12.07 of this book for the discharge rules.

[57] Bankruptcy Code § 1223(a).

[58] Bankruptcy Code § 1223(b).

[B]—Post Confirmation

The plan may also be modified after confirmation. The rules regarding modification of the plan after confirmation are interesting because they depart somewhat from the notion that Chapter 12 cases must be entirely voluntary. Chapter 12 cannot be commenced by a creditor, nor may a creditor file a plan; however, unsecured creditors (and the standing trustee) may propose modifications of the plan after confirmation. To this rather limited extent, a Chapter 12 debtor may be forced into a plan he or she does not want—or, more precisely, may be forced to chose between accepting and funding an unwanted plan, converting to Chapter 7, or dismissing the case altogether.[59]

A modification may be proposed by the debtor, an unsecured creditor, or the trustee at any time after confirmation but before completion of payments. The modification may (i) increase or decrease payments, (ii) extend or reduce the time for payments, or (ii) alter the distribution to a creditor to the extent necessary to take account of payments made outside the plan.[60] The plan must comply with the usual requirements.[61] Any secured creditor who accepted or rejected the original plan is deemed to have accepted or rejected the modified plan unless (i) the modification changes the creditor's rights and (ii) the creditor changes its previous acceptance or rejection.[62] Since unsecured creditors do not vote on the plan, their view of the modified plan is irrelevant. The modified plan becomes "the plan" unless it is disapproved after notice and an opportunity for a hearing.[63]

§ 19.10 Revocation of Confirmation

The rules regarding revocation of an order of confirmation must inevitably balance the interest in fairness to creditors with the interest in finality. Thus, the timing and the substantive basis for revocation are both limited. On request of a party in interest, and after notice and an opportunity for a hearing, the court may revoke confirmation if it was procured by fraud. The request must be made within 180 days after the date the order of confirmation was entered.[64] If the order of confirmation is revoked, the court may either convert or dismiss the case under section 1207.[65] or, if the debtor submits a modified plan, that modified plan may be confirmed.[66] If so, the proceeding continues under the new plan.

---

[59] The debtor always has the right to convert to Chapter 7 and nearly always has the right to voluntarily dismiss the case. Bankruptcy Code § 1208(a), (b).

[60] Bankruptcy Code § 1229(a).

[61] Bankruptcy Code § 1229(b)(1), (c).

[62] Bankruptcy Code § 1223(c).

[63] Bankruptcy Code § 1229(b)(2).

[64] Bankruptcy Code § 1230(a).

[65] Bankruptcy Code § 1230(b).

[66] Bankruptcy Code § 1230(b).

CHAPTER 20

Role of Professionals in the Proceeding

§ 20.01 Introduction

Bankruptcy matters usually involve at least a few professional persons—at a minimum, the lawyers for the debtor, the trustee, and the creditors. In a complex bankruptcy, there may be scores of lawyers. There may also be accountants, experts, and other professionals whose advice is necessary or at least useful to the proceeding. This advice is not cheap; neither is it always useful. There is a perception—not entirely without basis in fact—that complex bankruptcies are nothing but cash cows for bankruptcy professionals.[1] It is certainly true that some cases have yielded immense profits for a few lawyers and accountants. Millions of dollars in professional fees—even tens of millions of dollars—may be incurred in a major reorganization proceedings. Whether this is justifiable may reasonably be questioned. However, it would be impossible to conduct a difficult proceeding without people whose experience and expertise are sufficient to meet the challenges involved. Those few who possess the background and skill required for a complex case naturally demand a commensurate level of compensation. As is true throughout any free market economy, there is a tension between what the market will bear and what the public finds reasonable.

It is also necessary, when considering the proper role of a lawyer or other professional, to deal with potential conflicts of interest. Especially given the fees demanded, it is imperative that the estate be provided with a full equivalent value in services. Part of that value is complete impartiality. Ideally, the professional who represents the estate should be wholly disinterested yet wholly committed to pursuing the interests of the estate (and thus, indirectly, the interests of creditors as a whole). It is for this, as well as knowledge and experience, that the professional is being paid from funds that, after all, are the creditors'.

§ 20.02 Employment of Professionals; Qualification to Serve

The primary provision concerning the employment of professionals in the proceeding is section 327. It broadly authorizes the trustee/DIP (with the approval of the court) to employ attorneys, accountants, appraisers, auctioneers or "other professional persons."[2] There must be no conflict of interest; the professional must not have or represent an interest adverse to the estate; they must also be

---

[1] See, for example, Alexander L. Paskay & Frances Pilaro Wolstenholme, *Chapter 11: A Growing Cash Cow, Some Thoughts on How To Rein in the System,* 1 Am. Bankr. Inst. L. Rev. 331 (1993).

[2] Bankruptcy Code § 327(a). For the procedures involved, see Bankruptcy Rule 2014.

disinterested.[3] Similarly, section 1103(a) of the Code permits a Chapter 11 Creditors' Committee to employ "one or more attorneys, accountants, or other agents, to represent or perform services for" the committee.[4] The professional appointed by the Creditors' Committee must likewise be disinterested; she may not, during employment by the committee, "represent any other entity having an adverse interest in connection with the case."[5]

According to the legislative history, the primary determination of whether a person is disinterested is as follows: "A person is a disinterested person if the person . . . is not a creditor, equity security holder or insider; . . . and . . . does not have an interest materially adverse to the estate."[6] One aspect of this that comes up frequently is that the lawyers for the trustee or the debtor-in-possession should not be creditors of the estate. This can be a problem, particularly in a Chapter 11 case, because the law firm that seeks to represent the DIP in the case may well be the law firm that represented it prior to the case. The debtor may have unpaid bills from the firm; or, just as bad, may have paid those bills during the days immediately proceeding the filing and thus made a preferential transfer to the firm. The DIP has a duty to recover that preference; its lawyers have an equal interest in leaving it be. The only clear way for the law firm to continue representation of the debtor is to waive its right to payment for past-due fees and to return any payment received within the preference period.

As might be expected, the debtor's attorney is subject to especially strict scrutiny. Whether or not the debtor's attorney asks for compensation from the estate, the attorney must file with the court a statement regarding certain pre-petition transactions with the debtor. The statement must detail:

1. Compensation paid during the year prior to the petition for services related to the case,

2. Compensation promised during the year prior to the petition for services related to the case, and

3. The source of the compensation.[7]

If the compensation is found to be excessive, the court can order it to be returned.[8]

---

[3] Bankruptcy Code § 327(a). Remember that "disinterested" means neutral; this differs from "uninterested," which means indifferent.

[4] Bankruptcy Code § 1103(a).

[5] Bankruptcy Code § 1103(b). The Code's example of an entity with an adverse interest is a creditor "of the same class as represented by the committee." Id.

[6] H. R. Rep. No 595, 95th Cong., 1st Sess 310-11 (1977); S. Rep. No. 99, 95th Cong., 2d Sess 23 (197).

[7] Bankruptcy Code § 329(a); see Bankruptcy Rule 2017.

[8] Bankruptcy Code § 329(b).

§ 20.03 Fees

The payment of professional fees from the estate has long been one of the most irksome bankruptcy problems. Given that the creditors are very unlikely to be paid in full—and that "creditors" may include some people who have been gravely injured by the actions of the debtor and others who have not been paid the wages on which they and their families depend—there can be, and often is, some discomfort in dealing with demands from lawyers, accountants, and other professionals to be paid hundreds of dollars per hour for their work. Some years ago I sat in a room at the bankruptcy court full of lawyers and precariously supervised by a bankruptcy judge. The judge remarked, only half-facetiously and almost accurately, that he was the lowest-paid person in the room.[9]

In examining compensation, it is important to note that the Code's rules only apply to those who seek compensation from the estate. For example, a lawyer who is representing a creditor, and whose fees are not reimbursable from the estate, may (within the normal rules governing professional conduct) charge whatever the client is willing to pay. A lawyer who seeks compensation from the estate, and whose fee thus effectively comes out of the pockets of creditors generally, is subject to greater regulation. The usual rationale is the obvious one: the other creditors have not agreed to pay the lawyer anything, let alone what the lawyer is claiming. Even when there is a contract, however, such as an agreement with the trustee or the creditors' committee, the compensation provided for in that contract is subject to court review and the judge is not always obligated to award the amount provided for. "[T]he court may allow compensation different from the compensation provided . . . if such terms and conditions prove to have been improvident in light of developments not capable of being anticipated at the time of the fixing of such terms and conditions."[10]

Section 330 of the Code deals generally with compensation of professionals. They are entitled to "reasonable compensation for actual, necessary services rendered."[11] The court may award this compensation to the professional; it may also award "reimbursement for actual, necessary expenses."[12] Although in most cases compensation is awarded at or near the end of the proceeding or plan confirmation, the professional may request interim compensation. Generally, the request for interim compensation may first be made 120 days after the order for relief, and each 120 days thereafter.[13]

Application of these apparently simple rules has generated great controversy. One issue of considerable debate has been the degree to which the Code's standard for determining compensation diverges from the long-standing tradition of insisting on "economy of the estate." Under the old Bankruptcy Act, the courts tended to demand

---

[9] Actually I think that was an honor that I, a very junior associate, enjoyed.

[10] Bankruptcy Code § 32(a).

[11] Bankruptcy Code § 330(a)(1). See also, Bankruptcy Rule 2016.

[12] Bankruptcy Code § 330(a)(2).

[13] Bankruptcy Code § 331. The time period may be shortened by the court.

what amounted to the lowest possible fee for the service, on the theory that this would preserve as much of the bankruptcy estate as possible for the creditors. Critics of this approach deemed it penny-wise, pound-foolish since it could deprive the proceeding of the best qualified (and thus best-paid) professionals. The legislative history to section 330 was quite specific:

> Attorneys' fees in bankruptcy cases can be quite large and should be closely examined by the court. However bankruptcy legal services are entitled to command the same competency of counsel as other cases. In that light, the policy of this section is to compensate attorneys and other professionals serving in a case under title 11 at the same rate as the attorney or other professional would be compensated for performing comparable services other than in a case under title 11. . . "Notions of economy of the estate in fixing fees are outdated and have no place in a bankruptcy code."[14]

The difficulty is determining what level of compensation is necessary to attract the most able lawyers, accountants, and others without in consequence turning the bankruptcy into a proceeding solely for their benefit.

The 1994 Amendments greatly expanded the statutory guidelines for awarding professional compensation. Under these guidelines, the court must consider various factors, including the time spent, the rates charged, the need for and benefits of the services, and whether the services were performed "within a reasonable amount of time commensurate with the complexity, importance, and nature of the problem, issue, or task addressed."[15] The court is also explicitly told not to allow compensation for services that were unnecessarily duplicative, services that were not reasonably likely to benefit the estate, or services that were not necessary to the administration of the case.[16] How much difference these new guidelines will make is unclear. It is at least arguable, based on some of the language contained in the new version of section 330(a), that the "economy of the estate" concept has been reintroduced to the evaluation of fee applications.

A number of courts utilize test derived from a pre-Code Fifth Circuit case, *American Benefit Life Ins. Co. v. Baddock (In re First Colonial Corp. of America).*[17] As presently applied, this test requires that the judge "ascertain the amount of time involved and the rate at which the services should be compensated."[18] Another

---

[14] 124 Cong. Rec. H1109 (daily ed. Sept 2, 197) (statement of Rep. Edwards); 124 Cong. Rec. S17406 (Oct. 6, 197) (statement of Sen. DeConcini), quoted in Roger M. Whelan, Mandy S. Cohen & Christopher C. Thomson, *Professional Compensation Reform: New Ideas or Old Failings?*, 1 Am. Bankr. Inst. L. Rev. 407 (1993).

[15] Bankruptcy Code § 330(a)(3)(A) (1994 Amendments).

[16] Bankruptcy Code § 330(a)(4)(A) (1994 Amendments).

[17] 544 F.2d 1291 (5th Cir. 1977), cert. denied, 431 U.S. 904 (1977). For a fuller discussion of this case and its progeny, see Gregory W. Bachmann, Note, *Professional Fees in Bankruptcy: Tailoring the Johnson Factors to Suit Bankruptcy*, 1 Am. Bankr. Inst. L. Rev. 453 (1993).

[18] In re Gulf Consol. Services, Inc., 91 Bankr. 414, 417 (Bankr. S.D. Tex. 19).

method—or in the view of some, a variation of the *First Colonial* Method—used by some courts for calculating appropriate fees is the "lodestar."[19] This is also a method that predates the Code; it has been used for a generation by courts awarding attorneys' fees under statutes that provide for their recovery by the prevailing party. It involves calculation not only of the ordinary market price for legal services, and the allowable number of hours, but also for the upward or downward revision of the amount derived if the services were exceptional or deficient.[20] Yet another method, derived from the treatment of attorney's fees in class action suits, focuses on the success of the lawyers efforts—that is, how much property was obtained for the creditors.[21]

A recurring problem is the treatment of paraprofessionals, such as paralegals. The tradition was to treat the cost of everyone but a licensed professional as a mere clerical expense. The Code, however, explicitly recognizes that paraprofessionals are entitled to be treated on the same footing as professionals insofar as compensation is concerned; the court may award "reasonable compensation for actual, necessary services rendered by . . . any paraprofessional persons" who are employed by the professional.[22] Thus, the fees allocable to the paralegal are normally recoverable. Debate lingers, however, over whether this applies only when the paralegal performs functions distinct from those of "clerical" staff. A recent case discussed this issue at some length, and came to the conclusion that it did not:

> The bankruptcy court held that clerical services—those services not requiring the exercise of professional legal judgment—must be included in "overhead." We cannot agree that in all cases the general ability of a legal secretary to perform some particular task determines whether a paralegal or a legal secretary is the appropriate, read "most efficient," employee to perform it at any given instant. At times temporal constraints may foreclose the delegation option. At other times a paralegal—or, for that matter, an attorney—can more productively complete a clerical task, such as photocopying documents, than can a legal secretary. For example, the combination of the paralegal's effort in retaining and instructing a legal secretary with the legal secretary's effort in performing the task may exceed the paralegal's effort in performing the task alone. Or, a legal secretary may lack the judgment needed in selecting and collating the documents to copy, and the expense of having a paralegal or attorney first instruct the legal secretary and then review his or her work for thoroughness and accuracy combined with the legal secretary's time (albeit subsumed within overhead) may exceed the expense of having the

[19] For a fuller discussion of the lodestar, see Gerard Di Conza, Note, *Professional Fees in Bankruptcy: The Use of the Lodestar,* 1 Am. Bankr. Inst. L. Rev. 463 (1993).

[20] For a description of the lodestar approach, see In re UNR Industries, Inc., 96 F.2d 207 (7th Cir. 1993).

[21] See Christine Jagde & Mamie Stathatos, Note, *Professional Fees in Bankruptcy: Percentage-of-the-Recovery Method: A "Solvent" Response for Bankruptcy Proceedings?,* 1 Am. Bankr. Inst. L. Rev. 471 (1993).

[22] Bankruptcy Code § 330(a)(1).

paralegal or attorney personally perform the task in the first place. Or, a legal secretary may simply be unavailable in time to meet a pressing deadline.[23]

The debate over compensation, like so many bankruptcy debates, is ultimately incapable of resolution. The best lawyers will be attracted to bankruptcy only if bankruptcy practice is honored; which, as a practical matter means is well paid. If the bankruptcy bar is not to be what some have called an "under-bar," then there either must be conscription or (as is more appropriate in a free-market economy) compensation sufficient to attract volunteers.

[23] In re Busy Beaver Building Centers, Inc., 19 F.3d 33, 52-53 (3d Cir. 1994).

CHAPTER 21

International Bankruptcy

§ 21.01 Introduction

Insolvency is a problem by no means limited to the United States. Courts around the world, or at least around the free market world, must deal with it. In an era of international business, and multi-national businesses, this inevitably creates problems of overlapping legal systems and legal rules. As there is no overriding sovereignty to force any one nation's courts to defer to another's, either in procedural or substantive matters, the resolution of these problems is left to the vagaries of international law. For one reason or another, international lawyers and international tribunals have not shown the same interest in bankruptcy as they have in matters of war and peace. Indeed, in the words of a leading authority, "the legal treatment of troubled multinationals is primitive and chaotic."[1] There are thus few treaties or other agreements that deal with transnational insolvency.[2] This has left most issues to be resolved by what is colloquially known as the "grab" rule. Generally, every country will grab whatever assets are within its borders, and thus subject to its sovereignty, to administer them. This often means that the multinational insolvent will be administered piecemeal, in multiple proceedings with duplicated expenses and inconsistent results.

Although it is widely recognized that the grab rule is inefficient, it is likely to remain predominant. The most fundamental reason for this is that there is a wide divergence among countries about bankruptcy policy. The choices we have made in this country about the relative status of debtors, creditors, and owners are neither self-evident nor necessary to the continuance of a prosperous economy. Indeed, in the eyes of many, our bankruptcy laws are absurdly tilted toward debtors and impose huge and unnecessary costs on our economy. It is probably true that most of the world's insolvency professionals have no desire to adopt or work under laws substantively identical to those of the United States.

There are also parochial reasons for the grab rule. Local administration means not only local law, but local judges and local lawyers. Local creditors may get a better deal because of this, and the local bar is almost certain to get better fees.

In short, efforts to create a multi-national insolvency regime face two interlinked problems. One is the choice of law to be applied; in the absence of any generalized

---

[1] Jay Lawrence Westbrook, *Theory and Pragmatism in Global Insolvencies: Choice of Law and Choice of Forum,* 65 Am. Bankr. L. J. 457, 458 (1991).

[2] The most ambitious attempt has been made in the European Union (f/k/a/ the European Community, f/f/k/a the European Economic Community, f/f/f/k/a the Common Market). For a discussion of this attempt, and of the issue generally, see Donald T. Trautman, Jay Lawrence Westbrook & Emmanuel Gaillard, *Four Models for International Bankruptcy,* 41 Am. J. Comp. L. 573 (1993).

agreement about what bankruptcy law should do, it is difficult to obtain consensus about choice of law rules. The other is choice of forum. Broadly speaking, British creditors would rather be in British courts, French creditors in French courts, and American creditors in American courts, regardless of the law to be applied.

It is probably a fair statement that the U.S. bankruptcy system is slightly more internationalized than most. This internationalization expresses itself in two arguably contradictory ways. First, U.S. courts are more likely than others to attempt extraterritorial enforcement of their orders. Second, the Bankruptcy Code explicitly authorizes Bankruptcy courts to entertain domestic proceedings ancillary to, and thus governed by the rules of, a foreign proceeding. This second matter is dealt with at length in the following section.

§ 21.02 Ancillary Proceedings Under the Bankruptcy Code

[A]—Introduction

The United States Bankruptcy Code has made at least a minor attempt to deal with transnational bankruptcies without employing the grab rule. Under section 304, a representative appointed in a foreign insolvency proceeding[3] may petition for an ancillary proceeding in U.S. Bankruptcy Court. An ancillary proceeding is not a full-blown bankruptcy case; rather, it is a way of facilitating the foreign court's proceeding. For example, suppose that ABC, Ltd., an insolvent, is under administration in the British court. Although ABC is primarily a British company, it has a warehouse and a small inventory in New York City. If the U.S. Bankruptcy Court for the Southern District of New York[4] grants the petition for an ancillary proceeding, that court may:

1. Enjoin the commencement or continuation of actions against the property or against the debtor regarding the property,[5] or

2. Enjoin the commencement or continuation of the enforcement of any judgment against the debtor respecting the property, or any act or proceeding to create or enforce a lien against the property,[6] or

3. Order that the property, or its proceeds, be turned over to the representative,[7] or

---

[3] Note that the foreign proceeding need not be a "bankruptcy" proceeding in the U.S. sense, but it must be for the purpose of liquidation or reorganization, and it must be in the country where the debtor has its domicile, residence, principal place of business or principal assets. Bankruptcy Code § 101(23).

[4] Since this is fundamentally an action in rem—an action to determine rights to property—it is generally held that the proper court is the court of the district in which the property is located. See Collier on Bankruptcy ¶ 304.05.

[5] Bankruptcy Code § 304(b)(1)(A).

[6] Bankruptcy Code § 304(b)(1)(B).

[7] Bankruptcy Code § 304(b)(2).

4. Order other appropriate relief.[8]

In the example given, the court might order the warehouse and inventory sold, and the proceeds of sale turned over to be administered in the British case.

The court's involvement in a case ancillary to a foreign case may be very slight or quite substantial. To a certain degree, every ancillary proceeding is *sui generis.* The grant of power given by section 304 is rather like the Constitution's "necessary and proper" clause. It is deliberately designed to be open-ended and flexible, and thus to permit the court to fashion customized relief for the particular circumstances of each case. Section 304 proceedings are simply "designed to operate in aid of a principal proceeding abroad."[9] Filing a section 304 petition does not trigger the automatic stay. The foreign representative must affirmatively request injunctive or other available relief.[10]

Most of the disputes over section 304 have not concerned the court's power to take appropriate action if the petition is granted. Indeed, it has been said that in fashioning relief the court has a "near blank check."[11] The more difficult problem is the decision to grant any relief at all—the decision to allow the petition and commence the ancillary proceeding.

The court is given only broad guidance. It is to "be guided by what will best assure an economical and expeditious administration" of the estate.[12] A few factors are specifically identified. These are:

1. Just treatment of all holders of claims against or interests in the estate.[13]

2. Protection of United States claimants against prejudice and inconvenience.[14]

3. The degree to which the foreign proceeding protects against preferences and fraudulent transfers.[15]

4. Whether the foreign proceeding will result in the distribution of the estates assets in a manner that is "substantially in accordance" with the order of distribution required by the Bankruptcy Code.[16]

---

[8] Bankruptcy Code § 304(b)(3).

[9] Interpool, Ltd. v. Certain Freights, 878 F.2d 111, 112 (3d Cir. 1989), quoting Collier on Bankruptcy, ¶ 304.01.

[10] *Interpool, Ltd.*, 878 F.2d at 112. *Interpool* went on to note that the foreign representative has an alternative — filing a full-scale bankruptcy case under Bankruptcy Code § 303(b)(4). 878 F.2d. at 112 n. 4.

[11] In re Culmer, 25 Bankr. 621, 624 (Bankr. S.D.N.Y. 1982).

[12] Bankruptcy Code § 304(c).

[13] Bankruptcy Code § 304(c)(1).

[14] Bankruptcy Code § 304(c)(2).

[15] Bankruptcy Code § 304(c)(3).

[16] Bankruptcy Code § 304(c)(4).

5. "Comity," meaning cooperative goodwill between nations and their court systems,[17] and

6. If the insolvent is an individual, the degree to which the foreign proceeding provides an opportunity for a "fresh start."[18]

It has frequently been noted that these six factors are internally contradictory, and do nothing more than list some of the issues that inevitably arise in a transnational bankruptcy.[19] Factor 1 is at least facially neutral, and indeed may support an ancillary proceeding as providing the most consistent and economical method of dealing with the insolvency. However, even it may be used in a parochial fashion if the judge merely looks to U.S. law as the touchstone of what is "just." Factors 2 and 4 are wholly parochial; the former explicitly protects the interests of U.S. creditors, even at the expense of foreign creditors; the latter assumes that the Bankruptcy Code's distributional system is inherently better than any substantially different alternative. The third factor may be in part parochial, since there are somewhat different attitudes about whether certain types of transfers should be avoidable. Factor 5 is the only factor that unequivocally points toward granting the petition. Finally, factor 6 might best be characterized as none of our business; why should American courts care whether foreign countries give their own people a fresh start in bankruptcy?

Also note that the factors the court is supposed to use in determining whether to grant the petition for an ancillary proceeding operate as a sideways choice of law rule. On the face of it, section 304 is only a choice of forum rule. However, the decision to permit a section 304 proceeding involves the court obliquely in choice of law, because if the law that would be applied is too much different from American law, there will be no ancillary proceeding.

Given the highly equivocal guidance given to courts, it is perhaps surprising that, in general, bankruptcy judges have been reasonably sympathetic to section 304 petitions. As a general rule, the petition is likely to be granted unless there are serious concerns about the treatment of United States creditors. For example, if in the foreign proceeding a U.S. lien creditor would be treated as an unsecured creditor, thus losing the benefits of its security, the court may refuse to grant a petition to turn over the encumbered property.[20]

A couple of recent cases well illustrate the potential complexity of the court's decision to grant the section 304 petition. *Interpool, Ltd. v. Certain Freights*[21] involved the petition by the liquidator of an Australian company for an ancillary proceeding and dismissal of a pending Chapter 7 case against the debtor. The court denied the petition, focusing on the differences between Australian and American insolvency law. The court saw procedural problems regarding notice given to

---

[17] Bankruptcy Code § 304(c)(5).

[18] Bankruptcy Code § 304(c)(6).

[19] For a concise discussion of this, see Collier on Bankruptcy ¶ 304.04.

[20] In re Toga Mfg., Ltd., 28 Bankr 165 (Bankr. E.D. Mich. 1983).

[21] 102 Bankr. 373 (D.N.J. 1988).

creditors in the Australian proceeding. More importantly, the court saw a crucial difference in the substantive law. The case raised the possibility that there had been abusive actions by an insider. Under American law, this might cause the equitable subordination of the insider's claim against the estate.[22] However, Australian law apparently does not provide for equitable subordination.[23] In summary, in the court's view:

> Both the laws and the public policy of the United States will be violated if the case is permitted to proceed under Australian law. The claims of the creditors may have already been prejudiced by the dealings between the Liquidator and [the insider], and this Court does not intend to stand idly by while United States citizens and creditors are harmed.[24]

The phrasing of the court's decision may well suggest that this case represents nothing more than excessive parochialism from the United States Bankruptcy Court. It is hard to say that equitable subordination represents any fundamental bankruptcy policy. To be sure, it is recognized in the Bankruptcy Code. However, it is a doctrine that very rarely applies and is by no stretch of the imagination essential to bankruptcy law as other factors noted in section 304, such as preferences, fraudulent transfers, and a fresh start.[25]

More in keeping, perhaps, with the spirit of section 304 is the case of *In re Brierley.*[26] That case involved an English liquidator's section 304 petition. The court noted the long tradition of granting comity to other common law countries:

> The laws of the United Kingdom share the same common law tradition of our own system of jurisprudence. The federal courts have repeatedly granted comity to foreign proceedings where the foreign proceeding was in the United Kingdom or in a country whose laws were derived from the United Kingdom's laws.[27]

The court brushed aside the complaint that an American creditor would have to litigate in London. "One can surmise that there will be some delay and, if traveling to hearings in England is called for, possibly enhanced costs for Wertheim. But the prejudice and inconvenience of which Wertheim complains is typical of what every U.S. creditor in a sizeable domestic case encounters when it is forced to liquidate its claim."[28]

The court noted that the requested ancillary proceeding was part of a vast and complex transnational insolvency and that coordination was of particular

---

[22] For a discussion of equitable subordination, see § 10.05[C] of this book.

[23] *Interpool, Ltd.,* 102 Bankr. at 379.

[24] *Interpool, Ltd.,* 102 Bankr. at 380.

[25] For a particularly sharp and detailed criticism of Interpool, see Jay Lawrence Westbrook, *Theory and Pragmatism in Global Insolvencies: Choice of Law and Choice of Forum,* 65 Am. Bankr. L.J. 457, 474-78 (1991).

[26] 145 Bankr. 151 (Bankr. S.D.N.Y. 1992).

[27] In re Brierley, 145 Bankr. at 162, n.5.

[28] In re Brierley, 145 Bankr. at 163.

importance.[29] Finally, the court compared the relevant British law with the Bankruptcy Code. Rather than do what the Interpool court did—pick on a single relatively minor difference between the laws—the *Brierley* court looked at the broad structure and goals of the British insolvency law. It noted that the rights of creditors, and the duties of the administrator, were generally similar to the rights of creditors and the obligations of a trustee or debtor-in-possession under the Bankruptcy Code. It also noted that the distributional scheme under the British Act, although somewhat different from that under the Bankruptcy Code, was overall much the same. The standard it used, in short, was far different from the standard in *Interpool*: "Nothing dictates that the foreign law be a carbon-copy of our law; rather, the Insolvency Act must not be *repugnant* to American laws and policies, which it is manifestly not."[30]

[B]—Who May Be a Debtor

Broadly speaking, foreign law, rather than American law, determines whether a person can be a debtor under section 304. In the case of *Goerg v. Parungo (In Re Goerg),*[31] the court was faced with the question of whether an ancillary proceeding could be filed with regard to the insolvent estate of the late Heinz Guenter Kaussen, a West German citizen. Under West German law, a decedent's estate can be put in bankruptcy.[32] This is not possible under American law.[33] Focusing on the purpose underlying section 304, and noting that Congress could extend the Bankruptcy Code to insolvent decedents' estates, the court held that the term "debtor" in section 304 does not have the same meaning it has generally in the Code:

> Because the focus is on making United States processes available in aid of foreign proceedings, not actual bankruptcy administration, it would make little sense to require that the subject of the foreign proceeding qualify as a "debtor" under United States bankruptcy law . . . Indeed, in light of the comity concerns that induced Congress to enact section 304, it would make eminent sense for Congress to define expansively the class of foreign insolvency proceedings for which ancillary assistance is available.[34]

Goerg also stressed that the fact that a section 304 proceeding is very limited, with no automatic stay, no discharge, and potentially no relief at all.[35]

---

[29] In re Brierley, 145 Bankr. at 164.

[30] In re Brierley, 145 Bankr. at 165 (emphasis added).

[31] 844 F.2d 1562 (11th Cir. 1988), *cert. denied,* 488 U.S. 1034 (1989).

[32] Ingo A. J. Klocker, *Foreign Debtors and Creditors Under United States and West German Bankruptcy Law: An Analysis and Comparison,* 20 Tex. Int'l. L.J. 55, 90 and n. 224 (1985).

[33] In re Goerg, 844 F.2d at 1566.

[34] In re Goerg, 844 F.2d at 1568.

[35] In re Goerg, 844 F.2d at 1568.

[C]—What Law Applies/What Forum Adjudicates

The link between choice of law and choice of forum in transnational bankruptcies is well illustrated by *Koreag, Controle et Revision S.A. v. Refco F/X Associates, Inc. (In re Koreag, Controle et Revision S.A.).*[36] That case involved the attempt by the liquidator of a Swiss bank to recover funds that had been transferred from Switzerland to the United States. A transfer of those funds was requested under section 304(b)(2). The Court of Appeals held that, before granting the request for relief, the bankruptcy court should have determined whether the funds were in fact property of the bankrupt Swiss bank and that this determination should have been made under applicable New York state law. Quoting Collier on Bankruptcy, the court said: "'For purposes of section 304, the estate of a foreign debtor is defined by the law of the jurisdiction in which the foreign proceeding is pending, with other applicable laws serving to define the estate's interest in particular property."[37]

In response to this, the Swiss liquidator argued that even if local law was to be applied regarding ownership, the Swiss forum presiding over the insolvency case, and not a local U.S. bankruptcy court, should apply the law. It argued that adjudication of creditors claims in a United States court would deprive non-U.S. creditors of an effective opportunity to be heard. The court rejected this argument.[38] In essence, it held that section 304 contemplates that relief will be given pursuant to American procedural rules, by an American court.

[D]—Conclusion

The future of transnational insolvency law remains uncertain. At present, development is stunted by a combination of parochial interests (more bluntly, people who lend, borrow, and vote locally) and concerns about sovereignty. Progress has been very slow even within relatively united economic blocks such as the European Union. As more and more businesses operate internationally, however, pressure for a more uniform and efficient system is bound to grow. It is likely that there will some day be an international bankruptcy code subscribed to by at least a substantial number of countries. If and when this happens it will be at least as dramatic a change as was the 19th Century shift of American insolvency law from the states to the federal government.

In the words of one excellent commentary on international bankruptcy:

> The European Community has been a schoolhouse for the entire world for learning about international cooperation. Its extraordinary efforts have taught lessons in its failures as well as in its more frequent successes. The difficulty of achieving European agreement as to insolvency is a leading example. How can it be that governors and lawyers who have so skillfully overcome tradition, inertia, and parochialism in so many complex areas have made so little progress in matters of insolvency.[39]

---

[36] 961 F.2d 341 (2d Cir. 1992), cert. denied, 113 S. Ct. 188 (1992).

[37] In re Koreag, 961 F.2d at 348, *quoting* Collier on Bankruptcy ¶ 304.01.

[38] In re Koreag, 941 F.2d at 349-50.

[39] Donald T. Trautman, Jay Lawrence Westbrook & Emmanuel Gaillard, *Four Models for International Bankruptcy,* 41 Am. J. Comp. L. 573, 625 (1993).

Whatever the answer, in a world of ever greater international investment, trade, capital flows, and economic integration, the need for workable international solvency law is increasingly imperative. Speaking of and to bankruptcy professionals, the same commentary states: "we bear an especially great burden to adjust our thinking to a larger and more generous perspective, in the service of the great social and economic communities that sustain us and our work."[40]

[40] Id.

CHAPTER **22**

Special Uses of, and Problems in, Bankruptcy

§ 22.01 Introduction

Bankruptcy is a powerful tool in the hands of capable lawyers. It can do more than serve its most obvious function—the discharge of unpayable debt for the financially troubled. It can also be used as a tool to deal with many other difficult problems, particularly problems faced by business entities that are looking for a clean way out of difficulties. In this chapter, we discuss only a few of the most well-publicized creative bankruptcies. Keep in mind that every one of these specialized uses is, to say the very least, controversial. Indeed, to many they are not "uses" but "abuses" that ought to be curbed by court or, if necessary, Congressional action.

Some of the uses of bankruptcy discussed in this Chapter are new. Others, notably substantive consolidation, have a long history. Some are specifically provided for in the Code; other represent the use of existing bankruptcy tools to accomplish goals outside the traditional scope of bankruptcy proceedings.

§ 22.02 Mass Torts

Disaster is inevitable in any society. In an industrial society, it is equally inevitable that some disasters will occur because of the bad luck, incompetence, or bad faith of an industrial enterprise. A sedative may have teratogenic properties that cause thousands of disabling birth defects. A commonly used mineral—a mineral in fact once used in baby powder—may cause a fatal lung disease. An intrauterine device may cause sterility. A jumbo jet may crash. Any of these disasters may result in a "mass tort"—broadly speaking, a situation in which a single act, transaction, or product has generated hundreds or thousands of personal injury lawsuits.

Ordinary procedural law has few devices to deal with mass torts, and efforts to create more such devices have generally proved futile. In large measure, this is because of inextricable links between procedural means and substantive results. Most proposals for procedural reform include massive consolidation of actions; unified discovery, pre-trial, and trial,restrictions on the multiple award of punitive damages, and review of attorneys, fees. Each of these proposals is controversial in itself; put together, those controversies make it virtually impossible to create workable mass tort reform.

Attorneys, particularly plaintiffs' attorneys, chafe at the restrictions and the degree of judicial control that would be inevitable in any transformation of the tort process. Critics of this attitude claim that it is all rooted in the desire to obtain maximum fees for minimum effort. The opponents retort that tort reform is nothing more than a barely disguised effort to close off avenues of recovery for people who have been maimed by bad products peddled by incompetent or uncaring businesses.

Almost by default, bankruptcy has become a battleground in this struggle over tort reformulation. A bankruptcy is a collective proceeding; in most cases it provides debtor and creditors with a single forum in which all controversies can be decided before a single judge. True, that judge is (generally) unaided by a jury;[1] but the judge has the advantage of dealing with all matters concerning the debtor in one go. Moreover, the judge can provide for an even distribution of available assets among all claimants, thus avoiding the possibility that those claimants who sue early will collect in full while those who sue late will get little or nothing. In any event, there is nothing in the Bankruptcy Code that prevents a debtor from using it to attempt a global resolution of mass tort issues, and a number of companies have attempted exactly that.

In general, this effort has met with only limited success. It is not clear that either claimants or defendants are better off than they would have been if the mass tort had been litigated piecemeal. Although there are some savings from the consolidation of the proceeding, these are gained at heavy cost; the bankruptcy itself is extremely expensive and the management loses a measure of control over the debtor while the case is proceeding. From the standpoint of the claimants, bankruptcy may simply lead to further frustrating delay. In part this is because the bankruptcy must inevitably concern itself with matters far removed from, and far different from, the goal of the claimants. They only want compensation, but the bankruptcy court must also consider the interests of other creditors and the rights of the debtor. The tort victims' goal is compensation; the purpose of bankruptcy is financial rehabilitation. These are often in fatal conflict.[2]

§ 22.03 Collective Bargaining Agreements

Depending on one's perspective, a financially troubled company's union contract may well be something that the company unreasonably dislikes or of necessity must abrogate. Perhaps the workers are unreasonable, obdurate luddites, and uninterested in the continued survival of the business. Or perhaps they are themselves at tether's end, unconscionably subjected to devastating loss because of the ineptitude of a management that perhaps ought never have been hired and certainly ought now be fired. Those extremes at least describe the differing viewpoints of capital and labor.

This becomes an issue of bankruptcy law when the company decides to deal with its perceived labor problems in Chapter 11. Remember that a trustee or DIP has the power to reject executory contracts; remember too that a collective bargaining agreement is itself an executory contract. At this point, you are exactly in tune with the thinking of a number of corporate executives circa 1980. If a collective bargaining agreement has no status apart from that as executory contract, then, like any executory contract, it can be rejected. There will, of course, be a claim for breach,

---

[1] For a discussion of jury trials in bankruptcy proceedings, see § 5.04[F].

[2] For a detailed and skeptical review of one mass tort case ultimately resolved in bankruptcy, see Ronald J. Bacigal, The Limits of Litigation: The Dalkon Shield Controversy (1990).

but that claim is just another general unsecured claim, payable only in depreciated bankruptcy dollars.[3] If a debtor can cut its labor costs by $500,000,000, and is forced to pay only $50,000,000 to do so, it is still substantially ahead.

This is what led a number of companies to file Chapter 11 with an eye to rejecting their union contracts. This tactic aroused outrage, especially, but not exclusively, from organized labor. The Supreme Court, however, ruled that it was permissible; that nothing in the Bankruptcy Code or other federal law bestowed special bankruptcy privileges on union contracts.[4]

Congress, perhaps more receptive to labor issues, quickly responded with a compromise. It accepted the basic principle that collective bargaining agreements could be rejected. However, it decided that these contracts should be given special status and special protection. In effect, it made organized labor a preferred contract creditor in Chapter 11 bankruptcy proceedings. This preference is indirect; the debtor is not given any special treatment when it comes to paying claims, but it is preferred when it comes to determining which contracts the debtor must accept and which it may reject. Whether this compromise has in fact benefitted either reorganizing companies or their labor unions is open to doubt. Bankruptcy judges, who are sometimes called "liberal" but are perhaps more accurately described as "receptive to debtors' concerns," have not always been enthusiastic about the special status conferred on labor agreements. In doubtful cases they are perhaps more likely to concur with the debtor's claim that rejection of the contract is required for reorganization than the union's claim that rejection put too much of the reorganization burden on labor. It is, however, at least true that the new rules have forced both union and management to appear to conduct good faith negotiations over proposed changes in wages and working conditions.[5]

Congress' response to the collective bargaining agreement problem is embodied in section 1113.[6] Both substantive and procedural requirements are imposed. Broadly speaking, the procedural requirements force both sides to attempt negotiation of a mutually satisfactory new deal. In this respect, it reinforces the bargain model of both Chapter 11 and of collective bargaining law. If the bargaining process fails, then and only then may the debtor act unilaterally; if it does so, the substantive requirements force the court to decide whether a new deal is really necessary to save the debtor. In this respect, section 1113 models itself to a degree on the cramdown rules.

---

[3] For a discussion of the effect of rejecting an executory contract, see § 9.04[C] of this book.

[4] National Labor Relations Board v. Bildisco & Bildisco, 465 U.S. 513 (1984).

[5] See Daniel Keating, *The Continuing Puzzle of Collective Bargaining Agreements in Bankruptcy,* 35 Wm. & Mary L. Rev. 503 (1994). For an interesting empirical analysis of section 1113 cases, see Christopher D. Cameron, *How "Necessary" Became the Mother of Rejection: An Empirical Look at the Fate of Collective Bargaining Agreements on the Tenth Anniversary of Bankruptcy Code Section 1113,* 34 Santa Clara L. Rev. 841 (1994).

[6] Note also Bankruptcy Code § 1114, enacted under the Retiree Benefits Bankruptcy Protection Act of 1988, which has parallel provisions for dealing with the payment of insurance benefits to retired employees.

After the petition is filed, but before filing an application to reject a collective bargaining agreement, the trustee/DIP must make a proposal to the representative of the employees. This proposal must be based on the most complete and reliable information available; it must encompass those "necessary modifications" in the agreement as are "necessary to permit the reorganization."[7] The employees' representative must also be given all relevant information necessary to evaluate the proposal.[8] From that point on, the trustee/DIP and the employees will, it is hoped, negotiate; in the somewhat rosy scenario of the Code, "the trustee shall meet, at reasonable times, with the authorized representative [of the employees] to confer in good faith in attempting to reach mutually satisfactory modifications of such agreement."[9]

When those negotiations fail the trustee/DIP may seek to terminate the agreement unilaterally, and substitute new terms and conditions of employment. This requires court approval. The court approves only if (1) the requirements regarding the proposal and the negotiating process were met,[10] (2) the authorized representative of the employees has refused to accept the proposal without good cause,[11] and (3) the balance of equities "clearly" favors rejection of the agreement.[12] When weighing the equities, the courts have often considered six issues:

1. The likelihood and consequences of liquidation if rejection is not permitted,

2. The likely reduction in the creditors' claims if the agreement remains in effect,

3. The likelihood and consequences of a strike if the agreement is avoided,

4. The possibility and likely effect of employee claims for breach of contract if the agreement is avoided,

5. The cost-spreading abilities of the various parties, taking into account the number of employees covered by the agreement and how their wages and benefits compare with those of others in the industry, and

6. The good or bad faith of the parties in dealing with the debtor's financial problems.[13]

The degree to which this provision adequately addresses the problems of collective bargaining agreements is debateable. Labor organizations remain dissatisfied. In any event, the problems created by rejecting a collective bargaining

---

[7] Bankruptcy Code § 1113(b)(1)(A).

[8] Bankruptcy Code § 1113(b)(1)(B).

[9] Bankruptcy Code § 1113(b)(2).

[10] Bankruptcy Code § 1113(c)(1).

[11] Bankruptcy Code § 1113(c)(2).

[12] Bankruptcy Code § 1113(c)(3).

[13] Truck Drivers Local 907 v. Carey Transportation, Inc., 816 F.2d 82 (2d Cir. 1987).

agreement may outweigh the benefits; nothing in the Bankruptcy Code takes away the ability of disgruntled and demoralized employees to strike or requires them to give their best efforts to an employee whom they perceive as having betrayed them.

§ 22.04 "Single Asset" Proceedings

The 1980's and early 1990's witnessed one of the most spectacular boom and bust cycles ever in the long boom and bust history of real estate development. Spurred in large measure by tax laws enacted in 1982 (and perhaps in part by lax regulation of lending institutions), developers put up commercial and residential buildings at a dizzying pace. In 1986, however, the favorable tax treatment of passive real estate investments came to an abrupt end. This, coupled with the huge overhang of already built but barely needed property, brought on a savage collapse of rental and resale values. Problems were widespread, but were particularly acute in those areas, such as New England, Texas, and California, that had enjoyed the frothiest go-go markets.

Even the worst economic clouds enjoy at least one silver lining: bankruptcy. Insolvent developers and developments reached for their lawyers in an effort to stave off foreclosure. In many of these cases, the debtor had only one major asset, a building, and only one major creditor, the financial institution from which it borrowed to build. While at first many financial institutions were accommodating, this rapidly changed. Bad loans mean bust banks, and the collapse of the construction industry led inevitably to the immensely expensive government bailout of the financial industry. Banks and thrifts were taken over by the government in breathtaking numbers; for a time, at least, our financial system was in a precarious position ominously reminiscent of the early years of the Great Depression.

Under intense government scrutiny and financial pressure, lenders began to push their borrowers harder and harder. From the lenders' viewpoint, most of the bad real estate loans could be salvaged only in part and only by foreclosure. By contrast, many developers, still perhaps believing the line of patter with which they sold the bank on the project originally, stubbornly clung to the hope that eventually the market would rise and eventually the building would fill with well-paying tenants. It is this clash between hard-headed calculation and blind faith that is at the root of the controversy over the propriety of the single asset bankruptcy filed by the single asset debtor (who has inevitably become known as SAD).

There is no real definition of the single-asset bankruptcy; indeed, the name is a bit misleading. The following, however, is a fair paradigm:

> Lucky Ace Development, Ltd. (LAD), an affiliate of Lucky Star Development, Inc. (LSD), is a limited partnership that owns the 30-story Lucky Tower, an office building completed in 1988. Only 25% of the building's space is occupied, and only two-thirds of that is occupied by tenants who are current on their rent. To attract any tenants at all, LAD has had to accept bargain-basement rents. The rent per square foot is only half of what LSD had projected when it first set up LAD and promoted

the Lucky Tower project. Thus, total rental income is barely 10% of what had been anticipated. This is nowhere near enough to cover even the interest payments on the $20,000,000 construction loan made to LAD by River Bank. River Bank has a mortgage on the building for the full amount of the loan, plus interest; however, the building is now worth less than $8,000,000.

LAD has filed Chapter 11 bankruptcy. As things presently stand, LAD has, apart from the Tower, only about $35,000 in assets, although these are free of encumbrances. River Bank has a secured claim for the value of the building ($8,000,000), and an unsecured claim for the balance of the principal plus the pre-petition interest, a total of $15,000,000. LAD also owes $3,000 to Sanitation Management, Inc. (the company that cleans the building) and $250 to Ding-Dong Telephone Company, LAD's long-distance carrier.

River Bank refuses even to consider any plan of reorganization. The Bank now thinks that LAD's management is, at the very least, incompetent and, in all probability, corrupt; it wants the building, and believes it can veto any plan. LAD proposes a plan under which there are two classes of unsecured debt: Class 1 is River Bank's unsecured claim; Class 2 is the unsecured claims of Sanitation Management and Ding-Dong. Class 1 is to receive a distribution of 1%, payable in equal installments over 20 years. Class 2 is to receive a distribution of 99.99%, payable in full immediately upon confirmation. There is also a class of secured debt—River Bank's secured claim; it is to be paid off over 25 years, with 85% of the payments to come in years 20 through 25.

Although River Bank votes against the plan, LAD claims that its plan can be confirmed under the cramdown rules.[14] It is providing everyone at least the liquidation value of its claim, and one impaired class, Class 2, has voted for the plan. River Bank objects to confirmation and demands that the case be dismissed or, in the alternative, that the automatic stay be lifted.

In essence, River Bank and LAD are fighting over who will get the benefit of any future appreciation of the building. If the plan is confirmed, and the market improves, LAD (more precisely, LAD's owners) will benefit from that improvement. If River Bank gets to foreclose, and if it keeps the building long enough for the building to appreciate in value, River Bank will get the benefit of that appreciation. River Bank is also seeking to cut its losses. It may not want to keep the building, thus perhaps sending good money after bad, but if it gets the building it can at least sell it for its current value and obtain at least partial payment on what is at present a "non-performing" loan. This in turn may facilitate River Bank's efforts to repair its own financial status and improve its capital position. Such improvements may get River Bank out of hot water with the regulatory authorities and enable it to make new and it is to be hoped better loans.

---

[14] For a discussion of these rules, see § 17.15[D] of this book.

Prior to the 1994 Amendments, there was little in the Code that is designed to deal with this problem. The most obvious provision was, and is, section 1111(b), discussed in Chapter 17 of this book. However, that section does not address the real desire of the creditor—which is to terminate the bankruptcy, seize the collateral, and retain or resell it.

In consequence, a number of other attacks have been made on single-asset bankruptcies. We have already looked at two—attacks on the gerrymandering of a class of claims to vote for the plan[15] and attacks on the new value exception to the absolute priority rule.[16] More central is an attack on the whole proceeding; many creditors have asserted that the single-assets proceedings are in bad faith. It appears that to a large degree the creditors are winning this argument; it has become increasingly difficult for a true single-asset plan to be confirmed.[17] Perhaps more significantly, the real estate recession of the late 1980's and early 1990's is now fading, and with it much of the impetus behind single asset cases.

The 1994 Amendments added just a little additional ammunition to the creditors' arsenal. There is now a provision that tightens the time limits imposed on some single asset debtors. The provision applies only to so-called "single asset real estate" cases. These are narrowly defined as cases in which substantially all of the gross income of the debtor is generated by a single property or project (other than a property that consists of 1 to 3 residential units). In addition, the debtor must have aggregate noncontingent liquidated secured debts of $4,000,000 or less.[18] This narrow definition excludes large single asset cases, such as the one described in the hypothetical above.

The substantive restriction on the single asset real estate case is found in the automatic stay rules. Ordinarily, the court is to lift the stay on the secured creditor's foreclosure rights unless, within 90 days of the entry of the order for relief, the debtor has either filed a plan that has "a reasonable possibility of being confirmed within a reasonable time" or has commenced making monthly payments of interest on the secured claim.[19] The interest payments are pegged to "a current fair market rate," which apparently may be more than, equal to, or less than the amount provided for in the loan agreement.[20] Even this provision is not absolute; the court may, "for cause" extend the time period.[21] Whether this provision will reduce complaints about single asset cases remains to be seen.

---

[15] See § 17.11[E] of this book.

[16] See § 17.15[D][4] of this book.

[17] See generally, Symposium, 1 Am. Bankr. Inst. L. J. 1 (1993).

[18] Bankruptcy Code § 101(51B) (1994 Amendments).

[19] Bankruptcy Code § 362(d)(3) (1994 Amendments).

[20] Bankruptcy Code § 362(d)(3)(B) (1994 Amendments).

[21] Bankruptcy Code § 362(d)(3) (1994 Amendments).

§ 22.05 Consolidation

Except for spouses, who may file joint bankruptcy proceedings,[22] each individual or entity in bankruptcy is treated separately. This is ordinarily true even if related debtors go into bankruptcy at the same time. For example, real estate developers commonly set up many corporations and partnerships; typically each project will involve different companies, although all of them are under the direct or indirect control of the same developer. The failure of the developer may result in the developer's personal bankruptcy as well as the bankruptcy of several related companies. In most cases, each of those bankruptcies will be deal with separately, even though there is overlapping ownership, control, and debt. However, it is common to order "administrative consolidation" (also known as "joint administration" and "procedural consolidation"; the terms are used interchangeably). More significantly for creditors, under some circumstances, the court may order substantive consolidation of proceedings.

Administrative consolidation is, as the name suggests, simply a method of simplifying procedures to increase convenience and reduce costs. Bankruptcy Rule 1015(b) specifically permits the court to order a joint administration of two or more estates if the petitions are pending in the same court and the petitioners are spouses, a partnership and at least one of its general partners, two or more general partners of the same partnership or a debtor and an "affiliate."[23] "Affiliate" has the meaning prescribed by section 101 of the Code; broadly speaking, that definition describes various situations in which a person is likely to be in effective control of a business entity by reason of equity or property ownership. The most common situation described in the rule is ownership of at least 20 percent of the voting equity.[24] Thus, a closely held corporation is usually an affiliate of its primary owners; similarly, a subsidiary is an affiliate of its parent corporation.

However, the rule is very clear about the limited nature of joint administration. It does not consolidate the debts or the assets of the debtors, which remain separate. It merely permits such things as the appointment of a single trustee, the use of "a single docket . . . including the listing of filed claims, the combining of notices to creditors of the different estates, and the joint handling of other purely administrative matters that may aid in expediting the cases and rendering the process less costly."[25] Even these actions are permitted only to the extent that they do not materially affect the interests of the creditors of the different estates.[26] For example, in some cases

---

[22] See § 6.02[D] of this book. Note that the joint filing does not mean that the cases are substantively consolidated; substantive consolidation of joint husband-wife cases is analyzed in much the same way as substantive consolidation generally. See Reider v. Federal Deposit Insurance Corp. (In Re Reider), 31 F.3d 1102 (11th Cir. 1994).

[23] Bankruptcy Rule 1015(b).

[24] Bankruptcy Code § 101(2).

[25] 1983 Advisory Committee Note to Rule 1015.

[26] Bankruptcy Rule 1015 partially addresses this issue: "Prior to entering an order [for joint administration] the court shall give consideration to protecting creditors of different estates against potential conflicts of interest."

it might be necessary to have separate trustees because there are disputes between the debtors.[27] If a parent and subsidiary have both filed bankruptcy, and the sub is making a claim for damages against the parent, it would generally be inappropriate to have the same trustee for both, since the dispute would create a conflict of interest.

In short, administrative consolidation does not affect the fundamental legal separateness of the debtors. In the end, each debtor is liquidated or reorganized separately; each set of creditors receives payment from the assets or future income of the debtor against whom their claims are made. It is certainly true that in many of these cases each debtor will owe money to a largely similar group of creditors; and in some cases one debtor will be a co-obligor with another debtor; but the debts will be paid (or more likely not paid) by the debtor or debtors who actually incurred them, not by the group as a whole.

This is the key difference between administrative and substantive consolidation. Substantive consolidation entails the elimination of legal distinctions between entities. Debtor A and Debtor B and Debtor C lose their separate identity, and become, in effect, debtor ABC. All of their assets are combined, as are all of their obligations. A single liquidation or a single reorganization follows; all creditors of each entity are paid, if at all, by the consolidated entity.

Sorting out the exact dimensions of the consolidated estate can be tricky, in part because intragroup obligations are eliminated. For example, suppose that A has $10,000,000 in debt and $4,000,000 in assets; B has $12,000,000 in debt and $3,000,000 in assets while C has $1,000,000 in debt and $100,000 in assets. Of A's assets, $2,000,000 constitute a debt owed by B and $500,000 constitute a debt owed by C. Conversely, of B's $12,000,000 in debt, $2,000,000 is the obligation to A; and of C's $1,000,000 of debt, $500,000 is its obligation to A. These are netted out upon consolidation; an entity cannot owe money to itself. What remains are the groups "real" obligations (that is, the obligations to outsiders) and its "real" assets (its tangible property plus its claims against outsiders).

Netting out the intragroup transactions, A's assets drop to $1,500,000; B's debt drops to $10,000,000 and C's debt drops to $500,000. Upon consolidation, the new entity has $20,500,000 in debt. It also has $4,600,000 in assets.

Substantive consolidation is similar but not identical to the concept of "piercing the corporate veil." It extends to entities other than corporations; although most substantive consolidations do involve corporate affiliates, they can also draw in individuals and partnerships. Moreover, many piercing cases merely involve giving creditors of the corporation access to the assets of the corporation's owner. Substantive consolidation gives creditors of all the consolidated entities access to the assets of all the consolidated entities.

There is also a family resemblance between substantive consolidation and equitable subordination.[28] Under that doctrine, claimants who have engaged in misconduct may find their claims given a lower priority than they otherwise would have. Equitable subordination is a less drastic remedy than substantive consolidation

---

[27] See Collier on Bankruptcy ¶ 1100.47.

[28] For a full discussion of equitable subordination, see § 10.05[C] of this book.

because it leaves intact the legal identity of those involved. It also focuses more precisely than substantive consolidation on redressing misconduct; one of the difficulties of substantive consolidation is that it can have a severe impact on the rights of third parties who were in no way involved in the misconduct that gave rise to the remedy.

Given the long history of substantive consolidation, it is curious that there is no explicit authorization for it in the Code, nor are their any guidelines in the Code or the Rules for its use. Indeed, in the view of many critics, there is no cohesive theory of substantive consolidation. This lack of cohesion may be inevitable; substantive consolidation is arguably a remedy for dealing with several distinct problems. Sometimes substantive consolidation is in fact an extreme form of administrative consolidation; it is simply not feasible to administer the estates separately. Sometimes it is a method of dealing with abuse or fraud. Still other times it is voluntary. Although there is a good deal of overlap in the facts examined and the rationales used in these various circumstances, they are to at least some degree analytically distinct.[29]

Substantive consolidation because of administrative necessity arises when there is no feasible way to have a separate administration. Example: Able Company has two subsidiaries, Baker Ltd and Charlie Inc. The three companies are in exactly the same line of business, have a largely identical group of creditors, and have never kept separate books and records. Indeed, the invoices and purchase orders of the three companies have been used interchangeably. Nobody really knows who owns what or owes what. It would be impossible or at least extravagantly expensive to sort this out.[30] The court has no real alternative but to order substantive consolidation. Whether the actions of the companies were fraudulent or abusive (or merely incompetent) is not really relevant because there is no alternative.

Most of the serious disputes over substantive consolidation involve situations in which it is possible to have separate administration. The request for consolidation comes from creditors of at least one entity who argue that consolidation is the only way to save them from the effects of prior misconduct. Typically, these cases involve situations in which one or more of the debtors either (1) misled creditors about whom they were dealing with or (2) was grossly underfinanced by those in control of the debtor group. There are also cases in which there is outright fraud or the use of fraudulent transfers to conceal assets.

Misleading can occur, intentionally or unintentionally, when the debtor group has failed to make clear to creditors who exactly is obligated on debts. For example, consider a company, Maxwell Group, which owns a subsidiary, Maxwell Capital. Both parent and subsidiary use virtually the same letterhead for all documents, correspondence, and checks. The letterhead consists of the word MAXWELL, coupled with a very distinctive design. The name of the parent or the sub appears

---

[29] Note also a fourth category—the consolidation of a joint husband and wife bankruptcy. This issue is dealt with explicitly in the Code and is discussed in § 6.02[D] of this book.

[30] See, for example, Chemical Bank v. Kheel, 369 F.2d 845 (2d Cir. 1966) (estimated cost of untangling the financial affairs of affiliates might exceed the entire value of the estate).

only in very small type. In addition, both companies have the same address, telephone number, and virtually the same personnel. This type of situation, especially if coupled with other factors suggesting a failure to maintain the companies as separate entities, can lead to substantive consolidation.

Underfinancing can be illustrated by the following example, somewhat modified from an actual, though unreported, case. Pater Corp. is a holding company with two subsidiaries, Fabricator Co. and Vendor Ltd. Fabricator manufactures widgets. It sells all its widgets to Pater, which resells all of them to Vendor. Vendor then sells the widgets on the open market. Pater has set the prices it pays Fabricator and the price it charges Vendor so that Parent appears to make money, regardless of whether this causes the subsidiaries to make or lose money. In fact, the price it pays Fabricator is sometimes less than the cost of manufacture and the price is receives from Vendor is sometimes more than the widgets can be sold for. All three companies go into bankruptcy; because of Pater's practices, nearly all the unencumbered assets are in Pater and there is virtually nothing left to pay the unsecured creditors of Fabricator and Vendor. Creditors of both Fabricator and Vendor may seek substantive consolidation, claiming that Pater's actions amount to a misuse of its subsidiaries to the detriment of their separate creditors.

Although situations of these two types are found in most substantive consolidation cases, the courts have not singled out any one factor that is dispositive. Instead, they have resorted to lists. An early case, dealing with a parent/subsidiary consolidation identified the following factors:

1. The parent owns or controls the sub,

2. The corporations have the same directors or officers,

3. The parent provides financing for the sub,

4. The parent created (incorporated) the sub,

5. The sub has grossly inadequate capitalization,

6. The parent pays salaries and expenses of the sub, and subsidizes losses,

7. The sub conducts little or no business with any entity other than the parent,

8. The sub has few or no assets except those it received from the parent,

9. The parent refers to the sub as a department or division, rather than an separate corporation,

10. Directors and officers of the subsidiary act in the interests of the parent, and under the parent's orders,

11. Corporate formalities (such as separate books and records, shareholder and director meetings) are not maintained.[31]

[31] Fish v. East, 114 F.2d 177 (10th Cir. 1940).

Other cases have added to the list without necessarily increasing clarity. Additional factors identified include such things as fraudulent transfers between companies in the debtor group, intercorporate guarantees, the use of consolidated financial statements, commingled assets, and the difficulty of sorting out the property and debts of the various entities.[32] Although attempts have been made by scholars to articulate a precise rule, the courts have been resistant to the idea. Rather, they prefer to keep substantive consolidation an open-ended tool that can be used in a variety of circumstances to deal with what the judge perceives as unfair treatment of creditors.

There is however another side to the substantive consolidation coin. Whenever one part of the debtor group manipulates another part to its advantage, the creditors of the manipulator benefit. Remember the Pater-Fabricator-Vendor hypothetical—while it is certainly true that the creditors of Fabricator and Vendor would have been better off if Pater had not manipulated its subsidiaries the way it did, the creditors of Pater are in a better position precisely because of that manipulation. Indeed, although the cases often are written as if the wrongdoer was being stripped of ill-gotten gains, it is actually the wrongdoer's creditor's who suffer. For example, in the Pater-Fabricator-Vendor case, the only real argument was whether some of the assets otherwise payable to Pater's creditors would instead go to the creditors of Fabricator and Vendor.

This creates an extremely difficult problem for the court. Assume Pater's creditors had no part in and no notice of the misconduct, and further that they had extended credit based on Pater's own assets and cash flow. If the estates are consolidated, assets that Pater's creditors had believed would be available to them are taken away and given to other creditors. This explains why substantive consolidation often pits not debtor against creditor but rather one group of creditors against another.

The stakes can be substantial. Suppose that the Pater-Fabricator-Vendor group land in liquidation. Pater has $70,000,000 of unencumbered assets and $100,000,000 of general unsecured claims. By contrast, Fabricator and Vendor have negligible assets and $250,000,000 in claims. If there is no substantive consolidation, Pater's creditors will receive a 70% dividend, while the subsidiaries' creditors will receive virtually nothing. If the three estates are consolidated, then all creditors will receive approximately 20%—a considerable gain for Fabricator and Vendor creditors, all at the expense of Pater creditors. If the court is satisfied that Pater's creditors relied on Pater's separate financial status, and were not themselves involved in or aware of misconduct, the court may well refuse substantive consolidation, at least in cases where it is feasible to separate the assets and debts of the entities.[33]

There are other examples of potential unfairness. Consolidation can wipe out guarantees and security interests in stock of a consolidated entity. It can also have the effect of destroying intra-group claims for the very misconduct complained of. If any of this causes injury to a bona fide creditor, consolidation may be refused.[34]

---

[32] See Collier on Bankruptcy ¶ 1100.06.

[33] See In re Flora Mir Candy Corp., 432 F.2d 1060 (2d Cir. 1970) (holders of debentures issued by Meadors, a corporation subsequently acquired by Flora Mir, would be injured by substantive consolidation of Meadors and Flora Mir; since it was possible to separate the two entities, the injury precluded substantive consolidation).

[34] In re Gulfco Investment Corp., 593 F.2d 921 (19th Cir. 1979).

Creditors resisting consolidation may press for less drastic remedies that punish the wrongdoer without as drastic an impact on third party interests. The same conduct that can give rise to substantive consolidation might also justify equitable subordination or the recovery of fraudulent transfers. To return to our hypothetical, assume that much of the debt owed by Fabricator and Vendor is owed to the management of the group. Further assume that those managers have milked Fabricator and Vendor to obtain improper salary and bonuses. Creditors of Pater may argue that those loans should be subordinated and those salaries and bonuses recovered. Assume that, if this is done, the creditors of the subsidiaries will receive a 10% dividend. A court might well find it appropriate to do as Pater's creditors ask. This will provide a significant dividend to the subs' creditors, will impose no burden on Pater's creditors, and will impose the costs directly and completely on those who were responsible for the problem on the first place.

This does not mean that consolidation must or will be refused merely because it has a negative impact on some creditors. The courts' effort is to come up with some form of rough justice, recognizing here as throughout bankruptcy law that there are simply more meritorious claims than can be paid. However, it is broadly true that if consolidation would greatly injure a bona fide creditor, it is not likely to be ordered.

[illegible]

[illegible]

TABLE OF STATUTES AND REGULATIONS

[References are to sections and footnotes.]

[References are to sections and footnotes.]

Bankruptcy Code—Cont.

Section	Text Section
304(b)(3)	21.02[A]n8
304(c)	21.02[A]n12
304(c)(1)	21.02[A]n13
304(c)(2)	21.02[A]n14
304(c)(3)	21.02[A]n15
304(c)(4)	21.02[A]n16
304(c)(5)	21.02[A]n17
304(c)(6)	1.01[B]n8; 21.02[A]n18
321(a)(1)	4.06n26, n27
321(a)(2)	4.06n28
321(b)	4.06n30
321(c)	4.06n31
322	16.06n47
322(a)	4.06n32
323(a)	4.06n33
324(a)	16.06n46
327(a)	20.02n2, n3
329(a)	20.02n7
329(b)	20.02n8
330(a)	10.04[B]n53
330(a)(1)	20.03n11, n22
330(a)(2)	20.03n12
330(a)(3)(A)	20.03n15
330(a)(4)(A)	20.03n16
331	20.03n13
341(a)	4.09n49
341(b)	4.09n50
341(c)	4.09n51
343	4.09n54
344	4.09n60
361	19.05n25
361(1)	8.06[B][2]n83
361(2)	8.06[B][2]n85
361(3)	8.06[B][2]n87, n90
362	14.01n11
362(a)	6.03[G]n82; 8.02n5
362(a)(1)	8.02n6
362(a)(2)	8.02n8
362(a)(3)	8.02n11
362(a)(4)	8.02n16
362(a)(5)	8.02n17
362(a)(6)	8.02n12
362(a)(7)	8.02n18; 10.09n101
362(a)(8)	8.02n7; 8.03[C]n50
362(b)	8.03[B]n23
362(b)(1)	8.03[C]n38
362(b)(2)	8.03[B][1]n24
362(b)(2)(A)	8.03[B][1]n25
362(b)(3)	8.03[B][2]n28
362(b)(4)	8.03[C]n39
362(b)(5)	8.03[C]n39
362(b)(8)	8.03[C]n47
362(b)(9)	8.03[C]n49
362(b)(10)	8.03[B][3]n29
362(b)(11)	8.03[B][4]n30
362(b)(12)	8.03[C]n48
362(b)(13)	8.03[C]n48
362(c)(1)	8.06[A]n68
362(c)(2)	8.06[A]n70
362(d)	8.06[5][6]n117, [B][1]n76
362(d)(1)	8.06[B][2]n78
362(d)(2)	8.06[B][4]n109
362(d)(3)	8.06[5]n115; 22.04n19, n21
362(d)(3)(B)	22.04n20
362(e)	8.06[5][6][7]n119, n120, n121, n122, n123
362(f)	8.06[5][6][7]n124
362(g)(1)	8.06[5][6][7]n125
362(g)(2)	8.06[5][6][7]n126
362(h)	8.07[B]n132, [C]n138, n139
363	17.10[C]n94; 17.19n247
363(a)	9.03[B]n7
363(b)(1)	9.03[C][2]n18
363(c)(1)	9.03[C][1]n14, n15, n17
363(c)(2)	9.03[B]n8
363(c)(3)	9.03[B]n10, n11
363(c)(4)	9.03[B]n9
363(d)	9.03[D]n21
363(e)	9.03[D]n20
363(f)(1)	9.03[E]n22
363(f)(2)	9.03[E]n24
363(f)(3)	9.03[E]n25
363(f)(4)	9.03[E]n26
363(f)(5)	9.03[E]n28
363(g)	9.03[E]n30
363(h)(1)	9.03[E]n34

[References are to sections and footnotes.]

Bankruptcy Code—Cont.

Bankruptcy Code—Cont.

[References are to sections and footnotes.]

[References are to sections and footnotes.]

Bankruptcy Code—Cont.

[References are to sections and footnotes.]

[References are to sections and footnotes.]

Bankruptcy Code—Cont.

[References are to sections and footnotes.]

Bankruptcy Code—Cont.

Bankruptcy Code—Cont.

[References are to sections and footnotes.]

Bankruptcy Code—Cont.

Bankruptcy Rules

[References are to sections and footnotes.]

Bankruptcy Rules—Cont.

United States Code

[References are to sections and footnotes.]

TABLE OF CASES

[References are to sections and footnotes.]

A

B

C

D

[References are to sections and footnotes.]

[References are to sections and footnotes.]

[References are to sections and footnotes.]

[References are to sections and footnotes.]

[References are to sections and footnotes.]

INDEX

[References are to sections.]

A

[References are to sections.]

[References are to sections.]

[References are to sections.]

[References are to sections.]

[References are to sections.]

[References are to sections.]

[References are to sections.]

[References are to sections.]

[References are to sections.]

[References are to sections.]

[References are to sections.]

[References are to sections.]

[References are to sections.]

[References are to sections.]

[References are to sections.]

[References are to sections.]

[References are to sections.]

[References are to sections.]

I

J

[References are to sections.]

[References are to sections.]

[References are to sections.]

[References are to sections.]

[References are to sections.]